Essentials of Aviation Management

A Guide for Fixed Base Operators

Fifth Edition

J.D. Richardson
J.F. Rodwell
Peggy Baty

KENDALL/HUNT PUBLISHING COMPANY
4050 Westmark Drive P.O. Box 1840 Dubuque, Iowa 52004-1840

Aviation Management Series

UNITED STATES AIRLINES: Trunk and Regional Carriers, Their Operations and Management, Leo G. Fradenburg
AIR TRANSPORTATION, Ninth Edition, Robert M. Kane and Allan D. Vose
AVIATION LAW: Fundamental Cases with Legal Checklist for Aviation Activities, Fourth Edition, Gerald Pucci
ESSENTIALS OF AVIATION MANAGEMENT: A Guide for Fixed Base Operators, Fifth Edition, J.D. Richardson, J.F. Rodwell and Peggy Baty

Cover photos courtesy of Beech Aircraft Corporation.

Library of Congress Catalog Card Number: 95-78303

ISBN 0-7872-1026-X

Printed in the United States of America
10 9 8 7 6 5 4 3 2 1

Dedicated to
J.D. Richardson

1922–1983

Truly he searched for a way to help the fixed base operator.

Contents

List of Figures

Preface

The fifth edition of *Essentials of Aviation Management: A Guide for Fixed Base Operators* is being published at what hopefully is the close of a difficult period for many Fixed Base Operators (FBOs). A decrease in general aviation aircraft production starting in 1978 was followed by declines in certain types of flying, which impacted business volume and mix for FBOs. As the industry moves into the twenty-first century, certain types of flying will continue to shift. In particular, an increase in personal flying and an increase in business and executive travel are anticipated, especially in heavier and more sophisticated aircraft.

The FBO of the future must be a business person first and an aviation enthusiast second. *Essentials of Aviation Management* seeks to provide an overview of basic business practice with a focus on the FBO. It serves several levels of audience including the technical, vocational, graduate, and undergraduate levels as well as the individual in industry. For an in-depth study, it should be supplemented with additional trade and industry materials. There is a growing flood of business materials; the reader is referred to sources such as:

Ron Christy's and Billy M. Jones, *The Complete Information Bank for Entrepreneurs and Small-Business Managers* in cooperation with the Center for Entrepreneurship and Small Business Management, Wichita State University; and AMACOM, the American Management Association, New York, 1988.

In the aviation world the flow of informational materials also continues to grow. Membership in the National Air Transportation Association (NATA), the FBO industry's trade and professional association, provides excellent information about industry trends. Trade magazines such as "Airport Services" and "FBO" provide vital and timely insights into current events and issues. Additionally, the reader is encouraged to be aware of pertinent federal publications through use of such sources as the Federal Aviation Administration's "Advisory Circular Checklist."

This fifth edition's format of *Essentials of Aviation Management* is as close as possible to the fourth edition. However, some changes in content have been made in order to stay abreast of changing issues. Many useful suggestions were received from professors and instructors who contributed to Kendall/Hunt's telemarketing survey in the summer of 1994.

As with any "how-to" book, there are differing opinions on the best way to approach a problem. Many opinions presented here are synthesized from the teachings of experts in the various fields. Others are derived from my fifteen-year career as an aviation educator, pilot and industry consultant. Many forms of assistance went into this edition of the book and thanks are due especially to Frank Mitchell, Joe Sprague, and Bill Monroe, although the author takes full responsibility for the book's facts and opinions.

Dr. Peggy Baty
Parks College
Cahokia, IL

Chapter 1

The Role of the Fixed Base Operator in the National Aviation System

Objectives

- ✔ Explain the term "FBO," especially the role it plays in the general aviation community.
- ✔ Discuss the historical development of powered aircraft and why some believe we have come "full circle."
- ✔ Describe some of the trends and issues relative to the fixed base operator.
- ✔ Recognize the public awareness issues facing general aviation and impacting its future.

Introduction

This book is a small business text for the management of United States Fixed Base Operators (FBOs), who are the service stations of the aviation system. It addresses two audiences: the aviation student who may not have extensive managerial experience or training, and the fixed base operator owners, managers, and staff who are practitioners in the field with varying levels of formal business training.

In recent times there has been considerable industry discussion about the idea of changing the name "FBO" to some other term more meaningful to the nonaviation public. During 1988 *Airport Services Magazine* ran a reader survey that resulted in 80 percent of the respondents favoring "general aviation center" and 20 percent favoring an "aircraft center".[1] The FBO industry's trade association, the National Air Transportation Association, examined the idea of a campaign for a name change and decided that its priorities were elsewhere.[2] There are also those who objected to the term "general aviation" because it is a catch-all term that is neither a military nor a scheduled airline term. In 1993 a large company with several locations across the country elected to rename their businesses "Flight Support Operators." Feeling the name was more descriptive of the type of business they conduct, they hope others will follow suit. To the non-aviation public the term is probably more descriptive. Therefore, in coming years, we will likely see the introduction of several new terms. In this book we interchange the terms "FBO" and "general aviation center." The reader should assume they are synonymous.

This book's context places the FBO as part of the national aviation system. It reviews current small business practice and theory in areas such as business planning, marketing, financial strategy, human resources, and administration and information systems. It explores the principal areas of FBO activity; namely, flight line and front desk, flight operations, and aviation maintenance. The regulatory context of each area is summarized. Physical facility planning for FBO areas and other parts of the airport and environs are discussed. Finally, the book examines possible future trends affecting general aviation and FBO services.

Fixed Base Operators: Their Role

For many the term fixed base operator conjures up images of a gas station for airplanes. While providing quality fuel is a key service, it is far from the only contribution FBOs make to general aviation. They provide the repair and overhaul services needed by the aviation community, not only for routine maintenance but to meet the demands of aircraft that experience problems enroute. FBOs also provide other services, such as flight training and charter services, that help stimulate interest in general aviation and add to the public's understanding of another important segment, business aviation.

Since 1980, the number of individual FBOs has dwindled from about 10,000 to less than half that amount as many service providers have succumbed to the dual forces of recession and increasingly more costly environmental rules.

According to the FBO Resource Group, a Denver-based aviation consultancy, there were about 4,000 active FBOs operating within the U.S. in 1994.

Aviation Economic History

Aviation Pioneers and Economic Milestones

There are two primary approaches to aviation history. The first approach focuses on the technological advances, new records, and feats of endurance in aviation and space. This approach is well documented in numerous texts, one of which, *Air Transportation,* is used heavily as a reference here.[3] A second approach addresses the development of aviation as a significant component of the economy. This is the approach used in this text. There are fewer supporting materials using this point of view.

When human beings first began to build flying machines, particularly when they began to build powered craft, their primary preoccupation was to understand and master aerodynamics; potential markets for the technology were a secondary consideration. Orville Wright, even ten years after Kitty Hawk, felt there was almost no chance of successfully completing a transatlantic flight.[4]

Yet, the economic and transportation role of aviation was understood by some even in the very early days. Experimenters such as Samuel Langley did get financial backing from people interested in the large-scale practical uses of aircraft.[5] With Lindbergh's solo transatlantic flight in 1927, the perception of the market potential of aviation began to change. For airmail, it changed much earlier. From 1911 mail was carried by air in the United States in a system that must have had as many challenges and risks as the Pony Express in the first part of the nineteenth century. Mail does not present the same risk as human cargo in a crash, and it can withstand delay and rerouting more readily. The American public, however, waited for evidence of safety and reliability in airmail service before entrusting themselves as aircraft passengers.

Some acceptance of air travel resulted from the earlier lighter-than-air flying machines. The first controllable dirigible was built by Henri Giffard as early as 1852, and in 1909 Count Zeppelin started the world's first airline called DERLAG.

During World War I the Germans used dirigibles extensively for bombing. In the 1920s and 1930s several other nations became active in the development of passenger and military airships. This ended after a series of crashes. The last one was the explosion and crash of the Hindenburg in 1937. After this, airships were used only for military purposes.[6]

By the middle of the 1920s, especially in the United States, the capabilities of the heavier-than-air planes were apparent. As a result of changes in mail handling, passenger service became popular in the 1920s and 1930s. Between 1911 and 1927, the post office handled airmail in its own aircraft. However, the Airmail Act of 1925 enabled other air carriers to contract for mail service.

By early 1926, twelve contract airmail routes had been awarded. In 1927 the Boeing Airplane Company received a bid award (later transferred to Boeing Air Transport) and in the first two years of operation carried about 6,000 passengers as well as 1,200 tons of airmail. However, the general acceptance of aircraft as passenger carriers did not come about until the 1930s after several legislative changes designed to strengthen national airmail routes and encourage financially viable carriers. This was a stormy period in the development of commercial aviation; however, by the end of 1936 the air carriers were making more revenue from passengers than from mail.[7]

The Jet Engine: New Horizons

World War II military necessity gave the jet engine its impetus, although experimenters in this area had been working on it for decades.[8,9] The jet's greater speed and range opened up significant new horizons for aviation, especially in larger countries such as the United States and Canada. During World War II, jet technology became refined, and after the war commercial applications began. The implications of jet aircraft relate not only to speed but also to:

1. Range of flight without refueling.
2. Noise levels (with a few exceptions).
3. Runway length requirements. (With a few exceptions, the typical business jet requires 5,000 feet or more for landing, while the typical piston aircraft can operate with half that length.)
4. Fuel type requirements and comparative costs.
5. Fuel consumption.
6. Traffic mix in the flight pattern.

The subsonic jet is now state-of-the-art for most air transportation. Decreasing transatlantic or transcontinental travel time down to about seven hours and eliminating refueling stops were highly significant achievements for most of the flying public.

Although supersonic transports are in service in various parts of the world, there are currently serious questions in the United States about the acceptability and financial feasibility of these aircraft. Cutting transatlantic travel from seven hours to four hours may be a need for some, but the question that a reporter asked Tip O'Neill after his maiden flight on the Concorde, "What did you do with the time you saved?" must be weighed against the cost and environmental disadvantages of supersonic transports.

Rotorcraft: New Functions

The concept of a flying machine that could hover, land almost anywhere, and perform operations without even needing to land was a dream for many aircraft inventors over the years.[10] Its development has led to the design and use of very sophisticated machines with range, speed, and load capacity close to midsized, fixed-wing aircraft. Because of the need to eliminate a mile of runway, increasing numbers of corporations are turning to the use of rotorcraft. Their use has been of major importance in the development of offshore oil resources and servicing of rigs, in pipeline laying and patrol, in construction of tall buildings, and in search and rescue. They have also been important in activities such as logging, which previously required the construction of roads for access. Rotorcraft, though not a major portion of the total aviation fleet, do comprise a rapidly growing one.[11]

With the downsizing of the military in the late 1980's and early 1990's the supply of helicopter rated pilots available to meet the growing need by industry was an issue. However, with the introduction of new, relatively inexpensive, helicopters available for flight training, the numbers of civilian pilots earning their helicopter ratings has increased.

The Full Circle: Ultralights and Homebuilts

It has been said that if the Wright Brothers had had dacron and aluminum tubing available to them, they would have invented the ultralight. Certainly the appearance and handling of the first generation of ultralights (such as B1-RD and Kasperwing) is very similar to the aircraft in which the Wrights first undertook powered flight.

There has been a tremendous surge of interest in recent years not only in ultralights, but also in related heavier aircraft including the new category of Primary Aircraft approved by the FAA in 1993 and a great array of experimental and homebuilt aircraft.

General aviation hit its peak since WWII in 1978 with the largest number of general aviation aircraft shipped. In 1977 a total of 17,811 aircraft were shipped from the manufacturers, compared to an all time low of only 941 in 1992. A slight increase in 1993 found a total of 960 aircraft manufactured. With the passage of the Tort Reform bill in 1994, industry is hopeful this upward trend will continue.

According to a 1993 report from the General Aviation Manufacturers Association, a few years ago, the U.S. manufactured nearly all of the world's piston-engine airplanes. Today, the U.S. now accounts for only 75 percent of worldwide piston-engine airplane production. In 1980, there were 29 U.S. manufacturers of certified piston-powered airplanes and 15 foreign. Today, there are 9 U.S. manufacturers and 29 foreign, almost a complete reversal.

But on the other side of the ledger, homebuilt and experimental aircraft totalled 734 completions in 1993. The need by the flying public for new cost effective aircraft is still valid. Interest in general aviation continues to soar as evidenced by the attendance annually at aviation events around the country. In 1994 the annual convention sponsored by the Experimental Aircraft Association in Oshkosh, Wisconsin had over 850,000 participants. Over 12,000 airplanes were flown in from around the world to be on display for the convention.

Airline Deregulation

The Airline Deregulation Act of 1978 was a major economic milestone in the history of U.S. aviation because it established a basis for eliminating the industry's protected and subsidized role as an "infant industry."[12] Deregulation permitted the airlines to abandon unprofitable small points they were formerly required to serve. New, competitive subsidy processes for these small points were established under "essential air service." Many commuter carriers have been successful in bidding for this small community ser-

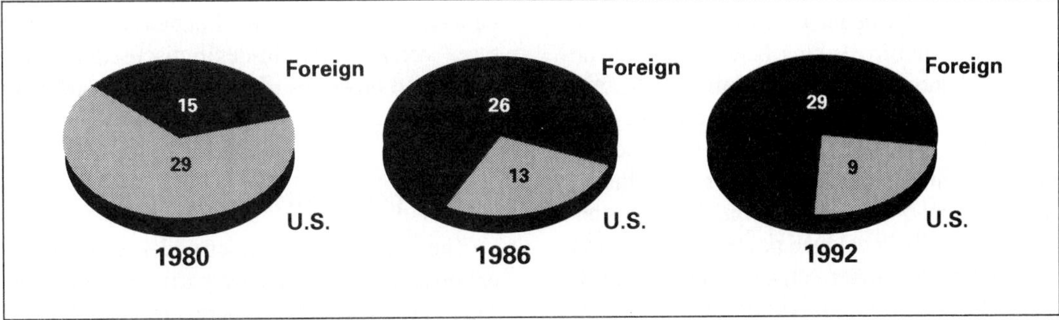

Figure 1.1. Number of Piston Airplane Manufacturers.

vice and receiving federal subsidies to assist them. While the Essential Air Service Program is now substantially reduced in scope, it provided an important boost to small carriers in the years after deregulation.

At the same time, rapid fuel cost increases, fare increases, intensive competition and, in some cases, overambitious expansion have resulted in major stresses for many of the larger carriers. This has led to numerous mergers and several bankruptcies. As a result, other new markets have opened up for commuters and former air-taxi operators. In the decades since deregulation, fewer and fewer scheduled service markets in the United States continue to have nonstop service. This is primarily due to the airlines' development of hub-and-spoke route systems. The economic impact of the deregulation act seems likely to continue and to result in new opportunity for not only scheduled commuters, but also for the traditional FBO charter and air-taxi services. One of the success stories resulting from the Airline Deregulation Act has been Southwest Airlines. With a marketing strategy of a "no frills" airline, they have steadily increased their market area. Beginning as a regionally based carrier, operating primarily in the southwest U.S., they have now expanded their routes to include over half the U.S.

A unique management style, designed to be both customer and employee oriented, has led to their success. Reducing operating costs by eliminating meal service (peanuts only), eliminating boarding passes (passengers are seated on a first come, first served basis), and quick turn around times at the gate were all factors contributing to their success. Other more established carriers initially thought Southwest would not survive long. It is interesting to note that now many of those same airlines are now trying to duplicate the successful strategies initiated by Southwest.

The start up of several new companies since deregulation has helped to keep fares low. The stiff competition has also led to the demise of several companies and has also resulted in several mergers.

The Modern Aviation Industry

Industry Development

In the beginning all aviation was experimental. But even before the 1920's there was evidence of market segmentation in the United States. Airmail flights were gradually becoming more sophisticated, thus triggering the development of coast-to-coast air navigation and airfields in the United States. This was the commercial development of the infant industry. Then there were the stunt flyers and barnstormers, who helped to popularize aviation by flying all over the country with their daring feats. The aircraft manufacturers persisted in seeking better and safer designs with more practical applications. The military use of aircraft played—and still plays—a major role in the research and development of new aviation technology. Then there were the airlines that first developed the airmail business and then eventually developed passenger transportation and carried other cargo. During the 1920s and 1930s (with the support of the WPA), there was great activity to develop the airport system. Without this network, no amount of aircraft technological and market development would have led to a viable air transportation system.

Although the history of the fixed-base operations system is not well documented, it seems that it must have gone hand-in-hand with the development of the airport system, for without fuel and repairs the aircraft could not function for very long. In 1911 when Calbraith P. Rogers made the first transcontinental flight across the United States, a special train was sent ahead of him with parts and repair facilities.[13] Therefore, as aviation developed, fixed-base operator services must also have grown in number.

Components of the Industry

Today's aviation system has evolved into a number of distinct areas:

- Pilots—at all levels of rating
- The airport system
- The air navigation system
- Aviation manufacturers
- Scheduled air carriers
- General aviation, including fixed base operators
- Aviation interest groups
- The governmental regulatory system

Many aspects of aviation are regulated by the Federal Aviation Administration. A list of the regulations is contained in Appendix I. The following sections provide a brief description of the national aviation system. Chapter 13 "The Future," offers a more in-depth discussion of key issues and problems affecting certain aspects of the system.

The Airport System

The airport system varies widely in its physical quality and the type of traffic it can handle. There are over 3,000 airports designated as essential to the national air transportation system. These airports vary from major international facilities with several runways and many services, to the single short runway with limited or no services. Nationally there are over 15,000 landing facilities. However, many of these are little more than fields or airstrips and are for private use or use by permission only. Most of them do not have any public services and may only have a tie-down. Of an estimated 6,865 public-use airports, over half are privately owned and operated by the owner or on contract to an FBO.

The nature of airport usage varies greatly. The most densely populated states are well served by scheduled service airports such as the Kennedy—LaGuardia—Newark trio in the New York area and the Los Angeles International—Long Beach—Burbank—Newport Beach—Orange County system in southern California. More rural parts of the country depend more heavily on general aviation airports; the most extreme example is the bush areas of Alaska, where many communities have no road access and hopping into a small plane is as natural as driving. In this instance the local airport may be a seaplane facility with floats used in summer and skis in winter.

There are four types of airports. The Conventional Takeoff and Landing (CTOL) airport is the one with which most people are familiar. It includes all of the hub airports and those serving general aviation. The Vertical Takeoff and Landing (VTOL) airport is designed to accomodate those aircraft which can operate in an area of 200–500 square feet. These are commonly referred to as heliports and used almost exclusively by helicopters. The Short Takeoff and Landing (STOL) airports have runways with lengths of 1,500–3,000 feet. Airplanes such as the Maule, JAAR's, and several of the newer kitplanes can operate safely at these airports. The Reduced Takeoff and Landing (RTOL) airports are being designed to accomodate aircraft that can carry 80–150 passengers and can operate from airports with runways from 3,000–5,000 feet. The idea is to locate these near large metropolitan areas, allowing for easier access to the overall airport system.

Airports in the United States are oftentimes put into one of four categories: large hub airport, medium hub airport, small hub airport, and small nonhub airport. The classification is based on the amount of civilian air traffic generated by the aviation community. A large hub contains 1.0 percent of total enplaned passengers, a medium hub 0.25 to 0.99, a small hub 0.05 to 0.24, and a nonhub has less than 0.05 of the nation's total.

Classification of airports is based on the Standard Metropolitan Statistical Areas (SMSA) requiring aviation services. A SMSA is a county that contains at least one city of fifty thousand population, or twin cities with a combined populations of at least fifty thousand, plus any contiguous counties that are metropolitan in nature and have a contiguous economic and population structure.

Individual communities fall into hub classifications, as determined by each community's percentage of total enplaned revenue passengers in all services and all operations of certificated route carriers within the United States.

The FAA issues a report annually (FAA Airport Activity Report) presenting the total number of enplaned revenue passengers. From the statistics gathered, specific airport information is received. Each airport's percentage of the total is tabulated and from this information, classification is determined. Typically the hub airports account for approximately 95% of the total number of passenger enplanements.

An airport's organizational structure can vary greatly depending on its size and ownership.

In a large metropolitan area served by several airports, one authority may have jurisdiction over all aviation operations or even an entire transportation system. Intermodal transportation agencies within government is a current trend. Even airports within this type of arrangement have a certain amount of autonomy. It does, however, permit the centralization of several airport functions. Examples of areas with large hubs include Atlanta, Los Angeles, and New York.

Medium hub airports are found in smaller metropolitan areas of the country, and, to a smaller scale, operate similarly to a large hub airport. Cities with medium hub airports include Portland, Oregon; Tampa, Florida; and Memphis, Tennessee.

Small nonhub airports on the other hand operate more independently and usually are smaller in terms of geographic size and aircraft operations.

The Air Navigation System

The civil airspace and its management come exclusively under the purview of the FAA. There are 21 Air Route Traffic Control Centers (ARTCCs) that cover the whole country and keep track of all traffic flying on Instrument Flight Rules. The ARTCCs transfer traffic to individual air traffic control areas. There are en route airways and navigational aids of various types and rules for en route and airport vicinity flying. The number of Flight Service Stations have been decreased. Remaining Flight Service Stations have been "automated" making them more efficient by use of computers and telephone voice systems. Pilots may now receive current weather information for their arrival, departure, and enroute phases of flight without speaking to a "live" briefer. The option is still there for those who want further clarification or who prefer the ability to converse with an FAA representative.

At the time of this writing, FAA Administrator David Hinson has announced the agency is scrapping its plan to upgrade the air traffic control computer system, integrating a voice automated system. After several years and many hundreds of millions of dollars, the project was still way behind schedule and progress was not plentiful. Part of the decision to halt the project is also due to the current talks on privatizing the air traffic control system in the U.S. Many aviation groups, commercial and general, oppose the idea.

Aviation Manufacturers

Many of the general aviation aircraft manufacturers and their suppliers are represented by the General Aviation Manufacturers Association (GAMA). Membership includes Cessna, Piper, Beech, Lear, and others. Some innovative manufacturers such as Rutan tend to operate more independently. The large aircraft companies include McDonnell Douglas, Boeing, and Lockheed. Makers of avionics and aircraft components are another important group. Much of the aircraft component manufacturing is now taking place overseas because of lower labor costs.

Scheduled Air Carriers

Since the Airline Deregulation Act of 1978, the hierarchy of air carriers has changed both in nomenclature and in role.[15] Airline aircraft in 1987 involved about 3,400 aircraft, or 1.5 percent of the civil aircraft fleet.[16] Commuters accounted for 1,600 aircraft, or 0.7 percent. The distinction between these two levels of carriers, which started in 1969, is fast disappearing. The new nomenclature for the carriers is majors, nationals, large regionals, medium regionals, and small regionals. The FAA has dropped the air carrier/commuter distinction for airports, and now they are simply commercial service airports of varying sizes. In this book, any reference to airlines means scheduled carriers of any size, as contrasted with nonscheduled air taxis.

General Aviation

General aviation comprises almost 97 percent of the civil aircraft fleet. As shown in figure 1.2, it also constitutes a very major portion of the system in terms of activities such as hours flown.

	1992	
Fleet	#	%
Scheduled Airlines	6,037	3.2
General Aviation	184,434	96.8
Total	190,471	100.0
Hours Flown		
Air Carrier	13.8 million	34.2
General Aviation	26.5 million	65.8
Total	40.3 million	100.0

Figure 1.2. General aviation's role in the system. (Source: *FAA Statistical Handbook of Aviation—1992*).

Additionally, although less easily measured, general aviation industry sources estimate that general aviation carries about one quarter of all air passengers in the United States.

The nation's fixed base operators provide the airport services to this major segment of the aviation system as well as servicing airlines at a number of the country's major airports. General aviation is a complete array of types of users and varieties of activity. Figure 1.5 suggests a method of organizing general aviation into a meaningful system. It divides general aviation activity into (1) methods of travel and (2) methods of undertaking an operation from the air. This second role of general aviation is a key distinguishing characteristic because airlines provide **only** transportation and GA provides much more.

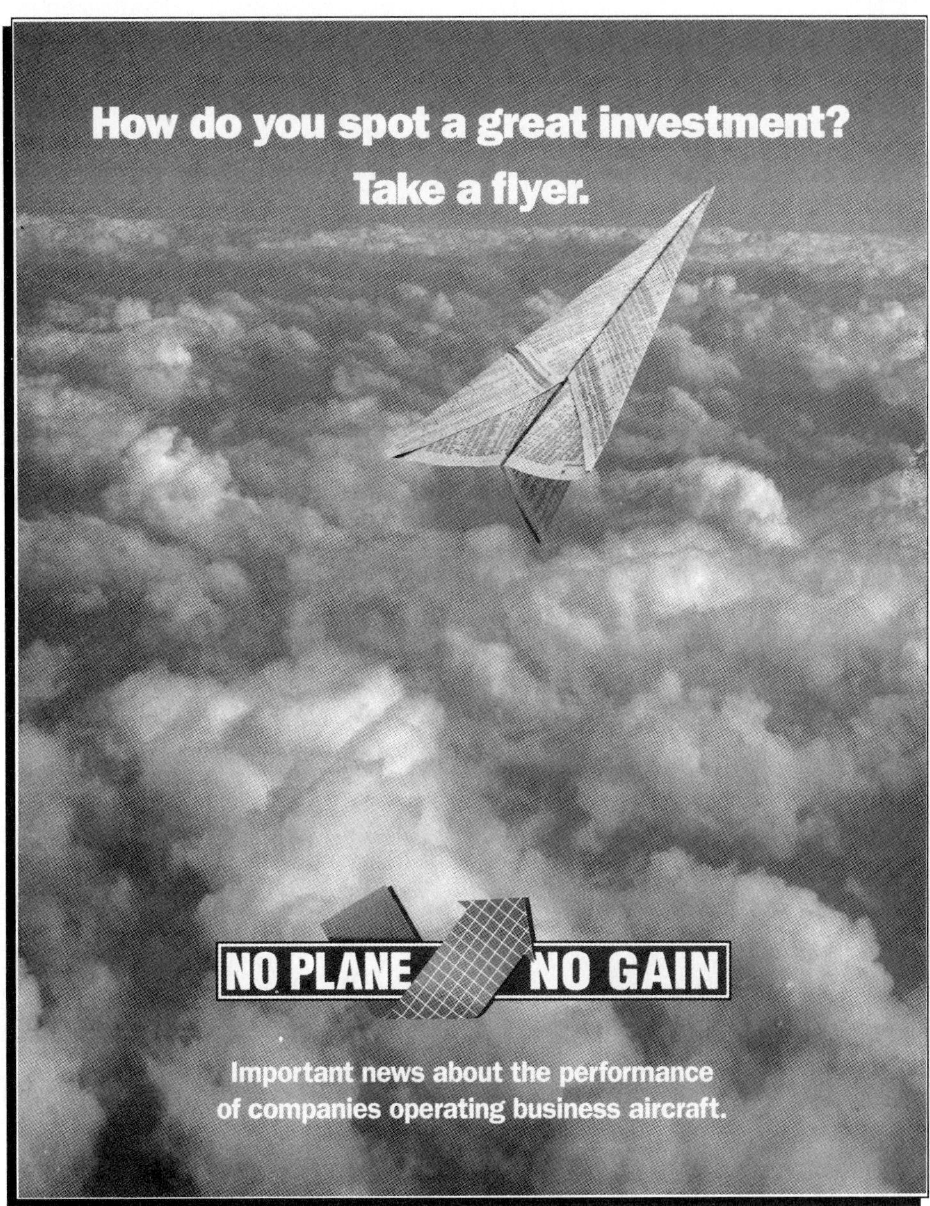

Figure 1.3. Courtesy of The General Aviation Taskforce.

No plane. Smaller stock market gains.

Savvy investors focus on total return over the long haul.

Do companies that operate aircraft perform as well as non-operators over many years?

The answer is: They perform better.

FORTUNE's honor roll— 92% own or operate aircraft

If there ever was an "honor roll" to which corporate management should aspire, it's *Fortune* magazine's annual list of 50 companies with the "Highest Total Return to Investors—10 Years."

These companies achieved an astounding 30 percent compound average return each and every year between 1982 and 1992, measured by stock price gains and dividends happily received by their farsighted shareholders.

This list is dominated by aircraft owners and operators. Forty-six out of fifty companies use business aircraft to gain time, flexibility and productivity, as well as generous gains for their stockholders.

What kind of company makes it to *Fortune*'s honor roll list? These are great companies. Focused, well managed and aggressive. But they're not necessarily huge multinationals, either. While some are household names such as Coca-Cola, Merck, Kellogg, Philip Morris and others, many are unfamiliar to the casual investor. Over half are smaller firms that rank between 250th and 500th in sales.

Indeed, the popular impression that only big companies use business aircraft is wrong. Many of these operators are lean, entrepreneurial, growth-oriented companies.

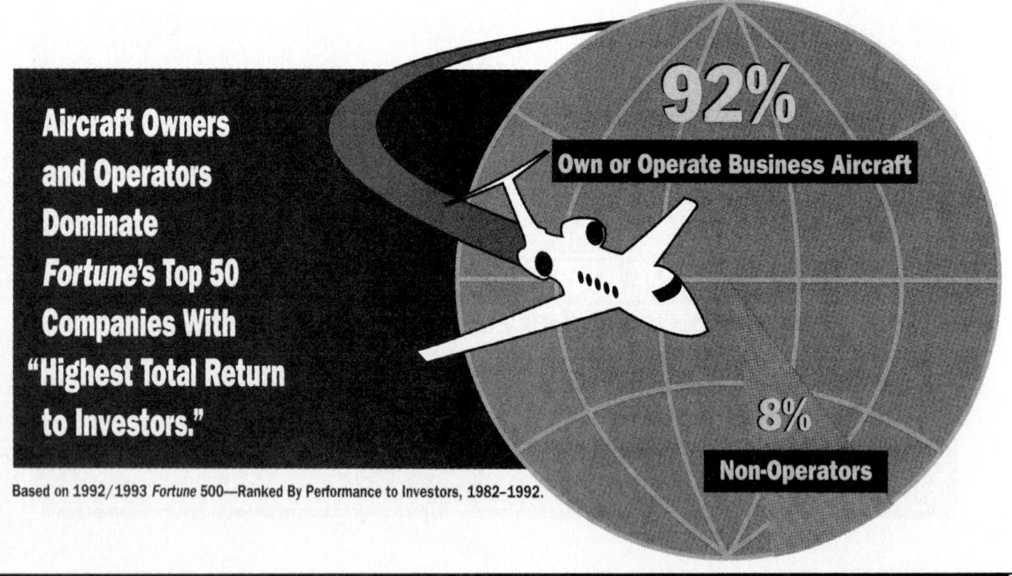
Aircraft Owners and Operators Dominate *Fortune*'s Top 50 Companies With "Highest Total Return to Investors."
92%
Own or Operate Business Aircraft
8%
Non-Operators
Based on 1992/1993 *Fortune* 500—Ranked By Performance to Investors, 1982-1992.

Figure 1.4. Courtesy of The General Aviation Taskforce.

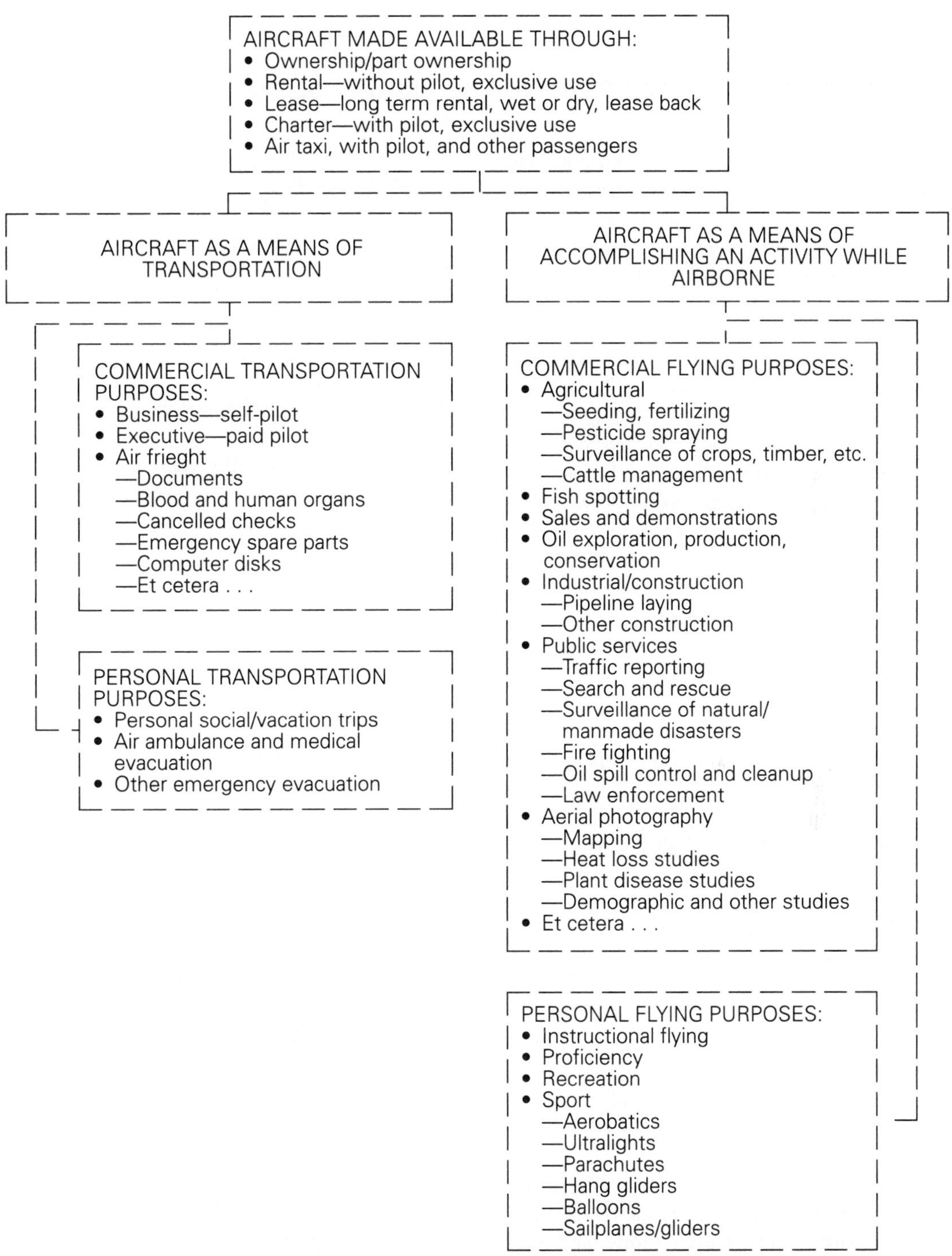

AIRCRAFT MADE AVAILABLE THROUGH:
• Ownership/part ownership
• Rental—without pilot, exclusive use
• Lease—long term rental, wet or dry, lease back
• Charter—with pilot, exclusive use
• Air taxi, with pilot, and other passengers
AIRCRAFT AS A MEANS OF TRANSPORTATION
AIRCRAFT AS A MEANS OF ACCOMPLISHING AN ACTIVITY WHILE AIRBORNE
COMMERCIAL TRANSPORTATION PURPOSES:
• Business—self-pilot
• Executive—paid pilot
• Air frieght
—Documents
—Blood and human organs
—Cancelled checks
—Emergency spare parts
—Computer disks
—Et cetera . . .
PERSONAL TRANSPORTATION PURPOSES:
• Personal social/vacation trips
• Air ambulance and medical evacuation
• Other emergency evacuation
COMMERCIAL FLYING PURPOSES:
• Agricultural
—Seeding, fertilizing
—Pesticide spraying
—Surveillance of crops, timber, etc.
—Cattle management
• Fish spotting
• Sales and demonstrations
• Oil exploration, production, conservation
• Industrial/construction
—Pipeline laying
—Other construction
• Public services
—Traffic reporting
—Search and rescue
—Surveillance of natural/ manmade disasters
—Fire fighting
—Oil spill control and cleanup
—Law enforcement
• Aerial photography
—Mapping
—Heat loss studies
—Plant disease studies
—Demographic and other studies
• Et cetera . . .
PERSONAL FLYING PURPOSES:
• Instructional flying
• Proficiency
• Recreation
• Sport
—Aerobatics
—Ultralights
—Parachutes
—Hang gliders
—Balloons
—Sailplanes/gliders

Figure 1.5. A taxonomy of general aviation flying. Courtesy of Rodwell Resources, Seattle, WA.

Fixed Base Operators

Definitions and Functions

According to the National Air Transportation Association (NATA), the industry organization representing FBOs, fixed base operator (usually shortened to FBO) is an elusive term applied to almost any general aviation business existing on an airport.

The first companies labeled fixed base operators were easily distinguished from their counterparts known as the field-hopping, post World War I "barnstormers." Although exciting and colorful, these transient characters had no fixed base of operations and were pilots first, last, and always. Those who started the first FBOs were also pilots. They became business people committed to providing stable, professional flight and ground services to all customers from a permanent, or fixed, base of operations.[18]

Although some airport authorities and state agencies seek to regulate the minimum services that an FBO can provide, there is great diversity. The array of possible aeronautical services listed by the Federal Aviation Administration is as follows:

- Charter operations
- Pilot training
- Aircraft rental and sightseeing
- Aerial photography
- Crop dusting
- Aerial advertising and surveying
- Passenger transportation
- Aircraft sales and service
- Sale of aviation petroleum products
- Repair and maintenance of aircraft
- Sale of aircraft parts

Specifically excluded by the FAA's definition are ground transportation (taxis, car rentals, limousines); restaurants; barber shops; and auto parking lots—although, of course, an FBO may operate such items.[19]

In terms of flight services alone, one Cessna dealer lists the following array:[20]

- Air ambulance
- Aerial inspection and patrol
- Aerial mapping
- Aerial photography
- Aerial pick-up and delivery service
- Air cargo in
- Air cargo out
- Emergency medical supply
- Fishing and hunting trips
- Holiday and vacation travel
- Management field inspection
- New business calls
- Out-of-town conventions and meetings
- Personal transportation to special events
- Plant-to-plant company transportation
- Regular sales calls
- Transportation of dated articles; newspapers, mail, reports, proposals, retail merchandise
- Transportation of perishables
- Trouble-shooting with tools
- Transportation to hub air terminals
- Ski trips
- VIP passenger service for clients, customers or prospects

Scale of the Industry

There are potentially, we may assume, over 6,000 airports with some type of FBO service because this is the number of public-use airports. In a unique study in 1978, the FAA wanted to find out more about FBO activity. It was hypothesized that the quality and service levels of FBOs could be a major determinant of the level of activity at an airport.[21] Preliminary contact with 6,521 airports resulted in responses to the survey from 4,406 FBOs. By the mid–1980s, according to NATA estimates, there were around 3,500 FBOs. There have been both closings and start-ups of FBO businesses in recent times. NATA estimates that its 1,000 or so members conduct 85 percent or more of the nation's FBO sales.[22] There is also a small number of very large FBOs, such as Van Dusen, MillionAir, Hangar One, Combs-Gates, FlightSafety International, SignatureAir, Air Kaman, and Beech Holdings that have branches or franchises at many airports.

Airport Management

FBOs who also have the responsibility for the management of the airport have a special, multifaceted role. The best interests of the FBO and the (publicly owned) airport may not always coincide. Little is documented about FBOs who wear dual hats; however, the previously mentioned FAA study showed the following:

- Airports managed by FBO — 1,526 — 34.6 percent
- Airports with public manager — 1,855 — 42.1 percent
- Other — 1,025 — 23.3 percent

Thus, many FBOs have dual roles with a potential for conflict. These figures do not distinguish between FBOs running airports for either a private or a public owner.

FBO Industry Trends and Issues

Maturity and Professionalism

Early aviation managers or businesspeople found themselves faced with many technical problems associated with simply keeping the plane airborne. The challenge of the job and the associated thrills kept them occupied. There appears to be a historical tendency for the general aviation businessperson to be primarily a flyer or aircraft mechanic who allowed love of aviation and preoccupation with technical problems to override sound business practices. Conventional wisdom indicates, almost without exception, that inventors and other creative geniuses make poor businesspeople, no matter what the field of endeavor. The early decades of technical genius in aviation were indispensable, but the industry has matured and also needs other skills.

The 1980's showed signs of being a transition era in the management of many aviation enterprises. The early flyer-turned businessperson, often a retired military pilot, is now becoming a manager with more awareness of the need for business skills. In many instances, the manager simply acquires this additional insight through training and the necessity for survival. In other situations the second generation in a family business has often influenced the business and accomplished changes. Additionally, there has also been an influx of new professional managers who are bringing new ideas to the general aviation field.

When viewing the general aviation business scene, one should bear in mind that most fixed base operators are very small businesses in a very competitive, volatile industry. Despite this smallness the FBO manager is called upon to provide a complexity of skills and services common to much bigger enterprises.

An examination of many general aviation businesses reveals four unsound business practices:

1. Continued investment of money in a business because of a love of flying rather than because of profitability.
2. Low rates of return for costly qualification training, capital investments, and operating expenses.
3. Lack of adequate record keeping and procedures for monitoring and evaluating performance.
4. Weak marketing and promotional activities.

The anticipated growth in general aviation, the need for high-quality aviation services and the competition for qualified labor are likely to mean that in order to survive in future years or even during the current slump in which general aviation finds itself, FBOs will become more professional and based less on the love of flying.

Public Awareness

When the different aviation markets are examined, it seems each acquires a different image. The airlines are commonly accepted forms of transportation, and over 70 percent of the adult population has flown at least once.[23] Air cargo traffic is beginning to be perceived by the public as a vital service, particularly as express package delivery grows in importance. But general aviation still seems to have the silk-scarf-and-goggles image of the barnstorming days. Even major general aviation airports have been referred to by planning officials as "just marinas for planes." Some elements of the flying community may heighten this frivolous image by taking unnecessary chances that can result in spectacular accidents and incidents. The negative image may also be enhanced because general aviation airports are often located in smaller communities. In such locations there may be a larger percentage of people who lack basic trust in aerodynamics and who lack awareness of general aviation's key role in the transportation system. As population growth has often brought residential neighborhoods in contact with airports, the negative responses of some of the population have been exacerbated by aircraft noise.

The public awareness questions affecting general aviation's future, and thereby the future of the FBOs, include:

- Pollution
- Noise
- Land use
- Community safety
- Transportation availability
- Allocation of the costs of the airway system in equitable fashion
- Access to the airport system for all users
- Product liability and other legal issues
- Image of general aviation

Many organizations have begun campaigns in the 1990s attempting to introduce more people to aviation. Of particular note are the Young Eagles program, Learn To Fly, and Project Pilot.

The Young Eagles program, initiated by the Experimental Aircraft Association in 1992, intends to introduce one million young people (ages 8–17) to the world of aviation by the year 2003, commemorating the 100th anniversary of powered flight. Members of the Association volunteer their time and airplanes to take the youngsters on an introductory airplane flight.

The Learn to Fly program, now under the auspices of the National Air Transportation Association (NATA), hopes to encourage more adults to learn to fly. NATA sees a definite advantage to its members, FBO owners and managers, by increasing not only their flight instruction business but also potential sales of new and used aircraft.

The Aircraft Owners and Pilots Association (AOPA) has been promoting its "Project Pilot" program, begun in 1994. Members of AOPA are asked to bring their friends to the airport, take them for a flight, bring them to a local pilot's meeting, etc. in the hopes of bringing another new person into aviation.

All of these programs are efforts to help market aviation to the general public. Obviously, the hope is that many of these individuals will go on to obtain pilots certificates and ratings, becoming "consumers" of aviation. But, the other benefit is an educated pro-aviation citizenry; local members of the community who will not complain about airplane noise or block expansion of their local airport, etc.

Technical Issues

Fuel prices and availability will periodically be major concerns for general aviation, as they will be for all transportation systems. The possible transfer to alternative fuels appears less easily achieved than for stationary fuel consumers. More fuel-efficient engines and lighter aircraft will continue to be major technical objectives. Quieter aircraft engines present another major technical challenge, although much has already been done in this area. Improved navigational safety and greater crash survivability seem likely to be substantial issues of the coming decades. The pioneers tackled the basic aerodynamic problems leading to successful flight, and the same kinds of innovation and technical skill will be needed to enable aviation to play its full role in the transportation system of the future.

Conclusion

The nation's fixed base operators are central to general aviation. The skill of their pilots and the FBO's sensitivity to the concerns of the nonflying public, as well as the way they bring new users and advocates into the system, will have much to do with the prosperity of general aviation in coming decades. Failure to develop a more understanding public will likely lead to more restrictive zoning, more lawsuits about noise, failure to pass needed bond issues and appropriations, restrictive leases, closure of airports, lack of business support in the community, and limited access for general aviation to the nation's airports and airspace.

Thus the nation's fixed base operators have more than just the challenge of running a profitable business in a tough economy. They have the wider obligation concerning:

- Technical improvement in the performance and safety of flight vehicles and equipment
- Improved standards of professionalism and business orientation throughout the industry
- Reduced fragmentation of the industry
- Wider public understanding and acceptance of the general aviation industry and its benefits to the public as a whole

Summary

A brief review of aviation history reveals a background of tremendous individual accomplishment in overcoming aviation, technical, and aeronautical problems. The civil aviation industry began to divide in the 1920s into scheduled passenger service and "general aviation." Particularly since the Airline Deregulation Act of 1978, airlines have functioned similarly to other big business by focusing on market opportunities and the bottom line. They have developed management practices as specialized and sophisticated as most other large organizations. By contrast, general aviation is still closer in spirit and functions to the exciting days of barnstorming and record breaking. The industry went through rapid growth until the late 1970s when a variety of factors caused a decline. Since that time, the surviving operators have achieved success largely because of their ability to evolve from aviation enthusiasts to professional managers. As the general aviation industry matures, these trends will likely continue, although there will still be a strong experimental and innovative aspect in general aviation design that will affect the whole industry. In short, general aviation will be predominantly a business activity, but there will also be a segment who fly just for the enjoyment.

Discussion Topics

1. Explain the importance of the human desire to fly in the development of aviation.
2. What did the Wright brothers achieve that was unlike previous successful flight?
3. Name five career pathways in the several elements of the aviation system that offer opportunity to a person with your aptitudes and training.
4. What are the three most important competences of an aviation manager?
5. What aspects of aviation are encompassed by the term "general aviation"? Can you think of a better term?
6. What is the future growth potential of the general aviation fleet? Why?
7. Why would a business person remain in a low-profit aviation activity?
8. Where does the term "Fixed Base Operator" come from? Can you think of a better term?
9. What are the major elements of the U.S. aviation industry?

Chapter 2
Management Functions

Objectives

- ✔ Discuss the four functions of management and how they specifically relate to the operation of an FBO.
- ✔ Recognize some of the common managerial errors found in business today and how to correct them.
- ✔ Describe the elements of a successful business plan.
- ✔ Understand the do's and don'ts of delegation.
- ✔ Show how good time management techniques relate to good business practice. And, demonstrate good time management concepts that you can implement now.

"Some are born managers, some achieve management, and some have management thrust upon them."[1]

Introduction

The Four Functions of Management

Management is getting things done through others. This means that a manager's primary responsibility is to keep his or her staff effectively occupied on the priority activities of the department or company. Its successful accomplishment may require different techniques for different tasks and people. It appears to be both an art and a science. The FBO owner/manager may be the only manager in the company, depending on its size. In a bigger organization the owner/manager will have other departmental managers reporting to him or her.

Management activities are traditionally divided into four functions:

1. Planning
2. Organizing
3. Directing
4. Controlling

The ways that these are interpreted and carried out will have major results on the success or failure of the enterprise. Management theory has been evolving rapidly in the last 10 to 15 years, and there are numerous books, articles, and professional associations that can assist the aspiring manager.[2] It is also sometimes useful to consider the traits of the *ineffective* manager so that they can be avoided.

Common Managerial Errors

There are a dozen problem areas that managers must overcome if they are to be successful.[3]

Failure to Anticipate Industry Trends

We are part of a fast-changing economy, and new technology in some other field may affect part of our sales. For example, the facsimile machine has been available since the mid 1970s, but it did not offer good quality until the late 1980s. Suddenly many information items are being "faxed" over telephone lines instead of being delivered by overnight small package air express. Any FBO depending heavily on the air courier market may be significantly affected by this trend, as well as by computer networking.

Lack of Priorities

We live in an increasingly overwhelming information environment, making it harder to decide what to read. Greater knowledge about the economy, about potential markets, and about new business tools can make the business owner feel indecisive about where to begin. As one business owner said, "I'm so busy doing the urgent things that there isn't time to do the important things." Going in all directions causes exhaustion and lack of results.

Indecisiveness

As some businesses grow, they resist the establishment of policies and procedures. The owner/manager thinks out how to proceed each time, even though similar situations arise again and again. Worse yet, the manager makes a decision, the staff starts implementing it, and a week or two later management revises it. Companies of any size need rules about who can make what level of decision, and standard occurrences need manuals and policy guidelines.

Poor Time Management

It is said that the average manager gets interrupted once every eight minutes. This means that even large tasks must be managed in less than eight minute segments and that the manager must be extremely disciplined about getting back on task after the interruption. Failure to do so is the most time-consuming consequence of interruptions.

Poor Communications Skills

Since the manager's results are manifested only through the work of his or her subordinates, then the ability to communicate clearly what one wants is crucial. This is discussed more fully in chapter 5.

Lack of Personal Accountability

Even though the manager delegates a task, he or she is still responsible for the result. If the delegatee failed to produce, it becomes the manager's responsibility, including finding a timely remedial action, so that the project can still be salvaged.

Failure to Develop, Train and Acknowledge People

A knowledgeable manager will often have a better understanding than his staff about what the proposed project should look like. Unless their people are given a chance to grow to the same level of knowledge, understanding, and initiative, the manager will not get results from them. More on how to "stretch" people is discussed below under "Delegation" and chapter 5 reviews training and recognition. Even modest performers need appreciation and acclaim.

Failure to Support Company Policy in Public

When talking to one's team, an attitude that says "we've got to do this even though we don't like it because the higher-ups say so" is very likely to engender reluctance rather than enthusiasm. Good managers express their reservations and concerns to bosses in private, and sometimes they are persuasive enough to get their way. If they lose the argument they support the boss's decision gracefully (or quit).

Failure to Acknowledge People's Workstyles

Numerous testing instruments divide people into four or more groups. Each group has a vastly different style of learning, working, and thinking. Effective bosses, regardless of their own style, identify the styles of their people and use this knowledge both in what they assign to whom and how they manage the assignees. A good manager knows this is the way to get the most out of everybody.

Failure to Focus on Profit

Ignorance of business results and lack of awareness about the comparative success of one's different products and services can be a major downfall. In most companies, sales and profits are the key objectives, and everything else undertaken must keep this in mind. Different workers may bring about profits in different ways; problems should be resolved primarily because lack of resolution will affect profits.

Failure to Recognize Needs People Meet from Working

Many studies about motivation indicate that people want to do a good job and to be shown greater challenges by a supportive boss. The manager who behaves unpredictably, or who manipulates people for his or her own ends, or who attempts to be a buddy with subordinates will generally create a counterproductive level of discomfort. By contrast, a boss who sets out clear expectations and plays fair will generally get more than adequate work from people.

Failure to Establish and Adhere to Standards

Standards permit all staff to be treated alike. In recurrent task areas, they must be established and then all violators treated the same way (see the discussion of the "red hot stove" rule in chapter 5). Incompetence must not be tolerated no matter who is the source.

Planning and Organizing

The Need for a Business Plan

The first two functions of management—planning and organization—are daily processes for the manager. Much can also be gained by formally structuring these processes into a written business plan. The aviation manager wears the many hats of the entrepreneur and does so in an organization that has more than the average number of different technical areas with varying levels of sophistication. The FBO manager must also cope with the very rapid rate of change that continually occurs in aviation. New equipment, changing regulations, advancing technology, and a volatile market all contribute to a rapidly changing environment.

A sound planning process is a necessity in this kind of environment. The effective utilization of a planning process becomes a way of life for the successful manager. Planning falls into two areas: objectives planning and operational planning. Objectives planning concerns the things the business owner wants to accomplish, and operational planning concerns the methods used to achieve them. Objectives planning deals with specific long- and short-range targets for the organization. It is the subject of the following paragraphs. Operational planning deals with the development of policy, procedures, rules, and standards used to run the business. This is the topic of chapter 6 entitled "Organization and Administration."

Some business owners will argue that in a changing world it is impossible to plan effectively, so it is better to simply seize opportunities as they present themselves and not formulate any kind of plan. Here are some considerations in relation to this approach:

1. If the business has not specifically selected a market niche, it will tend to pursue all opportunities without priority. Time and energy will be wasted pursuing activities that are not central to the company's strength areas. In the meantime, more valuable opportunities may be overlooked.
2. Customers who know the direction the company is going will tend to plan their own needs around the future availability of services. For example, a businessman thinking of learning to fly may choose a flight school based on the fact that starting next year it will be offering instrument instruction.
3. Customers who know your business and service area priorities will refer customers to you who need those services.
4. Setting ambitions through achievable goals is often a self-fulfilling prophecy. The very process of setting higher goals tends to shift the employees' "comfort zone" of what is attainable. Well thought-out goals seem to create a synergy of their own, and time after time, fortuitous occurrences will take place in support of these goals.
5. A business plan can be written for each and any new business project such as a new product line. Such analysis will help to make it very clear what time and money commitments will be needed to get the new line into place on a profitable basis.
6. Last but not least, any business that may ever need outside financing must have a written business plan in order to attract suitable lenders.

A business plan is only valuable if it is examined and evaluated frequently and its results compared to the original objectives. It is a living process, not a beautifully bound report on a shelf.

Most business experts place great emphasis on a written business plan. Even for a new company or one that is in a very volatile market, such as general aviation, it should be specific, written and made available to all managers, and periodically reviewed and updated. A suggested outline for a full business plan is shown in figure 2.1. The numbers after each section indicate the order in which to write the sections.

Mission Statement

The mission statement can be quite short such as the following:

- "To be the best quality repair, instruction, and flight service facility within a fifty-mile radius of xyz" or
- "To provide the lowest cost fuel and services and maximize transient traffic."

There can be different mission statements for each segment or profit center in the business. Another way of considering the mission statement is to answer the question "What business(es) am I in"? The functions enjoyed most by the owner may be neither the most needed nor the most profitable functions. The manager should consider why customers use aviation to meet their needs and whether the business is primarily service or product oriented. The mission statement should answer the questions "Who we are, what we do, and why we're different."

Values

The most successful businesses seem to be those that (1) stay close to the customer and (2) operate with real concern for employees.[4,5] A value statement combining these two concerns might be "Our top priority in xyz company is customer satisfaction, and our only means of achieving it is through each and every employee. We want happy employees so that we will have happy customers."

Other values could apply, such as quality, durability, reliability, speed of service, and friendliness. The important thing is to spell out the paramount value or values so that all members of the firm know what comes first. Companies with a strong "corporate culture" have a better chance of dealing with difficulties.

Market Niche and Goal

This part of the business plan should discuss the total market for the company's products or services, and the precise niche or segment of the market that this company hopes to serve. It will include whatever ways the company's products or services differ from those available elsewhere and should relate closely to the mission statement.

Company History and Background

This section, primarily for readers outside the company, can also be useful for orientation of new employees.

Industry Overview

The FBO may be in the mainstream of industry trends or may already have one or more specialty niches that are atypical of the industry. Periodic evaluation of major factors and trends affecting the whole industry are important. Also, it may be valuable to examine national economic and demographic trends that do NOT at first appear to have much to do with aviation, (e.g., the aging of the population). Some open-ended brainstorming on such issues may yield both threats and opportunities.

A. EXECUTIVE SUMMARY (12)
- —*Mission Statement*—definition of business purpose, product and market. Method of sales and distribution.
- —Values.
- —Brief description of management team.

For Seeking Capital or Loans:
- —Summary of financial projections.
- —Amount, form and purpose of money being sought.

B. COMPANY HISTORY AND BACKGROUND (10)
- —Date and state of inception, form of company.
- —Principals and functions of each.
- —General progress to date.
- —Successful strategies to date.
- —Most urgent issues to be addressed.
- —Other general context.

C. INDUSTRY OVERVIEW (2)
- —Current status and outlook for industry.
- —Specific industry-related issues (economic, social, technological, regulatory).
- —Areas of growth and opportunity.
- —Performance of primary participants.

D. PRODUCT(S) (1)
- —Description.
- —Research and development.
- —Future development.
- —Environmental factors.
- —Policies and warranties.

E. MARKETING ANALYSIS (3)
- —Market definition.
- —Market size.
- —Market trends.
- —Competition.
- —Competitive advantages/disadvantages.

F. MARKETING PLAN (4)
- —Potential target markets, estimated sales, market share.
- —Strategies.
- —Pricing.
- —Sales and distribution.
- —Suitable promotional methods and costs.
- —Promotional mix and total budget.
- —Evaluation/effectiveness plans.
- —Stationery, logos and image.

G. LEGAL REQUIREMENTS (9)
- —Legal structure of the business.
- —Licensing, trademarks, patents.
- —Certification.
- —Insurance.
- —Codes or zones affecting business.
- —Anticipated changes affecting business.
- —Company name.

H. PERSONNEL (6)
- —Number and type of employees.
- —Labor issues and compliance.
- —Sources of labor.
- —Changes anticipated.

I. OPERATIONS (7)
- —Location.
- —Plant and/or office facilities.
- —Equipment.
- —Methods of production and manufacture.

J. MANAGEMENT (5)
- —Organization.
- —Key people and resumés.
- —Strengths and weaknesses.
- —Professional advisors.

K. FINANCIAL INFORMATION (8)
- —Funding requested (if appropriate)
- —Desired financing.
- —Capitalization.
- —Use of funds.
- —Future financing needs.
- —Current financial statements.
- —Financial projections.

L. APPENDIXES (11)
1. Goals.
2. Objectives.
3. Functional Schedules, Gantt Charts, etc.
4. Information Systems.

Figure 2.1. Business plan outline. Courtesy: RODWELL/REDDINGTON, Seattle, WA.

Products

This section provides the opportunity to examine not just the present product and service mix, but also key technological, institutional, environmental, and market changes that may affect the product mix.

Marketing Analysis

The marketing analysis will likely be addressed separately for each product line. Some products and services may have a highly local market (e.g., a flight school). Others may have national markets, such as a maintenance shop certified to do major overhauls of specific types of aircraft engines.

Marketing Plan

Some new activities may not need much marketing. Perhaps something new is being offered based on "market research" in terms of customer feedback, which is an excellent way to find out what the existing client group wants. Then a way to market it may be simply to enclose a flyer with billings, tell each customer as they come in, and so on. But this will not develop a new clientele or sell a product if its need was identified in some other way. The choices of marketing and sales techniques are discussed more fully in chapter 3, and the precise approach will probably need to be developed on a case-by-case basis. It is useful to keep track of what worked or didn't in a promotional campaign so that the plan can be more finely honed the next time. Again, the plan requires segmentation into individual tasks with deadlines, quotas, and staff assignments.

Legal Requirements

In many cases, such as obtaining business licenses, legal requirements are a one-time process. However, the FBO should not assume that this is always so. A current example is the underground storage tank issue, where tough environmental requirements are causing FBOs (and others) to look very carefully at both past and future operations relating to fuel storage. The legal structure of the business should also be reexamined periodically as the business changes.

Personnel

Written organization charts and job descriptions are an important starting point, though in some cases they are only that. Staff in a small business may need to perform more than one job, and organizational structures are increasingly being supplemented by special task forces, quality circles, and the like. But even these more nebulous arrangements generally lend themselves to some kind of description and narrative. This topic is discussed more fully in chapter 6 "Organization and Administration" and chapter 5 "Human Resources."

Operations; Production Plan

This part of the business plan reviews physical requirements, supplies, materials, labor, office equipment, and other items needed to actually produce the goods and services. These areas are reviewed more fully in chapters 8 through 10 and in chapter 12. Plans describe the overall functions of each division of the firm, and tasks describe individual work assignments to that end.

Management

This may include a review of key people, strengths and weaknesses, and include on-going resources available such as a financial or management consultant used on retainer. These topics are crucial to any business plan seeking outside investment, but should not be ignored if the business plan is for internal use only.

Management information can have other uses such as selling company services to a major corporation and in public relations. A small brochure may be appropriate, especially one separate from the rest of the business plan document.

Ownership information may or may not be appropriate in a plan to be shared with all employees; in any case, it requires some consideration, especially in a very small and/or family-owned business where the sudden absence of key people might cause the firm to flounder. The succession needs to be spelled out clearly, and key-person insurance may be a consideration.[6]

Financial Information

In some cases it may be desirable to set up a financial plan for a period of 20 or 30 years, if this is the length of a new FBO lease or the anticipated retirement date of the owner. In other cases, a five-year period may be sufficient. In a new business, particularly one that is seeking financing, the first year should be presented on a month-by-month basis.[7] In the case of a new project or firm, the financial plan should include a profit-and-loss statement, a balance sheet showing assets and liabilities, and a cash-flow analysis showing the break-even time. This will also show the cumulative amount of cash needed before a positive cash flow begins. Another useful feature of the financial plan can be criteria for new expenditures (e.g., those related to production or sales volume). These topics are discussed more fully in chapter 4 "Profits, Cash Flow, and Financing."

Strategy and Objectives

For a long-established firm, the strategy for becoming established in a market niche may already have been accomplished. However, new market opportunities arise constantly; and if a decision is made to pursue them, a strategy is needed. The strategy statement must discuss the new product in terms of its features, benefits, and pricing, its means of production, the sales and promotional activity, and the cost of getting it launched. Setting objectives means choosing specific, measurable targets with dates attached.

Growth Strategy

Once the target level of activity is reached for a product or service, several growth strategies are possible for successive time periods. For example, the sequence or choice of strategies might be:

1. No growth. (Note that in a growth market this means declining market share.)
2. Maintenance of market share—growth at the pace of the total market.
3. Growth to a specific, higher dollar volume or market share by a certain year, with annual rates of growth till then.
4. Growth till some perceived point of diminishing returns. For example, a repair shop might grow only until utilization of the repair hangar reaches the maximum point, yet stopping short of the expense of a new hangar.

Growth will be limited by the competition, national trends in aviation, and by the business cycle. A detailed growth strategy will need to look carefully at the actual and potential profitability of each service or product, which is a topic discussed more fully in chapter 4 "Profits, Cash Flow, and Financing."

Functional Schedules

In the appendix section it may be appropriate to develop more detailed schedules than in the main text of the business plan by using PERT and Gantt charts as well as matrices that show the assignments of staff to tasks.

Information Systems

The best plan in the world is of little value if there is no way of telling whether it is being successfully implemented. Information on the competition, industry sales, new clients acquired, costs, productivity, profit by area, promotion results, and so on must be collected regularly and organized into quickly usable formats. As when flying a plane, the quicker you know you are off course, the easier it is to get back. And the sooner you know that turbulent times are ahead, the easier it is to enact contingency plans that will keep you safely aloft. This subject is reviewed in depth in chapter 7 "Information Systems."

Directing and Controlling

Managing Versus Doing

Poor delegation is probably the typical manager's greatest weakness when it comes to the second two management functions—directing and controlling. The more one is a manager, the more one must obtain results through others and the less by doing things oneself. And yet, some technical knowledge and interest in specific aviation activities is what brings a person into the business, and indeed, equips them to delegate with some knowledge about what it takes to do the job.

Most individuals start off in the working world by acquiring a technical skill or specialty. Most FBO managers start with an interest in aviation and some professional qualifications. Their career track may have included being a corporate pilot, mechanic, flight instructor, aircraft production worker, or simply a private pilot and aviation enthusiast. When the opportunity came along, they moved into managerial positions, either as owners or employees. Such a move required that they begin performing different activities, such as planning, organizing, directing and controlling the work of others, rather than doing wholly technical or line activities. In an FBO this tends to mean more office work and less time in a plane or a hangar. This changing role requirement is illustrated in figure 2.2.

Studies of successful and unsuccessful managers indicate that the successful ones are paying close attention to planning, organizing, directing, and controlling others. The less successful ones are spending most of their time doing other things.[7,8] In a 1960s study by the Small Business Administration, the success of a business was found to be in direct proportion to the owner's possession of these talents:[9]

- Alertness to change
- Ability to adjust or to create change oneself
- Ability to attract and hold competent workers
- 180-degree vision with respect to operating details
- Knowledge of the market—customers and their needs

A difficulty for the FBO manager in a very small firm, one with ten people or less, is that he or she never will be able to devote 100 percent of the time solely to managing, but must generally spend part of the time in line functions. This is because of the long hours most FBOs must be available and the mixed array of services they offer. Managers in such a position may need to consciously divide each day into "doing" and "managing" times and make sure that the precious and limited managerial time is assigned to top-priority issues.

Style of Delegation

There are many styles of delegation, and any that gets both short- and long-range results is successful. Much has been written about whether the autocratic or the democratic approach is most suitable. The choices appear to be on a spectrum, as follows:

- The manager makes a decision and announces it
- The manager "sells" a decision
- The manager presents ideas/decisions and invites questions
- The manager presents a tentative decision subject to change
- The manager presents the problem, gets suggestions, and then makes his or her decision

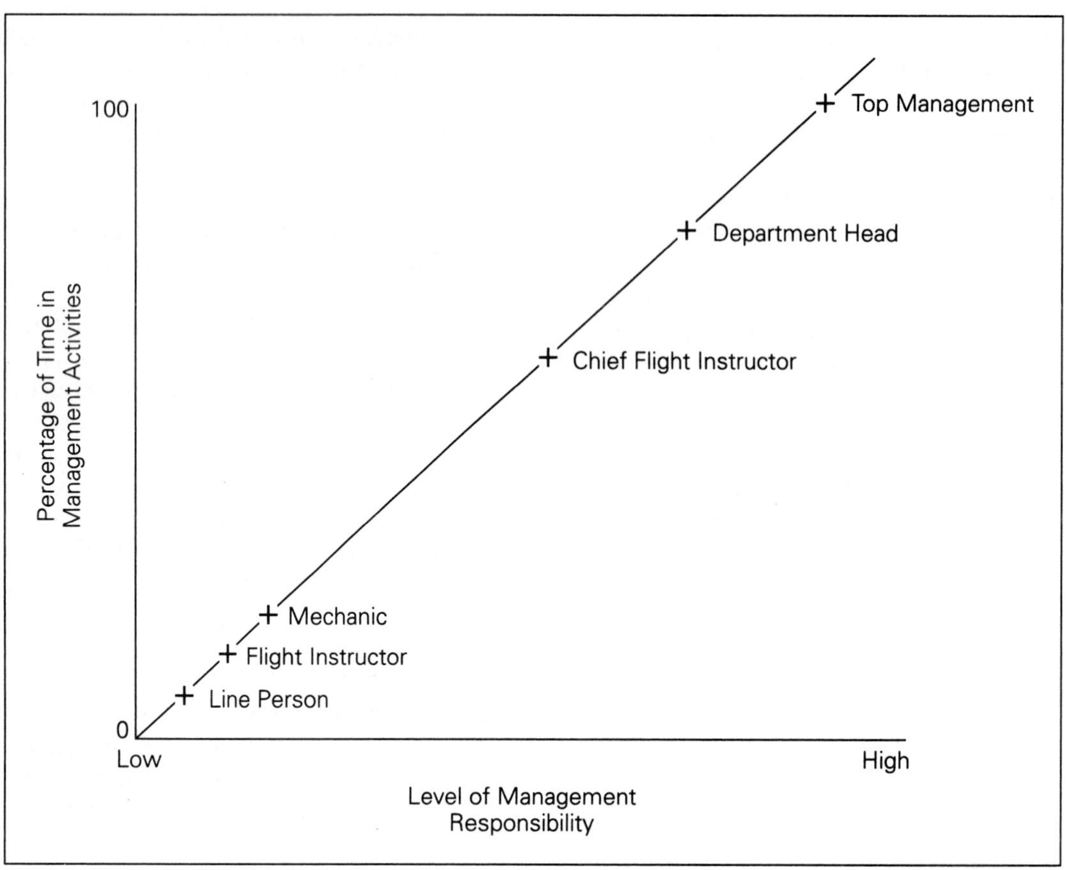

Figure 2.2. Managing versus doing.

In general, U.S. management appears to have shifted from the autocratic toward the participatory during the past three decades.

Objectives of Delegation

An autocratic view of management might be described as one set up with only the manager's immediate personal needs in mind; thus, its objective is mainly to free the manager's time for other important tasks. The staff is to do the manager's bidding, preferably carrying out tasks as closely as possible to the manner in which the manager would carry them out. This manager is happier the more closely his or her subordinates are able to function as "clones."

Another perspective is that "freeing up" the manager is only one of the purposes of delegation. A fuller list of the purposes of delegation includes:

- Leaving the details to others
- Getting the job done
- Allowing key management staff to take initiative
- Keeping things going in the boss's absence

- Raising the level of employee motivation
- Increasing the readiness of subordinates to accept change
- Improving the quality of all managerial decisions
- Developing teamwork and morale
- Furthering the individual development and growth in skills of employees

The degree of delegation depends on the level of skill available, the central or peripheral nature of the task, its urgency, and the manager's other priorities.

Managerial Control

Delegation of responsibility for a task does not mean giving away control or accountability. A manager in delegating work must:

- Spread the work realistically among available aides
- See to it that the job is done correctly
- Have enough time to take corrective action should something go wrong
- Develop the subordinates' talents and abilities

To accomplish these ends, a process of auditing the progress of the task is needed, but without constantly peering over the person's shoulder or being rigid about how the task is done. Choices for keeping track include:

- Verbal reporting at prearranged points or dates
- Written reports on progress
- Scheduled conferences
- Setting deadlines for results
- Checking results
- Measuring results in related areas (e.g., changes in the number of complaints)

When the task is clear from the outset, product inspection and deadlines, with some intermediate status reporting, may be successful. When the task itself still requires definition, the manager may assign various specific tasks to different people and schedule a conference at some reasonable future date to decide what the problem is and to design and assign a course of action. In the case of new problems or new employees, where untrodden ground is to be covered, it is advisable to delegate only small, highly specific tasks with short deadlines. Then one can evaluate quite soon the person's response to the issue, and whether supervision and other expertise is needed. Throwing people into the deep end to see how they do is usually unproductive and demoralizing. Also, it is easier to gradually give out more responsibility based on good results than it is to take it away once it has been given.

Choosing the Areas to Delegate

One of the most crucial questions for a small business is what areas to delegate on a consistent basis. Lower level managers constantly encounter the need for decisions ranging from a trivial to a serious nature. They would consume your entire day with questions if they did not have some basic guidelines. The general level of responsibility given to line managers must be tailored to each company, but some possible criteria include:

- The owner approves all decisions relating to spending the company's money (e.g., overtime, new promotions, equipment, or all decisions above some modest amount).
- The owner is the final decision maker on hiring and firing, or at least above a certain level of management.
- The owner decides about new services to be offered.
- The owner makes or approves all public statements to the media, politicians, and so on.

Do's and Don'ts of Delegation

One of the biggest complaints of managers is that they cannot "get the monkey off their back," that is, the task delegated to a subordinate is brought right back and for various reasons becomes the manager's problem again. Successful delegation requires that the delegatee actually perform most if not all of the delegated task. How can this be accomplished? One useful rule-of-thumb is the 85:15 rule. Delegate tasks to people who are 85 percent ready to handle them. Give clear instructions and establish mechanisms and timelines for checking how things are going. There will seldom be anyone who is 100 percent capable of doing the task. The autocratic manager *knows* that he or she is the *only* one really competent to do it. At 85 percent readiness, the person will handle most of the assignment, will grow in the process, will ask some questions, and will generally advance to virtually 100 percent readiness for next time. At 50 percent readiness, a person will be intimidated, overwhelmed, anxious, ask for help, and may make serious mistakes—or do nothing until right before the deadline. It is the manager's business to know how ready each employee is for specific new functions. Figure 2.3 offers some do's and don'ts for successful delegation.

The Decision-making Process

In an established enterprise where basic authority has been clearly delegated to certain people for certain things, few if any questions should arise about who should decide what. Indeed, nothing but routine decisions should be taking place. Such periods of stasis are, however, the exception rather than the rule in small businesses and in aviation businesses in particular. The need to react frequently to rapidly changing conditions is what one author considers the crucial difference between entrepreneurs and executives. (The latter are characterized as having a custodial role and temperament while caring for an existing empire.)[10]

A sound decision-making process involves seven steps:

1. Setting company goals and objectives as a context for the decision.
2. Diagnosing the problem or issue precisely —not the symptoms, but the causes.
3. Collecting and analyzing data about the problem or issue.
4. Developing an array of possible alternative solutions, including a do-nothing option. Through brainstorming, mindmapping, and the like, use the rule that "all ideas are good" at this stage.
5. Evaluating and weighing the pros and cons of each alternative, quantifying wherever possible, and perhaps combining elements of several alternatives into a new one.
6. Selecting and implementing the alternative(s) that best fit(s) with objectives and solve the problem.
7. Feedback—did it really work?

The manager may choose to involve the staff in all or none of these stages, depending on his or her theories of effectiveness. However, the numerous studies of group dynamics in recent years, coupled with motivational analysis, suggest that much better results will be obtained by involving key personnel in the process. They may have other interpretations of the performance data so that the problem may ultimately be defined quite differently. Their staffs may need to be enlisted to help gather better data on the problem, requiring both an understanding of what is going on and a time commitment. The process of developing alternatives almost always goes through several iterations. The manager might develop what he or she considers to be a complete array of possibilities and in a management conference find new options proposed. Similarly, when everyone has digested the issues and perhaps chatted with outsiders (e.g., with spouses and customers if appropriate) and presented the

Do's and Don'ts of Deregulation

1. Select the right person for the job. Don't just dump it on the first person that comes to mind. The right person will depend on how urgent the job is and whether you can afford the time to give the assignment to a less experienced employee. Urgent tasks must usually be assigned to old hands.
2. Set the climate for a comfortable briefing. Don't delegate on the run. Encourage the delegatee to ask questions.
3. Encourage the free flow of information. Don't forget to impart everything you know about the assignment, including any existing materials.
4. Focus on the results, the *what.* Don't stress the *how,* unless there's absolutely only one right way.
5. Delegate through dialogue. Don't do all the talking yourself.
6. Set firm deadlines, both interim and final. Don't leave due dates uncertain but work them out with delegatee's input, given other projects and plans. Interim dates allow time to rescue the project if necessary.
7. Be certain the person is pointed toward all the necessary resources. Don't leave them wondering where to start.
8. Turn over the entire job to one person. Don't give bits of it to several different people.
9. Give the person the full authority to do the job and make this clear to others through staff meetings, memos, and phone calls to peers in other departments. Don't set them up to fail.
10. Offer guidance without interfering. Don't fail to point out the minefields. Don't cross wires by making your own contacts with people you have told the delegatee to talk to.
11. Establish a system of controls beforehand. Don't do it as an afterthought. A written week by week schedule is desirable.
12. Support your people if they need help or in disputes. Don't leave them to succeed or fail on their own.
13. Follow up along the way. Set the task up to minimize surprises. Don't wait until deadline day to see if the job is done.
14. Give credit to the delegatee for a job well done. Put his or her name on the cover of the report; take him or her to the meeting with higher-ups to present the work, and praise the person to your bosses. Don't hog the glory.
15. The "Rodwell Rule" of delegation: to give away each and every task which someone on your staff is 85% ready to handle. Reserve for yourself only the tasks that you alone can do.

Figure 2.3. Do's and Don'ts of Delegation.

options to their own departments, it is almost a certainty that constructive and creative new alternatives and subalternatives will spring up on any big issue. In the task of quantifying the pros and cons of the possibilities, the staff's time and understanding may be needed. The manager may reserve the final selection of the best alternative; but if this is after a participatory process, then everyone will know why it is being done, why certain alternatives were rejected, and what is going to be involved. In this context it will be much easier to delegate the plan's implementation successfully.

The decision-making process just described can be accomplished in five minutes or five months, depending on the complexity and importance of the issue. One of its most difficult elements is the second step—being sure one has properly identified the problem, and one is not just treating symptoms. It is essential to define the root cause. Treating only the symptoms will not remove the problem. It is suggested that the problem-solving team seek to isolate the critical factor that has to be changed, moved, or removed before anything else can be accomplished.

The process of developing alternatives does not imply that these are necessarily "exclusive" possibilities. More likely they are "program packages" of compatible solutions to related issues. The selected alternative may include program elements from several other alternatives, as long as the program as a whole is internally consistent.

Decision-making Tools

Some decision-making tools are straightforward and commonsense applications of knowledge in an aviation business. Figure 2.4 depicts some typical problem areas and available techniques for decision making.

Other tools are more complex. The field of operations research is devoted to the study of management problem-solving tools. A few of the basic types of approach are summarized here.

Sampling theory involves the use of random samples to represent the population being considered. Sampling techniques can be of great value in an aviation business to conduct surveys of customer opinion regarding service, products, or potential business. Other applications include the sampling of inventory, work activity, or production quality.

Time distribution can be a useful piece of data when examining staffing shifts and hours of operation. Arrival time, service time, average wait time, maximum parking accumulation, and similar time-related data sampled over different days of the week and seasons can be a great help in making decisions about the best allocation of resources. A sign at the front desk about peak times of the week (as is done by the postal service) can even help customers with choices about their schedules.

Simulation of scenarios can be useful, particularly with today's microcomputers (but even manually for certain issues). Simulation of scenarios alters one factor at a time in an analysis to examine "what-ifs." For example, an analysis of acquiring a new aircraft might examine the consequences of different interest rates on monthly repayments. A drop in prices could be tested using different assumptions about elasticity to see what would happen to revenue in worst- and best-case situations. Using a computer, models can be built to test the results of changing several variables at once.

Decide Something!

"Not to decide is to decide," as the saying goes. That is, the world will not stand still even if you do—there will be changes to deal with as a result of not making a decision. This generally seems to hold true except for the most compulsive type of manager, who may benefit once in a while from letting things run their course for a few days. Serendipity sometimes steps in and resolves things without any action on the manager's part. However, even this approach means

Areas	Typical Problems	Available Techniques for Decision-Making
1. Human Resources	Selecting personnel	Application blanks, interviewing guides, tests, reference checks, job specifications, job descriptions.
	Evaluating employee performance	Job requirements, performance appraisal system and forms.
	Compensating employees	Job evaluation program, job surveys, performance appraisal system.
	Disciplining employees	Clear rules and regulations, positive discipline environment, progressive discipline system, grievance procedure.
	Organizing work activity	Organization chart, manual; planning goals, organization.
2. Financial	Determining profitability	Financial information system, financial analysis, goals and objectives.
	Capital investment problem	Analysis by pay-back, rate of return, present value, company investment requirements.
	Departmental development and control	Goals and objectives, budget, analysis of activity.
	Cash requirements	Cash budget, short-term loan source.
	Accounts receivable	Credit policies, credit application, account aging process, collection procedure.
3. Material	Supplies on hand Pricing material Maintaining physical assets	Inventory system, information system, goals and objectives. Pricing policy, pricing guidelines and procedures. Maintenance policy, preventive maintenance procedure.
4. Aviation Operations	Marketing activity level	Company goals and objectives, economic situation, product requirements, outside assistance with promotion.
	Flight activity guidelines	Operating procedure manual, pilot training and flight standards.
	Maintenance quality control	Statement of policy, guidelines and procedures, inspection check lists, inspector personnel.
	Fuel contamination	Company policy, rules, procedures, fuel sampling, clear markings, training.
	Safety	Policy statement, rules, regulations and procedures,reinforcement and recognition, involvement.

Figure 2.4. Practical decision tools for the aviation manager.

making a decision to address the issue next week, if it hasn't been resolved.

Time Management

"Work expands so as to fill the time available for its completion," says Parkinson's First Law. "Granted that work (and especially paperwork) is thus elastic in its demands on time, it is manifest that there need be little or no relationship between the work to be done and the size of the staff to which it may be assigned."[11]

While written in a whimsical vein, there is a very large measure of truth to these remarks. The converse is also true: an urgent project always seems to be done by the deadline no matter how few people are assigned to it. Witness how even the most lethargic organization always gets its paychecks out on time.

Sources of Time-management Problems

Various studies and books available on time management seem to agree on the key causes of problems:[12,13,14]

- Procrastination—because you dislike a task or it is overwhelming
- Telephone and other interruptions
- Failure to get back to the task being done before the interruption
- Meetings—too many, too long, too unspecific, no agenda
- Reports—too many, too many contributors, too long
- Unplanned visitors
- Lack of delegation; poor delegation
- Failure to make decisions on incoming items
- Preoccupation with operational crises rather than preventive activities
- Special requests—interruptions without adequate warning
- Delays
- Too much unfocused reading
- Lack of priorities

Learning to plan time is one of the tasks that all workers need to do, but managers need it most because they are not on a production line with tasks coming at them constantly, but rather must exercise a choice about how to spend every minute of the day.

Time Management Strategies

Clear delegation is the best means of gaining time. Moreover, all tasks should be delegated that someone else can handle, whether or not they can do them quite as fast, quite as well, or in exactly the same way as the manager would. As the mother whose three-year-old washed the supper dishes every night said, "Sure I could do it faster, but she enjoys it and has a sense of achievement; besides, it frees me up to do the things a three-year-old can't do, such as paying bills or vacuuming." It pains many managers immensely to delegate to people they sometimes feel have the competence of a three-year-old, but as long as the job gets done, the manager can get on with something else that *only* he or she can do. Also, the person given a task slightly ahead of their skill level will learn, feel pride, and be ready for even more difficult assignments.

Other recommended methods of better managing time include:

- Plan each day's activities; don't just stumble through.
- Use a "tickler" file to keep papers relating to future dates and projects.
- Sort tasks into priority 1, 2, and 3. Aim to do two to three top priority tasks a day. Many of the 2s and 3s will simply disappear.
- Work out six to seven goals with your manager.
- List the tasks that relate to the goals, along with start and finish dates.
- Transfer tasks on to "today's to-do" list when their start date arrives.
- Keep a notebook, pack of index cards, or pad for ideas or things to remember.

- Eliminate avoidable distractions—set up a routine where someone working for you handles them.
- Identify the long-winded, and set up short times to speak to them (e.g., just before a meeting or shift end).
- Communicate with "chatterers" in writing instead of orally and have them do the same to you.
- Use a desk needle for messages and calls to be returned/responded.
- Manage by wandering around and asking questions—forestall problems before they develop.
- Don't interrupt others but plan your use of their time.
- Stick to one task until it's done; try not to interrupt yourself.
- Keep your bosses posted on your results before they have to chase you down and ask you.
- Make sure your employees know their authority and discretion.
- Set up a section/division procedures manual so everyone knows what they should be doing and who to go to for help.
- Handle paperwork only once.
- Use the phone instead of going to see people.
- Use a written checklist for shift transfer issues.
- Set up "red flags" for certain personnel on things they *must* get help on.
- Graduate your people to fewer "red flags" as they learn new skills.
- Take advantage of the POSITIVE side of deadline pressure by getting adrenaline going and allowing less time for others to change their minds.
- For tasks that are done well under deadline pressure, set up more (artificial) deadlines to increase productivity.
- If a task *has* to be stopped in the middle, try to leave it where you know exactly what you were going to do next; write yourself a note.
- Do standardizable tasks in a standardized way.
- Coordinate errands and tasks together whenever possible.
- Delegate all possible tasks and set up reporting-back arrangements.
- Set goals for your people with check-up dates.
- Personal prime time—identify your best working time.
- Don't put in too long at one stretch on high priority tasks.
- Do low priority tasks at low-output periods of the day.
- Work somewhere else on key projects.
- If unable to reach a decision, examine the need for more information and delegate getting it.
- Divide overwhelming projects into small pieces and delegate parts.
- Do a first, appealing, or random small task on a big project to develop momentum and ideas and to get over the intimidation.
- Set intermediate milestones for big projects and acknowledge getting there.
- Identify why you are putting off a project and tackle the cause.
- Make all projects as simple as possible to get the job done—remember OPPORTUNITY COST.
- To get you started, do the task first that you like best; it'll be easier then to do the distasteful part.
- Use small parcels of time (e.g., while waiting to see someone) to check lists, add to lists, write someone a note, brainstorm a new assignment.
- Be assertive—assert the right to refuse more assignments.
- Exercise telephone discipline; be task-oriented.
- Reduce paper flow to essentials. Handle correspondence only once, including assigning it to someone else.
- Be selective in reading.

- Utilize travel time for catching up on projects.
- Finish one thing before starting another.
- Relax and recharge occasionally by attending conferences and meetings away from the office.
- Limit your reinvolvement in tasks already delegated.
- Use your worst times of the day for trivial matters and low priority items.
- Work somewhere else on key projects, away from the phone and visitors.
- Block out time several times weekly when you don't take calls or visitors except in dire emergencies. (If you were out of the office at a business meeting, people would put up with not being able to reach you, so be adamant.)
- Break big projects down into small manageable steps; delegate some parts.
- Write less and use the phone more. Not only do you get instant feedback, but some things are better floated as trial balloons without being committed to paper.
- If you get stuck in a useless meeting, work on something else.
- Don't go to meetings with ineffective chairpersons.
- Since meetings can be considerable time-wasters, meeting management skills should be a goal of everyone who ever has to call a meeting. Figure 2.5 shows meeting management pointers.

1. Don't hold a general meeting if two individuals can resolve the issue together.
2. Prepare a written agenda, get it out ahead of time, identify topics and OBJECTIVES of meeting on these topics. Consider specifying the time to be spent on each agenda item. Ask for missing items when the meeting begins, but reserve the right to save them for another time.
3. Call people 48 hours before the meeting to
   a. Remind them of time and place
   b. Refresh their memory on their role
   c. Ask for any other agenda items from them.
4. Substantial handouts should be distributed by the person responsible for that agenda item, BEFORE the meeting. Be sure any needed audiovisual aids are working properly.
5. Start on time. Have someone else take minutes. Record those present and absent in the minutes. Don't allow side conversations. End on time!
6. Listen to input but firmly steer discussion back to the subject if it wanders. Give the talkers tasks to do; invite involvement of the quiet ones.
7. Take action on every item, even if the action is not final. Assign responsibility for more research, for example, with products and deadlines.
8. Keep meetings to no more than one hour and specify finish time on agenda.
9. Use a place with no chairs to speed up meetings, if necessary.
10. Get minutes out promptly; highlight each recipient's new tasks and deadlines.
11. If votes are required or other formal protocol, establish rules (*Robert's Rules of Order*, for example).

Figure 2.5. Meeting management.

Summary

Management is defined as getting things done through others. It therefore involves the planning, organizing, directing, and controlling the work of others. A business plan can help the manager lay out the long-range activities and rationale of the business. The plan will contain many elements of the manager's job. In so doing, he or she is constrained by time in how much "doing" takes place. In a small business a manager wears many hats and spends significant portions of time delivering the goods or services of the business; however, this activity should be delegated as much as possible. Various styles of delegation and levels of decision making are available. The manager by these choices effects good or poor use of not only his or her own time, but also the time of all the staff.

Discussion Topics

1. Describe the manner in which a manager's functions will change as he or she advances up the promotion ladder.
2. Tasks should be delegated to the most junior staffer remotely capable of handling them. Discuss.
3. What subjects should a business plan cover? Why?
4. What are the pros and cons of preparing/ not preparing a written business plan?
5. What are some of the choices about styles of delegation? How should a manager set about deciding which to use?
6. What are the pros and cons of decision making by consensus?
7. What are the greatest causes of time mismanagement? How can they be dealt with?

Chapter 3
Marketing

Introduction
- Need for Marketing in Aviation
- Definition of Marketing
- Natural Markets
- Marketing Orientation

Market Research
- National Trends
- Understanding the Local Aviation Market
- General Aviation Organizations
- Forecasting Techniques and the Individual FBO
- Customer Needs and Identification of New Prospects

Product and Service Definition
- Total Product
- Product Classification
- The Competition
- Market Niche

Price
- Cost-based
- Demand-based
- Elasticity
- Pricing Policy

Place
- Location
- Distribution Systems

Promotion
- Advertising
- Direct Mail
- Referrals
- Institutional Promotion
- Consulting as a Promotional Tool

Sales
- Needs Assessment
- Alternatives
- Closing
- Collecting

Marketing Controls
- Marketing Plan
- Performance Evaluation
- Quality Control
- Contribution Analysis
- Budgeting
- Information Systems

Integrated Marketing
Marketing the Airport
Summary
Discussion Topics

Objectives

- ✔ Describe the reasons why a marketing plan aimed at the mass market would not be beneficial to an FBO manager.
- ✔ Understand how forecasting techniques are utilized, differentiating between controlled and uncontrolled factors.
- ✔ Show how businesses must be able to identify new prospects and relate that to customer needs.
- ✔ Discuss the differences between cost-based and demand-based pricing.
- ✔ Realize the importance of location and promotion to a marketing strategy.
- ✔ Describe three elements of distribution and how they function.

Introduction

Need for Marketing in Aviation

The aviation industry has evolved from being an experimental, exploratory, and record-setting sport into being an important element in everyday business. In its early years, the excitement created by air travel and its stunts was often enough to attract huge crowds of patrons. In today's world, the FBO cannot wait for people to come to the business; he or she must seek them out. If the customers are business travelers, they will constantly be evaluating other travel modes such as the scheduled airlines and the automobile. If they are recreational flyers, many nonaviation activities compete for their support and dollars.

Nor is the FBO in the position of having a captive audience. If the service is unfriendly or the desired fuel is not available, a pilot will certainly fly to another airport next time. Within metropolitan areas, studies have shown that pilots will travel some distance to hangar or tie down their aircraft at a favored field.

Aviation businesses must continually seek to improve their marketing skills if the business is to prosper. The most effective companies in the United States spend a good deal of time "staying close to the customer." A suggestion box may tend to gather only complaints, whereas training each and every employee to invite feedback will generate more discussion and ideas of a positive nature. Aviation customers, especially those who travel a good deal, are also excellent sources of information on innovations being tried elsewhere.

The entire business strategy must hinge upon anticipated sales. The money to run the business, make improvements, and to expand comes from gross sales. A realistic sales forecast must rest upon a planned schedule of daily and weekly marketing activities.

Modern aviation businesses are learning something the hard way: a specific marketing plan and its timely implementation are essential to a healthy business. This is an area of expertise where the manager and employees should be continually exploring and experimenting. Marketing is still as much an art as a science, and what works for one business or product may not work for another.

Definition of Marketing

Marketing, as treated in this chapter, covers the entire process of identifying customer needs, purchasing or producing goods and services to meet those needs, determining the price and place to dispense the items, prospecting, promotion, and selling. In short, it deals with the four Ps: product, price, place, and promotion.

The marketing function in a company may be handled by the owner/manager, or it may be handled by each department. For example, the maintenance manager might be responsible for planning sales in his area and the used aircraft manager might be responsible in his area, and so on. In a large company, the marketing function may be handled by a separate department, as shown in figure 3.1.

Whether these functions are handled by one individual as a part-time responsibility, or whether they are each handled by a separate person, they are all necessary functions in the marketing area.

FBOs are unusual in a number of ways. First, their entire function depends heavily on a piece of infrastructure over which they often have little or no control—the airport runway. Without this facility, there could be no FBO business. Its quality affects the FBO customers, even though there may be no direct quality control on the part of the FBO.

Second, FBOs are sellers of both products and services, and both types of goods encompass a wide array of choices. Even the smallest FBO generally caters to a variety of perhaps incompatible market segments (e.g., the corporate chief executive taking a charter and the euphoric six-

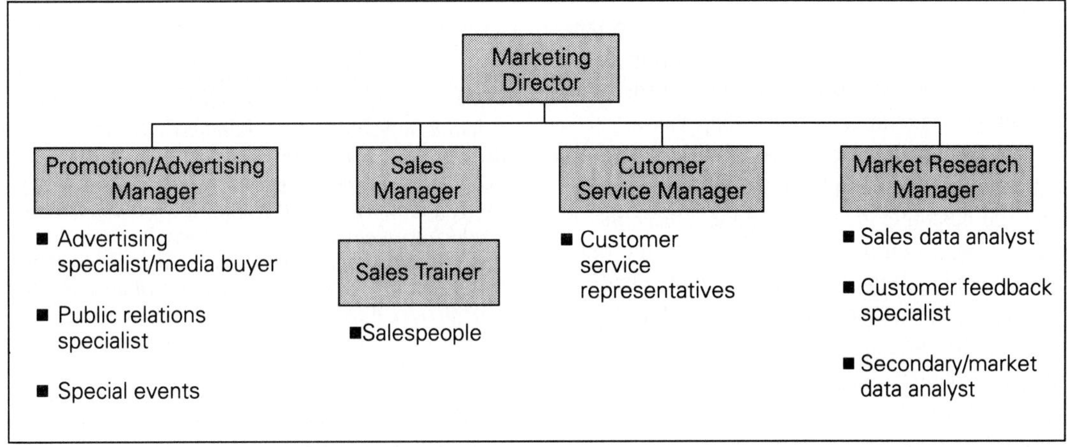

Figure 3.1. Typical marketing department—organization.

teen-year-old in half a T-shirt who has just soloed). The ambience and facilities of the FBO must accommodate both of these ends of the spectrum and an array of markets in between.

Since services are one product of an FBO, the word "product" is generally used here to refer to both products and services.

Natural Markets

One marketing expert describes the world as being generally divided into three markets:

1. The mass market—the 80 percent of the population that has discretionary income.
2. The young, upwardly mobile urban professional ("yuppy") market—about 25 percent of the population.
3. Certain cultural subgroups or the wealthy (over $100,000 household income; highly specialized markets); two percent or less of the population.[1]

Each of these market groups lends itself to different types of promotion.

What, therefore, is the FBO's natural market using this market division? An evaluation of some of the national statistics suggests that FBOs must generally target both the 2 percent market and the 25 percent market. The typical FBO is less likely to tap the mass market. The 2 percent market figure is derived from the fact that only a small percentage (about 0.3 percent) of the whole population are actually pilots. About one person in a thousand owns an aircraft.

The 25 percent market is derived from the fact that nonpilots traveling by air are thought to use general aviation about one quarter of the time.[2]

By contrast, mass markets and mass marketing techniques may simply not be appropriate for FBO businesses. The FBO is in the custom-tailoring business, at least on the service side, so that each client is treated differently and has different needs met.

Marketing Orientation

Having a *marketing orientation* in a business means running the entire business with a *focus on the customer*.[3] It is a viewpoint that recognizes the dependence of the business upon customers and the sale of products or services to them. The manager without a marketing orientation makes no real effort to attract customers and by many subtle indications actually suggests that customers go elsewhere. Such a manager's employees are likely to be reinforcing the same message. The manager with a marketing orientation is totally conscious of customers, their needs, and what it will take to attract and keep them.

Such a manager recognizes that the business depends upon sales and that the first step is getting the customer inside the door. Once inside and facing a company representative, the customer should continue to experience the positive marketing orientation of the business all the way through the conclusion of the sale and in subsequent encounters. The marketing-oriented manager sees to it that every single one of his or her employees behaves likewise, whether their job calls for dealing with customers and whether they know all the answers customers want.

Market Research

National Trends

Every FBO needs to be aware of national trends in aviation. Air travel is generally a "derived" demand and triggered by some other purpose rather than being an end. This means FBOs also need to be aware of overall business and recreational trends and competing products. Aviation tends to be substantially affected by the health of the overall economy. This suggests that if possible the mix of goods and services should be counter-recessionary in part (e.g., emphasizing the used—rather than new—aircraft market in lean times). The service department could likewise emphasize engine overhaul and rebuilding rather than the maintenance of new engines.

It would be impossible to review here the entire economy from the FBO standpoint; moreover, regional variations make such a task of doubtful value at the national level. However, the general aviation picture nationally is both well documented and a useful guide to local trends.

The Federal Aviation Administration's annual national forecasts in 1988 provided the following overview of general aviation trends:

"The general aviation industry is undergoing deep and broad structural changes. There are indications that the long-term growth of the active fleet and activity will be slowing down. For the past nine years, general aviation shipments have continuously declined from a peak of 17,811 units in 1978 to 1,495 in 1986. The major independent manufacturers have been taken over by conglomerates. Cessna and Piper have suspended production of most of their piston-engine aircraft. For the forseeable future, the large general aviation manufacturers will focus on the production of turbine-powered aircraft. Further, a majority of the companies have significantly reduced their work forces and consolidated plants. The decline in aircraft sales is complemented by decreasing numbers of private pilots. Between 1980 and 1985, the number of private pilots declined from 343,300 to 305,700. Between 1980 and 1985, the number of student pilots declined each year from 210,200 to 146,652. In 1986, however, the number of student pilots increased to 150,273.

"Foreign competition, here and abroad, has also created problems for the U.S. manufacturers. Foreign producers are making inroads into domestic markets, while exports experienced a protracted period of decline. Exports fell from 3,995 in 1979 to 354 in 1985, a yearly rate of decline of 33.0 percent. However, after declining for seven years, exports registered a 24.3 percent increase in 1986 totalling 440 units. The lower value of the U.S. dollar may be partially responsible for finally seeing some recovery in the export market. Ultimately, the shrinking stock of pilots and the slowing in the expansion of the general aviation fleet will reduce the rate of growth of activity at FAA facilities.

"General aviation has, to date, failed to respond to the current economic recovery, one of the most robust of the postwar period. Historically, the economic cycle of the general aviation industry has closely paralleled that of the national economy. The theories about the reasons for the decline in sales and pilots are diverse. Some cite high aircraft prices and the availability of low cost alternatives such as ultralights. Others hypothesize that high operating costs and interest rates have been responsible for depressing the industry. Still others allege that the changes in the tax laws and high product liability costs are responsible. To be sure, each one of these factors has had some effect. Numerous studies that have been conducted by the Office of Aviation Policy and Plans, by universities, and by the industry have shown that many of the economic factors cited above have outweighed the positive effects of a growing economy.

"Although the economics of the industry are important in affecting people's choices, we cannot overlook the fact that we may also be experiencing a fundamen-

tal change in the tastes and preferences of the population. In the long run, this could be more destabilizing and have a larger adverse impact on general aviation than the negative economic factors that have plagued the economic equations that have held for many years for the industry. If this phenomenon is occuring, then falling prices, operating costs, and real interest rates, accompanied by economic growth, may not be sufficient to revive the market. As a nation becomes wealthier, households can afford to pay the higher prices of specialized items, and a proliferation of varieties generally takes place. This intensifies the competition in specific types of markets. During the recent strong economic recovery, the demand for recreational flying in conventional aircraft has been rapidly declining, while the demand for relatively expensive cars, homes, and boats has been expanding. This lost market may be difficult to recover even if the economic forces shift in favor of aviation."[4]

In numerical terms, anticipated national growth is shown in figures 3.2, 3.3 and 3.4. Thus, it is apparent that the growth areas are turboprop and turbojet flight as well as rotorcraft (which is somewhat dependent on oil prices). Other segments of general aviation are predicted to be stagnant. FBOs wanting to expand in the slower-growing GA market must carefully consider their opportunities and strategies. Pockets of opportunity exist, but need to be ascertained and quantified before pursuing them.

These forecasts are by no means cast in stone and are revised every year; however, they are a reliable backdrop to any one FBO's situation. Historic trends in one sector of aviation can be a useful backdrop to the individual FBO situation. For example, general aviation aircraft production and sales began to fall off in the late 1970s. It was predictable from that time—though not widely observed—that FBO business in the early 1980s would fall off as a result.

Understanding the Local Aviation Market

More fine-grained analysis of the market can be obtained from other public studies such as the FAA'S Terminal Area Forecasts that contain airport-by-airport forecasts for every facility in the National Plan of Integrated Airport Systems. Individual airports also periodically conduct airport master plans, usually with the help of a consultant. These plans may provide a guide not only to demand for growth at a particular airport, but also capacity limitations that could affect those plans.

Trade magazines and newspapers provide a more detailed review of technology and market shifts. The major ones are listed in figure 3.5.

Another shift in markets that FBOs should anticipate is the "ripple effect" in metropolitan areas. As major airline airports become more congested, there is a tendency to encourage general aviation traffic to use reliever general aviation airports that in some cases lie further out in the suburbs of metropolitan areas. As these airports in turn become busier, the proportion of business traffic tends to increase, and the recreational and instructional flyers may prefer to go out to more rural airports where smaller, lighter aircraft dominate the pattern and where they are not constrained by the requirements of an air traffic control tower.

Location will tend to determine the market of an airport, and an FBO must be prepared for these shifts and adapt to them, unless he or she desires and is prepared to work against the current. The process of working downwards from national trends to local and individual business prospects is described in figure 3.6.

General Aviation Organizations

There are a number of organizations dedicated to the growth and support of general aviation. As a part of the business plan and marketing efforts of a fixed base operator, a working knowledge of those organizations and how they might support the goals of the local business can be a strategic part of the overall plan. The following are some of these organizations.

Aircraft Owners and Pilots Association. AOPA represents 300,000 general aviation aircraft owners and pilots who use their aircraft for non-commercial, personal and business transpor-

Active General Aviation Aircraft by Aircraft Type 1983–1992

Aircraft Type	1992	1991	1990[1]	1989[1]	1988[1]	1987[1]	1986[1]	1985[1]	1984	1983
Fixed-Wing—Total	**170,844 (0.7%)**	**184,620 (0.7%)**	**184.5 (0.5%)**	**190.8 (0.6%)**	**183.8 (0.5%)**	**190.5 (0.5%)**	**192.3 (0.5%)**	**184.7 (0.6%)**	**207,571 (0.5%)**	**200,831 (0.7%)**
Piston—Total	**162,117 (7.0%)**	**175,347 (0.7%)**	**175.2 (0.6%)**	**180.8 (0.5%)**	**175.0 (0.6%)**	**181.5 (0.5%)**	**182.5 (0.6%)**	**175.6 (0.6%)**	**197,442 (0.5%)**	**191,480 (0.7%)**
One Engine	143,580 (0.8%)	154,102 (0.8%)	154.0 (0.6%)	158.9 (0.6%)	153.7 (0.6%)	159.7 (0.6%)	160.3 (0.6%)	153.4 (0.7%)	171,922 (0.5%)	166,247 (9.8%)
Two Engine	18,451 (1.7%)	21,119 (1.7%)	21.1 (1.3%)	21.8 (1.2%)	21.2 (1.4%)	21.7 (1.3%)	22.1 (1.6%)	22.1 (1.5%)	25,258 (1.2%)	24.910 (1.4%)
Other Piston	86 (17.7%)	127 (22.2%)	0.1 (30.0%)	0.1 (33.8%)	0.1 (21.7%)	0.1 (25.0%)	0.1 (24.3%)	0.1 (20.9%)	262 (13.4%)	143 (9.8%)
Turboprop—Total	**4,704 (3.1%)**	**4,920 (2.7%)**	**5.3 (1.8%)**	**5.9 (1.5%)**	**4.9 (1.7%)**	**4.9 (1.9%)**	**5.6 (1.9%)**	**5.0 (2.1%)**	**5,809 (1.0%)**	**5,453 (1.7%)**
Two Engine	4,094 (3.5%)	4,398 (3.0%)	4.9 (1.8%)	5.7 (1.5%)	4.7 (1.8%)	4.7 (1.9%)	5.4 (1.9%)	4.9 (2.1%)	5,633 (1.0%)	5,311 (1.6%)
Other Turboprop	610 (3.0%)	522 (2.4%)	0.4 (7.0%)	0.2 (14.2%)	0.2 (7.1%)	0.2 (8.9%)	0.2 (16.2%)	0.1 (7.8%)	176 (8.5%)	142 (26.8%)
Turbojet—Total	**4,022 (2.4%)**	**4,353 (2.0%)**	**4.1 (2.0%)**	**4.1 (1.5%)**	**3.9 (2.0%)**	**4.0 (1.5%)**	**4.2 (2.2%)**	**4.1 (1.7%)**	**4,320 (1.6%)**	**3,898 (3.3%)**
Two Engine	3,790 (2.3%)	`4,066 (1.9%)	3.7 (2.0%)	3.7 (1.4%)	3.6 (2.1%)	3.6 (1.6%)	3.8 (1.6%)	3.6 (1.7%)	3,780 (1.3%)	3,447 (2.7%)
Other Turbojet	232 (15.3%)	286 (14.4%)	0.4 (8.2%)	0.4 (8.2%)	0.3 (5.5%)	0.4 (5.0%)	0.4 (16.2%)	0.5 (7.2%)	540 (26.9%)	451 (20.2%)
Rotorcraft—Total	**5,753 (3.8%)**	**6,292 (3.5%)**	**6.9 (3.0%)**	**7.0 (0.6%)**	**6.0 (3.6%)**	**5.9 (3.2%)**	**6.5 (3.1%)**	**6.0 (4.0%)**	**7,096 (3.1%)**	**6,540 (3.7%)**
Piston	2,211 (7.7%)	2,470 (7.6%)	3.2 (5.3%)	3.0 (1.2%)	2.4 (7.9%)	2.6 (5.0%)	2.7 (6.0%)	2.7 (7.0%)	2,936 (6.3%)	2,541 (7.5%)
Turbine	3,542 (3.9%)	3,822 (2.9%)	3.7 (3.1%)	4.0 (0.4%)	3.6 (2.7%)	3.3 (4.2%)	3.8 (3.1%)	3.3 (4.5%)	4,160 (2.8%)	3,998 (3.8%)
Other—Total	**7,837 (1.9%)**	**7,563 (2.9%)**	**6.6 (3.0%)**	**7.2 (2.4%)**	**6.4 (4.1%)**	**6.3 (3.4%)**	**6.5 (3.0%)**	**5.8 (3.3%)**	**6,275 (2.7%)**	**5,923 (3.5%)**
Total All Aircraft	**184,434 (0.7%)**	**198,475 (0.7%)**	**198.0 (0.5%)**	**205.0 (0.5%)**	**196.2 (0.5%)**	**202.7 (0.5%)**	**205.3 (0.5%)**	**196.5 (0.6%)**	**220,943 (0.5%)**	**213,293 (0.6%)**

[1]Revised to correct for nonresponse bias.
NOTE: Columns may not add to totals due to rounding and estimation procedures.
(Percent Standard error is shown in parenthesis)

Figure 3.2.

Active General Aviation Aircraft Total Hours Flown by Aircraft Type 1983–1992

Aircraft Type	1992	1991	1990[1]	1989[1]	1988[1]	1987[1]	1986[1]	1985[1]	1984	1983
Fixed-Wing—Total	**23,801 (1.7%)**	**26,851 (1.9%)**	**29,546 (1.8%)**	**29,327 (1.7%)**	**28,040 (1.8%)**	**28,391 (1.7%)**	**28,994 (1.7%)**	**29,085 (1.7%)**	**33,265 (2.1%)**	**32,558 (2.1%)**
Piston—Total	**21,251 (1.9%)**	**24,102 (2.1%)**	**25,832 (2.0%)**	**24,907 (1.9%)**	**24,291 (2.0%)**	**24,969 (1.9%)**	**24,805 (1.9%)**	**25,666 (1.9%)**	**29,194 (1.8%)**	**28,911 (2.3%)**
One Engine	18,074 (2.1%)	20,540 (2.3%)	21,883 (2.2%)	20,600 (2.2%)	20,326 (2.2%)	20,446 (2.0%)	20,260 (2.1%)	21,102 (2.1%)	23,506 (2.1%)	23,149 (2.6%)
Two Engine	3,172 (3.9%)	3,555 (4.1%)	3,897 (3.8%)	4,292 (3.3%)	3,943 (4.1%)	4,509 (5.2%)	4,535 (4.6%)	4,539 (4.1%)	5,585 (3.6%)	5,730 (5.3%)
Other Piston	4 (22.6%)	7 (33.5%)	53 (48.7%)	16 (67.3%)	20 (44.5%)	14 (33.3%)	10 (45.5%)	24 (34.6%)	102 (29.4%)	32 (31.2%)
Turboprop—Total	**1,478 (5.7%)**	**1,513 (5.3%)**	**2,319 (6.4%)**	**2,892 (5.0%)**	**2,195 (5.0%)**	**2,010 (5.0%)**	**2,661 (5.1%)**	**1,921 (4.6%)**	**2,506 (4.7%)**	**2,173 (7.1%)**
Two Engine	1,238 (6.5%)	1,359 (5.8%)	2,162 (6.8%)	2,776 (5.2%)	2,117 (5.1%)	1,841 (5.0%)	2,583 (5.3%)	1,862 (4.8%)	2,452 (4.7%)	2,090 (7.2%)
Other Turboprop	240 (10.2%)	154 (12.8%)	157 (10.9%)	116 (16.6%)	78 (14.9%)	169 (24.6%)	78 (14.1%)	59 (10.9%)	54 (25.9%)	83 (37.3%)
Turbojet—Total	**1,072 (4.2%)**	**1,236 (4.5%)**	**1,396 (4.1%)**	**1,527 (3.7%)**	**1,554 (4.4%)**	**1,411 (3.9%)**	**1,527 (4.7%)**	**1,498 (4.4%)**	**1,566 (4.7%)**	**1,473 (6.6%)**
Two Engine	1,030 (4.3%)	1,183 (4.7%)	1,279 (4.3%)	1,424 (3.9%)	1,434 (4.7%)	1,312 (4.2%)	1,446 (4.9%)	1,349 (4.8%)	1,328 (5.0%)	1,350 (6.8%)
Other Turbojet	42 (16.4%)	54 (15.1%)	117 (12.2%)	103 (12.2%)	120 (10.9%)	99 (10.3%)	90 (19.4%)	149 (10.6%)	237 (13.9%)	124 (25.0%)
Rotorcraft—Total	**2,283 (6.6%)**	**2,757 (7.5%)**	**2,209 (5.9%)**	**2,610 (0.9%)**	**2,507 (6.5%)**	**2,108 (7.4%)**	**2,424 (6.7%)**	**1,990 (7.7%)**	**2,495 (5.5%)**	**2,271 (7.0%)**
Piston	416 (12.4%)	585 (12.0%)	716 (10.2%)	692 (2.1%)	533 (11.6%)	602 (9.2%)	742 (12.8%)	521 (15.1%)	592 (11.3%)	572 (8.6%)
Turbine	1,866 (7.6%)	2,172 (9.0%)	1,493 (7.2%)	1,918 (0.9%)	1,974 (7.6%)	1,506 (9.6%)	1,682 (7.7%)	1,468 (8.9%)	1,903 (6.4%)	1,700 (8.9%)
Other—Total	**410 (6.0%)**	**459 (8.9%)**	**341 (7.0%)**	**396 (7.4%)**	**568 (24.2%)**	**384 (6.0%)**	**364 (7.6%)**	**382 (8.2%)**	**358 (6.7%)**	**420 (11.7%)**
Total All Aircraft	**26,493 (1.6%)**	**30,067 (1.8%)**	**32,096 (1.7%)**	**32,332 (1.6%)**	**31,114 (1.7%)**	**30,883 (1.7%)**	**31,782 (1.6%)**	**31,456 (1.6%)**	**36,119 (1.6%)**	**35,249 (2.0%)**

[1]Revised to correct for nonresponse bias
NOTE: Columns may not add to totals due to rounding and estimation procedures.
(Hours in Thousands)
(Percent Standard error is shown in parenthesis)

Figure 3.3.

Estimated Active Pilot Certificates Held December 31, 1983–1992

Category	1983	1984	1985	1986	1987	1988	1989	1990	1991	1992
Pilot—Total	**718,004**	**722,376**	**709,540**	**709,118**	**699,653**	**694,016**	**700,010**	**702,659**	**692,095**	**682,959**
Student[1]	147,197	150,081	146,652	150,273	146,016	136,913	142,544	128,663	120,203	114,597
Recreational[1]	N/A	N/A	N/A	N/A	N/A	N/A	N/A	87	161	187
Airplane[2]										
Private	318,643	320,086	311,086	305,736	300,949	299,786	293,179	299,111	293,306	288,078
Commercial	159,495	155,929	151,632	147,798	143,645	143,030	144,540	149,666	148,365	146,385
Airline Transport	75,938	79,192	82,740	87,186	91,287	96,968	102,087	107,732	112,167	115,855
Helicopter (only)[3]	7,237	7,532	8,123	8,581	8,702	8,608	8,863	9,567	9,860	9,652
Glider (only)[4,5]	8,157	8,390	8,168	8,411	7,901	7,600	7,708	7,833	8,033	8,205
Lighter-than-air[5,6]	1,337	1,166	1,139	1,133	1,153	1,111	1,089	[6]	[6]	[6]
Flight Instructor Certificates[7]	**62,201**	**61,173**	**58,940**	**57,355**	**60,136**	**61,798**	**61,472**	**63,775**	**69,209**	**72,148**
Instrument Ratings[7,8]	**254,271**	**256,584**	**258,559**	**262,388**	**266,122**	**273,804**	**282,804**	**297,073**	**303,193**	**306,169**
Non-pilot—Total	**413,199**	**426,802**	**395,139**	**410,079**	**427,962**	**448,710**	**468,405**	**492,237**	**517,462**	**540,548**
Mechanic[9]	288,335	298,028	274,100	284,241	297,178	312,419	326,243	344,282	366,392	384,669
Parachute Rigger[9]	10,074	10,194	9,395	9,535	9,659	9,770	9,879	10,094	7,916	8,163
Ground Instructor[9]	66,385	67,463	58,214	59,443	60,861	62,582	64,503	66,882	70,086	73,276
Dispatcher[9]	8,223	8,980	8,511	9,025	9,491	10,020	10,455	11,002	11,607	12,264
Flight Navigator	1,636	1,603	1,542	1,512	1,445	1,400	1,357	1,290	1,225	1,154
Flight Engineer	38,546	40,534	43,377	46,323	49,328	52,519	55,968	58,687	60,236	61,022

[1]Category of certificate unknown.
[2]Includes pilots with an airplane only certificate. Also includes those with an airplane and a helicopter and/or glider certificate.
[3]See table 7 for the total number of pilots with a helicopter certificate.
[4]See table 8 for the total number of pilots with a glider certificate.
[5]Glider and lighter-than-air pilots are not required to have a medical examination; however, the totals above represent pilots who received a medical examination within the last 25 months.
[6]Lighter-than-air type ratings are no longer being issued.
[7]Not included in total.
[8]Special ratings shown on pilot certificates, do not indicate additional certificates.
[9]Numbers represent all certificates on record. No medical examination required.
N/A Not available. Recreational certificate first issued in 1990.

Figure 3.4.

Aero Magazine, Macro-Comm Corp., P.O. Box 38010, Los Angeles, CA 90038.

Ag-Pilot International, 10 N.E. Sixth, Milton-Freewater, OR 97862.

Agricultural Aviation, National Agricultural Aviation Association, Suite 103, 115 D Street, Washington, D.C. 20003.

The Aircraft Flyer, Ziff-Davis Publishing Co., One Park Avenue, N.Y., N.Y. 10016.

Airport Services, Lakewood Publications, Inc., 50 South 9th Street, Minneapolis, MN 55402.

Air Progress, 10920 Ambassador Drive, Suite 518, Kansas City, MO 64153.

AOPA Pilot, 421 Aviation Way, Frederick, MD 21701.

The Aviation Consumer, P.O. Box 972, Farmingdale, N.Y. 11737.

Aviation Magazine, Brookfield, CN 06804.

Aviation Safety, 1111 East Putnam Avenue, Riverside, CT 06878.

Aviation Week and Space Technology, McGraw-Hill, 1221 Avenue of the Americas, NY, NY 10020.

Business and Commercial Aviation, Ziff-Davis Publishing Co., Hangar C-1, Westchester County Airport, Westchester, N.Y.

Canadian Flight, Canadian Flight Publishing, P.O. Box 563, Station B, Ottawa, Ontario, Canada, KIP 554.

FBO, Johnson Hill Press, 1233 Janesville Ave., Fort Atkinson, WI 53538.

Flight International, Business Press International, Quadrant House, The Quadrant, Sutton, Surrey, England, SM2 5AS.

Flight Training Magazine, 405 Main St., Parkville, MO 64152.

Flying, Ziff-Davis Publishing Co., One Park Avenue, N.Y., N.Y. 10016.

General Aviation News & Flyer, 5611 76th St., W., Tacoma, WA 98467.

Glider Rider Magazine, P.O. Box 6009, Chattanooga, TN 37401.

Homebuilt Aircraft, Werner & Werner Corp., Ventura Boulevard, Suite 201, Encino, CA 91436.

Light Plane Maintenance, 1111 East Putnam Avenue, Riverside, CT 06878.

Plane and Pilot, Werner & Werner Corp., Ventura Boulevard, Suite 201, Encino, CA 91436.

Private Pilot, Macro-Comm Corp., P.O. Box 2432, Boulder, CO 80322.

Professional Pilot, West Building, Washington National Airport, Washington, D.C. 20001.

Sport Aviation, Experimental Aircraft Association, Wittman Airfield, Oshkosh, WI 54903-2591.

Sport Flyer, Flyer Newspapers, P.O. Box 98786, Tacoma, WA 98498-0786.

Woman in Aviation, Inc. P.O. Box 40, Lake Ann, MI 49650,

Figure 3.5. General aviation publications.

tation. AOPA members constitute 60 percent of the active pilots in the nation.

American Association of Airport Executives. AAAE is a professional organization representing the men and women who manage airports which enplane 90 percent of the passengers in the United States.

Experimental Aircraft Association. EAA is a sport aviation association with a worldwide membership of over 132,000 aviation enthusiasts,

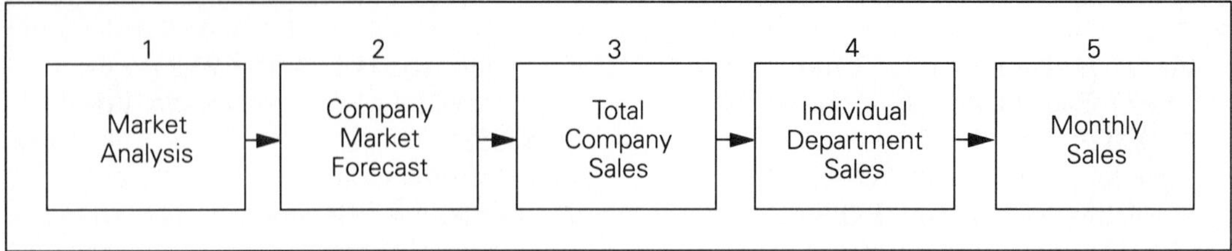

Figure 3.6. Market research and sales planning process.

pilots, and aircraft owners. The organization includes an active network of over 800 chapters.

General Aviation Manufacturers Association. GAMA represents 46 U.S. manufacturers of general aviation airplanes, engines, avionics, and related equipment.

National Air Transportation Association. NATA represents the business interest of the nation's general aviation service companies providing fueling, flight training, maintenance and repair, and on-demand charter service by more than 1,700 member companies with more than 100,000 employees.

National Association of State Aviation Officials. NASAO represents the state government aviation service agencies in all the states, as well as the aviation departments of Puerto Rico and Guam.

National Business Aircraft Association. NBAA represents the interest of over 3,200 companies which operate general aviation aircraft as an aid to business. NBAA members earn annual revenues in excess of $3 trillion and employ more than 16 million people worldwide.

Professional Aviation Maintenance Association. PAMA is a national professional association of aviation maintenance technicians, with some 4,000 individual members and 250 affiliated company members.

Women in Aviation, International. WAI is a professional organization representing the interests of women in all facets of aviation—genera, commercial, and military. The organization provides networking opportunities, educational outreach programs, and career development initiatives.

Forecasting Techniques and the Individual FBO

The individual FBO must examine the local and regional aviation market and determine what share of local sales will be captured for each area of service. National events and trends play a role, as well as the policy of the FBO. For example, suppose that a metropolitan area FBO has been heavily involved in providing flight instruction during the period that the V.A. was supporting this through the G.I. Bill. In the mid-1980s when the VA program expired, flight instruction was allowed to dwindle to a minor activity and revenue area for the company. Now let's suppose that Congress recognizes the lack of trained pilots and has re-instituted federally assisted flight training. Suddenly this market area looks promising. How promising? How long until the new program is approved and underway? What are likely to be the plans of other FBOs in the area? Is this a market that our FBO should pursue? Can flight instruction be sufficiently profitable under the new program? Some research and analysis will be needed before deciding that flight instruction sales will be *x* dollars this year. A contingency plan may even be appropriate. "If the new federal program reaches such-and-such a state of readiness by July of this year, we can initiate our program in September and this means by December we will expect to have twenty students enrolled." Sales will be forecast under several different startup scenarios.

Such forecasting is not very sophisticated because of factors outside of the FBO's control. However, this may be the most specific level of prediction feasible.

Other areas of the business may be more predictable. For example, let's suppose the FBO has a well-established maintenance shop that has increased its business by 5 percent per year over the past 5 years. Is it reasonable to predict that sales will be up five percent this year, too? Yes and no.

First, you need to know whether that history of 5 percent growth includes inflation. If the cost of labor and parts also went up five percent per year, then the actual volume of business stayed the same, even though the dollar volume went up. If the price went up *more* than 5 percent in a single year, then the volume of business actually declined.

Are there any reasons why the coming year might be other than "business as usual"? Is a competitor about to get into or out of the aircraft maintenance business? Or does the FBO have a good chance of winning a new fleet maintenance contract for a commuter airline or a corporate flight department? You must examine whether the total market "pie" is growing or shrinking in your market area and what share of that pie you can realistically expect.

It will be apparent from the above discussion that forecasting based on historic trends is a little superficial and risky unless some evaluation is made of the underlying causes of those trends and whether any of *them* will change. Nevertheless, predicting from historical trends if often done. This is most accurate at the large-scale level and least accurate at the individual company level.

Market share is another method of forecasting. In looking at individual airport-based aircraft operations, one approach is to use national forecasts and using aircraft per capita population, disaggregate to the local or regional level. This method requires a reliable national forecast and does not allow for local variations in aviation activity.

The most sophisticated approach to forecasting is to build a multiple regression model. The factors contributing to historical activity are identified, as well as the scale of each factor's contribution. The relationships that held in the past are postulated to hold true in the future. Future values for the causal factors, such as disposable income, fuel prices, and population by age group, are identified from published sources, and predictions developed.

Such a method still has weaknesses, especially since relationships *do* change over time; therefore, the time period over which a factor is examined may not be representative, and good forecasts may not be available for the variables considered relevant. Moreover, such a method is difficult to use for such a small unit as an individual FBO; it will be much more accurate at the regional level.

In summary, there is no perfect way to do aviation sales forecasts. They should be developed with as much knowledge as possible about what the competition is doing, with as much understanding as possible about national aviation trends and their causes, and with company goals and policies in mind. Forecasts can often become self-fulfilling prophecies.

Customer Needs and Identification of New Prospects

There are a number of ways to identify and sell to more customers, and for most businesses these ways must all be applied all the time. Every business continually loses clients through relocation, death, and changing needs. Therefore, every business requires new clients just to maintain current levels of sales. A growth plan requires more than this. Growth of the client base is possible to achieve in the following ways:

1. Maintain market share; grow or decline in step with the total market. The FAA said the GA fleet would decline through 1992 and then slowly start to grow again.
2. Obtain a bigger market share, that is, take business away from the competition.
3. Offer new products to existing clients.
4. Offer existing or new products to clients not previously in this marketplace (e.g., new general aviation enthusiasts attracted away from the airlines).

Effective ways of selling more or different items to the same clients include maintaining close rapport and seeking feedback in person, by surveys, by complaint forms, and by direct-mail advertising. It is recommended by most marketing experts that both a list and a wallmap of existing clients be maintained.

Lists of prospective clients served by competitors are obtainable from many sources. In today's sophisticated direct-mail market, lists of pilots and aircraft owners; and lists by area, income, and industry type (and thousands of other classifications) may be rented from list brokers in all major cities.

To attract customers who are not currently involved with general aviation, new techniques may be needed. For example, there is substantial evidence of a growing reliance on executive travel among the top companies (Fortune 1000). Armed with some of the statistics correlating company performance and use of general aviation aircraft, an FBO might present the benefits to business people at Chambers of Commerce, Jaycees, Kiwanis, and Rotary clubs.[7] NATA's "GAME" plan can assist in this respect. This is a major publicity program launched in 1988 to heighten the public's awareness and usage of General Aviation. (see figures 3.13 through 3.16 later in this chapter).

To encourage recreational flying and instruction, an FBO may need to publicize the contests organized by the General Aviation Manufacturers' Association as well as use other approaches.

While the overall economic climate for general aviation in the past decade has been discouraging, many enterprising FBOs nationwide have developed healthy markets in such areas as:

- Corporate aircraft maintenance
- Restoring antique aircraft
- Airline flight training
- Propeller balancing
- Airport hotels and motels
- Air charter
- Servicing airline aircraft, including de-icing
- Airport snow removal
- Overnight package express
- Air ambulance services
- Airport barbershops
- Pay telephones
- Retail merchandise[8–23]

For general public awareness of the benefits of the FBO's services and the airport, fly-ins, open houses, and air shows may be appropriate, although care should be taken not to present a barnstorming image if that is not the airport's target market. Appendix II of this book presents a list of other suggestions.

Product and Service Definition

The starting point of any business is the identification of the product it wishes to sell. In the aviation business, this means the identification of several products, such as transporting passengers, providing landing facilities, servicing aircraft, renting space, and so on. It is extremely important that the manager clearly identify each of the products that he or she expects to include as part of the business. Each product or service offered by a business must be identified because decisions on other marketing variables, such as promotion, will depend upon identification and knowledge of the product. In addition the manager may want to identify services that will be offered if requested but will not be emphasized. What such items are, for any one FBO, is hard to predict. They will be things that take more trouble in terms of training and special equipment than will normally prove feasible or profitable. For many businesses such an item might be banner towing or aerial photography.

By the same token, there may be activities that are in demand but the FBO might want to refer to another specialist in the field. Some examples include specialized avionics, radio work, and the whole maintenance function. Some FBOs do not pump fuel, except perhaps for their own use, because the municipality runs this operation or another FBO is better placed to do it profitably. Each FBO must decide its own service and product lines relative to what it perceives as its customers' desires and on the profit in each area.

Finally, there are some activities that although nonaviation are very profitable related areas. Examples include restaurants, car rentals, and limousines. A quality airport restaurant with good views of active aircraft may attract many nonflyers and help provide an introduction to the services and facilities at the airport as well as provide a positive public image.

Total Product

Even for consumer goods, the typical customer is not just looking for the product but for the experience of fulfilling a want. He/she is concerned with the total product, including the experience of obtaining it, as well as the assurance of related functional and aesthetic features. The typical customer is also concerned with necessary accessories, installation guidance, instruction, packaging, dependability, and assurance that good future service and maintenance is available. In making his or her purchase, he/she is looking for indications that all needs in regard to the item will be met.

Product Classification

Traditional marketing theory divides consumer goods into four categories:

1. *Convenience goods* are those the purchaser wants to buy frequently and with minimum effort; therefore, comparison shopping is not employed. An example might be aviation fuel, unless there is a discount fuel operator in the area.
2. *Shopping goods* are those items that shoppers do compare. Examples might be a used aircraft or a flight instruction course. The FBO will have to offer some special features of quality or price to attract customers.
3. *Specialty goods* are those items where the customer wants one specific brand name or custom item and will go to great lengths to obtain it.
4. *Unsought goods* are those items that the customer is not seeking and may not have thought he or she needed. New products, the savings realized from preventive maintenance, and novelty items fall into this category.

The Competition

Convenience goods will be sold to local customers and to transients who are at that point a captive market. If you have what they need, they'll buy it. Shopping goods are the subject of strong competition and there may not be any customer loyalty for these. Specialty goods can help an FBO to establish a reputation either as carrying a good inventory, or as being known to go to any lengths to find what a customer wants. Unsought goods require skills to make a potential customer aware of the benefits of something new.

Market Niche

Based upon the total market in the area and the competition's share of it, each FBO must seek to determine its own market niche or share. This will also require review from time to time. Questions to address are "What do we do?" and "Why are we different?"

Price

There are two basic methods of pricing: cost-based and demand-based. These are discussed in the following section.

Cost-based

Retail stores usually mark up wholesale prices about 100 percent; that is, an item costing ten dollars wholesale will be sold at twenty dollars retail. This markup is a cost-plus approach to pricing in which the overheads such as storage, retail showroom space, labor, bookkeeping, and financing costs are covered by a predetermined overhead rate. Assuming you purchase wholesale at competitive rates, and your overhead costs are within industry norms, you can price competitively using this method.

Cost-based pricing is a straightforward approach with a basic appeal to most aviation managers. There are, however, two typical difficulties which exist in many situations: (1) many managers are not aware of, nor do they have available, adequate cost data, and (2) even where some data are available, the manager may not adequately recognize the various ways that costs change. In order to use cost-based pricing, the manager must understand the following types of costs:

1. *Total fixed costs* is the sum of those costs that are fixed in total, regardless of output level. Typical fixed costs include rent, property taxes, insurance, depreciation, and administrative salaries. Such expenses must be paid even if business activity ceases temporarily.
2. *Total variable costs* is the sum of those variable expenses that are closely related to level of business activity. Variable expenses include materials used, wages paid, and sales commissions. At zero business, total variable cost is zero. As output increases, total variable cost increases.
3. *Total costs* is the sum of total fixed costs and total variable costs. With total fixed costs set, growth of total costs is dependent upon the increase in total variable costs.
4. *Average cost* is figured by dividing the total cost by the volume of business, the average cost per unit of business is then obtained.
5. *Average fixed cost* is when the total fixed cost is divided by the quantity of business.
6. *Average variable cost* is the total variable costs divided by the related quantity of business.

The following example illustrates the above cost structure for a line department engaged in aircraft fueling operations in an aviation business: Figure 3.7 illustrates the cost data for such an activity. Notice that the average fixed cost decreases steadily as the quantity of fuel increases and that the total variable cost increases when quantity increases. Note also that the average cost is decreasing continually. The behavior of the three average-cost curves (average variable, average fixed and average cost) have been graphed in figure 3.8. The aviation manager could use this type of graph in setting prices. First, he must include an element for profit either as a fixed amount in the total fixed costs, or as a fixed amount per unit in the average variable cost. The next step is to simply decide how many gallons of fuel the department will sell. If the goal is to sell 30,000 gallons, then by referring to the cost curve (Figure 3.7), the price is determined per

Quantity	Total Fixed Costs (TFC) (AFC)	Average Fixed Costs (AVC)	Average Variable Costs (TVC)	Total Variable Costs	Total Cost (TC)	Average Cost (AC)
5,000	4,000	.80	1.50	7,500	11,500	2.30
10,000	4,000	.40	1.50	15,000	19,000	1.90
15,000	4,000	.266	1.50	22,500	26,500	1.77
20,000	4,000	.20	1.50	30,000	34,000	1.70
25,000	4,000	.16	1.50	37,500	41,500	1.66
30,000	4,000	.133	1.50	45,000	49,000	1.63
35,000	4,000	.114	1.50	52,500	56,500	1.61
40,000	4,000	.10	1.50	60,000	64,000	1.60
45,000	4,000	.088	1.50	67,500	71,500	1.59
50,000	4,000	.080	1.50	75,000	79,000	1.58
55,000	4,000	.072	1.50	82,500	86,500	1.57

Figure 3.7. Costs at various levels of business (in dollars).

gallon. Therefore, for whatever quantity is desired, the price can be identified. The quantity selected can be related to previous levels of activity or to target goals for future periods; thus, it becomes a useful managerial tool.

Demand-based

Another method of pricing is simply to charge whatever the traffic will bear. As long as this is higher than the price arrived at by cost-plus, there will be a higher profit. For desirable or scarce items there will be a very considerable profit, which will bear little relationship to the actual cost of making that item available.

The addition of the Recreational Pilot certificate in 1989 was thought to be an answer to the declining number of new student starts. As of the end of 1993 the number of individuals who have completed this certificate totalled less than 200. The certificate requires less flight time than a private pilot certificate, allows the pilot to carry one passenger, but limits the distance flown. Although many point to the small number who have actually obtained the certificate, and deem the idea a failure, some believe that many more pilots actually began flight training intending to make it their first rating. But once into their flight training opted to complete the requirements for the private pilot certificate (an additional ten hours), giving them more privileges.

Another positive trend in terms of flight training has been the increasing percentage of pilots who are adding advanced certificates and ratings. The percentage of pilots with instrument ratings now totals 45%. This has been especially true of women pilots who have increased by almost 300% from 1983–1992, the number obtaining Airline Transport pilot certificates.

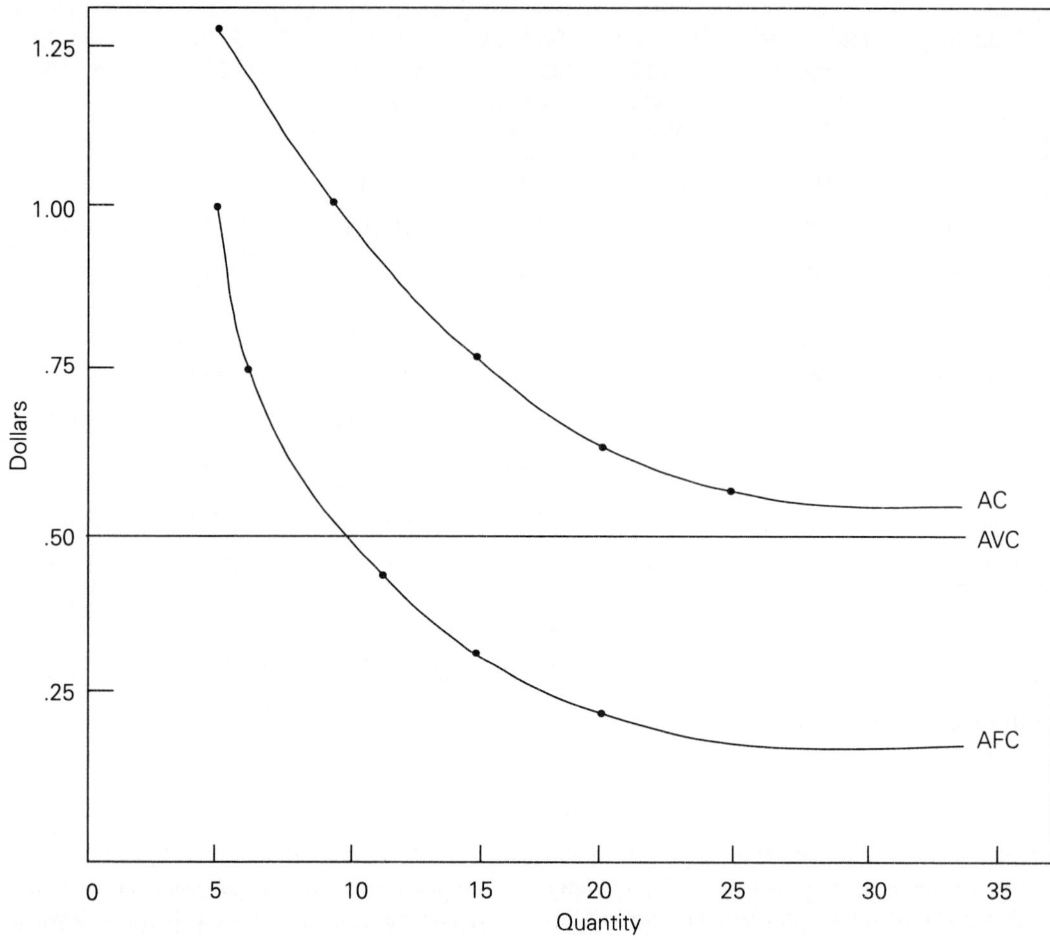

Figure 3.8. Shape of typical fuel cost curves when average variable cost is assumed constant.

Aviation examples are rare because of competition in the industry, but other examples abound like the Cabbage Patch dolls during the Christmas seasons of 1983 and 1984. These computer-designed dolls, supposedly each unique, were sold for $100 or more when their cost at mass production was probably under $10. However, Coleco, the manufacturer, has since declared bankruptcy. Therefore, pricing must bear some relation to both cost and value.

It is also very important to keep the latest technology in mind when considering marketing strategies and continued long term business. In the computer industry, a company on the cutting edge today can find their product basically obsolete in one or two years. The development of RNAV and Loran, which were the most advanced flight navigation systems in the 1980's are now considered "dinosaurs" by some in lieu of the latest GPS systems available.

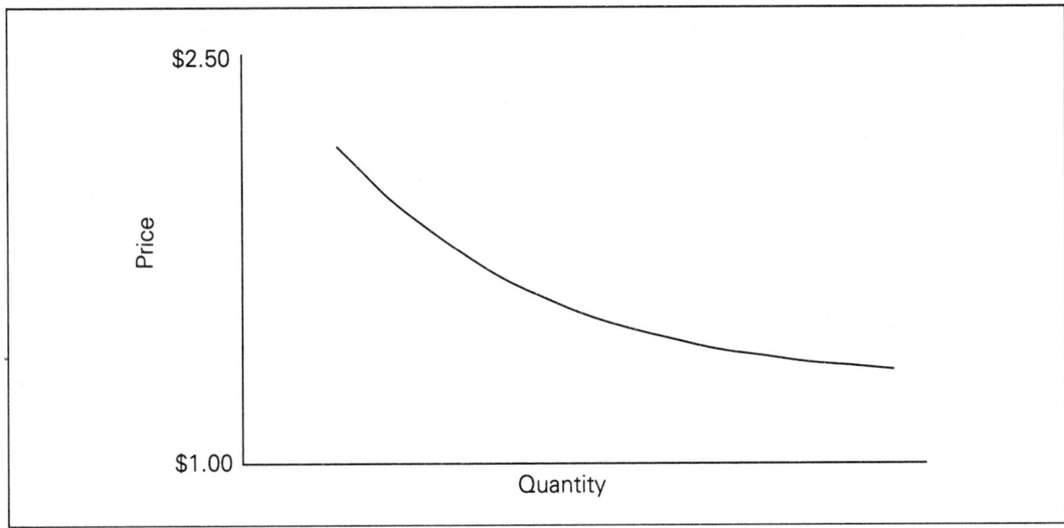

Figure 3.9. Demand curve for aviation fuel.

Elasticity

Pricing that reflects what the traffic will bear conforms to the economist's true pricing theory. That theory states that price is determined as the point at which the seller's supply curve and the buyer's demand curve intersect. As price goes down, the buyer is assumed to want more; and as the price goes up, the consumer wants less. For a price increase of 1 percent, a drop in demand of 1 percent would follow under conditions described as *unit-price elasticity.* Price elasticity is less than one or less than unit if demand goes down less than 1 percent for a 1 percent price increase. For example, it appears that price elasticity for aviation fuel is fairly low. Where price elasticity is small, a seller would have to lower prices considerably to sell more to the same customer.

In theory, each buyer has his or her own demand schedule for each product at different prices. This is expressed most commonly as a curve, as shown in figure 3.9. As a customer comparison shops for a product or service, it seems likely that his or her demand curve will shift depending on the asking prices of suppliers for various levels of quality.

The seller behaves in the opposite way. The higher the price of the product he/she is selling, the more he/she wants to sell. Such a supply curve is shown in figure 3.10. Where the buyer's demand curve and the seller's supply curve intersect is the price, as shown in figure 3.11. In practice most prices are not negotiated with each buyer but are predetermined and based on assumptions about regional aggregate supply-and-demand conditions. Moreover, in times of scarcity, when traditional economic theory would indicate raising price as the market's best form of allocating supply, there are usually regulations in effect about price gouging. Offering more of something for sale when prices go up is questionable because the *profit margin* probably will not go up at all. In order to remain competitive, an FBO most likely will pass on the higher cost to the customer. However, trying to make an exceptional profit when demand is high will probably alienate customers and be self-defeating.

Pricing is, therefore, an inexact science where basic economic theory must be combined with common sense and knowledge of the competition. Year-end or other sales to get rid of old inventory, as well as discount pricing for promotions, must be added to this complex picture before any calculations of revenue can be considered.

Pricing Policy

For the pricing practices of an organization to follow a logical pattern, for the employees to have a pricing guide to follow, and for the customer to experience understanding and goodwill toward the business, it becomes vital to have pricing policies on at least the following seven essential areas:

1. One price or flexible prices
2. Price level with respect to market
3. Pricing as related to the product life cycle
4. Pricing product lines
5. Promotional pricing policies
6. Geographic pricing policies
7. Marketing channel pricing policies

Most businesses set their prices according to some guidelines rather than allow the daily market pressures to determine price. One policy option is one price to all customers versus a flexible-price policy where different customers may pay different prices. The second policy deals with the decision to price at above or below the market level. Many factors must be considered in making this decision and in reviewing it for necessary changes. The next area deals with picking a policy that covers practices related to product life cycle. Will the prices be high initially in order to "skim" the market "cream" or will the prices be lower in order to "penetrate" the market and get a larger share? The fourth decision deals with creating policies in relation to the various product lines. Is the relationship between the various product lines a logical one? Are price classes to be set, rather than individual prices? The next policy area deals with promotional pricing, such as coupons, multiple unit pricing, loss-leader pricing, and introductory price setting. The last two policy areas deal with geographic and channel problems and are not major concerns for

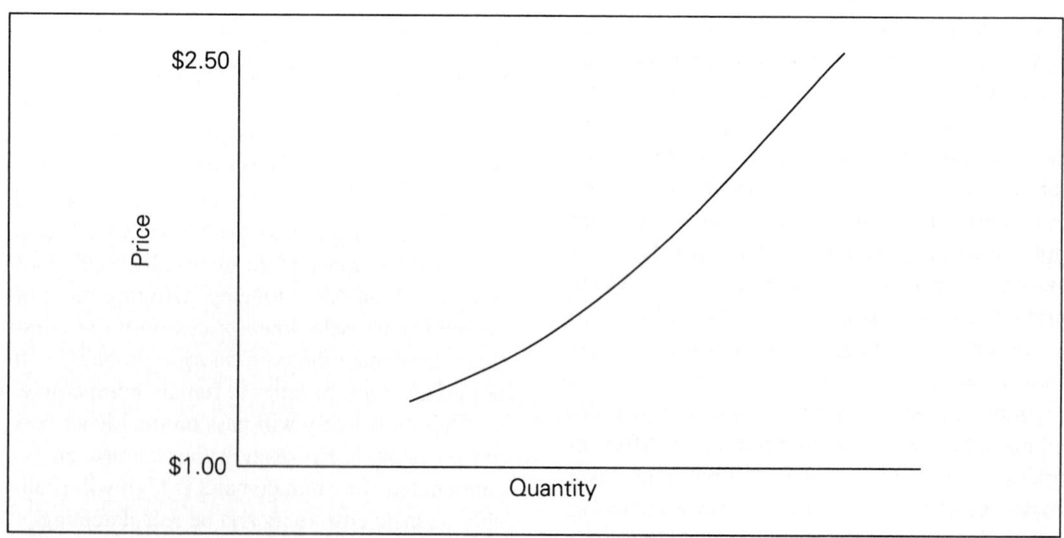

Figure 3.10. Supply curve for aviation fuel.

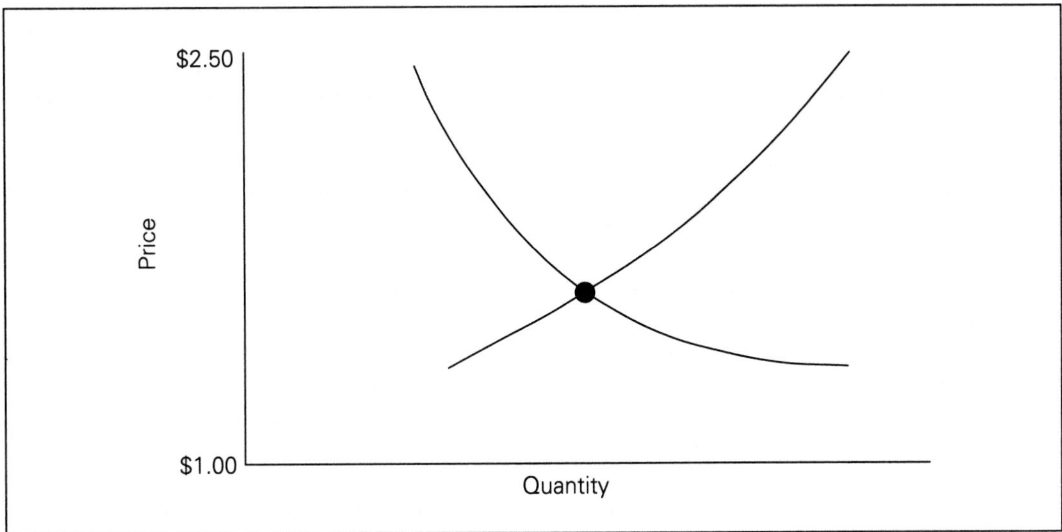

Figure 3.11. Equilibrium of supply and demand for aviation fuel.

most aviation managers unless they have widespread operations or strongly influence pricing throughout a marketing distribution channel.

In order to use pricing as a marketing tool, it is necessary to understand the need for pricing policies and to understand the operational opportunities in each of the above seven areas. The first policy area—fixed or flexible prices—can be applied to many aviation business activities. For example, let us consider the charter business. Will you charge $150.00 an hour for rental of a twin-engine aircraft, or will you promote a lesser rate ($125.00/hr) for the hours of midnight to five a.m. in order to enhance the utilization of the aircraft? Although some managers are reluctant to use flexible prices, others are quick to use such policies to their advantage.

Higher prices may well be associated with better quality products; lower prices with cheaper products. At the same time, the decision to price below market level may very well be influenced by the desire to increase the volume of business. Finally, your price level may well determine the level of support/services you may provide in your business for your products. For example, higher rates for maintenance labor may enable you to have better equipment and better qualified mechanics.

Pricing as related to the life cycle of a given product means normally that when the product is new and in great demand, the price may be higher. Later, when the product is not as new, or when competition has become plentiful, the price may, out of necessity, become lower.

Pricing by product line may be hard to introduce in the typical aviation business. For example, pricing fuel lower than competitors may help establish a low-price image for the entire business.

Promotional pricing activities are a familiar feature of the aviation business world. Coupons and bonuses have been used at many airports. Airline special or promotional rates are commonplace and accepted. Introductory price cuts by new businesses are sometimes used to speed entry into the market.

Geographic pricing policies may not have to be made by many of the smaller aviation businesses, but they are frequently the target of such policies set by large national distributors of aviation products. The main issue is who will pay the freight or how is it split between buyer and seller. FOB (Free On Board) pricing means that the closer you are to the source, the cheaper the product becomes. Zone pricing is used to to smooth out the delivered prices in sections of the country. Uniform delivered pricing means that there is one price to all customers, wherever they may be. Freight absorption pricing is another example of geographic pricing policy. This technique is used by businesses who are shipping their goods considerable distances. In those distant markets they may absorb some of the freight costs in order to allow their salespeople to become more competitive.

The last pricing policy area deals with marketing channels activities. Most aviation businesses do not set channel policies, but they should be aware of the approach. By viewing a marketing channel as a unit, they can consider applying many of the above policies to the channel as a unit. The secret to the success of this approach lies in every member of the channel feeling that commensurate profits are being realized.

Place

Location

No product is commercially valuable if it cannot be brought to the right place at the right time. The FBO business is one in which the customer comes to the business, rather than the other way around. Therefore, the location of the business is critical. But in another sense, the location of an FBO is fixed and relocation is difficult if not impossible. Place is a given for the FBO business. By contrast, aviation supply stores in shopping malls and mail-order avionics firms are much less tied geographically and have considerable advantage over an FBO in this respect.

Distribution Systems

Place also refers to the channels of distribution and the process that gets goods into the FBO's stock for use or sale. The channels between original producer and end consumer may involve no intermediaries (e.g., Beech Aircraft and Cessna sell factory direct and no longer use dealers). Or the process may require one or more wholesalers and the FBO as a retailer. Figure 3.12 shows these four basic channels of distribution.

The FBO as retailer must understand the distribution process for all the items sold, since it affects their cost, availability, and supply schedule. He or she must also be involved in merchandising, which means the display of retail goods to best advantage, and inventory control, which means keeping track of fast- and slow-moving items and setting up appropriate reorder schedules. These functions to some extent will also be necessary in the parts department, where display and merchandising can perhaps produce many more sales than many parts and service managers realize. Chapter 10 discusses how to calculate the "Economic Ordering Quantity" of a given item.

Computerized inventory control can in many cases be useful in keeping track of stock from the point of sale and preparing summaries of product turnover.

Promotion

The object of promotional activities is to inform, persuade, and remind existing and new customers about what the business offers them. Methods of promotion include television, radio, newspapers, trade publications, direct mail, novelty items, air shows, tours, signs, and referrals from happy customers (with or without incentives). Figure 3.13 shows a year-long promotional planning chart for a typical FBO.

Advertising

Advertising is but one method of promotion, and its cost-effectiveness is generally greater when it can be targeted more toward the right market. Thus, advertising in the mass media such

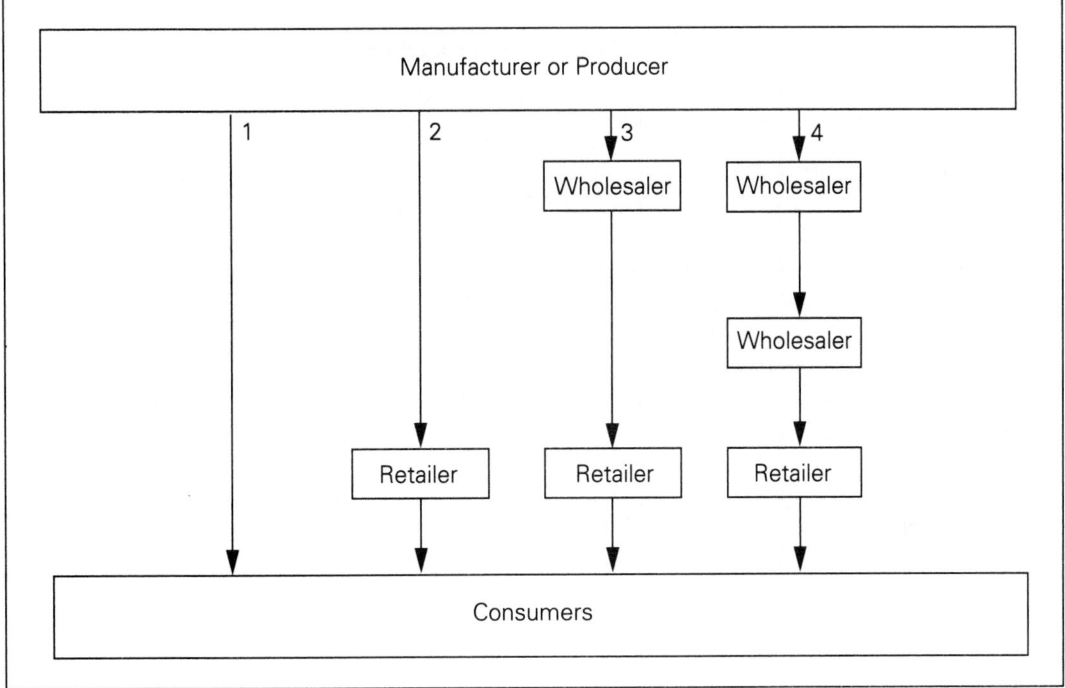

Figure 3.12. Four basic channels of distribution.

as radio and television may not be very appropriate for general aviation, whereas advertising in aviation publications may be. A relatively new targeted mode of advertising is cable television, where detailed information is available on what types of audiences are watching what types of shows.

Direct Mail

For general direct mail, such as to all households in certain zip codes, a "rule of thumb" in the industry is that a good result is two percent for most kinds of mass merchandise. The use of aviation mailing lists and preselected business lists could be much more successful than general lists for aviation purposes. Carefully designed and targeted direct-mail advertising with a no-risk "offer" to encourage response can be an excellent source of leads.

Referrals

Word-of-mouth and selling more to existing customers may be the most effective promotional tools in an aviation business. The individual FBO will need to test different concepts in limited ways before deciding which particular techniques work in each of his or her market segments. What appeals to the business market is more likely to relate to efficiency and quality, while price may be the overriding consideration for the flight instruction market. Follow-up with every customer should be a goal in order to identify negative feedback. With prompt followup, a negative experience for one of your customers can be turned around so that he makes positive referrals. If uncontacted, the unsatisfied customer will be persuaded by the competition the next time. Conversely, firms that get a reputation for dealing fairly and promptly with problems get good

Planning Chart

ACTIVITY		January	February	March	April	May
LINE OPS	PLAN		check line needs			
	ACTION			Refurbish line, exterior Paint, spruce		←
INSTRUCTION	PLAN	Plan Spring LTF Program Develop Prospect List Films - ETC			LTF Air cond. June + July	Local LTF Promotion
	ACTION	Advanced Ratings →	Go Twin LTF Two Time	High School Promotion	← National Adv. LTF → $5, $88.	solo
FLIGHT SVCS	PLAN					
	ACTION	← Twin Invitational →				
ACFT SALES	PLAN			Plan for Arrow II		
	ACTION	National Adv. Local Promotions Travel Analysis	Business Twins →		← Arrow II Nat'l Adv → Local Promotion PFC	
PARTS	PLAN					
	ACTION			Promote Pilot Supplies		←
SERVICE	PLAN					Plan programmed maint. Effort
	ACTION	Review Annual List	Promote Engine Work	Promote Radio Work		Promote Acft Clean-up
OTHER General	PLAN			Prepare Open House		
	ACTION	Review Plan For Year!!	Visit: News TV	Visit: Real Estate	Annual Open House	
OTHER	PLAN					
	ACTION					

Figure 3.13. Promotion planning chart for a general aviation organization.

June	July	August	September	October	November	December
—— Special	Service Program →			Winterize + safety Program		
	Plan Fall Instrument Rating Course	Plan PIP Trng. Fac.				
← LTF-Air Cond. →		Follow up LTF		Local Instr. course Go Twin NAT'L. ADV.	PIP New Model Acft	← Ground School
			Order Calendars Navajo Now!		Plan local Twin Promotion	PFC Refresher
Piper Nat'l ← Fortune	Adv 500 →			Navajo now!	Calendar mailing	'73 material + literature
			Prepare Xmas List			
—— Promote Cleaning	Materials →			December Gift mailing		
Piper Nat'l Adv. For Programmed Maint. Local Program		Maint. Seminar				
Movie Showings	Airport Promotion			Fall Fly-In	Dealer Meeting!!	

Figure 3.13. Continued.

word-of-mouth press that can continually strengthen their client base.

Institutional Promotion

Institutional promotion or advertising means the promotion of a positive image about the business without stressing any particular product or service. In many cases it is very successful because people want to buy an experience and some assurance of ongoing service rather than a product *per se*. Institutional promotion can use mass media or targeted marketing, depending on the situation. As FBOs begin to compete with airlines for business travel, they need to consider emulating airline institutional advertising techniques. A major step has been taken in this direction through the General Aviation Task Force's "GAME" plan that is promoting all aspects of general aviation flying through a national advertising campaign which supplies ad copy to individual FBOs. Examples are shown in figures 3.14 through 3.17.

Consulting as a Promotional Tool

In the aviation world a great deal of selling relates to the selling of aircraft, particularly to new business users that have been identified as a growth market. The general aviation manufacturers such as Beech, Cessna, and Piper offer to prospective buyers a pro forma analysis comparing current methods of travel for time and costs with travel by means of a corporate aircraft. The astute FBO can conduct this analysis on behalf of prospective buyers. The study helps the FBO achieve a better rapport with the prospective client and helps to specify exactly what type of aircraft will best meet the company's needs. Such a study will include:

- Current company travel patterns
- Current travel costs (including overnight costs and time spent by personnel)
- Percentage of past year's travel that could have been made more efficiently by general aviation
- Cost of making that travel by general aviation, including deductions for savings of time and overnight costs
- Costs of aircraft ownership minus tax benefits
- Net positive or negative position resulting from use of corporate aircraft, annualized

The study may be manual or computerized; the latter permits the testing of more assumptions. An FBO might offer to conduct such an analysis and refund its cost if the client buys an airplane.

Sales

Needs Assessment

"Staying close to the customer" should be interpreted in part as listening to what problem the customer is trying to solve or what benefit he or she is seeking. Particularly for major purchases, a first discussion should likely focus only on needs and not on products.

Alternatives

A second, or second-stage discussion will present to the prospect some alternatives that the FBO has available to address the needs already expressed. The dialogue will give the buyer the opportunity to comment about each alternative.

Closing

Closing may involve satisfactorily addressing objections raised by the customer and presenting the best alternative in terms that suggest a purchase. Much has been written elsewhere about sales techniques and much of the necessary skill appears teachable if the salesperson has the right attitude.[7,8] Selling should be a win-win proposition for the buyer and the seller, especially assuming that follow-up sales and service and pos-

HOW TRAVELING SALESMEN CAN DO MORE SELLING AND LESS TRAVELING.

It's simple. Just cover more ground in the same amount of time.

All it takes is a better means of transportation. One that combines the convenience of your car with the speed of flight.

You can charter a plane or learn to fly yourself. Either way, you're on the road to more sales calls— and more sales. To find out more, call:

FROM (DEALER NAME)

Call 000-0000

GAME Plan
Ad TBA - 7A

Figure 3.14. Courtesy of The General Aviation Taskforce.

THE ANSWER TO TOO MANY DAYS ON THE ROAD GOES RIGHT OVER MOST PEOPLE'S HEADS.

If you find yourself spending more time behind the wheel than in front of your clients, maybe you need a fresh perspective: Look up to General Aviation.

Whether it's chartering an airplane or learning to fly, you'll spend less time getting there. For less than you might think. To see how much less, just call:

FROM (DEALER NAME)

Call 000-0000

GAME Plan
Ad TBA - 4A

Figure 3.15. Courtesy of The General Aviation Taskforce.

ARE YOUR OVERNIGHT LETTERS GETTING BETTER AIR SERVICE THAN YOU ARE?

FLY SMARTER. THINK CHARTER.

When business demands that you absolutely have to be at a given place at a given time, counting on the scheduled carriers is like putting all your faith on a 25¢ stamp. Sometimes it's worth a bit extra, just to be sure. Sometimes it's smarter to air charter. For information, call: 800 "I-CAN-FLY" (422-6359).

OTHER HIGHLIGHTS

- *Also seen in The Wall Street Journal and USA Today.*
- *Combined 4th quarter media schedule delivered over 22 million gross impressions.*
- *Message received by 49% of GAME Plan's targeted audience (frequent business travelers) nearly 3 times each.*

As advertised in TIME Magazine.

Figure 3.16. Courtesy of The General Aviation Taskforce.

TO GET THERE FAST, CALL US FIRST.

FLY SMARTER. THINK CHARTER.

If your business can't afford to wait, you need to know about air charter.

Because if you're flying to more than one destination, or if your destination isn't a major hub, or if more than one of you is going, or if you hate standing in airport lines, charter can save you time and just maybe save you money.

Now, who should you call before your next business trip?

GENERAL AVIATION

FROM (DEALER NAME)

Call 000-0000

GAME Plan
Ad TBA - 10A

Figure 3.17. Courtesy of The General Aviation Taskforce.

itive referrals are desired. The same approach should be used whether the sale is large or small because the next purchase may be a major one.

Collecting

Payment is, of course, essential. Part of the sales process is to determine if the buyer is financially qualified for credit or is going to pay cash. Terms must reflect your costs of financing. Chapter 6 discusses credit policies and procedures.

Marketing Controls

Marketing Plan

The marketing effort must be part of the overall business plan, for it is that portion of business planning that helps estimate sales and hence revenue to the business. Measures of marketing effectiveness may include sales volume, area coverage, new clients, product establishment, or all of these.

Contribution Analysis

Contribution analysis allows the manager to examine what contribution each sale makes to profit or overhead. For example, each sale might cost sixty cents and yield forty cents to pay commission, overhead, and profit. If a certain advertising promotion results in another 100 sales, the advertising cost per sale can be calculated and the contribution to profit compared with previous results. In this way the merits of more or less advertising for that product can be calculated in terms of the return yielded.

Performance Evaluation

An important area is the collection and analysis of sales data. Routine analysis of sales data for selected operating periods provides benchmarks that can be used to measure progress toward the selected goals of the firm as well as to analyze some of the fundamental assumptions used in setting these goals. The focus may be on sales territory, individual product, salesperson productivity, or cost analysis.

Quality Control

Some pilots who have flown in many parts of the United States comment that in some regions there seems to be more of a "pro-aviation" attitude. When a plane arrives, there is a "follow-me" van right there. And a red carpet treatment that offers to check everything, to obtain ground transportation, and to do whatever is needed in the way of service and information. In other regions, flyers say that it is difficult to even find line help and get the basics. Quality is a constant goal in the best businesses.

Budgeting

The marketing budget is part of the cost of doing business and must be set up by product or by division of the firm on an annual or quarterly basis. Chapter 4 discusses budgeting in more depth.

Information Systems

In order to keep track of the sales of numerous products and services and organize these data into useful monthly or other summaries, good record keeping and analysis are essential. A microcomputer can be very beneficial in this regard. This and other data systems are discussed in chapter 7 "Information Systems."

Integrated Marketing

In order to realize the maximum potential in a given business, the marketing effort should be developed as an integrated, consistent, and systematic approach. The first step is to clearly identify the business goals, the products, and the market. All available tools should be utilized. Specific short-range objectives should be set. Budgeting may use a cost that is a percentage of past or forecast sales or may be based on other considerations such as matching competitors' spending or spending to achieve a certain sales goal.

Coordination of the marketing tasks to achieve the desired schedule is a key step. Work schedules, flowcharts, and similar tools may be helpful. Careful analysis at each step not only checks on progress, but also may suggest corrections and alternative marketing actions.

Marketing the Airport

Because of the FBO's dependence on the whole airport and not just on the part that he or she leases, the marketing function must address the question of creating and maintaining a positive image for the airport among nonuser neighbors who—as we have just seen—are likely to predominate over users. Even a privately owned airport must pay increasing attention to this because of:

- Land use and zoning decisions around the airport
- Property tax questions
- Availability of public federal funds for selected private airports
- Public actions needed to protect airspace
- The need for highway signs to the airport
- The need for support from the business community

The FBO relies on a good public image for the total airport, whether he or she owns the field or is a tenant. The FBO can do much to create a positive attitude about the airport.[9,10] For example, he or she can:

- Ensure that flight instructors and students know the noise-sensitive areas to avoid and the proper noise-abatement techniques for flight operations
- Set up a documented complaint system for airport neighbors and meet personally with any who are the victims of buzzing or other inappropriate flight behavior
- Invite airport neighbors to open houses and demonstration flights
- Present the operation of the airport as a business to business groups
- Invite local public officials to visit the FBO and make presentations to flight school classes
- Conduct tours for school children and others
- Organize a fly-in or airshow and invite the local community to attend
- Organize group meetings and seminars for local pilots or other groups including local business owners, letting them utilize airport facilities

Such activities are a form of institutional marketing except that the FBO will be trying to convey the value of the airport as a whole, not just the part of it he or she may lease. Even if other FBOs on the field are not willing to spend the time to do this, the FBO should try to make it a priority. As a result goodwill will flow to the business.

Summary

The successful aviation manager develops a marketing orientation; he or she operates the business with a major focus on the customer. Specific target customers and markets are identified. The product and service, price, place and promotion mix is developed to meet customer needs. To accomplish this effectively, the first step involves the collection of information on the market and the many variables that affect business activity. From these data, a forecast must be developed that will enable the manager to formulate a marketing mix to satisfy buyer needs. The product element is concerned with firm identification of the "total" product and the market-related concepts of product categories, demand curves, supply curves, and product planning. Place deals with physical distributions: getting the right product to the target market in order to provide the customer with the right time-place-possession utility. Promotion activities are designed to inform, remind, and persuade target customers about the available products and services. This may be done through personal selling, mass advertising, direct mail and other techniques. Price is based upon cost considerations tempered by pricing actions of competitors. Predicting market opportunities requires thorough study and constant vigilance for necessary adjustments resulting from economic and technological changes as well as changes in the competition. Marketing is more than sales; a sound marketing plan should guide the sales forecasting and implementation process through market research and strategy development.

Dicussion Topics

1. Why is a "marketing orientation" important to the aviation manager and how can it be acquired?
2. Identify three key activities associated with a comprehensive marketing strategy.
3. Identify the "four p's" of marketing and discuss the ways in which they are different for FBOs than for most other types of businesses.
4. Distinguish between (a) convenience goods, (b) shopping goods, (c) specialty goods, and (d) unsought goods. Identify aviation products and/or services in each category.
5. Why are demand and supply curves useful in relation to market planning?
6. Describe three elements of distribution and how they function.
7. What methods would one select for (a) mass marketing, and (b) personal marketing? How would each work?
8. What are three basic sales-related tasks that an FBO must carry out as a retail operation?
9. How can one determine the effectiveness of promotional activities? Discuss two methods.
10. What are the pros and cons of setting prices based simply on your costs plus a profit margin?
11. Identify five types of market-related input that can be obtained from either sales records or customer feedback. How can each be used?

Chapter 4
Profits, Cash Flow, and Financing

Introduction
- Historic Context
- Profit and Cash Flow Today

Definitions of Profit
- Reward for Effort
- Reward for Risk
- Return on Assets
- Profit to Sales Ratio

Profit Objectives
- Profit Maximization
- Satisfactory Profit
- Nonmonetary Profit
- Hobby/Business
- Social Responsibility

Profit Levels
- FBO Reports
- Aviation Industry Studies
- What Is Your Profit?

Realizing Profit
- Profit Orientation
- Planning
- Marketing Orientation
- Information System Design
- Records
- Depreciation Practices
- Inventory
- Bad Debts
- Managerial Decisions
- Cash Flow

Setting Your Cash Flow and Profit Goals

Part 1—Planning for Positive Cash Flow
- Forecasting Sales and Revenues
- Forecasting Expenses
- Month by Month Cash Flow Analysis
- Improving the Cash Position

Part 2—Planning for Profits
- Profit Objective
- Break-even Analysis
- Profitability Variations Among Product Lines
- Profit Centers
- Profit and Loss Statement/Income Statement
- Balance Sheet

Part 3—Budgeting
- Introduction
- Aviation Budget Development
- Steps in Budget Development
- Budget Operation and Control

Part 4—Other Considerations
- Tax Planning
- Competition
- Retained Earnings
- New Revenue Sources

Financing
- Types of Money
- Sources of Money

Credit Management
- Nature and Reason for Credit
- Creating a Credit Policy
- Functions of Credit Management
- Credit Process
- Terms and Definitions
- Cash or Credit Card?

Summary

Discussion Topics

Objectives

- ✔ Describe the meaning of the word "profit."
- ✔ Understand the relationship between social responsibility and profit in business decisions.
- ✔ Give examples of the differences between "fixed" and "variable" costs.
- ✔ Recognize methods of improving the FBO's cash position.
- ✔ Realize the conditions needed for effective budgeting.
- ✔ Describe the benefits and disadvatages of extending credit to customers.

"Lack of cash can drive a firm into bankruptcy even though its products are first rate and its operations are profitable"[1]

Introduction

Historic Context

The economy of this country has been built upon entrepreneurs who started out small, provided a vitally needed product or service, made often very large profits, and plowed them back into the business to finance further growth. Profits were the key to a successful business. In former times, profits provided cash flow for two reasons. First, it was much more a cash economy, and customers expected to pay cash on the spot. Second, it was a tremendous growth economy so that demand was always outstripping supply and "supernormal" profits were often possible.

While this statement is a major simplification of the United States economy in pioneer days, it contains some important concepts. The main concept is that cash flow was not much of an issue. A second concept is that businesses were less likely than today to seek outside sources of financing to support growth, since internally generated funds arrived copiously and fast.

Profit and Cash Flow Today

Due to slower growth in most markets and to virtually instant communications about the competition, "supernormal" profits are now only evident in new industries and evident only in the beginning. Due to the credit economy, cash flow lags are a major issue in almost every type of business. In many industries, customers expect at least thirty days to pay. Money has to be spent producing and delivering the goods well before the producer gets paid. Profits alone, when they are eventually collected, may not be sufficient to finance growth. Even if they are, financing may be needed to get a business out of seasonal or startup cash flow "holes."

One facet of cash flow is often not well understood: That the faster a company is growing, the greater its cash flow problems are likely to be. It may be growing fast simply because it has found a highly **profitable** market niche. Nevertheless, more raw materials, people, and other inputs are needed to respond to the growth market with quality and promptness. Costs go up fast; and even though receipts will eventually come in, any lag means a cash flow "hole."

A successful small business will do well to consider, therefore, that both positive profit **and** positive cash flow are essential for continued operation. Each is a necessary, but not a sufficient condition, for the survival of the business. Large amounts of outside financing channeled into an unprofitable business will only delay and not prevent its demise. Borrowing to ensure a positive bank balance will not be an adequate plan. Having more money coming in than going out does not alone mean a healthy business if this situation appears only on financial statements (in terms of receivables) and not in the checking account (in terms of receipts actually received). Figure 4.1 provides an illustration of the typical cash flow process in a small business and the ways that cash flow can be adjusted to keep the business solvent.

This chapter examines how a financial plan for an FBO business can deal with both profit and cash flow in such a way as to provide the basis for long-term viability.

Definitions of Profit

Reward for Effort

Some business owners regard profit as being simply what is left after all the bills are paid. It is a bonus on top of their salary. Some do not even take a salary but look on profit, if there is any, to be their compensation. Yet the theoretical economist will say that the very reason for anyone being in business is the "profit motive."

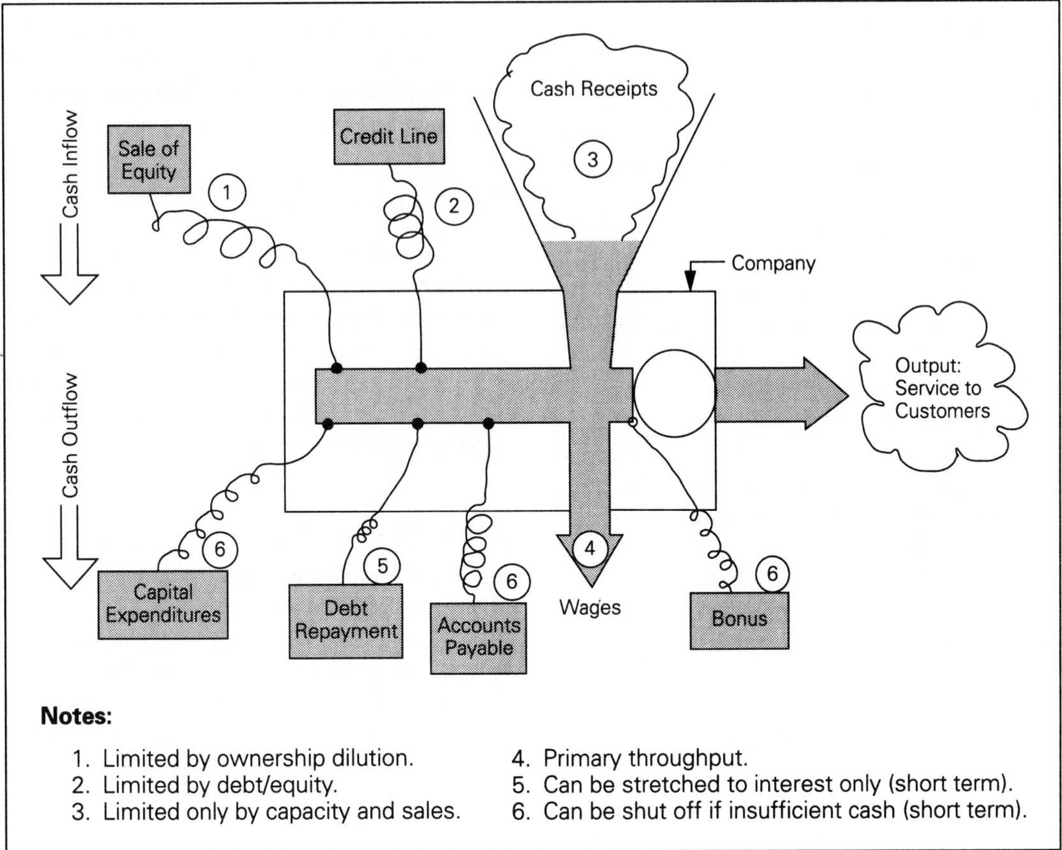

Notes:

1. Limited by ownership dilution.
2. Limited by debt/equity.
3. Limited only by capacity and sales.
4. Primary throughput.
5. Can be stretched to interest only (short term).
6. Can be shut off if insufficient cash (short term).

Figure 4.1. Cash flow process in a small business. By permission, John Moore, President, Electrotest Inc., San Ramon, California (unpublished staff training material, 1983.)

Is the possible chance of something being left over when the bills are paid a sufficient motivation?

Reward for Risk

A more precise definition of profit is *reward for the risk* of entrepreneurship. It therefore should be ranked with similar rewards from higher or lower risks that can be made with one's time and money. These range from speculating in highly risky but profitable investments to perhaps putting one's money in a passbook savings account at 5 percent. To be in business at all, says this school of thought, an owner should not only be earning as much in wages as he or she would get from being on someone else's payroll, but should also be getting a reasonable pretax return (which in today's market might be 8 to 10 percent) on his or her investment in the business.

Return on Assets

Profit measured in this way is examined as a percentage earned on the equity the owner(s) hold in the business. This ratio indicates whether the organization is realizing enough net profit in relation to dollars invested in assets. A business owner should be able to get at least as high a return on total investment as he or she could by investing elsewhere, or have some reasons why not.

Profit to Sales Ratio

This ratio is calculated by dividing the net profits of the business by its total sales. It indicates whether profits are appropriate in relation to total dollars brought into the company through sales.

However, if an aviation specialist develops his or her own FBO business rather than investing the funds elsewhere, it provides several other results in addition to a return on capital. For example:

- A full-time job and/or a vocation
- A paycheck
- The opportunity to build a highly successful, profitable, and salable enterprise

Profit ratios should be examined over time as well as used to compare the company with industry norms.

Profit Objectives

A business person has many possible choices regarding what plan for profits he or she wishes to pursue. The only inappropriate course would be not to plan for profit at all and just hope for the best.

Profit Maximization

In theory this is the only profit goal. The point of maximum profit can be calculated by examining the point of diminishing returns for the business's production; that is, the production volume at which the marginal cost of producing one more item exceeds the marginal revenue from selling it. In reality, production functions tend to go in steps. That is, new economies of scale might be realizable by expansion. This expansion—such as a new maintenance hangar—tends to come in large units. But for any given set of production factors there is a point of diminishing returns. In a labor-intensive business, this might be the point reached when everyone has worked 15 hours a week overtime and is getting too tired. More output will require new hiring, and unit costs will go up again.

Satisfactory Profit

More for the sake of more is less and less consistent with the lifestyle of many of today's managers, who may seek more leisure rather than ulcers. Setting a profit goal in terms of a certain satisfactory dollar level, whether or nor it represents maximum profits, is a choice that many managers may want to make.

Nonmonetary Profit

A variation on the theme of modest profit is that many people in aviation are in it as much for the fun and excitement as for the money. This is fine except that it will not pay the bills and will not provide the return on investment one could get elsewhere. But a conscious lowering of profit goals because of enjoyment of the business is a possible approach. Some managers are forced to settle for this level of profits because their competition is setting profit low (and hence prices) because of *their* love of flying.

Hobby/Business

A love of one's occupation to the point where profit is not a concern puts that enterprise in the category of a hobby rather than a business. If it fails to make a profit for three consecutive years out of five, and if there appears to be no real intent to make a profit, then the expenses associated with the activity *may* not be deducted from anything but the earnings of that activity. The loss is not tax deductible. If one's business is bordering on being a hobby, a consultation with a tax specialist would be in order. The 1986 Tax Reform Act tightened up these requirements in relation to hobby businesses.[2]

Social Responsibility

There is a body of opinion, which appears to be growing as a result of federal program cutbacks, that says that business has a duty to support the needs of the community in a very broad way. Most managers do show considerable concern for the social environment that affects their employees and the community at large. Some of the things a good manager does perhaps cannot be justified on the grounds of profitability alone. However, they build loyalty and goodwill as well as help to ensure a long range future for the airport. Such activities really come under the topic of enlightened self-interest and are a cost of doing business. As such they do not need to erode profit.

Profit Levels

In planning for profit, what guidelines should an FBO use? In addition to what he or she could get by putting his money in the bank, he or she may want to know how others in industry set their profit goals or what they actually realize.

FBO Reports

When a number of FBOs were asked what their profits actually were, these were some of the replies:[3]

- "I'm lucky not to be losing money"
- "Hope to break even"
- "One to three percent"
- "Five percent"
- "Ten percent"
- "Fifteen percent"
- "Twenty-five percent"

The range of the replies and an analysis of the respondents suggest several things. First, one group felt that it was lucky to be breaking even. These people were in the 1 to 5 percent rate of return category. These may be new businesses, marginal operations, those experiencing temporary setbacks or perhaps those that do not know their true profit.

Another group, in the 10 to 15 percent category, attempted to be realistic when comparing the aviation business with other possible investments for their money.

The last group (25 percent) was apparently concerned with the risky nature of the aviation business and felt that higher compensation for risk was appropriate.

It is difficult to obtain system-wide profit information on FBOs because of confidentiality, the competitive nature of the industry and the fact that some FBOs do not even keep adequate records to determine their profit.

Aviation Industry Studies

Some years ago, Piper Aircraft surveyed over 160 Piper dealers around the country.[4] One question asked was, "Do you regularly check the return on your investment?" Seventy-eight replied "yes." Forty-four replied "no." Forty did not respond. An additional question, "What is it now?" received so few responses that it was meaningless. However, at a Piper dealer seminar some time later, the consensus among 100 dealers was that the rate of return should be 20 to 25 percent because of the relatively high risk involved. Other Piper analysis found that the rate of return before taxes was 32 percent among dealers of various sizes, while a Cessna study found that their profitable dealers averaged 25 percent return on investment.[5]

What Is *Your* Profit?

It seems apparent from this discussion that there have been successful FBOs making 20 percent or more profit. It also appears that lack of effort to ensure profit may contribute to the failure in reaching such a level. In addition to being the reward for risk, a solid profit margin has the added advantage of providing a cushion if extra expenses are suddenly required, as well as being available for planned long-term development of the business. Each FBO must make its own profit target and then monitor to see if the desired results are being produced. Profit should be planned in the same way as fixed costs.[6]

Realizing Profit

Profit Orientation

Profit orientation refers to a positive attitude toward profit generation, the effective utilization of managerial tools and techniques in achieving desired profit levels, and the permeation of this orientation throughout the organization.

Key techniques used for this include breakeven analysis, financial statement analysis, budgeting, pricing and cost control. These are discussed in subsequent sections.

Planning

Planning for profit is part of the overall business plan; and within the business plan, it is part of the financial plan, which is another part of cash flow planning. An adequate accounting system to track and report all financial activity in the firm is necessary for this purpose.

Marketing Orientation

As discussed in Chapter 3, a marketing orientation is also essential to a healthy business and to profits. It includes:

- The customer is always right
- Knowing what the customer wants
- Service rather than product delivery

Information System Design

A poor information system design can prevent profits because the manager is not getting information needed to answer certain questions. The manager needs the right information at the right time, though he does not need data collection on everything. This topic is discussed more fully in chapter 7, "Information Systems."

Records

Record keeping is the first step in implementation of the information system. Poor quality or absent records can be a hidden weakness in the system. Examples include:

- Fuel readings not taken and recorded
- Sales slips not filed
- Maintenance charges not entered for company aircraft
- Accounts receivable not organized by age
- Balance sheets being available only many months after the period they cover

Depreciation Practices

It is possible to treat depreciation of capital items in a number of ways with each having different long-and short-run tax implications that can affect income after taxes for a given year. The advice of an accountant who understands aviation is ideal; such a person may not be available unless the FBO educates one.

Inventory

In calculating the business's assets and liabilities, inventory is often a major asset. However, it is important to know the true value of inventory, which may not be the same as what was paid for it. Replacement costs may change, and existing stock may deteriorate during storage due to obsolescence or decay. Storage and insurance costs must also be attributed to existing inventory.

Bad Debts

Not all accounts receivable—another major asset of most businesses—will be collected in full. Total losses and those where only a percentage is realized because a collection agency is involved must be subtracted from income. This can have a significant effect on profits. The manager will need to allow some estimate for the level of bad debts, based on past history and on policy.

Managerial Decisions

There are numerous other areas in which managers can affect profit without even realizing it. These may include:

1. Excess allocation of overhead could turn a profitable department into a loser.
2. A department receiving labor or supplies at cost is receiving a cash benefit. The department supplying it is losing because the same goods and services could have been sold outside at full markup.
3. "Pot mixing" or combining resources from several departments for a special project can make it hard to allocate overheads.

Cash Flow

When payments lag 30 to 90 days after delivery of goods and services, the resulting cash flow lag may require outside financing. If so, the cost of money can erode profits.

Setting Your Cash Flow and Profit Goals Part 1—Planning for Positive Cash Flow

Forecasting Sales and Revenues

For each product and service, an annual forecast of units sold must be made. This will be based partly on the past year's performance, partly on market research about needs and trends in the area, and partly on expectations about the economy. NATA periodically polls its membership about activity and plans and publishes findings.

After predicting volume for each item, the price must be multiplied by volume to get revenue for each line and total revenue must be calculated. (Pricing was reviewed in depth in chapter 3 and will not be discussed here.) Sales by month should be estimated using seasonal factors common to the area. December, January and February are much slower aviation months nationwide than the rest, and most activity shows peaking over the summer months.

Forecasting Expenses

Expenses are generally defined as *fixed*, which have to be met if the business even opens its doors, and *variable*, which go up as the volume of sales goes up. Fixed expenses or overhead include such items as:

- Rent
- Utilities
- Property Taxes
- Office supplies
- Labor
- Professional dues and publications
- Janitorial and routine maintenance
- Advertising (part)
- Inventory (part)
- Insurance

Of course when inflation is more than zero, so-called fixed expenses also go up, and while some are predictable, such as escalator clauses in a lease, some are not. A worst- and best-case figure may be appropriate.

Some fixed costs go up because of growth. For example, more space or inventory may be needed. Heavy use of office machinery may cause it to wear out faster, or more inventory may be needed. More personnel means new office furniture and other overheads, and if overhead costs are figured in the "retail" cost of a new person, it may be two to three times their salary. The costs of expansion must always be allowed for before deciding whether it is feasible. This is discussed in a subsequent section "Break-even Analysis".

Expenses and sales of all types should be calculated on a monthly basis.

Expenses of all types should be calculated on a monthly basis allowing for seasonality of production needs and variations in overheads such as heating and air conditioning costs.

Month by Month Cash Flow Analysis

Particularly in a new business, but also in any business where cash flow lags or is erratic, a monthly cash flow for at least a year is a very valuable tool.

Figure 4.2 sets out a sample cash flow analysis.

In Figure 4.2, the cash position shown in the bottom line tells whether and when the firm will get into a cash flow problem and how great the need for cash will be. It can also tell for a new business how many months will go by before the firm has a permanent positive cash flow. Some businesses swing from negative to positive cash flow and back each year. Such a case is the small airline serving an island resort. Practically all the revenue is made between May and September. The rest of the year the revenue is less because of much less activity producing much less income.[7] Borrowing and repayment are part of the year's plan.

	Jan.	Feb.	March	April	May	June	July. . .	7 months
Cash In								
Product 1	2,000	6,000	3,000	4,000	5,000	5,000	5,000	30,000
2	1,000	2,000	1,000	2,000	2,000	3,000	3,000	14,000
3	5,000	5,000	4,000	4,000	5,000	5,000	5,000	33,000
etc.								
Total cash in	8,000	13,000	8,000	10,000	12,000	13,000	13,000	77,000
Cash Out								
Materials	2,000	2,500	1,500	1,000	1,000	1,000	1,000	10,000
Labor	3,000	3,000	3,000	3,000	3,000	3,000	3,000	21,000
Other inventory	500	600	700	400	500	500	500	3,700
Subtotal variables	5,500	6,100	5,200	4,400	4,500	4,500	4,500	34,700
Management	3,000	3,200	3,200	3,200	3,200	3,200	3,200	22,200
Rent	1,500	1,500	1,500	1,500	1,500	1,500	1,500	10,500
Utilities	250	250	250	250	250	250	250	1,750
Marketing/ads	200	1,000	1,000	750	1,000	250	250	4,450
Subtotal fixed	4,950	5,950	5,950	5,700	5,950	5,200	5,200	38,900
Total cash out	10,450	12,050	11,150	10,100	10,450	9,700	9,700	73,600
Net Cash Out	(2,450)	950	(3,150)	(100)	1,550	3,300	3,300	3,400
Starting Cash	–0–	(2,450)	(1,500)	(4,650)	(4,750)	(3,200)	100	–0–
Cumulative Cash or Deficit "hole"	(2,450)	(1,500)	(4,650)	(4,750)	(3,200)	100	3,400	3,400

Figure 4.2. Monthly cash flow chart.

Figure 4.2 provides a dramatic illustration of how a business can show a profit ($3,400 over seven months) yet still encounter serious cash flow problems (a cash flow "hole" of $4,750 by April).

In order to test a variety of cash flow scenarios, a microcomputer may be used to change one figure at a time and automatically recalculate the bottom line. It is a good idea to make pessimistic assumptions about payment lags, bad debts and costs in order to see the difference in cash position between that and the most likely case.

Improving the Cash Position

There are a number of ways that a firm can improve cash flow lags, including:

- Cash on the spot for more services
- Advance payment for a percentage of the cost (e.g., a charter for several days)
- Larger deposits on aircraft sales
- Advance deposits from regular customers
- Memberships paid in advance of service delivery, such as annual flying dues
- Interest charges on accounts over 30 days past due
- Flight instruction courses paid in advance
- Factoring receivables—selling the accounts receivable to a factor
- Borrowing against receivables

A firm can also delay its own cash outflow by such techniques as:

- Buying supplies on consignment—only paid for if and when sold
- Negotiating more favorable terms for purchases including discounts and extended payments

However, putting off payment will not cure the problems in a firm that never has a positive cash flow and is basically operating at a loss. Payments should only be deferred until the cash position is expected to improve.

Part 2—Planning for Profits

Profit Objectives

The desired profit in percentage terms should be converted into dollar terms for the year so that a precise profit figure is part of the budget.

Break-even Analysis

Break-even analysis is the tool that identifies whether doing more business will result in more profit. The first few units sold by a business do not bring in enough to cover even fixed costs. As sales go up, first fixed costs, and subsequently variable costs, are covered. The point at which all costs are exactly covered (but no more) is the break-even point. Beyond that point, all revenue is profit. This is shown in Figure 4.3.

A break-even level of sales can also be calculated *after* insertion of a figure for profit. In this case, profit is treated just like any other expense:

break-even sales = fixed costs + variable costs + profit

When a business owner is trying to decide whether to expand, it is apparent that any expansion requiring only higher variable costs will be profitable because each extra sale must cover only the extra or *marginal* cost of producing that sale, not the full cost. For example, the aviation manager plans to sell model planes at a convention. He can purchase the planes at $2.00 each on consignment (with the privilege of returning all unsold models). The booth rental is $800.00 and payable in advance. He feels that he can sell the aircraft models at $4.00 each. Assuming he is not going to have any labor costs, how many models must be sold to break even (zero profit)?

Break-even sales = fixed costs + variable costs + profit

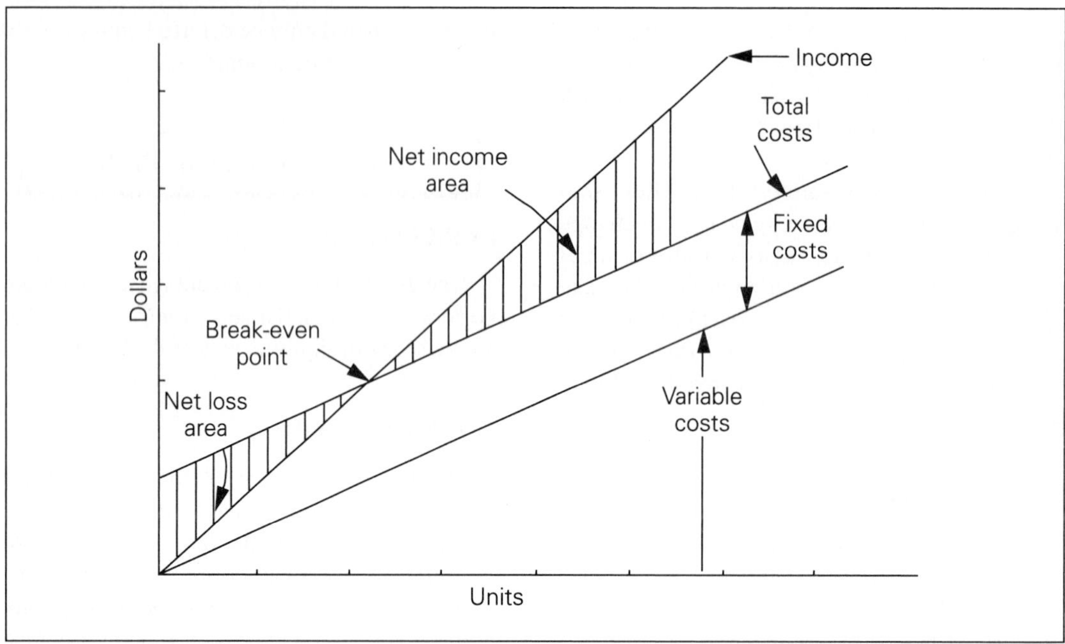

Figure 4.3. Break-even chart.

Let x = number of units to be sold to break even

$$\$4.00x = \$2.00x + \$800.00 + 0$$
$$2.00x = 800 + 0$$
$$x = 800 / 2$$
$$x = 400 \text{ units}$$

or in dollars:

$$x = \$1600.00$$

Three other important terms are the **Contribution Margin, Unit Contribution Margin, and Contribution Margin Ratio.** The Contribution Margin is what's left of revenue to contribute to fixed costs after variable costs have been subtracted:

contribution margin = revenue – variable costs

The **Unit Contribution Margin** is the unit selling price less the unit variable cost. The **Contribution Margin Ratio** is the unit contribution margin divided by the selling price. In the case just described it was .5 ($4.00/$2.00).

The Break-Even Point (BEP) in dollars is (fixed expenses + profit)/contribution margin ratio.

Breakeven analysis can be used for a single product line or department or for the business as a whole.It can apply to:

- Fuel servicing activity
- Billed service hours of a maintenance department
- Instructional hours of a flight department
- Activity volume of a parts department
- Revenue hours of air charter or air taxi work
- Route planning
- Acquisition of new operating equipment

A more complex example is the decision of whether or not to start a new flight school operation. The FBO has the following estimates:

Fixed expenses

- Building lease, utilities and taxes . . . . $ 10,800
- Aircraft insurance and depreciation . . . . $ 9,000
- Flight instructor base pay . . . . $ 7,500
- Subtotal . . . . $ 27,300

Variable expenses

- Aircraft operating expenses-$30/hr, for 2600 hours . . . . $ 78,000
- Instructor commission, $15/hr: . . $ 39,000
- Classroom time, 200 hours . . . . . $ 3,000
- Supplies/materials ($150/student, 75 students . . . . $ 11,250
- Subtotal $131,250
- Total Costs $158,550

Estimated income

- Ground School, 75 students @ $525 . . . . $ 39,375
- Flying Lessons, 2600 hours @ $67.50 . . . . $175,500
- Instruction Kit, 75 @ $300 22,500

Total income $237,375

Using these figures we can examine the breakeven point for each product:

- Ground school selling price, $39,375 / 200 hours; per hour $196.88
- Average variable cost per hour . . . $ 15.00
- Contribution Margin $181.88

Breakeven Point = Fixed Expenses/ Contribution Margin
$27,300/$181.88 = 150.09 hours
150.09 hours x $196.88 = $29,549.72

Thus, the ground school alone could pay for all fixed costs and for its own variable costs if $29,500 worth of enrollments or 56 students were mustered, compared with an estimated sales potential of $39,375 or 75 students.

Suppose the FBO decides to examine just added flying lessons without the ground school.

- Selling Price per Hour $67.50
- Average variable cost per hour ($30 + $15) $45.00
- Contribution Margin $22.50

Breakeven Point = Fixed Costs/Contribution Margin
$27,300/$22.50 = 1213 hours
1213 x $67.50 = $81,877.50 income

Thus the flying lessons must make $82,000 to break even compared with an estimated $175,500 in prospective sales.

Suppose now that all fixed costs are double the previous estimate:

Breakeven Point = Fixed Costs/ Contribution Margin
$54,600/$22.50 = 2427 hours
2427 x $67.50 = $163,823

This is a much more marginal proposal because 93 percent of forecast sales must actually be achieved just to break even, which leaves very little room for sickness, bad weather, lack of demand, and so on.

Profitability Variations Among Product Lines

In the above example, the ground school was more profitable than the flying lessons because one instructor was handling one class of 75 students, whereas the flying lesson is a one-on-one situation with substantial aircraft costs. It is possible to take all fixed expenses and allocate them between the divisions of the business and estimate which areas are most profitable. For example, one FBO may decide that they have ample extra space in the front desk area, he or she is going to emphasize the sale of aviation books and accessories, where the markup can be 100 per cent over wholesale for relatively little variable cost in handling. Another FBO may see their strongest profit line in aircraft sales, where even a few percentage points in commissions can mean many dollars because of the high value of the item. An FBO may decide not to even compete in such areas as specialty avionics because there is another operator on the field and the cost of startup would be so great for limited profit. Whatever the manager's inclinations, break-even analysis will provide the tools to find out whether something is really worth doing. Both breakeven and cash flow analysis should be applied to all prospective new ventures by using conservative assumptions.

Profit Centers

Owing to different profitability levels, it may be desirable to divide the various functions of the business into profit centers with each having its own profit goal. This avoids hidden cross-subsidies between areas, and also permits conscious cross subsidy of certain items that may bring in people to make greater purchases (e.g., washing aircraft, coffee, air and other "free" items).

Profit and Loss Statement/Income Statement

This is the operating income statement that represents the picture annually, monthly or quarterly. A skeleton income statement is shown in figure 4.4:

	19XX	19XY	19XZ
Sales			
Cost of Sales			
Gross Margin			
Marketing			
Management			
Engineering			
Administration			
Other			
Operating Profit			
Taxes			
Net Profit			

Figure 4.4. Income statement. (Source: *Entrepreneurship*, Steven C. Brandt.[8])

	19XX	19XY	19XZ
Assets			
Cash			
Inventory			
Accounts receivable			
Buildings, equipment			
Total Assets			
Liabilities			
Accounts payable			
Loans			
Net Worth			
Capital invested			
Earnings retained			
Total Liabilities and Net Worth			

Figure 4.5. Balance sheet.

Balance Sheet

A balance sheet tells not only about the operating account, but also about the capital account, as shown in Figure 4.5. It tells "What you own and what you owe."[9] Both the operating statement and the balance sheet need to be projected two to five years ahead.

Part 3—Budgeting

Introduction

There are some popular misconceptions about budgeting that have detracted from its use and effectiveness. Some individuals feel that a budget is a straightjacket; others feel that it is repressive; some people feel that it wastes time; and still others feel that it is a mechanical, futile activity. Many who have experienced the heavy end-of-year spending in order to make the budget appear accurate lose confidence in the process. Most of these misconceptions are the result of personal experiences in situations where budgeting was not handled properly or where the individual may have overreacted to the process.

Budgeting involves setting cost limits for each unit of the firm or profit center. These are based on the projected sales and profit desired for the line departments or with some reference to overhead as a percentage of business costs or sales for the administrative or staff departments. Budgets can be changed in the course of the year if circumstances warrant, and break-even analysis can help decide if a budget should be increased to capture a new business opportunity. The budget need not be a straightjacket but can achieve the following:

- Set specific goals for each department and the firm as a whole
- Establish limits within which managers know they are to operate
- Establish company needs and priorities during the budget period
- Foresee potential operational problems and allow preventive action
- Provide management with increased flexibility
- Inform line departments about improvements planned for later years
- Provide standards to measure performance and results

Aviation Budget Development

Developing a budget for an aviation business, like any other business, is really profit planning.[10,11] From a practical point of view, it is a technique for managing the business. It involves the formation of definite plans (budgets) for a limited future period. These plans are normally expressed in financial terms. A complete budget develops and includes standards to measure and evaluate the actual performance of management and the business.

In order for a budget to serve as an effective managerial tool, several conditions should exist. It is perhaps the absence of these conditions that creates the misconceptions mentioned. Advocates of the budgeting process suggest that the following are necessary:

1. There should be a suitable organization structure for the business activity.
2. An adequate accounting system should be in operation.
3. The budget should have the interest and support of top management.

Preliminary preparations for the budget include:

- Forecasting business activity
- Preparing budget proposals
- Assembling and approving the budget
- Using supporting budgets
- Budget operation and control

Steps in Budget Development

Preparing for the budget. The first and most important preparations are setting goals, defining objectives, and creating long-range plans for the organization. As was discussed in chapter 2 under planning, it is essential that the manager have a good grasp of the present organizational situation. He or she then develops a plan that is complete with goals and objectives. These goals and objectives should then be related to financial and other specific goals for the coming year. The objectives that are developed should express the desired results in specific measurable terms. Developing the long-range plan is considered an important prelude to the development of the budget, for there is obviously a very close correlation between the two. A budget may be considered the first year of a long-range plan—the implementation of that plan.

Forecasting business. Next, the manager develops some careful estimates or forecasts of business conditions that are expected to exist during the budget period. Although all external conditions are important, the critical task is the selection of conditions facing the individual business. Many managers feel that this is the chief difficulty in budgeting. They indicate major problems in: (1) obtaining meaningful figures in advance and (2) making good use of the information available. Forecasting future business is a fundamental and necessary process that must be accomplished for all businesses. It is not, however, an activity approached enthusiastically by all managers, partly because of unfamiliarity with the procedure, and partly due to apparent failures of past attempts.

It is felt that more meaningful figures can be developed by using a procedure which considers:

- Identification of the general economic situation
- Key regulatory factors that influence the business environment
- Recent industry developments
- Specific trend and forecast data that might be acquired
- The evaluation of business opportunities that may exist
- Local economic trends and factors
- Competitive elements facing the business

Budget preparation. With the forecast data in hand, the manager's next (and very important) step is the preparation of the budget. The development of the detailed blueprints showing how the company intends to reach the desired goals and objectives in the business conditions identified by the forecast is best accomplished in the following sequence:

1. Set a timetable for activity.
2. Develop a sales budget.
3. Formulate a purchases budget.
4. Develop an expense budget.
5. Formulate the income statement budget.
6. Calculate a balance sheet budget.

Timetable. It is very important to prepare a timetable for the development of a budget. Such a schedule is necessary because budgeting is a planning activity and is very likely to be postponed if not established on a fairly regular schedule. The following illustrates a timetable for a budget based on a calendar-year cycle. Of course, it should be recognized that a budget is a living, flexible document that must meet the variable conditions facing the business enterprise. The possibility and reality of change must become part of the timetable and the budgeting process.

Date	Activity
15 October	Develop plans and objectives
1 November	Complete business forecast
10 November	Develop preliminary budget
15 November	Final budget review
1 December	Budget acceptance and approval
1 January	Initial implementation
As required	Budget modification

Sales budget. The manager begins the development of this budget by working on the sales estimate. Since most of the activities of a business are geared to the level of expected sales, budget preparation begins with sales forecasting. The business forecasting procedures mentioned earlier should provide the basic material needed to start this first step. In some instances, it may even provide the exact information for a sales budget if the historical information is available and the forecast has been prepared in adequate detail. The initial step is a thorough market analysis. Normally, this is composed as an analysis of the overall marketplace (as is outlined in the earlier section on forecasting), salespeople's estimates of the market situation, general sales trends in the industry and the area, and a study of previous years' sales.

The second step is the development of the company market forecast. Using a great deal of the data acquired in step 1, a forecast is prepared for the company's market potential. The structure of the market in terms of types, units, time, and prices is set forth.

The third step involves pricing out the company forecast in order to acquire the expected total sales (revenue) of the business. Adjustments are made to reflect the goals and objectives of the business as well as the market situation.

The next step is the breakdown of total sales into the departments or work centers of the business. The expected incomes for parts, service, flight line, aircraft sales, instruction, and miscellaneous are estimated for the accounting year. Naturally, this reflects the forecast data used in the development of total sales.

The final step is the development of a monthly sales budget for each of the identified departments in the business. This enables the manager to identify and anticipate the monthly variations in sales due to seasonal and other fluctuations.

Figures 4.6 and 4.7 illustrate worksheets that may be used to calculate the sales budget for an aviation business. Figure 4.6 deals with the total and departmental sales budget while figure 4.7 is used for the monthly calculations. In using figure 4.6, the previous year's budget and actual sales are filled in for the total business and the departmental components. Using this as a guide along with the other elements for developing a forecast, the current year budget is projected. Figure 4.9 is a worksheet to be used in extending the annual sales budget on a monthly basis.

	Previous Year Budget	Previous Year Actual	Current Year Budget
Total Sales of Company			
Aircraft sales (300)			
Parts Sales (400)			
Service Sales (500)			
Flight Sales (600)			
Line Sales (700)			
Misc. Activity (800)			

Figure 4.6. Annual sales budget worksheet.

Procedure:

1. Fill in the current annual budget as prepared on the annual sales budget worksheet.
2. Allocate the annual sales figures among the months according to anticipated variations.

	Annual Budget	Jan.	Feb.	Mar.	Apr.	May	June	July	Aug.	Sept.	Oct.	Nov.	Dec.
Total Sales													
Airdraft Sales)													
Parts Sales													
Service Sales													
Flight Sales													
Line Sales													
Misc. Activity													

Figure 4.7. Monthly sales budget worksheet.

This will allow for calendar variations that result from a number of market-related elements (season, weather, and so on) that dictate or influence the monthly sales figure.

Purchases budget. Next is the development of the purchases budget. In order to achieve the desired sales level, it will obviously be necessary to purchase the products that will be sold to meet the sales budget goals. Figure 4.8 illustrates a worksheet for developing a purchases budget. Note that in calculating anticipated purchases that it is necessary to consider dollar volume of sales first. Then, the number of units or quantity of material needed to arrive at the right sales volume is calculated by using the markups for the various product areas. These annual purchase figures (which are expressed in dollars and units of quantity) are then divided into monthly allocations.

Expense budget. The manager next constructs an expense budget. Figure 4.9 illustrates a worksheet that may be used in this process. In this instance, the expense budget categories are identified as employment, aircraft, occupancy, and other. These four major groups are divided into subcategories, which are the expense accounts contained in the ledgers of the accounting system. In general, these expenses are incurred by operating the business. The worksheet is completed and the budget is formed by filling in previous-year expense figures and then projecting the current-year expenses. Of course, this projection is based upon anticipated sales and the effect upon expenses required to support the sales. The annual expense for each account is divided into a monthly expense item according to an appropriate system. It may be a straight percentage or it may be based on work load, number of people, borrowing schedule, marketing plan, or some other factor according to the elements that dictate or control the expenditures.

Income statement budget. The next key step in developing a complete budget is bringing the sales and expenses together into an income statement budget. Figure 4.10 suggests a budget worksheet. This form follows the income statement format and uses it for budgeting purposes with both previous year and current year figures. Sales, purchases, and expenses all come from the completed worksheets in those areas. The basic objective of this worksheet is to bring them all together with the primary focus on profit. At this stage, the goal is profit planning—budgeting for the desired net income for the operating period. This is the ultimate objective of budgeting: to identify planned operating profit.

Balance sheet budget. The final step in the budgeting process is to transfer the overall outcome of the operating budget to the balance sheet and to develop a projection for the total financial condition of the company. By using a worksheet comparable to those for sales, purchases and expenses, a budget can be constructed to show anticipated changes in assets, liabilities, and net worth. Desired business activities will influence accounts in each of these areas and a budget will assist in testing the feasibility of such action.

Budget assembly and approval. All the business activities should be represented in the budgeting process and in the various divisions of the budget. The final budget should be presented to identify clearly the organization's subdivisions and their assigned budget goals. The budget's figures should represent reasonable but not easily attainable goals. The personnel involved in and responsible for achieving business results should also be involved in the development of the budget. Back-up schedules should be developed as necessary features to augment the budget. The budget should not be developed with the expectation of cutting; rather, it should be considered a realistic contribution to achieving the overall company objectives.

In addition to these guidelines, the human aspects of budget building should be recognized and every effort made to create a structure as free from personal distortion as possible. Some of the

Guidelines:
Includes those goods that are the basis for the sales budgets. Materials on hand, plus units required for sales, resulting in the desired ending inventory needed for each product, by month.

Procedure:
1. Determine the total amount for each activity area, that is, sales, parts, service, and so on as a portion of the total sales volume.
2. Allocate this amount for the twelve months, making adjustments for seasonal variances.
3. Determine the units required for each month where appropriate.
4. Adjust annual budget as required.

		Annual Budget		Jan.	Feb.	Mar.	Apr.	May	June	July	Aug.	Sept.	Oct.	Nov.	Dec.
Aircraft	$														
Sales	#														
Parts	$														
Sales	#														
Service	$														
Sales	#														
Flight	$														
Sales	#														
Line	$														
Sales	#														
Misc.	$														
Activity	#														

Figure 4.8. Combined annual and monthly purchases budget worksheet.

EXPENSE BUDGET WORKSHEET

Procedure: 1. Fill in previous year annual expense figures
2. Based upon anticipated level of business activity, project the current year annual expense figures
3. Allocate the annual expense figures to months

		EXPENSES:		Annual Previous Year	Annual Current Year	Jan.	Feb.	Mar.	Apr.	May	June	July	Aug.	Sept.	Oct.	Nov.	Dec.
6	EMPLOYMENT	Salaries – Officers	20														
7		Salaries/Wages – Employees	21														
8		Commissions	22														
9		Taxes – Payroll	23														
10		Employee Benefits	24														
11																	
12																	
13																	
14		TOTAL EMPLOYMENT															
15	AIRCRAFT	Aircraft Delivery	30														
16		Aircraft Miscellaneous	31														
17		Depreciation – Aircraft	32														
18		Fuel & Oil – Aircraft	33														
19		Insurance – Aircraft	34														
20		Interest – Aircraft	35														
21		Inventory Adustment –Aircraft	36														
22		Maintenance – Aircraft	37														
23		Warranty	38														
24																	
25																	
26		TOTAL AIRCRAFT															
27	OCCUPANCY	Rent	44														
28		Depreciation/Amortization – Bldg.	45														
29		Taxes – Property	46														
30		Utilities	47														
31		Maintenance – Bldg./Land	48														
32																	
33																	
34		TOTAL OCCUPANCY															
35																	
36	OTHER EXPENSES	Advertising	50														
37		Bad Debts	53														
38		Depreciation – Other	56														
39		Donations & Dues	59														
40		Freight & Postage	62														
41		Insurance – Other	65														
42		Interest – Other	68														
43		Inventory Adjustment – Other	71														
44		Maintenance – Other	74														
45		Professional Services	77														
46		Supplies	80														
47		Taxes – Other than P.R./Prop./Inc.	83														
48		Telephone & Telegraph	86														
49		Travel	89														
50		Vehicle	92														
51																	
52																	
53																	
54		Miscellaneous	98														
55																	
56		TOTAL EXPENSES															

Figure 4.9. Expense budget worksheet.

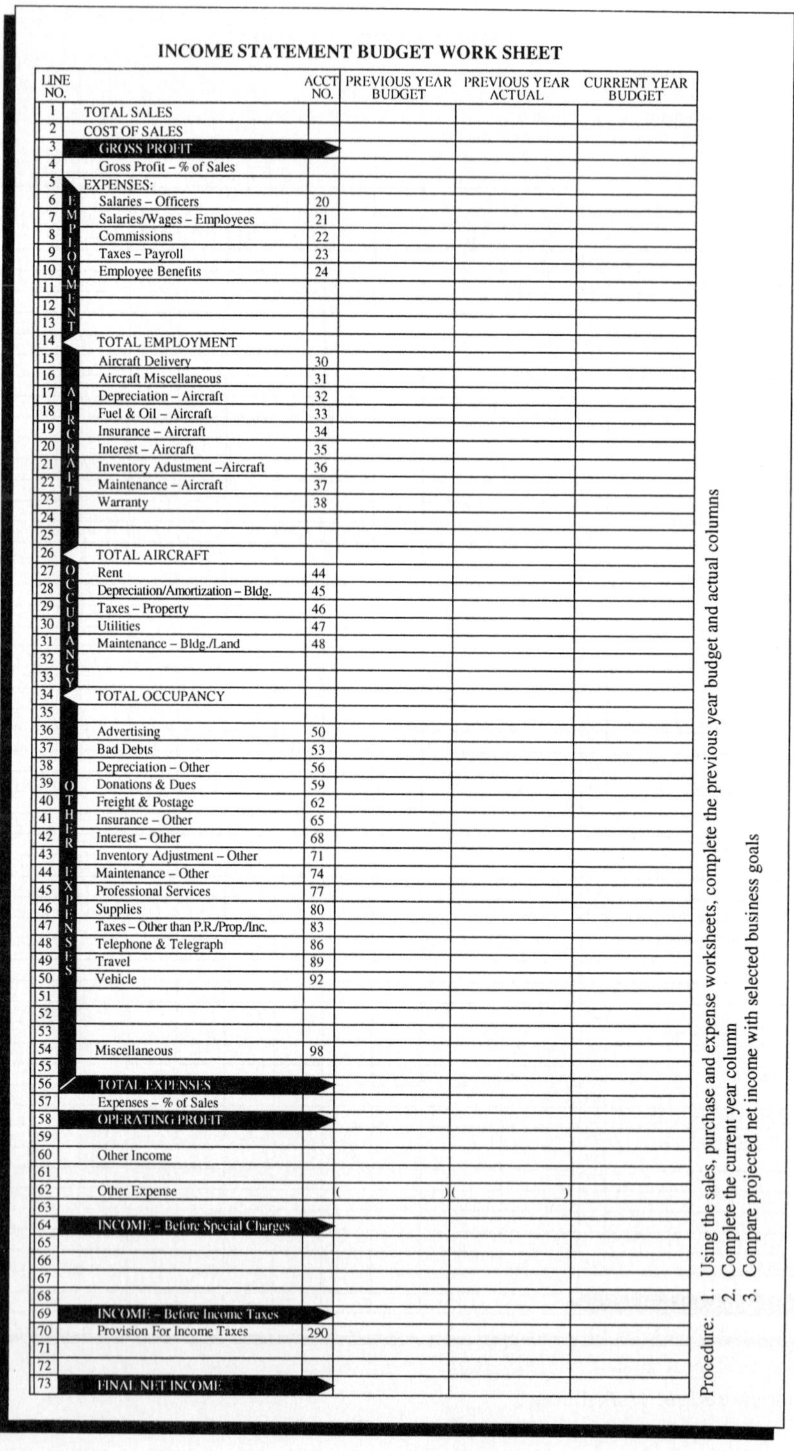

INCOME STATEMENT BUDGET WORK SHEET

LINE NO.			ACCT NO.	PREVIOUS YEAR BUDGET	PREVIOUS YEAR ACTUAL	CURRENT YEAR BUDGET
1		TOTAL SALES				
2		COST OF SALES				
3		GROSS PROFIT				
4		Gross Profit – % of Sales				
5		EXPENSES:				
6	EMPLOYMENT	Salaries – Officers	20			
7		Salaries/Wages – Employees	21			
8		Commissions	22			
9		Taxes – Payroll	23			
10		Employee Benefits	24			
11						
12						
13						
14		TOTAL EMPLOYMENT				
15		Aircraft Delivery	30			
16		Aircraft Miscellaneous	31			
17	AIRCRAFT	Depreciation – Aircraft	32			
18		Fuel & Oil – Aircraft	33			
19		Insurance – Aircraft	34			
20		Interest – Aircraft	35			
21		Inventory Adustment –Aircraft	36			
22		Maintenance – Aircraft	37			
23		Warranty	38			
24						
25						
26		TOTAL AIRCRAFT				
27	OCCUPANCY	Rent	44			
28		Depreciation/Amortization – Bldg.	45			
29		Taxes – Property	46			
30		Utilities	47			
31		Maintenance – Bldg./Land	48			
32						
33						
34		TOTAL OCCUPANCY				
35						
36		Advertising	50			
37		Bad Debts	53			
38		Depreciation – Other	56			
39	OTHER EXPENSES	Donations & Dues	59			
40		Freight & Postage	62			
41		Insurance – Other	65			
42		Interest – Other	68			
43		Inventory Adjustment – Other	71			
44		Maintenance – Other	74			
45		Professional Services	77			
46		Supplies	80			
47		Taxes – Other than P.R./Prop./Inc.	83			
48		Telephone & Telegraph	86			
49		Travel	89			
50		Vehicle	92			
51						
52						
53						
54		Miscellaneous	98			
55						
56		TOTAL EXPENSES				
57		Expenses – % of Sales				
58		OPERATING PROFIT				
59						
60		Other Income				
61						
62		Other Expense		( )	( )	
63						
64		INCOME – Before Special Charges				
65						
66						
67						
68						
69		INCOME – Before Income Taxes				
70		Provision For Income Taxes	290			
71						
72						
73		FINAL NET INCOME				

Procedure: 1. Using the sales, purchase and expense worksheets, complete the previous year budget and actual columns
2. Complete the current year column
3. Compare projected net income with selected business goals

Figure 4.10. Budget worksheet used to formulate complete budget.

likely distortions that might detract from the desired objectivity are:

- Preparing a low budget in order to play the role of the "successful, driving leader"
- Preparing a budget with excessive figures to get "my fair share" of the funds
- Allowing personal biases for a favorite aspect of the business to have too great an influence
- Allowing a "halo" effect associated with one department or business activity to distort the overall company budget beyond realistic expectations
- Distorting the sound budget concept into a game of trying to outguess the approving level of management

Using supporting budgets. In developing and utilizing a budget system, a manager will undoubtedly need to establish and use several additional supporting budgets to meet specific needs. He or she may need one for cash, one for people, one for fixed assets, or for a variety of items already in the budget as a single line but in need of support. One such budget with universal application and of special interest is a cash budget or a cash flow projection. Since cash flow is so very important to a business, we will review the cash budget in some detail. It is a schedule over time of cash inflows and outflows. This is used in an attempt to pinpoint cash surpluses and shortages so that the manager can always be certain to have sufficient money in the bank to cover obligations or have a plan to invest surpluses. There are a variety of uses of the cash forecast, including:

- Determining operating cash requirements
- Anticipating short-term financing needs
- Investing excess cash
- Planning reductions in debt
- Scheduling capital payments
- Taking advantage of cash discounts
- Supporting credit policies

The primary method of developing a cash flow forecast is through the receipts and disbursements comparison. This procedure generally adheres to the following pattern:

1. Develop forecasts for sales, purchases, expenses and related schedules.
2. Analyze the forecasts carefully to identify the cash receipts and payments of each particular period.
3. Using the cash budget worksheet (Fig. 4.11), list the receipts and disbursements for the periods that cash actually changes hands.
4. Review the projected results of the worksheet. Note the periods requiring additional outside funds and periods providing excess funds for use in retiring obligations or for investment.

With the cash position identified, the manager can take action to control the cash flow through day-by-day transactions. Three such actions are (1) speeding up collections, (2) controlling payables, and (3) controlling bank balances.

Budget Operation and Control

Once a budget period begins, the function of budgeting becomes one of exercising control over business operations as they progress. The word control, as used here, means making certain that actual performance is going according to plan. This usually requires:

- Periodic reporting of performance
- Comparing performance with the budget (plan)
- Pinpointing reasons for variations
- Taking action to correct unfavorable variances
- Reevaluating the original budget goals

Frequently, an examination of a budget in operation will suggest problems in the operation.

Procedure:

1. Identify the cash receipts and payments expected throughout the year.
2. List receipts and disbursements for the periods that cash actually changes hands.
3. Note difference between cash available and that required.
4. Plan for the source of needed funds or the utilization of excess.

Item	Jan.	Feb.	Mar.	Apr.	May	June	July	Aug.	Sept.	Oct.	Nov.	Dec.
1. Cash Balance, Beginning												
2. Add Receipts from Customers												
3. Total Available												
4. Less disbursements												
5. Payroll												
6. Aircraft												
7. Occupancy												
8. Misc.												
9. Income Tax												
10. Total Disbursements												
11. Difference between Cash Available and Required (Line 3 minus Line 10)												
12. Source or Utilization												

Figure 4.11. Cash budget worksheet.

When the budget is examined closely, one or more of the following deficiencies may be noted:

1. There has been a poor determination of budget standards.
2. Not all key business activities have been included in the budget.
3. The budget has not been revised when the need is indicated.
4. There is a lack of understanding of the budget process throughout the organization.
5. There is a lack of acceptance of the budget by management and employees.

The budget area should not be closed without at least a mention of the flexible or variable budget. The budgets discussed thus far are static in that the plan is geared to a single target level of sales. A flexible budget is geared to a range of activity rather than one level and will supply a more dynamic basis for comparison than will a fixed budget. As aviation managers and organizations become better versed in budgeting, they might like to use flexible budgeting for some or all of their needs.

Part 4—Other Considerations

Tax Planning

As mentioned, tax planning can affect cash outlays in a given year and in the amount, especially in relation to depreciation and tax credits. Taxes are an expense like any other but their prediction requires the skills of an accountant who not only sees you once a year, but also has helped to set up the books to collect the data needed for taxes and other purposes.

Competition

At all times an FBO must watch the competition and determine whether to match someone else's new service, reduce prices, or be innovative by trying something new. These contingencies should be allowed for in the business plan.

Retained Earnings

These are profits plowed back into the business or kept liquid for a rainy day. The cyclical nature of aviation suggests the desirability of retained earnings if only to even out the good and bad years.

New Revenue Sources

Many public airport owners are seeking new sources of revenue at airports and often finding that the most profitable ones are not aviation related. The feasibility of each depends on the size and clientele of the airport, but an FBO might be able to tap these just as readily as an airport manager. Recent studies found these possibilities:[12,13,14,15]

- Vending machines
- Luggage lockers
- Copying machines
- Stores and newsstands
- Coffee shops and restaurants
- Pay phones
- Car rentals
- Parking lots
- Rental of unneeded space for commercial use
- Agricultural (for example sale of hay, turf farming, worm farming)
- Video games
- Travel agent commissions

While leases may preclude some of these, any way to increase profits should be given consideration if little or no expense is involved.

Financing

Types of Money

There are basically four types of money for running a business: short-term cash, long-term cash, equity, and employee ownership. Each has different conditions. The last two involve giving away some of the ownership, and possibly control, to others in exchange for their cash or their willingness to give up cash.

Sources of Money

Family and friends. Many businesses start this way. It is important to be extremely specific about ownership, control, profit sharing, and inheritance where this approach is used. All loans should be written as if they were for strangers.

Accounts receivable financing. Accounts receivable financing, usually involving factoring, can help a business that is already operational but suffering from lags in collection. The factoring company normally takes title to invoices and collects directly from your customers. Rates charged by factors may be fixed or may vary with the collection period. However, your administrative costs can be cut or even eliminated; and once a relationship with a factor is set up, you can get cash at the time of invoicing.

Banks will also often finance accounts receivable. A bank will not buy the invoices. The business owner pays them into a special account from which the bank first pays itself and then any remainder goes into a business checking account. This will normally cost less than factoring, but the business owner is still responsible for collections.

Leasing. Leasing and lease purchasing are good ways to keep monthly costs down when compared with buying outright. Lease purchase terms, especially where the lessor takes care of maintenance, may be extremely cost effective.

Venture capital. Venture capital sources have been growing in recent years, particularly for high-tech areas, but for an FBO they remain an unlikely source. This is because investors are looking for five to ten times their investment within five years; also, they usually will only consider large potential sales. The dramatic growth path of any product in its early years is ideal for venture capital. One drawback is that ownership of 40 per cent or more of the business will pass to the venture firm.[16,17]

SBA. Small Business Administration (SBA) loans are actually usually loan guarantees. Being turned down twice for regular bank financing makes one eligible. Points above prime are charged, making this a very costly source of aid. Owing to the paperwork and conservatism involved in the banking industry, it is uncommon for new businesses to get SBA loans.[18,19]

Customers. A common practice among FBOs is to invite steady customers to place $500.00 on account with a bonus of $50.00 credit for doing so. The $50.00 retail may only cost $25.00 wholesale, so the $500.00 is being borrowed at an annual rate of only 5 percent. This method can encourage a close rapport with a set of regular customers and keep the bank balance healthy. However, the true cost of this financing depends on how fast the customer uses up his $500.00. If he uses it in a month, you have provided an annual rate of interest of 60 percent.

Banks. A bank will give a secured line of credit relatively easily for a few points above market rate. For an unsecured line of credit or a loan against receivables, they want to know everything about the business, its managers, and its performance. The more polished and detailed the presentation, the better chance of success. Also, it appears to pay to dress as a banker when making the request.

Public markets. Going public is complex and expensive, but some states have limited variations on full public ownership that could be feasible for an FBO.

Small Business Investment Companies (SBIC). These are companies licensed by SBA to provide equity capital or long-term loans to small businesses. They are restricted to businesses with a net worth of less than $6 million and a net income for past two years of less than $2 million. Rates and equity are determined by negotiation but the SBIC does not generally seek control.[20]

Credit Management

Nature and Reason for Credit

Credit is derived from *credo*. This means "I believe" or "I trust." Today, credit provides a measure of the trustworthiness of an individual to receive goods and services while deferring payment to a definite future time. The seller (creditor) recognizes this confidence or trust by allowing the customer (debtor) to receive the goods immediately, but to postpone payment until later.

The individual consumer uses credit to:

- Raise his standard of living or increase his enjoyment
- Realize the convenience offered by use of credit
- Meet the pressures of economic necessity

The manager or the business uses credit to:

- Enable the business to sell more goods and services
- Permit the business to purchase goods on terms that will normally allow the business to resell and thus gain funds for repayment and profit
- Provide the opportunity for cash loans from some financial institutions

Creating a Credit Policy

Every aviation business should have a credit policy that expresses the basic philosophy of the management and serves as a guideline for decision making throughout the organization. Although it may have many possible variations, a credit policy should consider the following areas:

- Authority for granting credit
- Terms of the sale
- Dealing with delinquent customers
- Classification of risks
- Helping customers obtain financing

Figure 4.12 contains a sample credit policy from The Conference Board publication on "Managing Trade Receivables."[20] Although your policy may not resemble the illustration, you should be aware that successful credit management comes from an efficient and well-coordinated program, which, in turn, comes from a sound basic policy.

Functions of Credit Management

The purposes of credit management include:

- To maximize sales and profits
- To minimize bad debt losses
- To achieve efficient utilization of invested funds
- To develop full coordination with the operating departments
- To establish an effective credit policy
- To set standards for credit operation
- To collect information on credit activity
- To analyze and evaluate credit activity information
- To make decisions on credit issues and matters
- To carry out the credit process

Credit Policy Statement

1. ***General policy.*** It is the policy of the company to extend credit and grant terms to customers in relation to the credit risks involved. The responsibility for implementation of this policy rests with the Vice President, Finance. Administration and control of this policy is centralized in the Credit Department.

2. ***Extension of credit and limits of authority.*** Credit may be extended to new customers as follows:

Extended value of each order	Authorized by
a. Up to $100	Any order-processing unit or salesperson
b. Up to $750	Division or Subsidiary Sales Managers
c. Up to $25,000	Credit Manager or his or her delegate in certain locations as specified
d. Over $25,000	Treasurer

3. ***Procedure***
   a. Credit approvals made by authorized personnel in paragraphs 2a and b must be reported to the Credit Department by memorandum, which will include customer name, address, class of trade, and amount of credit granted.
   b. Credit limits on specific customers will be established by the Credit Department and will be adjusted from time to time as conditions warrant.
   c. Orders received from customers with whom the company has had unfavorable credit experience must be cleared for credit approval through the Credit Department, regardless of the amount of the order, until such time as credit limits have been reestablished.
   d. Collection of accounts is the responsibility of the Credit Manager or his or her delegate. Other personnel may be asked to assist by the Credit Manager.
   e. Standard payment and discount terms are established by the Vice President, Finance and are published in sales literature and other documents. Deviations from standard payment and discount terms must have approval of Vice President, Finance or his or her delegate prior to granting such terms.
   f. All orders received from customers outside of the United States and Canada must be forwarded to the Credit Department for credit approval and determination of method of payment prior to release of the order for processing.

Figure 4.12. Sample credit policy. Courtesy of The Conference Board.

Credit Process

The total credit process in a business is made up of five elements:

1. Determining the acceptable credit risk
2. Setting the credit limits
3. Handling credit transactions
4. Maintaining controls and efficiency
5. Collections

Acceptable credit risk. In determining acceptable credit risk, the manager needs to answer two questions: "Can the customer pay?" and "Will the customer pay?"

In arriving at an answer to these questions, the manager frequently considers four key factors, known as the four *C*'s of credit. The credit risk is felt to be indicated by character, capacity, capital, and conditions (economic).

Credit Risk = Character = Capacity + Capital + Conditions

These four factors sound logical. Unfortunately, they are hard to determine in actual cases because they are difficult to identify through direct inquiry. There are, however, some credit qualities that can be investigated and used to infer a standing on the four *C*'s. Among the typical items reviewed are:

- Payment record
- Income level
- Employment history
- Residence: ownership and value
- Marital status
- Age and health
- References and reputation
- Reserve assets
- Equity in purchases
- Collateral available

In arriving at a decision on the acceptability of a credit applicant, the manager will normally make this decision based on information supplied by the applicant, information supplied by direct inquiry, and information supplied by in-house records.

The applicant must provide much of the credit evaluation data. The use of a credit application form similar to figure 4.13 shows a great deal of the needed information and should be included routinely as part of the process. An interview can be used to expand and verify the data received in the application and from other sources.

The organization should routinely check each applicant by making direct inquiry of all appropriate sources. This inquiry may be made by mail or by telephone and should include references, bankers, business associates, and previous credit sources. Credit bureaus and groups should also be considered and used if appropriate. They are a ready source of credit information and are designed for that specific purpose by having established procedures and sources.

In-house records may be used in many instances to either verify or obtain additional insight regarding the credit risk of an applicant. Records of previous business transactions (cash) are useful indicators to consider along with pertinent correspondence or business association.

One technique that has been found useful in evaluating an application for credit is the credit grading. By using a form such as the one illustrated in figure 4.14, each credit element or quality is consciously and separately reviewed and given its proper appraisal. Thus a higher degree of objectivity is achieved and a better overall decision is obtained. Measurement of a number of specific factors is likely to be more accurate than a single overall judgement. Credit quality is a relative evaluation, not an absolute measurement.

Setting the credit limits. Based upon evaluation of the risk and other factors such as economic environment, company position, and supplier policies, the manager must set a credit limit for the customer. This is normally expressed as a specific dollar figure and is used to guide admin-

PIPER Management Services

APPLICATION FOR CREDIT

Social Security Number ______

Full Name ______ Age ______

Spouse's Name ______ Single ______ Number of Dependents ______

Home Address ______ Own / Rent ______

______ Tel. No. ______

______ Zip ______ How Long ______

Previous Address ______ How Long ______

______

______

Employed By ______

Address ______

Position ______ How Long ______

Monthly Salary $ ______

Former Position ______ How Long ______

Landlord or Mortgage holder ______

Address ______

Nearest Relative (other than Husband or Wife)

______

Address ______

______

Personal Reference: ______

Address: ______

______

Banks: ______ Regular Checking ☐

______ Savings ☐

Loans ☐

Make of Car ______ Year ______

CREDIT REFERENCES

Name	Address	Type Credit

The above information is for the purpose of obtaining credit and is warranted to be true. I agree to pay all bills upon receipt of statement or as otherwise expressly agreed.

Date ______ Signature ______

Figure 4.13. Credit application form available to Piper Aircraft Dealers. Courtesy of Piper Aircraft Corporation.

CREDIT CHECK FORM

______________________ Date

______________________ Name

______________________ Address

Credit qualities	GRADE			Verified:
	GOOD 1	FAIR 2	POOR 3	
Income				
Employment				
Residence				
Marital Status				
Age				
References				
Reserve Assets				
Payment Record				
Reputation				
Summary – Overall				
Appraisal				

Decision: Accept ________ Refuse

Limit: $ ________ Single Item

$ ________ Monthly

$ ________ Total

Special Conditions: ________ ________ ________

________ ________ ________ ________

________ ________ ________ ________

______________________ Signed

______________________ Date

Figure 4.14. Credit check form.

istrative or accounting personnel responsible for monitoring the credit program. It is difficult to recommend any one method of fixing the credit limit. Some use the technique of limiting the account to a certain time (e.g., a month's purchases). Another manager might start with a low credit limit and raise its level with experience. Some organizations encourage the customer to fix his own limits (within bounds, of course).

Handling credit transactions. The actual handling of credit transactions involves identification, authorization, recording and billing. The first step is identifying the customer as an approved credit customer. This may be done through the use of a credit card, by signature, or by personal recognition. The approval or authorization of each transaction should be based upon the positive identification of the customer and a verification of the records indicating that he or she is an approved credit customer. This must be done by the salesperson at the point of sale.

Recording and billing are covered in chapter 7 "Information Systems".

Maintaining controls and efficiency. A successful manager should be concerned with maintaining positive control over the credit program to ensure that it is an effective one. There are a number of tests that can be applied by the manager in controlling credit activity. The generally accepted tests include:

- Review of bad debt loss record
- Analysis of credit sales
- Collection percentage records
- Days required to collect charges
- Turnover of receivables
- Number of new accounts
- Aging of accounts
- Cost analysis of credit program

The use of these techniques will greatly assist the manager in working toward previously determined goals and objectives.

Collections. Normally, collection problems are not major if sufficient attention is paid to the investigation and analysis of a credit risk. If, however, the credit analysis is weak, collection problems will multiply. There is a need for close supervision and administration of the collection policy. In accomplishing this it is desirable to understand the different types of debtors, to have a systematic collection system, to use the appropriate collection tools, and to understand the reasons for slow payment by customers.

Debtors vary considerably, but the different types can be classified as those who are prompt to pay, those who are sure but slow, and those who are undesirable risks because they are either dishonest or unfortunate. The process of collecting requires a systematic approach (steps and procedures) and a schedule to ensure timely action. Many organizations have found that a tickler file is most useful to ensure correct follow-up action.

The most frequently used collection tools in their sequence of normal use are:

- Invoices on transaction
- Statements on account
- Collection letters
- Follow-up notes
- Telephone reminders
- Personal visit
- Collection agency

Throughout the entire credit process there should be an awareness of credit problems and every effort should be made to spot trouble as soon as possible and to adjust the credit exposure.

Terms and Definitions

There are a number of terms and procedures that should be understood by those involved in developing and administering a successful credit program.

Credit period is the length of time allowed the buyer before payment becomes due. Usually computed from the date of the invoice.

Example: Net 30 (payment of the full amount within 30 days).

Cash discount is the deduction from the invoice amount allowed the customer for payment within a specified time prior to the expiration of the net credit period.

Example: 1% 10, Net 30 (payment within 30 days with a 1% discount for payment within 10 days).

Prepayment terms include COD—cash on delivery, CBD—cash before delivery, CWO—cash with order.

Individual order terms are the stated terms applying to each order individually and start with the invoice date.

Lumped-order terms are used when sellers allow buyers to accumulate obligations over a period of time, usually one month, and submit one payment after the end of each period.

Example: 10 keys EOM (invoice on last day of the month, payment due on the 10th day of the next month) Net 10th Prox (payment of all previous month's invoices on the 10th of the following month).

Cash discount value is the value of a cash discount and can be equated to the annual interest on the money involved.

Example:

1/2% 10 days, Net 30	9% per annum
1% 10 days, Net 30	18% per annum
2% 10 days, Net 60	14% per annum
2% 30 days, Net 60	24% per annum
2% 10 days, Net 30	36% per annum

Collection period is calculated by

$$\frac{365 \text{ x receivables}}{\text{collection period}} = \text{average annual net sales}$$

In general, the collection period should not exceed the net maturity indicated in the selling terms by more than 10 to 15 days.

Cash or Credit Card?

With increasing frequency, many aviation businesses are giving their customers only two alternatives in paying for products or services—cash or credit card. This trend stems from the realization that a small business is not as efficient as a credit agency. Without training, experience, procedures and volume, the real cost of extending credit is relatively high for the benefit received. As a result, many businesses have turned to credit cards from a few selected sources, such as fuel companies, MasterCard, and Visa. Some organizations still provide open credit for local and carefully screened customers of long standing, but these are at a minimum. The tendency has been to give the credit business to the "experts."

It should be recognized, however, that it costs the aviation business to use a credit card service. Typically the charge is expressed as a percentage of the sales with the actual percentage based upon the volume of business. This cost will vary, but for the small business it is likely to be around 4 to 6 percent. The actual figure may be negotiable, so the prudent manager will explore options.

When using credit cards, it is necessary to train issuing personnel in the correct procedures in order to minimize delays in receiving payment or the chances of error voiding a voucher.

It appears likely that the number of fuel companies with fuel credit cards or those accepting cards of other companies will be smaller in the future. This trend will reduce the options available to aviation businesses for extending credit and place a heavier burden on the remaining sources.

Summary

Business profits should be planned for and not left to chance. Planning techniques include ratio analysis, financial statement evaluation, budget projection, break-even analysis, and cash flow projection. The sales planning, pricing, and marketing orientation discussed in chapter 3 underlie sound profit planning. Profit levels vary in aviation businesses; a goal of 15 to 25 percent is not unrealistic given the high-risk nature of the industry. Nonmonetary profit measures such as "satisfactory" profits, social goals, and personal satisfaction may play an important part in setting the overall profit goal. The manager's job is to guide the organization to an explicit and acceptable level of profitability. In doing this he or she must also pay close attention to credit policies, bad debts, and the cost of finance.

Discussion Topics

1. What are some meanings to the word "profit"?
2. How should a business trade social responsibility against profit? Is it always an either/or situation?
3. Describe a manager with a "profit orientation."
4. What techniques should be used in profit planning?
5. What are the conditions needed for effective budgeting?
6. How should one distinguish between fixed and variable costs? Why does the distinction matter?
7. Why is cash flow important? How can it be improved?
8. What is breakeven point? How is it calculated, and what does it tell you about profit?

Chapter 5
Human Resources

Objectives

- ✔ Discuss labor market trends in aviation for the rest of this century and projections beyond.
- ✔ Realize some of the legal implications involved in hiring practices due to federal statutes.
- ✔ Realize a variety of methods utilized in recruiting qualified candidates for aviation positions.
- ✔ Identify issues that should be covered in an exit interview.
- ✔ Relate Maslow's hierarchy of needs theory to leadership styles.
- ✔ Describe the importance of having a personnel policy manual.

Industry Trends

Labor Market Trends in Aviation

Recent studies suggest that qualified labor for the aviation/aerospace industry as a whole, and general aviation operators in particular, is in short supply and in future years will become even shorter. A Blue Ribbon Commission was established by past president George Bush in 1991 to look at the needs for pilots and aviation maintenance technicians into the twenty-first century. The commission published its report in 1992 stating the need for both pilots and mechanics would begin to increase in the mid- and late 1990's based on a number of factors. First, the number of current employees who will reach retirement age in this time period will be on the increase. Additionally, due to downsizing of the military over several years, the readymade labor force, often relied upon by the general aviation industry, will not be available, at least not to meet the demand.

Mechanics. From a Bureau of Labor Statistics Report issued in 1993 the number of aircraft mechanics is expected to increase about as fast as the average for all occupations through the year 2005. A growing population and rising incomes are expected to stimulate the demand for airline transportation, and the number of aircraft is expected to grow. However, employment growth will be restricted somewhat by increases in productivity resulting from greater use of automated inventory control and modular systems which speed repairs and parts replacement.

Overall, the report indicated aircraft mechanics, especially those with experience, are expected to have excellent job opportunities since the number of job openings is expected to exceed the supply of qualified applicants. Growth in demand for the services of aircraft mechanics coupled with an expected large number of retirements should provide many job openings.

Job opportunities are likely to be best in general aviation. Since wages in small companies tend to be relatively low, there generally are fewer applicants for these jobs than for airline jobs. Also, some jobs will become available as experienced mechanics leave for better paying jobs with airlines or large private companies. Mechanics may face some competition for airline jobs because the high wages and travel benefits attract more qualified applicants. Mechanics who stay current with changes and technological advances in electronics, composite materials, and other areas will be in greatest demand.

In 1990 the median annual salary of aircraft mechanics was about $30,000. Mechanics who worked on jets generally earned more than those working on other aircraft. The top ten percent of all aircraft mechanics earned over $45,000 a year. (Refer to figure 5.1)

Earnings of airline mechanics generally are higher than mechanics working for other employers. Beginning aircraft mechanics employed by the airlines earned from $10 to $15 an hour in 1990, according to the Future Aviation Professionals of America.

Pilots. The Blue Ribbon panel stated in their final report a number of figures and projections related to the pilot population. The Department of Defense advised the panel that the 25,000 pilots and 95,000 technicians currently in the military would be reduced by 30 percent during the next five years. The military downsizing would adversely affect the air carrier pilot supply, because for some air carriers, 80 percent of the pilots are ex-military aviators who have undergone highly selective screening before their military training, are team-oriented, are knowledgeable of technically advanced equipment, have gained six to eight years of experience in mission-focused flying activities and, most importantly, require little extra investment.

The panel concluded that there are, and will continue to be, plenty of pilots who meet the FAA minimum requirements for a commercial rating.

Pilot Flight Pay (Hourly) National Average			
	High	Average	Low
Charter (Reciprocating)	$25.00	$18.73	$10.00
Charter (Turboprop)	$35.00	$23.42	$12.00
Charter (Jet)	$40.00	$33.88	$28.00
Flight Instructor (Single)	$25.00	$13.06	$ 7.00
Flight Instructor (Multi)	$35.00	$15.81	$10.00

Figure 5.1.

The more pertinent issue is the question of quality and the need to update the minimum training standards to ensure knowledge of computers, human factors, aeromedical issues, etc., in light of increasingly sophisticated equipment.

Under current standards, a civilian school graduate with 250 to 300 hours of flight time and a commercial certificate, multi-engine rating, and instrument rating has difficulty becoming employed by an air carrier until he/she has accumulated about 2,000 hours of flight time with perhaps 500 of those hours in multi-engine aircraft. Similar problems relate to career opportunities in corporate aviation.

Salary rates for general aviation pilots vary from as low as $7 per hour for beginning flight instructors to $40 or more per hour for charter jet pilots. (See figures 5.1 and 5.2.)

A GAMA study in the early 1980s suggested there could be pilot shortages because of declining student starts and because of the reduction of the ex-military labor pool as a source of airline pilots.[1] Even more acute shortages of aircraft technicians and toolers are already being felt. The

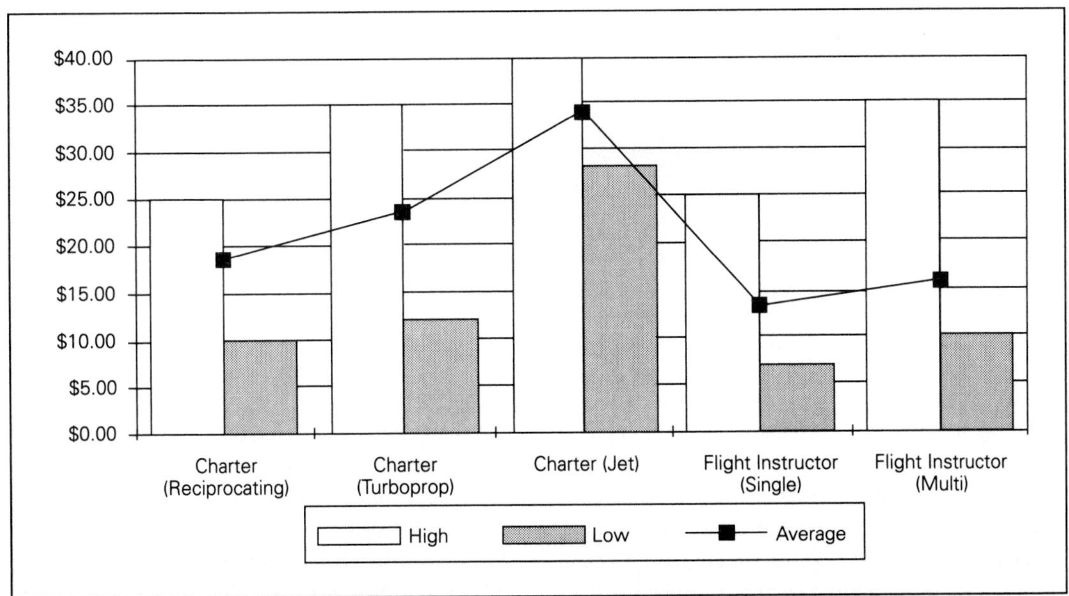

Figure 5.2.

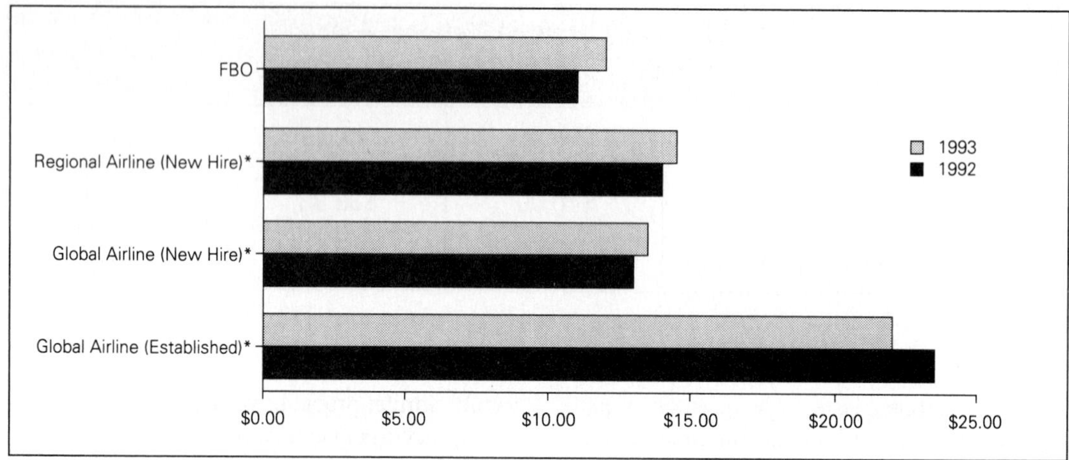

Figure 5.3. Mechanic *wage* comparison.

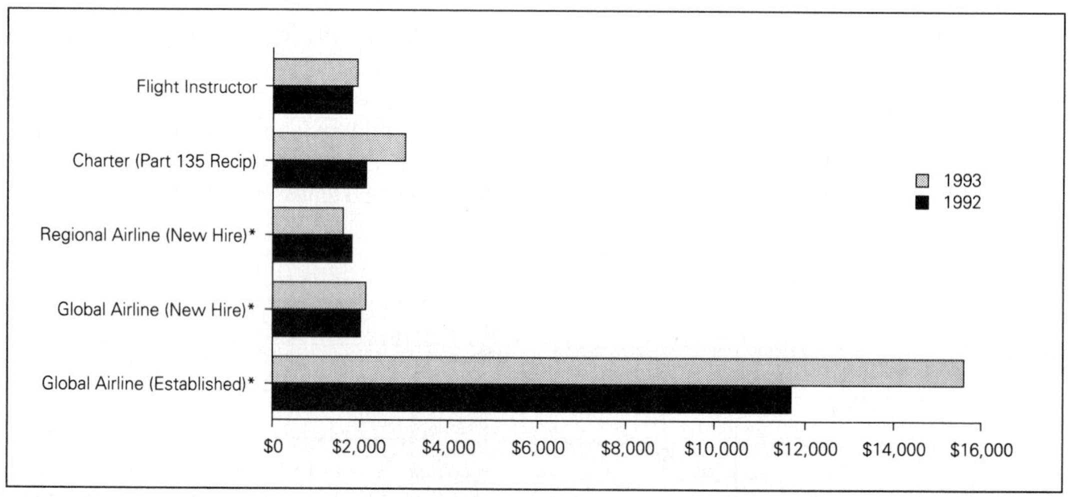

Figure 5.4. Pilot *salary* comparison.

shortage largely due to recruitment of these personnel into often higher paying nonaviation jobs. Existing schools are at 60 to 70 percent capacity. The study anticipated a significant shortage of Airframe and Powerplant (A&P) technicians in the 1990s. Serious shortages of avionics technicians and machinist/tooling specialists are also occurring. Compounding current shortages is the fact that individuals who will reach college and employment age in the 1990s have already been born. There were about 25 percent fewer eighteen-year-olds in 1992 than there were in 1977.

In addition, airlines commonly offer starting salaries as much as 20 percent higher to people with scarce skills, as illustrated in figures 5.3 and 5.4. As corporate aviation grows, another source of competition already faced by fixed base operators seems likely to become more acute.

Maturity and Professionalism

On the brighter side, tight labor markets spell good news for aviation students and suggest that working conditions and compensation must become more competitive. A career as an FBO may be a viable choice for even the best students, rather than just for the mediocre students or for those who find flying a paid avocation. Increased professionalism in terms of the quality of position and career ladder for employees is part of an increasing professionalism in the entire FBO industry.

During the 1980s, high insurance costs coupled with high costs of fuel and high interest rates caused a stagnation in aviation activity. Many FBOs went out of business during this period, leaving an area of great opportunity over the next few years for the remainder. Not only will FBOs have to operate with the highest standards of professionalism in order to compete for scarce skills, but also certain markets for FBO services will be strong enough for them to do so. The business and corporate aviation markets are likely to be particularly strong. Good employees will be key to meeting the demands of the market.

Pipeline Concept

A common tendency of small business owners is to assume or hope that staffing can be done just once and that stability will follow. This is an illusion brought about by the many pressures of the job and perhaps accentuated by the manager's discomfort in the personnel area.

A more realistic view, especially based on labor shortages, may be that most staff pass in a steady flow into, through, up, and out of the organization. Some degree of turnover is not only inevitable but can also be beneficial to both the company and the individual. Some individuals may not be adequate performers or may have insufficient interest in a career with an FBO. Others may have ambitions beyond what the FBO can offer. In any case, the FBO is better off when such employees choose to move on; managers may even have to terminate the person for the good of the company. An influx of new people means fresh ideas. The flow of personnel can be described as a pipeline with various spigots or control points along its length for the manager to operate. Controlling personnel matters is one of the many control functions that are an essential part of the management process. The pipeline is illustrated in figure 5.5.

Control Points

In dealing with the personnel pipeline, the manager has key control points for successfully operating the personnel management program. These points are:

- Identifying human resources needs
- Recruiting qualified candidates
- Selecting employees
- Communications
- Motivation
- Orientation and Training
- Compensation
- Evaluating employees
- Promotion
- Discipline
- Separation

This chapter considers all of these control points and the ways that they can be used to manage the flow of people through the company in the most beneficial manner.

The pipeline is a good description of the career course for some percentage of a company's employees, but it is neither desirable nor inevitable for all personnel. People work for reasons other than advancement and money. For example, they also work for a sense of belonging to a team that produces quality products and services. Shared values about the goals of the company and a perception of its overall direction and purpose, along with recognition and rewards, job security, and continued challenge can be reasons

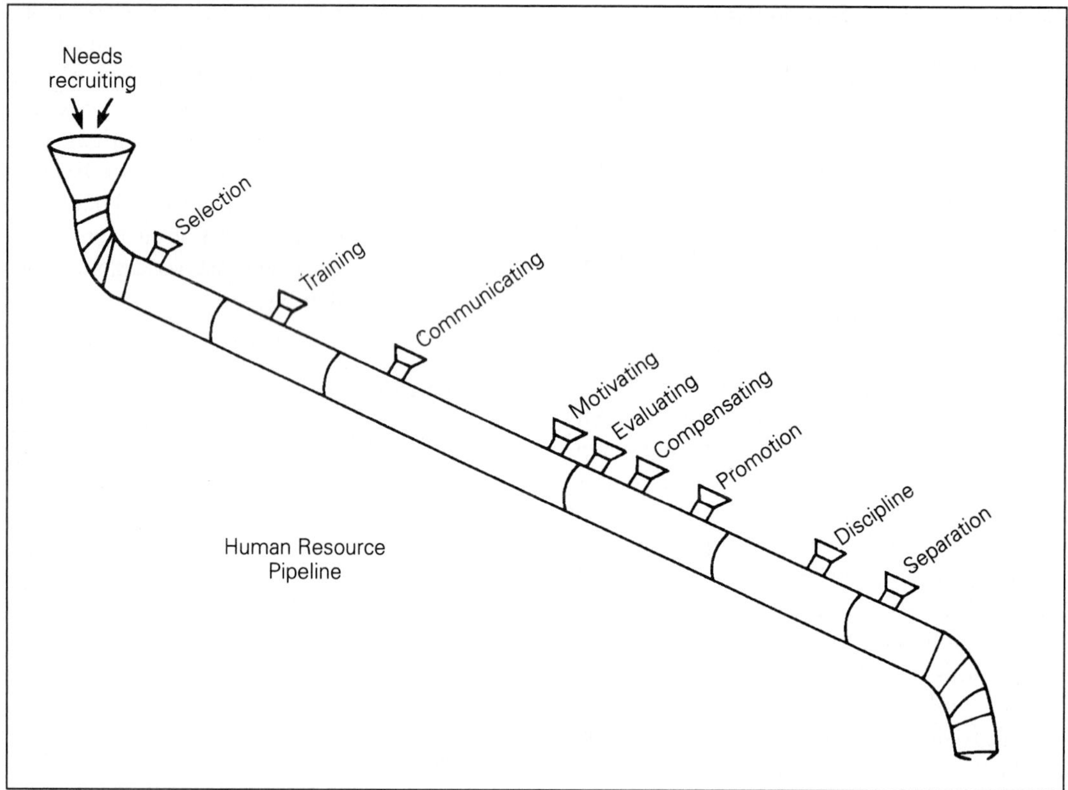

Figure 5.5. Human Resource Pipeline.

why a person might spend his entire working life in the same company.[2] Some of the ways in which these qualities have been developed in a company's staff include democratic, consensus-oriented decision making, interchangeability of most staff between the jobs in the business, and a willingness from top management to encourage the best contribution from even the less able workers in the firm. In a small FBO particularly, there may indeed be little choice but to run the firm this way. Its positive aspects need to be considered.

This chapter also discusses personnel matters in the context of related laws and regulations. It discusses how the key control points are combined into a personnel policy manual and considers appropriate ways to handle separation and employee organizations. For each of the topics the manager needs to have information on currently accepted tools and procedures, which are referenced in the text.

Identifying Human Resource Needs

The Human Resources Component of the Business Plan

Like the rest of the business plan, the personnel issue should be considered when the manager first gets into the business and then should be updated periodically. In a fast-changing enterprise it will not be possible to predict needs more than a few months ahead; in a static operation more advance planning may be possible. In most small FBOs, the personnel function is complicated by the fact that many or all of the staff must have more than one function. The industry also tends to be characterized by extensive use of part-time labor and in many parts of the country by large seasonal variations. Nevertheless, at any given time the manager needs to know the likely personnel needs, the skills and training required to meet these needs, the probable cost for each position, and some likely places to find new talent.

The overall company planning behind the human resources strategy includes:

1. Determine company objectives.
2. Formulate policies, plans, programs, and procedures designed to attain these objectives.
3. Develop a budget which will serve as a short-range plan of operations to meet the objectives.

With the plan, specific objectives and the means for achieving goals established, the next step is the process of relating the selected plan to human resource needs. The following questions should be asked:

1. What types of personnel are needed?
2. What will each person be required to do?
3. What number of personnel is required? full-time? part-time?
4. What skills will be required of each employee?
5. When will the new staff be required?
6. How long will each position be required?
7. What potential for development is desirable?
8. Can the type of person needed be attracted?
9. Can the type of person needed be afforded?
10. Are the types and numbers of personnel desired available?

Permanent or Temporary Needs

Where a need for extra help may be short-lived, the business may benefit from using temporary help. This may be from a temporary agency, a nearby college, or simply by hiring with the understanding that the job is of limited duration.[3] Depending on the workload, the tasks, and whether or not overtime is paid, an estimation of whether to hire from outside or have existing staff work longer may be worthwhile. Many companies are increasingly using contracted labor obtained through an agency. Such personnel are employees of the agency, not the place where they work.

Skills Required

The traditional approach to job skills is to look at the tasks performed by the organization, group them together into job descriptions, and seek people that appear to match them. Recent management literature suggests otherwise.[4] In his book *Entrepreneuring: The Ten Commandments for Building a Growth Company,* Steven Brandt presents the fifth commandment as "Employ key people with proven records of success at doing what needs to be done in a manner *consistent with the desired value system of the enterprise.*"

In addition to a concern with values, an employer may also look at a prospective employee's transferable skills from other jobs. In a world that is going to change more and more rapidly, an ability to transfer one's experience into a new context may be more valuable than years of doing the same thing over and over.[5] Such an approach does have implications for training, as discussed later.

Job Descriptions and Specifications

Each position requires specific tasks and definite functions that are all related to the overall plan. The following suggests an approach to be taken when determining the requirements of specific positions in an aviation activity.

Figure 5.6 describes the types of tasks that different aviation positions might require, and figure 5.7 describes briefly the skills needed for each. Figure 5.8 offers some guidelines for a detailed job description for any position.

Special activities. In addition to traditional flightline, flight operations, and aircraft maintenance functions, there are many other and varied activities for aviation businesses, such as auto rental, property rental, insurance, airline baggage handling, airline fueling, limousine service, auto parking, coffee shop or restaurant administration, and bar operation. Each of these activities calls for a separate position with individual responsibilities to fit the specific functional areas.

Most aviation managers in a small organization are well aware of the necessity for individuals to have a high degree of flexibility and efficiency in order to perform several positions. There are simply not enough people employed to compartmentalize each activity neatly and positively. This problem should not, however, overshadow the need to think through each functional area and consciously plan for its satisfactory completion. It is not desirable to create artificial, impassable barriers around separate positions. This reduces the incentive of the personnel as well as the overall flexibility of management and the organization.

Laws and Regulations

The Fair Labor Standards Act

The Fair Labor Standards Act was originally passed in 1938 in an attempt to eliminate conditions detrimental to the health, efficiency, and well-being of workers and to eliminate unfair competition based on these conditions. The Act covers:

- Minimum wages
- Overtime pay
- Employment of children
- Prohibition of wage differentials based on sex

The current provisions are covered in a brochure published by the Department of Labor, which should be consulted regarding specific situations.[6] In general, the following are exempt from minimum wages and overtime:

- Executive, administrative and professional employees
- Employees of certain small service establishments

The following are exempt from any overtime restrictions:

- Commissioned aircraft salespersons
- Airline employees

The child labor laws that could affect an FBO include:

- Those people under 18 years old may not undertake hazardous work.
- Children 14 and 15 years old may work no more than three hours on a school day or eighteen hours in a school week.
- Children under 14 years old may work for parents in their solely owned nonfarm business.

Equal pay provisions prohibit wage differentials based on gender for employees in the same establishment on jobs that require equal skill, effort, and responsibility, and on jobs that are performed under similar working conditions. An

Midmanager This position is required to accomplish a wide variety of activities depending upon the size of the business, its specific functions, and its organizational structure. Typical situations could include:

1. Serving as the manager in his or her absence
2. Performing specific, delegated duties for the manager
3. Representing the manager at certain functions
4. Being responsible for assigned technical or functional areas of the business; for example, department head or area manager
5. Serving on coordinating, developmental, or special project committees

Accountant This position is typically required to establish a bookkeeping and information system, to ensure that the system is performing to the organization's needs, to develop the desired reports, and to provide information and guidance of a financial nature to management.

Office Manager/Administrator This position is responsible for directing the administrative activities of the organization. This includes filing, record keeping, duplication, lease administration, insurance programs, reports, and the various activities of a clerical nature that might also include personnel programs.

Front-Desk Manager This person is responsible for reception of visitors, answering questions and directing personnel, scheduling aircraft, and telephone answering. In meeting the responsibilities of dealing with the public, this person must be knowledgeable about the internal organization, services and activities of all departments.

Line Service Personnel These employees are responsible for meeting, directing, servicing, and seeing-off aircraft that land and taxi into the ramp area of the business. They are responsible for operating various aircraft support vehicles and equipment and dealing with aircrew personnel of visiting aircraft. They are usually responsible for fueling.

Flight Instructor This person is responsible for: (1) the type aircraft used for instruction, (2) the required maneuvers and flight information, (3) instructional techniques and testing, and (4) administrative and promotional activities relating to the functions of flight instruction. These responsibilities vary with the size of operations and the type of instruction, such as private, multiengine, instrument, jet, helicopter, and so on.

Aircraft Pilot This person may be engaged in charter work, ferry, aerial application, cargo flights, forest or pipeline patrol, or other similar activities. Pilots are responsible for conducting flights safely and efficiently.

Aircraft Mechanic This position is responsible for a broad range of duties dealing with the inspection and repair of aircraft, maintaining records, completing administrative functions, and assisting customers.

Electronic Technician This person is responsible for servicing the various communication and navigation equipment used in aircraft. Also he or she is responsible for test equipment, necessary records, and administrative activities.

Engine Mechanic This position is responsible for the maintenance of reciprocating and turbine aircraft engines and related accessory equipment such as propellors, starters, generators, fuel pumps, carburetors and fuel-injection systems.

Custodial Worker This person has a variety of duties that will be determined by the needs of an individual location. A typical worker would be responsible for a number of duties related to security, cleaning, upkeep and repair, and, in some instances, vehicles and support equipment.

Sales Personnel Sales personnel can be new or used aircraft salespeople, ticket salespeople, parts salespeople, flight training salespeople, or flight store sales personnel. They are responsible for functions associated with selling. These include product knowledge, determining customer needs, explaining benefits, closing sales, and the administrative or support activities associated with selling.

Figure 5.6. Tasks required in FBO positions.

Position	Skills Needed
Midmanager	Knowledge of the overall business and the specific technical portion assigned. Managerial skills of planning, organizing, directing, and controlling to achieve specific objectives.
Accountant	Technically qualified in training and experience to provide the level of accounting services required by the business. Includes normal accounting training, skills in aviation accounting, information system development and financial reporting.
Office Manager	Qualified to direct the administrative office. Normally requires skills in personnel programs, insurance, record keeping, filing systems, duplication, and perhaps lease administration.
Front Desk Manager	knowledge of the internal organization and the activities of all departments. Skillful in meeting and dealing with the public. Normally must possess a radio operator's license and be skillful in radio operation and dispatching.
Line Service Personnel	Technically qualified to operate the assigend fueling and support vehicles. Knowledgeable about the systems and requirements of the aircraft to be serviced. Skilled in dealing with aircrew personnel of visiting aircraft.
Flight Instructor	Must possess a certificate for the type of instruction assigned. Must be skillful in communicating with and training students.
Pilot	Qualified in the assigned aircraft. Must possess the required operational experience and the technical knowledge of the type of flying, such as cropdusting, power line patrol, and so on.
Maintenance	Skill requirements depend upon the level of maintenance accomplished by the organization. Generally it will include knowledge related to airframe, powerplant, electronics, propeller and other specific qualifications. FAR Part 65 includes specific requirements for these and other positions.
Custodial	Skill or knowledge requirements vary dependent upon the job as developed. Generally includes skills in minor facility repair, security, cleaning and painting, and after-hour duties.
Sales Personnel	Must have knowledge of the specific product being sold, be skillful in selling and in the marketing and administrative activities related to selling.
Combination Positions	Skills necessary to meet the minimum requirements of the various jobs most likely to be assigned.

Figure 5.7. Skills required of various FBO positions.

Date ______________________

Organization ______________________

1. *Job Identification:*
   A. Job Title ______________________
   B. Department ______________________
   C. Employee Type: Exempt Nonexempt
   D. Reports to ______________________
   E. Job Number ______________________
   F. Grade ______________________
2. *Work Performed:*
   A. Summary Statement: (A statement of the job duties sufficient to identify the job and differentiate the duties that are performed from those of other jobs.)
   B. Major Duties: (Should indicate (a) what employee does, (b) how he or she does it and (c) why he or she does it. The description should indicate the tools and equipment employed, the material used, procedures followed, and the degree of supervision received. May also include relationship to other jobs.)
3. *Working Conditions:*
   (General physical environment under which the job must be performed. May include such things as lighting, degree of isolation and conditions such as hot, cold, dusty, or cramped. Job hazards identified.)
4. *Equipment Used:*
   (Identifies the equipment to be used in the performance of normal duties.)
5. *Job Requirements:*
   A. *Education:* (May include the minimum formal education, including special courses or technical training considered necessary to perform the job.)
   B. *Training and Experience:* (Minimum amount and type required in order that employee hold a job, expressed in objective and quantitative terms such as years and months.)
   C. *Initiative and Ingenuity:* (Identifies the degree, level and importance to the job and the relationship to others.)
   D. *Physical Demands:* (Identifies the amount of physical effort required and the length of time such effort must be expounded. Normally includes: walking, stooping, lifting, handling or talking.)

This statement reflects the general details necessary to describe the principal functions of the job identified and shall not be construed as a detailed description of all the work requirements that may be necessary in the job.

Approved by: ______________________

Figure 5.8. Job description format.

employer's desire to pay fair wages to all employees is likely to stem as much from a desire for harmony and a sense of fair play among workers as from legal requirements; however, anyone needing to know the exact situation on pay laws should consult an appropriate agency or legal expert.

The Civil Rights Act

The Civil Rights Act of 1964, implemented by the Equal Employment Opportunity Commission, prohibits discrimination in employment practices on grounds of race, color, religion, sex, or national origin.[7] The law applies to all aspects of employment: recruiting, hiring, training, promotion, job assignment, benefits, discipline, and termination. The ability to demonstrate that all employees are treated equally is a sound reason for a Personnel Policy Manual, as described toward the end of the chapter. If certain characteristics are essential to the job, such as heavy lifting or the ability to pass an FAA Medical for a pilot's job, these more stringent requirements prevail, so long as they are applied to all candidates.

Age Discrimination

Public Law 90–202, the Age Discrimination in Employment Act of 1967, as amended, prohibits job discrimination against applicants between the ages of forty and seventy.

The Handicapped

Federal law prohibits discrimination against the handicapped.[8] This means the essential physical and mental capabilities for a particular job should be clearly evaluated and documented in the job description. There may also be ways to adapt a job so that a handicapped person can perform it. These are often highly motivated individuals.

OSHA

The Occupational Safety and Health Act of 1970 controls working conditions.[9] Its purpose was "... to assure, so far as possible, every working man and woman in the nation safe and healthful working conditions and to preserve our human resources."

Businesses with eight or more employees are required to record work-related illnesses or injuries. Other OSHA requirements are detailed, complex, and variable depending on the nature of the worksite and work. Consultation with OSHA or state department of labor representatives is advised. There are now at least 20 states or territories with, or considering, state-administered OSHA-certified plans including: Washington, Oregon, Alaska, Hawaii, Nevada, Utah, Arizona, Wyoming, Minnesota, Iowa, Michigan, Indiana, Kentucky, Tennessee, North Carolina, South Carolina, Vermont, Puerto Rico, the Virgin Islands, Virginia, and New Mexico.[10] In these states, therefore, contact with the state labor department is recommended, as the implementer of the OSHA requirements.

Payroll Taxes and Deductions

An FBO is advised to obtain the help of an accountant in establishing the books and maintaining the proper deductions. It is vitally important that the business and financial plan for the company include adequate funds for the required items. In summary the likely items will include:

- Withholding of employee income tax
- Social Security and FICA
- Unemployment taxes
- Medicare taxes

Employee Access to Records and Fair Information Practices

Although there are no federal laws standardizing employee information practices, there are a number of states (e.g., California, Connecticut, Illinois, Maine, Michigan, New Hampshire, Oregon, Pennsylvania, and Wisconsin) that in recent years have established laws in regard to employee access to, and ability to change, data in personnel files.[11] There has also been increasing attention to the issue of employee privacy and the possible misuse of personnel data (e.g., in relation to credit, medical or other agencies). The personnel policy manual should contain a section on employee data, its use, and the company's policy on access to files by employees and their supervisors.

Recruiting Qualified Candidates

The recruiting function for an FBO business will vary in its scope and complexity with the degree of specialization involved. If the business needs a bookkeeper or file clerk, then local general business sources of candidates will be appropriate. If a very senior aviation technical position requiring current licenses is necessary, sources for bookkeepers will normally be inadequate and a more far-reaching search will be necessary.

Industry Contacts

For a position requiring aviation skills and knowledge, likely sources of qualified candidates include:

1. Friends of existing personnel (some businesses value this approach so much that they will pay several hundred dollars to staff that provide contacts leading to a new hire).
2. Managers in competing businesses who may not be doing as well as you (the risk being that they will recommend their worst people).
3. Personnel offices in competing businesses.
4. Professional and business associations, either general business or aviation related.

Whether your pursuit of these channels is local, regional, or national depends on the urgency, uniqueness, and scarcity of the labor required. Such a search, if extended into a large network, may become almost a full-time job. It's something that a business owner or even a full-time personnel director can not do with other normal demands on his or her time.

Recruiters

Recruiters and executive search or "headhunter" agencies are usually national businesses that for a fee of 15 to 25 percent of the first year's salary will seek out qualified specialists, screen them by phone, in writing, and even (if you pay) in person. Out of dozens of possibilities, they present you with three to five people to interview over the phone and then see in person. While this is a costly process, a reputable recruiter will present only interested candidates who have met all of your criteria. All that is left for you to do is pick the person with whom the rapport is best. You pay the fee, any travel costs, and the cost of relocation, if necessary. Normally you would have about 30 days to change your mind and pay nothing if the person does not work out. In the interest of self-preservation and good business ethics, a good recruiter will not make the first move to recruit that person again.

Employment Agencies

Employment agencies operate in somewhat the same manner as recruiters, except that the candidate, not the employer, pays the fee. Their labor pool tends to be more local. Agencies tend to work in regional or metropolitan labor markets and deal with more general types of skills such as office workers, accountants, purchasing agents, and computer specialists who have reasonable transferability of skills from one industry to another. There is often intensive competition between agencies. When you let a need be known, numerous candidates may be sent for interviews. Employer-paid fees are growing more common, and it may be advantageous to work with just one person in one reputable agency in cases where the national, specialized labor pool of the recruiter is not necessary.

Colleges and Trade Schools

These facilities are often one of the best sources of personnel for specialized aviation positions. The school's curriculum and national standing are available to you as a guarantee of consistent quality before you even see a specific individual. The faculty will, in time, begin to know the type of person you like and the functions you need to staff. School schedules often facilitate student employment as well as part-time and seasonal hiring, which can accommodate an FBO's varying personnel needs. An advantage of hiring student labor is that a person can be tried out for a considerable period of time before a permanent commitment is made.

Cooperative education (usually referred to as co-ops) and internships are another excellent way to utilize college and university students. Co-op programs can be set up with an option for payment or non-payment. Oftentimes the student receives college credit from his or her institution and the benefits of working in an industry environment while earning college credit is excellent. Again, it gives the employer an opportunity to preview a prospective employee with little investment.

Advertising

Many employers consider advertising as a last resort. Although it is not expensive when compared with some of the alternatives, its results can be very time-consuming. Typically, many people respond who are not qualified. The advertisement may run a day or more after you have selected someone, yielding responses that cannot be used. Ways to get the best results from advertising follow:

1. Use only major newspapers or trade periodicals.
2. Use only a box number and do not totally describe the firm so a person can guess its name.
3. Ask all respondents to fill out an application form: Only the interested will do so.
4. Use a very specific job description and skill requirements to screen candidates prior to interviewing them in person.

Selecting Employees

To a certain extent, the business manager is always looking for suitable talent whether there is a specific opening or not. Efficient handling of casual or unsolicited inquiries requires a selection process that existing employees must know about and can help to implement.

Preliminary Screening

The preliminary screening or initial interview provides a ten minute opportunity to determine whether the individual is a qualified prospect. Figure 5.9 is a screening guide based on Cessna Aircraft Company's Pilot Training Management Manual.[12] If this preliminary process suggests that the person is suitable, he or she can be told about any available positions and asked to fill out an application form. If, on the other hand, the preliminary screening suggests the candidate is definitely unsuitable because of qualifications or attitude, the person can be told that the firm will contact him if a suitable situation arises.

Screening Guide To Help In Hiring

Date ____________________
Phone ____________________

Name ____
Address ____
No. Street City State Zip Code

Ask the following questions; but stop if the applicant gives a wrong answer.

1. How long have you lived at this address? ____________________
   (Must be at least a month.)
2. What experience have you had? ____________________
   (Not important unless you want an experienced person.)
3. What kinds of work have you done? ____________________
   (Is this what you need?)
4. How much pay do you expect? ____________________
   (Is this too much?)
5. Are you willing to work evenings? _____Yes _____No; Saturdays? _____Yes _____No;
   Sundays and holidays? _____Yes _____No; Split hours?_____Yes _____No.
   (Can you use this person?)
6. Do you want full-time work? _____Full-time _____Part-time _____Hours per week
   (Can you use this person?)
   Are you willing to attend training programs conducted by our suppliers? ____________
7. (If he or she seems young) Are you over eighteen? _____If you are hired, you'll need to provide proof of your age. Will you be able to do that? _____Yes _____No
8. Do you have a job now? _____Yes _____No; (If no:) How long have you been out of work?
   (Must be less than 2 months.)
   How did that happen? ____________________
   (Reason must be very good—such as sickness, school, etc.)
9. What other experience have you had? ____________________
   (Will this be helpful?)
10. What experience have you had with aircraft? ____________________
    (Will this be helpful?)
11. Can you drive a car? _____Yes _____No; (if yes:) What kind of driver's license do you have?_____(OK?). May I see it?_____ Out-of-date,_____ Up-to-date; What notations are there on the license? ____________________
    (Is this person a safe driver?)
12. Can you fly? _____Yes _____No; (If yes:) What kind of license do you have?
    ______________(OK?)

If the applicant **won't do** because the answers to any of these questions means you can't use him or her or because you feel the person won't fit in with yourorganization, **say,** "I'm sorry but you don't seem to be the person we need right now. However, I have your name and phone number and I'll be glad to give you a call if we can use you some other time. Thanks a lot for talking with me."

If the applicant seems OK, say, "Fine, I'd like you to fill in an applicaiton. You can do it right here. Would that be OK?"

Figure 5.9. Screening guide.

The Application Form

The primary value of an application form is its systematic and impersonal collection of data. It establishes a consistent data base for all applicants and represents one step in equal opportunity. It also provides the means, through names of former employers and references, of conducting a more detailed investigation on a person before hiring them. It should be tailored to your own needs but will probably contain at least:

- Name, address and phone
- Previous employer's address, immediate supervisor, starting and ending salary, reason for leaving, dates of employment
- Education, formal and informal
- Social Security Number
- Height, weight, physical limitations, (if applicable to job)

The application form provides a basis for interview questions and, on occasion, may be a further screening mechanism leading to a decision not to further interview the person. If the person is hired, the form becomes a useful background item in their personnel file. Figure 5.10 is an application blank based on one developed by Piper Aircraft in selecting flight instructors.

The Interview

A full interview may last an hour or more and should probably never last under 20 minutes if an offer is going to be made. Some experts strongly recommend that more than one interviewer be brought into the process, especially when the manager has a poor record of picking good staff, and/or where he or she has a tendency to pick people like themselves, regardless of the job. A number of studies in recent years suggest that philosophy, style, and values may be as critical as technical skills in causing an employee to fit well and be productive. It is important for the employer not to ask leading questions in such areas, as the candidate may try to present only what he or she thinks is wanted. If certain skills, licenses, or education are prerequisites for the job, it may be appropriate to develop a checklist for use with every candidate. The interviewer should guard against forming such a liking for the candidate that he or she forgets to go over all the key issues. It will not pay to hire a likable incompetent! The following principles should guide most interviews:

1. Make a checklist of questions to ask, preferably including questions about how the person would handle problems and crises that typically appear in your business.
2. Set up a quiet atmosphere with no interruptions.
3. Put the applicant at ease and give him or her your full attention.
4. Keep the discussion at a level suitable to the applicant.
5. Listen attentively.
6. Never argue.
7. Observe style and manner, for example, ability to answer directly.
8. Provide the applicant with pertinent information about the job.
9. Note key replies and concerns.

Figure 5.11 provides twelve key factors to look for in interviewing or screening. Note that none of the factors relates to technical skill or training.

Application for Instructor Position

(All information treated confidentially)

Date ______________

Name (print) ______________ Telephone number ______________ Is this in your name? ______

Present address ______________ How long have you lived there? ______
No. Street City State Zip

Previous address ______________ How long did you live there? ______
No. Street City State Zip

Business address ______________ Business telephone number ______
No. Street City State Zip

Are you a citizen of the U.S.? ☐ Yes ☐ No Soc. Sec. No. ______________

Why are you applying to this Company? ______________

1. What influenced you to enter general aviation? ______________

2. Do you plan a general aviation career? ☐ Yes ☐ No

Education								
Type of School	Name of School	Courses Majored In	Check Last Year Completed				Graduate? Degrees Received	Last Year Attended
College			1	2	3	4		19
Other			1	2	3	4		19

Jobs While in School and During Summer

Scholastic standing in H.S. ______________ In College ______________

(Designate top 25%, middle 50%, lowest 25%)

Awards and honors received ______________

Favorite subjects ______________ Least liked ______________

Extracurricular Activities (exclude racial, religious, or nationality groups)

In high school ______________

Offices held ______________

In college ______________

Offices held ______________

What scholarships or fellowships have you received? ______________

What hobbies do you have? ______________

Service in U.S. Armed Forces

What is your current military service status? ______________

If exempt or rejected, what was the reason? ______________

Have you served in the U.S. Armed Forces ☐ No ☐ Yes; (if yes) Date active duty started ______ 19__

Which force? ☐ Army ☐ Air Force ☐ Navy ☐ Marines ☐ C.G.:

What branch of that force? ______________ Starting rank ______________

Overseas: Date(s) ______________ Location(s) ______________

Date of discharge ______________ 19___ Rank at discharge ______________

What citations and awards have you received? ______________

What special training did you receive? ______________

Figure 5.10. Application blank.

Work History

Include (a) self-employment and (b) secondary or moonlighting jobs (mark the latter with an asterisk)

Beginning with the most recent, list below the names and addresses of all your employers: a. Company name b. Address and telephone number	Kind of Business	Time Employed				How was Job Obtained?
		From		To		
		Mo.	Yr.	Mo.	Yr.	
1. a. ____ b.						
2. a. ____ b.						
3. a. ____ b.						
4. a. ____ b.						
5. a. ____ b.						

Indicate by number______________ any of the above employees whom you do not wish us to contact.

In the last 5 years, how much time have you lost from work? (Illnesses, leave of absence, or other conditions)__________

Have you ever drawn unemployment compensation?__________ Date(s) ______________________________

Please give specific experience . . .

Have you had sales experience? ☐ Yes ☐ No

If "yes" please specify type sales: (Big ticket, over the counter, delivery sales, route sales to homes, technical sales, specialty sales—tangibles; books, etc.; intangibles: insurance or services)

List employer(s) for whom you sold:

Name	Address	Lines Sold	Year(s)

If necessary, are you willing to work nights?_______Weekends? ______________________

Personal References (Not former employers or relatives)	Address	Phone Number
1.		
2.		
3.		

Health

Date of last FAA physical exam. ________________

Class ______________________

Restrictions ______________________

Figure 5.10. Continued.

Work History

Include (a) self-employment and (b) secondary or moonlighting jobs (mark the latter with an asterisk)

Nature of Work at Start	Earnings Per Month at Start	Nature of Work at Leaving	Earnings Per Month at Leaving	·Reason for Leaving	Name of Immediate Supervisor
					Name Title
					Name Title
					Name Title
					Name Title
					Name Title

Flying Experience

Certificate and Ratings: (Give Date Each Acquired)

A. ______ D. ______ G. ______

B. ______ E. ______ H. ______

C. ______ F. ______ I. ______

Flight Schools Attended **From** **To** **Course** **Graduation**

______

______

______

Pilot Experience (Other Than Instructor Time)

Pilot In Command ______

Copilot Time ______

Instrument Time ______

Multi Engine Time ______

Night ______

______

Instructor Experience (Hours)

Total Instructor Time ______

Private ______

Commercial ______

Night ______

Instrument ______

Multi Engine ______

Aircraft Flown: (Give Approximate Hours In Each)

A. ______ E. ______ I. ______

B. ______ F. ______ J. ______

C. ______ G. ______ K. ______

D. ______ H. ______ L. ______

Figure 5.10. Continued.

Personal Instruction Activity:

			% Passed FAA Exam
A.	Number of Pilots Instructed.	______	______
B.	Number of Commercial Pilots Instructed.	______	______
C.	Number of Instrument Pilots Instructed.	______	______
D.	Number of Multi Engine Pilots Instructed.	______	______
E.	Number of Instructors Instructed.	______	______
F.	Number of ATR Pilots Instructed.	______	______
G.	Number of Glider Pilots Instructed.	______	______
H.	Number of Float Plane Pilots Instructed.	______	______

Accidents:

Date:________

Circumstances: ______________________________

____

Damage or Injury: ______________________________

____

Forced Landings:

Date:________

Reason: ______________________________

Damage or Injury: ______________________________

____

Has your pilot certificate ever been suspended or revoked? ______________________________

____

Other Statements

Are there any experiences, skills, or qualifications which you feel would especially fit you for work with this Company?

____

What are your plans or aims for the future? ______________________________

If your application is considered favorably,
on what date will you be available for work?______________________________19 ____
How much notice will you require? ______________________________ Days

Signature ______________________________

*Not to be asked unless job related.

Figure 5.10. Continued.

1. Has applicant done some homework about the company?
2. Is applicant dressed properly for the interview?
3. Did the person arrive alone for the interview?
4. Did they arrive on time?
5. How did they greet you?
6. Are they assertive and confident?
7. Are they argumentative?
8. Do they present a positive attitude about their most recent employer?
9. Do they have a positive attitude about this company?
10. Do they seem to be observant and learning during the interview process?
11. Do they project enthusiasm, confidence, energy and dependability?
12. Do they project loyalty, honesty, pride in work and a desire to offer work and service for pay received?

Figure 5.11. Twelve steps to assessing a job candidate's suitability.

It is necessary to avoid asking discriminatory questions. The only issues that are pertinent relate to the person's ability to do the job. For most pilot positions a current medical would be adequate, although temporary disabilities such as a broken limb or pregnancy could be pertinent. It is not illegal to let the candidate volunteer information that would be illegal to request.

Some questions which may seem harmless enough can be interpreted as discriminatory. For example, asking a potential employee if they rent or own their own home, whether or not they are married or have any children, which organizations or societies they belong to (other than professional organizations), or their age are all potentially risky discriminatory questions.

Testing

In many cases testing for FBO jobs will not be necessary as long as checking is done to confirm that all claimed qualifications are current. For typing, a speed and accuracy test may be appropriate. However, in almost all cases, the quality of technical skills can best be assessed by discussion with former employers, clients, or teachers.

Personality testing is another matter. People do not always know themselves very well; they may have picked a technical area of training that does not fit ideally with their basic temperament, or they may have personality and managerial skills well beyond the level they envisage for themselves. Various personality style testing instruments are available. They generally group people loosely into four categories: leaders, influencers, detail workers, and supporting types.[13,14,15,16] Each of us has characteristics of each category but are predominantly one type. Someone who loves to manipulate numbers all day and is shy should not be put on the front desk to greet people. Someone friendly should be on the line or the desk so long as they are also results-oriented and can successfully juggle several clients. Technical skills are generally more teachable at any stage in life than personality traits. Personality traits can be improved but never radically changed. A person is happiest and most productive when both personality and technical skills are well-used. A good manager needs strength in all the personality styles and the ability to "switch gears" from one style to another as needed for the situation.

Testing requires money and time ($50.00 and up and several hours). If it is carefully used, it can lead to more successful screening and deployment of personnel. If existing personnel take the test, much will be learned that will be a permanent guide to personality assessment.

Background and References

Reference checking is critical prior to making a job offer. The most valuable contacts are generally those who have known the person in a business rather than personal context. Any personal references listed have probably been specifically selected because of their pleasant remarks. Previous employers, business associates, and clients are usually willing to give a candid appraisal of a person's strong and weak points (everyone has both) once they know the type of job and company for which a person is being considered. If a negative comment comes up that is unexpected or contradicts the candidate, it may be desirable to give him or her a chance to clarify. Telephone reference checking is generally more reliable than written requests because it provides an opportunity to ensure that the person being asked really remembers the candidate and is not just looking up file information. It also allows questioning and prompting on the part of the reference checker. Figure 5.12 provides a form for use in telephone reference checking. Many companies no longer allow their employees to give references because of legal liability; however, they will verify employment. Despite this difficulty, references should always still be pursued prior to hiring.

Credit checks may also be a means of obtaining information on a prospective employee and are particularly appropriate for jobs involving money. In this, as in all hiring matters, it is crucial to use consistent procedures. The request for a credit report must be communicated to the applicant; it is desirable to seek the candidate's permission.

The Physical Examination

With the exception of pilot positions, where a current medical may be sufficient to ensure that the applicant can handle the job, a physical examination can be important in hiring. Physicals should especially be used when the job requires features such as:

- Strength
- Good vision
- Ability to stand continously
- Freedom from allergies
- Unusual stamina
- Other qualities above the average

It is advantageous before considering hiring to know about such matters as:

- Physical limitations
- Contagious diseases that could put other employees at risk
- Potentially high rates of absenteeism due to poor health or previous injury
- History of substance abuse

The type of examination to be used should be determined with the help of qualified physicians. Figure 5.13 provides an example.

The Job Offer

The job offer may be made in person, by letter, or by phone. It should include not only the position, but also the compensation, hours, fringe benefits, the supervision, and general working rules to the extent that any of these have not already been discussed. Some firms use a job contract that both parties sign. Most people offered a job ask for a few days to decide, and a deadline for a decision should be established. Do not send out regret letters to anyone else until your chosen candidate has accepted or even started work. This is an important courtesy because later you may want to offer the other candidates jobs.

Communications

Basic Elements

Considerable successful communication has already occurred when a new member of a firm has been recruited, screened, selected and hired.

Telephone Reference Check on Applicant ______________________

Name of Applicant

____

Person Contacted | Position

____

Company | City and State | Telephone Number

1. I wish to *verify* some of the information given to us by Mr. or Ms. (name), who has applied for a position with our firm. Do you remember him or her? What were the dates of his or her employment with your Company?
   From ______ 19 ______ To ______ 19 ______
   Do dates check?

2. What was he or she doing when she started?
   ____
   Did she exaggerate?

   When she left?
   ____
   Did she progress?

3 She says she was earning $____ per____ when she left. Is that right?
   ☐ Yes. ☐ No; ______________________
   Did she falsify?

4. How much of this was salary?
   $____________Commission? ____________

5. How was her attendance?
   ____
   Conscientious? Health problems?

6. What type of instructing did she do?
   ____
   To whom?

7. How did her efforts compare with others?
   ____
   Industrious? Competitive?

8. Did she supervise anyone else?
   ☐ No, ☐ Yes; How many? ______________________
   Does this check?

   (If yes) How well did she handle it?
   ____
   Is she a good leader?

9. How closely was she supervised?
   ____
   Was she hard to manage?

10. How hard did she work?
    ____
    Is she habitually industrious?

11. How well did she get along with other people? her students?
    ____
    Is she a troublemaker?

12. Did she have arguments with customers?
    ____
    Does she like selling? Can she control her temper?

13. What did you think of her?
    ____
    Did she get along with her superiors?

14. Why did she leave?
    ____
    Good reasons? Do they check?

15. Would you rehire her?
    ☐ Yes, ☐ No; Why not? ______________________
    Does this affect her suitability with us?

16. What are her outstanding strong points?
    ____

17. What type of work do you feel she would do best?
    ____

18. What are her weak points?
    ____

Checked by ______________________ Date ______________

Figure 5.12. Telephone reference check guide.

Physical Examination Record
(Drivers)

Name ______________________ No. _____ M ____ F ____ Height _________ Weight ______

Medical History ____

____

Surgical History ____

When was a physician last consulted? ____________________ For what? ______________

Ever suffered any injuries? __________ When? ____________ Extent ______________

Ever have any "fits" or convulsions? ____________________ Tuberculosis? ______________

Eyes: Vision Rr 20/_______ Lt 20/ _______ Both _______ Near Rr J/ _______ Lt J/ _______

Accomodations Lt_______ Distance_______ Binocularity ____________________

External right eye ______________________ External left eye ______________________

Use of glasses _____ Corrected vision Rt 20/_____ Lt 20/_____ Near Rt J/_____ Lt J/_____

Color perceptions normal_____; deficient in red _____ green_____ blue_____ yellow_____

Ears: Internal_________ External_________ Hearing: Rt_________ Left_________

Nose________________ Throat________________ Mouth and Gums ________________

Teeth Condition ______________________ Care ______________________

Neck ______________________ Goiter ______________________

Lungs ____

____

Heart ____

____

Blood Pressure ______________________ Pulse rate ______________________

Abdomen ________________ Scars ________________ Hernia ________________

Location of_________ Duration_________ Genitalia_________ Ing.-Adenopathy_________

Urinalysis: Color___________ S.G.___________ Alb___________ Sugar___________

Sacroiliac ____

Joints: (Describe abnormalities, congenital or acquired) ______________________

____

Varicose Veins________________ Flat Feet________________ Deformities________________

Passed_______ Rejected_______ Reason for Rejection____________________

Comments ____

____

Date____________ Medical Examiner ______________________

Figure 5.13. Driver's physical examination form. Courtesy of Dartnell Corp., Chicago, IL.

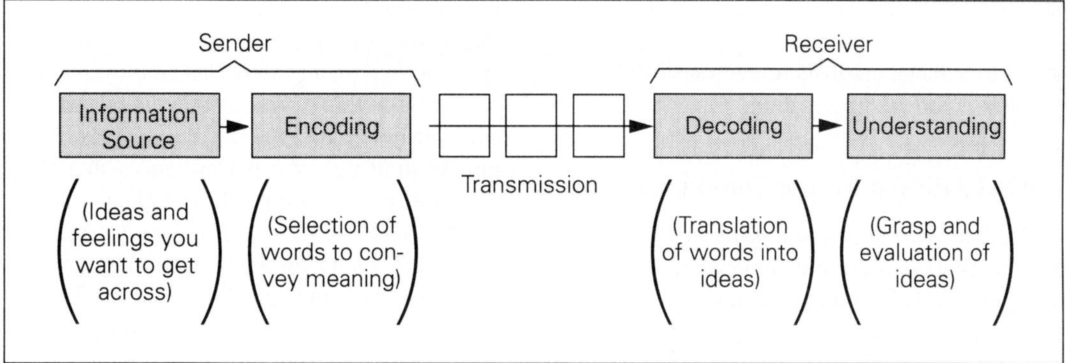

Figure 5.14. Model of the communication process.

But even the strongest candidate has to learn to communicate in various ways about new tasks with new colleagues in order to be successful on the job. Communication skills are starting to be specifically taught in schools and business seminars. Their acquisition and continual improvement is a necessity for every employee.[18]

Communication occurs whenever information is transferred from one person to another and understood so that it may be correctly acted upon. Information goes through five phases:

1. Encoding—expressing the idea in written, oral or gestural form.
2. Transmission—by sound waves, paper, light waves, and so on.
3. Reception—by the correct party in a timely manner.
4. Decoding—translation of the material into ideas.
5. Understanding—evaluation and analysis of meaning.

Figure 5.14 shows this process.

Communication can fail because of a problem with any one of these steps. If a supervisor fails to ascertain whether an employee, especially a new employee, has understood a message, then that supervisor has not communicated adequately. People new to an organization may require training in its vocabulary and style of communication. The amount of time it takes for them to pick this up depends not only on their intelligence, but also on their cultural background and the amount of their previous adaptation.

Barriers to Effective Communication

These problems in the communications process are often referred to as barriers to effective communication. The most common ones are:

- We hear what we expect to hear.
- We ignore information that conflicts with what we already "know."
- We judge the value of information by its source.
- We are influenced by our group bias.
- Words mean different things to different people.
- Groups may have their own "argot" or insiders' vocabulary.
- Our emotional state conditions what we hear.
- We don't know how the other person perceives the situation.
- We fail to listen.
- We ignore body language.
- We try to convey too much at once.
- The receiver is not "tuned in."

- Understanding is assumed rather than ascertained.
- Intermediates involved in the transmission filter or amend information.

Verbal and Non-Verbal Communications

Verbal communication skills are the most commonly discussed in communications. However, non-verbal communications can be just as important in sending a message. In fact, if the non-verbal cues being given conflict with the verbal message, more often than not the non-verbal message will be the most powerful.

Good verbal communication skills include not only the words used to convey the message but other factors as well. For example, the tone of voice being used can imply a variety of messages. Using a matter of fact tone versus a sarcastic one will certainly leave different images of what the sender is trying to say, even if the words are exactly the same. The rate of speech delivery, the volume of voice, and pitch all relate to how the message is received. And, silence sends a powerful message all its own, depending on how it is used.

Non-verbal communication includes everything from eye contact to gestures, from facial expressions to pacing. A person who stares at the ceiling while talking with someone is generally perceived to be untruthful. Good eye contact helps instill trust in the listener and implies honesty. Raising your eyebrows or rolling your eyes while shaking someone's hand and saying how pleased you are to meet them, sends the opposite message to the person you are meeting. A good manager should be be aware of non-verbal cues, not only to ensure they are consistent with the verbal message sent, but also to watch for the non-verbal cues of others.

Improving Communications

One of the most useful texts in recent years for improving communications in the workplace is *The One-Minute Manager.*[17] Its first recommendation is the joint development by manager and employee of a goal for that employee's work performance that can be written down and takes a minute or less to read. The manager gives "one minute praisings" for performances that shine and "one minute reprimands"—ending with a reminder of the value of the person being reprimanded. Thus people know what they are supposed to be doing and know they will hear immediately when they do something well or poorly. The manager doesn't just save up grievances or praise for annual review day.

A basic set of tools for improving communications includes:[18]

- Utilizing feedback to make sure the message was not only received but understood
- Developing sensitivity to the receiver
- Being aware of the symbolic meaning of words
- Timing messages carefully
- Reinforcing words with action
- Using simple, direct language
- Introducing the proper amount of redundancy

Utilizing feedback means being constantly on the alert for clues to whether one is being understood or not. Feedback from the recipient of the message may take the form of a "yes." It could be an understanding look, an attentive nod, or the desired action. Lacking any of these, the communicator should try again. Good supervisors actively encourage questions to make sure the instructions are clear.

Sensitivity to the receiver means attempting to adjust to the receiver's needs, especially possible interpretations of the message. Cultural and emotional factors must be considered.

Awareness of symbolic meanings is important because words can have meanings in the mind of the receiver that distort and interrupt the communications effort.The communicator should avoid such words once they are identified.

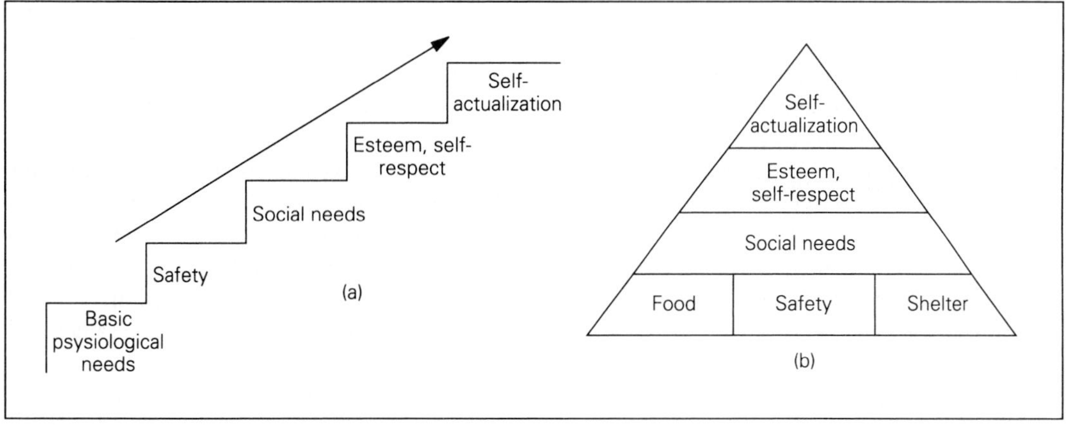

Figure 5.15. Maslow's hierarchy of needs: Two views.

Careful timing of messages is important because the receiver must be ready and able to handle the new input. Poor timing can include times when the receiver is already busy on a task, is overloaded with new input, is tired, or has become preoccupied with a distracting problem. It can also include times when prior events mean the person's mind is already made up on an issue. The message sender should anticipate these situations and adjust accordingly.

Reinforcement of words by action will greatly increase the chance of a communication being accepted, as well as the expectation of action based on past events.

The use of simple, direct language will enhance good understanding. Don't use technical terms and long tangled statements.

The proper amount of redundancy is important. Good teachers know that their ability to convey a new idea often depends on their ability to rephrase the same thing in as many different ways as necessary until all the class members have discovered its meaning in their own terms. Sales people are often taught that it takes six different exposures to the product before people are generally ready to respond. This repetition of ideas, often in different forms, is needed until it is clear the message has been understood.

The use of communications training can be important. Many people do not know the ways they communicate until they see themselves in role playing, on videotape, or hear a tape recording. Guided practice and feedback can almost always be part of a manager's personnel training program. Last but not least, it is the job of the message sender NOT the recipient to make sure the message has arrived.

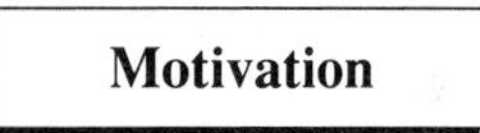

Motivation

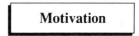

Array of Needs

Some four decades of thinking about motivation have been based on a hierarchy of needs first described by Maslow.[19] His theory (1) gave recognition to the fact that motivation comes from within and (2) depicted the driving forces as a hierarchy with simple physical needs for food, shelter and safety at the bottom. The person's attention goes to social needs once the basic needs are met. Then their needs become more sophisticated, and esteem and self-respect become the primary motivators. Finally, at the top of the hierarchy—and attended to only if or when all preceding needs are met—is the motivator of self-actualization. This hierarchy or staircase of needs is depicted in Figure 5.15.

More recent analysis by several management experts suggests that what motivates people can be any and all of these factors at the same time.[23,24] As society becomes more mobile and close-knit, family networks are harder to maintain and the workplace often becomes the primary social outlet. Everyone who works is motivated to a greater or lesser extent by money, or the need for more money; however, this is not usually the sole consideration for most people. Job satisfaction takes other forms.

Needs Satisfied by Working

Some companies appear to be arranged only to meet people's lower level needs. Executives and factory operators alike put most of their creative energy into diverse hobbies outside the workplace, requiring elaborate equipment and planning. However, *In Search Of Excellence* found that the excellent companies were "organized to obtain extraordinary effort from ordinary human beings"[25] The same feature of motivating even mediocre employees to be the best they can be is a feature of the larger Japanese companies, which in many cases offer lifetime employment so that they *must* find ways of motivating all personnel.[26] Some of the needs that can be met in the workplace include: autonomy and a sense of control over one's situation, being part of a team or a sense of belonging, public recognition and rewards, and a sense of responsibility for vital functions.

Creating a Motivating Environment

If these are the non-monetary rewards that people seek from their work, how can managers arrange working conditions so that these rewards occur?

Autonomy and control mean training a person to know he or she is empowered in specific areas. An atmosphere of trust can be generated by such techniques as abolishing time clocks in favor of an honor system, using flextime, allowing as much freedom as possible over workspace arrangements, and, in general, treating people as adults.

Recognition in the best companies seems to involve several steps. First, clear and specific performance goals are set up. They are set deliberately quite low so that almost everyone can be a winner. Reaching the goal is praised publicly and with varying levels of celebration. Praise and rewards are instant, specific, consist of things important to the performer rather than the rewarder, and may be sporadic and unpredictable, the result of the manager wandering around and particularly looking for things people are doing right.

Money is only one of many factors contributing to job satisfaction. Other important factors include participation in decision making, challenging assignments, positive feedback from one's superior, and the chance for advancement.

Most employees are highly motivated by recognition and acknowledgement. The precise mode of giving recognition will vary with the style and value system of the company. Some considerations to include in the design of the recognition system are:[20]

1. The award must have meaning for the recipient.
2. The recipient must understand why the award is being given.
3. The presentation must be dignified, sincere, and conducted before peers and supervisors.
4. The award must have intrinsic value and uniqueness.

Being part of a team of winners in a corporate family is another technique deliberately fostered by the excellent companies. The ways of achieving this include knowledge about each employee's personal situation, company trips and outings, and acceptance of the individual's uniqueness. Some companies have a store of myths and stories about the business—especially perhaps in its early days—which help to perpetuate the sense of belonging to something special. A strong and often repeated corporate philosophy stated in simple ways, such as "product quality and customer service" can be a major contributor. Some firms shift their personnel among functions, and this can strengthen corporate pride because people learn to understand the whole, rather than just a part of the business. It also gives managers a hands-on appreciation of the issues and problems facing many divisions of the company.

Finally, delegation means responsibility. If someone is put in charge of a task, then they must be allowed to carry it out in their own way without the boss constantly interfering. Specific results by specific dates mean specific success or failure. These milestones allow the boss to re-delegate the task differently if all is not going well by using the opportunity to communicate in more detail some of the "how" as well as the "what." Judgement must be used in giving responsibility commensurate with ability; this is one of the key tasks of a manager, since one seldom has at hand exactly all the right talents embodied in one person.

Leadership

Leadership is one of the major functions of a manager. In a small or new business, it may be almost without effort that the owner/manager conveys to the staff the excitement and drive that motivate him or her. In a bigger or older company, it may take more conscious effort. As mentioned, one author recommends first that people with appropriate values be the only ones hired. A set of values for one company is described as follows:[27]

- Any and every company problem is your problem (Don't pass the buck or point the finger).
- Glitter on your own time (Don't worry about status symbols or showing off on the job).
- We price and sell service, not technology or products.
- Let the customer take advantage of you.
- Finish and put your name on every task you start.
- Bake the incentives into the work itself.
- Pace company growth to staff growth.
- Simplicity rules.
- Know your customers' shoe size.

Such values, or minor variations on them, could probably fit almost any company. The same authors recommend that new employees be given at least eight hours of value orientation during their first three months on the job. The successful leader is one who wants others to be successful in the business and who is a super-coach, most of the time, rather than a star player.

One myth of leadership is that leaders are born. People are born with a degree of health and intelligence, but leadership can be learned. Another myth says you can learn to lead by being a good follower. On the contrary, leadership is learned by leading.

The following is intended to be a basic introduction to some basic leadership styles and their definitions. It is by no means a thorough examination of this topic.

Authoritarian Leader. This type of leader claims power, not through personal endorsement, but through the position they hold. This is often referred to as "situational" leadership. Characteristics of an authoritarian leader include:

1. Adheres to a schedule
2. Likes things in their proper place
3. Planning is very important (everything worked out ahead of time)

The only creativity allowed is that brought about by the leader. The leader presents directives, not alternatives. Others are eliminated from making decisions. People who are insecure like this kind of leader.

Therapeutic Leader. This type of leader does not want to make anyone mad and fears hurting anyone's feelings. This leader would rather form a committee than make a decision personally. In the end no one is satisfied. Characteristics of a therapeutic leader include:

1. Personable—wants to be everyone's friend
2. Spontaneous
3. Adaptable to change (ideas are usually those of the last person spoken with)

This type of leader does not concentrate on theirself, but rather on their subordinates. However, this is often due to a poor self-esteem. Again, this leader is more concerned that people like him/her personally.

Charismatic Leader. Eleanor Roosevelt and John F. Kennedy are usually mentioned when listing people with charisma. There is narcissistic charisma which can be either good or bad, and the autonomous charismatic who tends to stay in seclusion. Characteristics of this type of leader include:

1. Invites others to identify with them
2. Protects others (makes them feel strong)

Some people capitalize on their charisma while others are charismatic in spite of themselves. Freud said, "The charm of a child lies in a great extent to his narcissism." They can shut everything out and rest in themselves.

Each of the three styles of leaders has implications for the decision-making process and the managers's role as a change agent. No one fits neatly into any one of these styles. There are fragments of all of them in all administrators. Any kind of leader is accepted by some and rejected by others. It depends on the needs of the followers or, in the case of a business, employees at the time.

If the employees are in need of inspiration they will want a charismatic leader. If answers are needed the authoritarian leader will be preferred. And, if understanding is the major need, a therapeutic leader will be considered best. The good leader needs to fit all these needs. This is what makes it so difficult for a leader to be truly effective.

Orientation and Training

New Employees

New employees need orientation in order to develop a sense of belonging, as well as to know whom to turn to for help in the early days. Some firms assign a colleague for the first few days until the newcomer knows the way around. Existing employees should be apprised that hiring is in process and informed of the newcomer's status and functions. The manager needs to be sensitive to fears that a new person will diminish someone else's importance.

Orientation will usually involve both written materials and person-to-person review of tasks. In larger companies, the personnel department usually has a role, for example, in telling about the history of the firm, its values and goals, the fringe benefits, and the company-wide activities and information systems. If this is how things are to be done, ideally new employees should report on the first day to the person that hired them, be taken to meet the senior managers, and then go for orientation with personnel. Then they will be ready to start work with their new colleagues and not be pulled off new assignments in order to attend to the administrative aspects of orientation. A checklist of possible items to cover in orientation includes:

- Company history, policies and practice
- Company values and goals
- Facilities
- Organizational structure
- Employee conduct and responsibilities to the company

- Company responsibilities to employees
- The compensation program
- The benefits program life insurance, medical, pension, profits, and so on
- The evaluation program
- Promotion policy
- A tour of premises and the employee's own department
- Introduction to fellow employees
- Safety and security program
- Training opportunities
- Hours and pay schedule
- Work assignments

The process should also involve a check-back after about three days to answer any new questions that arise. On the first day someone should be assigned to make sure that the new employee does not have to eat lunch alone.

Training

Training involves three areas: training in the job for which the person was hired, training for more advanced functions in the company, and training to address social and economic changes that affect the way the company must operate. All employees need training for one or more of these areas. There are four basic modes of providing training:

1. On the job, by supervisors
2. Classroom activity at the workplace (e.g., during less busy periods of the week, with inside or outside instructors or vendors)
3. Apprenticeship
4. Special courses, seminars and classes off the premises, provided by specialists outside the firm

Training may include both technical and human resource development areas.

On-the-Job Training

On-the-job training is the basic training system used by all FBOs to some degree. Its success is strongly related to its being a hands-on process. It generally requires that the immediate supervisor become an effective teacher. One effective program for this is the Job Instructor Training (JIT) which was developed during World War II.[26] Its major elements are:

How to Get Ready to Instruct

Have a Timetable

How much skill you expect the person to have?
By what date?

Break Down the Job

List important steps
Pick out the key points

Have Everything Ready

The right equipment, material and supplies

Have the Workplace Properly Arranged

Just as the worker will be expected to keep it

How to Instruct

Step 1: Prepare the Worker

Put him or her at ease
State the job and find out what the trainee already knows about it
Get him or her interested in learning the job
Place in correct position

Step 2: Present the Operation

Tell, show and illustrate **one important step** at a time
Stress **each key point**
Instruct clearly, completely and patiently, but no more than the student can master

Step 3: Try Out Performance

Have the trainee do the job; correct errors
Have the trainee explain **each key point** to you as he or she does the job again
Make sure he or she understands
Continue until you know the trainee knows

Step 4: Follow up

Put the trainee to work alone
Designate to whom he or she goes for help
Check frequently
Encourage questions
Taper off extra coaching and close followup

If the worker hasn't learned, the instructor hasn't taught.

Developing Supervisors and Managers

Some people are natural managers, some can acquire the necessary skills, and some would prefer to spend their careers without getting into management. Given the difficulty of attracting experienced talent and the value of seasoned personnel who know **your** business, it may often be advantageous to bring in entry-level people and train them for management after a period of evaluating their suitability for advancement. The selected management training process should foster self-development, be tailored to individual needs and educational gaps, and should be a long-range concept.

Virtually by definition, management training will involve more than on-the-job training. Although working with someone on selected tasks is one approach, it will probably need to be supplemented by seminars, courses, workshops, and conferences provided by such organizations as:

- Aircraft manufacturers
- Aviation associations such as the National Air Transportation Association (NATA), the National Business Aircraft Association (NBAA), state associations of airport managers and other aviation groups
- Chambers of Commerce
- Colleges and universities
- Banks and other service organizations
- Professional education groups such as the American Management Association
- Small Business Administration
- Training consultants and vendors

Who pays and whether or not the programs are undertaken on company time must be resolved and preferably in advance. The management trainee can perhaps be encouraged to choose between several courses with any of them covering the needed material. Some firms retroactively pay a percentage of tuition costs for any relevant program completed by any employee. Other firms pay for tuition and time in exchange for having the trainee teach the new material to the other staff.

The concept of lifelong learning applies to virtually every profession in our society today. In an industry like aviation, it is ever important to stay abreast of new technologies, revising regulations, and market trends. The term "lifelong learning" encompasses everything from attending college courses to professional workshops and conferences to reading industry-related periodicals.

Training to Keep Abreast of Social and Economic Change

The world is changing at an ever-increasing pace and this can affect the marketplace for an aviation business. If it becomes harder to make a profit from the sale of fuel or aircraft, perhaps other products and service lines need to be emphasized. If so, different personnel may be involved and need guidance on merchandising and promoting the new items. If the airport operator is receiving a growing volume of noise complaints from certain areas in the flight pattern, then flight instructors need to be trained in more depth on noise issues and abatement procedures. Then they, in turn, can teach this in the air and in the classroom. If the business is investing in a microcomputer for accounting purposes, perhaps all the staff would benefit from a short presentation by the computer vendor about other functions that could be performed on the system. The manager must stay current with trends both within and beyond aviation, and the manager must determine how much of the staff's time to allot to briefings, reading of trade and general business publications, and formal classroom activities.

Evaluating the Training Program

Any training takes time away from revenue-producing work. Although theoretically it will pay off by reducing mistakes and increasing productivity and motivation, this consequence is not automatic. A training program must have before and after measurements. Measurable items in an aviation business include:

- Complaint rate
- Appreciation rate
- Invoice errors
- Accident rate
- Absenteeism
- Personnel turnover
- Repairs brought back to be done over
- Time required to perform a task
- Cost per task
- Scores on formal written tests
- Volume of sales
- New clients

The measures selected for evaluation of the training program must be items readily collectable or already routinely being collected.

Compensation

General Aviation Pay Levels and Systems

Most smaller FBOs have a variety of pay systems that range from minimum wage for line personnel through hourly commissions for flight instructors and hourly wages for repair personnel. Some build in a bonus system for instructors so that they earn more per hour with more bookings. Many FBO employees wear several hats. People on the flight line may also work on flight desk and maintenance assignments; the secretary may also pump gas, order parts, and do bookkeeping; and, of course, the owner/manager is often a jack-of-all-trades who fills in for anyone who is unavailable.

Perhaps the single biggest issue in the area of FBO personnel matters is that many of the people in the business are in it for their love of aviation. They settle for low and sometimes erratic pay patterns for a few years until the need to be more financially established takes them into other areas of aviation. These other areas, such as corporate pilot or mechanic, airport manager, airline pilot or mechanic, and positions in aircraft manufacturing tend to offer better pay, substantially better fringe benefits, and often greater job stability and better working conditions. As the FBO industry becomes more mature and more professional, it will have to address the issues of pay levels in competing areas and the questions of high turnover and high levels of part-time involvement that have traditionally characterized smaller FBOs. A comparison of typical 1994 FBO employee wages can be found in figures 5.16 and 5.17.

Comparable Worth

The issue of comparable worth means equal pay for jobs of comparable difficulty. The concept had its start in the mid-1970s when a landmark study in the state of Washington reviewed state salaries and found that on average women earned 20 percent less than men for comparable jobs.[21] In 1981 a Supreme Court ruling supported this finding. The criteria used by comparable worth studies may be of value in reviewing jobs for any purpose. They include:

- Skill, knowledge and education required
- Effort (e.g., mental demands, latitude, judgement and difficulty of problems)
- Accountability—scale of executive decisions
- Working conditions

Hourly Wages Paid *Full-Time* Employees By Job Classification, By Gross Sales (Average) and By National Average						
Job Classification	**National Average**	**Less than $1.49MM**	**$1.50MM to $2.99MM**	**$3.00MM to $4.99MM**	**$5.00MM to $9.99MM**	**$10.00MM or more**
Line Technician	$ 7.53	$ 6.99	$ 7.48	$ 7.49	$ 7.91	$ 8.91
Customer Service Representative	$ 7.93	$ 7.44	$ 7.97	$ 7.59	$ 7.15	$ 9.51
Mechanic (with A&P)	$11.83	$10.94	$11.47	$11.95	$13.09	$13.77
Mechanic (without A&P)	$ 8.65	$ 7.92	$ 8.21	$ 8.03	$10.11	$ 9.56
Avionics Technician	$12.69	$12.03	$12.81	$10.81	$13.52	$12.77
Inspector	$15.10	$15.39	$13.91	$12.23	$17.15	$15.39
Parts Clerk	$ 8.70	$ 7.33	$ 8.58	$ 8.52	$ 8.82	$ 9.56
Accounting Clerk	$ 9.29	$ 7.67	$ 9.88	$ 9.16	$ 8.95	$ 9.91
Bookkeeper	$ 9.60	$ 8.11	$10.48	$10.03	$ 9.55	$11.77
Secretary	$ 8.55	$ 7.71	$ 8.24	$ 8.20	$ 8.69	$ 9.84
Custodian	$ 7.14	$ 5.92	$ 6.89	$ 5.77	$ 7.75	$ 7.66
Dispatcher	$ 9.47	$ 9.14	$ 9.36	$ 8.00	$ 9.75	$10.37

Figure 5.16.

Each of these four factors is given a weight and the sum total of these weights ranks the job with all other jobs having the same weight, regardless of whether there is any similarity in jobs. Positions with extremely desirable ancillary conditions, such as free or almost free air travel if one works for the airlines, would get a negative weighting for that factor.

Job Definition

The first step in developing an equitable pay system for a business involves job definition.

One way to clarify what each employee's job actually is to have them fill out a simple form stating:

- Job title
- Reporting relationship
- Specifications
- Primary function
- Main duties
- Other duties
- Job requirements
- Technical/administrative complexity
- Responsibility for dollar results
- Responsibility for supervision and training of others
- Unusual working conditions

Some employees may turn out to be doing more or different tasks than thought, and more than one may claim primary responsibility for the same thing. These and other such issues may arise. The review process should also allow you to determine what functions may need to be covered by new staff.

Job Evaluation

Using the task information just collected and some criteria about responsibility levels, the jobs now have to be evaluated in relation to one another. One method for doing this is *simple ranking*, which ranks and groups the jobs by their value to the firm. Then the groups of jobs are arranged in a series of pay levels.

Job Classification	National			Regional							
	Low	Average	High	NE	EA	SO	GL	CE	SW	NW	WE
Line Technician	$ 4.57	$ 7.53	$16.80	$ 8.08	$ 7.86	$ 7.29	$ 7.60	$ 7.11	$ 7.30	$ 7.39	$ 7.97
Customer Service Representative	$ 5.00	$ 7.93	$20.00	$10.92	$ 8.14	$ 7.25	$ 9.26	$ 9.13	$ 7.30	$ 7.41	$ 8.34
Mechanic (With A&P)	$ 5.00	$11.83	$25.00	$13.68	$12.62	$11.55	$11.15	$11.18	$11.45	$11.83	$12.44
Mechanic (Without A&P)	$ 4.50	$ 8.65	$20.00	$ 8.50	$ 8.32	$ 8.44	$ 9.09	$ 7.25	$ 7.84	$ 9.15	$ 9.25
Avionics Technician	$ 7.00	$12.69	$25.00	$16.09	$12.22	$12.85	$12.13	$15.54	$10.97	$11.57	$12.00
Inspector	$ 5.65	$15.10	$28.00	$14.25	$13.49	$16.73	$14.27	$16.08	$16.10	$13.63	$15.03
Parts Clerk	$ 5.00	$ 8.70	$16.00	$ 9.60	$ 9.05	$ 8.15	$ 9.42	$ 7.03	$ 8.12	$ 9.08	$ 9.31
Accounting Clerk	$ 5.00	$ 9.29	$16.83	$11.89	$ 9.88	$ 8.73	$ 9.77	$ 7.98	$ 8.23	$ 9.76	$ 9.12
Bookkeeper	$ 5.50	$ 9.60	$19.00	$ 9.54	$ 9.03	$ 9.71	$10.01	$ 8.35	$ 9.00	$ 9.41	$11.28
Secretary	$ 4.00	$ 8.55	$15.00	$10.33	$ 8.86	$ 8.30	$ 9.01	$ 6.30	$ 8.23	$ 7.86	$ 9.08
Custodian	$ 4.25	$ 7.14	$16.00	$ 5.88	$ 6.31	$ 7.41	$ 7.62	$ 7.44	$ 6.00	$ 8.50	$ 7.89
Dispatcher	$ 4.25	$ 9.47	$17.00	$ 8.67	$ 8.54	$ 9.36	$10.36	$ 9.45	$13.46	$ 8.55	$10.68

Hourly Wages Paid *Full-Time* Employees
By Job Classification and By Region
National (Low, Average, High) and Regional Average

Figure 5.17.

Pay Ranges

Ranking the jobs in order of their value to the firm takes into account only the internal situation. The salary that people in these jobs can command elsewhere must now be investigated. Possible sources of such data include:

- Trade and professional groups such as NATA, which conducts an annual salary survey
- Chambers of Commerce
- Major firms in the area
- U.S. Bureau of Labor Statistics
- American Management Association
- Employment agencies
- Newspaper want-ads

In analyzing pay in your area and comparing it to your company's jobs, be sure to compare actual job descriptions and not just job titles. Based upon the average pay for each type of position developed from your market survey, a midpoint pay level for your own company can be constructed for each position. Commonly the low point in each range will be 85 percent of the mid-point and the high will be 115 percent. Such a range will enable employees to join your firm at the bottom of the pay range for that position and get 30 percent in raises without promotion to a higher job category. A more fine-grained breakdown of each pay range may also suit your purposes.

Fringe Benefits

Most full-time positions carry with them an array of non-salary benefits such as medical insurance, life insurance, pension plans, profit-sharing plans and other supplementary compensation. The primary advantages of these are:

1. In the event of the employee's death or disability, the dependents are provided for in a planned manner.
2. Group purchasing enables the employer to buy more benefits for the same dollar than employees could alone, particularly in insurance.

Most companies offer certain items on a mandatory basis, such as a minimum level of life insurance, and then provide optional additional benefits such as disability insurance. There may be choices of medical plans with varying levels of coverage and varying levels of employee participation in payment. The trend in this area is the "cafeteria" approach in which the company determines a fixed dollar amount or percentage of salary to be used for fringe benefits, and each employee chooses precisely and only that package of services that he or she really wants.[22] As more and more households involve both a husband and wife working for different employers with different benefit options, this ability to custom-design one's benefits is a great advantage. Computerization of benefits processing is the technology that makes this approach possible.

For most businesses, the typical scale of fringe benefits is in the range of 37 percent of basic pay.[23] Benefits have been rising faster than wages and salaries in the past two decades so that ways to control these costs are clearly important. The flexible benefits approach can give employees more of what each really needs without increasing total costs to the company. (See figures 5.18 and 5.19.)

Administration of the Total Compensation Plan

Many employees are unaware of the total dollar value of their salary plus benefits. When hiring new staff it is desirable to be able to cite lower and upper limits for the value of the total compensation package. Administration of the compensation plan will probably also involve periodic activity to stay current with what competing businesses are doing. It should involve a clear and consistent policy about raises, promotions, merit increases, bonuses, and the like. The plan needs to give the manager the flexibility to take quick steps to prevent the loss of a key employee without causing problems with the other staff. It must provide the freedom to bring in specialized talent at the going rate while not slighting long-standing, loyal employees. It must allow a visible career ladder within the firm so that staff can envisage their long-range futures. If pay levels and changes are soundly based on market competition, clearly set out, and fairly administered, it will go a long way toward minimizing trouble in what can otherwise be an ongoing source of discontent.

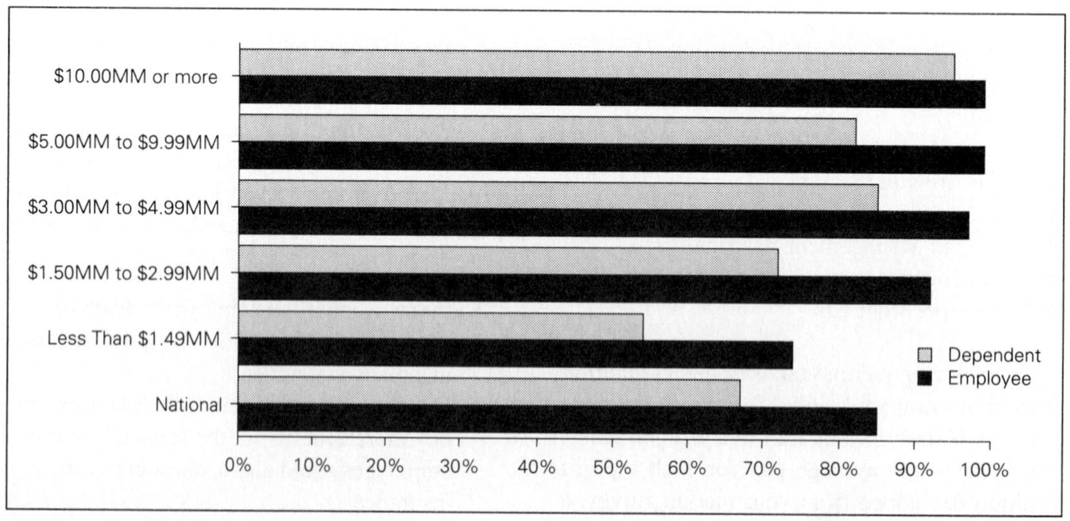

Figure 5.18. Percent of companies offering employee and dependent insurance benefits (by national average and by gross sales).

Percent of Companies Offering Employee Insurance Benefits Who Pay 100% Of the Premium (By Coverage, By National Average and By Gross Sales)						
Coverage Category	**National Average**	**Less Than $1.49MM**	**$1.50MM to $2.99MM**	**$3.00MM to $4.99MM**	**$5.00MM to $9.99MM**	**$10.00MM or more**
Hospital & Medical	49%	52%	49%	52%	46%	37%
Major Medical	49%	56%	48%	48%	48%	35%
Group Life	66%	65%	69%	80%	60%	57%
Accidental Death & Dismemberment	63%	67%	63%	67%	62%	61%
Long Term Disability	52%	52%	29%	62%	70%	67%
Dental	31%	26%	30%	44%	36%	23%
Vision	23%	25%	26%	33%	0%	14%
Weekly Sickness & Accident Benefits	25%	18%	12%	25%	50%	50%
Loss of License	5%	7%	0%	17%	0%	0%

Figure 5.19.

Evaluating Employees

The process of employee discipline and evaluation may be best accomplished primarily in the style of *The One-Minute Manager,* that is, by the one-minute reprimand about a specific thing done wrong, but including a reassurance to the employee about his worth.[24] This is as an alternative to the "gunny-sack" approach in which all the bad things, along with the good, are dumped out on the conference table once every six months or every year at performance evaluation time. The principle of tackling little errors promptly when they occur is aimed at ensuring that big errors do not have much of a chance to happen. Nevertheless, periodically the manager will need to sit down with each of his staff and review how things are going. This may or may not be tied to periodic merit, cost-of-living, or other pay increases.

An effective employee appraisal plan will:

- Achieve better communication between the manager and employee
- Relate pay to work performance and results
- Provide a standardized approach to evaluating performance
- Help employees better understand what is expected of them and how they can improve

The appraisal process should consider the following and should be reviewed with all supervisors doing reviews so that there is a reasonably consistent approach to applying these factors:

- Results achieved
- Quality of performance
- Volume of work
- Effectiveness in working with others in firm
- Effectiveness in dealing with customers, suppliers, and so on
- Initiative
- Job knowledge
- Dependability
- Enthusiasm

A sample performance appraisal form utilized by Midcoast Aviation is shown in figure 5.20.

MIDCOAST AVIATION, INC.

NONEXEMPT
PERFORMANCE APPRAISAL / IMPROVEMENT PROFILE

Name: ______________________________

Job Title: ______________________________

Department: ______________________________

Date Assigned to Present Job: ______________________________

Date of This Review Period: From: ______________ To: ______________

Reviewed By: ______________________________

INSTRUCTIONS:

This form is to be completed for each salaried nonexempt employee:

- Annually.
- On an interim basis, as necessary, to review the Employee's performance.

This report covers all important aspects of the past performance of the employee, a summary of his/her current status, and a discussion of potential for growth and development. In addition, the report provides a vehicle for your personal discussion of the appraisal results with the employee. Carefully consider the employee's performance during the review period based on assigned duties and level of responsibility. Check the appropriate block in each category which best identifies the employee's current performance. Next, check the block indicating the change in performance since the last evaluation.

Figure 5.20. Sample performance appraisal.

Performance Factor	Current Evaluation					Since Last Evaluation		
	Unsatisfactory	Acceptable	Competent	Competent Plus	Outstanding	Reverse	Same	Improved
1. **ATTITUDE:** Consider the employee's work attitude including overall appropriateness of behavior towards the environment, fellow employees and supervision. Is the individual willing to accept new assignments, policies and procedures? Is he/she flexible in meeting changes, additional requirements, etc.								
2. **ORGANIZATION:** Consider the individual's ability to effectively organize his/her work load and establish priorities. Does the individual properly plan out work including coordinating with others as required?								
3. **PRODUCTIVITY – QUANTITY:** Consider the individual's overall productivity in terms of quantity of work produced in timely basis. Consider the individual's ability to meet or exceed job requirements.								
4. **PRODUCTIVITY – QUALITY:** Consider the individual's ability to produce neat, accurate work on a timely basis. Does the employee possess acute attention to detail when it is an essential factor?								
5. **INITIATIVE:** Consider the employee's ability to work without constant supervision and his or her ability to begin and/or follow through with assignments.								
6. **TECHNICAL OR JOB COMPETENCY:** Consider the individual's overall technical knowledge and job competency, and the employee's ability to put this knowledge into practical application.								
7. **ATTENDANCE:** Consider the individual's attendance record. Does the individual attempt to adhere to policies concerning lunch hours and work breaks? Does the individual notify his/her supervisor of absenteeism or tardiness?								

Figure 5.20. Continued.

OVERALL PERFORMANCE SUMMARY

Indicate the performance level that most closely reflects how the employee's overall performance measured up to what should normally be expected from an employee with similar experience at this level.

☐ Unsatisfactory	☐ Acceptable	☐ Competent	☐ Competent Plus	☐ Outstanding
Doesn't meet objectives, falls short of required performance, consider trial (probationary period), transfer to a more suitable job or termination.	Usually meets objectives, areas for improvement noted in appraisal, level of performance is less than expected but acceptable.	Consistently meets objectives, full utilization of ability and experience to produce the desired results expected from a qualified employee.	Consistently meets objectives and actively contributes to achievement of overall company goals. Superior performance in some aspects of job. Performance above the competent level.	Consistently exceeds objectives, actively develops teamwork and cooperation, seeks new and better ways to accomplish tasks, extremely capable and versatile in adjusting priorities to current needs, an effective communicator.

PRINCIPAL JOB DUTIES DURING REVIEW PERIOD. Briefly describe the principal work assigned to the individual. List and number specific job objectives and goals established.

Signatures and Dates:

Appraised by:	Director, Human Resources
Department Head	Employee

Figure 5.20. Continued.

JOB PERFORMANCE STRENGTHS (Summarize the employee's most significant strengths.)

DEVELOPMENT PLANS (Summarize the activities such as special coaching, special assignments, off-the-job training, etc., that are planned to help this employee improve job performance during the next appraisal period.)

IMPROVEMENT NEEDS (Summarize the employee's most significant areas needing improvement.)

ADDITIONAL COMMENTS:

EMPLOYEE COMMENTS:

Figure 5.20. Continued.

Disciplinary Problems

Conflict Resolution

Because most businesses involve operating under time pressure with a diverse group of personalities, most job situations lead periodically to disagreements on how something should be, or should have been done. An autocratic manager or boss who rules, "In the future we'll do it *my* way, and that's the end of the matter," is losing in several ways:

1. Resentful employees may consciously or unconsciously seek other ways to undercut their boss's authority. Morale will drop.
2. Good suggestions from employees on how to improve the company's methods will not be heard, and this will tend to stifle future problem-solving ideas and activities.
3. Junior staff are not given either recognition or the ability to grow, thereby heightening the chance of future inadequacies.

If, instead of an autocratic approach to disagreements, the manager is willing to be more open minded, the guidelines in figure 5.14 can be helpful in achieving a satisfactory solution.[25]

Administering Discipline

Positive discipline through motivation and self-control is what makes most companies work well most of the time. Negative discipline—punishment of some type—may only result in behavior adequate to avoid punishment, not in real correction of the problem. However, even under the best of conditions with trained and loyal employees and excellent leadership, someone is bound to violate the rules now and then so that there are serious negative consequences. When this happens, there is a need for some generally accepted principles to guide management. In administering discipline, two conflicting goals—protecting the rights of the individual to be disciplined, and preserving the interests of the organization as a whole—must be reconciled. Within this context the following guidelines are generally considered desirable:

1. Provide definite policies covering discipline.
2. Establish reasonable rules and standards.
3. Communicate rules to all concerned.
4. Investigate each case thoroughly.
5. Ensure consistency.
6. Provide a logical sequence of progressive penalties.
7. Establish a right of appeal.
8. Document all disciplinary matters in writing with dates and names.

The "Red-Hot-Stove" Rule

A practical approach to discipline is the "red-hot-stove" approach in which the consequences of a misdemeanor are **immediate, consistent and impersonal.** The act and the discipline seem virtually like one event. This involves:

1. Having advance warning—knowledge of the rule and the consequences of breaking it.
2. Immediate and painful results from the violation.
3. The same results for everyone, no matter what their status.
4. The result is not because of who you are, but what you did.

This process may be difficult to apply in every case, but persistence will pay off at least in part because of its deterrent effect.

The Troubled Worker

Stress and fragmentation of our lives occur not just in the workplace, but also in the rest of life as well. The above descriptions of how to handle normal disagreements and infractions may not be

A. *When Something Happens That Upsets You/Makes You Mad*

1. Ask the person involved for a specific time to talk over something; tell him/her what you want to discuss.
2. Set a mutually agreeable time and place.
3. Prepare. Make notes or run through in your mind what seems to have happened and why you're angry about it.
4. Do it soon. Don't put the other person in suspense overnight or over a weekend, unless it can't be helped.

B. *Holding the Discussion*

5. Do it in private.
6. Allow no interruptions.
7. Finish it. Don't leave until both feel clear a resolution has been reached.
8. Acknowledge the other may have had a good reason (to him/her) for doing what he/she did, regardless of how stupid it seems to you. Ask for clarification.
9. Listen, interpret, and clarify.
10. Stick to the issue. When discussing what A did, don't get sidetracked by discussions of the times B has done the same thing.
11. Use "I" statements; be accountable for your own feelings.
12. Allow your own anger.
13. Expect and acknowledge the other's anger but don't take responsibility for it.
14. Don't let the other person's anger make you angrier; you are not the target.
15. Stick to one issue at a time. If necessary, set another time and place for other issues or agree to continue then and there.
16. Don't gunnysack ("twice is always").
17. Don't walk away.
18. Don't interrupt.

C. *Concluding the Discussion*

19. Completion and clarity on the issue; mutual understanding of how to be deal with it.
20. Reassurance and reaffirmation of the other person.
21. Let it go. Don't bring it up again or blame others. What's done and resolved is over. Be friends again.

Figure 5.21. 21 steps to fighting fairly.

applicable when the worker in question is in some kind of non-work trauma. This could be death, divorce, serious illness of oneself or a loved one, problems with children or step-children, substance abuse, domestic violence, financial worries, or a number of other causes. While the truly professional worker will attempt not to bring these problems to the workplace, sometimes the situation is so severe that effects will show at work.

The supervisor's or manager's role is very sensitive in such situations. Discussions with the employee must be restricted to the problem's effect on job performance. It is not the supervisor's business to become a diagnostician or a counselor. If the issue is not resolved satisfactorily through a supervisor and employee discussion, it may be necessary to seek outside help. Many companies are now contracting with "Employee Assistance Programs" or EAPs, where the troubled worker can obtain expert counsel and, if needed, referral to a detoxification program or other treatment facility. As in all cases of disciplinary action, careful documentation of the steps taken, the commitments made, and their schedule must be retained. This is vital if the employee must later be fired because it will provide ample documented evidence.

Particularly in the case of drug and alcohol abuse, the supervisor must carefully monitor behavior and deal with the deterioration in work performance before it poses a threat to the safety or productivity of other workers.

In 1988 the federal government adopted requirements for drug testing of certain personnel in aviation. Aviation employees with safety or security related responsibilities are subject to drug testing. Part 135 companies of any size are required to develop and submit a plan to FAA that includes random drug testing. It also requires pre-employment and post-accident testing. While employers are not required to offer rehabilitation, they are encouraged to consider such plans in establishing the total compensation plan. Employers must designate a physician as the Medical Review Officer for administration of the drug testing plan.

Personnel Policy Manual

This chapter has touched on numerous aspects of personnel management, particularly as it affects the small FBO business. It assumes that the company has no personnel manager, and that the company manager and various supervisors must carry out personnel activities as part of their jobs. Since consistency is such a major feature of so many personnel issues, there is a need for a written manual. The manual will likely contain at least the following:

- Purpose
- Authority of the manual
- How to use the manual
- Responsibilities of department heads, supervisors, and employees
- Employee relations policy
- Recruiting and selection policy
- Training and development policy
- Working schedules and hours
- Compensation policies and procedures pay and fringes
- Promotions, transfers and layoffs
- Attendance, punctuality and absenteeism
- Safety and security programs
- Operational rules
- Profit awareness
- Complaint and grievance procedures
- Communications
- Labor relations
- Personnel forms

Manual Style

The manual can be anything from a formal, legalistic compendium of all current policies (perhaps in a loose-leaf binder), to a small, perhaps humorous brochure. In many companies it may be appropriate to have both—a reference book with all the detail, and something short for each employee. New employees should be required to study the book and ask questions. The manager also needs to decide whether they alone will update the policies, or whether they will seek advice from supervisors or assign the full responsibility to someone else for recommending updates.

Personnel Records

A number of record sheets will accompany the personnel manual. A typical list of needed sheets is presented in figure 5.22. Examples of some of these have been presented earlier in the chapter.

Personnel Forms and Records	
Activity	**Form**
1. Researching or studying various jobs to obtain information necessary in developing the organization.	Job Analysis
2. Clearly describing a given job in terms of its contents and tasks involved.	Job Description
3. Describing the requirements of a job in terms of skill, effort, responsibility needed by the person on the job.	Job Specification
4. Advising the personnel office or the employment agency of the type person you are recruiting for a specific job.	Requisition
5. Recording biographical, training, experience and personal information about a job applicant.	Application Blank
6. Conducting an interview with a job applicant.	Oral Interview Guide
7. Checking job applicant's references and data to insure validity and gain additional information.	Reference Check (a) Telephone (b) Letter
8. Conducting a physical examination of applicant to insure ability to handle job and determine overall physical condition.	Physical Examination
9. Orienting or inducting new employees into the organization.	Orientation Check List
10. Recording all necessary data and activities on each employee.	Employee Personal Record or Folder
11. Recording attendance and results from various training programs.	Training Records
12. Evaluating and recording the performance of employees.	Performance Rating Form
13. Recording disciplinary situations and action taken.	Disciplinary Forms: (a) Warning (b) Layoff (c) Dismissal
14. Providing a means of handling employee complaints and grievances.	Grievance Forms
15. Providing a means of obtaining employee suggestions.	Suggestion Forms
16. Collecting information and data from all personnel leaving the company.	Exit Interview Form

Figure 5.22. Personnel forms and records.

Employee Organizations

A significant percentage of American labor is unionized (about 20 percent). Although unionism is not as prevalent in FBO operations, it ranges around 5 percent in most parts of the country. The financing and power behind the nation's major unions means that if unionization begins, a single business owner would be unable to resist.[26] In recent years some traditionally non-union areas such as office workers have become increasingly unionized. The usual reasons for unionization can often be addressed by fair and reasonable personnel policies. These reasons may include:

- Changes in management
- Pay system problems
- Elimination of promotional opportunities
- Sudden work-force reductions
- Unsatisfactory or more restrictive working conditions
- Poor or inconsistent supervisory practices
- Desire for greater voice
- Desire for better income and working conditions
- Desire for control over benefits

Impact on Management

The existence or introduction of a union has an impact on the entire organization. This impact can include:

- Competition for loyalty of employees
- Possible challenge to management decisions
- Use of time at work to discuss union issues
- Stimulation of more careful personnel practices
- More rigid working rules
- Possible threats to flexibility and efficiency
- Centralization of personnel decisions
- Introduction of outsiders to the management-employee relationship
- Higher labor costs

Every manager should consider very carefully the reasons that contribute to the formation of employee organizations, the impact that such an organization would have upon the business, and develop a managerial philosophy and action program accordingly.

Separation

Whether voluntary or involuntary, there should be some standard procedures for termination. The departing employee may become a vendor, a source of referrals to the business, or may even at some point be rehired. A person who does not fit the company's present needs may still have desirable skills in changed circumstances. In all cases, an exit interview is recommended to seek information from the outgoing employee about concerns and issues and to provide management with ideas for changes to benefit the remaining staff. A second purpose of an exit interview is to stimulate the maximum self-esteem and positive feeling about the company in the mind of the departing employee. A sample form for exit interviews is presented in figure 5.23.

EXIT INTERVIEW

____
Interview Date

Employee's name ______________________
Job______________ Employment date ______________
Department ______________________
Reason for Separation ______________________
Departure Date ______________________

Information received from departing employees can be very useful in analyzing problem areas and in providing for organizational improvement. The key to successful exit interviewing is to encourage the employee to talk as freely as possible. Establish yourself as a sympathetic listening post so that his true feelings and opinions may be obtained. The following questions covering basic areas should be used to set the interview pattern. Other topics, appropriate to individual cases should be explored as indicated.

Reason for termination? ______________________
Do you have another job?__________Where?__________Pay?__________
Did you like the work you were doing? ______________________
How were the working conditions?______________________
When you first started here
Was your job fully explained? ______________________
Were you introduced to co-workers?______________________
Did you enjoy pleasant relationships with co-workers?______________________
______________________Exceptions?______________________
Did you like your supervisor? ______________________
Did your supervisor seem to know his/her job?______________________
How well did your supervisor handle gripes or complaints?______________________

Was it easy to communicate with him/her?______________________

Do you feel your pay was fair? ______________________

Were benefits satisfactory? ______________________

Was there sufficient opportunity for advancement? ______________________

Do you know how you stood as far as work performance was concerned? ______________________

What suggestions do you have for improving policies, procedures, work situations, etc.? ______________________

What are your plans for the future?______________________

Others? ______________________

Explain benefits and future relationships with company. ______________________
Comments: ______________________

Interviewer ______________________

Figure 5.23. Exit interview form to be used with the departure of each employee.

Summary

The success of an aviation business can largely be attributed to its personnel. Human resource programs are instrumental in providing an environment that stimulates people to contribute their best effort. Programs are designed to provide and service a steady flow of personnel into the organization. This flow is like a pipeline with various control points along its length: identification of needs, recruiting, selecting, orientation, training, development, compensation, evaluation, discipline, promotion, and separation. The areas of communications and motivation are especially critical to the organization's success and should receive special managerial attention.

Discussion Topics

1. What is meant by the "pipeline concept"?
2. Identify and briefly discuss five "control points" instrumental to the success of human resource management programs.
3. Identify the key steps involved in the selection of employees.
4. What issues should be covered in an exit interview?
5. What are the key elements of orientation and why are they important?
6. What are some factors that could cause complaints about discrimination in the hiring and managing of personnel?
7. How does Maslow's hierarchy of needs relate to the ways a manager can choose to supervise his or her team?
8. What are three reasons for having a personnel policy manual?

Chapter 6
Organization and Administration

Objectives

- ✔ Draw a distinction between formal and informal organizations.
- ✔ Discuss the organizational principles of specialization and decentralization.
- ✔ Recognize that the exact number of people a manager can effectively supervise depends on a number of underlying variables and situations.
- ✔ Recognize the advantages and disadvantages of various business organizations: sole proprietorship, partnership, and corporation.
- ✔ Understand the difference between "line" and "staff" positions.
- ✔ Demonstrate the logic of organizing and its relationship to other managerial functions.

Introduction

Once the workload of an enterprise grows beyond what a single person can do, organization becomes necessary. Various tasks must be assigned to different people and their individual efforts must be coordinated. As the business expands, this process leads to departments and divisions with each having its own particular mission. One should consider the resulting organization as a complex machine—like an airplane designed for airline service. Each part of the plane performs a necessary function—supplying power, providing lift, heat, control, communications and so forth. The different parts are carefully balanced and fitted together in order to meet the stringent demands placed upon such a vehicle. A change in any one of the parts will frequently call for an adjustment in several others.

A manager of an aviation enterprise must view the organization in a like manner. It is composed of several parts or elements that must be carefully balanced in order to achieve the desired goals. To accomplish tasks the manager must utilize both technical and social tools of organizing. The techniques of structure, procedures and manuals must be appropriately used in a social setting that recognizes the influence of individuals and groups on the ultimate outcome of business efforts. The organization must be developed to accomplish the job, and a social structure must be built to meet the needs of the people doing the work.

Goals and Objectives

Basically speaking, when the manager sets about organizing business efforts, there are two major initial considerations: (1) what are the goals and objectives, and (2) what resources are available to achieve these goals? With these two elements firmly in mind, the manager can organize the efforts of the business to pursue the desired goals.

Determining goals and objectives, as discussed in chapter 2, is the necessary first step managers must take. Naturally, some consideration is made of the resources available so that restrictions may be noted. Care should be exercised, however, that the resources or apparent resources do not limit the potential of the business. Certain goals may warrant extending the present resources to a point not previously considered possible.

Determining available resources means simply identifying the financial means available, reviewing the personnel capabilities, and surveying the physical assets of the organization. A careful examination of these areas is a necessary first step in developing an organizational structure, because the business must have the required resources available, or else develop a structure more compatible with the ready resources.

Answering the following questions methodically and carefully should provide the manager with an idea of what resources are available:

General

1. Do you have a written plan for arranging and relating resources to meet planned objectives?
2. Do you have a firm estimate of the resources required?
3. Do you have an inventory of resources on hand?
4. Are additional resources available?
5. Do you have a plan for obtaining additional resources?

Financial Area

1. Do you have current, accurate financial statements?
2. Do you routinely compare your present financial status with your past record?
3. Do you project your financial needs into the future?

Personnel

1. Do you have a current list of your present personnel indicating qualifications, skills, history, and performance?
2. Do you have an ongoing training and development program for your present personnel?

Physical Assets

1. Do you maintain an accurate listing of buildings, equipment, vehicles, aircraft, and real estate?
2. Does your listing indicate value, physical state, and operational capabilities?

Having clearly identified the existing resources of the organization, the manager should determine the capacity for the business to acquire additional resources. Some insight into this capability can be gained by answering the following questions:

1. Is additional capital available either in the form of equity, loans or credit?
2. Can the labor market provide additional personnel of the type required?
3. Can additional physical resources in the form of real estate, buildings, or operating areas be acquired?

The next step is to establish goals and objectives. The framework for this activity was presented under the managerial function of planning discussed in chapter 2. Here it becomes the structure that guides the day-by-day organizing activity of the manager and the total business.

Organizational activity develops a structure that will facilitate and encourage the achievement of these goals.

Legal Structure

The manager has several forms of business organizations available. By carefully selecting the appropriate form, he or she can increase profit, decrease taxes, provide for orderly growth of the business, and balance the resources against the challenges provided by the competitive world of business. The following basic types of business organizations are available:

- Sole proprietorship
- Partnership
- Corporation

There are variations in partnerships and corporations, but we will consider only these three major categories. It should be noted that any one specific form of business organization need not be considered permanent. As the business grows, it will change in its operations and needs, and the financial and tax situations will more than likely also change. Likewise, statutory, legal, and tax developments may change the characteristics and advantages of the various business structures available. In view of the changing business world, the manager should re-examine at regular intervals the business framework most suitable for a certain situation.

Let's consider the major advantages and disadvantages of the three principal forms of legal structure.

Sole Proprietorship

The sole proprietorship is usually defined as a business owned and operated by one person.[1] In community property states, the spouse also has an ownership interest. To establish such a business, all that is required is any local business licenses.

Advantages include:

1. Ease of formation and dissolution
2. Sole ownership of profits
3. Control and decision making vested in one owner
4. Flexibility
5. Relative freedom from regulation and special taxation

Disadvantages include:

1. Unlimited liability for business debts that may affect all the owner's personal assets Additional problems of liability such as physical loss or personal injury may be reduced by proper insurance
2. An unstable business life, highly dependent on the health and welfare of the owner; potential lack of continuity
3. Less available capital in most cases; relative difficulty in obtaining long term financing
4. Relatively limited viewpoint and size, and a lack of "sounding boards"
5. Difficulty in building equity in the company for sale or retirement purposes

Partnership

A partnership is an association of two or more people for business purposes.[2] Written articles of partnership are customarily executed, and one expert in this area suggests each prospective partner write out their desires and goals from participation in the enterprise before any formal negotiation.[3] This will clarify, for example, any conflicting ideas about time to be put in versus compensation taken out. Written articles normally address:

- Name, purpose, domicile
- Duration of agreement
- Nature of partners (general or limited, active or silent)
- Contributions by each (at inception, subsequently)
- Business expenses (how handled)
- Authority of each partner to make decisions
- Chief Executive Officer
- Separate debts
- Books, records and methods of accounting
- Division of losses and profits
- Draws or salaries
- Rights of a continuing partner
- Death of a partner (dissolution and winding up)
- Employee management
- Release of debts
- Sale or transfer of partnership interest
- Arbitration
- Additions, alterations or modifications of agreement
- Settlement of disputes
- Required and prohibited acts
- Absence and disability

It is recommended that partners be mutually subject to intensive background, credit, and character investigation because most new ventures founder because of disagreements between partners.[4]

Advantages of partnership include:

1. Ease of organization
2. Minimum capital required
3. More capital available
4. Broader management base and continuity

Disadvantages include:

1. Conflicts between partners
2. Less flexibility owing to the need for consultation
3. Unlimited liability, as with sole proprietorship
4. Size limitations
5. Capital restrictions
6. Firm bound by actions of just one partner
7. Difficulty of transferring partnership interest

Incorporation

The corporation has a separate legal life from its members; it is "an artificial being, invisible, intangible, and existing only in contemplation of the law."[5] Corporations are usually formed under the authority of state governments. Multistate or out-of-state corporations are more complex because they must comply not only with various state laws, but also with the requirements of interstate commerce.

Advantages of corporations include:

1. Limitations of the stockholder's liability to the amount invested, with respect to business losses (though not with respect to damage suits, and so on)
2. Ownership is readily transferable
3. Separate legal existence, even with the demise of all current owners, can be inherited
4. Relative ease of obtaining capital
5. Tax advantages, including owner's fringe benefits and other considerations
6. Permits large size
7. Easy expansion
8. Delegated authority
9. Potentially broader skill base

Disadvantages include:

1. Close regulation
2. Cost and complexity to set up
3. Activities limited by charter
4. Manipulation of minority stockholders
5. Double taxation—on corporate net income and on individual salaries and dividends

This last feature may be overcome by establishing Subchapter S status.[6] The purpose of Subchapter S (IRC 1371 1379) is to permit a small business corporation to have its income taxed to the shareholders as if it were a partnership. One objective is to overcome the double taxation feature; another is to permit shareholders to offset business losses against their other income.

Some conditions for subchapter S are that the corporation have ten or fewer shareholders, all of whom are individuals or estates, that there be no nonresident alien shareholders, that there be only one class of outstanding stock, that all shareholders consent, and that a specific portion of the corporation's receipts be derived from active business rather than enumerated passive investments. No limit is placed on the size of the corporation's income and assets.

Given the choices of structure, many businesses may want to advance gradually to more complex forms as they grow. The benefits of incorporation may be particularly strong for family enterprises.[7]

Organizational Principles for Internal Organization

No matter what the legal structure of the firm, it has numerous choices of internal structure. In the past decade or even the past five years, internal business organization seems to be undergoing some radical change. Most FBO businesses are quite small—the 1988 NATA Wage and Salary handbook reported that the average member firm had thirty-one full-time and seven part-time employees.[8] This means that little latitude for research and experimentation and learning from industry at large, may be an important means of keeping a modern approach.

The Rational Model vs. Some New Approaches

Adam Smith, in his classic *The Wealth of Nations,* set the stage for the success of the industrial revolution by addressing the issue of division of labor, and therefore, specialization.[9] A twentieth-century prophet in the same vein was Frederick Taylor, who pioneered the idea of motion study; namely, each task has only one best way to do it, and finding this best way will lead to efficiency and profit.[10] The advancement of statistical tools of analysis, together with the ability to process large amounts of quantitative information using computers, seems to be a continuation of this school of thought.

But several studies of Japanese productivity and of highly successful U.S firms seem to lead to a new view of business organization as requiring both technical and analytical tools **and** human qualities.[11,12,13,14] The talents required for custodianship of an existing corporate leviathan may now include creativity, innovation, adaptation to change, and high quality.[15]

Explicit Corporate Philosophy

One tool of management and organization that seems to be gaining ground is the statement of corporate values and goals.[16] Examples include Caterpillar's dedication to parts shipped anywhere in the world within 48 hours, Frito-Lay's 99.5 percent reliability of daily calls to all stores, McDonalds' stress on hygiene, Hewlitt-Packard's emphasis on *sufficient* profit to finance company growth and provide the resources needed for other corporate objectives, and many others.[17,18] Such a statement can provide the backdrop and value system for all that goes on in the company, and it can help to explain the nuances of structure and provide guidance where the structure does not state anything specific.

Organizational Culture

The effectiveness of an organization is also influenced by the organization culture, which affects the way the managerial functions of planning, organizing, staffing, leading, and controlling are carried out.

As it relates to organizations, culture is the general pattern of behavior, shared beliefs, and values that members have in common. Culture can be inferred from what people say, do, and think within an organizational setting. It involves the learning and transmitting of knowledge, beliefs, and patterns of behavior over a period of time, which means that an organizational culture is fairly stable and does not change fast. It often sets the tone for the company and establishes implied rules for the way people should behave.

Many slogans give a general idea of what a particular company stands for. Here are some examples:

- Delta describes its internal climate with the slogan "the Delta family feeling."
- The Disney Corporation refers to its customers as "guests" and its employees as "characters" (implying they are all considered to be *on stage* while working).
- United Airlines used the promotion "Fly the *friendly* skies of United" to describe its culture.

In similar ways Maytag wants to be known for its reliability, Ford for quality, Amway for opportunity, and so on.

Managers, especially top managers, create the climate for the enterprise. Their values influence the direction of the organization. Changing a culture may take a long time, even 5 to 10 years. It demands changing values, symbols, myths and behavior. This is important for a new manager or business owner to keep in mind.

Specialization and Job Rotation

A general overview of U.S. history suggests that great strides were made in producing larger quantities of goods at lower cost partly because of specialization. As the number of an employee's duties became more limited, he or she became an expert in a narrow area.

Evidence from Japan and elsewhere suggests that there may be limits to this approach. Some problems include:

- Monotony and boredom

- Lack of ability to see or understand the whole enterprise
- Lack of pride in products, as a person only carries out one small task on each item
- High absenteeism
- High turnover

By contrast, where entry-level managers are rotated to every key part of the firm and have to learn every job, they relate well to the big picture and to the problems of other departments. When senior management has been through this apprenticeship there is more contact with the technical realities of the job. Likewise, when employees on the line are organized so that they see the total fruits of their labors, quality and satisfaction go up. When line employees are asked for help on improving the processes (e.g., quality circles), they often contribute enthusiastically and constructively.

Decentralization and Decisions by Consensus

The rational model indicated that the owner/manager should reserve all major decisions. The new approach is more oriented toward making all decisions at as low a level as possible; that is, as close as possible to the people who will be putting them into effect.[19]

Decentralization does not refer to specialization of the work itself, but to the division of the managerial work and assignment of specific duties to various department heads or executive levels. The key issue becomes: how much of the managerial work, the planning, organizing, directing, and controlling shall be done by the president, or manager, and how much should be assigned to other personnel? This allocation of managerial work is one of the most critical and most sensitive aspects of the organizing process. The amount of decentralization reflects many considerations such as importance of work, individual capabilities, and managerial desire to decentralize. In many situations the executive finds a need to decentralize out of sheer necessity in order to lighten the work load. Often it is found that such action results in improved morale, better local coordination, and faster action on important matters.

A manager should look closely at the work load in deciding what part or parts of his total job should be transferred to executives at lower levels. He or she should remember that delegating responsibilities is:

1. Assigning duties
2. Granting authority
3. Creating an obligation on the part of the subordinate

These three elements have been compared to the legs of a three-legged stool. All three are required for the whole to exist effectively. Assigning duties without the necessary authority over resources to accomplish the duty illustrates the need for all three elements if the manager is to successfully decentralize.

In deciding how much decentralization to attempt, or where to place authority and obligation in an organizational structure, the manager might consider the following guides:

1. Who knows the facts, has the technical ability, and can get them together most readily?
2. Who has the capacity to make sound decisions?
3. Is it necessary that speedy, on-the-spot decisions be made?
4. Is it required that local activity be carefully coordinated with other units?
5. How significant are the decisions in the area under consideration?
6. What is the existing work load for managers?
7. Will morale and initiative be significantly improved by decentralization?

When the manager decentralizes the operation in the process of developing an organizational structure, he or she should recognize the importance of this action and the change that will be required in his or her manner of personal operation.

Experience has shown that planning is the most critical of the managerial functions if decentralization is to be effective. The process of identifying problems and deciding the correct action to take as a plan of work is something the manager is loath to release to others; it is something he is prone to supervise closely himself. The functions of organizing, directing, and controlling are very important, but they tend to depend upon how the planning duties have been allocated.

Management by Walking Around

A phrase apparently coined by Hewlett-Packard called management by walking around means the owner/manager gives himself a direct, unscheduled view of what is going on, including stopping to ask junior staff what they are doing and what the obstacles are to doing it better.[20] Great tact, of course, is required in order not to undermine the authority of the immediate supervisors. The chief executive should take up any observed problems privately with them and be sure to give them a chance to explain why they took their chosen course. In a tight line/staff organization of any size, management by walking around is the only way the owner/manager can keep in touch with what's happening on the floor. Rather than relying on reports from the five to ten department heads and aides who report directly to him, he or she sees it.

Management by Results

The ultimate result of any business is profit, and the intermediate results are quality and customer satisfaction. Management by results is a variation of management by objectives that explicitly gives the people responsible the necessary latitude to decide for themselves what techniques to use to obtain desired results (within the ethics and quality standards of the firm).

Span of Control

Span of control is a concept used in organizational activity that is based largely on a theory of human limitations. Ideally a particular manager in a specific situation can directly and effectively supervise a limited number of subordinates. There is considerable controversy over the nature and implications of the span-of-control concept. No one denies the existence of the idea. There has to be some limit, but the exact figure varies, and the figures cited in various studies are either suggestions based on experience or reports of actual practice.

A practical approach may be to realize that the correct span of control is affected by a number of factors and to try to organize the business structure with these factors in mind. In following this practice one would consider:

- The complexity of the work being controlled
- The degree of similarity to other work
- The degree of interdependency with other work
- The stability of the organization and situation
- The degree of standardization
- The caliber of the manager, including the span of attention, energy, and personality
- The caliber of the subordinates and their motivation

The "correct" span for one manager in one situation at a particular time may vary widely from that of another manager, situation, and/or time. Ralph Davis, in his classic 1951 study, suggested that if a manager is supervising subordinate managers and the work is difficult, then the span should be limited to approximately three to nine. If one is supervising operative employees, acceptable spans are from ten to thirty.[21]

The specific determination of the span of control must be decided on an individual basis by remembering that the outcome determines the supervisory relationship between superior and subordinate and the shape of the organizational structure. The manager must remember, too, the basic human needs and the primary needs of the organization for an effectively coordinated and controlled effort.

Effective Work Groups

Just as there are individual personalities and differences, there are also group personalities and differences. Organizational activities tend to create and influence the development of work groups. By knowing something about groups, their characteristics, and their behavior, the manager can improve his management. He can develop more effective work groups. He must accept the work group as an integral component of the total organization.

Rensis Likert has said, "An organization will function best when its personnel function not as individuals but as members of highly effective work groups with high performance goals."[22] Because of the group's importance to the organization, we will attempt to understand how it works, how its structures and procedures can influence business results, and how it can be used, as well as misused, in advancing the organization's interests. A starting point is the determination of the characteristics of the group. By considering these characteristics, a manager can plan his organizing activity to achieve goals or measure progress from the past. The key characteristics of a group and some important concepts or guidelines from the manager's point of view are shown in figure 6.1. The manager needs to recognize these characteristics of a group and

Characteristics	Concepts
Group Goals	Group members are more dedicated to goals they help establish than to those imposed upon them by others.
Structure	There is both formal and informal structure in small groups.
Size	Should be large enough to obtain sufficient ideas yet small enough not to hamper free communication and inhibit participation.
Leadership	Indications are that every group requires some "central focus."
Participation	Group size, power and status structure and style leadership are determinants of the nature and extent of participation.
Cohesiveness	Determined largely by the degree to which group goals help satisfy individual needs. If cohesiveness is obtained for official, task oriented groups, the organization stands to gain through increased cooperation and motivation.
Norms	There is a tendency for the behavior of group members to coincide with group norms.
Agreement	Pressures toward group norms tend to produce agreement. Most business groups prefer to work toward a consensus. Acceptance without necessarily approving personally.

Figure 6.1. Key characteristics of a group.

utilize the pertinent concepts to his or her advantage in order to develop the organizational structure.

Staff Support

In designing an organizational structure, most managers utilize some sort of staff. The staff is normally separated from the primary chain of command to produce economy and effectiveness of operation. The concept of staff refers to a supportive unit not directly involved in the end product of the organization. Serving in the normal fashion, staff units typically:

1. Give advice—The personnel office may offer advice to the manager of the maintenance department on the interpretation of selection screening devices used by the company.
2. Perform services—The accounting department in developing an analysis of the costs involved in conducting flight instruction is providing a service for the flight department.
3. Provide information—In many instances the staff provides information on personnel, on employment data, on tax questions, and on many areas in the technical competence of the specialist.

It should be recognized that the terms line and staff and the distinction between the two represent an oversimplification. The real relationship in terms of authority, influence, and control is much more complicated. Instead of the departmentalization that is seemingly emphasized by the concept, the real focus should be on the high degree of interdependence required if the major systems in the organization are to function at maximum effectiveness.

Without cooperation and coordination in the pursuit of joint goals, conflict is likely to emerge in line-staff relationships. This will lead to many operational problems and ultimately to the need for managerial corrective decisions.

Human Factors

One factor that becomes a major element in organizing a business is the recognition of the human aspects of organization. A good starting point is the realization that people work to satisfy needs and that the design of the organizational structure makes a tremendous impact on the achievement of these needs.

Our primary concern at this point is meeting human needs through the organization, since the structure of a company defines an environment of formal rules, job descriptions, and communication networks during working hours. This environment can satisfy needs or block them. It can develop good attitudes or bad attitudes, and it can partly determine what people think and learn. Structure becomes a highly important element in getting results. It can contribute to or detract from the satisfaction of human needs. The following are a number of ways that organization design can contribute to human needs:

Small units. By assigning workers to small groups of three to ten, social satisfactions are greater.

Non-isolated jobs. One should not break down work into such extremely specialized and independent parts that a person lacks the opportunity to interact with fellow workers.

Broad responsibilities. A very narrow area of responsibility tends to create a situation of always giving and never receiving. To satisfy social needs, a person's relationships with others must be reciprocal.

Place or status. The place or status of the individual in the organization may create pride in the position and even in the title itself.

Job enlargement. Narrow specialization or division of the work into extremely small components may diminish worker satisfaction and affect the employee's opportunity for growth. By enlarging the job many companies have realized benefits, including increased worker satisfaction.

Decentralization. Increasing the freedom of action of the subordinate and the opportunity to satisfy the need for self-expression are two benefits of decentralization.

New Approaches to Organization

Organization is a management tool—a most powerful tool—designed to fulfill specific needs. As the needs change, new ways are required to satisfy the changing conditions. There is an interaction between the manager's knowledge and skill level, the organization's existing situation, and the impact of the environment and its changing demands. The combination of these elements results in the identification of an existing organizational situation.

Change is inevitable in the business world, so the manager has a real concern for the application of new approaches to organization that will make it easier to meet the demands of change. In one situation, it may mean simply the introduction of a formal organizational chart and structure in order to achieve a degree of stability. In another, it may mean identifying the need to relate more strongly to the customer. In still another way, it may require being aware of the special needs resulting from complex problems, special environmental issues, or technological changes. Each of these situations suggests the need for a new approach to organizational design. Some of the new directions that have been suggested include:

1. Hiring "idea" people to promote innovative ways of approaching and developing answers to problems
2. Hiring individuals who are manifestly "different" from those normally hired in order to ensure fresh ideas
3. Focusing management control on the outcome of work rather than the way work is done
4. Increasing rotation among jobs
5. Increasing employee participation in decision making
6. Encouraging professional association involvement so that people identify with a group outside the organization
7. Using project teams whenever feasible
8. Including formal consumer representation
9. Decreasing the number of supervisory levels or eliminating the superior and subordinate relationship
10. Implementing individual profit centers
11. Providing compensation based upon results achieved
12. Allowing freedom of access to information
13. Encouraging mobility of individuals
14. Increasing individual rights
15. Supporting continued education

A prototype organization for the business of the future has been suggested. It may not be completely realistic, but it should stimulate additional thought and action in developing the new form needed for the business of tomorrow. This proposal has four major features:

1. Hierarchical and bureaucratic structure is reduced to an absolute minimum.
2. Most middle-level jobs are conceived of as temporary.
3. Individual employees are assigned to competence centers or profit centers.
4. Career development is emphasized by the introduction of many varied programs.

Internal Structure Design

In developing an organizational structure in a certain business, the manager should consider such factors as departmentalization, decentralization, delegation, specialization, managerial resources, staff capabilities, and the specific types of business activity involved. Managers need to use each of these concepts in developing an effective total organizational structure. The determination of the overall structure is based upon four major considerations:

1. What balance and emphasis should be given to the various departments?
2. How can the span of control or supervision of each manager be effectively utilized?
3. How can the creation of dynamic change be provided for?
4. How can organization be integrated into the other phases of planning, directing, and controlling?

The answers to these questions provide direct assistance in identifying the desired organizational structure.

Formal and Informal Organization

The formal organization consists of the official, authorized relationships prescribed by management. Informal organization consists of the myriad relationships, unofficial and unauthorized, created by the many individual personalities and groups within the formal structure. These relationships spring up spontaneously, inevitably, and continually. There is no choice whether to have an informal organization; it is a fact of organizational life.

Formal Internal Structure

In developing the formal structure of the organization, the manager has three basic formats to consider: functional, line, and line and staff. Since many aviation businesses need to utilize elements of all three business structures, it is recommended that the manager understand the terms and be able to use all three concepts in organizing a business.

Functional or Matrix Management

In a traditional sense, the functional organization has a supervisor in charge of each function rather than in charge of specific employees. Each of these supervisors is a specialist and has the final decision for that functional area. Although the functional structure has difficulties, the small aviation business frequently finds itself operating on a functional basis. As the owner/manager hires an assistant or supervisor, this person is normally placed in charge of a specific function and all employees receive guidance from him or her in that one area. As additional supervisors are added with functional specialities, the employee must move from supervisor to supervisor (function to function) as he or she performs different physical tasks. This is one source of difficulty with the functional organization; employees become confused, conflicts develop, and problems arise in evaluating quality of work and performance on the job. Figure 6.2 depicts a possible functional organization chart for a small aviation activity. On the other hand, temporary functional assignments such as task forces can have great value.

Line Organization

The second type of formal organization structure is the pure line organization. In this type of structure, the supervisor is in charge of a specific operational unit and the time of all people assigned to work in that unit. This is frequently thought of as the military form of organization. The line organization has one person in charge of another person, who in turn is in charge of other persons. (See figure 6.3)

Line and Staff Organization

For companies that have grown beyond the direct supervision stage, the line and staff organization becomes the most feasible form of structure. It differs from the straight line because

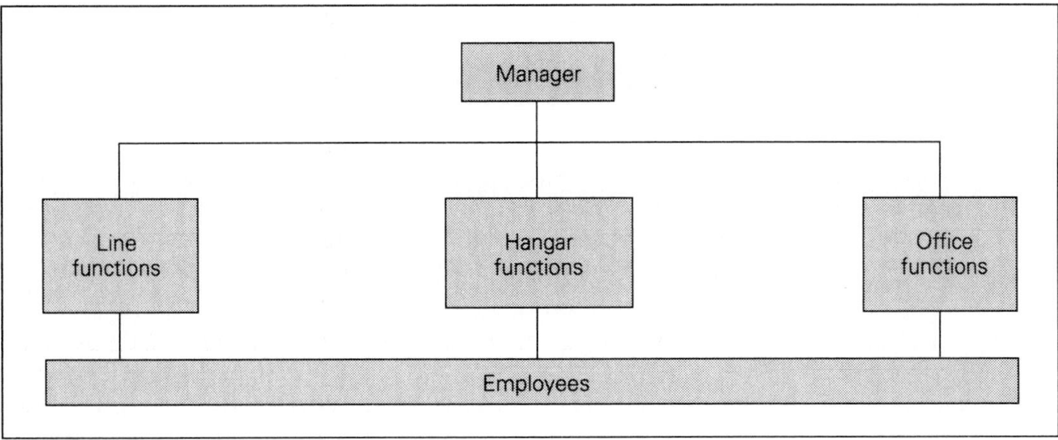

Figure 6.2. Functional organizational chart.

a staff element has been added to the structure. In regards to actual operations, the structure operates similarly to the line structure. However, the staff element is there to advise the line manager on the technical features of that staff specialty, thus assisting that manager in getting the job done. The staff unit is normally designed to provide advice, information, and services to line managers. Figure 6.4 suggests a line and staff structure for an aviation business. In this type of structure, the supervisors in sales, instruction, service, and flight have the responsibility for getting the job done in their individual areas, but the staff personnel in administration and finance have the task of advising and assisting in their areas of specialty. For example, accounting might advise on the necessary records and budget guidelines, or administration might advise on OSHA requirements and coordinate report deadlines.

The aviation manager should be aware of all three types of organizational structures and recognize that there are elements of each in every business. When a business starts, it may be functional, then become a line structure, and then, with size, assume the characteristics of a line and staff structure.

Informal Internal Structures

Whereas the formal organizational structure consists of the official and authorized relationships prescribed by management, the informal structure consists of all those unofficial and unauthorized relationships created by the many individual personalities and groups within the formal organization. Since it exists regardless of the manager's approval, it is advantageous to examine its advantages and disadvantages.

The informal structure is the source of many positive values that can contribute to the organization. Management's chief concern in this area is to achieve positive feelings and identification, which will provide a maximum benefit to the organization's efforts. Although this goal may depend strongly on the individual manager's skillful use of organizational tools (including the ability to direct and control), it also includes the ability to achieve a high level of harmony without eliminating the value of individual freedom and dissent.

Advantages

1. It fills in gaps and deficiencies in the formal structure.

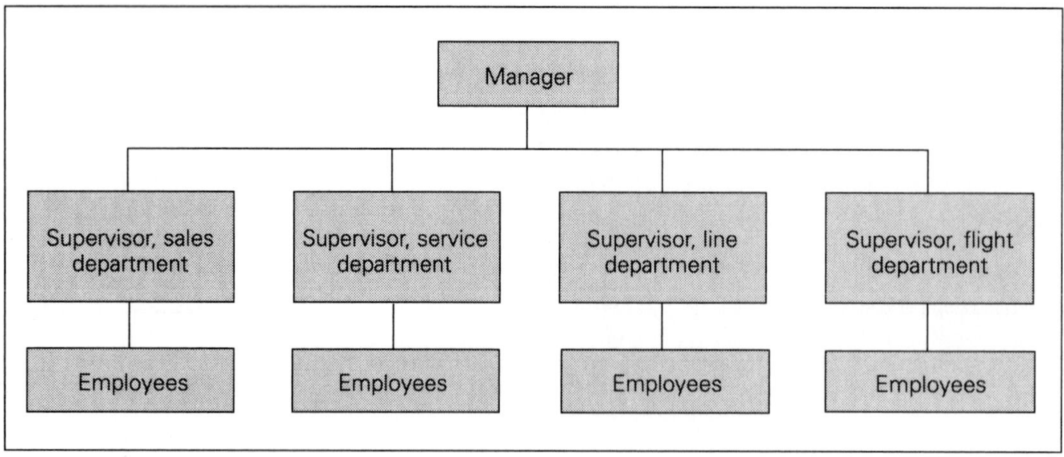

Figure 6.3. Line organization.

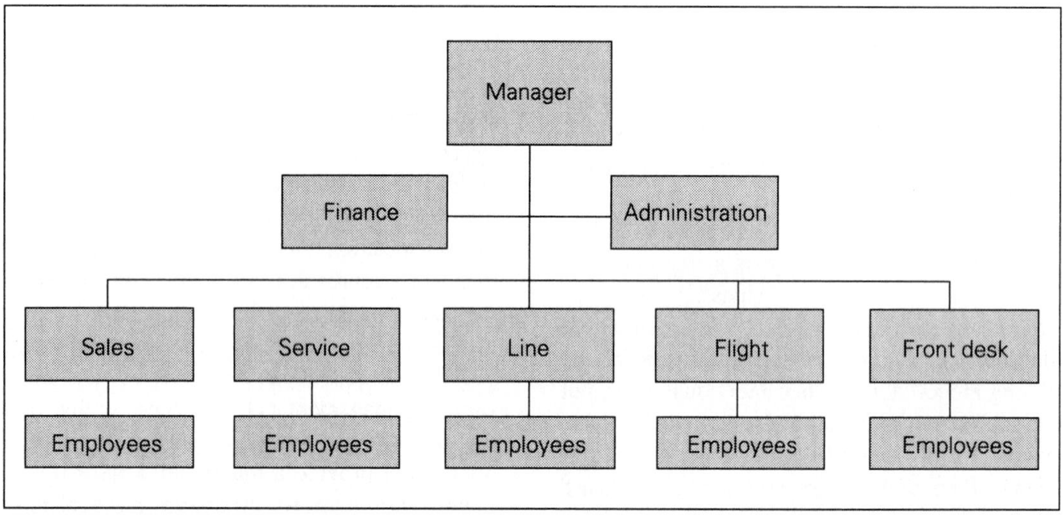

Figure 6.4. Line-staff organization.

2. It facilitates the majority of the organization's work.
3. It lengthens the effective managerial span of control.
4. It compensates for the violation of formal organizational principles.
5. It provides an additional channel of communications.
6. It stimulates better management.

Disadvantages

1. Informal activities may work counter to organizational goals.
2. There is less ability to predict and control outcome of informal group activity.
3. There is less interchangeability of individuals within groups, thus reducing managerial alternatives.

4. There are higher costs of maintaining a positive, informal set of relationships.

The informal organization can be identified and charted using sociometric techniques. The most common applications of this procedure develop: (1) a chart depicting actual contacts between particular people, (2) a chart reflecting the feelings of people toward each other, or (3) the influence-of-power chart, which depicts the level of influence of each member in the group. Each of these techniques provides the means for gaining some insight into the informal structure and provides additional information to supplement the organizational efforts of the formal structure.

Informal work groups are an inevitable fact of life in any organization. Managers who do not understand group behavior and attempt to break up groups are frequently frustrated when new alignments form and present continuing problems. The successful manager is one who understands the nature of group forces, who is perceptive to group needs, and who can successfully blend the group goals with those of the formal organization.

The informal group selects a leader who reflects the views of the group toward the formal structure. Even if this leader is removed as a troublemaker or malcontent, the difficulty is not solved because the group will simply select another representative who, in turn, will present the same views. The manager can work with the group leader to obtain full cooperation from the group. This does not mean that he or she should channel orders through the leader or attempt to make him a member of the management team. When this is attempted the usual result is the identification of a new informal leader. The manager can, however, devote a little extra attention to winning the support and approval of the group leader when the need arises, or perhaps on a continuing basis.

The informal organization can be used to supplement the formal channel of communications. The informal structure has been recognized as being fast, but at the same time, prone to being full of distortions. It can, however, be utilized to gain input on group discontent or pending problems and be of tremendous help to managers. In most instances it is considered wise to utilize the informal communications network and to deal with the informal leader in a delicate and discreet manner.

Quality Circles

Quality circles are another feature borrowed from the Japanese, although it was an American who introduced the Japanese to quality planning. A circle of workers is jointly responsible for a finite, complete product and—in addition to being on the production team together—meets regularly to iron out problems and make improvements. Various circles doing the same thing may become quite competitive. Posting weekly performance can be an incentive toward high results.

Task Forces

Good task forces may be short-lived and interdepartmental. Many companies use them to brainstorm a problem on an intensive basis, and some firms use an annual weekend retreat to do much the same thing.

Social Structures

Some firms deliberately encourage and even subsidize sports teams and other clubs with the intent of mixing all types of employees together in informal settings. A superior's usual aloofness can be set aside for a period. Parties and picnics can do some of the same things, depending on how they are run. Public celebration of work achievements is sometimes part of these functions, or the public recognition "hoopla" may be reserved for other times.

Other Networks

Special-interest professional groups of all types can give senior staff members the exposure that they might not otherwise get to junior staff members. They also help to convey directly the corporate values and culture to all levels of employment. Remoteness of senior officials is not necessarily the only means to power.

External Pressures on Choices of Structure

In designing the structure of an aviation business, consideration is given, consciously or unconsciously, to the pressures of external elements—pressures that suggest or dictate certain patterns to your organizational structure.

Industry Norms

The overall aviation industry, as the major environmental element of small aviation businesses, creates a pressure toward an organizational design somewhat common throughout the industry. Hangar design, ramp location, services requested by the customer, and competitor activity all tend to pressure the manager to conform to the general industry organizational structure.

The companies supplying the major aircraft product lines (Piper, Beech, Cessna, Grumman, and so on) provide a degree of pressure through franchises or other agreements, which results in the development of a structure suggested by the company and similar to others in the organization. These standard structures have generally been found to be successful and have been promoted in order to achieve standardized operations and successful businesses.

Geography

Geographic influences have had a definite impact on organizational structures and managers should recognize them. Environmental features influence the type of aviation activities, the type of structures erected, and the physical layout. Each of these, in turn, directly influences the shape of the organization required to meet customer needs.

Government

Governmental activity at all levels plays an important part in structuring aviation businesses. By requiring reports, manuals, and procedures and by offering financial support, federal, state, and local regulations cause the manager to structure the organization in a certain fashion. For example, OSHA requirements have caused many managers to write procedures, appoint safety directors, and in some instances reorganize the business. For those managers involved with Part 135 operations, this type of business activity has required operating manuals and routine periodic checks that create certain organizational structures. FAA, VA, and state educational agencies have created requirements for flight schools that literally determined organizational structure for aviation businesses engaged in instruction. Aviation maintenance as stipulated by the FAA and equipment manufacturers very effectively contributes to the structure of aviation maintenance activities.

Practical Applications

Guidelines

Thus far the primary focus has been on basic concepts and principles and planning the organizational effort. Now the focus is on the practical task of dividing the business into functional areas and assigning these separate functions to specific individuals.

In organizing, the manager is constantly balancing two factors: the desired structure and the available personnel. Does he or she design the structure and then attempt to find or train personnel to do the work, or does he or she utilize the available human resources and work with the resulting organization? He or she will undoubtedly work with a combination of these two approaches, although the successful manager apparently sets his organizational goals and then works to build the structure that will achieve these objectives. This topic was considered in chapter 5 "Human Resources."

In a practical sense organizing is the basic process a manager uses to unite the efforts of different people to achieve company goals. There are two elements present in the process of organizing: (1) dividing work into separate jobs and (2) ensuring the separate areas of work are combined into a total team effort. Let's now consider the various steps that become part of this practical organizing activity.

First, identify the basic or recurring pattern of work that takes place in the business. The best approach is to group work on the basis of geographical areas, products, customers, or functions. Many aviation organizations can and do utilize all four groupings. This is evidenced by companies who have regional salespeople, who distinguish employees working on Piper aircraft from those working on Beech aircraft, who classify customers by income level and assign salespeople to each major category, and who group work on a functional basis such as service, sales, or charter. This first step becomes an effort in understanding the activities that will take place within the business.

The second step is *describing the relationships that will exist between the various groups within the business.* This can be done through a chart on paper, a written description of the working relationships that exist, or both. Typically this is achieved through an organization chart and organization manual.

Define precisely what each unit will do as a portion of the overall organization. In identifying units, the basic principles of specialization, decentralization, span of control, work groups, staff activity, and human factors should be kept in mind.

Assign business activities to specific individuals and units of the organization. This may be done casually in conversation or formally by charts, job descriptions, operations manuals, meetings, or joint understanding.

Provide for the means of tying the organization together and for developing integrated, cooperative action in the day-by-day transaction of business. Normally this is accomplished through communications, procedures, rules and controls.

In summary, the organizing process involves:

- Identifying the kinds of work that take place
- Describing the relationship between work groups
- Defining precisely what each group will do
- Assigning activities to specific individuals or groups
- Developing integrative action between work groups

Problems

The practical activity as just outlined represents the minimum that should be included in the organizational process. It is actually an oversimplification of the procedure. Realistically, the manager should recognize that there are many problems inherent in the process and should try to avoid these difficulties. Some of the problems frequently experienced are:

- Lack of clearly defined duties and resulting friction
- Expansion of activities beyond assigned areas by overzealous managers
- Desire to create a situation in which the unit reports high up the administration chain
- Failure to adapt to necessary changes
- Failure to integrate with the other functions of planning, directing, and controlling

The Organization Manual

As mentioned earlier, one of the most effective tools for developing a business structure is the organization manual, management manual, or handbook. This particular manual does not follow a specific format or content outline, but provides a flexible technique for meeting individual organizational needs. As usually visualized, this document is a centralized source for policies, organizational structure, relationships, responsibilities, rules, and procedures. Properly designed, implemented and maintained, it becomes an extremely valuable tool in organizing the business. It becomes a source for individuals in the organization in order to guide them in day-to-day operations and a source for training new employees. Primarily, it is a means for creating and maintaining the desired organizational structure and activity.

Manual Outline

Although the contents of an organization manual should vary in order to meet the needs of each organization, usually one finds the following subjects covered:

1. Introduction, philosophy
2. Organization structure
   a. Authority
   b. Responsibility
3. Departmental organization
   a. Activities
4. Staff activities
   a. Personnel
   b. Financial

Summary

Organizing the business is a continuing challenge for the aviation manager. Both the external legal structure and the internal practical structure must be established to support the goals and activities of the company. The choice of ownership structure should be made consciously and reviewed periodically. Internal organization should recognize the needs of the various company departments as well as the informal structures that help a company function. External pressures and industry norms may need to be considered.

Discussion Topics

1. Name two initial considerations the manager reviews when organizing the business.
2. What are the key advantages and disadvantages of the three legal structures?
3. Distinguish between the formal and informal organization. How can they work in harmony?
4. Discuss the organizational principles of specialization and decentralization.
5. What is span of control and how can the business choose appropriate spans?
6. What approach would you recommend in balancing (1) the desired organizational structure and (2) the available personnel?
7. Why is an organizational manual useful? Name three elements in it.

Chapter 7
Management Information Systems

Objectives

- ✔ Understand the necessity of a business information system.
- ✔ Relate the requirements of an effective business information system to an aviation business.
- ✔ Recognize the problems in maintaining an effective records system in an aviation business.
- ✔ Demonstrate the origins, pathways and use of the four key elements for an aviation business.
- ✔ Describe the factors to consider in automating a business operation.

Introduction

A management information system is one that supports managerial decision making by supplying relevant information when required. This chapter discusses the types of data needed in the typical fixed base operator business, the formats and flows involved, the analysis and use of performance data for keeping the company on the right track, and the choices of tools for data processing. Finally the chapter looks at information collection in relation to what the books indicate about the business, as opposed to what is really going on.

In the 1990s, significant factors affecting FBO management information systems will include the following:

1. The availability of special-purpose computer hardware and software designed to keep track of every aspect of an FBO's business with a growing number of vendors and applications.
2. Increased numbers of FBO franchises and FBOs with multiple locations sharing a centralized approach to information procedures, including standardized forms and customized computers systems. Franchises are expensive investments. As a result, it is less easy than in the past to access the forms and business methods of the leading aviation service companies.
3. Despite the availability of more sophisticated information management systems, "garbage in" still produces "garbage out." A muddled or haphazard approach to management information produces muddled results even if one obtains a state of the art computer system, the best-designed forms, and the most expert advice.

System Purposes

There are a number of reasons for keeping good records on a regular basis for any small business. These include:

- Financial survival
- Performance improvement
- Special reports
- Taxes and legal obligations
- Check on reality

Financial Survival

Knowing how much is being sold, whether it has yet been paid for, the cash on hand, the cost of opening the doors each day, and the break-even level of activity are basics for the survival of any business. Even a small business will involve more than the manager can carry in his head. It is particularly easy to overlook upcoming expenses. Any plans for expansion will also require a knowledge of unit costs, potential profits, and the market picture. Most important, a small or new business cannot wait until the end of its fiscal year to find out how it is doing. Monthly status reports are essential, and in some cases, weekly or daily posting of results may be appropriate.

Performance Monitoring and Improvement

Good information systems permit the examination of the whole business and also subareas such as projects, sales territories, individual employees, profit centers, and cost centers. Such data can then permit the manager to initiate actions to correct any problems. Accurate comparative data on employee performance, such as productivity, hours worked, and absences can be important in establishing a clear and fair case for promotion or termination. The earlier that it is reported that a certain area is "off-course," the sooner and easier it is to make "course corrections." Good management entails almost constant course corrections in all areas of the business.

Special Reports

Apart from monthly postings of a regular nature, good records can permit special reports on specific subjects as the need arises. These might include five-year trends in parts costs compared with maintenance labor costs in order to determine a policy on sale of parts to self-repairers. The analysis would examine whether the profit is greater on sale of parts or on labor and how the two are likely to relate in the future, based on past trends. Or a special analysis might look at the allocation of time of a certain group of employees between tasks. Jobs might be reorganized to use less costly personnel for less profitable areas of activity. A look at seasonal and daily peaks might change marketing and work shift strategies, and so on. The manager's ability to have special reports prepared depends on knowledge of the readily available data in the firm and what those data can reveal if used intelligently. Much more can be found from data kept for accounting purposes than is generally intended.

Taxes and Legal Obligations

A good data system can not only assure that required reports and payments are made on time, but it can also flag upcoming events so they can be anticipated.

Checks on Reality

Good paper records of inventory, cash in hand, receivables, and volume sold can check against employee laxness or actual theft. A company where the boss regularly checks records against what is observable in the stockroom and elsewhere will establish an atmosphere in which pilfering or fixing the books is less likely. If an employee or customer is stealing, good records are essential both for prosecution and for insurance claims.

System Processes

Integrated Flow

Data systems all begin with the recording manually or on a computer of all data at its point of origin. The flow from that point on should be virtually automatic. The data should flow freely from user to user, with repetitive work and human intervention minimized. This means the initial data should be collected in a format that suits the needs of its final users and perhaps with more detail being recorded than is needed for intermediate purposes.

Requirements of an Effective System

In all the diverse areas where information should be collected, there are a number of common requirements. The management information systems set up to address these requirements must be **timely,** must **aid in the allocation of resources** and must **improve decision making** by assisting in the selection of alternatives. They should be **adequate** to fit the needs of the particular business without being **overdesigned** and should address the **total operation** of the company, not just accounting and financial records. They should be understandable and operational and adhere to the existing organizational structure but also be flexible. Most importantly, they should flag problems or deviations from the norm and indicate corrective action.

First Steps

In developing the information systems, the manager can either use an ad hoc approach or develop a master plan that covers the basic requirements and stands in readiness when additional needs are identified. First steps include:

1. Establish long-range objectives for the data system.
2. Define the information currently being collected and its adequacy, using chronological or input-output flow and, if appropriate, relating information flows to floor layouts.
3. Make short-range improvements that are consistent with long-range plans.
4. Establish the schedule and responsibility for the long-range plan.
5. Implement the plan.

The long-range objectives for the data system may be drawn from the overall company business plan (see chapter 2). Specific data requirements will need to consider:

- Data source
- Frequency of occurrence
- Batching versus transmitting as data comes in
- Time period for complete information cycle
- Lags between event and its report to manager in meaningful form
- Format of data after tabulation or analysis
- Adequacy of existing data: Is enough data being collected in a useful form to actually provide guidance to management?

Aviation Management Information Systems

Human Resources

Many personnel issues arise not on a regular basis, but in relation to changes in personnel and personnel requirements. A few, however, occur on a regular basis. These include time sheets or cards, punctuality records, sick time, and leave taken. These records will likely be kept by the employee on a daily basis and submitted on a weekly or biweekly basis for payroll processing. For employees wearing more than one hat or belonging to more than one profit center, time records will report not just time on the job but time by project. It can be useful to break down the manager's own time between such activities as marketing, public relations, administration, other overhead, and direct revenue-generating time, if it exists in any area.

Figure 7.1 shows the complete array of probable human resource data requirements, sources, and controls.

Financial

The cash and cash needs of the organization are shown in figure 7.2.

Material

Material covers all the tangible assets of the business such as buildings, aircraft, vehicles, inventory, shop, flight school, and office equipment. Information is needed on the condition, contribution, and replacement of these assets, as well as flags for scheduled preventive maintenance. Figure 7.3 summarizes these assets and their information sources and controls.

Aviation Operations

This topic is crucial because it represents the areas where the business makes its money. Some of the information needed in these areas originates elsewhere in the system and must be converted or transferred for managerial decisions about operations. Figure 7.4 summarizes these data areas.

Activity	Source of Information	Control Measure
1. Identifying human resource requirements	Inventory of company's human resources Job requirements	Company goals, objectives Organization requirements
2. Recruiting	Examination of practices Review of results	Turnover goals Stability desired Training needed
3. Selection	Personnel records Performance results	Organization requirements Position requirements
4. Training	Training records	Training requirements Individual needs Defective rate
5. Using human resources	Personnel records Time cards Job orders	Turnover rate Tardiness rate Labor productivity Organization requirements

Figure 7.1. Human resource data needs.

Activity	Source of Information	Control Measure
1. Obtaining adequate funds	Organization requirements Financial statement analysis	Goals Comparative data
2. Accounting for funds	Accounting record Routine reports	Accounting standards Comparative data
3. Utilizing funds	Financial analysis	Organization goals Historical data Industry data

Figure 7.2. Cash needs of an organization.

Legal and Tax Information

The accounting system yields data on the various taxes due and the schedules for payment. Legal information may be more sporadically generated and is vitally important. It must be well organized and complete.

Market Information

Information about industry trends and about what the competition is doing comes from many sources, as discussed in chapter 3 "Marketing." The manager must decide how to monitor and assemble this information so that it is readily accessible.

Activity	Source of Information	Control Measure
1. Aircraft	Physical inspection Profit records Customer indications	Organization goals Historical records Industry data
2. Inventory	Routine inventory records Profit records Customer indications	Goals Historical records Industry data
3. Physical plant	Physical inspection Preventive maintenance records Engineer reports Customer indications	Company goals Historical records Comparative data
4. Equipment	Physical inspections Preventive maintenance records Customer indications	Company goals Historical data Manufacturer requirements

Figure 7.3. Summary of business assets.

Technological Information

Aviation technology is constantly changing, and decisions have to be made about whether to try new manufacturers, product lines, and methods. The success or failure of each test should be documented, as should requests from customers for something new.

Analyzing Business Activity

Sometimes described as financial analysis, this task is a combination of checking over the accounting data and critically reviewing the operating procedures and accomplishments. Accounting data provide the measures of actual activity and management expertise, as expressed through the business plan, must be used to set up performance standards to measure those results.

General Procedure

Sources of performance standards to apply to the business can come from:

- Results from a previous operating period
- Contrasting two previous operating periods
- Industry averages, from National Air Transportation Association (NATA) or other national sources
- Competing businesses, as obtainable
- Similar businesses, as reported in trade press articles or in advertising

Analyzing the Business as a Whole

The purpose of this activity is threefold—to determine whether goals and objectives are being met, to identify areas with potential for improvement, and to suggest possible corrective actions.

Activity	Source of Information	Control Measure
1. Line operations	Gas/oil sales records Related sales Customer indications Personnel reports Profit records	Volume goals Profit objectives Historical data
2. Maintenance	Volume of work Customer indications Work redone Labor allocation FAA inspection	Volume goals Profit objectives Historical data Industry data
3. Instruction	Volume of work Customer indications Profitability Instructor and aircraft utilization records FAA inspection	Volume goals Profit objectives Historical data Industry data
4. Flight services	Work volume records Customer reports FAA inspections Profit records Utilization	Volume goals Profit objectives Historical data Industry data
5. Sales	Sales volume records Profitability Customer indication Sales reports	Unit goals Historical data Industry data
6. Miscellaneous (Rental, parking, and so on)	Specific activity reports Profit analysis	Predetermined goals Historical data

Figure 7.4. Aviation operations data.

Specific tasks will include:

- Comparison of financial statements with budget and financial projections
- Comparison of current financial statement with previous years' statements
- Comparison of financial statement with those of similar businesses, if possible

Specific measures should include:

- Net income
- Return on equity
- Qualitative considerations
- Community considerations
- Balance of different departments within the firm

After an examination of the financial statement/balance sheet as a whole, it is appropriate to examine the individual items on it. They should also be compared with expectations, previous results, industry, and even general business norms. The help of an accountant or banker may be appropriate.

Secondly, the income statement should be examined in the same way. It is particularly useful to express income in each department as a percentage of the total. Gross and net profit by department should be calculated, and profit centers ranked.

The final step in the analysis of the overall business through financial statements involves the use of ratios. Ratios are developed to show the relationship of key areas identified on the statements. They may be classified according to their source data as balance sheet, income, and mixed ratios. They may also be classified according to the purpose of the ratio comparison:

- Liquidity measures
- Managerial efficiency
- Leverage measures
- Profitability measures

Prior to examining key ratios in each of these areas, certain basics regarding the use of this technique should be considered. A ratio is most useful when compared to previous ratios, to industry ratio averages, and to generally accepted standards. Ratios based upon poorly prepared statements are practically worthless and may be misleading to the unsuspecting analyst. Finally, ratios indicate business situations in a general sense; they indicate positions that may require further investigation in order to analyze and understand the situation adequately.

Liquidity ratios. These ratios describing liquid assets are helpful in analyzing the ability of a business to meet its debts and liabilities and to move rapidly in meeting unexpected business opportunities.

Current assets: current liabilities. Figures are taken from the balance sheet for this calculation. The value of aircraft in inventory will greatly influence this ratio.

Fixed assets: tangible net worth. Figures are taken from the balance sheet. Tangible net worth excludes "goodwill" or similar accounts. Dunn and Bradstreet suggests that a desirable figure is under 75 percent. Figures over 75 percent suggest the operation has too much invested in fixed assets and may be weak in operating assets or may not be flexible or liquid enough to meet changing business conditions.

Inventory: net working capital. Net working capital is considered as current assets less current liabilities. Once again, Dunn and Bradstreet has suggested that a desirable ratio is something less than 80%. A business with a higher figure is felt to have too much in inventory. The organization is not considered "liquid" enough to meet the rapidly changing conditions of the business world.

Ratios of managerial efficiency. Ratios in this category are designed to analyze the efficiency with which managers handle the assets of the organization. Specific ratios cover the various assets of the business.

Receivables: sales per day. The accounts receivable collection period measures management's efficiency in handling the assets tied up in outstanding accounts. The soundness of the accounts receivable and the credit policies of the company are indicated by this relationship. It is generally felt that a collection period of between 30 and 45 days is optimal. If collections take longer than 45 days, it may be that customers are "using" the funds of the organization or, in other words, credit policies are too lenient.

Cost of sales: average inventory. Inventory turnover reflects the efficiency of management's use of the assets represented by the inventory. The desirable turnover must be identified through experience, nature of the product, industry averages, and other factors such as shortages.

Leverage ratios. Ratios in this area reflect the balance of borrowed funds and ownership funds. They provide an indication of management's ability to "lever" funds into additional assets by way of increased borrowing. The existing leverage provides a measure of the support and faith lenders have in the organization and the existing management.

Total debt: tangible net worth. If the relationship is over 100 percent, the equity of the creditor exceeds that of the owner. It has been suggested that if this relationship is over 80 percent, the organization is facing possible difficulty. Of course, higher leverage allows a greater return on ownership. It also becomes a weakness when there is a decline in earnings.

Current debt: tangible net worth. This ratio reflects leverage through the amount of current debt that can be acquired with respect to the existing net worth of the organization. It reflects the trust that creditors place in the management of the organization as well as the management philosophy.

Total debt: total assets. This ratio reflects again the leverage that exists in the value of the assets and in the management of those assets.

Profitability ratios. Ratios in this area are designed to provide a measure of the profitability of operations. Earnings or profits are compared with key indicators of ownership to reflect the profitability of such activity.

Earnings before taxes: total assets. This ratio, normally referred to as return on investment before taxes, reflects the relationship between annual profits and the investment in assets committed to this profit. Indications are that with the aviation business community this return should be around 30 percent.

Net profits: net worth. With this ratio, the owners are provided with a measure of the earning power of their investment. The desirable return will depend upon the alternatives available, the risk tolerance of the investor, and industry averages. Considering the risk element in the aviation business and relatively secure alternatives, the owner's return should be approximately 15 percent.

Net profit: sales. The profit for a period as related to the sales for that period offers an indication of profitability as well as a measure of the efficiency of the business.

Special-purpose ratios. There are a large number of items in the financial statements that can be evaluated through ratio analysis. Individual expense items can be related to sales. Income categories can be compared with total sales. Ratios of this type are useful in period-to-period comparative analysis, for comparison with industry averages, and for budgetary control work.

Management Audit

The management audit is the second procedure that may be used by the manager in analyzing the overall business. This process uses a number of the same tools and techniques employed in financial analysis, but the general concept is different. What is a management audit? By definition, it is a systematic checklist approach to the analysis of a business, its functions, operations and decisions. By carefully reviewing each of the functional and operational areas of a business, and comparing existing conditions with previously identified goals and required or desired standards, some measure can be obtained of strengths and weaknesses and corrective action suggested. By examining the entire business in this manner, an auditor is really examining management, hence the name "management audit."

Appendix III to this book contains an Aviation Management Audit. It is designed as a self-audit, one that can be conducted by the management team. To do this as it should be done requires a thoughtful, objective point of view. Of course, the audit can be expanded and made much more beneficial when administered by an impartial third party such as an aviation management consultant. By having such an outsider conduct the audit, a higher degree of objectivity and more penetrating questions can be developed. The audit can also be used in a seminar setting to achieve a higher level of management awareness and an exchange of information by the participants. A typical seminar has a small group of 18 to 25 aviation managers in attendance. Each has received an audit manual and has been requested to complete the self-audit prior to arrival. The seminar reviews the audit manual with individual replies, group comparison, and leader comments and analysis of each of the items. Further benefit could be received by the tabulation of accumulated audit responses and perhaps even the preparation of nationwide norms and standards.

The management audit is not an accounting or financial audit, but a review of the overall business as well as the individual departments. A thorough audit provides management with invaluable information and advice regarding the organization; consequently, it is considered a valuable supplement to the regular information system portrayed throughout this chapter. Conducted at regular intervals, one audit can serve as a bench mark for successive audit reviews and promote successful change.

Analyzing Departmental Activity

Introduction

The normal tools used in analyzing departmental activity are:

- Plans and objectives
- The budget
- Operating controls
- Financial records

Although each is a separate technique, they combine as a sequence that forms a method of analyzing department activity. The process is described so that the manager may consider the major elements of each step.

Plans and objectives. Identifying plans and objectives represents the first step in conducting a thorough review of departments or profit centers. Without a definite business objective, it becomes difficult to determine whether the activity of that portion of the business is successful. To paraphrase the Cheshire cat from "Alice in Wonderland," "If you don't know where you're going it doesn't matter which way you go, and you won't know if you get there." The following are questions that should be asked in this first step:

1. What are the objectives of the department? List.
2. Are the objectives definite and clear-cut?
3. Are they attainable?
4. Are the objectives understood and accepted by those involved in their attainment?
5. Are the department objectives compatible with and supportive of overall company objectives?

By using these questions, a manager should be able to develop an initial set of standards to measure a business success or failure.

Budget. Practically speaking, a budget is a quantitative expression of the plan or objectives of the department. As such, it becomes an aid in coordination and implementation. It is indispensable in grappling with uncertainties. Its benefits exceed its costs. Budgets should be positive vehicles for progress and improvement.

Operating controls. These controls are used as guidelines to prevent excessive spending, to provide ample supplies, to monitor personnel and aircraft utilization, etc. For the parts department, the control may be inventory limits; for aircraft sales there may be a unit dollar limit; for service there may be a desired level of billed mechanic time; for credit, a total outstanding accounts receivable in each of 30, 60, 90 and 120 days; for flight instruction, a desired level of flight hours per instructor; and for passenger activity, a mandatory procedure for briefing and debriefing with each flight.

A series of general questions should help in the examination of a department's operations:

1. What is the true worth of departmental assets? List them.
2. What is the extent and character of departmental liabilities? List.
3. Is there the ability to earn a fair return?
4. What is the capacity to withstand setbacks?
5. What is departmental labor efficiency?
6. How efficient is the utilization of equipment?
7. Is departmental and company-wide space utilized properly?
8. Are the departmental records maintained accurately?
9. Do the activity indicators reflect constant action (e.g., sales calls, and inactive student follow-up)?
10. Are salaries adequate? Too high? Too low?
11. Do expenses appear in line? Do they match budgeted figures?
12. Is the department inventory maintained accurately? Is it adequate? Excessive?
13. Are the department-generated receivables too high? Too low? What is the bad debt experience?
14. Prepare an analysis of departmental income by key categories.
15. Develop a break-even analysis for the department. Determine key indicators.

Financial records. The financial records for this purpose are the income statement and various supplements used to amplify or explain indications of the statement. Figure 7.5 illustrates the departmental income and expense form used by Piper dealers. Using this form as a guide, a manager may conduct a review of a department's activity. The manager should examine each subject category on the statement line by line to determine whether departmental objectives have been achieved, operations are efficient, and problems exist.

As an illustration, suppose a review is made of several of the lines on the income statement. The following analysis shows possible comparisons to make:

- **Line 1—Total sales.** Compare with budgeted figure on a monthly and year-to-date basis. Analyze the various components of the total sales figure (new, used, geographic, demographic) to determine relationship of previous marketing action and to suggest possible future activity.
- **Line 2—Cost of sales.** Consider efficiency of buying practices. Identify possible weaknesses and means for improving methods.
- **Line 3—Gross profit.** Compare with budgeted figure and with data for similar periods of operation. A large difference would suggest further examination and analysis.
- **Line 4—Gross profit: Percent of sales.** Compare with budget and other projections. Compare with similar businesses (will vary by department).
- **Line 7 and 8—Salaries and commissions.** Compare with budget projections, historical data, and other businesses. Examine job requirements and consider impact on incumbents in the job.
- **Line 9—Taxes, payroll.** Compare with budget projections. Ensure compliance with federal and state regulations.

INCOME STATEMENT | **DEPARTMENTAL INC**

For ________ Months Ending

________________ 19 ____

LINE NO.			ACCT NO.	TOTAL OPERATING INCOME AND EXPENSE — MONTH	TOTAL OPERATING INCOME AND EXPENSE — YEAR-TO-DATE	AIRCRAFT SALES 300 (3/C) — MONTH	AIRCRAFT SALES 300 (3/C) — YEAR-TO-DATE	PARTS 400 (4/D) — MONTH	PARTS 400 (4/D) — YEAR-TO-DATE	
1		TOTAL SALES								1
2		COST OF SALES								2
3		GROSS PROFIT								3
4		Gross Profit – % of Sales								4
5		EXPENSES:								5
6	EMPLOYMENT	Salaries – Officers	20							6
7		Salaries/Wages – Employees	21							7
8		Commissions	22							8
9		Taxes – Payroll	23							9
10		Employee Benefits	24							10
11										11
12										12
13										13
14		TOTAL EMPLOYMENT								14
15	AIRCRAFT	Aircraft Delivery	30							15
16		Aircraft Miscellaneous	31							16
17		Depreciation – Aircraft	32							17
18		Fuel & Oil – Aircraft	33							18
19		Insurance – Aircraft	34							19
20		Interest – Aircraft	35							20
21		Inventory Adustment –Aircraft	36							21
22		Maintenance – Aircraft	37							22
23		Warranty	38							23
24										24
25										25
26		TOTAL AIRCRAFT								26
27	OCCUPANCY	Rent	44							27
28		Depreciation/Amortization – Bldg.	45							28
29		Taxes – Property	46							29
30		Utilities	47							30
31		Maintenance – Bldg./Land	48							31
32										32
33										33
34		TOTAL OCCUPANCY								34
35	OTHER EXPENSES									35
36		Advertising	50							36
37		Bad Debts	53							37
38		Depreciation – Other	56							38
39		Donations & Dues	59							39
40		Freight & Postage	62							40
41		Insurance – Other	65							41
42		Interest – Other	68							42
43		Inventory Adjustment – Other	71							43
44		Maintenance – Other	74							44
45		Professional Services	77							45
46		Supplies	80							46
47		Taxes – Other than P.R./Prop./Inc.	83							47
48		Telephone & Telegraph	86							48
49		Travel	89							49
50		Vehicle	92							50
51										51
52										52
53										53
54		Miscellaneous	98							54
55										55
56		TOTAL EXPENSES								56
57		Expenses – % of Sales								57
58		OPERATING PROFIT								58

LINE NO.		ACCT NO.	MONTH	YEAR-TO-DATE	FINANCIAL RATIOS		PERSONNEL	FULL TIME	PART TIME	
59										59
60	Other Income				Current Asset/Liability		Manager			60
61					Net Worth-Total Liability		Supervisor			61
62	Other Expense		( )	( )	Pre-Tax Income - % of Sale		Salesman			62
63					Adm. Expenses - % of Sale		Pilot			63
64	INCOME – Before Special Charges				Parts Inventory Turnover		Accounting			64
65					Return on Investment		Mechanic			65
66							Parts			66
67							Clerical			67
68							Line			68
69	INCOME – Before Income Taxes									69
70	Provision For Income Taxes	290								70
71										71
72										72
73	FINAL NET INCOME									73

Page 2

BE SURE TO SHOW NUMBER OF PERSONNEL

Figure 7.5. Income portion of statement developed by Piper Aircraft Corporation for its dealers.

DEPARTMENTAL INCOME AND EXPENSE

LINE NO.	ACCT. NO.	SERVICE 500 (5/E) MONTH	SERVICE 500 (5/E) YEAR-TO-DATE	FLIGHT 600 (6/F) MONTH	FLIGHT 600 (6/F) YEAR-TO-DATE	LINE 700 (7/G) MONTH	LINE 700 (7/G) YEAR-TO-DATE	800 (8/H) MONTH	800 (8/H) YEAR-TO-DATE	ADMINISTRATIVE 900 (9/Z) MONTH	ADMINISTRATIVE 900 (9/Z) YEAR-TO-DATE	
1												1
2												2
3												3
4												4
5												5
6	20											EMPLOYMENT
7	21											
8	22											
9	23											
10	24											
11												
12												
13												
14												14
15	30											AIRCRAFT
16	31											
17	32											
18	33											
19	34											
20	35											
21	36											
22	37											
23	38											
24												
25												
26												26
27	44											OCCUPANCY
28	45											
29	46											
30	47											
31	48											
32												
33												
34												34
35												
36	50											OTHER EXPENSES
37	53											
38	56											
39	59											
40	62											
41	65											
42	68											
43	71											
44	74											
45	77											
46	80											
47	83											
48	86											
49	89											
50	92											
51												
52												
53												
54	98											
55												
56												56
57												57
58										( )	( )	58

LINE NO.	OTHER INCOME	ACCT. NO.	MONTH	YEAR-TO-DATE	OTHER EXPENSES	ACCT. NO.	MONTH	YEAR-TO-DATE	
60	Gain on Sale of Assests	900			Loss on Sale of Assets	900			60
61	Discounts Earned	901			Discounts Allowed	901			61
62	Interest	902				902			62
63	Rent	903				903			63
64	Bad Debts Revocered	904				904			64
65	Commissions	905				905			65
66	Vending Machines	906				906			66
67									67
68					Officer's Life Insurance				68
69	Miscellaneous	909			Miscellaneous	909			69
70									70
71									71
72									72
73	TOTAL OTHER INCOME				TOTAL OTHER EXPENSES				73

Page 3

Figure 7.5. Continued.

- **Line 57—Expenses:** Percent of sales. Will vary with the department. Compare with budget projection, historical data, and with departments in similar businesses.

In like manner, each line should be examined by the manager to first determine the general situation and then identify problems that may exist. In conducting this type of analysis, he or she must remember that the income statement is:

- The result of facts
- The result of accounting conventions
- The result of personal judgments and evaluations

Analysis supplements. Special supplements to the financial statement are tremendously valuable in examining the various operational activities and developing insight into possible cause-and-effect relationships.

Tables, charts, graphs, and worksheets can be prepared for a variety of departmental activities and will present specific, detailed data for the desired business activity. The supplements may be practically applied to the activities of service, sales, parts, flight, passengers, line, or other departmental activities. Typical supplements of interest to managers include:

- Accumulated aircraft sales per salesperson
- Monthly parts sales compared to projections
- Aircraft utilization by aircraft and by type flight
- Charter sales by month
- Student completion rates
- Instruction hours per month
- Daily, weekly, and monthly fuel sales
- Fuel inventory records
- Transient aircraft count
- Passenger analysis
- Employee training records

Postanalysis action. Such action may be corrective, reinforcing, or perhaps even innovative. The general objective is to improve the efficiency and profitability of departmental operations and ensure that they contribute to the achievement of overall organization objectives.

Taking Action

The analysis of information-system data should point toward some selected action. Normally there are two alternatives: (1) to revise or adjust the basic plan of the organization for the specific area under consideration, or (2) to adjust the business activity that is taking place. Of course, there is a third alternative available—do nothing and hope things will improve. Chances are that they will worsen if ignored, so this alternative is not realistic. Typically, the action taken is to make some adjustment in the current business activity.

Selling might be accelerated, hours changed, layout altered, personnel added, or a similar activity undertaken to help meet an objective of the organization. In some situations the objective or plan of business must be revised in order to meet new circumstances, but normally the manager makes some change in the business activity to achieve the selected goals. Figure 7.6 might well be typical of actions taken by an aviation manager after completing the analysis and finding that:

1. Analysis of aircraft revenue passenger seats indicates a 50 percent utilization.
2. Gross profits as a percent of sales is found to be 30 percent.
3. The return on investment (before taxes) is reported at 6 percent.

In each of the areas a careful analysis must be made and then a decision reached on the appropriate action. A later section of this chapter is devoted to specific techniques used in analyzing the overall business as well as the individual

Analysis	Action Taken
Instruction hours low	Promote additional students by telephone
Low fuel sales	Revise target volume of sales
Maintenance profits low	Reduce overhead
Parts sales low	Direct mail advertising campaign
Accounts receivable high	Special collection letter
Weak liquidity position	Obtain additional credit reserves

Figure 7.6. Management analysis and action.

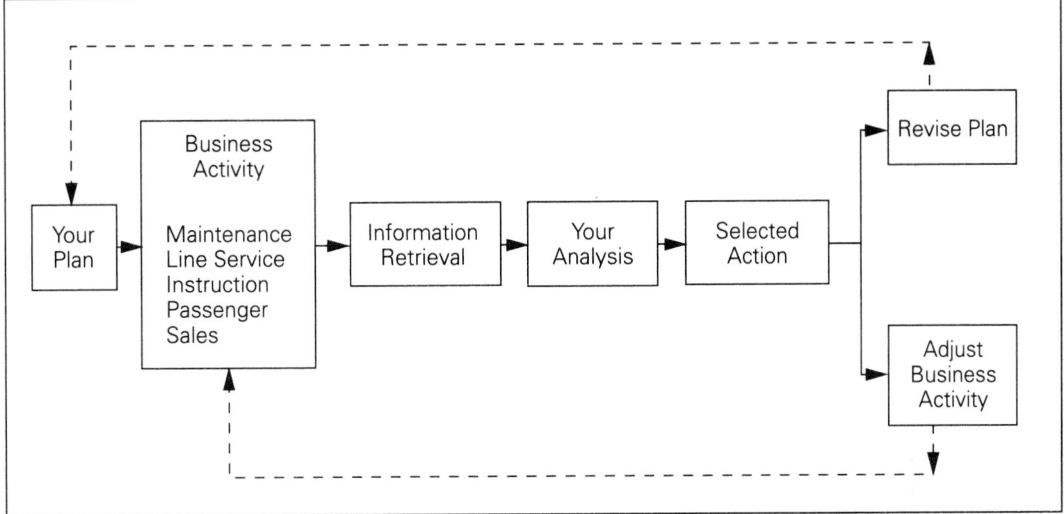

Figure 7.7. Information cycle.

departments. Special attention should be given to the material because it is an important expansion of this section on information-system utilization.

The entire sequence of events involved in the use of the information system by a manager is depicted in figure 7.7.

Controlling the information flow in an aviation activity is no easy task. It implies much more than just having information. The manager controls both the availability of information **and** the action taken as a result.

Records and Record Keeping

Although records and record keeping are obviously important, many aviation firms fail to do an adequate job. Record keeping is almost a nuisance, and hiring personnel to do it generates expensive overhead. For the manager who yearns to experience the thrill of flying, record keeping becomes an unpleasant task, especially for the individual who lacks appreciation of its benefits and who has an inadequate background in some of its fundamental concepts.

Good records are really required. Bankrupt aviation businesses typically have failed to record adequate information. Conversely, successful businesses have been found to have effective record systems. Good records, as identified in the earlier section on the components of an overall management information system, are necessary in achieving better control over operating results. They are also desirable in supporting credit applications to bankers and other creditors and are necessary in filing tax returns and making reports to regulatory agencies. Internally, a good record system makes possible the detection of employee frauds, material waste, errors, spoilage, and other losses requiring prompt correction. It may also pinpoint employee skill deficiencies as well as internal organization problems.

Records Design

The design of records and record keeping systems is seldom done very well by the amateur. In setting up a system, careful attention must be given to the achievement of the objectives mentioned earlier in the chapter. System requirements associated with the three areas of managerial concern—people, money, and material—should be identified and included in the design of the system. The design of efficient, economical forms is very important. They should be prepared so that completion time is minimized while necessary information is provided. Each form should clearly state its purpose in its heading. The form size should be suitable for both filing and entering into posting and bookkeeping systems. Forms should be kept simple and capable of being completed by either hand or typewriter. Recurring information should be preprinted on the form. All prospective users should check each new form to ensure that it contains the desired data.

Printed material and form-handling equipment are available from suppliers to service a wide variety of needs. Many forms for use by today's aviation businesses are computer forms—either generated on the screen or preprinted and completed on the computer printer. In addition to material, suppliers can frequently provide valuable assistance in analyzing a system and its needs. They can adapt and work up special forms to fit individual company needs. Many of these forms are the practical source documents that guide personnel in correct operational procedures as well as provide financial data.

Correspondence

Correspondence or letter writing is undoubtedly the most prevalent form of office paperwork. It is the principal way of conducting business and over the last few decades has increased quite dramatically in volume and diversity. This expansion has led to the need to improve and control correspondence procedures as well as develop new techniques. Given the average cost of a letter—reading, drafting, typing, editing, and mailing, it is apparent that correspondence should be a great economic concern to the aviation manager.

Two basic approaches may be taken to improve the correspondence handled by a front office: (1) training the letter writers and (2) lowering correspondence costs. Letter writing, like other skills, can be improved by training and practice. Training can increase the readability of correspondence, reduce the length of letters, reduce the number of rewrites, and increase the number of letters per writer. There are many sources for this kind of training.

Reducing the costs of correspondence primarily involves improving the rate of production. These improvements can be achieved by the following methods:

Reducing planning time. Planning the correspondence frequently takes more time than writing the letter itself. Writing letters that are short and easy to read and using form letters, guide letters, and other prepared kinds of correspondence can substantially reduce the planning time.

Reduce reading time. Correspondence that is poorly conceived and written is frequently difficult to understand and takes longer to read. By improving the readability of letters, the reading time of recipients and the subsequent time devoted to clarifying telephone calls and correspondence is reduced.

Reducing writing time. The time taken to prepare a 175-word letter will vary depending upon its manner of preparation. The average time for a handwritten letter is 59 minutes, for a dictated letter 30 minutes, and for a form letter 3.5 minutes. To reduce the writing time for correspondence, the following guidelines are useful:

- Greater use of form and guide letters
- Greater use of dictating equipment
- Fewer rewrites
- More judicious use of telephones
- Greater use of the informal reply
- Greater use of routing slips
- Reduction of hand-drafted letters

Reducing reviewing time. The average letter receives three reviews prior to being mailed. More care in preparation or the use of form or guide letters may reduce or even eliminate the review completely. Reviews for inspection by the author or approval by top officials can be reduced in this manner. Delegating signature authority, routing courtesy copies, and eliminating perfunctory approvals will all reduce reviewing time.

Reducing word processing time. By writing shorter letters, using form and guide letters, following a simplified format, and using window envelopes, word processing time can be noticeably reduced.

Reducing delivery time. The time from preparation to delivery can be reduced by cutting the number of reviews, lowering the signature level, improving accuracy in addressing and in maintaining efficient messenger routes and timely mail delivery schedules.

Reducing filing time. Filing time can be cut substantially by using good judgment as to what should be filed and what should not be filed. For those items that require filing, only the necessary copies should be prepared and filed. The use of a subject line or filing key by the author will greatly reduce the filing time of the clerk or office manager. Another quick way to file is to keep one set of correspondence in a chronological file and another set in a subject file. Files should be purged at least annually and only key legal and financial records saved.

Using supplies and equipment effectively. Office productivity can be improved by the efficient use of computers, fax machines, dictating equipment, and printing and mailing supplies such as self-mailers, postcards, brief printed messages, and continuous stationery.

It should be recognized that most business activity is accomplished through words, and many of them are written or typed. The better the manager writes, the better the job is done and the more successful the organization. The goal of correspondence management is the achievement of these objectives.

Records Management

Records have been described as the working tools of management, the memory of the organization, and the source of many kinds of valuable information that's needed in the process of making business decisions. The tremendous increase in the volume of business records in the past few years has created a challenge to the organization—a challenge that grows with each passing year and with organizational growth. The reason for this growth is clear. Rapidly developing technology, a changing economy, the use of photocopying, and the increasingly complex aviation business all contribute to the growth of records and to the problems identified through the terms "red tape," "information explosion," "flood of forms," and the "paper-words jungle." The challenge to management is to bring the tidal wave of records under control and to create a system that serves the needs of the company as efficiently and economically as possible.

Record identification. For most aviation businesses the following records are normally part of the business routine:

- Correspondence, including letters and memos
- Business forms
- Reports and summaries
- Standard organizational instructions and procedures
- Handbooks and manuals

One can also consider records in the two categories of administrative and operational records. The administrative records, which make up 10 to 15 percent of the total, include rules and regulations, policy and procedures manuals, financial and planning records, articles and by-laws, and agendas and minutes. The operational records, which make up the remaining 85 to 90 percent, are made up of purchase orders and requisitions, claims, bills of lading, personnel records, construction records, invoices, cancelled checks, and maps and blueprints.

All of the records follow a similar path or cycle in their existence. They are (1) created, (2) classified, (3) stored, (4) retrieved when needed, and (5) returned to storage or destroyed. Each of these steps must be understood and controlled as part of an active records management programs.

Records management program. There are many approaches that could be taken in the identification of the various components of records management. On a practical basis, records management encompasses all those activities dealing with the creation, maintenance, and disposition of records. The following are parts of a well-rounded records-management program:

- Control of reports
- Control of administrative directives
- Control of paper forms
- Control of paperwork procedures
- Microfilming
- Mail service controls
- Files control
- Records retirement
- Records storage
- Reviewing requests for space and equipment for records

The control of reports becomes a major concern to the manager when he or she views the number of internal and external reports required in the operation of an aviation business. The necessity for a reports-control system to monitor important areas and to ensure that all external report commitments are met on schedule can become critical to the success of a business. Internal reports should also be monitored and controlled with the same concern, since the organization originates many of these reports. It is necessary to avoid duplication and overlapping of data and to cull unnecessary reports.

The control of administrative procedures and directives is another internal problem that increases as the organization grows and is stimulated by the complexity of the typical aviation business. In order to control this area effectively, it is necessary that directives and guidelines be developed for the organization and that their implementation be administered consistently. The content of this framework will vary depending upon the needs of the organization's size, diversity of activity, number of personnel, geographic locations, and management pattern. It may range from a simple system of working procedures and informal memoranda to a more complicated structure with a formal manual that specifies the complete system of procedures and directives and their administration.

The control of forms used in an aviation business becomes an extremely important part of a records management program because of the many requirements for information and records pertaining to passenger statistics, student activity, maintenance progress, and fuel allocations as well as internal departmental activities and analysis. They are necessary to transmit information and instructions and to record data. Forms are carefully designed papers that perform, simplify, and standardize office work. They accumulate and transmit information for reference or decision-making purposes. They may be classified in various ways, but a typical system classifies them according to their business functions such as purchase forms, sales forms, correspondence forms and accounting forms. There are three objectives in forms control: (1) to eliminate as much unneeded information and as many business forms and records as feasible, (2) to combine as many of the business forms as possible, and (3) to simplify the forms in content, arrangement, and method of preparation. With these objectives in mind, the manager can utilize the following three principles in the standardization and control of forms:

1. A form should exist only when there is a need for it.
2. The size, quality, and color of paper used in all forms should be standardized to reduce costs and confusion.
3. The design, use, and replacement of business forms should be centrally controlled.

One effective method of attaining the desired objectives and achieving efficient and economical forms is through the use of a design checklist. Such a checklist can be used in reviewing existing forms or in developing new forms.

The control of paperwork procedures is another key element in a complete management program. With rising costs in every portion of the business, the manager must control the use of personnel involved in handling paperwork. Clearcut procedures allowing maximum productivity of the personnel will result in the best possible results. A logical flow diagram of the various steps involved in the use of paperwork will help the manager visualize the complete procedure and control the process. For larger organizations with many personnel engaged in paperwork, work standards can be utilized successfully. In some aviation businesses a program of work measurement is beneficial.

With the relatively low cost of today's personal computers and the myriad of software programs available to assist business and accounting functions standardization of forms is easily performed via computer. Computers actually reduce the amount of paperwork generated through the utilization of E-mail and other electronic communication means.

Mail-service control should be reflected through a system that is tailored to meet the particular needs of each organization. Accuracy, speed, and economy are the three key criteria. Mail-service procedures will be quite different in various organizations, depending upon size and type of business activities. Since mail is one of the communication links of an aviation business with its customers and suppliers, the mail office should be equipped, organized, staffed, and supervised to do the job effectively. Management should provide for practical organization, up-to-date equipment, written procedures, planned layout, informed personnel, and controlled costs. Each of these areas needs to be carefully reviewed by management, and action taken to ensure that the desired level of mail service is being achieved. The responsibility for mail service must be assigned and fixed. The proper equipment to expedite the handling of mail should be identified and obtained. The procedures for handling internal, as well as external communications, should be planned and written for reference purposes, for compliance and update information. The layout or arrangement of a mail room varies depending upon the size of the activity, but the primary emphasis is on efficiency. Mail service personnel should be trained to understand and handle their mail service for the company. They should be knowledgeable about company policies, mail procedures, and postal regulations, as well as dependable, accurate and thorough. The costs of mail service must constantly be reviewed. There are many specific ways to cut costs without reducing service. Alert and trained personnel using the proper equipment in an efficient layout can identify these opportunities and take advantage of them. In today's world of high-speed communications, many FBOs are finding the need to supplement mail service with facsimile machines (FAX). There are many choices of product.

Files control includes the identification and development of an appropriate filing system, the acquisition of supplies and equipment, the training of personnel, and the development of working procedures that will result in the filing activity needed by the organization. The operational adequacy of the filing system can be examined through the use of a file audit like the following one. This audit is a systematic examination of day-to-day internal operations in a particular filing operation. The following checklist illustrates the technique of auditing the filing system and the records-management activity:

1. Are files under central control?
2. Is there a records manual? Is it up to date and adequate?
3. Are files neatly maintained?
4. Is filing kept up to date?
5. Are personnel adequately trained?
6. Are all records marked with a retention period?
7. Are obsolete records destroyed?
8. Are records adequately protected?
9. Has provision been made for expansion?
10. Do different files duplicate records? Is this necessary?
11. Is employee handwriting of records legible?
12. Has microfilming been examined to determine its feasibility?
13. Is provision made for the transfer or removal of inactive records?
14. Is there an inventory of all records?
15. Have records been classified in terms of being vital, required, routine, and so on?
16. Are control reports required and submitted?
17. Is there an on-going program of evaluation and follow-up?
18. How much is records maintenance costing?

Through this kind of critical examination and its implied follow-up activities, the files of an organization can be developed and maintained at the desired level of capability. As with other administrative or support functions, the level of sophistication will vary with the size and complexity of the business. The full file audit can be of tremendous value to any organization.

Records retirement or retention is another extremely important element of administration. The number of records required to manage an aviation activity today has reached gargantuan proportions. This has resulted in stuffed files and the necessity for a planned program for record retirement. Various records are kept or disposed of according to different requirements such as the Statutes of Limitation and the stipulations of different regulatory agencies. To assist in evaluating records for retirement, the manager might consider the following:

1. Value for administrative use
2. Value for legal use
3. Value for policy use
4. Value for fiscal use
5. Value for operating use
6. Value for research
7. Value for historical use
8. Supporting value (Is the record necessary to support other records of importance?)
9. Physical duplication (How many copies are available?)
10. Duplication in content (Is the content duplicated in some other record?)
11. Volume of file. (The value of all records should be weighed against the volume of the file in terms of equipment, floor space, and resultant maintenance cost.)

The *National Fire Protection Association* has developed a record classification system that should be helpful to aviation businesses in developing a retirement/retention program.[1]

Vital. Those records that underlie the organization and give direct evidence of legal status, ownership, assets, and liabilities. The loss of them would seriously affect continuing a business.

Important. Those records that are essential to the business and could be reproduced from original sources only at great expense.

Useful. Those records that have routine significance. The loss of them would cause temporary inconvenience but they are not essential to continuing a business.

Nonessential. Those records of no present or future value that should be destroyed.

As a guide to everyday activity, many organizations have developed a schedule covering the retention period of their records. This schedule should be adjusted to meet the needs of individual businesses and the changing requirements of federal, state, and local laws. When records have served their purpose, they may be disposed of by tearing, shredding, or burning. These techniques are useful when the contents are confidential and mutilation is necessary. It is good management to account for the destruction of all important papers and to have a system that provides for the retirement of the others. As mentioned earlier, microfilming can possibly play an important part in the records retirement and retention program. Although the emphasis is normally placed upon the immediate dollar savings resulting from reduced storage requirements, the importance of preserving business experiences and history should not be overlooked. Information regarding motives and reasons for making decisions can become useful in later years.

Records storage can be considered in two forms: operational storage and inactive storage. The key governing factors in maintaining a proper balance in storage are availability, cost, and organization. Operational storage, as mentioned earlier under files control, is concerned primarily with material being used daily, weekly, or on some regular basis. Of course, records that are not valuable should be destroyed before they reach the files for storage. A retention guide will greatly assist an organization in identifying what to retain in storage and for how long. Most organizations retain far more paperwork than is necessary. It has been estimated by the National Records Management Council that 95 percent of all corporate paperwork over a year old is never used as a reference. Considerable savings can be realized by carefully screening records according to a retention list and transferring only those necessary valuable records to a low-cost storage location. Storage facility requirements vary considerably. Generally they should offer protection from fire, dust, dirt, moisture, and vermin, and should provide reasonable accessibility.

A dynamic organization will undoubtedly experience a continuous need for additional filing space and equipment. Requests for such additional capability should be considered carefully. When the file cabinet overflows, it may be time to get rid of some records through storage or elimination, rather than buying another file cabinet.

Communications

Success in an aviation business depends increasingly upon communications. Managers need to study the techniques and devices that make communications as successful as possible. Communication problems are troublesome and businesses should consequently give them careful attention.

The first step in developing a satisfactory communication plan for an aviation business is to analyze and identify both the internal and external needs of the organization. Careful consideration should be given to such factors as types of communications, internal layout, types of employees, work flow, customer distribution, and economic concerns. Such an analysis will consider the following areas:

- The number and kinds of communications that are transacted internally and externally
- Frequency, duration and timing of internal and external communications
- The relationship between cost and service level
- The importance of speed
- Whether the responsibility for communication is fixed
- The importance of exact understanding and accuracy for some or all communications
- Whether there is a need for direct communication hookups to branches, suppliers or customers
- What the key internal communication system needs are
- The communicative ability of organizational personnel

The second step is acquiring and installing the desired communications equipment and techniques to meet the internal and external needs of the organization. Bulletin boards, correspondence, newsletters, booklets, meetings, suggestion systems, attitude surveys, e-mail systems, intercom systems, messenger systems, pagers, walkie-talkies and closed-circuit TVs are examples of primary internal communications equipment. The external methods of communication include electronic and regular mail service, telecopiers, facsimile machines, and telephones. Each of these areas contains a wide variety of possibilities and each should be considered carefully to ensure that organizational needs are being met as completely and economically as possible. Communications equipment sales personnel or service representatives can greatly assist in identifying needs and matching these needs with available equipment.

The third step in creating an adequate communication network is training personnel in the communication process and in how to use available communication equipment. Training in communication is a continuous effort that should include all personnel and should focus on eliminating problems that plague oral and written communications. A great deal can be accomplished through the use of lectures, training sessions, practice, demonstrations, bulletins, illustrative literature, and instruction sheets.

Duplicating Information

Office copying machines have improved so much in recent years, and the price has decreased so much that other office copying systems, such as carbon paper, stencils and mimeograph, are virtually things of the past. Considerations in regard to photocopying equipment include:

- Whether to rent or buy
- Automatic feed or handfeed
- Collate manually or automatically

There are machines of every level of power and capacity. For the best quality, when several hundred copies are required, offset printing will be less expensive.

Aviation Accounting

Accounting is simply maintaining a record of business activities. It is the systematic recording of the financial transactions and facts of a business so that periodically the status of the business and the results of its operations can be presented correctly and understandably in statement form. A businessperson needs to know almost on a daily basis about whether the business is profitable. Which lines of aviation activity are the most or least profitable? What are the cash needs? What are the working capital requirements? The business owner can get reliable information like this only if there is a good accounting system, which is a key component of the Management Information System (MIS). The manager or owner of an aviation business is normally very knowledgeable about the technical aspects of the business. However, frequently he or she does not have a background in accounting, but is an aviation enthusiast first and a businessperson second. As a result, the typical manager avoids accounting and continually delegates it to others. Ultimately, he or she becomes unable to use it as a managerial tool. Because of this tendency, the following material points out the relative simplicity of aviation accounting, which can lead toward a more successful business.

Accounting Flow

The manager accounts for business activities with financial statements such as balance sheets and an income statements. Essentially, a balance sheet shows business (assets), what it owes (liabilities), and the investment of the owners in the business (net worth) at a certain point in time. The income statement, on the other hand, is a summary of business operations for a certain period, usually between two balance sheet dates. It indicates the financial results of the company's operations for the selected period of time. In very general terms, the balance sheet tells where you are, and the income statement tells how you got there. Accounting includes the "systematic recording of financial transactions and facts of business." The first step in this process is the completion of the source documents—a record of individual business transactions. These transactions include sales, purchases, payroll, and obligations such as depreciation, insurance, and taxes. From the source documents the accounting information flows through the system and becomes input to the financial statements. Figure 7.8 graphically depicts this flow of information through the accounting system. The manager should be familiar with this flow of information and the various records involved. In order to more fully understand the flow of accounting information, each step in the process is examined.

Source Documents

For the typical aviation activity, the normal source documents are sales invoices, journals, general ledger, and financial statements.

Sales Invoices will be from the following areas:

- Aircraft
- Charter
- Passenger
- Flight Instructions
- Service
- Line activity
- Parts
- Rental
- Cash receipts
- Checks
- Vendor invoices
- Time cards
- General journal vouchers

Figure 7.8 shows a sample computerized invoice.

Appendix IV to this book illustrates typical forms used as source documents for these kinds of business activities. The development of individual forms to meet specific business requirements should be done with great care. Forms control is an important responsibility of the central office.

Journals

Information from the individual source documents is entered into the journals—the first accounting record of the transaction. These books are frequently called the "books of original entry" and they represent a chronological record of all transactions conducted by the business. A

MILLER AVIATION CORPORATION

Box 4 Edwin A. Link Field
Johnson City, New York 13790-9724
Phone: (607) 770-1093
Telex: 703-522

INVOICE

PAGE NUMBER	1
DOCUMENT NUMBER	28706
DATE	9/29/87

Spare Parts Distribution

******************** Think of Miller Aviation for: ********************
GOODYEAR TIRES, GILL BATTERIES and CHAMPION PLUGS and FILTERS!!

** AOG ***AOG ***AOG ***
A/C S/N 310R01234
945

** AOG ***AOG ***AOG ***
** AOG ***AOG ***AOG ***

BILL TO
Flight Group Inc.
R D # 3
Pottstown/Limerick Airport
3310 W Ridge Pike
Pottstown PA 19464

SHIP TO
Aero Tech
Smoketown Airport
Smoketown, PA 17576

WALTER

TERMS	REFERENCE NUMBER	SHIP VIA	ORDER NO.	ORDERED	REQUESTED	SHIPPED	CUSTOMER REPRESENTATIVE	
Net 30 Day	P/0 #12345	FED-1 DROP SHIP	27341	9/29/87	9/29/87	9/29/87	Walter Rittenhouse	Open Account

LN NO.	ITEM NUMBER	ITEM DESCRIPTION	ITEM REFERENCE	BO	TAX	QUANTITY PER	PRICE PER	QTY. SOLD	LIST	DISCOUNT	NET	EXTEND. NET
5	9910070-1RX X	MOTOR - EXCHANGE	S/N 1234	Y	N	Each	Each	1.00	320.00	10.0%	288.00	288.00
6	9910079-1RX C	MOTOR - CORE		Y	N	Each	Each	1.00	300.00	NET	300.00	300.00
7		PLEASE RETURN CORE ASAP FOR										
8		POSSIBLE CORE CREDIT.										
9	AM4-31	BOLT		Y	N	Each	Each	3.00	.82	19.5%	.66	1.98
13	AM1021125FP	FILTER S/S	1250704-3	Y	N	Each	Each	1.00	75.00	15.0%	63.75	63.75
14	MAS1103-22D	BOLT S/S	MAS464-3-22	Y	N	Each	Each	2.00	.74	20.0%	.56	1.12
15	FREIGHT	INSURED ABC FED-EX		Y	N	Each	Each	1.00	.00	NET	6.58	6.58
16	INSURANCE	U P S INSURANCE AT $.25/$1.00		Y	N	/$100	/$100	6.00	.25	NET	.25	1.25
											Subtotal:	662.85
											Freight:	21.00
											TOTAL	683.85

Figure 7.8. Courtesy of Miller Aviation Corporation, Edwin A. Link Field, Johnson City, NY 13790.

journal is simply a financial diary. A typical aviation accounting system has the following journals:

- Cash receipts and sales journal
- Purchase and cash disbursements journal
- General journal
- Payroll journal

In order to ensure the flow of accounting information, administrative procedures must be established that ensure the accurate completion of all forms and the timely submission of all completed forms to the accounting office. At the end of an accounting period, the column totals of all journals are balanced and posted to the general ledger. The use of a computer can automatically and rapidly take care of this flow.

General Ledger

The ledger is a loose-leaf binder or computer file made up of the accounts identified in the business. A separate account is maintained for each type of asset, each type of liability, and each element of equity. The data transferred from the journals is entered into the appropriate ledger account. The balances in the ledger accounts are then reflected in the financial statement when it is prepared. Any transactions during the operating period result in increases or decreases in assets, liabilities, and owner's equity.

Financial Statements

As previously mentioned, business activity is summarized and presented in the two financial statements—balance sheet and income statement. Figures 4.4 and 4.5 in chapter 4 illustrate a simplified version of these two reports. A more detailed version of aviation statements will be utilized later in this chapter to illustrate the process of analyzing business activities. Accounting records and books of a business are not directly involved in decision making; however, they are used by the accountant to prepare financial statements and special supporting documents that are used by the manager in decision making. Since the preparation and handling of data, documents, and records has a tremendous influence on the outcome as represented by the financial statements, it is essential that the manager have a thorough working knowledge of the system and be involved in some of the decisions in designing and administering it.

Accounting Activity Flow Chart

The complete flow of accounting information from the source documents to the financial statements is depicted in figure 7.9 and is broken down into individual areas in Appendix IV. This illustration suggests the basic outline of an aviation business accounting system and is not intended to be all-inclusive. Source documents can be expanded or contracted, journals realigned, or ledgers developed to meet specific business needs. Although the balance sheet and the income statement are considered the two major products of the accounting system, there are other system products that are extremely valuable to the manager, such as the material for income tax returns and the various information schedules used by the manager in making operational decisions on a continuing basis.

A major managerial function is organizing. This normally includes the development of an organizational structure and the allocation of functions and duties to organizational units and to individuals. The manager's primary objective is to establish work teams that can function efficiently and profitably. As a part of this effort, it is necessary to develop a flow of information pertaining to each work team or activity center in order to ascertain the actual business results. This information flow is needed to measure progress and provide direction for future management activity. A clear picture of how records are processed. (Who does what? And when?) is necessary for training personnel in the process.

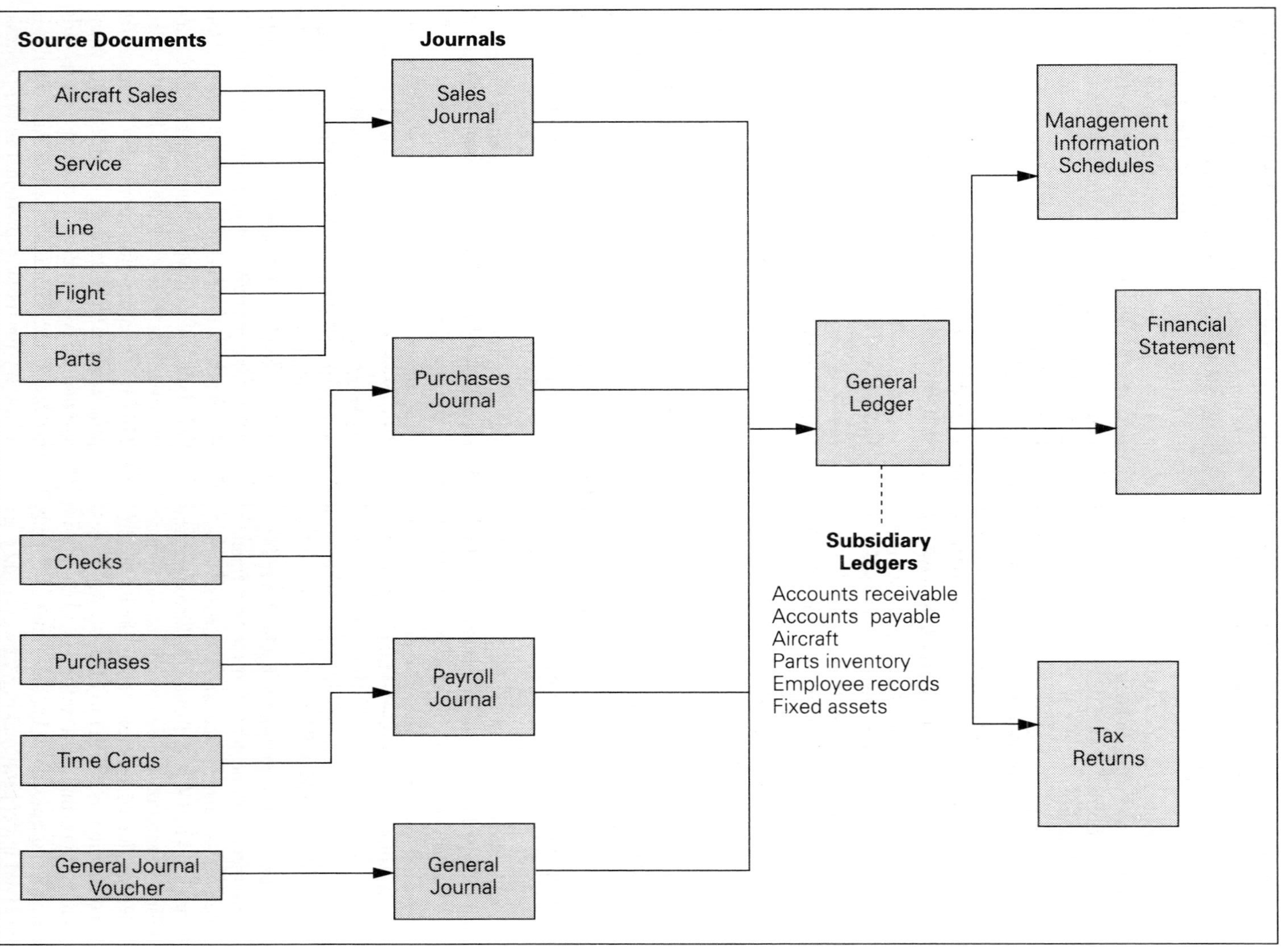

Figure 7.9. Information system activity flow chart.

Variations undoubtedly exist from business to business, but the general framework should be like the one presented in Appendix IV. Management must ensure a logical, efficient flow of information, provide for necessary personnel training in the use of the system, and maintain a system of checks and controls to guard against a loss of resources through inefficiencies or theft.

The Accounting System

Each account is given a number that serves as its identifier and as the means of guiding and controlling the flow of information through the accounting system. At a minimum, the accounting records should provide information on:

- Assets, including real estate, equipment, inventory, receivables and cash
- Liabilities to banks, suppliers, employees and others, including income taxes due
- Owner's equity in the firm
- Sales, expenses and profit for the accounting period

In developing a system to meet these requirements and the needs of his organization, the aviation manager can take one of several approaches. With the help of a local accounting firm, he or she can (1) develop his or her own system, (2) turn to one of the many large accounting firms that have an aviation accounting system available, (3) solicit the help of large printing houses that have developed complete systems, or (4) obtain assistance from one of the aircraft manufacturers that has developed complete systems for its dealers. In view of the difficulties and problems encountered, it would obviously be better to acquire a system designed specifically for an aviation business and to avoid the problems of developing one from the very beginning. There are now many vendors of aviation accounting software; however, this is a rapidly changing service. As already discussed, you must be careful to select the appropriate vendor.

The system developed by Piper Aircraft Corporation for the outlets in its distribution system is an excellent example of a financial information system designed specifically for the aviation business community. The total system is made up of the following components:[2]

- Financial statements
- Chart of accounts
- Source documents
- Accounting system
- Accounts receivable portion
- Accounts payable portion
- Payroll section
- General ledger

All the components are fully integrated, with each keyed to the chart of accounts. The statements, source documents, and the accounting system are preprinted with the appropriate account numbers to facilitate efficient operations. It is a compact structure with the capacity for flexibility and growth. A nonautomated accounting system is a *Post Rite*, or pegboard system, developed and provided by Reynolds and Reynolds of Dayton, Ohio.[3] As the aviation organization grows, it can shift to partial or full electronic accounting programs by still using the same basic chart of accounts, source documents, and record-keeping procedures. Indeed, automation is next to impossible if the existing system is disorganized.

Source documents comprise an integral part of the accounting system. They are designed specifically for aviation businesses and are coded with account numbers to facilitate their use and reduce transfer errors.

The accounting system as developed by Piper is basically a pegboard system designed for firms that keep their books by hand. Under the pegboard system, a business transaction needs to be recorded only once, and the original entry of data is recorded simultaneously on all relevant records. This is achieved by using a board with a flat, hard surface and carbon papers or carbonless duplicating forms. All records requiring an entry are placed on the board, one on top of the other. Proper alignment is determined by pegs affixed to the board. After each posting, the records are advanced on the board one notch. The distinct advantages of pegboard accounting are readily apparent. The entry of a business transaction on all relevant records is done with one writing, thereby reducing records-handling time, eliminating errors in transcription, and providing many of the advantages of machine bookkeeping without the high initial cost. With this foundation of an aviation-oriented chart of accounts, keyed-in source documents, financial statements, and the basic accounting system, it becomes relatively easy to move to a more sophisticated electronic accounting when the volume of business allows it.

Profit Center Accounting

The typical aviation business is engaged in many types of activities: selling aircraft, providing service, giving flight instruction, providing air transportation, selling parts, pumping fuel, renting aircraft, leasing space, as well as other related enterprises such as car rentals. In order to properly operate each of these activities, the manager needs to have current information on the profitability of each. He/she needs an accounting system that will properly allocate the income and expenses of each business activity to that activity so that the worth of each as a profit center can be judged. The system will also allocate company-wide overhead on a percentage basis to each profit center.

In order to develop and administer a profit center accounting systems, it is necessary to understand and implement the following:

Responsibility accounting recognizes various activities in an organization and traces costs, revenues, assets, and liabilities to the individual managers who are primarily responsible for making decisions for that activity. Ideally, revenues and costs are recorded and traced to the one individual in the organization who shoulders primary responsibility for the area.

Controllable costs are critical to responsibility accounting. These costs are directly influenced by a manager within a given time span. Thus, we must identify the manager of a specific activity and delineate the time span under consideration.

It is hard, however, to determine whether an item is controllable or uncontrollable, or what degree of control is available. There is the additional problem of trying to assign clearly the sole responsibility to one person. Perhaps several individuals exert influence over a cost center. The question is: "Who is the one person in the organization with the most decision-making power over the item in question?"

Uncontrollable costs are generally excluded by a selected manager from his performance report. However, the opposite point of view suggests that each manager should be assigned some of these costs to become more aware of the operational problems of the total organization.

Cost allocation is an inescapable problem in nearly every organization. How should the costs of an aviation business be split among the flight department, line department, service department, and so on? How should staff costs, computer, advertising, and equipment be allocated? These are tough questions and the answers are not always clear. We need to gain insight into these problems to do a more acceptable job of dealing with profit centers and to increase the overall business profit.

Three major aspects of cost allocation include:

1. Delineating the cost center; that is, the department, product, or process.
2. Choosing and accumulating the costs that relate to the cost center: material, labor, overhead.

3. Choosing a method for specifically relating costs to cost centers. This normally means selecting an allocation base for the individual costs.

The cost centers of primary concern are those departments or work areas that have been identified by the accounting system.

Choosing and accumulating the costs to be analyzed are basic concerns of the manager and of the information system. The system should identify the key costs and provide the mechanism for accumulating and transporting them to the manager in usable form. The actual method of relating costs to business areas will vary, depending upon the criteria selected for making decisions. Possible criteria include:

- Physical identification
- Services used
- Facilities provided
- Benefits received
- Ability to bear costs
- Fairness or equity

Allocation bases for overhead. There is a tendency to aggregate overhead costs in pools and use one allocation base for each pool. The following bases are widely used:

- Physical units produced
- Direct-labor hours
- Machine hours
- Direct-labor costs
- Direct materials

The major problem in choosing a proper base is relating overhead to its most closely related cause. At the same time, the base factor that is easiest and cheapest to apply should be selected.

In allocating costs to properly develop an organization for achieving objectives, the administration must select an allocation system that influences employees and managers to take the correct action. The best system measures cause-and-effect relationships of business activity. The fully allocated versus partially allocated cost question can never be answered with one solution for all situations. There are many variables that influence the decision to fully allocate all costs. Among those frequently considered are:

- The size of the line organization
- The sophistication of the information system
- The relative cost of the allocation
- The importance of cause-and-effect relationships
- Managerial awareness of the concept
- Anticipated personnel reactions

Existing cost systems in many businesses are crude. However, tremendous improvement can be realized through the intelligent use of averages, the development of the "best possible" system, and the tendency toward full allocation of costs.

A suggested procedure for allocating costs is contained in the following steps:

1. Use the income statement for the business as the starting point.
2. Determine initial policy on allocation, that is, full or selective.
3. Review each item in the total income and expense columns.
4. Determine allocation unit and method of allocation.
5. Extend the selected allocations for several financial periods.
6. Analyze and compare the consequences.
7. Ask the question: Does this system provide me with the necessary profit-center evaluative data?
8. Consult with managers of the individual departments on the appropriateness of the selected system.
9. Identify additional requirements.
10. Resolve any difficulties.
11. Implement the allocation system.
12. Communicate and educate.
13. Evaluate the system after a period of operation. Modify as required.

Contribution concept. The term contribution or contribution margin is an expression used in accounting but frequently not understood by managers. It is important to the successful application of the profit-center concept and ultimately to an analysis of departmental and overall business activity.

The *contribution margin* is considered the excess of income over the variable expenses. It can be expressed as a total, as an amount per unit, or as a percentage. To more easily present the concept, let us develop a graphical presentation of contribution margin. The three components used in the graph are variable expenses, fixed expenses, and income. These elements are used in a graph where the horizontal axis represents the number of units handled or the volume of services delivered. The vertical axis is graduated in dollars and will be used for dollars of expense or income. The first step is to add the variable expenses, those costs that increase with increasing volume. Next, add the fixed expenses, those costs that remain constant over the volume range being considered in the chart. Finally, add the income or revenue as reflected by varying sales volume. The combination provides the cost/volume/profit chart—better known as the break-even chart. Figure 7.10 is an expanded version of the chart. It identifies the components just described as well as the contribution margin. This is the same chart used in chapter 4 (see figure 4.4).

By using the definition of contribution margin as the excess of income over variable expenses, we can see from the graph that below the break-even point (BEP) that we still have a contribution (to the organization) of dollars toward the fixed costs incurred by that department or activity. The manager's goal is to sell enough

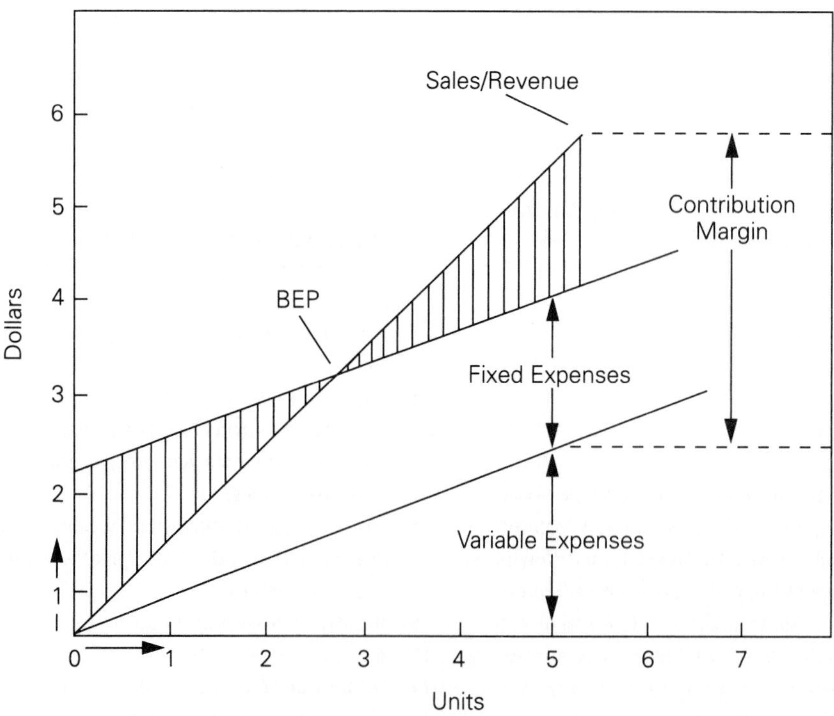

Figure 7.10. Contribution margin as graphically illustrated in a break-even chart.

units so that each department or activity realizes a profit. But in the event a profit is not realized, he or she should recognize the "sunk cost" aspects of fixed expenses and appreciate that some portion of those costs are being offset by that business income. More importantly, in the event that business income is eliminated, the remainder of the business activity has to shoulder those expenses.

Information System Tools

Manual Systems

There is a major distinction between management information and the way it is recorded, tabulated, and analyzed. Until the late 1970s most smaller businesses never gave this distinction much thought. The most obvious tools were pencil, green eyeshade, eraser, and ledger book or spreadsheet. Sales receipt books with carbon paper copies were another important tool. Paychecks were typically written by the bookkeeper and signed by the owner/manager.

This system is perfectly adequate; and because it's simple, it lends itself to good order and timely postings. However, no small business management book of the 1990s is complete without a discussion of computers, particularly personal and multi-user small computer systems.

The Pros and Cons of Automation

Computers are to manual accounting systems as the horse is to the automobile. You can get there faster so you save time. But you find different ways to spend that saved time by going places you never could before. That is to say, a manager should not expect to reduce personnel or other administrative costs with a computer. He or she **will** find however, that after the start-up phase, existing functions can be accomplished more efficiently and that all kinds of new information storage, tabulation and analysis are possible. This opens up new horizons for better managerial control and faster reaction to problems.

By the early 1990s the typical office is no longer buying the IBM Selectric type of machine, since for about the same price a microcomputer will do the same things faster and offer some new things a Selectric cannot do.[4] At present the only typing jobs a **computer** cannot easily do is fill out someone else's forms. Given the current pace of technological innovation, this will no doubt soon be resolved.

There are many choices of computer system, and these are discussed below.

Considering Automation

The considerations for automation are much the same as those for making any substantial change in a manual system. What is the data collection? What does it cost? Is it adequate? Are there some gaps to close? Any new functions? What are you prepared to commit in terms of time and money to make the changes? The switch to computers will require adjustment of the staff, perhaps duplicate operations for a few months, and substantial managerial attention.

Computer selection. This chapter cannot provide a detailed review of all the issues surrounding the purchase of your first computer, but these are the key considerations:

1. Decide what things you want to automate and pick the software that can do it.
2. Select the hardware compatible with initial and future software.
3. Consider the expansion possibilities of your system; for example, in the future would it be useful to do graphics? If so, can your system be upgraded?
4. Consider other software compatible with your system.
5. If you have identified special aviation or

other software, make sure your system can run it.

6. Compare the degree of "user friendliness" of your system with the degree of computer literacy of your personnel. Some systems have easy to use software because of prompts and questions on the screen, but manuals that are almost unintelligible to a beginner.
7. Establish the degree of training and support the vendor will provide.
8. Clarify the warranty and repair arrangements, including what happens if the system is "down" (temporarily nonfunctional).
9. Select a vendor with a trade record. How long have they been in business? Do they offer revised software? As users, do they make suggestions?

Computer Service Bureaus

Service Bureaus take your raw data such as:

- Checks
- Sales slips
- Receipts
- Journal entries
- Payroll data—names, hourly rates, hours worked, withholdings

Then they use their own computer, staff, and time to contract and produce reports and other products such as:

- Paychecks
- Cash receipts journals
- Check registers
- Payroll registers
- Sales journals
- General journals
- General ledgers
- Receivables ledgers
- Payables ledgers
- Property ledgers
- Balance sheets
- Income statements
- Aged accounts-receivable listings, with customers' statements
- Inventory status reports
- Payroll reports, including those to be filed with government agencies
- Budget reports
- Operating ratios

If your computer service bureau is also your bank—a common trend—then they will even pay your bills, issue checks, and deduct the funds from your account. Your company's personnel do not need to know anything about computers, though they will still have to know something about accounting to check things over. Of course, sending everything out can be expensive. Also, the necessary turnaround time means that you cannot get instant answers and must plan ahead.

Mainframe Computers

The first computers of recent decades fall into this category. They are typically bought by large companies that custom design what they want. Most FBOs would have little interest in owning such systems, although costs, as well as size, are down since their introduction.

Time-sharing

By purchasing or leasing a terminal and a modem (direct phone link) to someone else's mainframe computer, you can rent time on a powerful system without having to buy it. Some of the available systems also involve data banks that are constantly kept current. As the types of data banks proliferate, there may be some of interest to aviation businesses. Several users can be working on a mainframe at the same time because it has such a huge memory; however, there can be perceptible and annoying delays at peak times. But you can get instant results to data questions. Someone in the office will need some training to use such a system.

Minicomputers

Minicomputers may be defined as costing from $7,000 to $20,000 for the hardware, plus any custom programming. This may be a suitable machine for a larger business, but it is an unlikely suitable **first** computer. A larger company with little or no "computer literacy" should probably buy a microcomputer such as IBM and its "clones," DEC Rainbow or Macintosh, the next time the office needs a new typewriter. Then the manager should find through hands-on experimentation and study of the manuals what else the computer can process. The main advantages of a minicomputer are:

1. It's yours, which means a greater degree of confidentiality is possible.
2. It is a multi-user system—everyone in the office who needs one can hook in through a terminal.
3. Because of this feature, every part of the business using a terminal can feed into the same data bank. For example, the repair shop and front desk can simultaneously use it for a cash register/inventory control program, and daily reports on receipts and inventory can be tabulated.

On the other hand, if a minicomputer is down, it's down. Also, it may need a special dust- and static-free room.

Microcomputers

The first microcomputers (other than those in use by hobbyists, who generally built their own) appeared in about 1975. The market was initially the home/game market, but the introduction of an electronic spreadsheet, VisiCalc, changed that, and the business world became very interested in what micro, "desktop," or "personal" computers could do.

A microcomputer can conduct all the accounting functions that might be done manually by the bookkeeper or sent out to a service bureau. In addition, the following can be done with ease and speed:

1. Form letters, individually typed, with salutation and as many references to the individual as you may want in the text
2. Sorting, for example of mailing lists by zip code, date of last purchase, aircraft owner or not, and any number of other criteria
3. Alphabetizing lists
4. Printing invoices
5. Printing shipping documents
6. Retrieval and display of a customer's account and credit status
7. Contracts or leases with standard text plus one-time insertions
8. Conditional printing, causing a paragraph to go in a document only if certain conditions are met
9. Cash register functions
10. Automatic inventory tally and reorder reminders
11. Budget projections including any number of "what-ifs"
12. Break-even analysis
13. Special reports on any data collected on the computer, for example, productivity, allocation, and cost trends
14. Forecasts using linear regression
15. Spelling checkers
16. Tracking of projects and programs

Figure 7.11 shows the various office machines and functions that can be replaced by a microcomputer (or two or three). Figure 7.12 shows one software vendor's program for keeping track of aircraft maintenance projects. There are a growing number of aviation-tailored programs. Available now on floppy disks and cd rom are copies of FAA documents including federal aviation regulations (FARs), the Airman's Information Manual (AIM), service bulletins, etc.

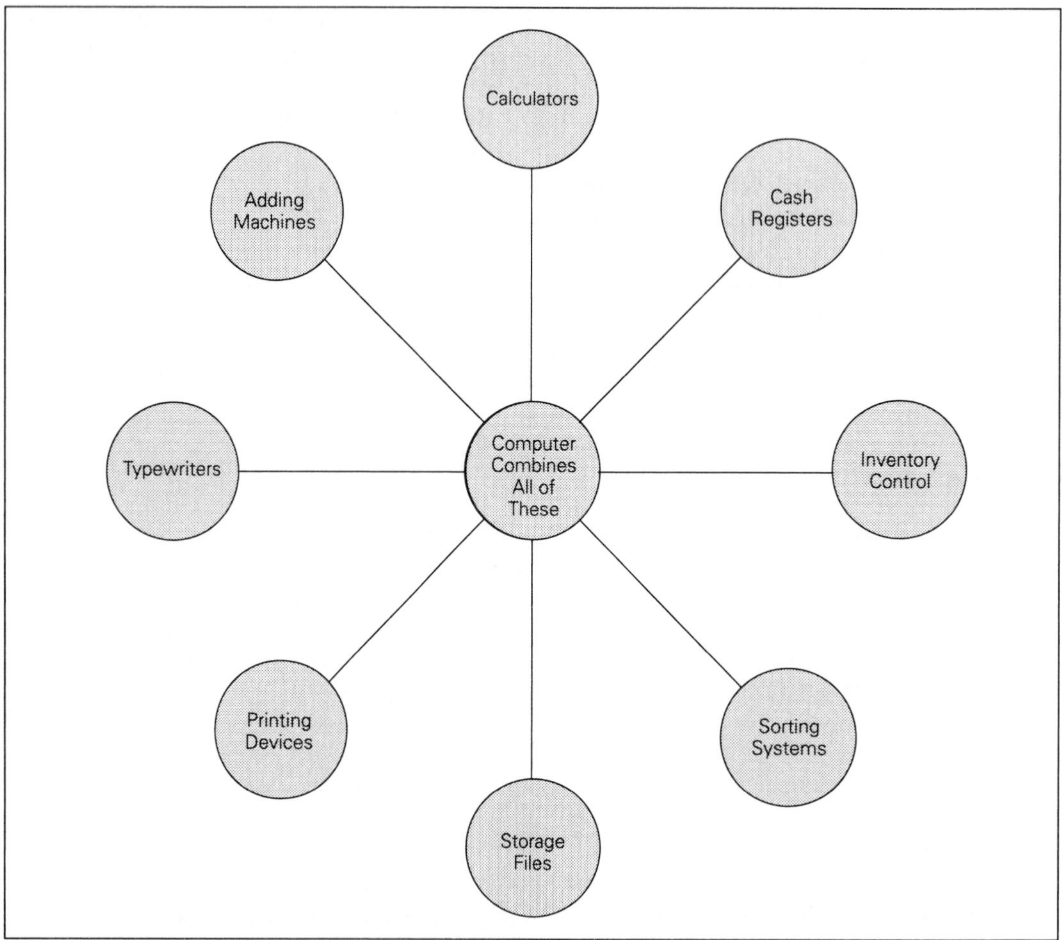

Figure 7.11. Office machines and functions that can be replaced by a microcomputer.

Of note here is the decision by the FAA to eliminate written test exams for pilots and aviation maintenance technicians by the end of 1995. All testing will have been converted and made available solely by computer linkage. Fixed base operators used to giving paper and pencil FAA written exams in the past, have had to make the decision to invest and switch to computerized testing or withdraw from that part of their business.

Other software may be purchased and even produced by your own office to suit your own needs. But the number of existing programs is vast and growing so rapidly that a small business can go many years without needing to do any programming. In the past few years many vendors have entered and then left the industry of providing computer services to FBOs. It is, therefore, impossible to provide an up-to-date list; FBOs considering computerizing one or more areas of operations should review current literature and advertising in the aviation trade publications such as *Airport Services* and *FBO*.[5,6,7,8] Considerations to include when select-

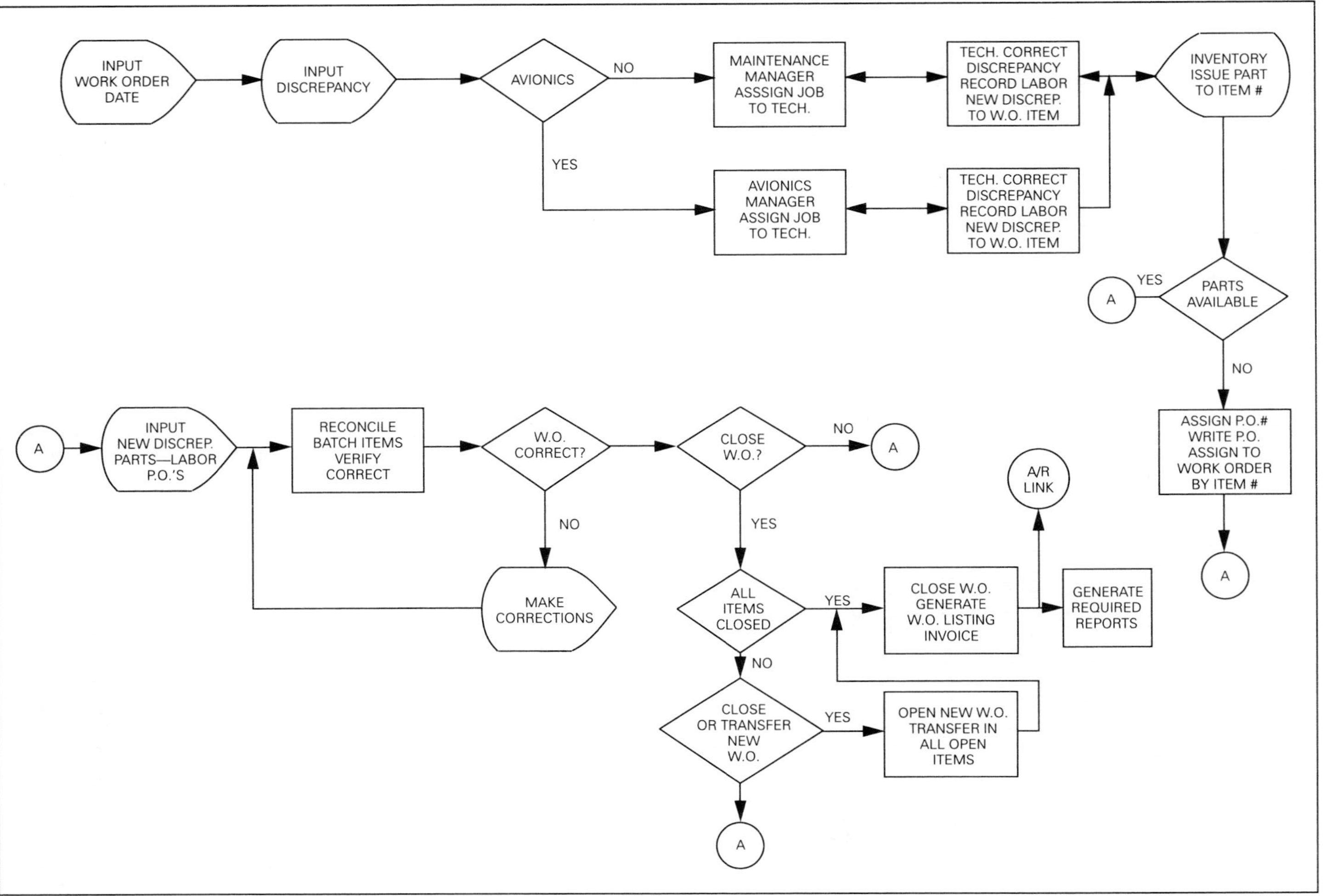

Figure 7.12. Computerware's aircraft maintenance system. By permission, Jerry Hamill, Director, Product Services, Computerware, Inc. Dallas, Texas.

ing a vendor are similar to those when selecting a mainframe computer.

Microcomputers are generally individual machines that can only be used by one person at a time. But if you have several identical machines and one goes down, the work can be done on another. Only one letter-quality printer is needed, though if you use microcomputers for cash registers, you will need at least a dotmatrix printer for each station. Some managers have completely abandoned handwritten reports or dictation and now use a microcomputer to do drafts, and then give their secretary the disk to edit, spellcheck, print, file, and mail. It is also increasingly common to set up microcomputers in a network.

There is concern about losing records through computer or operator failure. Financial records such as monthly statements should be printed on paper. All computer work should have a backup file, which is created automatically by some systems. For really important data, a duplicate disk should be stored somewhere. No computer should cause the manager to abandon previous good habits of saving all basic records—such as register receipts—for at least three years. Power aberrations should be guarded against with a surge protector ($25 and up). Using these precautions, the risk of losing computer data is no more likely than it is for other kinds of office records. One risk from computerization is the computer "virus." This is most likely to be "caught" when one's computer system is connected to other systems. New "virus" problems occur, however, as fast as they are fixed, and this phenomenon must be taken into account.

Other electronic devices available to managers today include fax machines (although most minicomputers, including notebook and laptop versions, come installed with fax/modem capability), cellular telephones, portable electronic appointment schedulers, and beepers. All of these devices are great time savers and help managers stay organized.

Business Security

Confidentiality and Control of Information

Even the smallest business will probably need to keep some information for the manager's use only. Locked file cabinets or keeping key information in a safe or at home are possibilities. With a computer there are controls on the system. For classified information, the user must provide a proper user code or password before the file is made available. Computer "hackers" are forever finding ways to beat such systems and computer manufacturers are forever making them more elaborate. If the company contains a computer hobbyist or fanatic, some monitoring may be advisable. Other personnel probably lack the means or persistence to bother with trying to beat the system.

Types of Losses

Every employer needs to watch for the possibilities of employee theft (as opposed to simple curiosity). Embezzlement is "the fraudulent appropriation of property by a person to whom it has been entrusted."[9,10] Theft can include many levels of sophistication and value including:

- Taking home office supplies
- Giving unofficial "discounts" to friends and relatives
- Making personal toll calls
- Using company time for personal business
- Receiving cash for sales and keeping it
- Lapping—the temporary witholding of receipts, with progressively larger amounts being taken from subsequent payments
- Check-kiting—depositing business funds in a personal account and covering the checks before the bank clears them
- Payroll fraud
- Dummy suppliers and fictitious purchases

- Kickbacks from vendors—purchase of goods at inflated prices with employee and vendor splitting the profit
- Padding of expense accounts
- Charging personal items to the company
- False vouchers for use of petty cash
- False overtime claims
- Use of company postage and photocopiers for personal business

Methods of Combatting Losses

No system where delegated authority exists is foolproof. By definition, other people are in positions of trust. Criminal and credit records can be checked before hiring but that will not identify the potential thief. What employers can do includes:

1. Set a scrupulous example.
2. Establish a climate of accountability.
3. Design an accounting system with sufficient internal controls.
4. Separate the duties of employees so that the same person does not handle incoming checks and cash as well as enter them into the accounts receivable record.
5. Obtain operating statements at least monthly, compare them with previous months, and clarify satisfactorily any anomalies.
6. Look for clues—an employee who scarcely ever leaves the desk and does not take vacations, increases in returned goods, unusual bad-debt write-offs, declines in cash sales, inventory shortages, profit declines, increases in expenses, and slow collections. These items are not necessarily indications of theft, but could be. The manager's close scrutiny of all these areas will act as a deterrent.

Summary

The information system in an aviation business, as in any business, plays a key role in helping management determine whether the business is developing according to plan. As the business grows, information systems will likely need updating. Information should be kept on four subject areas: (1) human resources, (2) financial, (3) material, and (4) aviation operations. Records and record keeping are necessary components of the information system, and they should be tailored to the needs of the individual business. Appendix IV illustrates the forms and source documents likely to be needed. Many computer vendors are now offering systems that can serve all aspects of FBO operations; before embarking on computerization, some analysis of choices and the readiness of the existing system should be considered. Many forms can be produced by computer and potentially save storage space.

The task of analyzing business activity to measure progress should be undertaken regularly. Both financial analysis and a management audit (shown in Appendix III) are useful tools for this; they should be applied to individual profit centers or departments as well as to the business as a whole.

Discussion Topics

1. Name three reasons why a business information system is needed. Which is the most important reason, and why?
2. Outline the principal requirements of an effective business information system for an aviaiton business.
3. What are the major problems in maintaining an effective records system in an aviation business?
4. Outline in a flow diagram the origins, pathways and use of the four key elements of aviation business information.
5. Identify the purpose of each of the following ratios: (a) liquidity, (b) efficiency, (c) leverage, and (d) profitability.
6. Describe at least two examples of the ratios discussed in the preceding question.
7. What is a management audit? Give some reasons why it is not more widely used.

Chapter 8

Operations: Flight Line and Front Desk

Objectives

- ✔ Distinguish differences and similarities in the flight line and the front desk.
- ✔ Describe the various functions of the flight line operation.
- ✔ Give examples and explain the difference between internal and external customers of a fixed base operation.
- ✔ Recognize the areas, issues, and functions aided by a procedures manual.
- ✔ Recognize the factors inherent in making the flight line a profit center for itself and other parts of the operation.

The flight line and the front desk are both show windows and nerve centers for the organization. Operating the two efficiently will contribute tremendously to the success of the business. Efficient and safe operation comes from a clear identification of the functions, positive organization of the resources, and thorough training of assigned personnel.

Introduction

The two operational activities, flight line and front desk, are extremely important in establishing the desired image of the business and in contributing to the efficient flow of business activity. The flight line is that portion of the organization that deals with the customer in or around the aircraft. The front desk is the visible nerve center of the business that deals with the customer who comes into the organization by aircraft, as well as those who drive or walk to the business. The physical location of the front desk is normally in the lobby or reception area of the business and close to the administrative offices.

The two activities, flight line and front desk, are considered as separate entities in this chapter. In many businesses they are clearly separate, while in others one can find a variety of mergers and combinations. To management, it is important that the two be organized according to the physical layout and the overall objectives of the business. In addition to the material in this chapter, job descriptions and necessary skills are described in chapter 5 "Human Resources."

Flight Line

The flight line is that part of the business that greets, services, and sends off transient aircraft traffic; services local tenant customers; and supports other departments of the organization. It normally provides temporary parking for transients, fuel and oil, minor maintenance, and flight servicing for larger aircraft. In the process of performing these duties, the line department may operate fuel trucks, ground power units, tugs, "follow-me" vehicles, pre-heaters, aircraft tow bars, vacuum sweepers, pressure washers, snow removal or ramp sweeper equipment, and lavatory service equipment. They may provide gas and oil trucks, high pressure air, air conditioning (heating and cooling), oxygen recharging, passenger and cargo access ladders, baggage vehicles, lavatory service equipment, water- and food-servicing equipment, de-icing equipment, servicing ladders, and block heaters for aircraft engines.

For local customers, aircraft parking services are generally purchased on a monthly or annual lease. Fuel, oil, and other services are much the same for both transient and based aircraft. In a fully departmentalized organization, the line department may also provide services to the company's own flight department and the maintenance department by parking, fueling, and washing aircraft, as well as providing similar services. Even in smaller organizations, where departmentalization is not complete, it is beneficial to identify any other parts of the business receiving line services.

It is important to recognize at the onset that line operations are primarily a service. The activity is not a product sales business, but a service business. With some exceptions, the price of fuel, oil, etc. is much the same at any airport; the service received is the main selling point and the primary reason for repeat sales. There is a wide variation in the size of line operations at the various airports around the country, the number of aircraft passing through or based at the facility, and the volume of fuel pumped. Indeed, in some businesses the flight line activities are the predominant source of income. Regardless of the difference in size and the contribution of the flight line to total company sales, it should be operated as a profit center. This is accomplished through the application of managerial functions of planning, organizing, directing, and controlling.

Aviation businesses must be concerned first with the pilot and passengers as customers. The customer views your line operation as the entrance to the airport and your business. The image created by the initial contact with the business is likely to be lasting and will be extrapolated to the entire operation. Since the flight line is such a critical part of the business, we will consider the key elements that contribute to the initial image: line layout, line operations, training of personnel, record keeping, and profitability.

Line Layout

To the transient pilot (or local customer) taxiing into a aviation operation, the **line location and layout** will contribute to that important "first" impression. Will the ramp be visible and easy to identify? Will the line be operational and easily accessible? Are signs legible? Do ramp markings stand out adequately? What is the general appearance of the line? Is it neat and orderly or does it look like a graveyard for relics of World War II? Does it appear modern and up-to-date, or does it sprout faded advertisements on the side of aged buildings, misspelled signs, and disorder?

These questions may be answered by the simple process of reviewing the operation through the "eyes of a visitor." The next time you taxi into your ramp, review it critically to see if the layout meets the criteria of being:

- Operational
- Easy to visualize by a transient
- Positive in image
- Practical to support

Naturally, the size of the ramp layout varies depending upon the volume of business and the services offered. Regardless of size, there is a great deal that can be done to develop and maintain a line that is efficient for the volume of business and that presents a neat, clean, attractive image. The physical layout of the flight line or ramp varies drastically with the number and size of aircraft involved. A small airport that's concerned primarily with light training aircraft will probably provide fixed fuel pumps, a hard surface upon which to taxi for service, and tiedown points for the aircraft. A larger facility may have a parking spot adjacent to the main terminal for discharging passengers and improved hard surfaced tiedown areas for the aircraft. Service is provided to the aircraft in either location by fuel trucks. There are three basic considerations that govern the size and configuration of the ramp:

1. The size of the loading area required for each type of aircraft.
2. Aircraft parking configuration; nose in, angled nose in, nose out, angled nose out.
3. Mix of based and transient aircraft.

Within these ramp requirements, aircraft can be grouped adjacent to the terminal in four basic parking systems:

1. **Frontal or linear system.** Aircraft are parked in a line immediately adjacent to the terminal building.
2. **Open-ramp or transporter system.** Aircraft are parked in groups away from the terminal building.
3. **Finger or pier system.** Fingers or protrusions extend out from the terminal building

Aircraft ramp and hangars. Courtesy Beech Aircraft Corporation.

into the ramp area, allowing additional aircraft to be parked using the frontal system.

4. **Satellite system.** Small buildings are located on the ramp and connected to the terminal by means of a tunnel. Aircraft are parked around each satellite building.

At larger airports, aircraft need to be serviced at their respective gate positions. Fueling may be accomplished by trucks, fuel pits, or hydrant systems. Other servicing may be accomplished through fixed installations; mobile equipment is also widely used. Lighting, ramp marking, blast protection, passenger comfort, security, communications, and safety are concerns at all flight lines, and they become even greater concerns with larger aircraft, larger numbers of aircraft, and more passengers.

Line Operations

The operation of a flight line differs according to the size of the airport. The same functions of greeting arriving aircraft, directing, and servicing will be accomplished at any location. As an example of the sequence of events in a line operation, consider what typically happens at a medium-sized airport.

A visitor's initial contact with an organization could be via the UNICOM, a direct radio link between the aircraft and the service organization. This could be via either frequency 122.7 or 122.8 Megahertz (MHz) when there is no tower or on 123.0 MHz when there is a tower in operation. Through the UNICOM the incoming aircraft, while still airborne or on the taxiway, can request fueling assistance, parking directions, inquire about ground transportation facilities and service and obtain other assistance. In general, early communications can greatly facilitate the service stop of an aircraft at a given location.

The ground usage of radio can do much to create an initial favorable impression on the visiting travelers and provide the organization with the information needed to do a superior service job.

The second point of contact with the line may be a vehicle marked "Follow Me" for the larger operations or the line service representative for the smaller ramps. The "Follow-Me" vehicle enables ramp personnel to cover a larger area. The vehicle may have the capacity to provide for immediate transportation of personnel, luggage, or supplies to the hangar or terminal. After assisting in parking the aircraft, the line representative creates a favorable impression by greeting the potential customer, inquiring about needs, and doing as much as possible to facilitate requests. Of course, the basic function of line service personnel is taking orders for fuel, oil, service, and other business needs. This is the primary reason for his or her presence. This, then, is also the ultimate measure of their success.

The layout, construction, and facilities of the flight line deserve the special attention of the manager. The following considerations should be reviewed periodically from an operations standpoint to see if the needs of the organization and the customers are being met.

1. Is the line layout operational from the incoming pilot's point of view?
2. Is the design and construction of the line itself adequate in regards to size, parking areas, safety in access and egress, pavement markings, weight bearing capacity of ground or hard surface?
3. Is the designated traffic flow evident?
4. Are the facilities of the line adequate for the level of activity being serviced adequate number of available and proper size chocks, and adequate tie-down facilities?
5. Are there adequate service facilities to meet expected customer needs? Different types of customers will need different equipment, as described at the start of this section.
6. Is the operational safety of the flight line given special emphasis? Are safe parking

Two line attendants chock the plane and roll out the red carpet. Courtesy Flightcraft, Inc.

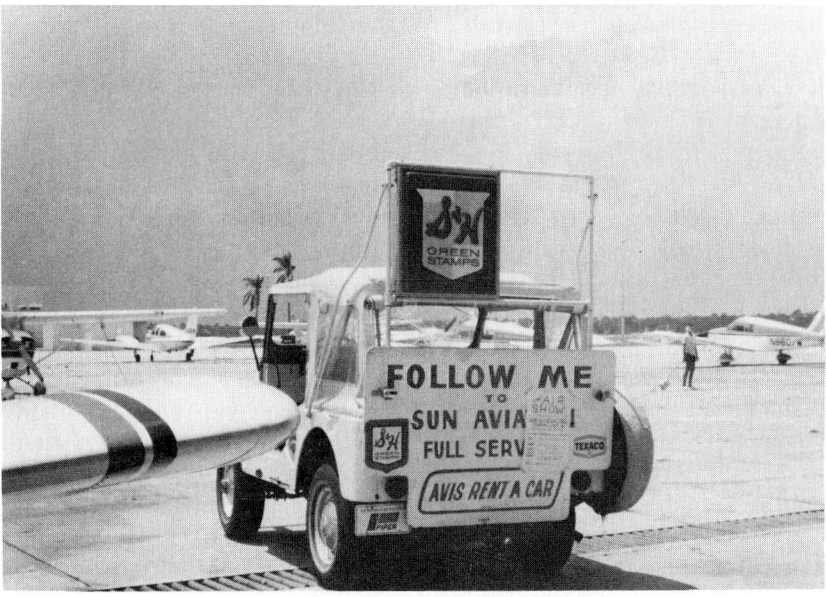

Follow-me vehicle for directing incoming aircraft. Courtesy Sun Aviation, Vero Beach, Florida.

Moving corporate aircraft on the ramp. Courtesy Flightcraft, Inc.

areas for fuel trucks identified and utilized? Are adequate fire extinguishers available, and required grounding facilities present and in use?

7. Are line personnel receiving adequate ongoing training in customer service and safety?

Transportation arrangements for passengers, luggage and cargo will naturally vary, dependent upon the size of operation, the volume of each, and the ramp parking system. Passengers cross the ramp by foot or by vehicle. Smaller airports tend to rely completely on foot passage from the airport to the terminal or hangar. A red carpet is provided at many FBOs. This is especially important for outbound passengers because its role as a doormat helps keep the aircraft clean.

Baggage and cargo handling facilities will likewise vary from motorized ramps, trains, or carts to wheeled luggage racks that the pilot or passenger uses to push luggage to the parking lot. Some of the smaller airports have golfcart-type luggage and personnel carriers or a van or bus to carry passengers and luggage from the distant aircraft—particularly in inclement weather. Many passengers handle their own luggage.

The actual handling and servicing of aircraft by flight line personnel is important to the customer and to the aviation manager. These activities must be accomplished to the customer's satisfaction as well as efficiently and safely. Aircraft handling and servicing can be viewed as several distinct operations. Each requires an organizational structure, personnel training and a high level of safety. The major flight line activities are:

- Directing the movement of aircraft
- Parking aircraft
- Tying down aircraft
- Towing aircraft
- Taxiing aircraft
- Fueling aircraft
- Servicing aircraft systems (oxygen, food, coffee, water, lavatory, and so on)

Procedures are needed in order to prevent injuries to personnel and damage to aircraft as well as to create and maintain an efficient and profitable activity that meets the customers' needs. Federal Aviation Administration Advisory Circular NO: 00- 34A on *Aircraft Ground Handling and Servicing* contains useful data with generally accepted information and safety practices for many of the flight line activities listed above.[1]

Line Administration

The administration of the flight line becomes a critical element in the eyes of the customer and in the ultimate success of the operation. The term administration is used here to embrace both the internal administration of the flight line operation and the overall coordination of the flight line with the total organization. The overall coordination is frequently the responsibility of the "front desk." This important function will be covered in detail in later portions of this chapter.

The administration of the flight line is examined here. The most critical element when a plane arrives at the airport is the impression created by the actions and attitudes of the line personnel. The visual and mental image created by these individuals can do much for the company. The desired image is a friendly, courteous, efficient, and concerned individual that's interested in the welfare of the customer.

During the customer's stay, one way of enhancing efficiency and accomplishing successful servicing of the customer's aircraft is through the use of a simple order form. Figure 8.1 depicts a typical form that may be used for this purpose. This form serves as a reminder to the service personnel, provides specific written instructions, and may be used to obtain additional information about customers and their needs.

The order form becomes a method of ensuring that the desired service has been performed and provides a basic record of what was accomplished. The internal paperwork to record and charge the customer for all services rendered will vary depending upon the method of payment. Cash, charge, or credit card may be used to settle the bill.

One method of handling this transaction is through the use of a Line Invoice as illustrated in figure 8.2. This form is provided by Piper Aircraft to meet just this need.

The third phase of handling a flight line customer is the "send-off." The departure of a customer, although frequently not recognized as it should be, is as important as the other phases of the visit and should be specifically recognized by the organization and by the line personnel.

Every effort should be made to ease and facilitate the departure. Rolling out the red carpet, baggage help, last minute check on the adequacy of the service, help with chocks and tie-downs, start up, taxi assistance, and a cheery wave will all influence the customer to return for future business.

Training Line Personnel

The flight line is often the place where entry level personnel and part-timers are employed, because of the menial nature of some of the work—washing aircraft and pumping fuel. Because it is generally the customer's first contact with the FBO, it is critically important that these junior-level staff are trained to be professional service providers.

Two key areas of training are needed—safety and customer service. Additionally, line service personnel need training in dealing with unexpected contingencies and obtaining more senior help as necessary. A number of fuel companies and other organizations offer detailed training manuals for the safety purpose.[2,3] An individual FBO should consider its level of training needs and select accordingly from such sources. At air carrier airports, recent changes in Federal Aviation Administration requirements under the Code of Federal Regulations, Title 139 mean that FBO line employees must undergo specific training.[4]

MILLER AVIATION, INC.
LINE SERVICE REQUEST

REGISTRATION NUMBER ______________ ARRIVAL TIME ______________________ DATE ____ / ____ / ____

AIRCRAFT TYPE ______________ ESTIMATED DEPARTURE TIME __________ DATE ____ / ____ / ____

NAME / ADDRESS OF REGISTERED OWNER: ______________

FLIGHT CREW NAME(S): ______________

LOCAL CONTACT: ______________

LOCAL PHONE: ______________

METHOD OF PAYMENT: ____ EXXON ____ MULTI SERVICE ____ AMERICAN EXPRESS ____ VISA ____ MASTER CARD ____ CHECK ____ CASH

FEDERAL EXCISE TAX EXEMPT NUMBER: ______________ SALES TAX EXEMPT NUMBER: ______________

FUEL REQUIREMENTS

TYPE: ____ 100LL ____ JET 'A'

PRIST ____ YES ____ NO

QUANTITY ________ GALLONS INTO ________ TANK

QUANTITY ________ GALLONS INTO ________ TANK

QUANTITY ________ GALLONS INTO ________ TANK

QUANTITY ________ GALLONS INTO ________ TANK

OIL REQUIREMENTS

TYPE ______________ WEIGHT ______________ QUANTITY ______________

PARKING REQUIREMENTS

FROM ____ /____ /____ THROUGH ____ /____ /____ ____HANGAR ____TIEDOWN

DEICE

________ HEATED HANGAR ________ HOT GLYCOL

I hereby authorize the deicing of the Aircraft #________ with a deicing solution containing a hot mixture of 50% glycol and 50% water. I understand that deicing is not anti-icing, and that I, as the pilot of the above aircraft and/or the duly authorized representative of ______________ have final responsibility to check wings, control surfaces, and fuselage of the aircraft to determine whether all snow, slush, and ice has been removed. This will acknolwdge that I have done so and that the deicing has been performed to my satisfaction.

Pilot Signature or Authorized Representative ______________ Invoice # ________

OTHER SERVICES REQUIRED

____ CATERING ____ AUTO RENTING ____ LIMOUSINE ____ TAXI

____

MAO59A KAC 11/27/87

Figure 8.1. Courtesy of Miller Aviation Corporation, Edwin A. Link Field, Johnson City, NY 13790.

LINE INVOICE

PIPER
Aviation Center

AIRCRAFT NO. N–	MAKE	NON-SCHED. AIRLINE	TACH.
NAME			CR. CARD NO.
ADDRESS			METER STOP
CITY	STATE	ZIP	START
			TOTAL

WRITTEN BY	DATE	LINE INVOICE NO.	N-CONTROL NO.	KEY
	/ /	10833	0000	I

QUANTITY		DESCRIPTION	KEY	ACCT. NO.	AMOUNT	KEY
80	100	KERO				
		GALS. AVGAS @ ¢	C	700		−
		GALS. AVGAS-FLT. DEPT.	C	701		−
		QTS. AVIATION OIL ______ WT. @ ¢	C	700		−
		QTS. AVIATION OIL ______ WT.-FLT. DEPT	C	701		−
		GALS. GAS-TRUCK @ ¢	C	701		−
		GALS. GAS - COURTESY CAR @ ¢	C	701		−
		QTS. OIL-TRUCK WGT. BRAND @ ¢	C	701		−
		QTS. OIL - COURTESY CAR WGT. BRAND @ ¢	C	701		−
		NIGHTS-TIE DOWN @	C	706		−
		PILOT SUPPLIES	C	707		−
			C			−
			C			−
		TAX		228:		−
CHARGE SALES – CUSTOMER NO.			I	111:		+
RECEIVED BY:		SOURCE 210 CHARGE 330 CASH				S
X		CASH ON HAND		105:		+

FORM PI-137 THE REYNOLDS & REYNOLDS CO., CELINA, OHIO LITHO IN U.S.A.

Figure 8.2. Line invoice form developed by Piper Aircraft Company for its dealers.

The supervisors must go through an approved fuel service course and must then, in turn, train other line employees.

Customer Service Training. Everyone within the organization must realize that they play a part in customer service. Whether it is the line-person fueling the airplanes, the receptionist, or the FBO owner—customer service must be first and foremost in everyone's mind.

One important concept of customer training is defining the customer. Too often we think only of the individual coming through the door, or taxiing up to the ramp to utilize our business, as the customer. Customers can also include vendors, visitors, and other employees. Other employees are usually considered the "internal" customers.

Example: If the chief mechanic has procrastinated in completing the paperwork on an aircraft repair, thereby delaying the airplane's return to the line, this can impact the flight instructor and student pilot who intended to use it for a flight lesson. Not only is the student pilot, usually considered a typical or "external" customer, affected, but the flight instructor who works for the same company has been impacted as well.

Employees who are rude to each other or who do not honor each other's deadlines and time schedules, impact the entire operation.

Telephone skills are an important element in customer service training. Being polite, friendly, and professional on the telephone requires a certain amount of practice, but the benefits can be tremendous. Knowing how and when to put people on hold, how to take a good message, how to tactfully deal with an angry or upset customer, are all important skills to know.

Whether general aviation is in a down period, with few people actively engaged in flight activity, or the industry is blooming and business is brisk, customer service can be the one element ensuring customer satisfaction, which means repeat business.

Service Array and Profitability

The ability of a flight line to generate profits for the organization varies depending upon many factors, such as size, volume of aircraft traffic, competition, management, operative personnel and the general economy. Regardless of these factors, the flight line should be operated as a profit center. On the smallest field, the records should reflect the income-cost profit picture for the line operation. During past periods of economic depression, experience has proved that for the large majority of general aviation businesses around the country, the fueling operations of the flight line provided the "bread and butter" income that enabled them to survive. Large metropolitan airports have found that it is difficult to operate a general aviation activity without a fuel concession. Where the airport authority or city retained the fueling rights for themselves, the airport has frequently been plagued by a turnover of general aviation businesses.

Line operations and fuel service can be profitable if properly managed. The area is becoming more competitive in terms of self-service fuel: and customer courtesies, such as coffee, restrooms, and magazines. Quality service seems likely to continue as the most important consideration. This means that good administration, good layout, and good employees rather than gimmicks will assure consumer satisfaction.

Fueling

The fueling activities perceived by the aviation customer are only the tip of the iceberg when the whole process of supplying safe fuel in a safe manner is considered. Owing to a number of recent changes in the fuel situation, this topic requires special attention. Numerous publications by the National Fire Protection Association, the American Petroleum Institute, and the Federal Aviation Administration address guidelines on the safe handling and storage of fuel at airports. Certain economic aspects are summarized here.

Trends in Autogas Use

The FAA has gradually approved the use through Supplemental Type Certificates (STCs) of cheaper autogas in more and more reciprocating engines to replace 80 octane avgas.[5] Some aircraft, such as ultralights, were designed from the outset to use auto gas or "mogas."

The trend toward mogas is good news for aircraft owners because of cost savings. But it has been bad news both for FBOs and for government agencies collecting flowage fees or fuel taxes. The declining demand for 80 octane fuel (caused by many factors) means that many airports have the greatest difficulty in obtaining fuel suitable for light aircraft, thus strengthening the market for alternatives such as auto gas.

If the number of auto gas users goes up, there will be an increasing economic effect unless procedures change at airports. The volume of auto gas being brought by car or truck to airplanes and the increasing numbers of pilots transferring it by diverse means from car to plane represent a growing safety hazard at airports. Some FBO owners are now providing auto gas as a fuel sale alternative.

Self-fueling

The trend towards self-fueling is not just represented by ultralight operators bringing five gallons at a time to the airport in their cars. More and more corporations with based aircraft are starting to supply their own fuel.[6] The Federal Aviation Administration's guidelines and individual public airport requirements in regard to airport minimum standards can be used to ensure that these operations are safely run.[7] But the FAA's requirements with respect to competition at federally funded airports means that as long

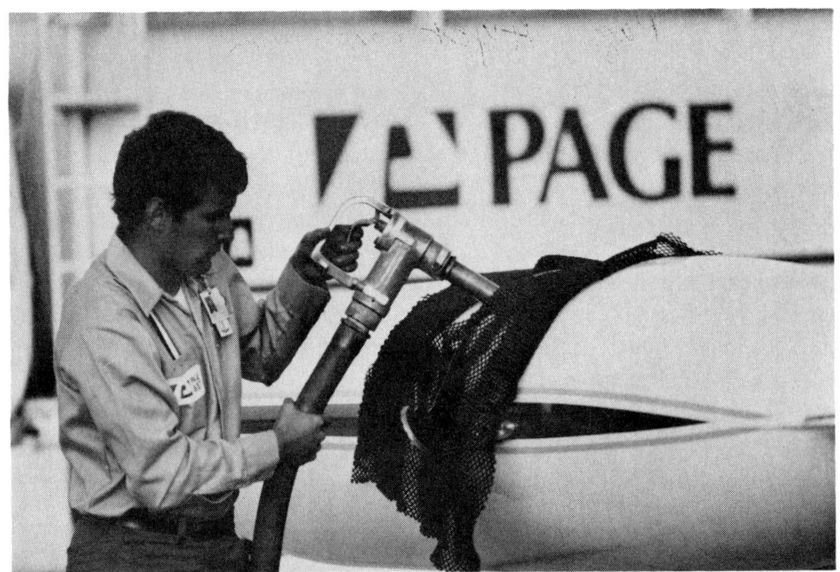

Careful fueling of a plane. Courtesy Page Avjet Corporation.

Fueling the plane with great care. Courtesy Flightcraft, Inc.

as standards are met, corporate or other self-fueling must be permitted.[8]

A survey by NATA revealed that of 286 FBOs polled 31 percent identified 247 self-fueling operations at their airports.[9] Some 61 percent of the respondents indicated that over 50,000 gallons of fuel were being self-pumped. This constitutes losses of $50,000 per year in revenues and $15,000 in profits.

An NATA Task Force polled 112 corporate self-fuelers asking their reasons for the change and found the following results:[10]

- Better price—87%
- More control, avoid misfueling, invoice errors, lack of detail—65%
- Lack of timely service—49%
- Better aircraft security—43%
- No turbine fuel, had to install own—19%

Only 42 of the 112 consulted with the FBOs at the field before deciding on self-fueling. Clearly, FBOs need to present a better customer service image to their corporate clients.

The FBO seeking to persuade an airport-owner landlord not to permit self-fueling may be able to present the best case by demonstrating the company's high level of expertise and quality facilities. Early discussions with each corporate-based aircraft owner—staying close to the customer on needs, frustrations and plans—are also very important.

Front Desk

The front desk is the nerve center of the aviation organization. As such, it represents the organization to the customer, to the public, and to the employees. It deals with the individual who comes into the organization by aircraft as well as the person who drives or walks into the business. As the hub for all business conducted by the company, it is the reception desk and the public relations center for the company. It coordinates business transactions with all the departments and strives to see that the customer receives the most efficient and courteous service possible. Its secondary goal is to ensure that all company procedures and guidelines are followed in achieving a successful front-desk operation.

As with many other aspects of the aviation business, the functions of a front desk must be provided for by every organization. The very small "mom-and-pop" operation may not have a formal reception desk, but individuals find that they serve the same function. The majority of middle-sized airports and most general aviation businesses of any size have a front desk. The very large airport will have a passenger terminal and then each fixed base operation will have its own front desk.

Procedures

As the hub of the business operation, one goal of the front desk is to ensure adherence to all company procedures and guidelines. This can be achieved very efficiently by developing and providing a front desk procedures manual. In Appendix V, the outline of such a manual is shown.[11]

Transient Traffic

From time to time an FBO should conduct customer surveys. These may relate to satisfaction and performance, to new products or services and how they are viewed, or to problems such

Front desk. Courtesy Beech Aircraft Corporation.

as noise-sensitive areas. The FBO might seek to identify key users of the airport as a first step in assessing its contribution to the local or regional economy. Whatever the purpose, based aircraft owners and other local customers, such as regular charter customers, are usually easy to identify from tie-down lists, etc. But transient operators may not be so easily identified. For this reason it is strongly recommended that a detailed transient log be kept specifying:

- Company, if applicable
- Phone number, address of pilot in command
- Number of people in flight
- Where from today
- Where to when leaving
- Trip purpose at this airport
- Comments on service quality

The log book should be placed prominently at the front desk, and personnel should be trained to ask all transient pilots to complete it. If many pilots do not enter the building, then the line staff should have a similar log for them to fill out at the same time as fuel orders. The log can also provide the manager with day-to-day information on activity and possible problems, allowing a quick follow-up with appropriate staff or customers.

Flight line airplane preflight. Courtesy Parks College.

Related Services

Many FBOs make part of their revenue from activities other than direct aviation services. If this is the case, the front desk staff will likely be the information-givers, schedulers, and coordinators of these services. Predominant non-aviation activities include rental cars and auto parking, followed by small stores and restaurants. More FBOs are entering the hotel/motel business; a hotel near the Teterboro, N.J. airport caters specifically to aviation and offers such items as weather information at the hotel.

FBOs who do offer only aviation services will still find themselves being asked for help on how to find ground transportation and places to stay, to eat, and places to be entertained. Many merchants give discount coupons and display materials for visitor use; the front desk may be a good place for these.

Flight Planning and Services

Pilot Services. As front desk services become more competitive, some FBOs are extending their range of accomodations to pilots and passengers. Traditionally, an area with chairs for flight-planning purposes is offered. A telephone link to the Flight Service Station will generally be provided. It is becoming more commonplace to also offer computerized weather information.

Flight Service Stations

Pilots are able to avail themselves of flight conditions on various radio stations especially catering to aeronautical and nautical weather, and they may also receive in-person briefings from FAA Flight Service Stations (FSS). Pilots not within reach of the nation's FSSs may get weather briefings and file flight plans by phone or computer by contacting a FSS.

The ground support systems for weather and flight planning will change substantially over the next 15 years as part of the National Airspace System Plan (NAS).[12] A consolidation of flight service stations into just 61 automated stations is almost complete. Many of the new stations will not be at the same locations. Most pilots using the FSS system will do so not on a walk-in basis but through remote terminals or by phone.

Weather Information Systems

This planned substitution of indirect contact for direct contact under the FAA program is already being supplemented by the private sector. Advances in this sector are substantially altering the FBO role in flight planning and preflight weather information. A number of private vendors have developed weather automated systems for private clients, and increasing numbers of FBOs are offering these services.

Other Pilot and Passenger Services

Some FBOs are now offering additional attractions such as exercise rooms, sleeping rooms, meeting and conference rooms, and clerical support services. As business/corporate/private aircraft travel increases, growth in specialized high quality front-desk services will continue.

Facility Appearance

The general appearance and upkeep of the facility and its surroundings can say a lot about the business. A lobby or lounge that is not kept clean and in a general state of disorder does not give a good first impression. Maintenance shops where spare parts litter the floor and tools are left out in the open in a haphazard matter, do not instill confidence in aircraft owners as to the type of work done in that shop. A prospective new student pilot who is met by individuals in the office who are indifferent, and who notes that the airplanes on the ramp look like they have not been washed in months, may be reluctant to learn to fly at this operation, if at all.

Poor appearance can and does have tremen-

General aviation waiting area. Courtesy Beech Aircraft Corporation.

dous detrimental effects on potential business. Thus it should not be treated lightly or dismissed.

Example: Students from an aviation management class at a university in Atlanta, Georgia were asked to select an FBO in the metropolitan Atlanta area and critique it. In submitting their written and oral reports to the class, the majority of students were amazed at the poor customer service attitudes and the general condition of the facilities they visited. One student saw incidents of unsafe fueling, lack of preflighting, a dissatisfied aircraft owner returning an aircraft radio he had brought in earlier for repair that still did not work, and ran into a student whose lesson had just been cancelled because the flight instructor had elected to take a charter flight instead. And, all of this occurred in a one hour visit!

Summary

The flight line and front desk are the first points of contact for aviation customers arriving by air and by ground. The impression created by each is strongly influenced by the physical layout, the level of upkeep, and the knowledge and friendliness of the personnel. Three factors generally create a strong impression: (1) the initial reception, (2) the provision of service, and (3) the sendoff. These characteristics affect the ultimate profitability of the whole business, since the flight line and front desk not only serve customers directly but also refer prospective clients to other parts of the business such as the repair shop.

In many aviation service businesses the true "hub" or nerve center of the operation is the front desk. The individuals serving here coordinate many customer-related activities as well as other aspects of the total business. The functions of the front desk should be based on a procedures manual that ensures a consistent level of quality regardless of who is on duty, and that contains rapid reference to key company policies on how to deal with various customer and other transactions.

Discussion Topics

1. Distinguish between the flight line and the front desk. What do they have in common?
2. Name six functions of the flight line. Discuss the importance of each to the customer.
3. What are the pros and cons of different aircraft parking layouts?
4. What should be the principal objectives of a flight line training program? Why?
5. What kinds of employees are typically assigned to the flight line and what problems does this create?
6. What factors will enable the flight line to generate profits for itself and other parts of the business?
7. What areas, issues, and functions can be aided by a procedures manual? By operations checklists?
8. What is meant by saying that the reception desk is the nerve center of the aviation business?

Chapter 9

Flight Operations

Objectives

- ✔ Understand the requirements necessary for an air taxi operator to be approved for Part 135 operations.
- ✔ Recognize the differences between air taxi and commuter operations.
- ✔ Discuss the problems and opportunities inherent in a flight instruction program.
- ✔ Describe several opportunities involving actual flight operations to ensure a profitable business.
- ✔ Explain the role flight simulators play in a flight instruction program, including cost benefits to both the business and the student.

Introduction

Types of Flights

Flight operations refer to the provision of aircraft and/or personnel for flight services and the monitoring of these activities to ensure profitability. The reader should refer to the "Taxonomy of General Aviation" shown in chapter 1, figure 1.4. The following types of flight service occur:

Air Transportation

- Charter
- Air taxi
- Aircraft rental
- Aircraft leasing
- Aircrew and ferry services
- Air cargo
- Air ambulance

Use of Aircraft for an Activity While Airborne

- Flight instruction
- Aerial patrol—powerline, pipeline, forest, highway, border, and so on
- Aerial advertising—banner towing
- Aerial application such as crop dusting, seeding, fertilizing
- Sight-seeing services
- Helicopter operations
- Gliding and sailplaneing
- Ballooning
- Parachuting
- Ultralights
- Aircraft demonstrations
- Medical evacuation
- Search and rescue
- Fish spotting
- Aerial photography

These lists show only some of the types of flight service that may be offered. Each must be considered in terms of what types of client are involved—business and executive, other commercial clients, flight students, or sport and recreational flyers.

Market Trends

Flight operations constitute a key profit center for many FBOs. Numerous services can be offered, some highly compatible with one another and others perhaps less so.

In the late 1970s and 1980s, the U.S. general aviation industry saw a massive reduction in aircraft shipments and a decline in active aircraft. Some causes were discussed in chapter 1. As a result, the profitable FBO must constantly be alert for new flight operation market opportunities. In recent years FBOs around the country have become involved for the first time in such diverse areas as:

- Air ambulance
- Airline aircraft servicing
- Aerobatics
- Aircraft management
- Aerial fire fighting
- Air taxi service
- and many others.

System Issues Affecting Flight Operations

The nation's busiest airports and airspace have become more congested in the 1990s. This is due to airline traffic growth, fewer air traffic controllers, airline schedules focused on peak periods, and hub development that causes more landings and takeoffs per passenger trip. As a result, various pricing and management strategies have evolved to reduce the access of general aviation aircraft to certain airports and airspace areas in order to reserve space for airline aircraft. This trend particularly affects business aviation, where passengers often seek the same major city destinations as the airlines. Rural and recreational general aviation is less severely impacted. The general aviation industry and flight operators such as FBOs, need to be cognizant of this trend in order to ensure that general aviation continues to have access to the aviation system.

Choosing What Services to Offer

Certain types of flight operation will be in heavy demand at a certain airport. For example, an island or resort community may have a strong demand for air taxi and sight-seeing trips. A metropolitan airport may have a high level of business charters and rentals, whereas a rural airport may be extensively involved in aerial patrol and agricultural application. Because of the varied types of aircraft required for many of the more specialized functions, the FBO will have to be selective about what services to offer. Where several FBOs are on the same field, they may each specialize in specific areas and avoid direct competition. Also, on many fields small specialized operators handle just one type of activity, such as a parachute center, glider service, aerial photography, crop dusting, etc. Whether these single-service operators can be defined as FBOs is debatable. FAA guidelines do not specify a minimum amount of services in order to justify the title, but some individual airport minimum standards do.[1] The choice of what to offer depends on the clients' needs, the services offered elsewhere on the field or in the region, the owners' preferences, and the expected profit from each area.

Organization

Organizing the aviation business for safe, profitable flight operations is one of the most important aspects of the entire company. Goals and objectives must be identified, structure formulated, responsibilities assigned, duties outlined and understood, rules, regulations and procedures established, and controls provided in order to ensure that flight operations goals are achieved safely and profitably.

For each of the major flight categories listed above, this chapter reviews the nature of the operation and its requirements.

Air Transportation

Benefits

The use of private business aircraft as a means of transportation is increasing faster than many other segments of general aviation. Since the Airline Deregulation Act of 1978, scheduled passenger service, while increasing in quantity, has diminished in terms of available non-stop flights. The reason for this is the adoption by major and national airlines of a "hub-and-spoke" system of operation.

While some airlines such as Delta have been using the hub-and-spoke concept for over 40 years, for many others deregulation triggered the growth of this concept.[2] At the time of deregulation, the major carriers had less than 50 percent of their total domestic capacity devoted to hub flying. By 1987 these same carriers allocated over 80 percent of their domestic seat miles to hub-and-spoke flying.[3]

Reasons from the airline point of view for hub development include:

1. Scheduling efficiency—fewer aircraft to serve the same points.
2. New market synergy—one new spoke added to a hub adds many new markets.
3. Market control—connections more easily made on the same carrier through the same hub point.
4. Market fragmentation—less service available for small points and greater number of connections to complete the trip.

In addition to hub and spoke implications, the initial reduction in airline fares after deregulation has generally been replaced by substantial fare increases. The cost is especially greater when the ticket is booked without much advance notice, as many business trips are.

These factors such as hub development and higher air fares combine to make private air transportation comparatively more appealing to the busy executive. Therefore, airline deregulation appears to have been a major factor behind the growth of corporate aircraft ownership and air taxi and charter activity in many parts of the country.

Many feature articles have been written in the past few years that address the benefits of business flying. These benefits include:

1. Increasing the executive's effective time by as much as 100 percent.
2. Permitting en route business conferences to be held in privacy.
3. Reducing overnight hotel and meal costs by eliminating awkward airline connections and circuitous routing.
4. Ability to access over 10,000 small communities compared with a few hundred by airline and far fewer with nonstop flights.
5. Ability to increase contact between managers through ease of travel between branches.
6. Ability to run an enterprise with fewer corporate staff because of mobility to all divisions.
7. No lost baggage or missed flights.

For many corporations, the gradual increase in use of private business aircraft follows this progression:

1. Airline trip is made involving multiple connections, take-off delays, and overnight stops to accomplish business.
2. Urgently needed business trip is required and business traveler cannot get there in time and back using airlines.
3. Charter flight is booked through local FBO.

For several years, **Business and Commercial Aviation** has reported studies of aviation use by the nation's top companies—the Fortune 1000. Year after year, the aircraft-using companies, which now number about half the group, have about 80 to 90 percent of the gross sales, the profit, and the return on investment and about twice the labor productivity. The nonaircraft operating half of the group have only 10 to 15 percent of the performance. There appears to be a causal connection.[4] To the aviation business, capturing the local demand for business air travel can be a rewarding and profitable activity.

Charter and Air Taxi

Charter operations are the nonscheduled flights that carry passengers or cargo when the party receives the exclusive use of the aircraft. Charter agreements may be negotiated by certificated air carriers, as they often are for tourist flights, or by general aviation businesses.

Air-taxi flight activity describes the semi-scheduled and nonscheduled commercial flights of general aviation businesses. Individuals purchase air transportation as they would a taxicab. Light-to-medium weight aircraft are used to carry passengers and cargo to and from the small communities that do not have enough traffic for scheduled airline service and where scheduled airlines cannot serve the needs of the customer.

Aircraft. The aircraft utilized for charter work varies from a large jet transporting a group on an intercontinental trip to a light, single-engine aircraft carrying two business people from one community to another. Air taxi flying is normally accomplished with light-to-medium general aviation aircraft, normally twin engine types.

Rules and regulations. Basic operating procedures for charter and air taxi flights are regulated by the Federal Aviation Administration. General aviation businesses conduct charter and air taxi flights as a form of commercial flying regulated primarily by Part 135 of the Federal Aviation Regulations (see Appendix VII, sample, *Air Taxi Operations Manual*). However, the rules for Part 135 Operations are becoming much closer to the Part 121 requirements, and this trend is expected to continue.[5]

In charter operations, the manager is selling air transportation to meet a customer's specific need. The aircraft and pilot are provided to the customer according to agreement for his exclusive use. For example, Allied Petro-Chemical may call and charter a Cessna 401 to carry and return two of its sales executives on a vendor call from Memphis to Nashville. In complying with Part 135 and other pertinent regulations, the manager must ensure the following:

1. The receipt of an air taxi/commercial operator (ATCO) operating certificate.
2. A current manual for the use and guidance of flight, ground operations, and maintenance personnel in conducting operations.
3. Procedures for locating each flight for which an FAA flight plan is not filed.
4. Exclusive use of at least one aircraft that meets the requirements of the operations specifications.

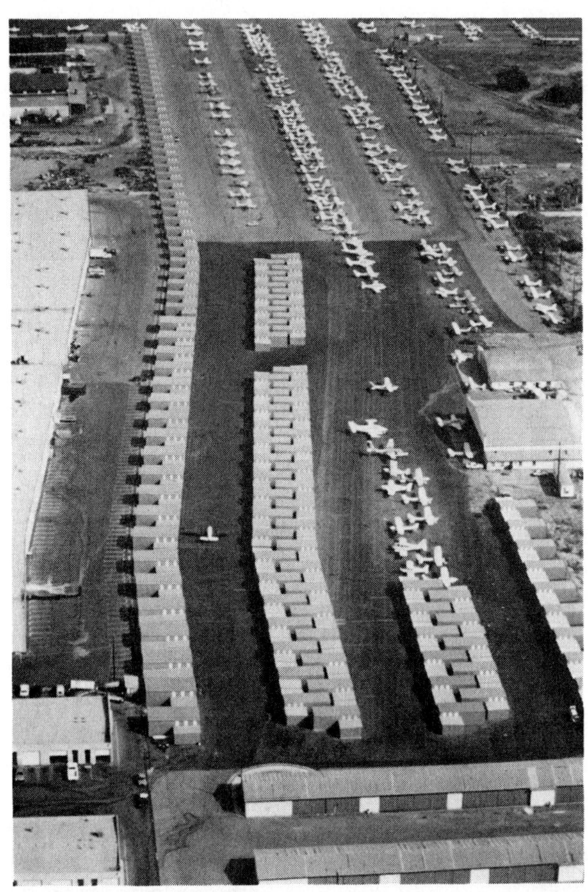

Ramp and tiedown area showing portable modular T-Hangars. Courtesy Port-a-Port, Inc.

5. Qualified aircrew personnel with appropriate and current certificates and the necessary recency experience.
6. Maintenance of required records and submission of mechanical reliability reports.
7. Compliance with the operating rules prescribed in FAR Part) 91 and 135, including:
   - Airworthiness check
   - Area limitations on operations
   - Available operating information for pilots
   - Passenger briefing
   - Oxygen requirements
   - Icing limitations
   - Night operations
   - Fuel requirements, VFR and IFR
   - VFR operations
   - IFR operations

These requirements reflect only a summary of the pertinent sections of Part 135. The reader is referred to the Federal Aviation Regulation for complete details of the requirements.[6]

Aircraft Rental

In this kind of flight operation, the manager is engaged in renting aircraft to the customers who provide their own pilot for the flight. All types of planes may be rented, although most businesses utilize light- and medium-weight general aviation aircraft. In providing and controlling rental activity, the manager is primarily concerned with:

1. Establishing rental rates that will cover all costs and provide a planned profit.
2. Clear and adequate hull and liability insurance.
3. Providing administrative procedures for handling rental activity.
4. Positive renter-pilot identification.
5. Evidence of renter-pilot qualification and competence:
   - Past experience and proficiency
   - Valid pilot certificate
   - Current medical certificate
   - Flight checkout.

Accounting procedures to control income and expenses.

Leasebacks

The Economic Recovery Tax Act of 1981 established new incentives for business equipment acquisition. As a result there was a period where it was advantageous for a business aircraft owner to lease his aircraft to an FBO and rent it back when needed. This situation has changed and expert tax advice should be obtained to address the pros and cons of a leaseback for a given situation. It may help an owner who does not need his aircraft all the time. For the FBO, the advantages include not having to invest large sums in new aircraft and the ability to keep later-model aircraft on the flight line.[7]

The requirements to qualify for this are precise, and anyone considering it should consult with a tax specialist. In cases where it is feasible, it provides unique advantages for both owner and FBO.

Aircrew and Ferry Services

Providing aircrew services to the customer may take various forms. They range from an occasional trip with a non-instrument-rated pilot customer who needs instrument capability for a specific trip, to the corporate customer who has a large twin (but no pilots) and contracts for full crew (pilot, co-pilot and flight attendant) to meet his schedule. In providing this kind of service, the aviation manager should regard it as a specific business opportunity to be approached on a sound economic basis.

Operational guidelines and procedures should be developed, as well as administrative methods and controls, adequate insurance coverage, and a provision made for the routine flow of information on income and costs that can be examined regularly to ensure its profitability.

In addition to providing pilot services, the business may offer to completely maintain and operate an aircraft for the customer. For the nonpilot business person, this may offer an economical way of operating his aircraft while at the same time enabling the aviation business to obtain greater utilization of its personnel and facilities. To assure a smoothly working arrangement, the manager should develop a contractual relationship that will clearly delineate the responsibilities of both parties.

Air Cargo

Air cargo (freight and mail) is important to all levels of air transportation providers, and there are a number of all-cargo scheduled airlines. General aviation plays a key role in this area with activities such as transporting cancelled checks, shipping urgently needed factory parts to keep a production line going, express small package delivery, and so on. The size of aircraft may range from the single-engine prop to a plane able to accommodate containers. Very often small amounts of freight or mail will accompany passengers in the same compartment.

This appears to be a growing market for any cargo that is high-value/low-bulk or any cargo that is time-sensitive, such as documents and perishables. An air taxi operator may coordinate with a metropolitan courier service to provide door-to-door small package service in markets that are already covered for passenger service.

Air Ambulance/Medical Evacuation

This area has been growing rapidly due in part to the disparity in quality of medical care between rural facilities and metropolitan hospitals, some of which are unique in the nation for their specialized research and equipment. Custom-remodeled aircraft that can take stretchers and supply in-flight medical care are required. This type of operation is becoming subject to increasing scrutiny and regulation.

As medical care becomes increasingly sophisticated and specialized, and as hospital competition grows, services are a growing market area for the FBO. Not every FBO will want to enter this market.

An example of an FBO initiating air ambulance service is Seattle Flight Service's development in the early 1980s of flight support for Airlift Northwest. Seattle Flight Service, now defunct, and its successor, Seattle Jet Center, also defunct, were instrumental in contracting with a group of Seattle hospitals—Harborview Medical Center, University Hospital, Providence Hospital, Children's Hospital and Virginia Mason Hospital and Medical Center—to provide air ambulance service throughout Washington, Montana, Idaho and southeastern Alaska. The service agency, Airlift Northwest, is now contracting with Seattle Jet Center's successor for flight support from several fixed wing and helicopter craft, and the organization has grown to about 65 employees. This service is unique in the region and enables burn and trauma victims from outlying places to reach state-of-the-art medical care within hours.

Other Commercial Flight Operations

Aerial Patrol

Flight operations for the purpose of pipeline, powerline, forest, highway, and border patrol are fairly widely used, although the actual flight activity is normally restricted geographically and seasonally. Forest patrols cover specific wooded areas and are most active in a dry season. Power and pipeline patrols cover designated lines and may be most active following heavy rainfalls and inclement weather. Highway and border patrol flights are assigned specific sectors and normally have missions related to traffic, construction, illegal entry, and so forth. Many of these flights are flown by uniformed police or border patrol personnel in aircraft owned by a federal or state agency. There is, however, an opportunity for general aviation businesses to provide maintenance services under a contractual arrangement with enforcement agencies for the support of these aircraft.

One opportunity for conducting flight activities that many aviation businesses consider is the Aerial Fire Detection Services for the United States Department of Agriculture (USDA) Forest Service. The various national forests throughout the United States develop air detection plans for their areas of responsibility. These plans establish the procedures covering air operations, including the base of operations, pilot and aircraft requirements, required flight patterns, flight frequency, the fire season, and general flight operating procedures.

The Aerial Fire Detection Requirements are advertised by the contracting officer for the particular area and the detailed specifications are identified. A typical contract covers the following items:

- Scope of contract
- Descriptions of operation base
- Flight paths
- Flight speed
- Observer personnel
- Governmental furnished equipment
- Aircraft specifications
- Pilot qualifications
- Flight duty limitations (pilot)
- Flight time requirements
- Inspection and approval of aircraft and pilots
- Safety requirements
- Flight time measurement
- Method of payment

A regional air officer of the Forest Service must inspect and approve the successful bidder's aircraft and pilots. The contracting officer or his or her representative will authorize and regulate the standby and flight time schedule. Actual flight time will be entered on Forest Service Form 6500–122, Daily Flight Report and Invoice, and submitted by the contractor. The typical contract will contain a minimum guarantee per year in dollars, an hourly bid rate for flight time, and the rate allowed for standby time.

Power line and pipeline patrol activity are normally conducted under contractual arrangements similar to those used by forest patrols. They are typically low-level flights providing visual inspection of cross-country pipelines or electric power lines. Patrol activity of this type is normally accomplished in high-wing aircraft with good visual capability. Relatively slow speeds are desirable with adequate power for emergency needs. Frequently the Super Cub, Cessna 182, and the Helio Courier are used for this type of work, although other model aircraft are being used, including helicopters.

The aviation manager in this situation is concerned with equipment selection, pilot selection and training; procedures for scheduling, conducting, and controlling flights, insurance requirements, administrative paperwork, and the profitability of the operation.

In many cases of aerial patrol, the helicopter can be an asset because of its ability to safely handle low-altitude flight, hovering, and landing in restricted areas. The decision to invest in helicopter rental or charter equipment is a major one because of the substantially higher cost of the aircraft and the high level of skill needed to operate it.

Aerial Application

Agricultural flying is a term used to describe the use of aircraft in the interest of agriculture, forestry, fishery, and public health, where its use is primarily a tool for making observations or applying product. Most agricultural flying is aerial application: the distribution from an aircraft of agricultural chemicals or seeds. The aerial applicator is one of the most versatile and highly trained specialists. He must be a business person as well as a top-flight pilot who is knowledgeable in chemistry, physics, agronomy, entomology, farming, engineering, meteorology, and cost accounting. A great deal of agricultural application work is done at a height of 5 to 10 feet above the target, with concern for the following factors:

1. Accurate marking for successive straight swath runs.
2. Application rate, or the total quantity of material applied per acre, depending on the:
   - output of each nozzle
   - number of nozzles
   - width of swath
   - ground speed.
3. Distribution of the spray liquid on the target, determined by:
   - droplet size
   - number of nozzles
   - flying height and speed
   - swath width
   - meteorological conditions.
4. Operational influence of wind, rain, temperature, and humidity on the aircraft procedures and the distribution of material.

Aerial application is used for spraying chemicals such as insecticides, fungicides, herbicides, defoliants, and desiccators; and for spreading solid materials such as seeds, fertilizer and lime. Other activities, such as minnow seeding, are also undertaken by aerial applicators.

Aircraft characteristics. Aircraft used in early agricultural application work were designed for other purposes and then converted for this use. Currently most aircraft doing aerial application work are specifically designed for their job. Those qualities desired in an agricultural aircraft include:

1. Good performance from small, unprepared strips.
2. Safe operating speed of 60 to 100 m.p.h.
3. Maneuverability.
4. Docile handling characteristics.
5. Good field view from cockpit.
6. Protection and comfort for pilot (in a crash).
7. Fire protection: fuel tanks away from pilot.
8. Simplicity in construction and maintenance.
9. Resistance to corrosion by agricultural chemicals.

The size and power required of the aircraft varies according to the type of operation and the working conditions. Most aircraft are single engine with 150 to 600 horsepower and a capacity to carry 600 to 3,000 pounds of material.

Rules and regulations. Agricultural application by aircraft is one of the most thoroughly and tightly controlled aviation activities in the United States. Rules, regulations, and codes have been established by the Federal Aviation Agency, the United States Department of Agriculture, the United States Food and Drug Administration, the Environmental Protection Agency, and state departments of aviation, agriculture, and public health. Feed-processing companies, as well as chemical and food industry groups, provide additional regulations.

Primary aviation control is provided through Federal Aviation Regulations, Part 137—Agricultural Aircraft Operations. This regulation covers the following:

- Definition of terms involved in agricultural aircraft operation
- Certification rules for an operator's certificate
- Operating regulations
- Aircraft requirements
- Personnel requirements
- Required records and reports

In addition to demonstrating a knowledge of

the performance capabilities and operating limitations of the aircraft, the applicant for an agricultural aircraft operator's certificate will be tested on:

1. Steps to be taken before starting operations, including survey of the area to be worked.
2. Safe storage and handling of poisons and the proper disposal of used containers and rinsate for those poisons.
3. General effects of poisons and agricultural chemicals on plants, animals, and people, and the precautions to be observed in using poisons and chemicals.
4. Primary symptoms of poisoning, the appropriate emergency measures to be taken, and the location of poison control centers.
5. Safe flight and application procedures and a demonstration of:
   - Short-field and soft-field takeoffs
   - Approaches to working area
   - Flare-outs
   - Swath runs
   - Pull-ups and turnarounds.

Profitability. As with other flight activities, the aerial applicator is concerned with the profitability of the operation. Assuming the existence of adequate financial, accounting, and operational information, the manager must carefully determine all costs, both fixed and variable, add the desired amount of profit, and market the service to ensure a successful level of operation. The following is a detailed list of the typical expenses incurred in an aerial agricultural operation:

- Pilot wages
- Other wages, for example, flagman
- Officer wages
- Officer salaries
- Radio repairs
- Equipment repairs
- Airplane repairs
- Shop and equipment supplies
- Truck and automobile rent supplies
- Airport and office rent
- Room rent
- Dues and subscriptions
- Donations
- Travel
- Advertising
- Flags
- Airplane insurance
- Employee insurance
- Other insurance
- Airplane depreciation
- Truck and auto depreciation
- Radio and equipment depreciation
- Other equipment depreciation
- Interest (loans)
- All utilities
- Airplane gas and oil
- Vehicle gas and oil
- Office and administrative
- Property taxes
- Unemployment taxes
- Individual insurance
- Licenses and taxes
- Airport Maintenance
- Chemicals

These individual expense items are normally grouped into categories for regular review and analysis by the manager.

The major concern to the manager is ensuring a positive margin of profit between the earnings of the aircraft and the total cost of operating. Two basic alternatives are available—to raise the price for aerial application services or to improve the efficiency of the business. The latter can be achieved through the reduction of those items that constitute the direct and indirect costs of operation and through increased aircraft utilization. Still another target of the manager is the improvement of the work rate capability of the operating aircraft. The key factors are ferry distance, payload, swath run, speed of flight, turning time, and loading time. These elements strongly influence the work rate or the number of acres serviced per hour. By improving the efficiency of operation, the work rate can be increased and the actual cost per hour reduced. Profit will be improved by the increased acres per productive flight hour.

Aerial Advertising

Another profit potential in flight activity and another way to extend the utilization of existing aircraft is through banner towing. By making this unique advertising medium available to a wide range of businesses, additional flight-service revenue can be generated.

Aircraft selection. With a maximum recommended top speed of 80 mph (banner drag and wear increase rapidly above this speed), the aircraft used must have adequate engine cooling and positive flight control at low speeds. Be sure all spelling is correct on the banner!

Fish Spotting

The use of small aircraft to spot fish shoals is of great importance to commercial fishing operations in certain areas and in some cases to those involved in recreational fishing. Fish spotting is particularly used in locations such as the Alaska coast, where the salmon season is controlled to the minute and good timing is important. The aircraft pilot uses a radio to direct fishing boats. Although highly seasonal, this activity can be lucrative for an FBO because of the high value of the potential catch and the fact that no special equipment is needed for the aircraft.

Aerial Photography

Aerial photography has at least five important applications:

1. High level vertical photos for photogrammetry and mapping.
2. Low-level photos for advertising, site planning and development.
3. Low-level infrared pictures for heat-loss study.
4. Plant disease study.
5. Demographic study.

Few general aviation businesses are involved in the sophisticated areas of aerial photography because of the equipment and skills required. High-level vertical photos, for example, require a camera mounting in the floor of the plane as well as oxygen, since heights may be 20,000 feet or more. Infrared photography also requires special cameras. The likely level of involvement for most general aviation businesses will be in conducting occasional flights for realtors, land developers, news reporters, city and state planners, and engineers and commissioners who usually make their own observations and take their own pictures.

Flight Instruction

The Changing Market

The cost of flying has risen rapidly in the last few years so that now an hour in a Cessna 150 with an instructor costs more than $70.00. More flight students are learning to fly for career reasons and fewer are learning just for fun. Those who are learning it just for fun and are probably also in the market for skiing, scuba, recreational vehicles, and tropical vacations. Thus these activities all compete for financing with the same discretionary dollars.

Training Programs

Some flight programs involve an integrated program of ground school and in-flight instruction. This method of learning to fly is valuable for the student who wants to have some theoretical understanding of aerodynamics, navigation, and safe procedures before taking the controls.

Others are best able to learn by doing, and may attend ground school later or not at all. There are many self-study courses available to help such students prepare for the FAA written exams. In view of different needs, an FBO may offer in-flight instruction on demand, but only periodically offer ground school. It may be best to run each service as a separate profit center for this reason.

Ground school instruction comes in a myriad of forms today, including not only the traditional classroom style taught at the airport or a local college or university, but also situations where technology is playing more of a part. Video tape series can be purchased to help prepare individuals for the written and flight tests for virtually any flight rating or certificate.

Computer based training is another alternative, with various programs available, for almost any personal computer. With the introduction of computerized testing, computerized ground school has become much more attractive recently.

Instructional flight operations include the formal training that leads to private, commercial, instrument, multiengine, airline transport pilot rating (ATP), instructor, glider, and balloon licenses and ratings. They also include instruction that leads to type ratings, such as specific aircraft checkout, aerobatics, and agricultural aircraft operation.

In establishing flight training programs, the manager is normally concerned with the requirements expected of graduates of the program, an effective and efficient syllabus, competent instructors and the profitability of the instruction. The major source of guidance in determining pilot requirements for various certificates and ratings is the Federal Aviation Administration. The requirements for the following certificates and ratings are contained in the indicated sources:

- Student pilot FAR 61.3
- Private pilot FAR 61.81
- Commercial pilot FAR 61.11
- Instrument rating FAR 61.35
- Instructor rating FAR 61.17
- Multiengine rating FAR 61.15
- Air transport rating FAR 61.14
- Glider category rating FAR 61.15
- Lighter-than-air category rating FAR 61.15

Part 61 of the Federal Air Regulations is very important to all pilots because it deals with pilot qualifications, privileges and limitations. It is equally important to the manager who is responsible for ensuring that his aircraft are being handled by qualified personnel.

To ensure that the student pilot achieves the level of proficiency stipulated by the FAA or other sources, the manager should ensure the adequacy of the training program for the certificate or rating involved. The private pilot flight training program is the most prevalent in the United States. There is an abundance of training programs. They range from the most fundamental topical ground and flight outline to sophisticated syllabi with audiovisual materials. Learning programs that the manager can consider acquiring and installing at the business include:

- Aero Products Research, Inc.—"Air Learn System"
- Beechcraft—"Beechcraft Private Pilot Ground and Flight Training System"
- Cessna Pilot Center—"Integrated Flight Training System"
- Diamond Aircraft—Horizons Systems International
- Institute for Aeronautical Education—Flight and Ground Syllabus
- Piper Flite Center—"Piper Instructional Program"
- Jeppesen/Sanderson

Other programs are available from various developers and publishers. In addition to complete flight and ground school programs, there are numerous manuals published to help student

Classroom instruction. Courtesy Auburn Flight Service.

pilots master private pilot subjects, instrument topics, and multiengine concepts. These manuals can be obtained from a number of aviation publishers and suppliers.

There are many flight training organizations throughout the United States that have developed their individual program and syllabi for the various ratings. These schools may be of some assistance to the manager intent upon opening a training center. Of course any aviation business that plans to open a flight school should study *FAR Part 141—Pilot Schools* very carefully. This regulation prescribes the requirements for becoming a certificated pilot school and provides for the approval of pilot training courses offered by certificated schools. Federal Aviation Administration Advisory Circular 14–1—Pilot School Certification sets forth guidelines to assist persons in obtaining a pilot school certificate and associated ratings under the Federal Aviation Regulations, Part 141. Advisory Circular No. 140–2J—List of Certificated Pilot Flight and Ground Schools contains a list of those schools that have been recognized as approved by the Federal Aviation Administration.

Instruction Administration

The administration of a flight instructional program presents many challenges to the manager. There are procedures to develop, rules to establish and follow, schedules to make and carry out, personnel to manage, progress checks to administer, and controls to monitor. The training program may become large enough to become an independent department with the full organizational structure of a school. The administrative procedures established should provide for:

- Registration of students
- Curriculum identification and improvement
- Scheduling the utilization of aircraft, instructors and students
- Identifying and coordinating aircraft maintenance
- Student progress checks
- FAA and state approval of flight school
- School operational guidelines and procedures
- Maintenance of flight training records
- Accounting system
- Flow of information and economic analysis of school activity

Several organizations have recognized the need to develop a complete package for the management of a flight school, and quite a few are available today. One of the most thorough and complete is the Cessna Pilot Center System developed by Cessna Aircraft Company. This system was developed to provide "a total package with which to conduct a profitable flight training business." The management manual for the Cessna integrated flight training system provides a well structured and comprehensive approach to flight training through the identification and application of the following system components:

- Integrated flight training curriculum
- Management system for operating a flight school
- Management training
- Instructor curriculum training
- Consultation services by Center specialists

A review of these components clearly indicates the Cessna approach to be well structured

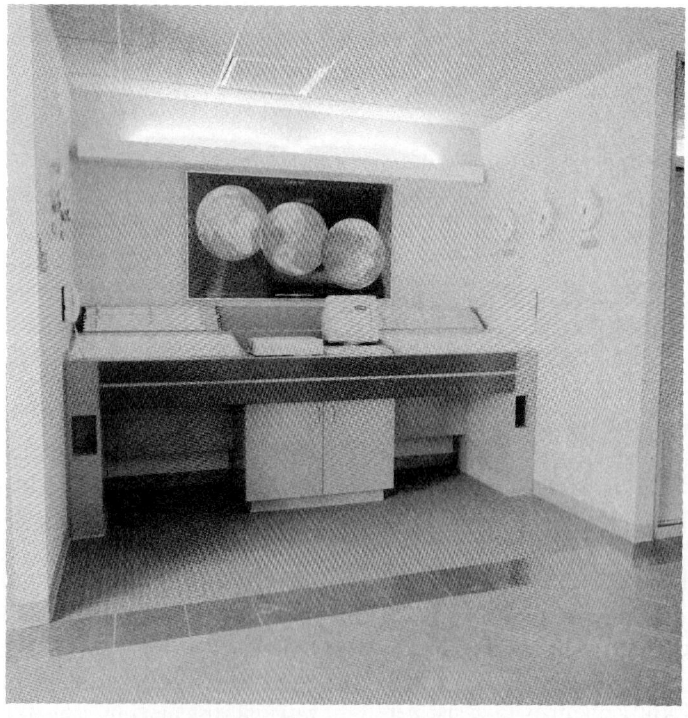

Flight planning area. Courtesy Beech Aircraft Corporation.

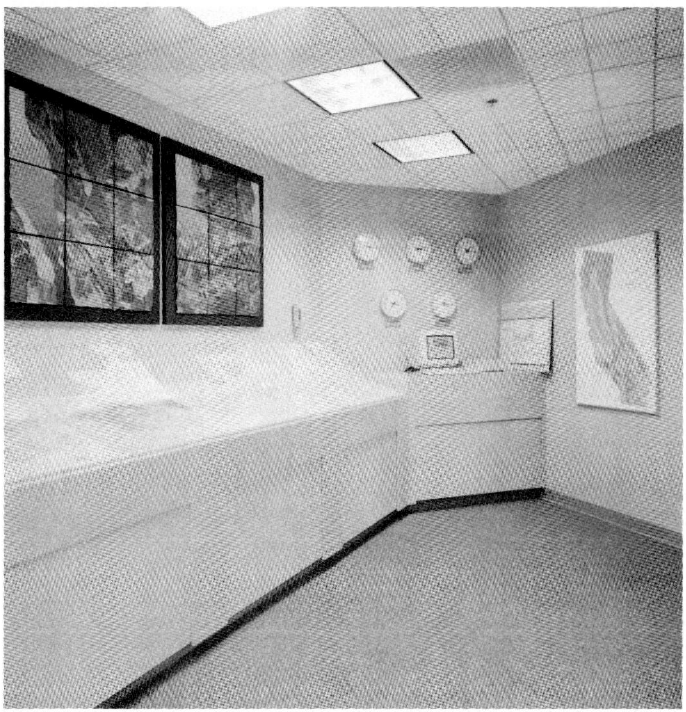

Student flight planning area. Courtesy Flightcraft, Inc.

and comprehensive. The operational elements in the management system include:

- Flight counter procedures
- Student enrollment forms
- Flight training agreement
- Appointment cards
- Student record folders
- Flight scheduling forms
- Aircraft maintenance schedule
- Instructors work schedule
- Instructors scheduling card
- Aircraft rental agreement
- Flight line procedures
- Facility appearance guidelines
- Equipment utilization
- Accounting system
- Financial analysis
- Tax considerations
- Human resources programs
- Reports and controls

The total package from the Cessna Pilot Center System is designed as an integrated program with coordinated supplies, records and procedures. The core of the system is the integrated flight and ground curriculum. Other companies have approached the development of flight instruction along the same lines. These companies include Piper, with the Piper Flite Center; Beech, with the Aero Club; and the Air Learn System of Aero Products Research, Inc.

Flight Instructors

Flight instructors are perhaps the most critical element in the development of successful flight instruction activity. The desired image of an instructor is professionalism. He or she should be well qualified technically, possess the desired teaching skills and motivation, and demonstrate the ability to implement these skills. In many real-life aviation businesses, there are several problems associated with flight instructor selection and utilization that create difficulties for flight department manager: (1) poor selection procedures, (2) no company orientation program, (3) lack of training, (4) rapid turnover of instructor personnel, (5) low salary scale, (6) lack of a career orientation, (7) fluctuating seasonal demands for labor, (8) lack of marketing orientation and (9) a weak identification with the organization.

It has been observed that many aviation businesses do a poor or indifferent job of selecting their flight instructors. Many managers have fallen into the practice of having their office call the next name on the availability list when another instructor is needed. Too much emphasis is often placed on the possession of an "instructor's ticket," and little attention is given to other qualifications that the organization might find desirable in their instructors. This approach appears to be caused by the lack of management's ability either in time or knowledge to engage in careful identification of personnel needs and then to exercise care in the selection of new instructors.

As discussed in chapter 5 "Human Resources," many aviation organizations as small businesses lack time or interest in developing adequate personnel structures. The first and obvious step is the development of a position description to describe the job of an instructor as needed in that organization. From this description, a job specification can then be developed that identifies the qualifications the prospective employee must possess. Chapter 5 contains information on the functions and skills needed for the position of a flight instructor.

After an active recruiting program to ensure an adequate number of candidates for job openings, the next step can be the utilization of an application blank for all potential flight instructors. Such a form can be very effective in screening candidates and identifying those pilots best suited to the needs of the organization. Figure 5.6 in chapter 5 depicts the form developed by Piper Aircraft corporation for the use of their Flite Centers. This form is very comprehensive, provides a great deal of information on the applicant, and should be extremely useful in selecting new flight instructors.

At some point in time, it will become necessary to interview the candidate in order to verify or amplify the data contained in the application blank and at the same time provide the candidate with information about the position and the organization. An interview form is very useful to busy managers. Such a form is somewhat like a pre-takeoff checklist in that it serves as a reminder to the interviewer and helps evaluate the candidate. An example is shown in chapter 5.

Instructor Training

Training of flight instructors should include those elements that will enable the person to perform the total job more effectively. This would mean training in:

- Flying
- Instructional skills
- Marketing
- Administrative duties
- Organizational responsibilities

Historically, primary emphasis has been placed on flying skills, and minimal emphasis has been placed on instructional and educational skills. Frequently, due to wages being based upon the number of hours flown at an hourly rate, other responsibilities were minimized or not included, and skills or talents in other areas were never developed. More and more organizations have realized the advantage of hiring instructors on a full-time basis, providing training in broader organizational responsibilities, and realizing additional benefits from airborne and ground activities of instructor personnel. There must be an adequate student load and related business activity to economically justify the individual instructor.

Freelance Instructors

Just as some FBOs must contend with tailgate mechanics and so-called gypsy operators, so too the freelance instructor is another possible source of unfair competition. Any pilot with a Certified Flight Instructor (CFI) rating can give lessons legally as far as the FAA is concerned. However, the owner of a based aircraft who gives lessons at someone else's airport is probably in business without a lease or operating permit. Since he pays no rent or other overhead, such an operator can invariably undercut the FBO's prices. But he does not offer the student the guarantees of high-quality instruction, the use of facilities for classroom time, or backup aircraft. Because of low-budget maintenance and lack of regulation on the field, such operators can also be a safety hazard that could also make the FBO liable despite his or her not being directly responsible.

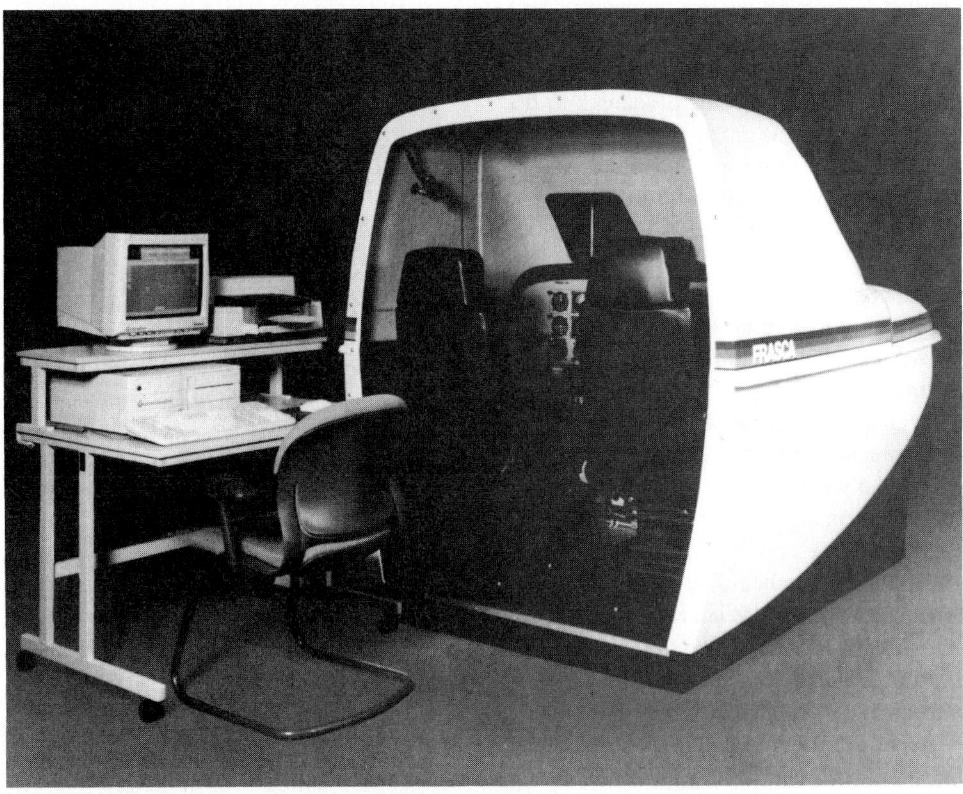

Frasca Model 142 Wide Simulator and Station w/Gist, exterior right view of.

Simulator Usage

Simulators have been designed for use in flight training to assist in training for basic flight, for instrument work, and for specific aircraft and equipment checkouts. It has been said that the worst possible place to give flight instruction is in the air because of the noise, the distractions of many physical sensations, and the inability to stop the machine and talk about a mistake. To help overcome these problems, a wide variety of simulators have been developed.

When a ground trainer or simulator is being used as part of a training course, the extent of its use should be clearly stated in the syllabus. FAR Section 141.41(a) prescribes the requirements used to obtain the maximum flight training credit allowed for ground trainers in approved courses. FAR 141.41(b) provides for the use of ground trainers that do not meet the requirements of Section 141.41(a). The training course must clearly show that the simulator being used meets the stated goals of the syllabus and adheres to the guidelines of 141.41(a) or (b).

The simulator can be a valuable adjunct to a flight training program by accomplishing the following:

1. Reducing the calendar time required for a given training program.
2. Providing additional utilization of flight instructors.
3. Providing a means for sustaining student interest and proficiency during periods of inclement weather.
4. Providing an improved training environment.
5. Facilitating the scheduling process of the organization and the student.
6. Providing a less expensive training opportunity for the student and for the organization.
7. Providing a means for the student to overcome specific learning obstacles.
8. Saving fuel.

The Federal Aviation Administration has recognized the usefulness and effectiveness of the simulator in instrument training by allowing credit for instrument rating experience to be completed in an acceptable instrument ground trainer. Other ratings also recognize and accept simulator time. Most airframe manufacturers have recognized the advantages of simulators for instructing and qualifying pilots in the more sophisticated aircraft. Here the emphasis may be on the operation of complicated systems and emergency procedures as well as on the actual operation of the aircraft.

Simulators used to be expensive for a small FBO, though their comparative cost-effectiveness has improved as fuel costs have increased. Today's micro-computers have opened up a whole new simulator technology. A student with most brands of personal computer can now purchase software to use at home as well as at the flight school.

Sport and Recreational Flyers

Gliders and Sailplanes

Where terrain and climate provide good thermal currents, this is often a popular activity. It may go well with business-oriented FBO services because it is largely a weekend activity. However, the mix of slow unpowered aircraft in the traffic pattern can be a hazard. Some fields are dedicated just to this type of activity. The main revenue to an FBO will come from fuel sales to the tow plane and tow fees to the glider pilots. Many glider owners transport their aircraft to and from the field in special containers, so the potential for tie-down income is limited. This aspect of general aviation continues to experience modest growth in suitable locations however, it is a very small contributor to national FBO income.

Parachuting

Like gliding, parachuting can present problems at a field with a heavy traffic pattern. The jump landing zone needs to be isolated; departing pilots in other aircraft need to watch for the drop. However, owing to slow speed and high visibility, descending parachuters do not present a major hazard. This too tends to be a weekend activity. It can generate important revenue from bystanders as well as participants.

Ultralights

The first ultralight fly-in was in Florida in 1974; thus, ultralights have now been around for two decades. But the rest of the general aviation industry still seems very uncertain about how to handle them. Ultralights require only a few hundred feet of landing area, go at very slow speeds, and so far the pilots are not required to be licensed or pass any course of instruction. Since they use auto gas and mostly do their own repairs, they do not appear to generally offer a source of profit to FBOs and are often viewed as a hindrance to the regular customers. Whether they use separate landing areas within existing airports or completely separate fields, they may in certain locations present a new opportunity for FBO services.

The FBO owner/manager who is able to harness the enthusiasm and dedication of these avid flyers, may find them an asset rather than a liability. Some of these pilots may be interested in obtaining their pilot certificate at some point and/or renting or purchasing a more traditional airplane.

Experimental and Home-built Aircraft

This facet of the general aviation industry appears to be growing more vigorously than personal flying in conventional aircraft. A major reason is the substantially lower cost to both operate and own such aircraft. In 1994 there were over 850,000 people in attendance with close to 12,000 airplanes from all around the world at the annual fly-in of the Experimental Aircraft Association in Oshkosh, Wisconsin. The organization also boasts a network of over 800 local chapters.[8]

As was mentioned in chapter 1 of this book, the number of experimental aircraft completed in 1994 was 734, compared to the 960 general aviation factory built airplanes in the U.S.

Balloons

Ballooning is very popular in some areas, but it does not need an area the size of an airport or an FBO to function, although it can add to the glamor and excitement of an air show. Conflicts with other recreational uses frequently cause ballooning to be sited at airports rather than parks.

Helicopters

Helicopter ratings have become more attractive in the 1990s. This is due, at least in part, to the availability of the new Robinson R-22 helicopter. The R-22 was designed primarily as a training helicopter, much like the Cessna 150 for airplane flight training. A lightweight, two passenger aircraft, the Robinson is also a more affordable helicopter. Although still more expensive than learning to fly in a small two seat airplane, the Robinson is a very affordable helicopter, at an average range of $125–$160 per hour for instruction, not including the instructor.

Helicopter flight training can occur at an airport offering fixed wing flight training without undue burden to either operation. Typically, the helicopters fly at a pattern of 500 feet above ground level, versus 800–1,000 feet for airplanes. And, because helicopters are not restricted to taking off and landing on runway surfaces, they can initiate their own traffic pattern, parallel to or away from the fixed wing traffic.

Sight-seeing

Flying customers around the city, over scenic areas such as the Grand Canyon, or along the ocean front so that they can view the panorama has long been a popular part of aviation. In general, it requires something scenic to view and normally is seasonal work, peaking in summers, vacation periods, or even on sunny, pleasant weekends. With few exceptions, this type of business is conducted with existing, standard aircraft almost on a pick-up basis. Aside from the usual aircraft and pilot insurance requirements, there are some special concerns for the manager, such as safety on the ground and in the air, pilot training, passenger briefing, and specific flight time and route controls. With care, this type of flying can improve aircraft utilization, provide additional income, and stimulate interest in aviation that may lead to business in flight instruction and aircraft sales. The notion of whether or not aircraft should be allowed to fly over national parks was up for discussion in 1994. The final ruling by the FAA, at the time of this printing, disallows flights over many national parks.

For most FBOs recreational aviation of various types is not an important element of their business. At some airports such activity is discouraged because of conflicts with faster, heavier traffic. The more innovative types of recreational aviation such as ultralights, tend to be volatile, with many operators and manufacturers leaving the industry each year. Insurance for some aspects of sport and recreational aviation is either unavailable or a prohibitive expense. Nevertheless, for the right FBO in the right location, this industry segment may provide a previously overlooked market.

Aircraft Sales

New Aircraft

Aircraft sales are the largest item of business for some FBOs, while for others it is not significant. NATA surveys show that in the 1990s, the percent of members in the aircraft sales business has been shrinking. This is particularly true for the sale of new aircraft. Selling aircraft requires the financial ability to carry an expensive inventory for unpredictable amounts of time. It also requires substantial showroom space. The average time in inventory is generally longer for new aircraft than for used, according to studies conducted by NATA.[9]

The percentage of FBOs who are franchised aircraft dealers has risen steadily in recent years, from 57 percent in 1981 to 84 percent in 1984.[10]

A significant change in terms of aircraft sales relates to the number of foreign aircraft being sold in the U.S. Many companies such as the French-based Aerospatiale, Canadian-based Dimona, and Swiss-owned companies are doing good business in the U.S. As mentioned in chapter 1, aircraft manufacturing has definitely shifted to a global marketplace, with the number of American-owned companies diminishing.

Used Aircraft

As with auto sales, used aircraft may be taken as trade-ins. Usually the FBO refurbishes and checks out the aircraft before resale, which involves some costs that must be included in calculating the selling price. Inventory times are typically shorter for used aircraft.[11]

Brokerage

Selling aircraft as a broker means that one does not have to carry the inventory or finance the sale, but simply act as a matchmaker between buyers and sellers. The commission on this activity can be worthwhile. About 5 percent of FBOs in the NATA survey were brokering in the 1980s. Some FBOs also sell aircraft on consignment; that is, they do not pay the seller until the aircraft has a new buyer.

Demonstration Flights

Although not usually time-consuming, these flights are key to a successful sales operation, and they should be made by the personnel best suited to presenting the aircraft's features and benefits.

Flight Operations Manual

A flight operations manual has various meanings in different organizations. In many small businesses, it refers to a general guide for conducting flight operations that attempts to set the tone for the overall business and its related activities. Such a manual contains both policy and specific rules and regulations. In an effort to indoctrinate all employees in the philosophy and procedures selected by the organization, the manual becomes required reading. It also provides specific guidance to key operating personnel, including those at the front desk, on the flight line, instructors, and pilots. Appendix VII of this book contains a sample of such a manual.

In some aviation organizations the term "operations manual" refers specifically to the publication that is required in order to operate air taxi aircraft under the authority of *FAR Part 135—Air Taxi Operations and Commercial Operation of Small Aircraft.*

Summary

Flight operations form the core of the aviation business. The other activities such as maintenance, aircraft storage, parts supply, and administration develop from the need to keep aircraft in flightworthy condition. Flight activities may be grouped into those involved simply in transporting people or products between two points, such as charters, air taxi, business aircraft operation and air ambulance; and those activities involving conducting a business operation as an intrinsic part of being airborne. The second group consists of flight instruction, agricultural applications, aerial photography, fish spotting, survey and patrol work, construction and many others. Each of the various activities requires specific aircraft and flying skills. Each possesses characterisitics that must be identified and understood by the FBO if they are to become profitable elements of the business. An understanding of the key elements involved in each activity, identification of the type of aircraft and other equipment needed, knowledge of the rules and regulations governing that type of flying, and awareness of the primary economic considerations are all part of the aviation manager's job. Finally, the use of internal operating procedures and guidelines to assist in achieving established goals facilitates a consistent and streamlined operation in the flight department.

Discussion Topics

1. What requirements must an air taxi operator meet for Part 135 operations?
2. What are the differences between air taxi and commuter operations?
3. What are some of the built-in problems and opportunities of flight instruction?
4. How does climate affect the market for flight operations?
5. What are some of the technical requirements facing the agricultural operator?
6. What procedures should be used to ensure the profitable operation of such activities as aerial photography, sightseeing and banner-towing?
7. Identify five FBOs within a 100-mile radius and determine (1) what percentage of their revenues comes from flight operations, and (2) how the flight operations revenue is divided between the various flight operations areas. Which flight operations areas have they chosen and why?
8. Assume you are entering the aircraft rental business. What questions must be addressed for each rental transaction?

Chapter 10
Aviation Maintenance

Objectives

- ✔ Identify and describe the four subdivisions usually found in the organizational structure of a maintenance department.
- ✔ Explain the certification process necessary to earn an FAA airframe and powerplant certificate.
- ✔ Describe the facilities and equipment necessary to open and operate an aviation maintenance shop.
- ✔ Understand the implications of product liability on an aviation maintenance operation.
- ✔ Recognize the advantages and disadvantages of subcontracting out all maintenance work.
- ✔ Discuss the concept of Flat-rate-pricing.

Introduction

The maintenance field must be viewed through FAA requirements, personnel, shop facilities and equipment, parts and supplies, quality control, subcontracting, product liability, marketing, administration, pricing and profitability. In this chapter we will review all of these aspects of maintenance, emphasizing the manager's role in guiding the activity toward established objectives.

Maintenance activities are not undertaken by all FBOs; where they are part of the service, they are basic to its success. Good maintenance provides reliable aircraft, ensures customer satisfaction and aircraft utilization, increases the stature of aviation in the public's eye and leads to further development of the industry. Without the support of good maintenance, the reverse happens; business dries up and the industry stagnates, regardless of the products manufactured. Maintenance activity at a general aviation business started when the flyer/manager found that he had to maintain his own aircraft in an airworthy status in order to stay in business. With the arrival of privately owned aircraft on his field, the manager found that he was performing maintenance on these additional aircraft. This represented a mixed blessing; for although he now spread his costs over a wider base, he was also in the maintenance business. With most aviation businesses today, maintenance work is done for company aircraft as well as for external customers. In some larger full service operations, where maintenance is a separate profit center, the shift has been so complete that internal company requests for maintenance must compete with external customer requests for available shop time and are also billed at standard rates.

Maintenance Activity

The aviation manager entering the maintenance business needs to understand the structure of this complex field, to understand the rules and regulations and to know the equipment and personnel needed for the various levels of maintenance activity. The Federal Aviation Regulations provide the major guidance and control for the operation of aviation maintenance facilities.[1]

This guidance is contained primarily in:

1. Part 43—Maintenance, Preventive Maintenance, Rebuilding and Repair.
2. Part 65—Certification: Airmen Other Than Flight Crew Members.
3. Part 145—Repair Stations.
4. Part 147—Aviation Maintenance Technician Schools.
5. Related Advisory Circulars covering many aspects of aviation maintenance.

Maintenance activity at an aviation business can be described in terms of the various levels of work accomplished. The following definitions of the key service or maintenance activities outlined by the Federal Aviation Administration:

1. "Maintenance" means the inspection, overhaul, repair, preservation and replacement of parts, but excludes any preventive maintenance.
2. "Preventive maintenance" means simple or minor preservation operations and the replacement of small standard parts not involving complex assembly operations.
3. "Major repair" means repair (a) that if improperly done might appreciably affect weight, balance, structural strength, performance, power plant operation, flight characteristics, or other qualities affecting airworthiness; or (b) that is not done according to accepted practices or cannot be done by elementary operations.
4. "Major alteration" means an alteration not listed in the aircraft, aircraft engine, or propeller specifications that might appreciably affect weight, balance, structural strength, performance, power plant

operation, flight characteristics or other qualities affecting airworthiness; or an alteration that is not done according to accepted practices or cannot be done by elementary operations.

Part 43—Maintenance, Preventive Maintenance, Rebuilding, and Alteration prescribes rules governing the maintenance, preventive maintenance, rebuilding and alteration of aircraft having a U.S. airworthiness certificate and the airframe, aircraft engine, propeller or appliances of such aircraft. These rules identify the persons authorized to perform maintenance, preventive maintenance, rebuilding and alterations, or to return an aircraft or component to service; the form of maintenance records; the guidelines for performing maintenance work (methods, techniques and practices); and the identification of specific operations classed as major alterations, major repairs, and preventive maintenance.

The persons who may perform maintenance, preventive maintenance, rebuilding and alteration are:

1. The holder of a mechanic certificate, as provided in Part 65.
2. The holder of a repairman certificate, as provided in Part 65.
3. Individuals working under the supervision of a mechanic or repairman.
4. The holder of a repair station certificate, as provided in Part 145.
5. An air carrier, as provided in Parts 121, 127 or 135.
6. The holder of a commercial operator certificate as provided in Part 42.
7. The holder of a pilot certificate issued under Part 61 who may perform preventive maintenance on any aircraft owned or operated by him that is not used in commercial air service.
8. A manufacturer operating under a type of production certificate.

Organization

Maintenance activity by an aviation business is generally accomplished in accordance with the Federal Aviation Regulations. To assist in achieving the business's objectives, most concerns are organized specifically for this purpose. The typical organizational structure of a maintenance or service department would look like that in figure 10.1. Even if the organization is small and the personnel are few, the functions represented by this organizational chart are accomplished when the business provides service support for aircraft, power plants and electronic equipment. The chart enables the business manager to identify the various functions provided and the relationships between them and a framework for future growth of the maintenance activity. The components of the structure are responsible for the following:

1. **Manager, maintenance department:** Responsible for the overall operation of the department including profitability of service, coordination, technical competence, compliance with rules and regulations, quality of product and highest possible safety standards, and hiring and training.
2. **Administration:** Provides administrative support to the department by maintaining department records, maintenance manuals, Airworthiness Directives (ADs), job orders, and required reports.
3. **Power-plant division:** Responsible specifically for service activity dealing with power plants, propellers, fuel systems, and related engine accessories. This includes trouble-shooting, repair and replacement of the equipment authorized by the FAA.
4. **Airframe division:** Provides support for the authorized maintenance of composite and all-metal construction aircraft as contained in the FAA authorization.

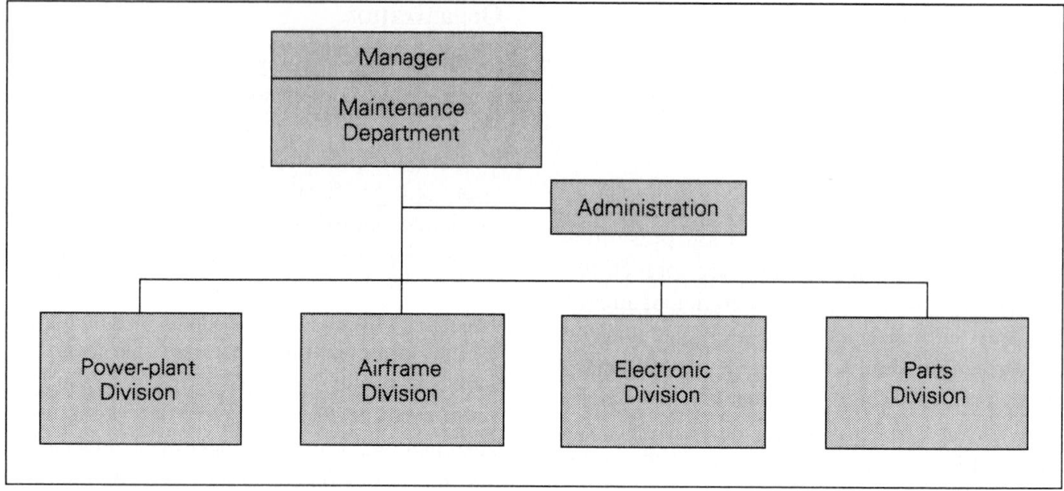

Figure 10.1. Typical organization of a maintenance department.

5. **Electronics division:** Responsible for maintenance activities dealing with communication equipment, navigational equipment, radar, and instruments. Frequently this includes accessories such as starters, magnetos, and electronic systems. The approved activities are identified in the FAA certificate.
6. **Parts division:** Provides the parts, material, and logistics support for the department. Procures, stores, and maintains the inventory necessary to maintain the best economic balance for the business.

Certification

Aviation businesses must be identified as facilities qualified to conduct aircraft maintenance. Part 145—Repair Stations prescribes the requirements for obtaining a certificate as a repair station that authorizes aircraft maintenance work. This part prescribes the requirements for such a certificate, the procedure for obtaining the permit, general operating rules, and the various ratings issued. An applicant for a certificate applies on a form and in a manner prescribed by the FAA and forwards its inspection procedures manual, a list of any maintenance functions to be performed by others under contract, and a list of propellors and accessories to be maintained, if those ratings are requested. Figures 10.2 and 10.3 illustrate the application form used for a repair station certificate and the certificate itself. The domestic repair stations may seek the following ratings:

Airframe ratings:

- Class 1: Composite construction of small aircraft
- Class 2: Composite construction of large aircraft
- Class 3: All-metal construction of small aircraft
- Class 4: All-metal construction of large aircraft

Power plant ratings:

- Class 1: Reciprocating engines of 400 horsepower or less
- Class 2: Reciprocating engines of more than 400 horsepower
- Class 3: Turbine engine

US Department of Transportation
Federal Aviation Administration

APPLICATION FOR REPAIR STATION CERTIFICATE AND/OR RATING

Form Approved
OMB No. 212-0010

If additional space is required for any item, attach additional sheets of paper

1. REPAIR STATION NAME NUMBER, LOCATION & ADDRESS

A. OFFICIAL NAME OF STATION	REPAIR STATION NUMBER
	PHONE NUMBER

B. LOCATION WHERE BUSINESS WILL BE CONDUCTED

C. OFFICIAL MAILING ADDRESS OF REPAIR STATION *(Number, street, city, state, and ZIP code)*

2. REASON FOR SUBMISSION

	ORIGINAL APPLICATION FOR CERTIFICATE AND RATING
	CHANGE IN RATING
	CHANGE IN LOCATION OF HOUSING AND FACILITIES
	CHANGE IN OWNERSHIP

OTHER *(Specify)*

3. RATINGS APPLIED FOR		CLASS	LIMITED
	AIRFRAME		
	POWERPLANT		
	PROPELLERS		
	RADIO		
	INSTRUMENT		
	ACCESSORY		
	SPECIALIZED SERVICE		

4. LIST OF MAINTENANCE FUNCTIONS CONTRACTED TO OUTSIDE AGENCIES

5. APPLICANT'S CERTIFICATION

NAME OF OWNER *(Include name(s) of individual owner, all partners, or corporation name giving state and date of incorporation)*

I hereby certify that I have been authorized by the repair station identified in item 1 to make this application and that statements and attachment hereto are true and correct to the best of my knowledge.

DATE	TITLE	AUTHORIZED SIGNATURE

FOR FAA USE ONLY	**RECORD OF ACTION REPAIR STATION INSPECTION**	*Reports Identification Symbol FS 8320-5*

6. REMARKS *(Identify by item number. Include deficiencies found, ratings denied)*

7. FINDINGS – RECOMMENDATIONS

	A. STATION WAS FOUND TO COMPLY WITH REQUIREMENTS OF FAR 145
	B. STATION WAS FOUND TO COMPLY WITH REQUIREMENTS OF FAR 145 EXCEPT FOR DEFICIENCIES LISTED IN ITEM 6
	C. RECOMMEND CERTIFICATE WITH RATING APPLIED FOR AN APPLICATION BE ISSUED
	D. RECOMMEND CERTIFICATE WITH RATING APPLIED FOR ON APPLICATION *(Except those listed in item 6)* BE ISSUED

8. DATE OF INSPECTION.

9. OFFICE	**SIGNATURE(S) OF INSPECTOR(S)**

10. SUPERVISING OR ASSIGNED INSPECTOR

ACTION TAKEN		CERTIFICATE ISSUED	INSPECTOR SIGNATURE
	APPROVED AS SHOWN ON CERTIFICATE ISSUED ON DATE SHOWN →	NUMBER	
		DATE	TITLE
	DISAPPROVED		

FAA Form 8310-3 (1.83)

Figure 10.2. Federal Aviation Administration application for repair station certificate.

UNITED STATES OF AMERICA
DEPARTMENT OF TRANSPORTATION
FEDERAL AVIATION ADMINISTRATION

Air Agency Certificate

Number

This certificate is issued to

whose business address is

upon finding that its organization complies in all respects with the requirements of the Federal Aviation Regulations relating to the establishment of an Air Agency, and is empowered to operate an approved

with the following ratings:

Sample

This certificate, unless canceled, suspended, or revoked, shall continue in effect

By direction of the Administrator

Date issued:

This Certificate is not Transferable, AND ANY MAJOR CHANGE IN THE BASIC FACILITIES, OR IN THE LOCATION THEREOF, SHALL BE IMMEDIATELY REPORTED TO THE APPROPRIATE REGIONAL OFFICE OF THE FEDERAL AVIATION ADMINISTRATION

Any alteration of this certificate is punishable by a fine of not exceeding $1,000, or imprisonment not exceeding 3 years, or both

FAA Form 8000-4 (1-67) SUPERSEDES FAA FORM 390.

Figure 10.3. Federal Aviation Administration certificate used for designating repair stations.

Propeller ratings:

- Class 1: All fixed-pitch and ground-adjustable propellers of wood, metal or composite construction
- Class 2: All other propellers by make

Radio ratings:

- Class 1: Communication equipment
- Class 2: Navigational equipment
- Class 3: Radar equipment

Instrument ratings:

- Class 1: Mechanical instruments
- Class 2: Electrical instruments
- Class 3: Gyroscopic instruments
- Class 4: Electronic instruments

Accessory ratings:

- Class 1: Mechanical accessories
- Class 2: Electrical accessories
- Class 3: Electronic accessories

The specific requirements for each of the ratings and the included classes are established in Part 145. The applicant is expected to provide the equipment and materials necessary for efficiently performing the identified job functions. Appendix VIII contains the job function required for each rating.

Personnel

Maintenance personnel are the key to success in the aviation maintenance business. In order to ensure that the maintenance department is successful and contributes to the profitability of the overall business, the manager should be as knowledgeable as possible about the qualifications required of maintenance personnel, the training procedures, the process of certification, and the capabilities and limitations of maintenance personnel. Growing shortages of qualified aircraft maintenance personnel mean all possible steps should be taken to recruit and train people who will stay.

Qualifications

The Federal Aviation Regulations, Part 66, prescribe the requirements for an aviation mechanic and associated ratings and set forth the general operating rules for holders of the certificate. Subpart D of Part 66 specifies the eligibility requirements for a certified mechanic as follows:

1. At least 18 years of age.
2. Able to read, write, speak and understand the English language.
3. Has passed all the prescribed tests within a period of 24 months.
4. Meets the requirements for the specific rating requested.

A mechanic certificate can be obtained with an airframe or power-plant rating or both, if the applicant meets all the requirements. These requirements include knowledge as demonstrated in a written test, practical experience in the rating area sought, and skill demonstrated in an oral and practical test. The knowledge requirement calls for the applicant to pass a written test covering the construction and maintenance of aircraft appropriate to the rating he or she seeks and the regulations as contained in Parts 43, 65 and 91. The experience requirements may be met through completion of a certificated aviation maintenance technician school; or satisfactory evidence of eighteen months of practical experience in constructing, maintaining, or altering airframes or power plants, or thirty months of practical experience concurrently performing duties appropriate to both ratings. The oral and practical tests cover the applicant's basic skill in performing practical projects on the subjects covered by the written test for the rating.

Federal Aviation Regulation Part 147 was modified dramatically, effective in 1994. Of significance was a reduction in the number of hours required for learning about radial engines, fabric covering of aircraft, and woodworking. However, the new requirements added to the curriculum include information about composite materials manufacturing and repair, avionics and electronics, as well as turbine and jet knowledge.

Training

The training or experience requirements of an aviation mechanic are usually fulfilled by completing of a certificated aviation maintenance technician program. A review of the requirements for such a program will provide some insight into the training given an aviation mechanic. The following are the major elements of the curriculum required by the FAA:

- Airframe—1,150 hours (400 general plus 750 airframe).
- Power plant—1,150 hours (400 general plus 750 power plant).
- Combined airframe and power plant—1,900 hours (400 general plus 750 airframe and 750 power plant).
- Coverage of the following subject areas is included:
  - General curriculum
    - Basic electricity
    - Aircraft drawings
    - Weight and balance
    - Fluid lines and fittings
    - Materials and processes
    - Ground operations and servicing
    - Cleaning and corrosion control
    - Mathematics
    - Maintenance forms and records
    - Basic physics
    - Maintenance publications
    - Mechanic privileges and limitations
  - Airframe curriculum
    - Structures
    - Wood structures
    - Aircraft covering
    - Aircraft finishes
    - Sheet metal structures
    - Welding
    - Assembly and rigging
    - Airframe inspection
  - Airframe systems and components
    - Aircraft landing gear systems
    - Hydraulic and pneumatic power systems
    - Cabin atmosphere control systems
    - Aircraft instrument systems
    - Communication and navigation systems
    - Aircraft fuel systems
    - Aircraft electrical systems
    - Position and warning systems
    - Ice and rain control systems
    - Fire protection systems
  - Power plant curriculum
    - Power-plant theory and maintenance
    - Reciprocating engines
    - Turbine engines
    - Engine inspection
  - Power plant systems and components
    - Engine instrument systems
    - Engine fire protection systems
    - Engine electrical systems
    - Lubrication systems
    - Ignition systems
    - Fuel metering systems
    - Engine fuel systems
    - Induction systems
    - Engine cooling systems
    - Engine exhaust systems
    - Propellors

The curriculum must:

- Include practical projects
- Balance theory and other instruction
- Show a schedule of required tests
- Provide at least 50 percent of the total curriculum time should be in shop and laboratory instruction.

The majority of maintenance technician training is accomplished in FAA certificated schools using the recommended and approved curriculum of study. The FAA maintains a directory of all certificated schools that can be used in locat-

Aircraft maintenance hangar. Courtesy Flightcraft, Inc.

ing and selecting a school. This directory is published as Advisory Circular 147–2.[2]

Training in specific aircraft, power plants, parts and accessories is available from manufacturers or distributors of the various products. This training is most beneficial in enabling the maintenance technician to meet the FAA requirements and to understand the requirements of the manufacturer and the maintenance manuals for the equipment concerned. The maintenance manager must contact the manufacturer or his representative for a schedule of schools and programs and arrange attendance at the sessions needed by his personnel. The variety is too great and the schedule changes too numerous to attempt a listing here.

Certification

A candidate for an aviation mechanic's certificate must apply for the certificate and associated rating on a form prescribed by the Federal Aviation Administration. After review of the application and the supplementary documents indicating successful completion of the requirements in the knowledge, experience and skill areas, a certificate and the appropriate ratings will be issued by the FAA.

Capabilities and Limitations

A certified mechanic is authorized by the FAA to perform certain functions, so long as he or she meets specified requirements. He or she may perform or supervise the maintenance or alteration of an aircraft or appliance, or part thereof, for which he or she is rated. If he has an airframe rating, he may approve and return to service any airframe, or any related part of appliance, after he has performed, supervised, or inspected its maintenance or alteration—excluding major repairs and major alterations, or after he has completed the 100 hour inspection required by Part 91. If he or she holds a power-plant rating, he or she may accomplish the same for a power plant, propeller, or any related part or appliance. To exercise these privileges, the mechanic must meet the following requirements:

1. He or she must have satisfactorily performed the work concerned at an earlier date, showed the FAA his/her ability to do it, or accomplished the work under the supervision of a certified mechanic who has had previous experience.
2. He or she must understand the current instructions of the manufacturer and the maintenance manuals for the specific operation concerned in order to exercise the privileges of his/her certificate and rating.
3. He or she must have had recent experience in his/her field. The FAA must have found within the preceding 24 months that he or she is able to do the work or that for at least six months he or she has served as a mechanic, technically supervised other mechanics, or supervised in an executive capacity the maintenance or alteration of aircraft.

Inspection Authorization

The next level of experience and responsibility for aviation mechanics is obtaining an inspection authorization. The holder of this authorization may inspect and approve for return to service any aircraft or related part or appliance (except those under a Part 121 or 127 continuous airworthiness program) after a major repair or major alteration. The holder of this authorization may also perform an annual inspection and perform or supervise a progressive inspection.

The candidate for an inspection authorization must meet additional requirements to qualify for this position. He or she must have been a certified mechanic for at least three years. For the last two years he or she must have been actively engaged in maintaining aircraft; have a fixed base of operations; have available the equipment, facilities and inspection data necessary to properly inspect aircraft; and pass a written test on his ability to inspect according to safety standards for returning aircraft to service after major repairs, major alterations, and annual and progressive inspections. The inspection authorization expires on March 31 of each year. To be renewed, the holder must show evidence that he or she (1) performed at least one annual inspection for each ninety days that he held the authority, (2) performed inspections of at least two major repairs or major alterations for each 90 days that he or she held the authority, or (3) performed or supervised and approved at least one progressive inspection in accordance with prescribed standards.

Repairmen

A repairman certificate may be issued to personnel employed by a certified repair station, a certified commercial operator, or a certified air carrier that is required by its operating certificate or approved operations specification to provide a continuous airworthiness maintenance program according to its maintenance manuals. These personnel must be specially qualified to perform maintenance, be employed for a specific job requiring those special qualifications, and be recommended for certification by the employer. Additional requirements include 18 months of practical experience and English language qualifications.

A certified repairman may perform or supervise the maintenance of an aircraft or its components for the job that he or she was employed and certified, but only for his/her employer. He or she must perform these duties in accordance with the current instructions of his employer, the manufacturer of the article being maintained, and appropriate maintenance manuals.

Facilities and Equipment

A manager with the desire to operate a maintenance department must meet specific FAA requirements for facilities and equipment in order to qualify for a repair station certificate and rating. The facilities requirements include the following:

1. Housing for necessary equipment and material.
2. Space for the work to be accomplished under the rating.
3. Facilities for properly storing, segregating, and protecting materials, parts and supplies.
4. Facilities for properly protecting parts and subassemblies during disassembly, cleaning, inspection, repair, alteration, and assembly.
5. Suitable shop space where machine tools and equipment are kept and where the largest amount of bench work is done.
6. Suitable assembly space in an enclosed structure where the largest amount of assembly work is done. The space must be adequate for the work on the largest item covered by the rating requested.
7. Suitable storage facilities used exclusively for storing standard parts, spare parts, and raw materials. This area must be separated from the shop and working space, organized so that only acceptable parts and supplies will be issued for any job, and follow standard good practices for properly protecting stored materials.
8. Adequate storage and protection for parts being assembled or disassembled or awaiting work in order to eliminate the possibility of damage.
9. Suitable ventilation for the shop, assembly area, and storage area so that the physical efficiency of workers is not impaired.
10. Adequate lighting for all work being done so that the quality of the work is not impaired.
11. Temperature and humidity of the shop and assembly area must be controlled so that the quality of the work is not impaired.
12. For an airframe rating, there must be suitable permanent housing for at least one of the heaviest aircraft within the weight class of the rating.
13. For a power-plant or accessory rating there must be suitable trays, racks, or stands for segregating complete assemblies during assembly and disassembly.
14. A station with a propellor rating must provide suitable stands, racks, or other fixtures for proper storage of propellors.
15. For a radio rating there must be suitable storage facilities to assure protection of parts and units from dampness or moisture.
16. An instrument shop must be reasonably dust free, preferably air-conditioned.

The equipment requirements specified by the Federal Aviation Regulations for a repair station include the following:

1. The equipment and materials necessary to efficiently perform the functions of the ratings held (see Appendix VIII for a listing of these functions).
2. The equipment and materials required must be those that can efficiently and competently do the work. All inspection and test equipment shall be tested at regular intervals to ensure correct calibration.
3. Equipment and materials required for the various job functions must be located on the premises and under the full control of the station unless related to an authorized contract.

Managerial Concerns

The manager of a maintenance facility must be concerned with additional requirements in developing and operating the business. Included are (1) a concern for the economic efficiency of the facilities and equipment, (2) the working environment for all employees concerned, (3) the image presented by the facility to the customers

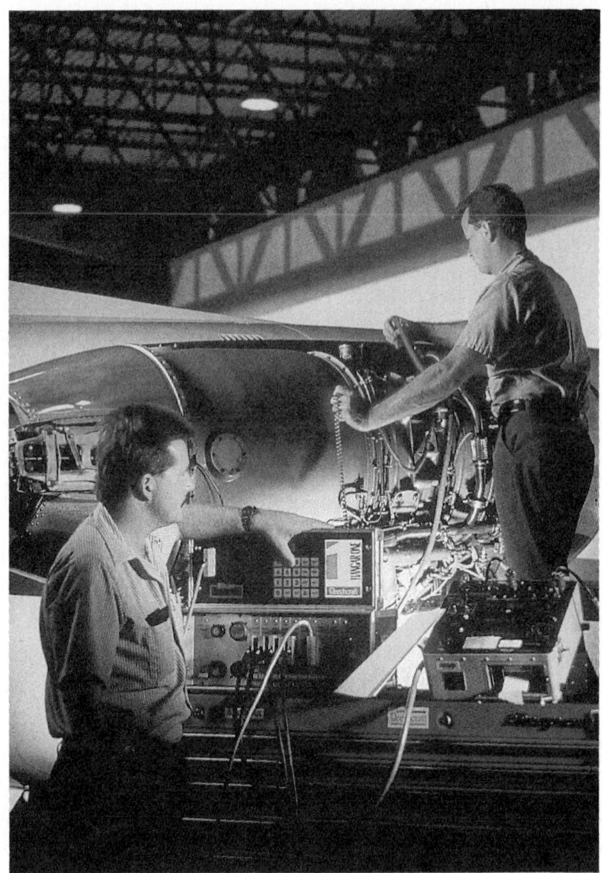

Aircraft and avionics repair shop. Courtesy Beech Aircraft Corporation.

and the general public; (4) fire, safety and construction laws promulgated by city, state and federal agencies; (5) requirements of manufacturers and distributors, if operating under a franchise arrangement; and (6) special requirements that may be generated by the manager or other source.

The equipment needed to furnish a maintenance shop for business represents a large capital investment and is a major concern, especially in view of the industry's rapidly changing technology and the resulting changes in aircraft construction, components and systems. Practical problems in this area include (1) determining the acquisition and inventory of test and repair equipment, (2) control of equipment and tools, (3) replacement and repair of facilities and equipment, (4) maintenance capability and capacity, (5) the utilization of facilities, and (6) whether to make the necessary investments to establish an avionics shop or whether to refer or contract these needs to other FBOs.

Parts and Supplies

The inventory of maintenance supplies and parts provides another challenge to the manager, the maintenance department, and the entire organization. The goal is to maintain the proper balance between capital invested in supplies and parts, utilization of the mechanic's labor time, and customer satisfaction. An unlimited inventory of parts and supplies enables the manager to efficiently utilize maintenance labor and provide maximum customer satisfaction through rapid repair work. Such an investment level in inventory is prohibitive to any business. The cost of maintaining such an inventory far outweighs the advantages and results in a financial drain on the organization.

On the other hand, a minimum inventory results in an inefficient utilization of shop personnel and sharp customer dissatisfaction. A minimum inventory results in needed items not being available locally. Consequently, shop personnel experience shortages, frequent waiting, and poor utilization of shop space. Customers find themselves waiting for parts to be located, ordered and delivered. The longer they wait, the greater the dissatisfaction. All these elements would strongly influence the profitability of the overall maintenance activity.

The manager, as part of his responsibility, must consider all these factors and take the appropriate action. He must establish guidelines to be used in the operation of the parts department, identify the criteria to be used in evaluating the operation, and establish controls to be utilized in maintaining direction.

Inventory Control

A good system of control for parts and supplies will greatly improve the buying and selling activity and result in a more efficient service activity. A good system will provide information on the following:

1. The right quantities to buy
2. Items no longer popular
3. The amount of a given item sold
4. The season or time a given item sells
5. The time to stop buying seasonable goods
6. The kind of goods customers want
7. The time to display and promote certain items
8. Articles that are slow movers
9. Particular items for which demand is declining
10. Best buying sources
11. Best buying prices
12. Price preferences of customers
13. Possibilities for new lines or kinds of goods
14. Whether stock is in proper balance

A system that provides this kind of information to the manager will eliminate many inventory problems and contribute to the success of the maintenance shop. Efficient and profitable control of the inventory of parts and supplies does not have to be difficult, complex, or expensive. Many manufacturers, agencies and associations can furnish good inventory systems to aviation businesses. Most of these systems are economical, simple, and easy to operate. They are easy to install, can be expanded or contracted to fit the business need, and can be handled in a few minutes each day by personnel with little special training. Typical of the systems available to aviation businesses is the inventory control system made available by Piper Aircraft Corporation to the organizations providing service to Piper aircraft. Figure 10.4 illustrates the preprinted inventory card that is part of the basic system.

There are three common methods of securing the information needed for inventory control in an aviation activity: observation, physical check, and perpetual inventory. Observation is used by the smaller aviation businesses and may be sufficient where the number of items is not large, the flow of sales is fairly constant, and the manager is in close daily contact with all the suppli-

PART NO. ______ ITEM ______ MIN. ______ LOCATION ______

MFGR ______ STD. PAGE ______ MAX. ______ LIST PRICE ______

DATE	ORDERED	RECEIVED	SOLD	BALANCE	DATE	ORDERED	RECEIVED	SOLD	BALANCE	

PART NO. ITEM

Figure 10.4. Piper Aircraft inventory card.

ers. The physical check of the inventory does become desirable, or even necessary, when the rate of sales varies on some basis or when there are some higher-valued items included in the inventory. This kind of periodic stock-taking is basically a physical count of the parts and supplies at a given time, which can then be compared to the number received and sold in the past in order to arrive at an estimate of the amount needed to replenish the stock. The perpetual inventory record, as illustrated in figure 10.4, enables the manager to know at all times the amount of goods that should be on hand.

Economic Ordering Quantity. (EOQ) In maintaining a sound inventory control, a manager must determine the most economical ordering quantity for the various materials in the aviation parts department. The most economical amount of material to purchase at one time and at a given price is that quantity where the total cost per unit is at a minimum. This low point occurs when the unit cost of preparing the purchase order for that quantity is equal to the unit cost of carrying the material in the supply room. In other words, the costs of inventory acquisition (ordering) must be balanced against inventory possession (storing). Figure 10.5 graphically presents the basic EOQ formula. The fundamental cost relationships may be expressed by the following formula:

$$Q = \sqrt{\frac{2RA}{P}}$$

Q = Quantity
R = Annual Requirements
A = Acquisition costs per order
P = Possession costs of holding one unit of inventory for one year

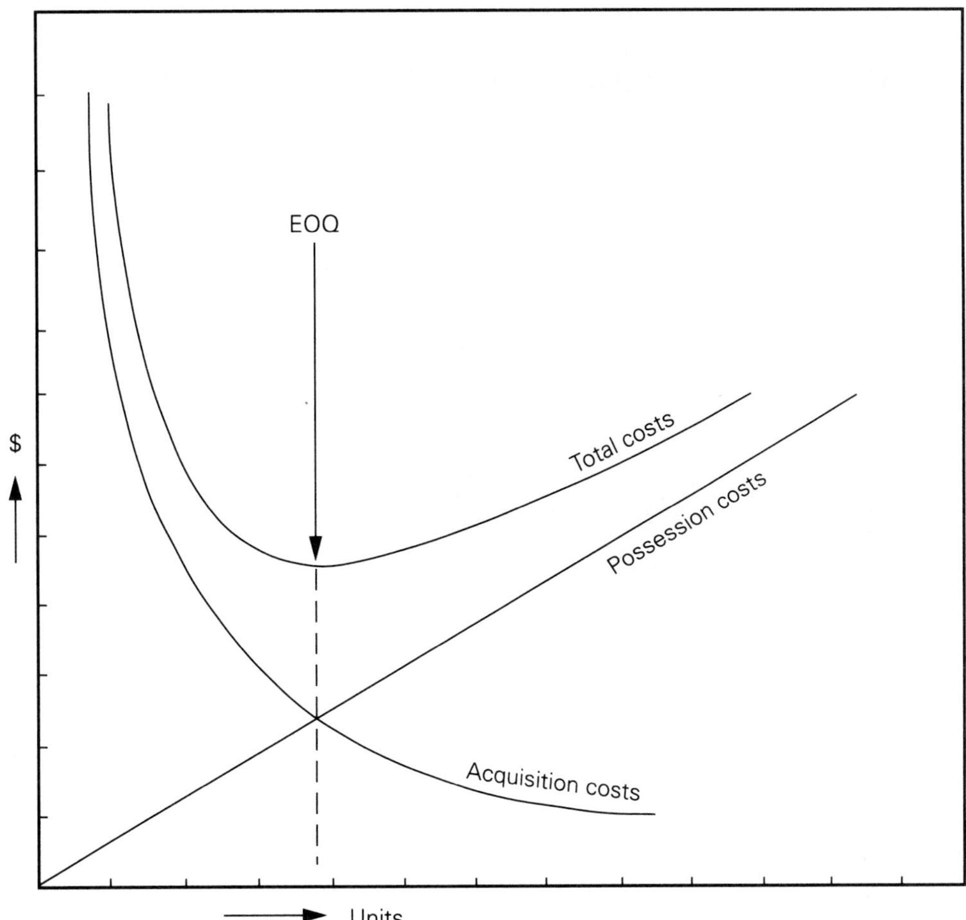

Figure 10.5. Basic EOQ graph.

When maintaining good inventory control, it is important that the manager know when to order the material as well as the correct quantity to order. In determining the correct reorder point it is necessary that two factors be considered: (1) the consumption rate in units and (2) the time required for procurement. Normally, since an out-of-stock situation is costly, the manager adds a buffer of a minimum safe inventory level to the theoretical ordering point in order to arrive at the actual reordering point. The following example illustrates this procedure with spark plugs of a particular type:

1200	Spark plugs used annually
2	Weeks reorder time
46	Theoretical reorder point (1200 ÷ 26)
25	Average one-week safety level
46 + 24 = 71	Actual reordering point

More and more businesses are using Just-In-

Aircraft maintenance hangar. Courtesy Flightcraft, Inc.

Time (JIT) ordering of inventory, where less is maintained in stock because required items can be obtained very fast and often overnight by air express. The items touched upon in this section represent the major elements of inventory control—the inventory records and a replenishment system. To realize the benefits listed at the beginning of this section, the manager must install the system and utilize the data represented by the records. Careful analysis of accumulated inventory data leads to decisions that keep inventory within bounds.

Quality Control

Producing good maintenance is desired primarily in order to secure customer satisfaction. Quality control is a key method for ensuring that a maintenance department consistently produces a product that results in high customer satisfaction. Although the term **quality control** may produce an unpleasant image in some minds—akin to that of police officer or monitor—the concept actually should be much more agreeable and supportive. The best quality control is achieved when the work environment lets individual employees know that good work is desired and expected, and they strive to achieve this as a personal as well as an organizational goal. Fortunately, there are some specific steps a manager can take to develop this attitude throughout the maintenance organization:

1. Provide training in the specific procedures to be followed and requirements to be met for each maintenance operation.
2. Provide checklists and guidelines to facilitate quality work.
3. Provide for the inspection of finished work by a person other than the one doing the work, and create an environment in which this procedure is totally accepted as desirable.
4. Ensure the recognition of quality work and of the individuals responsible for its accomplishment.

Training

Aviation mechanics that graduate from certified technical schools have a sound educational basis for their job. Throughout their training the need for quality work is emphasized. There is a need for continued training in the specific procedures to be followed and in the requirements of quality maintenance, repair, and alteration. This continued training is necessary for new procedures; new materials such as composites, new equipment, new requirements; and as a refresher course. Some of this training can be accomplished on-site in the local shop, while other training must be accomplished at plants, schools, or in training seminars. The organization's emphasis on quality will develop the desired attitude toward a quality product.

Checklists

A great deal of aviation maintenance work includes lengthy procedures with many safety checks and requirements. To ensure that all the required work is accomplished in the proper sequence with the desired safety checks and with the proper level of quality, checklists and guidelines have been developed. Figure 10.6 illustrates a typical list developed to ensure that all necessary items were checked on the inspection of a new aircraft after its first 50 hours. Operating and maintenance manuals frequently use checklists and procedure guides to ensure that disassembly, repair, and assembly are accomplished in proper sequence. One problem in the use of checklists is the tendency for some individuals to work from memory, and then later sign off the checklist as having been completed. Unfortunately, since this practice can lead to items being overlooked and subsequent difficulties, it is highly desirable that individuals and the organization strive to develop work patterns that utilize checklists and guides as a standard procedure.

Inspection

In the regulations dealing with maintenance personnel and maintenance procedures, the Federal Aviation Administration has provided for inspectors and inspection procedures. Quality of work and safety of flight are of primary importance, and one way to ensure them is to provide for the inspection of work by a person other than the one doing the work. It is hoped that this procedure will provide a degree of objectivity and an alternative viewpoint that will catch items overlooked or not completed correctly. Of course, the success of an inspection procedure will depend largely upon the qualifications and thoroughness of the inspecting personnel. The attitude of employees and the working environment must be such that the inspection procedure be universally accepted.

Recognition

One important aspect of obtaining quality work by a maintenance unit is the prompt recognition of high-quality work and of the individuals who have produced that work. This recognition can take many forms, ranging from personal praise, unit recognition, and publicity to financial incentives. Of course, the recognition must be sincere. Acknowledgement of low-quality work must also ensure that it does not become the accepted standard. Verbal reminders, corrective action, discipline, and even firing may be used to point out that low quality is not acceptable.

Balance

Quality control, like other business activities, is costly. Additional quality can be obtained with additional training, more checklists and guidelines, more inspectors, and lavish recognition programs. At some point the question must be asked: "How much quality is desired—and how much can we afford?" The manager must obvi-

PIPER AIRCRAFT CORPORATION

INSPECTION REPORT

THIS FORM MEETS REQUIREMENTS OF FAR PART 43

MAKE	MODEL	Serial No.	Registration No.
PIPER CHEROKEE	PA-28R-180 PA-28R-200		

Circle Type of Inspection (See Note)

50 100 500 1000 Annual

Perform inspection or operation at each of the inspection intervals as indicated by a circle (◯).

DESCRIPTION	50	100	500	1000	Inspector
A. PROPELLER GROUP					
1. Inspect spinner and back plate (See Note 5).....	◯	◯	◯	◯	
2. Inspect blades for nicks and cracks..................	◯	◯	◯	◯	
3. Check for grease and oil leaks..........................	◯	◯	◯	◯	
4. Lubricate propeller per lubrication chart............	◯	◯	◯	◯	
5. Check spinner mounting brackets......................		◯	◯	◯	
6. Check propeller mounting bolts and safety (Check torque if safety is broken.)....................		◯	◯	◯	
7. Inspect hub parts for cracks and corrosion........		◯	◯	◯	
8. Rotate blades of constant speed propeller and check for tightness in hub pilot tube.................		◯	◯	◯	
9. Remove constant speed propeller, remove sludge from propeller and crankshaft...............			◯	◯	
10. Inspect complete propeller and spinner assembly for security, chafing, cracks, deterioration, wear, and correct installation.......		◯	◯	◯	
11. Overhaul propeller...				◯	
B. ENGINE GROUP					
CAUTION: Ground Magneto Primary Circuit before working on engine.					
1. Remove engine cowl..	◯	◯	◯	◯	
2. Clean and check cowling for cracks, distortion and loose or missing fasteners.........................		◯	◯	◯	
3. Drain oil sump (See Note 2).............................	◯	◯	◯	◯	
4. Clean suction oil strainer at oil change (Check strainer for foreign particles.)............................	◯	◯	◯	◯	
5. Clean pressure oil strainer or change full flow (cartridge type) oil filter element (Check strainer or element for foreign particles)........................	◯	◯	◯	◯	
6. Check oil temperature sender unit for leaks and security..		◯	◯	◯	
7. Check oil lines and fitting for leaks, security, chafing, dents and cracks (See Note 4)............	◯	◯	◯	◯	
8. Clean and check oil radiator cooling fins...........		◯	◯	◯	
9. Remove and flush oil radiator...........................	◯	◯	◯	◯	
10. Fill engine with oil per lubrication chart.............	◯	◯	◯	◯	
11. Clean engine...		◯	◯	◯	
CAUTION: Do not contaminate the vacuum pump with cleaning fluid. Ref: Lycoming Service Letter 1221A.					
12. Check condition of spark plugs (Clean and adjust gap as required, adjust per Lycoming Service Instruction No. 1042.)..........................		◯	◯	◯	
13. Check cylinder compression ref: AC43. 13-1		◯	◯	◯	
14. Check ignition harness and insulators (High tension leakage and continuity.).......................		◯	◯	◯	
15. Check magneto points for proper clearance (Maintain clearance at 0.016.)..........................		◯	◯	◯	
16. Check magneto for oil leakage.........................		◯	◯	◯	
17. Check breaker felts for proper lubrication..........		◯	◯	◯	
18. Check distributor block for cracks, burned areas or corrosion, and height of contact springs			◯	◯	
19. Check magnetos to engine timing.........................		◯	◯	◯	
20. Overhaul or replace magnetos (See Note 3).........				◯	
21. Remove air filter and tap gently to remove dirt particles (Replace as required.)...........................	◯	◯	◯	◯	
22. Clean fuel injector inlet line screen (Clean injector nozzles as required.) (Clean with acetone only)...	◯	◯	◯	◯	
23. Check condition of injector alternate air door and box..	◯	◯	◯	◯	
24. Check intake seals for leaks and clamps for tightness..		◯	◯	◯	
25. Inspect all air inlet duct hoses (Replace as required.)..		◯	◯	◯	
26. Inspect condition of flexible fuel lines..................		◯	◯	◯	
27. Replace flexible fuel lines (See Note 3)..............				◯	
28. Check fuel system for leaks................................		◯	◯	◯	
29. Check fuel pumps for operation (Engine driven and electric.)..		◯	◯	◯	
30. Overhaul or replace fuel pumps (Engine driven and electric (See Note 3)...................................				◯	
31. Check vacuum pump and lines...........................		◯	◯	◯	
32. Overhaul or replace vacuum pump (See Note 3).				◯	
33. Check throttle, alternate air, mixture and propeller governor controls for travel and operating condition...		◯	◯	◯	
34. Inspect exhaust stacks, connections and gaskets (Refer to PA-28 Service Manual, Section III. Replace gaskets as required.).............................		◯	◯	◯	
35. Inspect muffler, heat exchange and baffles (Refer to PA-28 Service Manual, Section III.).......		◯	◯	◯	
36. Check breather tube for obstructions and security.		◯	◯	◯	
37. Check crankcase for cracks, leaks and security of seam bolts..		◯	◯	◯	
38. Check engine mounts for cracks and loose mountings..		◯	◯	◯	
39. Check all engine baffles......................................		◯	◯	◯	
40. Check rubber engine mount bushings for deterioration (Replace as required.)............................		◯	◯	◯	
41. Check firewall seals...		◯	◯	◯	
42. Check condition and tension of alternator drive belt (Refer to PA-28 Service Manual.).................		◯	◯	◯	
43. Check condition of alternator and starter............		◯	◯	◯	
44. Check fluid in brake reservoir (Fill as required.)..	◯	◯	◯	◯	
45. Lubricate all controls...		◯	◯	◯	
46. Overhaul or replace propeller governor (See Note 3)..				◯	
47. Complete overhaul of engine or replace with factory rebuilt (See Note 3).................................				◯	
48. Reinstall engine cowl..	◯	◯	◯	◯	

Owner 508

230 259 710111

Figure 10.6. Aircraft maintenance inspection checklist. Courtesy Piper Aircraft Corp.

Circle Type of Inspection (See Note)
50 100 500 1000 Annual

Perform inspection or operation at each of the inspection intervals as indicated by a circle (◯).

C. CABIN GROUP

	DESCRIPTION	50	100	500	1000	Inspector
1.	Inspect cabin entrance, doors and windows for damage and operation		○	○	○	
2.	Check upholstery for tears		○	○	○	
3.	Checks seats, seat belts, security brackets and bolts		○	○	○	
4.	Check trim operation		○	○	○	
5.	Check rudder pedals		○	○	○	
6.	Check parking brake and brake handle for operation and cylinder leaks		○	○	○	
7.	Check control wheels, column, pulleys and cables		○	○	○	
8.	Check landing, navigation, cabin and instrument lights	○	○	○	○	
9.	Check instruments, lines and attachments		○	○	○	
10.	Check gyro operated instruments and electric turn and bank (Overhaul or replace as required.)		○	○	○	
11.	Replace filters on gyro horizon and directional gyro or replace central air filter		○	○	○	
12.	Clean or replace vacuum regulator filter		○	○	○	
13.	Check altimeter (Calibrate altimeter system in accordance with FAR 91.170, if appropriate.)		○	○	○	
14.	Check operation of fuel selector valve		○	○	○	
15.	Check condition of heater controls and ducts		○	○	○	
16.	Check condition and operaton of air vents		○	○	○	

D. FUSELAGE AND EMPENNAGE GROUP

	DESCRIPTION	50	100	500	1000	Inspector
1.	Remove inspection plates and panels		○	○	○	
2.	Check baggage door, latch and hinges		○	○	○	
3.	Check battery, box and cables (Check at least every 30 days. Flush box as required and fill battery per instructions on box.)	○	○	○	○	
4.	Check electronic installation		○	○	○	
5.	Check bulkheads and stringers for damage		○	○	○	
6.	Check antenna mounts and electric wiring		○	○	○	
7.	Check hydraulic pump fluid level (Fill as required.)	○	○	○	○	
8.	Check hydraulic pump lines for damage and leaks		○	○	○	
9.	Check for obstructions and contamination in inlet of back-up landing gear extender actuator inlet head	○	○	○	○	
10.	Check fuel lines, valves and gauges for damage and operation		○	○	○	
11.	Check security of all lines		○	○	○	
12.	Check vertical fin and rudder surfaces for damage		○	○	○	
13.	Check rudder hinges, horn and attachments for damage and operation		○	○	○	
14.	Check vertical fin attachments		○	○	○	
15.	Check rudder hinge bolts for excess wear (Replace as required.)		○	○	○	
16.	Check stabilator surfaces for damage		○	○	○	
17.	Check stabilator, tab hinges, horn and attachments for damage and operation		○	○	○	
18.	Check stabilator attachments		○	○	○	
19.	Check stabilator and tab hinge bolts and bearings for excess wear (Replace as required.)		○	○	○	
20.	Check stabilator trim mechanism		○	○	○	
21.	Check aileron, rudder, stabilator, stabilator trim cables, turnbuckles, guides and pulleys for safety, damage and operation		○	○	○	
22.	Clean and lubricate stabilator trim drum screw			○	○	
23.	Clean and lubricate all exterior needle bearings				○	
24.	Lubricate per lubrication chart	○	○	○	○	
25.	Check rotating beacon for security and operation		○	○	○	
26.	Check security of AutoPilot bridle cable clamps		○	○	○	
27.	Inspect all control cables, air ducts, electrical leads, lines, radio antenna leads and attaching parts for security, routing, chafing, deterioration, wear, and correct installation		○	○	○	
28.	Reinstall inspection plates and panels		○	○	○	

E. WING GROUP

	DESCRIPTION	50	100	500	1000	Inspector
1.	Remove inspection plates and fairings		○	○	○	
2.	Check surfaces and tips for damage, loose rivets, and condition of walk-way		○	○	○	
3.	Check aileron hinges and attachments		○	○	○	
4.	Check aileron cables, pulleys and bellcranks for damage and operation		○	○	○	
5.	Check flaps and attachments for damage and operation		○	○	○	
6.	Check condition of bolts used with hinges (Replace as required.)				○	
7.	Lubricate per lubrication chart	○	○	○	○	
8.	Check wing attachment bolts and brackets		○	○	○	
9.	Check fuel tanks and lines for leaks and water		○	○	○	
10.	Fuel tanks marked for capacity		○	○	○	
11.	Fuel tanks marked for minimum octane rating.					
12.	Check fuel cell vents		○	○	○	
13.	Inspect all control cables, air ducts, electrical leads, lines and attaching parts of security, routing, chafing, deterioration, wear, and correct installation		○	○	○	
14.	Reinstall ispection plates and fairings		○	○	○	

F. LANDING GEAR GROUP

	DESCRIPTION	50	100	500	1000	Inspector
1.	Check oleo struts for proper extension (N-2,75 in. /M-2.0in.) (Check fluid level as required.)	○	○	○	○	
2.	Check nose gear steering control and travel		○	○	○	
3.	Check wheels for alignment		○	○	○	
4.	Put airplane on jacks		○	○	○	
5.	Check tires for cuts, uneven or excessive wear and slippage		○	○	○	
6.	Remove wheels, clean, check and repack bearings		○	○	○	
7.	Check wheels for cracks, corrosion and broken bolts		○	○	○	
8.	Check tire pressure (N-30 psi/M-27 psi)	○	○	○	○	
9.	Check brake lining and disc		○	○	○	
10.	Check brake backing plates		○	○	○	
11.	Check brake and hydraulic lines		○	○	○	
12.	Check shimmy dampener		○	○	○	
13.	Check gear forks for damage		○	○	○	
14.	Check oleo struts for fluid leaks and scoring		○	○	○	

Figure 10.6. Continued.

Circle Type of Inspection (See Note)
50 100 500 1000 Annual

DESCRIPTION	50	100	500	1000	Inspector
15. Check gear struts, attachments, torque links, retraction links and bolts for condition and security		O	O	O	
16. Check downlock for operation and adjustment.					
17. Check torque link bolts and bushings (Rebush as required.)			O	O	
18. Check drag and side brace link bolts (Replace as required.)				O	
19. Check gear doors and attachments		O	O	O	
20. Check warning horn and light for operation		O	O	O	
21. Retract gear – check operation		O	O	O	
22. Retract gear – check doors for clearance and operation		O	O	O	
23. Check anti-retraction system		O	O	O	
24. Check actuating cylinders for leaks and security		O	O	O	
25. Inspect all hydraulic lines, electrical leads, and attaching parts for security, routing, chafing, deterioration, wear, and correct installation		O	O	O	
26. Check position indicator switch and electrical leads for security		O	O	O	
27 Lubricate per lubrication chart	O	O	O	O	
.28 Remove airplane from jacks		O	O	O	

Perform inspection or operation at each of the inspection intervals as indicated by a circle (◯).

DESCRIPTION	50	100	500	1000	Inspector
G. OPERATIONAL INSPECTION					
1. Check fuel pump and fuel tank selector	O	O	O	O	
2. Check fuel quantity, pressure and flow readings	O	O	O	O	
3. Check oil pressure and temperature	O	O	O	O	
4. Check alternator output	O	O	O	O	
5. Check manifold pressure	O	O	O	O	
6. Check alternate air	O	O	O	O	
7. Check parking brake	O	O	O	O	
8. Check vacuum gauge	O	O	O	O	
9. Check gyros for noise and roughness	O	O	O	O	
10. Check cabin heater operation	O	O	O	O	
11. Check magneto switch operation	O	O	O	O	
12. Check magneto RPM variation	O	O	O	O	
13. Check throttle and mixture operation	O	O	O	O	
14. Check propeller smoothness	O	O	O	O	
15. Check propeller governor action	O	O	O	O	
16. Check engine idle	O	O	O	O	
17. Check electronic equipment operation	O	O	O	O	
H. GENERAL					
1. Aircraft conforms to FAA Specification	O	O	O	O	
2. All FAA Airworthiness Directives complied with	O	O	O	O	
3. All Manufacturers Service Bulletins and Letters complied with	O	O	O	O	
4. Check for proper Flight Manual	O	O	O	O	
5. Aircraft papers in proper order	O	O	O	O	

NOTES:

1. Both the annual and 100 hour inspections are complete inspections of the airplane – identical in scope. Inspections must be accomplished by persons authorized by FAA.
2. Intervals between oil changes can be increased as much as 100% on engines equipped with full flow (cartridge type) oil filters – provided the element is replaced each 50 hours of operation.
3. Replace or overhaul as required or at engine overhaul. (For engine overhaul, refer to Lycoming Service Instructions No. 1009.)
4. Replace flexible oil lines as required, but no later than 1,000 hours of service.
5. Inspect in accordance with Piper Service Bulletin 309.

REMARKS:

Signature of Mechanic or Inspector	Certificate No.	Date	Total Time on Airplane

230 290

Figure 10.6. Continued.

ously determine the desirable balance between the costs involved and the acceptable level of quality, and then strive to maintain that balance.

Competition

Nonexclusive Rights

Airports that have been federally funded or that hope to be are obligated to permit all aeronautical operators who can be accommodated to use the field, provided they meet certain standards.[3] Thus existing FBOs are constantly under the threat of new competition at federally funded airports. While this in some ways is in the public interest, at small fields it makes it difficult to achieve a reasonable profit.

Referrals

As a result of the competitive environment facing many FBOs, some prefer to refer their maintenance and repair work out to other operators on the field or elsewhere. This referral process will probably work well in both directions until there is a change in the performance of the other business. In this case not only does the FBO have very little control over his clients' maintenance needs, but also the poor service from the maintenance operator may drive them to another field for all their needs.

Subcontracting

Aviation managers frequently find themselves considering the feasibility of subcontracting some, or all, of their maintenance or avionics work. It may be that the light maintenance work load does not warrant having a shop or that it is not adequate to support the purchase of some special and expensive test equipment. Also it may not be sufficient to acquire and utilize the necessary skilled maintenance technicians. Any of these concerns might cause the manager to subcontract maintenance work. The decision of when to subcontract is normally based upon a consideration of the points just identified.

The use of financial comparisons may also be valuable in arriving at a decision on subcontracting. In each situation it becomes necessary to accumulate all the cost and income data related to the decision while being as objective as possible. There may be a number of factors that cannot be easily quantified but still must be considered, such as available human resources, management capability, space utilization, time to accomplish maintenance, control over quality, and customer reaction. All these elements should be considered in a rational decision-making process as described in chapter 2 "Management Functions."

When maintenance work is subcontracted, the amount should be recorded, and periodically the volume of work and the overall situation should be analyzed in order to verify the decision to continue subcontracting. This analysis should be done to identify the point when it becomes economically or strategically feasible to acquire the people, equipment, and space and financing needed to accomplish the maintenance work within the organization.

Problems. There are several problem areas that are related to subcontracting that should be identified by the manager, considered in the decision-making process, and monitored on a day-by-day basis. Included are:

1. Negotiating an equitable contract and monitoring its operation.
2. Handling warranty questions to the satisfaction of the customer and the contractor.
3. Dealing with liability situations in the legal environment.
4. Providing for customer satisfaction and customer identification with the primary business as well as the subcontractor.
5. Ensuring that the subcontracting operation is profitable on a direct job-basis and on a long-range basis.

Recognizing these problem areas and striving to overcome their potential difficulties becomes the responsibility of the manager and a challenge to administrative skills.

"Through-the-Fence" Operations

This type of activity refers to FBOs who are not airport tenants but own or lease adjacent land and access the airport through a real or imaginary fence at the property line. They can siphon off business from the FBO(s) on the field who are paying for the operation of the airfield, taxiways and other public areas. Where a new through-the-fence proposal is made, there are some safeguards recommended by FAA for protecting existing tenants. A copy of these appears in Appendix IX. But where the situation has existed for many years, as often seems to be the case, it can periodically become very troublesome. The airport owner has no real control over such an operator, except denying access until acceptable financial and performance arrangements are established. In a case where a through-the-fence operator has an existing access easement with the airport owner, it may be difficult to negate or tighten its terms. Ideally an access fee should be charged for use of the airport.

As available land on public airports becomes more scarce, the public airport system seems likely to receive more requests for through-the-fence rights, and the semiactive through-the-fence operator may become more of a challenge also. FBOs whose airports have potential or actual sites for through-the-fence activity need to make their own interests and concerns clearly known to the public airport operator.

Tailgate, Shade Tree, and Gypsy Mechanics

As costs of repairs go up, more people are repairing their own aircraft. As long as they comply with the required inspections, this is a legitimate activity. However, commercial repair services unofficially operating in individual hangars or other locations are not legitimate. All aeronautical operators providing services for sale on a public airport must have permission and an appropriate lease. Illegal operators may be doing poor work that the legitimate FBOs may later have to correct, even to the point of liability for aircraft originally sold but never maintained. The "gypsy" operator conveniently disappears when trouble starts. Thus as with through-the-fence operators, the FBO must be ever diligent in reporting such activities and insisting on enforcement of the same minimum standards for all.

Corporate and Other Self-maintenance

Like self-fueling, this is a growing trend for economic and other reasons and is permitted under the nonexclusive rights provisions at federally funded airports. The FBO may still be able to capture some of these repair dollars for specialized work, FAA inspections, and the sale of parts.

Administration

The administration of a maintenance department and its associated paperwork is another area requiring specific attention by the manager. These functions can consume a fair amount of time. The following activities are included in the term "maintenance administration":

1. Developing, understanding and administering the overall maintenance organization and system.
2. Developing and maintaining the necessary maintenance procedures, records, and library.
3. Complying with the necessary records and entries required in accomplishing maintenance repair or alteration.

4. Maintaining the necessary internal records associated with accounting, budgeting, job orders and time cards.
5. Dealing with FAA regulations, procedures and inspections.

These major activities will vary in content and meaning from business to business. Normally, they are included in the package known as administration. The first area is primarily the job of efficiently organizing the department and then developing the administrative structure and procedures for effective operation. The second activity deals with the need to develop, maintain, and administer: (1) the operating procedures and guidelines to be followed in effecting maintenance, repair and alteration, (2) the necessary technical records that must be maintained, and (3) the manuals and data that must be available in the department library. The third activity area includes compliance with regulations and the completion of various FAA and manufacturer records required when doing maintenance work. The final activity area for shop administration deals with the completion of the necessary internal business records. Included are the records dealing with accounting, budgeting, personnel, processing shop job orders, employee time cards, purchase orders, and safety reports.

Flat-rate Pricing

Pricing determinations for the products of the maintenance department normally include all the considerations mentioned in chapter 3 on marketing. These considerations must recognize the three cost components of material, labor, and overhead.

In many instances the traditional methods of determining prices for aviation maintenance work, assigning work loads to mechanics, and compensating individual employees have not resulted in an efficient operation. The organization might find itself with a poor utilization of maintenance labor and a departmental profit center that is not profitable! One suggested solution to this problem has been the development and application of a flat-rate price structure to aircraft maintenance. The technique is not new; it has been used in the automobile industry for years. Use of a flat-rate manual in the aviation industry is growing. Its procedures, advantages, and problems are included here. The operating procedure when using a flat-rate billing structure is as follows:

1. A flat-rate manual covering the type of maintenance service to be offered is acquired or developed.
2. The job to be accomplished is positively identified.
3. The manual is used to obtain the standard time suggested for accomplishing the job.
4. The work is accomplished by assigned personnel.
5. The individual completing the job is compensated according to the time schedule in the flat-rate manual, not how long it takes to actually complete the work.
6. If the job is returned for rework or correction, it is accomplished by the person doing the initial work, on his or her time, and without additional compensation.

When an aviation business begins operating under a flat-rate manual procedure, the following advantages are normally experienced:

1. Maintenance employees become work-oriented and time conscious.
2. The maintenance department experiences increased productivity and efficiency.
3. The quality of maintenance work improves and produces better customer satisfaction.
4. The flat-rate process tends to up-grade the level of employees with the marginal or less motivated leaving voluntarily.
5. The maintenance employees operating under a flat-rate manual experience a 10 percent to 20 percent increase in compensation.

The most frequent concerns regarding operating a maintenance facility under a flat-rate procedure have been:

- "My mechanics will never go for that procedure!"
- "Quality of work will go down, and we cannot tolerate that in aviation!"
- "I have no flat-rate manual for aircraft in my geographic area."

The first concern regarding mechanic reaction is best handled by a knowledgeable and determined manager who convinces his employees of the advantages of the procedure. As for the second concern, experience in several operations suggests that poor quality does not result from the system itself. Once the work force has stabilized under a flat-rate system, the quality seems to improve; perhaps the workers with higher qualifications are striving to do a better job and prevent rework and correction. Of course, the normal quality-control procedures and inspections continue in order to maintain the desired level of work.

The final problem is obtaining a flat-rate manual that adequately covers the type of aircraft serviced by a particular business in its unique geographic location. Since the various aircraft makes (Piper, Cessna, Beech, Bellanca, and so on) are constructed differently, it is necessary to have a manual for each plane. The climatic differences around the country with varying ranges in temperature and working conditions, influence the time involved in accomplishing repair operations. These differences must be recognized when establishing a manual for a location.

One illustration of a successful application of the flat-rate procedure to aviation maintenance work is Southwest Air Rangers of El Paso, Texas. There, a flat-rate manual was developed for use primarily on Piper aircraft. The manual was prepared initially from the analysis of a large amount of accumulated historical data on maintenance activity. Several revisions to the manual have been made as additional experience and data have been acquired. Figure 10.7 illustrates a page from the Southwest Air Rangers flat-rate manual. Additional information on the operation of the system and copies of the complete manual may be purchased from the management in El Paso.

Computer-assisted Maintenance

As aircraft have grown larger and become more and more sophisticated, it has become increasingly difficult for the manager to keep up with the myriad of details associated with keeping modern aircraft operational on a tight schedule. Many businesses have turned to the computer for assistance in ensuring that maintenance is scheduled and completed efficiently.

A number of organizations have developed complete computerized aircraft maintenance programs that they provide as a service to aircraft operators. These programs include a recommended maintenance schedule that can be adapted to individual needs. After the required data has been entered into the computer, the following reports are printed for the customer:

- Monthly aircraft status report
- Monthly maintenance due list
- Monthly aircraft history report
- Annual budget performance and reliability summary
- Inspection and services summary

Part of the system includes maintenance requirement cards that contain the latest acceptable maintenance procedures.

In addition to being valuable to many aircraft operators, the system is indicative of the part that the computer can play in maintenance work.

Profitability

As mentioned earlier, the focus of an aviation business should be on generating the desired

Job Description	18	23-4	23-250	23-AT	23-LT	24	24-T	25	28-4	28-6	28-R	30+39	30+39-T	31	31-P	31-T	32-260	32-300	34	36
Absolute pressure controller (cowl off)				1																
Actuator—brake	1	1	1	1	1	1	1	1	1	1	1	1	1	1			1	1	1	
Actuator—flap (hydraulic)		3	3	3	3															
Actuator—gear door (hydraulic)		1	1	1	1									1						
Actuator—landing gear (hydraulic)		3	3	3	3						1			4						
Actuator—waste gate (cowl off)				2																
Adapter—oil filter														4						
Adjust electric trim solenoid									1 1/2	1 1/2	1 1/2						1 1/2	1 1/2		
Aileron	1	1 1/2	1 1/2	1 1/2	1 1/2	1 1/2	1 1/2	1	1 1/2	1 1/2	1 1/2	1 1/2	1 1/2	1 1/2			1 1/2	1 1/2	1 1/2	
Aileron hinge or bearing (1 aileron)		2	2	2	2	2	2		2	2	2	2	2	2			2	2	2	
Aileron hinge doubler (1 aileron)									4	4	4						4	4	4	
Air box—carburetor (cowl off)	3/4	1	1	1					1	1							1			
Air filter—central (during insp)		1/4	1/4	1/4	1/4	1/2	1/2		1/4	1/4	1/4	1/4	1/4				1/4	1/4		
Air pressure pump		1 3/4	1 3/4	1 3/4	1 3/4									1 1/4						
Air—propeller (service ea)		1/4	1/4	1/4	1/4							1/4	1/4	1/4						
Align wheels (on jacks)		3/4	3/4	3/4	3/4	3/4	3/4					3/4	3/4	3/4						
Alternate air cable (complete)			10	10	10	2	2		2	2	2	10	10					3	10	
Alternate air cable (core)			2	2	2	1	1		1	1	1	2	2					1	2	
Alternator (cowl on)			2 1/4	2 1/4	2 1/4	1 1/2	1 1/2	1 1/2	1 1/2	1 1/2	1 1/2	2	2	1 1/2			1 3/4	1 3/4	3	
Alternator (cowl off)			1	1	1	1	1	1	1	1	1	1	1	1			1	1	1	
Alternator or generator belt (prop off)	1/4	1/4	1/4	1/4	1/4	1/4	1/4	1/4	1/4	1/4	1/4	1/4	1/4	1/4			1/4	1/4	1/4	

Figure 10.7. Sample page from an aviation flat-rate manual. By permission, Southwest Air Rangers, El Paso, Texas, 1985.

level of profits. The goal of the maintenance department should be to contribute its share to the overall business profitability. All of the material presented in this chapter should assist in the managing of the department and in achieving the desired profits. Additional assistance can be obtained through the development and use of an information system, the analysis of all relevant data, and finally the application of control techniques to assure the accomplishment of goals.

Chapter 7 "Information Systems" is devoted to an in-depth examination of the development and use of information systems. Since this section is designed only to illustrate some aspects of maintenance profitability, the one area that should be clearly identified is the charge for service labor. It is important the charge made to the customer cover all of the costs incurred by the organization plus a component of profit.

Information

It is imperative that a service manager receive operational information on the various aspects of the department and that this information be received in a timely manner. Data and costs on income are needed in great enough detail to cover jobs, aircraft, individuals, and so on. Data must be provided as fast as possible in order to analyze and take corrective action immediately.

Analysis

The analysis of reported service data can be accomplished using several techniques. Included here are: (1) comparison with established goals, (2) comparison with previous operating periods, (3) comparison with other similar businesses, and (4) comparison with generally accepted measures of efficiency. The typical maintenance data subjected to this type of analysis would include:

- Total maintenance revenue generated
- Revenue generated by each major working area
- Labor utilization
- Volume of rework
- Net profit as a percentage of sales
- Indirect expenses

Control

Control is a continuation of the analysis. It is the final stage of the comparison process that identifies the desired corrective activity and then implements that activity. For the maintenance manager, it may mean reducing personnel, increasing inventory, establishing a new inspection procedure, or engaging in a concentrated effort to promote annual inspections. The activity will be specifically related to the suggestions that resulted from the analysis and might be adjusted later in order to achieve desired goals.

Techniques

There are numerous procedures and techniques that utilize information, analysis and control that can be useful in gaining and maintaining the desired level of profitability for the maintenance department. Several practical illustrations follow.

Budgeting. There are various applications of budgeting that may be utilized in achieving the desired level of operating profits. Sales are first estimated for the 12 monthly periods. Then, using the historically developed and desirable percentages for cost of sales, gross profit, expenses, and operating margin, the anticipated dollar values for each of these items is calculated for the monthly sales projections. As the operating months are completed, the actual cost of sales, expenses, gross profit, and operating margin are entered in the second line for each month, and the actual percentages for each are calculated. In this manner the budget assists in monitoring sales and maintaining the desired relationship of cost of sales, gross profit, expense and operating margin. Trends can be identified and corrective ac-

Productivity			
Mechanic	**Hours Paid**	**Hours Billed**	**Percent**
1	184.7	160.6	87
2	176.0	171.3	97
3	169.2	164.3	97
4	193.0	123.6	64
5	169.9	145.0	85
6	198.4	165.2	83
7	175.6	157.4	90
8	184.9	175.2	95
9	160.0	152.8	96
10	160.0	160.0	100
	1771.7	1575.4	89

Figure 10.8. Individual and shop productivity.

tion can be taken on a monthly basis to ensure the desired operating margin.

Productivity. A second practical technique for measuring the efficiency of a shop is through the examination of its productivity. Figure 10.8 illustrates the calculation of individual and shop productivity measures. The goal is to bill out as many of the mechanic's working hours as possible. Realistically, this can seldom be 100 percent because there is administrative, training, and other overhead time that should not be directly billed to the customer. In this illustration, the manager should investigate the low productivity of number 4 mechanic (64 percent) and the high productivity of number 10 (100 percent).

Figure 10.9 illustrates a technique for reviewing and controlling the overall shop productivity. This chart shows that the break-even point for this shop at 100 percent productivity is three mechanics. The relationship of number of personnel, their productivity, and maximum income are illustrated. By applying the shop productivity of 89 percent for the ten employees in figure 10.8, you can tell at a glance how the department is doing. This concept can be very valuable in analyzing the overall situation and considering the need to reduce or increase the number of employees, develop additional business, or improve internal efficiency.

Ratios. Another very practical technique to use in monitoring the progress of a shop and its financial success is through ratios in monitoring the income statement. Financial ratios, or the relationship of one element of the income statement to another element, can provide a means of measuring the progress of the maintenance department and determining its degree of success or failure. A ratio can be used in comparison with an earlier ratio for the same department, in comparison with departments in other businesses, in comparison or with standards generally considered acceptable. Some of the key ratios in use and the normally accepted standards are shown in figure 10.10.

These techniques—budgeting, productivity review, and ratio analysis—are only a few of the many techniques available to the manager in

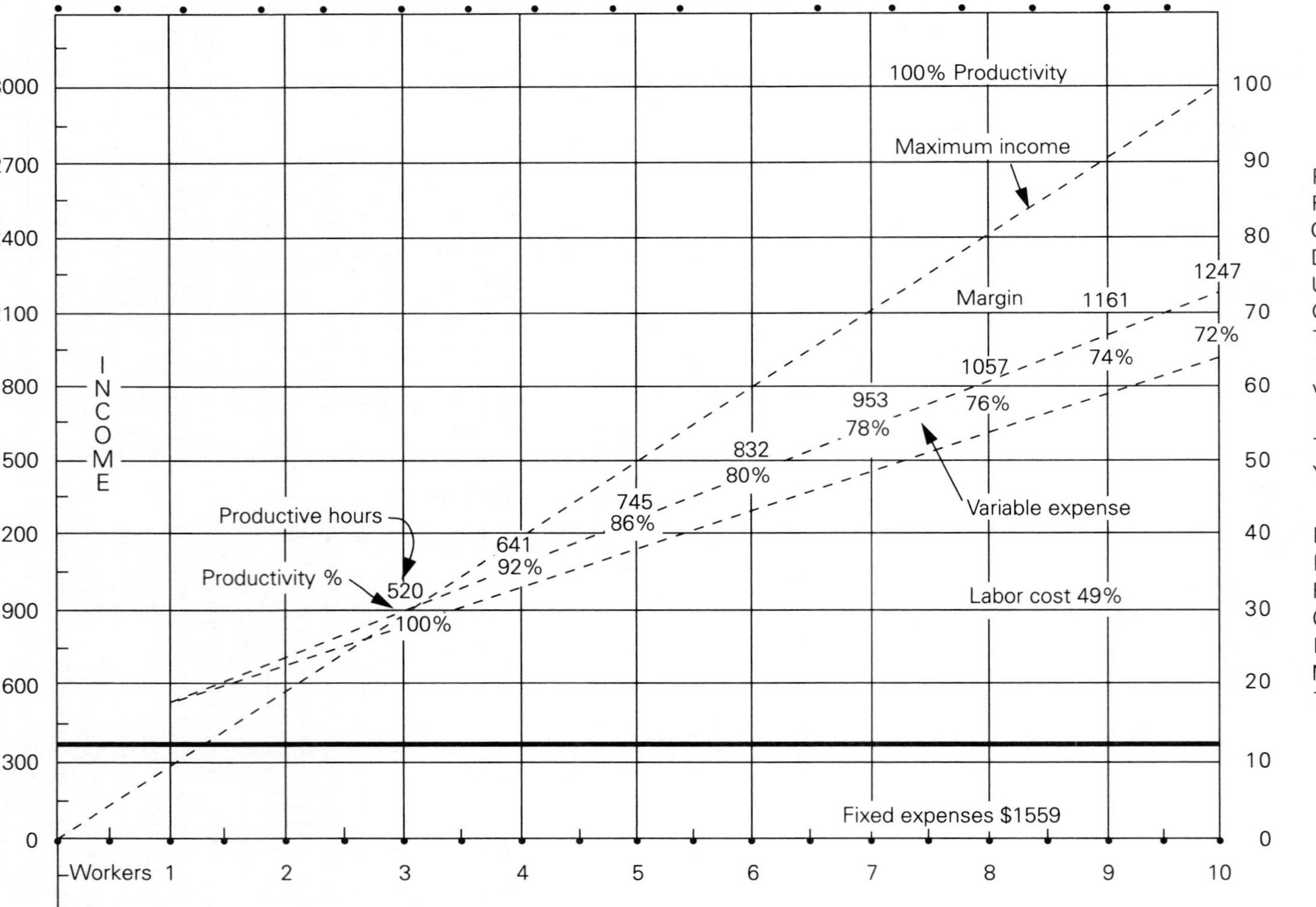

Figure 10.9. Break-even chart used for controlling overall service shop productivity. Courtesy of Robert Varner, Lane Aviation, Columbus, Ohio.

	Type	Acceptable Range
Ratio:	Gross profit as a % of sales	
	Service	45 to 47%
	Parts	18 to 22%
	Electronics	28 to 30%
Ratio:	Expenses as a % of sales	
	Service	44 to 46%
	Parts	13 to 17%
	Electronics	26 to 28%
Ratio:	Operating profit as a % of sales	
	Service	1 to 3%
	Parts	5 to 9%
	Electronics	2 to 4%

Figure 10.10. Key ratios and normally accepted standards for maintenance departments.

maintaining the profitability of the department. However, constant surveillance of maintenance activity and decisive action are the two managerial functions most necessary to ensure a successful maintenance department.

Professional Maintenance Organizations

There are three primary maintenance-related aviation organizations. They include the Aircraft Electronics Association (AEA), Aviation Technical Education Council (ATEC), and the Professional Aviation Maintenance Association (PAMA).

- **Aircraft Electronics Association.** AEA represents over 900 FAA Part 145 Certified Repair Stations as well as most manufacturers of general aviation avionics equipment and airframes.
- **Aviation Technical Education Council.** ATEC represents aviation educators and professionals.
- **Professional Aviation Maintenance Association.** PAMA is a national professional association of aviation maintenance technicians, with some 4,000 individual members and 250 affiliated company members.

Avionics Repair Stations

Avionics repair stations located at fixed-base operations may operate independently or as an integrated part of an existing maintenance operation. As aircraft become more sophisticated and avionics becomes a part of the operating system, there will be a greater need for integrated shops and people who are competent to do both kinds of jobs.

Summary

Managing an aircraft maintenance facility is a separate business or profit center requiring the same business management tools as other segments of the company. A comprehensive organizational structure is key, as is the quality of personnel. Careful attention must be paid to the selection, training, certification and utilization of mechanics, inspectors and repairpeople. Many aspects of repair shop facilities and procedures are controlled by FAA. Identification and compliance with requirements must be done carefully.

Whether as a section of the maintenance department or as a separate unit, the parts and supplies department contributes directly to the success of the maintenance shop. Keeping the optimum parts inventory on hand is a key concern to the service manager.

Quality control depends on the individual mechanic and on the entire organization. It may be achieved through training, procedures, inspection, and recognition. Other areas of concern for the service manager are subcontracting, liability, marketing, administration, and pricing. The key activity is the surveillance of departmental profitability and the use of information, analysis, and controls to assure the attainment of desired profit goals.

Discussion Topics

1. Identify four subdivisions frequently encountered in the organizational structure of a maintenance department and discuss their responsibilities.
2. How would an interested person become a certificated aircraft maintenance technician with an airframe and power-plant rating?
3. What facilities and equipment are needed to open and operate an aviation maintenance shop?
4. How would one set about identifying a practical inventory level for a new aviation service shop? For a shop that has been in business for some time?
5. "Quality control expenditures must be carefully weighed against the benefits thereby obtained." Discuss.
6. What are three implications of product liability for an aviation maintenance facility?
7. What considerations weigh in favor of subcontracting out all maintenance work? Against?
8. "The manager must be involved in setting and maintaining an adequate profit level for a shop." Identify and discuss these managerial activities.
9. Discuss the advantages and disadvantages of flat-rate pricing.

Chapter 11
Safety and Liability

Objectives

- ✔ Explain the difference between "risk management" and "risk transfer."
- ✔ Describe the "deep-pocket" theory.
- ✔ Recognize the advantages and disadvantages of self-insurance.
- ✔ Discuss the specialized areas of insurance typically found when dealing with aviation.
- ✔ Understand the implications of product liability on the FBO owner/manager.
- ✔ Describe the differing roles of the Federal Aviation Administration and the National Transportation Safety Board in relation to aircraft accidents.

Introduction

All types of business enterprise are exposed to some degree of risk. This chapter discusses normal business risks, the special risks of an aviation business, and the process of risk management through risk reduction and risk transfer. Finally, it discusses what must be done when something goes wrong.

The Need for Risk Management Procedures

Risk management consists of two related areas: *risk reduction,* which is accomplished through careful conduct of each aspect of the business, and *risk transfer,* whereby the business owner passes some of the risk to another entity through the purchase of insurance. The more effective the risk reduction, the less expensive the risk transfer. Risk reduction consists of the application of good management techniques by leaving only unforeseeable occurrences to be insured against. Insurance premiums tend to be lower with good risk reduction techniques.

An FBO needs to address the risk management area with great care partially because of the numerous other factors involved in airport services and facilities. There is often a lack of clarity in airport-leases and other operating agreements as to who is responsible for which functions and areas. This can blur the distinction between FBO liability and airport operating liability. There are two reasons for this: (1) FBOs frequently have contract responsibility to provide airport management functions, and (2) airports themselves frequently provide the same or similar functions as FBOs.

An adjunct of this mixed responsibility is the "deep-pocket" approach. This means litigants generally sue the most wealthy party, regardless of whether they're negligent. Other parties involved in aviation, including airport owners, pilots, aircraft owners, and others may not carry sufficient (or any) insurance, so the FBO must also be adequately covered against the deficiencies of others.

Interaction of Safety and Liability

Steps to run a safe, secure airport operation with adequately trained staff are a top priority in risk management. Negligence in an area quite unrelated to a particular claim may be cited as evidence of overall poor attention to detail. A well-run airport operation not only reduces the risk of accidents, but also assists in achieving favorable insurance rates.

Risk Exposure

Normal Business Exposure

The typical business is exposed to at least these risks:

- Fire
- Theft by employees and others
- Vandalism, problems arising from unauthorized access

Severe weather and "acts of God"

- Security of personnel, facilities and equipment
- Product liability
- Third party or non-employee liability
- Employer's liability and workers' compensation
- Automobile liability
- Loss of key person or persons
- Business interruption due to any of these events

Aviation Risk Exposure

In an FBO operation, additional risk occurs because of the nature of the goods and services involved and the high degree of skill required for many of the operations. In addition, several highly incompatible products may be found in different parts of the operation. These include fuel and oil, oxygen, welding materials, electrical equipment, and paint.

Areas of traditional concern to an FBO include:

- Aircraft hull damage
- Bodily injury and property damage to third parties resulting from travel in FBO aircraft
- Nonownership liability—for occurrences in aircraft flown by other than FBO personnel
- Premises and product liability, including aircraft and parts
- Fueling safety
- Hangarkeeper's liability

Relatively new areas that FBOs must concern themselves with in addition include:

- Underground fuel-storage tanks: potential leakage and contamination
- Agricultural chemicals used by crop-dusters: their storage and disposal

- Other hazardous and toxic wastes such as used motor oil
- New rules and more stringent inspections for Part 135 charter flight operations
- Emergency crash, fire and rescue (CPR) response capability at air carrier airports
- Employee exposure to hazardous products on the job
- Greater concern with security and crime prevention

In short, the regulatory context and insurance needs of the typical FBO are increasing, and this trend seems likely to continue.

Risk Reduction

Normal Risk Reduction

Risk management involves active risk reduction as well as risk transference through insurance. It is not simply the purchase of insurance for protection in case of loss. An adequate insurance program is only a partial part and not the ultimate goal of risk management. Actions taken by management before insurance is negotiated, during the life of a policy, and after a loss occurs are all part of risk management. They influence the premium costs to the business as well as the total loss experienced. In each risk area, there are specific organizational actions to reduce the risk and the ultimate costs involved. Additionally, in today's insurance marketplace where deductible amounts tend to be much higher than in previous decades, risk management is vital to cost control.

Fire Risks. Much can be done to reduce the risk of fire, including the use of fire resistant material and protective devices, such as automatic sprinklers and fire extinguishers and training personnel in housekeeping practices, fire prevention, and fire fighting. Figure 11.1 illustrates typical fire-risk reduction procedures.

Crime Risk. One of the most serious threats to business property today is the security threat—burglary, robbery and theft. Managing this threat becomes an important aspect of risk management. Insurance is only one part of managing this risk; reduction and prevention are also extremely important. As small businesses, many aviation operations are prime targets for the burglar and robber. However, many things can be done to reduce this risk by using protective devices, sound operating procedures, and employee training. Protective devices include silent central station burglar alarm systems, burglar resistant locks and equipment, and indoor and outdoor security lighting. Effective operating procedures might include daily bank deposits using an armored car, and using different routes and different times. Another possible safeguard is the transfer of excess cash from register to safe periodically throughout the day.

New technology is available to assist in the area of airport security. Electronic devices may be installed in aircraft that transmit a signal when unauthorized tampering occurs. Sophisticated computerized monitoring and alarm systems are available for the premises. Better quality locks can be installed on aircraft doors. Additional precautions, such as removing the distributor cap, may be advised when the aircraft stops at an unknown field. Local police do not always realize the value of aircraft and FBO equipment, and it's useful to actively keep them informed so that their speedy assistance is available.

A business person must deal with an occasional dishonest employee and dishonest customer. As for the dishonest employee, the manager's first problem is identifying the amount of the loss. Fidelity bonds can be obtained on those employees who have access to large amounts of money. Inventory shrinkage resulting from employee pilferage and other dishonest acts is substantial for many organizations. Risk management in this area includes the reduction or prevention of losses by the careful screening and selection of personnel, an effective

Emergency Preparation

- ☐ Fire organization posted
- ☐ Fire drill held regularly
- ☐ Fire exits well marked and unobstructed
- ☐ Fire alarms well marked and unobstructed
- ☐ Aisles and stairs clear
- ☐ Evacuation procedures posted
- ☐ Procedures for handling fuel spills posted
- ☐ Emergency equipment well marked, in place, and ready for use

Hangars and Buildings

- ☐ Hydrants and water supply checked and serviceable
- ☐ Sprinkler system checked and serviceable
- ☐ Foam and CO_2 systems checked and serviceable
- ☐ Fire doors checked and serviceable
- ☐ Fire extinguishers well marked, in place, checked and tagged
- ☐ Hose stations checked and serviceable
- ☐ Electrical circuits identified, enclosed, and provided with proper overload protection
- ☐ Gas systems checked and serviceable
- ☐ Fuel pumping equipment in good condition and free of leaks (extinguishing equipment adequate and available)

Maintenance Equipment

- ☐ Spray booths clean and properly ventilated and sprinkler heads protected from overspray
- ☐ Power tools and accessories, wiring in good condition
- ☐ Pressurized bottles properly connected and secured
- ☐ Mobile equipment extinguishers well marked, in place, and serviceable
- ☐ Powered equipment properly grounded
- ☐ Test equipment free of leaks, wiring in good condition

Management

- ☐ General housekeeping adequate
- ☐ Changes (alterations, processes, methods, and procedures) first cleared with Fire Marshall
- ☐ Floors clean and free of flammable fluid spills
- ☐ Storage of material orderly and in accordance with regulations
- ☐ Aircraft fueling in accordance with regulations (NFPA 407)
- ☐ Spray painting in accordance with regulations (NFPA 33)
- ☐ Welding and other open-flame operations in accordance with regulations (NFPA 410)
- ☐ Ramp and grounds clean and free of debris
- ☐ Proper disposal of soiled shop towels and rags

Figure 11.1. Fire inspection checklist. From "Aviation Ground Operation Safety Handbook," copyright 1977 by National Safety Council, Chicago, IL 60611. Used with permission.

accounting system, and varied control methods. Safeguards to be considered include (1) the use of outside auditors, (2) countersignatures on all checks, (3) immediate deposit and duplication of all incoming checks, (4) bank statement reconciliation by employees other than those who make the deposits, (5) joint access to safe deposit boxes, (6) "professional shopper" checks on cash register operating procedures, and (7) ensuring that all employees handling money take regular vacations.

The dishonest customer represents to the manager the additional perils of shoplifting and bad check passing. Retail operations expect to lose a percentage of their merchandise through shoplifting. Although most FBO operations do not include many retail functions, office supplies, maintenance supplies, and retail inventory are at risk. This kind of loss can be reduced by constant vigilance, special equipment, and sound operating procedures. Equipment such as two-way and convex mirrors and closed-circuit television, coupled with wide aisles, clear vision, and alert employees will help prevent the loss of much merchandise. Prominently displayed warnings against shoplifting and rules that provide customer guidance will deter the would-be offender in many instances.

Bad check losses pose a problem that can be minimized through sound procedures and well-trained employees. Proper identification should be requested before accepting checks, and then only for the amount of the purchase. The identification procedure should include a photograph along with a sample signature; or, in lieu of this, two forms of identification may be required. Postdated, illegibly written, or two-party checks should not be accepted. Employees should be trained in following the procedures selected and in identifying potential bad-check passers. A computerized check authorization bureau may be a worthwhile service.

Aviation Risk Reduction

As evidenced by the many types of aviation insurance and liability suits, there are many exposure or risk elements in the aviation operating areas. Poor maintenance, bad housekeeping, nonexistent or vague guidelines and procedures, inadequately trained personnel, low quality standards and lack of emphasis on safety, and poor supervision all can lead to accidents and costly legal conflicts. The aviation business is faced with potential threats from a wide variety of consumers who feel that they have been injured by a variety of "products." Business and financial risks in this area are also influenced by such specific actions as selecting parts for installation on an aircraft, "signing off" work as having been completed, or returning an aircraft to flight status. These and other similar actions should be considered carefully and steps should be taken to avoid unnecessary exposure or risk.

Because of concerns with the scale of claims for general aviation related accidents and injuries, various aviation groups have been securing product liability legislation that provides some relief. In late 1994, a new bill was signed into law by President Bill Clinton, providing a statute of repose for aviation manufacturers. The new 18-year liability limit provides some relief from potential legal action and is expected to help revitalize general aviation. Product liability insurance costs are 30 percent or more of new aircraft costs and up to $70,000.00 per aircraft, making aircraft ownership very expensive. A decline in aircraft ownership affects FBO businesses of all types. FBOs have additional risk exposure because of repairing a part of an aircraft engine or airframe; they, too, may be part of a lawsuit when an accident occurs.

Good operational risk management will:

1. Select and train qualified aviation personnel.
2. Provide adequate operational guidelines and procedures.
3. Insist on good housekeeping practices.

4. Place a high emphasis on safety.
5. Require consistently high quality standards for services and products.
6. Provide the supervision and maintenance necessary to ensure that these elements routinely take place.

Insurance companies recognize the relationship that exists between an efficient, well-managed, safe aviation organization and a low accident rate and minimum risk exposure. Prior to insuring against some of the aviation risks, many companies will survey the organization carefully, checking all the key operational areas and developing some concept of the premium rate structure. Low premiums have been awarded to those groups of aviation businesses that have demonstrated good organizational practices and procedures, and higher premiums have been assigned to the others. The practices, procedures, and recommendations of this book should assist the manager in identifying and correcting some of the operational risk exposures and should result in lower insurance premiums. The Operational Procedure Guide and the Operational Manual that appear as Appendices to this book should be especially useful when dealing with some of the flight operation areas. The chapters dealing with human resources and maintenance will also provide assistance in those areas.

Aviation Safety Regulations and Guidelines

There are a number of FAA Advisory Circulars about safe aviation operations in such areas as fueling, aircraft handling, and the condition of premises.[1,2] Along with airport certification requirements and the regulations for FAA-approved maintenance, instruction, and other FBO operations, these provide a very detailed set of requirements and suggestions on how to run a sound operation.[3]

Additionally, FBOs must also deal with EPA regulations and OSHA requirements regarding various hazards, including federal and state requirements about hazardous products handling and disposal. In addition, such organizations as the National Safety Council and the National Fire Protection Association provide a number of aviation and other booklets.[4,5,6] Individual airport minimum standards may provide another set of requirements for safe FBO operations in various areas. In the words of an aviation lawyer, this is how to regard the FAA documents:

"Rest assured that a plaintiff's attorney will acquire the Advisory Circulars and that the lawyer (and probably a jury) will fault an airport for any area in which its facility is deficient according to the Advisory Circular recommendations, even though these are not mandatory."

Airport Risk Audit

This lawyer recommends a self-applied risk audit where the airport operator, or in this case the FBO, goes over every area of activity to see if it is up to FAA and other standards. The Management Audit shown in Appendix III is a good starting point.

Procedures Manual

The safety procedures applied by the FBO should be written and referenced as appropriate by the Advisory Circulars and other standards. This document should be used for training and for recording the dates of risk audits and corrective actions.

Documentation

If a suit is ever brought against an FBO, then clear and dated documentation of standards, training, corrective action, and follow-up will be an asset in presenting evidence of a risk-preventing attitude. Lack of documentation will permit the plaintiff to go unchallenged.

Inclement Weather

Weather exerts a tremendous influence on aviation operations. The level of activity and safety of personnel, equipment, and facilities are influenced by inclement weather, and they are a major management concern. Of course, the primary concern is for the welfare of personnel, equipment, and facilities. The secondary concern is for the reduction or curtailment of aviation operations. High winds, torrential rains, heavy snows, dust storms, or floods can all injure people, damage aircraft, disable equipment, and ruin physical facilities.

A well-developed weather response plan includes evacuation schedules (aircraft, vehicles and personnel), protection of inventory, supplies and records, security of utilities, and procedures for getting the facility back into operation. As with other inclement weather situations, the primary concerns are knowing the situation, obtaining early warning, having a plan to follow, making the decision to act, and then following through as needed.

Risk Transfer

Principles of Insurance

The principle of insurance is to pool risk with others in similar situations so that in the event of a problem some protection is obtained. Risk is not eliminated by taking out insurance; there will still be some risks covered only by the operator (deductibles or ineligible areas); and some high-risk situations may call for such high premiums that the FBO chooses to buy only partial coverage. In some cases the owner has such a large internal risk pool that it is less expensive (or at least it is thought to be less expensive) to self-insure. This situation occurs, for example, in some states that own several airports, as it does with some large corporations.

Insurance Regulations

Some insurance is optional; some is mandatory. Workmen's compensation falls into the latter category and, in most cases, airport owners require some level of insurance for operators on their airport. This most likely will be spelled out in the airport's minimum standards and also in the lease.

Recent Developments in U.S. Insurance Markets

Industry as a whole. In the 1980s insurance costs of all types rose greatly and many types of insurance became virtually unavailable. This situation began in 1980 when both inflation and interest rates were climbing rapidly. For a period of time the prime rate was over 20 percent. As a result, tremendous investment yields became available, providing a strong incentive for insurance companies to acquire cash—by selling more policies. The enthusiasm for growth in insurance sales led to insurance price competition, so that comparatively good amounts of coverage became available for lower rates; and more insurance sellers were in the business.

As a result of this price competition, by 1981–82 prices for many types of insurance (especially commercial, property and casualty), were crashing down for a broad spectrum of the U.S. insurance industry. By 1982 the loss and expense ratio was often well over 100 percent which meant there were losses in the insurance sector of many companies; however, overall balance sheets still looked very healthy because of the excellent investment income results still being obtained.

By 1983 many companies had loss and expense ratios over 110 percent. By this time, overall profits were declining—due to underwriting losses on the underpriced policies written since 1980, and to falling interest rates. The industry as a whole still made a profit in 1983, but it was down from the previous three years. By mid-

1984, price increases were a necessity for many companies; and by the end of 1984, prices were generally rising.

Much of the insurance written in the United States is reinsured. By passing on part or most of the exposure to other insurers, a company can reduce its overall risk of being insufficiently covered for a major claim from one source. The ultimate reinsurer is Lloyds of London. The same economic forces were affecting the reinsurance market over this period. Companies that had entered the reinsurance business because of lucrative investment opportunities were getting out again by the end of 1984.

During the course of 1985, four consequences of the earlier phenomena occurred:

- Insurance prices jumped to much higher levels than before
- Some types of insurance became unobtainable
- Some levels of coverage became unobtainable
- Fewer choices of insurer became available

These conditions have continued into the early 1990s.

Aviation insurance. Aviation insurance is almost totally a reinsurance business, so that the sources of insurance have decreased even more than for most types of coverage. In the late 1970s there were 25 to 30 insurers offering various types of aviation coverage, and a decade later there were less than a dozen.

Not all of these offer all types of coverage. There may be only one offeror for a particular need. In addition to these 11, there are others who have been unable to complete their treaty agreements with Lloyds, and may not reappear in the aviation marketplace.

Within aviation, the most buying power is held by the airlines. However, general aviation has only 2 percent. Within general aviation the highest risk areas are:

- Old aircraft
- Homebuilts
- Ultralights and other experimentals
- Proposed primary aircraft
- General aviation after-market modifications

With the decline of aviation insurance availability, the lowest risks tend to be the only ones able to get coverage. This applies to new policies as well as renewals.

The effects are as follows:

- For small FBOs, coverage is almost non-existent
- Publicly owned airports can still get coverage, but at rising cost
- Underwriters are seeking limits of $100,000 per seat—virtually useless for a fatal or severe accident, given court settlement levels, which in the United States are the highest in the world and often over a million dollars

Everyone remotely involved in a claim resulting from an accident may be sued under "joint and several liability" considerations—the aircraft manufacturer, the most recent FBO that worked on the plane, the maker of parts, the airport, and so on.

One effect of the insurance and claims situation is the cost of product liability insurance. This is due to the value of many recent liability suit settlements, as well as to other trends in the insurance industry. For example, Bob Martin, general counsel of Beech Aircraft, estimated that product liability claims against Beech, Cessna, and Piper exceeded $1 billion. This was approximately twice the net worth of these three companies combined.

These companies are currently forced to spend $12 to $18 million annually to defend themselves against product liability lawsuits. Such lawsuits, which are successfully defended in 90 to 95 percent of the cases, may involve settlements of $1 million or more per person for wrongful death.

The costs of product liability insurance are a part of the cost of each year's production of general aviation aircraft. In 1978 when over 17,000 aircraft were shipped, each bore a smaller fraction of the total insurance for the product line cost. Today, with shipments of under 1,000 aircraft, the insurance cost burden per aircraft is many times higher. Liability costs often represent more than 30 percent of the price of the aircraft. Liability costs have also raised FBO prices for repair and maintenance of aircraft.

The new product liability bill passed in 1994 provides an 18-year liability limit for general aviation aircraft. This, however, does not modify all liability issues for FBO owners. In the past, there has been about a three-year cycle in the insurance industry. However, since Lloyds uses a three-year bookkeeping cycle, the results of any year are delayed. Moreover, the high levels of aviation accidents in 1983 and 1985 did not show up on underwriting losses until 2 to 3 years later because of the time it takes for legal proceedings. Thus the decline has taken longer than usual to turn around. It would appear that aviation insurance will continue to have a negative effect on general aviation growth although the new liability limit should help level off some insurance costs in the near future.

Normal Business Insurance

In general, the following types of insurance are available to the aviation manager:

1. Fire and general property insurance—covering fire losses, vandalism, hail, and wind damage.
2. Public liability insurance—covering injury to the public, such as a customer falling on the property.
3. Product liability insurance—covering injury to the customer arising from the use of materials or service bought at the business.
4. Burglary insurance—covering forceable entry and theft of merchandise, equipment, or cash.
5. Consequential loss insurance—covering loss of earnings or extra expenses in case of suspension of business due to fire or other catastrophe.
6. Fidelity bond—covering theft by an employee.
7. Fraud insurance covering counterfeit money, bad checks, and larceny.
8. Workmen's compensation insurance—covering injury to employees at work.
9. Life insurance—covering the life of the owners, key employees, and other personnel.
10. Plate glass insurance—covering window breakage.
11. Boiler insurance—covering damage to the premises caused by boiler explosion.

These specific types of insurance can be classified into four general categories:

1. Loss or damage to property owned by the business.
2. Bodily injury and owners property damage and liability.
3. Business interruptions and losses resulting from fire and other damages to the premises.
4. Death or disability of key executives.

The aviation business is concerned with these basic risk areas and the insurance that will serve to protect it. The list just described includes the typical operations, facilities, and resulting exposures of any business. A second area includes those exposures associated primarily with aviation businesses and their unique needs.

Loss or damage of property. The average aviation business has a considerable investment in buildings, furnishings, and inventory. These investments should be protected against fire and other perils such as smoke, wind storms and hail, riot, civil commotion, explosion, and damage by aircraft or motor vehicles. The latter form of risk insurance, or extended coverage, can be added to the basic fire insurance policy at little additional cost. Vandalism, malicious mischief, earthquake, and boiler explosion can also be added to the policy. In the beginning, the manager is concerned with the determination of insurable value and the approach to be taken. There are two basic measures: actual cash value and replacement cost value. Replacement cost means that the cost of replacing the facility with a similar structure of a like kind and quality at present-day prices. Actual cash value is based on replacement cost and is generally considered to be replacement cost minus depreciation. In planning for property insurance, the manager should consider accepting a coinsurance clause, as it may result in a substantial reduction in premiums. Under the provisions of a coinsurance clause, the manager agrees to maintain insurance equal to some specified percentage of the value of the property (80, 90, or 100 percent) in return for a lower premium rate. Payment is made under the coinsurance provision on the basis of the following formula:

$$\frac{\text{amount of insurance carried}}{\text{amount of insurance agreed to carry}} \times \text{amount of loss} = \text{amount paid}$$

If, at the time of loss, the insured organization has failed to maintain the specified percentage, it cannot collect the full amount of its loss, even if the loss is small. It is important to note that the coinsurance clause is applied at the time of loss and that the insured has the responsibility for maintaining the proper amount of insurance.

Under recent inflationary trends, building costs have increased rapidly, almost doubling in the last two decades. Thus replacement costs are much higher and have resulted in a tendency for older buildings to be underinsured. The manager should check frequently to see that facilities are adequately insured. Insurance companies frequently offer assistance in determining replacement value by means of an "appraisal kit," which includes multipliers to apply to the original cost, based on the age and location of the facility.

Legal liability. Legal liability is potentially the greatest risk that a general aviation manager faces. The loss associated with business property is limited to the value of the property. However, in liability exposure there is no fixed loss limit, and a judgment against the business in a personal injury or property damage suit may be a far higher amount. The size of damage suit awards has risen sharply in recent years, and today liability coverage of $1 million or more is not considered high or unreasonable. "Wrongful death" settlements, for example, range from $500,000.00 to $1,000,000.00 and up in recent U.S. aviation cases. Without liability insurance, a single judgment might strip an organization or put it out of business completely. Consequently, liability insurance is considered essential.

There are four types of liability exposure: (1) employer's liability and workmen's compensation (2) liability to nonemployees (3) automobile liability and (4) professional liability.

Employer's liability and workmen's compensation. Under common law as well as under workmen's compensation laws, an employer is liable for injury to employees at work caused by failure to (1) provide safe tools and working conditions, (2) hire competent fellow workers, or (3) warn employees of an existing danger. Employee coverage and the extent of employer liability varies from state to state.

Non-employee liability. Non-employee liability, general liability or third-party liability is insurance for any kind of bodily injury to nonemployees except that caused by automobiles and professional malpractice. This includes customers, pedestrians, delivery people, and the public at large. It may even extend to trespassers or other outsiders even when the manager exercised "reasonable care."

Automobile liability. Cars and trucks are a serious source of liability. Such liability is encountered primarily in vehicles owned by the business, but can be experienced under the doctrine of agency when the employee is operating his or her own or someone else's car in the course of employment. In this instance, the business could be held vicariously liable for injuries and property damage caused by the employee. If it is customary or convenient for an employee to operate his or her own car while on company business, the business is well advised to acquire non-ownership automobile liability insurance.

Business interruptions and losses. Although losses resulting from property damage may be covered by insurance, there are other losses that may be the consequence of property damage or that are indirect. For example, a fire may force the business to move to another location or to actually cease operations temporarily. Business interruption insurance can be purchased to cover the fixed costs that would continue if the business were forced to cease operations temporarily, extra expenses incurred in moving, and estimated profits lost during the period.

Death or disability of key people. The death or disability of a "key person" in the organization can cause serious loss to the business. If one person is critical to the success of the company, his or her death or disablement may result in the demise of the company. Even if the key person is a non-owner employee, his or her disability can be extremely serious to the company, for the person's services may be lost, yet the obligation to pay that person's salary continues. These risks can be minimized by acquiring life and disability insurance on the key person(s) payable to the company in amounts that will permit the business to operate and survive.

SMP—Special Multiperil Policy. The commercial risk insurance field has a comprehensive policy similar to the homeowner's policy. It is called the Special Multiperil Policy. Under this policy, the manager can purchase one insurance policy to cover most of the risks that normally would require separate underwriting agreements. The only ones not included in the package are workmen's compensation and automobile. By combining the policies into one package, policy writing and handling costs are reduced by creating savings reflected in reduced premium rates. This procedure can result in as much as a 25 percent savings in insurance costs and can cause the manager to consider his risk and insurance problem as one, rather than several individual difficulties. The likely end result is avoiding overlapping coverage and developing a program that covers the important risk exposures.

Special Aviation Coverages

Aviation is a very specialized area of insurance; general aviation, in particular, lacks buying power in the insurance market place. Therefore, it is vital to choose a knowledgeable agent. The following is a guide.

The aviation organization, in addition to the normal exposures of business, is faced with the special exposures and problems of the aviation world. These risks must be recognized and handled in a manner similar to other risks. Because of the magnitude of the risks, the premium costs involved, and the potential impact on the business if adequate protection is not provided, special emphasis and attention should be given this area by the manager. The major insurance coverages in aviation include:

- Aircraft hull
- Aircraft liability
- Airport liability
- Workman's compensation
- Aviation product liability
- Underground tank coverage
- Hazardous waste

Aircraft hull coverage may normally be written to cover two basic types of coverage: "all risks" and "all risks, vehicle not in flight." The "all risks" coverage is a broader form of insurance and protects the owner against damage to, or physical loss of, his or her aircraft while on the ground or in flight. It is frequently written with a deductible clause that applies to all losses except fire, lightning, explosion, vandalism, transportation, and theft. This deductible is frequently varied for the "not in motion" exposure and the "aircraft in motion" risks. The size of the deductible has a direct bearing on the premium and is one of the factors considered by the manager in planning his insurance coverage and risk management. The "all risks, vehicle not in flight" is a coverage that protects the physical aircraft against loss or damage while on the ground. Deductibles follow the same pattern as for "all risks" coverage.

Aircraft liability insurance covers the insured's legal liability that results from ownership, maintenance, or use of the aircraft. There are many exposures that must be considered in this area, including:

- Passenger bodily injury
- Bodily injury excluding passengers
- Property damage
- Medical payments—passenger and crew
- Voluntary settlement coverage
- Non-ownership liability

In general, the liability of aircraft owners and operators for injury or damage to persons or property conforms to the state laws applicable to damage suits stemming from accidents that occurred on the land or water. The basic legal principles applied are the common law rules of negligence—that is, the burden is upon the person who has been damaged to prove fault as a proximate cause of the accident. This has been expressed as a failure to exercise the requisite degree of legal care owed to the damaged plaintiff. The coverages included in bodily injury, property damage, and medical payments are self-evident from the terms. The limits of the coverage, especially because of the catastrophic nature of aviation hazards, are a primary concern. It is extremely difficult to select adequate limits in these three areas for the exposure involved. The trend over the last few years has been toward higher and higher limits because of larger court settlements.

Voluntary settlement or admitted liability insurance is available in conjunction with passenger legal liability. It is written on a limit-per-seat basis. Regardless of the legal liability, it offers to pay on behalf of the insured the prearranged sums for loss of life, limbs, or sight suffered by passengers in the aircraft. When voluntary settlement payment is offered a passenger, a release of liability against the insured must be obtained. In the event the claimant refuses to sign a release, the offered payment is withdrawn and the passenger liability coverage applies.

Non-ownership liability arises when the individual or corporation utilizes rented, borrowed, or chartered aircraft. Generally the owner's policy does not protect the user, so additional coverage is obtained through non-ownership policies or policy clauses that covers the use of other aircraft or substitute aircraft.

Airport liability insurance is designed to protect the owner and/or operator of a private, municipal, or commercial airport against claims resulting from an injury to any member of the public or damage to property suffered while on the airport. Owners and operators are liable for all such damage caused by their failure to exercise reasonable care. This liability extends to lessees, airplane owners, passengers, and persons using the facilities of the airport as well as to spectators, visitors, and other members of the general public who may be on or about the premises. Airport operators owe a duty to a wide range of people, and litigation may arise from a wide variety of events occurring on and off the airport.

The principal areas where litigation might take place can be summarized under the following headings:

Aircraft operations (liability to bailees, tenants and invitees)

- Aircraft accidents
- Fueling
- Hangar keeping
- Loading services
- Maintenance and service
- Rescue

Premises operations (liability to tenants and invitees)

- Automobile parking lots
- Elevators and escalators
- Police and security
- Slip and fall
- Special events
- Tenants and contractors
- Vehicles

This list is not inclusive nor complete. It does, however, suggest the variety of occurrences where the airport manager has a legal duty. The hangar keeper's legal liability endorsement provides coverage for another exposure of concern to airport owners or operators.[7] Damage to aircraft in the care, custody, or control, but not owned by the facility operator is normally not covered in the standard airport liability policy. Many claims have been directed against airport management for aircraft loading-stand accidents, although the majority have been against air carriers and ramp-service companies. Rescue operations, if conducted negligently, may lead to legal liability for damage to persons or property. Aircraft maintenance contracts can also be the source of claims for liability and damages.

Activities on the airport premises include a number of occasions and events that have led to legal action and judgments. Among these are automobile parking lots, stairs, elevators and escalators, police and security actions, airport special events, airport tenants and contractors, and vehicle operations. These areas are similar risk areas for many business activities and are not peculiar to aviation. The law follows the general rule that the operator has a legal duty to keep the premises in a reasonably safe condition for those persons who either expressly, or by implication, come to the facility by invitation.

Workman's compensation under common law, as well as the laws of the various states, considers an aviation employer liable for injury to employees at work caused by his failure to:

- Provide safe tools and working conditions
- Hire competent fellow employees
- Warn employees of an existing danger

Although employee coverage and the extent of the employer's liability varies from state to state, most states require employers to pay insurance premiums either to a state fund or to private insurance companies. The funds generated in this manner are used to compensate the victims of industrial accidents or occupational illness. Premiums are based on rates that reflect the hazards involved and safety program effectiveness.

Aviation product liability coverage is another area of great concern to aviation managers. The rapidly increasing number of products liability claims and the substantial costs incurred in defending these suits, as well as paying for adverse judgments, have dramatized the need for sound insurance protection in this area. Typical claims have arisen from incorrect fueling, poor maintenance, and deficient design or construction of airframe, engine, or components. There are some who feel that the products liability claim area poses such a threat to general aviation manufacturers that the entire industry faces severe restrictions, unless positive steps, such as a national aviation accident insurance program, are taken. Such a program would provide for a legislated compensation (a flat sum and/or documented losses) to those who have suffered a loss as a result of an aircraft accident.

Product liability law works in curious ways and has created a growing problem for the aviation business. The airplane manufacturer, as a larger corporation, is a frequent target for product liability suits. In these suits, where the product is alleged to be defective, it is easy under our judicial system to find the jury applying present-day standards in judging the safety of a product built many years ago. Coupling this with the humanitarian impulse—the feeling that someone has been hurt and should therefore be helped—juries are inclined to provide recovery from those best able to pay, rather than those responsible for causing the damage. An illustration of this is a suit brought by a widow against an airframe manufacturer. She claimed the aircraft in which her husband crashed was defective. He was a VFR pilot who, after an evening on the town, loaded his plane above gross takeoff weight, flew into a raging snowstorm without checking the weather, iced up, and subsequently crashed. The jury awarded $1,000,000 which was paid by the aircraft company's product liability insurance policy. When a juror was later asked why the jury made the award when the fault was clearly the pilot's, he responded: "Well someone was hurt, so we felt someone had to pay." This trend is further illustrated by a California jury who awarded punitive damages of $17.5 million against Beech Aircraft Company—an amount that was about 40 percent of Beech's net worth at that time. The rising cost of product liability has been reflected in the price tag placed on new aircraft. Today, the price of a new single engine retractable includes several thousand dollars to cover the cost of product liability insurance. This cost is ultimately absorbed by the consumer, just as though it were an item listed on the bill of sale. The insurance cost varies with the size of the plane and the price tag attached.

Aviation businesses engaged in maintenance, fueling, sales, or similar activities have been engaged in product liability suits. One aircraft service company, which had contracted to perform a 100-hour inspection, was sued because a broken valve stem was the cause of an accident. The company was alleged to be negligent in failing to discover the defect that caused the accident.

In another case, the underlying cause of an accident was determined to be the installation of bolts and bearings that did not meet specifications and an inadequate inspection that failed to reveal this condition. Damages in this case were awarded at $1.4 million.

Manufacturers and installers of aircraft components can be subject to legal action. There have been court cases involving fuel pumps, nose gear actuating cylinders, cylinder barrels, and propellor controls. Both the manufacturers and the aviation business using the products are involved in legal actions of this type.

The sale of used aircraft is also subject to this type of legal action, as evidenced by a case where the court held the seller liable for latent defects affecting the airworthiness of the aircraft.

Fueling activities have led to several accidents and resulting products liability suits for aviation businesses. Using de-icing fluid instead of ADI fluid, and jet fuel instead of aviation gasoline are two actions that have led to many aircraft crashes and resulting court cases.

Underground storage tanks. A relatively new area for FBO concern is underground fuel storage tanks. Many older tanks have corroded and begun to leak, risking contamination of water supplies and other hazards. The EPA has issued stringent requirements for inspection and, if necessary, removal of tanks. One aspect of the new rule is that FBOs and others with underground tanks must provide a $1 million or more bond as assurance of their ability to handle any tank problem. For most FBOs this results in a need for new insurance coverage.[8,9,10]

Hazardous wastes. EPA regulations regarding the handling, storage, disposal and disclosure of hazardous wastes have several effects for FBOs with maintenance shops and the more specialized agricultural operator.[11,12,13,14,15]

FBO/Landlord Agreement

When an FBO is a tenant, it is best to obtain a written agreement with the airport owner/landlord regarding responsibilities on the airport. This should relate to area, functions, and information flows between the two. As much risk as possible should be shifted to the airport owner. This document should be reviewed, if not prepared, by a lawyer.

Selection of Aviation Insurance

Knowing what kind of insurance to carry and how much to purchase are important aspects of good risk management. Here are some guidelines of risk management and insurance selection.

1. Consider carefully:
   The size of the potential loss
   Probability of loss occurring
   Resources to replace the loss should it occur
2. How much the business can afford to lose
   If the loss is likely to produce serious financial impairment or bankruptcy, then the risk should not be assumed
3. Consider the scale of the risk in relation to insurance costs
   A large loss may be protected by a small premium
4. Consider the probability and the size as potential losses
   Repeated losses are predictable and typically small
   Small losses can be assumed and budgeted as a cost of business
5. The following risks can be covered by insurance:
   - Loss or damage of property.
   - Personal injury to customers, employees, and the general public.
   - Loss of income resulting from interruption of business because of damage to the firm's operating assets.
   - Loss to the business from the death or disability of key employees or the owner.

Selection of Aviation Insurer

Care is needed in selecting a knowledgeable, reliable, and resourceful aviation insurance broker. One aviation group recommends asking these questions about the insurance provider:

1. Will the person responsible for my policy be an aviation expert with authority to bind coverage on behalf of his/her company?
2. Will I see my representative on a regular basis?
3. Will all coverages be handled in one simple policy?
4. Can I have an itemized monthly billing showing the cost of each aircraft plus other endorsements and coverages?
5. Will premiums cover only the actual number of days I own an aircraft with no short-rate penalty or finance charge?
6. Is my policy continuous, eliminating the annual problem of filing certificates to lienholders and others?
7. Is my policy flexible enough to handle special needs the business may become involved in, such as banner towing, pipeline patrol, and so on?
8. In the event of a loss, will an outside adjuster be called, or does my representative have authority to settle claims?
9. If an aircraft is damaged or a total loss, will I have to wait weeks or months to receive payment?
10. Is my policy tailored to my exact needs and usage?

Accident Policy and Procedures

In the event that an accident does occur on the FBO's property, to one of his passengers or to his aircraft, there are not only insurance claims to be filed, but also a number of other regulatory agencies with which to coordinate. Moreover, the following of proper procedures in handling accidents can reduce risk at the time and maintain a higher level of confidence on the part of your insurer for the next time.

Federal Reporting Requirements

Both the National Transportation Safety Board (NTSB) and the FAA are required to be involved in aviation accident investigations, depending on the nature and severity of the accident. A description of each agency's role and requirements follow.

The National Transportation Safety Board (NTSB) is the federal agency responsible for determining the probable cause of all U. S. civil transportation accidents. This responsibility is vested solely in the Safety Board and cannot be delegated to any other agency. If during the course of its investigation of accidents, the Board discovers facts, conditions, and circumstances that in the interest of public safety require corrective action, it may issue safety recommendations calling for remedial changes in any phase of civil aviation. The knowledge gained from accident investigation is used to prevent additional accidents. The Board also generates safety recommendations from the findings of special studies.

In carrying out its responsibility to determine the cause of all U. S. civil aviation accidents, the Board has issued United States Safety Investigation Regulations (SIR). Part 830 of the Regulations specifies rules pertaining to aircraft accidents, incidents, overdue aircraft, and safety investigations. It is important for managers and pilots to be familiar with and comply with the provisions of this regulation.[16] Important sections of Part 830 follow.

An accident. The National Transportation Safety Board has defined an "aircraft accident" as an occurrence associated with the operation of an aircraft that takes place between the time any person boards the aircraft with the intention of flight until such time as all such persons have disembarked, in which any person suffers death or serious injury as a result of being in or upon the aircraft or by direct contact with the aircraft or anything attached thereto, or the aircraft receives substantial damage.

Serious injury means any injury that:

1. Requires hospitalization for more than 48 hours, commencing within seven days from the date the injury was received.
2. Results in a fracture of any bone (except simple fractures of fingers, toes, or nose).
3. Involves lacerations that cause severe hemorrhages, nerve, muscle, or tendon damage.
4. Involves injury to any internal organ.
5. Involves second- or third-degree burns or any burns affecting more than 5 percent of the body surface.

In November 1980, changes were made to NTSB rules involving accident notification responsibilities. The definition of a "fatal injury" was revised to include any injury that results in death within 30 days of an accident. Added also was the definition "incident," which is an "occurrence other than an accident, associated with the operation of an aircraft that affects or could affect the safety of operations."

Substantial damage means damage or structural failure that adversely affects the structural strength, performance, or flight characteristics of the aircraft and that would normally require major repair or replacement of the affected component.

Rules Pertaining to Aircraft Accidents, Incidents, Overdue Aircraft, and Safety Investigations

Immediate Notification. The operator of an aircraft shall immediately, and by the most expeditious means available, notify the nearest National Transportation Safety Board, Bureau of Aviation Safety Field Office when:

1. An aircraft accident or any of the following listed incidents occur:

   Flight control system malfunction or failure
   Any required flight crew member is unable to perform his normal flight duties as a result of injury or illness
   Turbine engine rotor failures occur
   In-flight fire occurs
   Aircraft collide in flight
2. An aircraft is overdue and is believed to have been involved in an accident.

The notification shall contain the following information, if available:

1. Type, nationality, and registration marks of the aircraft.
2. Name of owner and operator of the aircraft.
3. Name of the pilot-in-command.
4. Date and time of the accident.
5. Last point of departure and point of intended landing of the aircraft.
6. Position of the aircraft with reference to some easily defined geographical point.
7. Number of persons aboard, number killed, and number seriously injured.
8. Nature of the accident, the weather and the extent of damage to the aircraft, so far as is known.
9. A description of any explosives, radioactive materials, or other dangerous articles carried.

Manner of notification. The most expeditious method of notification to the National Transportation Safety Board by the operator will be determined by the circumstances existing at that time. The National Transportation Safety Board has advised that any of the following are considered examples of acceptable notification.

- Direct telephone notification
- Notification to the Federal Aviation Administration, who would, in turn, notify the NTSB by direct communication—that is, dispatch or telephone.

Reports. The operator shall file a report on NTSB Form 6120.1 or 6120.2, available from the National Transportation Safety Board Field Offices, or the National Transportation Safety Board, Washington, D.C.:

1. Within ten days after an occurrence for which notification is required.
2. When, after seven days, an overdue aircraft is still missing.
3. Upon request of an authorized representative of the National Transportation Safety Board.

If physically able at the time the report is submitted, each crew member shall attach thereto a statement setting forth the facts, conditions, and circumstances relating to the accident or occurrence as they appear to him or her to the best of his or her knowledge and belief. If the crew member is incapacitated, he or she shall submit the statement as soon as physically able.

Where to File the Reports. The operator of an aircraft shall file with the Field Office of the National Transportation Safety Board nearest the accident or incident any report required by this section.

The Safety Board is a relatively small organization and has delegated to the Federal Aviation Administration the task of investigating nonfatal minor crashes involving light aircraft grossing under 12,500 pounds, with the exception of air-taxi aircraft and helicopters. The Safety Board still determines the cause of these minor crashes after evaluating the FAA's investigation findings.

The Federal Aviation Administration has the investigative role mentioned, as well as other related safety concerns. A statement of the FAA's investigative role has been given as follows:

FAA's responsibility in accident investigation is of a two-fold purpose: to assist the National Transportation Safety Board in carrying out its prime investigative task and to determine whether there may have been a breakdown in any of the following areas of responsibility charged to the FAA under the Federal Aviation Act of 1958:

- Violations of the Federal Aviation Regulations
- Operation and performance of air navigational facilities
- Airworthiness/crashworthiness of FAA-certified aircraft
- Competency of FAA-certified airmen, air agencies (such as repair stations and flight schools), commercial operators or air carriers.

If no one were hurt in a small (less than 12,500 pounds) plane accident and the damage was minor, the FAA investigation consists of little more than calling for a written report from the pilot in command at the time of the accident. Chapter 8 "Flight Line and Front Desk" and chapter 9 "Flight Operations" contain guidelines on developing safety-conscious operations and complying with existing regulations.

State and Local Reporting Requirements

State roles in accident investigation vary. Some states have staff who work with FAA (and NTSB, when applicable) to locate downed aircraft, keep onlookers away, and assemble evidence. Some states issue their own reports of probable cause, generally much faster than NTSB. Local police and municipal chief executives may also be required by law to be informed, or this may be just a courtesy in the interest of good airport public relations. The FBO should be apprised of all local requirements.

Crash, Fire and Rescue (CFR) Procedures

Airports operating under FAR Part 139 are required to have CFR equipment and procedures. Some extensive debate and study has taken place in the last few years about how small an airport needs to be to be exempt from CFR rules. General aviation airports do not have any federal requirements, but good management suggests that the FBOs and the airport owner should have a joint plan and periodic drills. There has been some debate about whether smaller airports should also have specific CFR procedures and FBOs at smaller airports should monitor this issue.

Airports other than certificated airports that maintain fire fighting and rescue services will find the guidelines contained in FAR Part 139 and AC 139.49–1 very useful.[17] Airports that do not maintain fire fighting services might benefit from these sources as well as from the bibliography contained in the appendix of this circular. In addition, the Advisory Circular 150.5200–15 is a valuable document.[18]

Availability of the International Fire Service Training Association's (IFSTA) Aircraft Fire Protection and Rescue Procedures Manual and the Advisory Circular 150/5200–16, Announcement of Report AS 71–1 "Minimum Needs for Airport Fire Fighting and Rescue Services" should be of value and interest to the aviation manager concerned with providing adequate facilities.[19] Fire fighting training is now required for FBO employees.[20]

Flight Security

Risk management and risk transfer through insurance may apply to other risk areas such as aircraft theft, drug trafficking, hijacking, and so on. Perhaps unlikely events for the typical FBO to witness these could be very serious threats to life if they occur.

Widespread criminal and terrorist activities directed against the aviation community have increased in occurrence and in intensity in recent years. Congress passed Public Law 93–366 in 1974 which contained Title II—Air Transportation Security Act of 1974. This act directed the Administrator of the FAA to prescribe or to continue in effect reasonable regulations requiring that all passengers and all property intended to be carried in the aircraft cabin in air transportation or interstate air transportation be screened by weapon needed in selecting or facilities employed or operated by employees or agents of the air carrier prior to boarding the aircraft.

The main impact of airport and aircraft security regulations occurs at air carrier airports. However, some of this impact is felt at feeder airports where scheduled air-taxi operators had customers who were "through" passengers, connecting with Part 121 carriers. In order for the ATCOs (Air Taxi Commercial Operator) to discharge their passengers into secure concourses, they are required to develop and maintain security programs that meet the minimum acceptable standards. After approving the security program, the FAA District Office issues the operations specifications covering the program.

Search and Rescue

Some states handle this one way, others another. The state police, national guard, or aeronautics agency may each be the lead agency, and these are not the only possibilities. The FBO may be actively involved by taking steps such as loaning aircraft, coordinating Civil Air Patrol (CAP) spotters, providing a communications base, or may choose to limit his or her involvement.

Summary

Aviation safety and liability issues are similar in many cases to those arising in any business. The four general categories of insurance—(1) loss or damage to property, (2) bodily injury and property damage liability, (3) business interrruptions and losses resulting from fire and other damage to the premises, and (4) death or disability of key executives are as much applicable to an aviation business as any other. Because of the nature of operations, there are also other insurance needs stemming from the specific risks faced in aviation. The discussion is divided into three sections: risk exposure and how to minimize it; risk transfer in an aviation business, and accident policy and procedures to follow if needed.

Discussion Topics

1. Distinguish between risk management and risk transfer. What would be the drawbacks of a risk management plan that had only the first of these elements? Only the second?
2. Explain the "deep-pocket" theory.
3. What are the pros and cons of self-insurance?
4. What are the problems associated with reducing insurance costs by using a high deductible?
5. What are the four main types of risk exposure and which is the hardest to obtain adequate coverage against?
6. What are five types of insurance coverage particular to aviation?
7. Discuss trends in product liability suits and their effect on the typical FBO.

Chapter 12
Physical Facilities

Objectives

- ✔ Explain the role of the FBO owner/manager in promoting the airport.
- ✔ Describe the major parts of an airport master plan.
- ✔ Recognize some of the issues to be aware of when negotiating financing for developments on leased airport land.
- ✔ Discuss major environmental issues relevant to airport properties and businesses.
- ✔ Understand techniques used to help reduce noise levels around airports, including the possible impact on the FBO operator.

Introduction: The Four Levels of FBO Involvement in Physical Facilities

FBOs need to be concerned with four levels of airport physical facilities. These are:

1. The national and international airport systems.
2. The community affected economically and environmentally by the operation of the FBO's local airport.
3. The airport itself: runways, taxiways, ramps, terminal buildings, parking lots, and so on.
4. The FBO's own facilities.

Each of these four levels must be well-planned and safely operated for the individual FBO to run an efficient, profitable business. Yet only the last, the FBO's own facilities, are under FBO control. At publicly owned airports, even the use of premises is subject to many obligations and restrictions. An important part of running a successful FBO involves monitoring and interacting with the other entities responsible for operating the four levels of the physical facility.

The National Airport Hierarchy

The Airport System

Chapter 1 discusses the national airport hierarchy and its operation. To recap:

1. There are about 15,000 landing fields nationwide.
2. About 12,000 are publicly owned and about 3,000 are privately owned.
3. Of the 15,000, about 6,000 are for public use and the rest are for private restricted use by permission only.
4. Of the 6,000 for public use, about half are privately owned and half publicly owned.
5. Of the 6,000, about 3,200 are considered key to the national aviation system and feature in the National Plan of Integrated Airport Systems (NPIAS).[1] All 3,200 are eligible for federal grants for planning and construction.
6. Of the 3,200 airports in the national system, about 200 are privately owned.
7. Of the 2,800 or so privately owned public use airports **not** in the NPIAS some are run by their owners and some are run by FBOs on contract.

Figure 12.1 explains this hierarchy.

Publicly owned airports have government funding opportunities not always available to privately owned fields—with some exceptions since 1982. The private fields usually compete for the same aviation market as public airports and need to have an understanding of their position in the marketplace. Among the nation's key airports, facility planning includes the use of federal funds.

The Airport's Wider Environment

Common Problem Areas

The role of the national general aviation airport system is little understood except by those directly involved. While most people have at some time flown on an airline or expect to do so and appreciate its availability, most do not hold the same expectation for general aviation. General aviation's negative or frivolous image derives from barnstormers, the silk-scarf and goggles set, jetset playboys buzzing around on weekends, and so forth. The GA airport is seen as "a marina for planes" at best, or at worst, simply a public nuisance.[2]

Many small airports were sensibly built outside of towns. But the towns have spread in all directions and now often surround the airport. At the same time the airport traffic has often grown heavier and more frequent; and if jets are involved, it's often significantly noisier.

The early phase of airport master and system planning in the 1970s often led to confusion in the public mind. For example, the term "reliever airport" (defined by legislation as general aviation airports relieving general aviation traffic from airline airports) is still often misconstrued by the public to mean that their little suburban airport may start serving jumbo jets.[3] It doesn't matter that there is not room for the necessary runways and that airline logistics preclude split operations except at the biggest hubs. Such misinterpretation over the years has led to substantial community fears about airport growth, noise, and safety.

Poor land use planning and zoning to protect

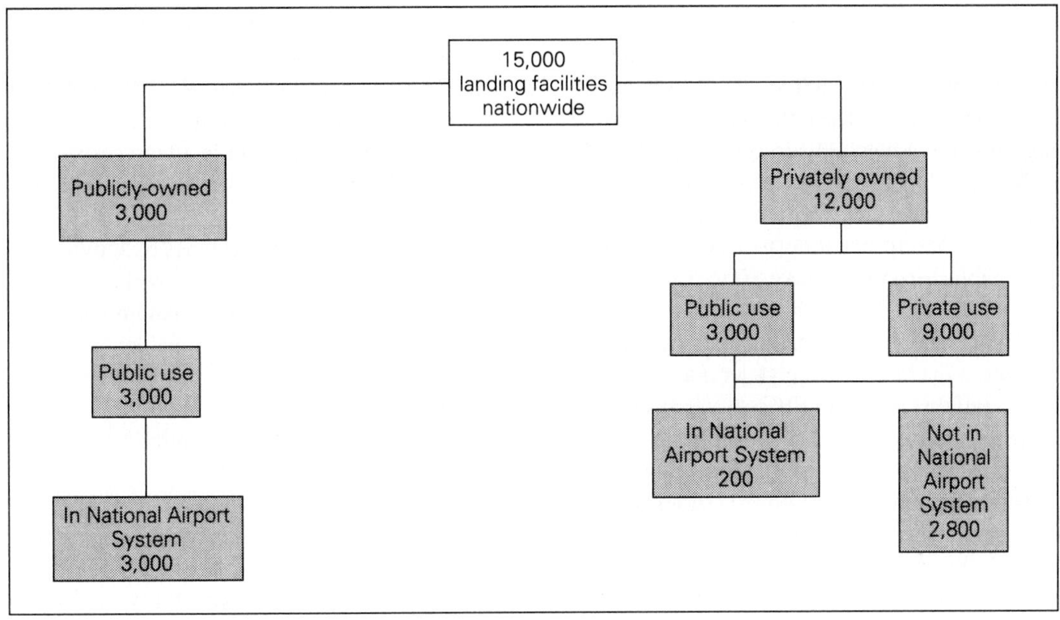

Figure 12.1. National airport hierarchy (in round numbers).

small airports are still a problem. Incompatible developments, such as housing, are still often permitted adjacent to airports. Some of the most avidly anti-airport organizations are in communities still permitting incompatible developments next to the runway or under the flight path.

Yet the airport system is virtually finite; therefore, it needs preserving. Even a small new airport requires at least one mile of flat land with road and utility access as well as unobstructed approaches. Such prime real estate, if it can be found, cannot serve major metropolitan and urban centers unless it lies close to the developed areas. An inherent conflict exists between airports and communities.

A study in the late 1970s showed that the private airport system is the main source of new airport facilities.[4] A private restricted field may open, may eventually become a public-use field, and eventually offer a full array of aviation services and facilities. But the privately owned airports, the historic source of airport system growth, are the most threatened airports in the system for such reasons as:

1. There is no guaranteed succession when the founder/owner dies or retires.
2. As private facilities they are often required to pay property taxes from which their publicly owned counterparts are exempt.
3. They must finance all capital improvements—even those for which fees cannot be directly charged—from internal funds. Public airports, on the other hand, can be 90 percent subsidized. (Note exceptions since 1982)
4. As private businesses, they may not get the support of local decision makers for needed land use and airspace obstruction controls.

At the same time that the privately owned airports are coming under such pressure, the public system has its own problems. Because of fears about noise, safety, and unlimited expansionism, it is becoming increasingly difficult to obtain (in full) all the necessary approvals for a new publicly owned airport. The NPIAS anticipates building only a few new GA airports in the next decade, a 2 or 3 percent growth compared with the expected 30 percent growth in the number of GA aircraft.[5,6] From inception to ribbon cutting, a new public airport can take 10 to 15 years and cost millions of dollars.[7,8]

This means it is becoming increasingly important to the health of the general aviation system—and that means to FBOs—to preserve and enhance the viability of the airport system that already exists. To accomplish this requires an intensive two-pronged nationwide strategy. These two prongs are (1) noise abatement and (2) convincing the neutral or hostile airport neighbor of the economic importance of that local airport to his or her community.

The Three Types of Aviation Noise Control

Source control means quieter aircraft technology by controlling and reducing the amount of noise emitted. Major steps have been taken in this direction; however, it is largely outside the control of FBOs and will not be discussed further here.

Operating controls mean flight techniques to reduce noise around airports. This can include such steps as:

1. Use of a preferential runway system—a runway whose flight path lies over the least noise-sensitive areas, used in as many wind conditions as possible.
2. Displaced landing thresholds so that arriving planes are at higher altitude over noise sensitive areas and land farther along the runway.
3. Longer runways so that departing aircraft can start their take-off roll further back and achieve greater altitude before being over sensitive areas.
4. Turning away early out of the flight pattern to avoid sensitive areas after departure.
5. Cutting back the throttle after a certain altitude or when airspeed has been reached after departure.
6. Limitations on certain types of activity during certain hours of the week.
7. Limitations on take-off or landing noise levels above a certain decibel level (set with guidance from FAA and applied consistently).
8. Reversal of the landing pattern to avoid sensitive areas.

While such operating restrictions may be frustrating to pilots, in some places they may be essential to the continued availability of that airport, and cooperation must be required by the FBO. This can be done by such actions as:

1. Teaching noise-abatement techniques in ground school and flying lessons.
2. Requiring renters to sign a promise to follow the FBO's operating procedures.
3. Maintaining a clear and responsive process for receiving and dealing with complaints, even if the problem was not caused by the FBO's aircraft.
4. Close coordination with the airport owner/landlord on what is happening on the rest of the field in terms of noise abatement and complaints.

Land use controls consist of various mechanisms to reduce or stabilize the number of noise-sensitive activities around the airport. In fully developed areas this approach has sometimes involved the purchase of homes and schools and their relocation or demolition.[9,10]

Other tools include soundproofing existing buildings and the construction of berms, walls, and run-up pits to contain noise on the airport. In some cases it is possible to purchase an avigation easement to the title of a house so that the owners and their successors forgo their right to complain about noise in exchange for a fee.

Where land is not yet developed there is more opportunity to prevent problems. However, this is often accompanied by less urgency, until one day someone realizes that a new nursing home or elementary school is under construction off the main runway. Available land use controls for undeveloped areas include:

1. Transfer or sale of development rights to the airport owner.
2. Aviation easements.
3. Soundproofing as part of the airport area building code.
4. Zoning restrictions, for example, in an "overlay" airport zone that adds more stringent conditions to existing zoning, or a complete rezone that eliminates incompatible land uses entirely from the airport area zoning. Where this is perceived as "downzoning" to a less commercially desirable use, there can be a question of "taking" private property.
5. Full disclosure of the airport's proximity in leases of new buildings.

The noise report of the Oregon Aeronautics Division provides sample legal language for these and other techniques and several FAA publications are also available.[11,12,13]

FAR Part 150

This portion of the Federal Air Regulations deals with aviation noise. It provides for a percentage of each year's Airport Improvement Program to be allocated to noise studies and to land acquisition for noise-abatement purposes.[14]

The noise study requirements include the preparation of a noise map showing present or future noise sensitive areas. Once this map is accepted, the next step of a Part 150 study is an abatement plan that evaluates all possible operational and land use strategies and presents a plan that will achieve the most effective results for that particular airport area. If appropriate, federal grant funds are available to purchase land for noise-abatement purposes. Smaller airports may not be able to get funding for noise activities, even though they may have noise-sensitive neighbors.

Continuous Noise Abatement Strategy

A noise study will not, in one step, eliminate noise and the threat it can pose to an airport's future. Indeed, in many cases the opportunity to be heard encourages airport neighbors to mobilize in opposition to the airport. Prevention, rather than cure, is the best strategy. Prevention means setting up good operational techniques before they are demanded. It means making sure that chronic complainers are invited to see the positive side of the airport in every way possible. It means keeping the business community and town leaders aware of the corporations the FBO serves and the way they depend on these services to do business in the community.

Airport Economic Impact

In the past, there have been two basic approaches to documenting the economic benefits of general aviation airports. One is heavily statistical and seeks to quantify every component of impact generated directly or indirectly by the airport—airport operator, FBO and airline salaries, taxes paid, income from airport users, spending in the community by air travelers, and multiplier effects.

The other approach is more qualitative or journalistic and presents profiles of key airport users and what they produce by showing how the airport is vital to their business.

The former approach can become immersed in data so it is hard to "see the forest for the trees." The latter approach may not contain enough hard facts to convince the sceptics.

Therefore, a middle ground may be the best. Regardless of the airport owner's activities in pursuing such studies, it is advantageous for marketing and public relations if the FBO makes its own ongoing effort in this regard. The FBO should know who its aircraft tenants are, and why and how much they use the airport. Employment and payroll figures should be readily available. The FBO should keep a good transient log and, periodically, when a new company signs in, should call to find out if there will be regular visits, and who they are coming to see. The FBO should be active in at least one local business group such as Kiwanis, Jaycees, Rotary, or Chamber of Commerce so that the facts about the FBO operation—and the role of the airport—reach ears other than those in the aviation community. FBOs should become involved in airport economic studies sponsored by others in order to maximize their own favorable publicity.

Airport and Aviation System Planning

The single airport has no value; it must be part of a system. The FBO who recognizes this and is aware of the changing roles of competing airports, changing markets, and demographics is positioned to take advantage of new opportunities. Periodically state and regional planning agencies undertake regional and systemwide aviation studies. The FBO should be aware of the opportunities these present to express opinions on aviation concerns beyond the individual airport's boundaries.

Facilities on the Airport

Introduction

Some FBOs are owners of the airport and control all the facilities. Others may manage a private or public airport on contract or may simply be one of several tenants. The state of facilities on the field requires constant monitoring and feedback, especially in those functions where the FBO does not have direct control.

Facilities on the airport affecting the FBO's operations may include the following:

- Runways and taxiways
- Air traffic control tower
- Terminal buildings
- Lights, radio, and so on
- Navigational aids such as NDB, ILS, Glide slope, and VASI
- Utilities
- Maintenance
- Auto access and parking
- Space leased to other FBOs

The Airport Master Plan

Airports in the National Airport System Plan are eligible for federal planning and construction grants under the Airport Improvement Program (AIP).[15] Eligible airports are encouraged to prepare a full Master Plan about every five years and to keep track of intermittent changes to facilities and activities. Smaller airports may not do a full Master Plan but rather an Airport Layout Plan (ALP) that shows the ultimate layout of the airport as it expands over the next 20 years. The ALP is also a key end product of the full Master Planning process, but it is supported by more analytical detail explaining how the chosen ALP was selected. Smaller airports with fewer complexities may not need all this documentation.

A full Master Plan involves the following steps[16]:

1. **Inventory**—of facilities, of activity and of financial performance.
2. **Forecasts of demand**—usually over 5-, 10-, and 20-year time frames. Forecasts are generally prepared for based aircraft, operations and passengers, by aircraft type (for noise analysis), and by year, peak day (for noise), and peak hour.

3. **Demand/Capacity analysis**—looking at the difference between existing facilities and what will be needed in the future, based on peak-hour demands. Traditionally this topic has been examined mainly in terms of runway capacity, but at many general aviation airports, the limits of aircraft-basing capacity will be reached long before runway saturation, so that **basing capacity** may become a key variable.
4. **Development alternatives**—different layouts and changes to accommodate the forecasted demand. These can include land acquisition and runway expansion, though not necessarily so.
5. **Financial plan**—an examination of capital and operating accounts and revenue sources to examine how to pay for the needed capital improvements. Increasingly, too, this task will examine how the operating account can be improved, for example, by new revenue sources.
6. **Noise and environmental analysis**—to see whether any growth and expansion will be within acceptable environmental limits. Certain topics may require a full Environmental Impact Statement (EIS) at federal and/or state level.
7. **Implementation program**—how to stage the desired improvements, usually including a phased capital improvement program for the 5-, 10-, and 20-year periods.
8. **Public participation program**—usually at two levels, a technical committee that will receive advance copies of the study reports and review them, and a public process. Certain proposals, such as runway extensions, also require a formal public hearing with legal notice periods, a transcript, and a formal schedule. In today's world, no such formal end to a study should take place without all interested parties having input into draft concepts. There should be no surprises on either side at a public hearing.

FBO Participation in Master Planning

The FBO, air-taxi operator, commuter, or other aeronautical provider at a public airport should actively seek participation in the technical level process of a master plan. What is done to the public portions of the airport and the decisions that are made about how to allocate still-vacant land at the airport can vastly affect the FBO's prosperity. An FBO may have prospective clients who are being held back by lack of another 500 feet of runway, by lack of the right fuel, or other deficiencies that the federally supported planning and construction process could remedy. There may be inadequacies in the condition of existing facilities—the runway needs a crack seal job, the taxiway needs widening, snow plowing is getting done too slowly, or a host of other possibilities for which the master plan will set budgets and priorities. The master plan will address what role the airport is to play. Will it serve primarily single engine trainers? Does the airport owner see a major corporate twin and jet market? Are capacity limits looming up that will inhibit growth for the FBO's business?

The FBO should seek a full role in the study. Airports are unique in the national transportation system because now they rely on teamwork between public and private sectors to keep them viable. The master plan is a key opportunity to audit and alter this symbiosis.

Private Airports

Since the AIP legislation of 1982, certain private airports have become eligible for AIP funding. They must fit the following criteria:

1. Any privately owned reliever airport, OR
2. Any privately owned airport which is determined by the Secretary of Transportation to enplane annually 2,500 or more passengers and receive scheduled passenger service of aircraft, which is used or to be used for public purposes.

The following conditions also apply:

1. The airport must continue to function as a public-use airport during the economic life of the federally funded facilities (at least ten years).
2. The airport must comply with the other grant conditions made to all sponsors (summarized here in figure 12.2).

Funding Levels for Small Airports

The Aviation Trust Fund was established in 1970. It provides the funds for airport planning and construction. From the beginning, the larger airports through passenger ticket taxes have generated most of the revenue. They have also been allocated most of the grants. The current legislative program provides most of the funds to pri-

1. The airport will be available for public use on fair and reasonable terms and without unjust discrimination (all like users shall have like rates and terms).
2. No exclusive right shall be granted for the use of the airport by any person providing aeronautical services to the public (the providing of services by a single FBO is not considered as an exclusive right if it should be unreasonably costly, burdensome or impractical for more than one FBO to provide such services, and if allowing more than one FBO would require reduction of space leased to an existing FBO).
3. The airport shall be suitably operated and maintained, with due regard to climatic and flood conditions.
4. Aerial approaches to the airport must be adequately cleared and protected.
5. Appropriate action, including the adoption of zoning laws, has been or will be taken, to the extent reasonable, to restrict the use of land adjacent to or in the immediate vicinity of the airport to activities and purposes compatible with normal airport operations.
6. Facilities will be available for the use of United States aircraft.
7. The airport owner will furnish to the government, without cost, any land needed for air traffic control, air navigation, or weather services.
8. Project accounts and records will be kept in accordance with prescribed systems.
9. The fee structure will permit the airport to be as self-sustaining as possible.
10. The airport owner will submit financial reports as requested.
11. The airport and its records will be available for inspection.
12. Revenues at public airports will go to aviation purposes.
13. Land acquired for noise control with federal funds will, when resold, retain restrictions making development on the land compatible with the airport.

Source: Public Law 97-248, September 3, 1982, paraphrase of Section 511. For precise conditions see P.L. 97-248 itself.

Figure 12.2. Grant conditions under Airport Improvement Program.

mary airports, those enplaning 0.01 percent or more of national passenger enplanements (about 30,000).

Small airports, even though key to the national airport system, must compete against one another for very limited funding compared with the primary airport system.[17]

During the 1980s and 1990s, the available funds for airport improvements have accumulated much faster in the Aviation Trust Fund than expended. Pressure is mounting for a higher level of funding, especially for larger airports. If this does not occur, the passenger ticket tax will be cut back to reduce the balance in the trust fund, even though national airport needs far exceed available funds. Tenants and operators at small and large airports alike need to ensure that these airport improvement funds continue to be available at appropriate levels.

Airport Revenue Planning

One component of the airport master plan is a financial plan. It typically examines needed construction costs compared with available federal, state, and local revenue sources. It also examines future operating revenues and rates to see if reserves can be set aside to cover the construction plan. Some airports have general funds or bonding powers available. Funds are often sought directly from the airport—the FBO leases and concession fees. The FBO, therefore, needs to be very close to policy-making in this area and be prepared to explain the costs and revenues of the business, especially if he or she believes that higher rates will be self-defeating because of lost demand.

On the other hand, as discussed in chapter 3, many profitable areas for new aviation and nonaviation business may be overlooked by the FBO and airport owner. The FBO's knowledge of these areas and their break-even levels may help to refocus the search for more money away from raising rates and toward provision of new services.

The FBO's Own Facilities

An FBO on a public airport is not only a tenant renting certain physical space, but is also involved in an operating agreement that provides certain rights and obligations relating to how the business is run. FBO facility management and lease development is thus somewhat more complex than the usual commercial lease.

The FBO in a full-service operation normally leases or owns the following: (18)

- Aircraft parking
- Tie-down areas
- Hangars
- Administrative space, front desk and waiting area
- Maintenance shop
- Aircraft showroom

Data Collection

The FBO will have considerable data on hand about current facilities and activities and should keep this in a current and usable format. Data on market trends, new opportunities, and the likely growth in demand for existing services are discussed in chapter 3 "Marketing." Data on existing activities should include:

- Number of based aircraft, by corporate and personal ownership, by equipment type and amount of use
- Identity of frequent transients (see chapter 8 for a discussion of a useful transient log)
- Seasonality and time-of-day peaking
- Noise complaints and responses given
- Revenue by area
- Profit by area
- Activity of any concessions or ancillary operators such as car rental, restaurant, vending machines, industrial parks

Data on existing facilities should include maps, plans and condition of:

- Navigational Aids under FBO control
- Buildings
- Ramps
- Tie-downs
- Hangars

The FBO may find it useful to review his database with the airport owner to see if other information would assist in the overall airport planning process.

Planning a New Airport

A study done in the late 1970s suggests that the newest airports entering the system are airports on private land.[19] Such facilities may be as simple as a farmer rotating which field he uses for crop-dusting flights, or they may from the outset be planned as public use facilities. Any new landing area requires FAA approval and in most cases either approval or at least registration with the state aviation agency.[20] In addition, since airports are often not permitted uses under municipal or county zoning, there may have to be zoning approvals or variances. There could also be requirements for compliance with state and/or local environmental regulations.

Facility Expansion

The decision to build a second maintenance hangar will depend on break-even analysis as discussed in chapter 4. In addition, it will almost certainly require approval from the landlord even if the site has already been leased.

Facility replacement may likewise require approvals. Design control may be involved, and certainly compliance with all FAA requirements on obstructions and setbacks will be necessary, as will compliance with local building codes and possibly airport requirements beyond the municipal code. Many states also have regulations affecting airports that will need to be considered. For his own purposes, the FBO will, of course, have to develop a staging plan for continuation of business during construction in order to minimize disruption.

Preventive Maintenance

Preventive maintenance—repairing and maintaining physical facilities **before** they collapse—is a key to good facility planning. Prevention versus after-the-fact repairs is a trade-off between forestalling unnecessarily frequent crises that disrupt service and the cost of a 100 percent prevention program. One aviation expert suggests a split of the maintenance budget into 70 percent preventive maintenance and 30 percent crisis troubleshooting.[21] The 70 percent may have a proportionally larger labor element because it involves such things as a planned schedule for replacing lightbulbs, while the 30 percent may involve the sudden purchase of major equipment to replace that which has unexpectedly collapsed, such as the furnace or the air-conditioning system.

Scheduled Replacement of Plant and Equipment

The expected life of all well-maintained equipment provides the basis for a planned replacement schedule that may extend over as much as 20 years. Each year various major items are replaced. This must be part of the facilities budget. The replacement schedule will only be adjusted when the unexpected premature collapse of a major item occurs. Even then the preventive maintenance budget should ideally be able to handle such needs, rather than the long-range equipment budget. The deferral of major replacement tasks is to be avoided, if possible, because every delay increases the risk of several major collapses close in time that could seriously disrupt the smooth operation of the business. Regular inspection of facilities will help make any appropriate changes in priorities as the years go by.

Zoning and Other Local Controls

Zoning regulations are varied and may not necessarily be aimed at fostering compatible uses around the airport. Where existing zoning restricts something an FBO would like to do, he or she has the choice of either seeking a variance for the one special case, or of seeking a rezoning of all pertinent parcels. The latter is usually a more major undertaking than an FBO might want to attempt, but if a rezone has already been initiated he or she may want to have input into the process. He or she may also want to have input to any zoning changes in the immediate airport neighborhood, since approval of some types of land use will simply favor the climate for new noise complaints.

In addition to zoning, developments the FBO may want to undertake will be restricted by local fire and building codes as well as any state requirements, FAA setback, and clear zone considerations.[22]

Leases

The right to operate an aviation business at a particular airport may be obtained through ownership of the land or through a lease arrangement. Most operations exist today under the contractual obligation of a lease. As the instrument that provides the basic parameters of the business and establishes a framework for success or failure, it is absolutely necessary that the manager understand the process and be able to obtain as favorable an arrangement as possible. Of course, from the onset the manager should recognize that it is necessary to obtain the services of an attorney to assist in moulding the contractual arrangement, and it is also best to find one familiar with the aviation business or be prepared to spend time acquainting him or her with the technical implications and operational difficulties of the problems involved.

Initial considerations. Prior to dealing with the contents of a lease and the typical framework of the contract, one should clearly identify the following considerations:

1. The aviation lease is a composite agreement, a combination of a **real estate lease** as it is normally understood by lawyers and nonprofessionals, and **an operating agreement** that sets forth the obligations, duties, and restrictions that apply to the manner in which the aviation business shall be conducted on the leased premises. Some specialists recommend making the operating agreement a separate document, incorporated into the lease by reference.
2. The pre-lease situation is normally one in which the lessor and lessee (land owner and aviation manager) are in a bargaining situation. It is not a precast, fixed situation. Guidelines are available, but each lease is different, representing the local situation and various local and state laws.
3. The contractual relationship between the base operator and the owners of the airport has an enormous impact upon both parties and more importantly upon the community they both serve. Because of the economic impact upon the community, the lease should attract a competent aviation organization and provide the opportunity for an adequate margin of profit on the required investment of time, money, and experience. It should cover a long enough period of time to sustain the financing required to establish and operate the business.
4. Developing a lease is not a one-time or periodic activity. A lease is a living instrument that controls a constantly changing relationship and as such should be under constant review. This is reflected in the comment "start working on your second lease the day after signing your first one."

5. Developing a lease is in reality developing a plan. As such, the plan should include those elements that will ensure success for both parties. A basic concern in creating the plan is the need to set the terms and length of the lease with full consideration of the requirements of the potential lenders, who will supply the large financing required of the proposed investment. In the eyes of the lender, the amount loaned will be limited to an amount that can be adequately amortized from the funds expected to be generated by the business during the term of the lease. Therefore, a 25 year or longer lease will be needed for many financing purposes.
6. To meet the requirements of business flexibility and frequently the lending institution's needs, there is a basic interest in the assignability provisions of the lease. Normally the lessee should be empowered to assign or sell the lease for financing purposes upon written notice to the lessor, with approval thereof not unreasonably withheld. The lessee should typically have the right to sublease part of the space covered by the lease, provided the sublessee is subject to the same conditions and obligations as those in the basic lease. Furthermore, it is desirable that the lease state the lessee has the right to sell without restriction to any corporation formed by it, consolidated, or merged with it, provided, however, that the purpose of the surviving organization is to perform under the lease.
7. An understanding of local and national economic aviation trends is important in projecting FBO sales over the life of the lease as well as anticipating increases in lease payments.

Preliminary Planning. Prior to any actual negotiations over the terms of the lease, considerable planning needs to be accomplished. Achieving a successful lease and ultimately a profitable business will depend to a major degree on the thoroughness of the planning efforts. In this plan you should:

1. Become acquainted and on social terms with the airport board and airport manager.
2. Review and study the lessor's previous agreements with parties operating similar businesses.
3. Review and study lessor's agreements with any airlines serving the airport; such contracts may have direct and indirect influences upon proposed general aviation businesses.
4. Develop a prospectus for the business and make financial projections for the future. This information is vitally necessary to the lessee for making decisions on the lease costs that can be accepted without compromising legitimate profit objectives. The airport board, in acting on the bid for a lease, has the right to probe into many personal and business financial issues to satisfy itself of the FBO's ability to perform.
5. Determine exactly what lease terms will be acceptable to the specific lending institutions expected to provide financing.
6. Obtain the advice of the intended fuel supplier on the lease agreements dealing with fuel-storage facilities, fuel handling, and the related fee structure such as the fuel flowage fees.
7. Determine through a title search that the lessor has clear title to the property being considered and is empowered to lease it to you.
8. Determine that the individuals negotiating the lease as lessors have the legal capacity and authority to represent the community or agency having actual title to the property.
9. Review the master plan for the airport and determine whether the future projections are in harmony with the proposed lease and

the included business and financial projections of the aviation business. Be sure that the areas you plan to lease will not be harmed by future facility developments elsewhere on the field.

10. In a new lease, review such issues as the underground storage tank conditions on the leased property; the airport noise situation and community relations; and whether the airport is in compliance with FAA requirements, OSHA requirements, local fire codes and other pertinent regulations and what is needed to maintain this compliance.
11. Review existing and future liability and insurance needs for the leased property, and examine coverage held by the airport operator to determine that there are no nebulous areas of liability between lessor and lessee.

Procedural steps. The normal procedural steps followed in negotiating and awarding a lease are:

1. The development and release of an invitation to bid by the lessor. The invitation is aimed at soliciting responses from all interested and qualified parties and contains the basic information necessary to identify the property, the desired services, and the basic leasing arrangement. In order to ensure coverage of desired items and an element of standardization among prospective lessees, a sample lease bid is usually included in the bid announcement, along with any applicable airport minimum standards that serve to screen out unqualified bidders. Bonding capability is a likely requirement.
2. The interested lessees then prepare and submit lease bids to the lessor. These are usually closed bids with simultaneous bid opening for all respondents.
3. All proposals received by the owners are evaluated fully through a detailed analysis of the major elements in each proposal. An airport board may establish a lease committee for this purpose.
4. Negotiations are conducted with the bid respondents submitting the most acceptable proposals in order to assure complete understanding of the proposals submitted and to reach any modifications deemed necessary.
5. The bidder offering the most acceptable final proposal is identified.
6. The detailed lease and operating agreement will be completed and agreed upon.
7. The final lease proposal is agreed upon and the unsuccessful bidders advised and released from their offers.

Appendix X contains a sample lease as suggested by the National Air Transportation Association. It may provide a basis for a final lease document to address a specific situation.

Major lease components. Most aviation leases follow a format similar to the one contained in Appendix X, and since there are certain basic concerns, they cover common elements. The major components in a lease are:

- Site location
- Terms of the lease
- Options
- Termination before expiration
- Rights after termination (reversion)
- Lease release
- Lease disputes and how they will be handled
- Rights and obligations
- Rent and conditions under which it will be increased

Let us examine these components, identify each, and consider elements of primary concern.

Site location. The premises being considered should be described clearly, fully, and accurately with the official plot plan and survey drawing of the properties attached and incorporated by text reference.

First right of refusal for adjacent areas to the site should be accorded to the lessee.

The privilege to use all general public airport facilities and improvements such as landing areas, runways, taxiways, parking areas, aprons, ramps, navigation facilities, and terminal facilities should be identified.

Term of the lease. The lease term should be established by setting the dates for the beginning and end of the lease period.

Provisions should be included for the extension of the term of the lease.

Term of the basic lease should be long enough to permit the amortization of loans made for physical improvements on the property and the erection of hangars and other installations. Financiers will be reluctant to make loans for longer periods than the basic lease even if renewals are available.

Options. Provision for extending the lease for an additional term should specify the length of the term, the maximum amounts by which rents, fees, and payments can be increased during the option period; and the basis on which those increases are to be calculated, as with, for example, the local cost of living.

Allowance should be included for appropriate extension of the term of the lease in the event of interruptions due to causes beyond the control of the lessee. In lieu of such extension, the lease should provide for a moratorium on rent payments under such circumstances.

Termination before expiration. The rights of both parties must be clearly set forth in the lease to cover the contingency that the lease may be terminated before its stated expiration date.

The lessor can usually terminate for one or more of the following reasons:

1. Substantial nonperformance or breach of contract.
2. Failure of the lessee to observe and conform to the terms of the lease and his or her continuing failure to bring his operations into compliance within 30 days after receiving notice from lessor to do so.
3. Failure of the lessee to pay the rent when it is due. The lease should set a period of time (usually 30–60 days) during which the lessee may remedy the fault.
4. If the lessee becomes bankrupt.
5. If the lessee makes a general assignment of the lease for the benefit of creditors.
6. If the lessee abandons the premises. Under this circumstance the lessor generally has the right to remove the lessee's abandoned effects without being liable for damages.

The lessee may terminate the lease prematurely for the following reasons:

1. If the lessor fails to perform substantially under the terms of the lease. Termination may require written notice to the lessor and the lapse of a stated period of time (usually 30 to 60 days) before the actual termination.
2. If the lessor commits any act or engages in any activity that prevents the lessee from doing business for a period of time (normally specified in the lease).
3. The lease might provide that the lessee can terminate the lease in event of civil commotion, acts of the military, acts of God, damage to runways, court orders restraining the use of the airport, or similar events that may interrupt normal business for a specified period of time. In lieu of premature termination of the lease, there may be a provision for a moratorium on

rent payments during such interruptions and/or the extension of the primary term of the lease during such time period.

4. If the lessee is hindered by the lessor or unreasonably prevented from doing business in accordance with the terms of the lease, he or she has recourse to the courts and may receive compensatory damages.

Rights after termination. The lease should contain provisions covering the rights of both parties after termination. Some leases call for reversion of title of the lessee's premises to the lessor. The lessee may or may not have first rights of renewal of the lease.

Some leases provide that the lessor has a purchase option on improvements to the real estate at a depreciated value.

Depreciation schedules should be spelled out in the lease and provisions included for handling property under early termination conditions.

Reversion. When an airport tenant builds facilities on public airport land, the most common form of agreement is that after an amortization period of 25 or 30 years, the facilities' title will revert to the airport owner. Usually the tenant will have rights of first refusal to become the renter of the facilities and at a rate to be negotiated. If the FBO in question has not been maintaining a quality operation, the airport operator may, not unreasonably, seek to use the end of the lease period as a means of getting a better operator into the premises. Because of the growth in aviation in the 1950s and 1960s, reversions are increasing in the 1980s and 1990s, and many FBOs must address whether (1) they are operating in such a way as to ensure their rights of first refusal are in good standing and (2) what is a reasonable rent for the 25- or 30-year-old buildings that they now must start to lease? The monthly cost may be higher than the mortgage, given 1950s or 1960s construction prices and interest rates. Some FBOs have torn down their hangars rather than rent them from the airport.[23]

Lease release. The lease may also be terminated before the date of expiration in a mutually acceptable release.

By a subsequent written agreement, both parties can agree to terminate the original agreement. For example, both parties may agree to terminate the lease if performance becomes impossible or impractical due to causes beyond the control of either party.

The lease can be written so that all obligations shall be held in abeyance during the period of interruption, and when operations under the lease are resumed, the term of the lease is extended for a period equal to the period of interruption.

Lease disputes. Even the most thoroughly prepared lease may not cover all problems, and disputes may arise. The lease should include a means for settling such disputes. One method provides for a three-person arbitration committee, with one arbitrator picked by each of the parties to the lease and the two selected arbitrators picking a third disinterested party. The selected means should be agreed to and specified in the lease.

Rights and obligations. Both parties to the lease must clearly understand their respective rights and obligations. A "right" is what the lease says *may* be done, an "obligation" or "duty" is what *must* be done. This section of the lease is actually the basic operating contract because it specifies what the lessee shall do and the functions to be performed in order to satisfy the requirements of the lessor. Likewise, the rights and obligations of the lessor should be identified. It is extremely important that the terms of the lease be designed to give the lessee sufficient latitude to operate the business profitably. The rights and obligations of each party, if the other fails to perform, should be spelled out. The following items are frequently included in an aviation lease under rights and obligations:

Covenant not to compete. Assuming the lease covers a business operation, there should be a provision that the lessor will not compete with the lessee; or if there is competition, its extent and character should be specifically identified. An example of this (and something to avoid) would be the airport manager (lessor) employed by the city and also engaged in a general aviation business in competition with the lessee. Another example would be both the lessor and the FBO having the right to sell fuel.

Operation. The lease must give the lessees and their customers the right to ingress, egress, and have free access to the premises, as well as "peaceful possession and quiet enjoyment" thereof. There should also be an assurance that the lessor will continue to operate the airport as a public airport consistent with government regulations and that there will be no restrictions to normal operations or contingent restrictions that might apply to the proposed leasehold operation during the term of the lease.

It is usual for a lessor to require indemnity insurance holding the public airport harmless from all claims, risks, accidents, or injuries caused by lessees or their employees acting in the airport's behalf in the operation of the leasehold business. The amount of such insurance coverage should be negotiated after competent consideration of all factors.

Duty to make improvements. The lease frequently requires the lessee to provide physical improvements and installations on the premises. Examples of this requirement could include the erection of hangars, shop facilities, office facilities, landscaping, paving, parking areas for motor vehicles and aircraft, creating and paving taxi strips, ramps, aprons, and erecting advertising displays and signs. The lessee might also be required to install fixtures, decorations, and equipment as well as to construct specific facilities for the use of the public. The lessee should know the requirements of the lease before negotiating or awarding any construction contracts.

Right of prior approval. A lease gives the lessor the right to approve or disapprove all architectural plans and designs for required improvements and require the lessor's prior approval of the contractor selected to perform the improvements. For this obligation, it is recommended that the lessee take every precaution to prevent the development of arbitrary or capricious demands or restrictions by the lessor. It is far better to set forth clearly and carefully the required improvements in the proposed plan and specifically consider the design or implementation requirements during the negotiations.

Minimum criteria. Many leases specify that the lessee comply with certain minimum criteria in meeting the requirements for improvements. Some specify a minimum fiscal expenditure, some describe the requirements in terms of space (for example, 200,000 square feet for a hangar), and others identify that the lessee must abide by the regulations promulgated by the authorized officials of federal, state, county, city, and airport officials. The lessee should carefully review the implications of these types of requirements and ensure his or her capability and interests. As in other areas, the advice of an attorney is beneficial, if not essential.

Deadlines. Deadlines for required improvements should be clear and feasible. There is a possibility that the lessor will want a deadline for any construction and improvements required in the leasehold. Clauses requiring completion "within 120 days of signing the lease" or stating that "construction must be complete within six months of design approval," are typical of this type of provision. They may be extremely difficult for the lessee, especially when noncompletion penalties are involved. In negotiating these kinds of lease clauses, it is desirable that the lessee obtain as much flexibility as possible in schedules for completing hangers, buildings, and other physical improvements. It is also desirable that the lessee be protected where there are delays caused by such events as fire, earthquake, flood, military action, civil strife, strikes, picketing, or other intervening causes beyond the control of the lessee.

Equipment and fixtures. It is desirable that the lessee have the right to install (at his own expense) the equipment and fixtures required to perform the functions of the business and the right to remove them at any time (also at his own expense). In some instances the lessor's prior approval is required before removal of equipment; in these cases, provision should be made to ensure that it will not be unreasonably withheld. Under removal circumstances, the lessee is normally expected to restore the premises to a condition satisfactory to the lessor.

Maintenance and repair. The lease should clearly specify which party shall be responsible for repair and maintenance of the leased facilities. In normal situations, the lessor pays for structural repairs and specific major items, and the lessee pays for maintenance needed because of ordinary wear and tear. Under these circumstances, if the lessee does not perform the necessary maintenance and repair, the lessor is normally given the right (after a specified time delay) to enter the premises and perform the necessary work at the lessee's expense.

Fire loss. Most leases require the lessee to replace buildings or facilities destroyed by fire and to return them to the pre-damaged condition so that the replacement is equivalent in value to the original facilities. The following provisions are normally made in this area:

1. Seventy-five to 80 percent fire and extended coverage and hangar keeper's liability coverage is usually required with the lessor approving the insurance company.
2. The lessor and any mortgage holders are normally named on insurance policies as additional insured.
3. The abatement of rent while facilities are not in use due to the fire should be considered.

Ownership after termination. The normal provision for ownership after termination of the lease indicates that title to the improvement shall remain with the lessee during the term of the lease, but passes to the lessor at the end of the lease. This would allow the lessee to have depreciated the property and liquidated the debt incurred with his financial supporters. The lease, and both parties, should ascertain the rights of lenders in the event the lease is prematurely terminated.

Other lease provisions might stipulate that the property title might pass to the lessor as soon as construction is completed, or alternatively remain with the lessee even after the lease is terminated. These arrangements have advantages and disadvantages that should be considered when developing the lease.

Removal at termination. Lease negotiations should cover the question of removing tenant improvements, fixtures, or equipment from the site at the termination of the lease. Normally a "reasonable" time is given to the lessee to exercise his opinion to remain. If the option to renew is not exercised and the lease is thereby terminated, the lessee should be given the authority to remove certain clearly defined fixtures or equipment within a stated time (for example, sixty days) or otherwise title of these will revert to the lessor.

Relocation of site. From time to time lessors may need the leased premises for the expansion or further development of the airport. The lease should include provisions for this contingency. One possible arrangement indicates that the lessor has the right on six month's notice to relocate or replace at lessor's expense the lessee's facilities in substantially similar form at another generally comparable location on the airport. If this is done, the lessee's loss of income during the transition period must be considered, and all contingencies covered such as abating the rent and/or extending the period of the lease. If not covered in the lease, it should be remembered that the public authority owning the airport has the right of eminent domain and has the inherent right to condemn the leasehold and improvements in the usual manner provided by law.

Performance bonds. The lease frequently includes the provision requiring the lessee to furnish bonds for the "full performance" under the terms of the lease for such items as facility construction, guarantee of wages, and payment of contracts.

Rent. The remaining lease component of rent will be covered fully in a later section of this chapter dealing with lease payments.

The operating agreement. A major portion of the lease constitutes an *operating agreement* between the lessor and the lessee. The earlier portions of this material are common to most real estate leases, but this area is unique to the lease dealing with aviation businesses. Since many of the following topics are not understood by people outside the aviation industry, care should be exercised in selecting legal advice and in negotiating items in this portion of the lease. The typical aviation business lease provides coverage of the following topics in the operating agreement:

- Permitted sales
- Permitted flight operations
- Permitted line service
- Signs and advertising
- Service charges
- Lessor inspection
- Security
- Snow removal
- Uniforms
- Fuel sales and charges
- New functions
- Collection of any fees on behalf of the lessor
- Motor vehicle parking
- Vending machines
- Maintenance, repair, and overhaul
- Subleases
- Taxes or payments in lieu
- Towing disabled aircraft
- Business practices
- Exclusive rights
- Collection of landing and parking fees
- Subleases
- Vending and game machines

A review of each of these operating topics with special emphasis on its application to the aviation business is desirable.

Insurance. Because of the complexity, cost, and increased deductibles in today's aviation insurance market, an important consideration in the FBO's operating agreement with the airport owner is who is responsible for what liability in the event of a problem. This requires the attention of an expert in aviation insurance, as does the premises insurance.

Sales. The lease should specifically permit the lessee to sell (retail and wholesale) new and used aircraft, new and used radio and electronic equipment, aircraft parts, navigation equipment, and pilot supplies and equipment. In addition to the sale of aircraft, equipment, parts, and accessories, the lessee should have the right to finance such equipment, to insure aircraft and contents, or to act as agent for another party for these purposes.

Flight operations. The lessee should be specifically given the right to engage in flight operations that may include:

- Demonstration of aircraft for sale
- Charter flights
- Air taxi activity
- Commuter airline operations

- Flight training (primary and advanced)
- Aircraft leasing
- Aircraft rental
- Test flights
- Sight-seeing flights and other miscellaneous flight activities
- Aerial application

In some instances the lessor may feel that certain flight activities, such as primary flight training, should not be conducted at the airport. Here the lessee should not be prohibited from conducting such flight activity away from the airport. For example, the lessee should not be prohibited from transporting the primary student by air to an outlying airport or practice area. Normally it should be acceptable for the lessee to have the right to conduct advance, recurrent or periodic flight training of licensed pilots at the airport. Some activities such as aerial application will entail special requirements on the part of the lessor.

Maintenance, repair and overhaul. The lessee in an aviation business should have the right to maintain, repair and overhaul all types of aircraft, engines, instruments, radio and electronic gear and to remove, install or re-install such equipment in aircraft in his or her care, custody, and control. Dependent upon the circumstances, it may be desirable to indicate in the lease that the lessee has the right to maintain, repair, and overhaul motor vehicles used in his business.

Line service. It is highly desirable that the lessee have the right to conduct aircraft fueling and line-service activities. In many instances this should include the right to service the large aircraft operated by scheduled carriers who do not maintain their own servicing equipment on the airport and the servicing of military aircraft under government contracts. The location of fueling and line service operations should be clearly defined in the terms of the lease. The lessee should have the right to load and unload passengers and cargo and to transport passengers from transient aircraft parking areas to the terminal and other areas of the airport.

Service charges. The lessee on an airport must have the right to assess charges and fees to customers for services rendered. The lessor may periodically be given the right to review the schedule of fees and charges. Some leases provide that the lessee must set charges at levels that are reasonably competitive with those in the surrounding area.

Towing disabled aircraft. The lessee should be given the right to tow disabled aircraft from or about the airport. The stipulation that this also be an *obligation* of the lessee should be considered carefully due to equipment requirements. If the obligation is necessary, perhaps it would be wise to limit the size of the aircraft to less than 12,500 pounds.

Security. The lease will probably require the lessee to prevent unauthorized persons from transiting the facilities or entering into restricted flight or loading areas. This probably will mean that the lessee has the additional responsibility of providing fencing of a size and quality acceptable to the lessor and personnel practices and procedures which will ensure control of visitors and customers.

Snow removal. The lease should be clear regarding the duties and obligations of both parties to remove snow (and like hazards) and should include a specific description of the various areas of responsibility. An FBO tenant may accomplish faster snow removal by contracting with the airport to remove the snow.

Uniforms. Some leases stipulate that the lessee's employees are to wear uniforms at the lessee's expense, and that this sometimes requires the prior approval of the lessor regarding design.

Motor vehicle parking. The lease must also provide for the identification of adequate space for the parking of motor vehicles. Provisions must be made for vehicles operated by lessee, lessor, customers, employees and the public at large. This should include vehicles operated on the normal vehicle roadway as well as the airport ramps and taxiways.

Vending and game machines. The lessee should be given the right to operate vending and game machines on leased premises. If such machines are not owned by the lessee, their installation may be subject to the approval of the lessor and their income may be included in the calculation of the rent for the facilities.

Signs and advertising. The lease should specifically provide the lessee with the right to install signs and advertisements promoting the business name and the brand names of any aircraft, fuel, and other products or services. If the lease provides that the lessor's consent be required prior to sign installation, it should also specify that such consent will not be unreasonably withheld or that unreasonable criteria will not be established. Procedures should be established that provide for the removal of signs after the termination of the lease or affiliation with the manufacturer or supplier of products or supplies.

Subleases. When desirable, the lease should authorize the lessee to operate ancillary businesses on the leased premises, such as rental car agencies, giftshops, restaurants, barbershops, newsstands, and so on. It should also authorize the subleasing of space to provide under-one-roof services such as electronic repair-related businesses, corporate office, or aircrew spaces.

Taxes/payments in lieu. The tax burden of a lessee is primarily the responsibility of the business, not the responsibility of the lessor. It should be remembered that a leasehold has a value as personal property and frequently is used as the basis for personal property taxes. To protect the lessee from financial overburden, it is recommended that the following clause be made part of the lease:

Lessee shall be liable for any and all taxes, penalties and interests thereon assessed, levied or charged by any governmental agency against lessee's tangible personal property situated on the lessor's premises; however, rentals to be paid by the lessee to the lessor shall be reduced by an amount equal to the ad valorem taxes against the lessee's leasehold improvements under this agreement.

Lessor inspection. The lessor may desire provisions in the lease that will give the lessor rights to inspect the leased premises and to review and audit the records and accounts of the lessee's business. If these rights are included in the lease, it is recommended that the lease specify that such rights be exercised reasonably, that they not be used improperly to harass the lessee, and that the expenses of such reviews, inspections, and audits be borne by the lessor. Extreme caution should be taken in this area to ensure that lessor rights are not created that will result in an unfavorable business situation for the lessee. If the lessor or a subsidiary business is in competition with the lessee, the lease should be designed to prevent an unfair advantage through intimate knowledge of the lessee's day-by-day operation of his books and records.

Business practices. The lease should provide the lessee with broad latitude in exercising his own judgment in areas of normal business activity. Lease terms requiring lessor's approval of price and discounts should be avoided. The lessee should have broad latitude in establishing charges and in the inventory to be maintained and sold. He should avoid lease terminology that forces him to invest in slow-moving items of merchandise, including some grades of aviation fuel. The lease should also provide that the lessee may engage in other aviation—or aviation related businesses—not specifically covered in the lease by making a request in writing to the lessor, and that approval will not be unreasonably withheld.

Exclusive rights. An airport is a limited geographical area, and investors providing funds for a business in this space would normally like protection to limit the chance of cutthroat competition. Frequently, a clause is requested for the lease that would prevent additional aviation businesses from entering the airport for a specified period of time. Such clauses will *not* normally be permitted at airports that have received federal funds.[24] However, the FAA's Advisory Circular on Minimum Standards can help an FBO combat competition from unqualified operators such as "tailgate mechanics" and free-lance flight instructors.[25]

Minimum standards. Any FBO on the field may have to comply with minimum standards set by the airport owner. FAA provides guidelines on these.[26] High minimum standards may help to keep out underfinanced operators who would likely "skim the cream" of aviation business for a short time and then perhaps move on. The FBO already on the field can encourage stringent standards for his/her own protection but must, of course, be prepared to comply with them himself.

Collection of landing and parking fees. Leases vary, and frequently the lessee is required to collect landing and parking fees as an agent for the lessor. Naturally it would be desirable if the lessee were compensated for this service. The question of parking fees for aircraft awaiting or undergoing maintenance should be anticipated and normal business latitude be provided the lessee in such matters.

Lease payments. In exchange for the privilege of operating an aviation business and receiving the benefits of such activity, the lessee normally agrees to some form of lease payment to the lessor. The calculation of this payment and the rate of payment vary widely from lease to lease primarily according to local conditions, the value of the lease, and the bargaining power of the two parties. The typical aviation operation is potentially a complex, multi-business operating in a volatile and sometimes erratic environment. The goal of airport owners, developers, and managers should be the best possible aviation facilities for the use of the aviation public and the general public as well. The economic balance of a lease is very delicate with a need to consider two major factors: (1) adequate economic incentive to support and motivate the lessee in providing satisfactory aviation services and (2) minimum cost to the lessor in meeting the obligation to provide these services. Because of wide differences in the economic potential of airports, there have been some leases that paid the lessee to manage the airport while others have provided substantial returns to the lessor. It is important to recognize the existing situation and develop a lease that has the correct balance. The lessee must be able to operate at a reasonable profit level and not be forced out of business. The lessor (normally a public agency) has to meet the need for providing adequate public aviation services and for doing this as economically as possible.

Lease payments are normally considered in three categories: (1) rent on real estate by cents-per-square foot, (2) fees based on the lessee's unit sales, such as cents-per-gallon of gas sold, and (3) percentage of gross sales. Frequently the lease provides for all three sources, rents, fees, and revenue percentage payment. Rents and fees are fairly straightforward, whereas the percentage of gross may result in an excessive burden to the lessee if not kept within prudent bounds. The areas of concession fees and revenue percentages are full of pitfalls for both parties and should be explored carefully. The tendency of the lessor to extract heavy payment from the lessee must be guarded against in order to have a dynamic business that meets the needs of the growing aviation public. All three forms of payment may be combined into one rate per square foot, which then allows comparison with FBO rates on similar fields.[27]

Real estate rent. Rent is the fee charged for the use of real property where the business operates. Real property is normally identified in the lease as unimproved property, improved property, buildings, office space, terminal building space, aprons, and ramps. Establishment of the rental rates is a bargaining process, and the lessee must determine whether the proposed rates are competitive and within the business potential for the location. Rates are constantly changing because of the economic pressures being exerted upon the airport operators. The trend of the last few years is toward higher rentals. This trend has continued, as would be expected. Since rentals are competitive, there is considerable variation among airports. The figures at least provide some guidance and a departing point in calculating the existing competitive situation.

Comparable figures should be obtained from other airports, as well as from other leases on the lessor airport. Also, when examining a given rate structure, a lessee should consider the entire lease because it is possible that a low rate in one area will be offset by a high rate in another area. Individual rates can be raised by the lessor using different lessees to achieve a higher overall rate. Frequently, a sliding scale of rentals is developed for the benefit of a new aviation business. In the early years of operation the rate is low, and it increases over time as the business grows. This arrangement encourages the growth of a stable business that can provide necessary services rather than maximizing the immediate cash flow for the lessor. It is realistic for both parties to anticipate that as the business grows, the lease may include provisions for increases in future rentals.

Percentage of the gross. Many aviation business leases provide for rent schedules based upon a "percentage of the gross," with fixed minimum rental payments. Some calculate the rental upon a real estate schedule and then provide for additional rental through the payment of a sum based upon a percentage of the gross. Regardless of the percentage used, this manner of rental payment calculation can be critical to an aviation business because it may establish a system of charges so high that the lessee cannot operate at a profit. Many general aviation businesses operate at a 2 1/2 percent to 3 percent margin and cannot possibly survive if the lease requires a 3 percent to 5 percent of gross sales rental payment.

If the lessor insists upon using gross sales revenues as an index for establishing rents, the lessee may maintain some balance by striving for a reduced schedule for the fixed real estate rental and for the use of an "adjusted gross formula," which is defined as the gross income, less taxes, less bad debts, less fuel flowage fees, and less aircraft sales.

Aircraft sales. Some lessors strive to obtain payments on a percentage of the gross or net revenue from aircraft sales. For the typical aviation business, however, it is felt that aircraft sales should be encouraged by not taking a direct percentage on any sales (wholesale or retail), presuming that a long-range benefit will result from more aircraft operating hours, more maintenance, storage, fuel, and other related businesses.

Fuel sales. Payments on the sale of fuel through the imposition of flowage fees should receive careful consideration by both parties to the lease. Fuel is part of the line service, which is expected and provided in the support of transient aircraft. The income from fuel sales often provides the revenue base that contributes to the development of a stable organization. It tends to support a business when sales or other revenues may not be forthcoming. Where the public body (city, county, and so on) retains fueling rights without providing other services, transients are frequently discouraged by the arrangement, service is not as responsive, and the aviation businesses tend to be weak with higher failure rates. Fuel flowage fees range from one-half cent to a few cents per gallon on fuel pumped by the lessee. Flowage rates above this level create a heavy economic burden on the lessee and may cause additional burdens as fuel prices increase, controls become heavier, and customer reaction becomes stronger.

If fuel flowage fees are included in the lease, it is desirable that the following practical guidelines be followed:

1. The lessee has the right to fuel the business's own aircraft without flowage charges.
2. The lessee has the right to fuel aircraft operated by the local, state or federal government without charge.
3. Air carrier aircraft with "turn-around" fuel contracts should not reflect a charge.
4. Fuel fees should be based upon fuel sold and not on volume delivered into the storage facilities.
5. The fuel fee should be based upon a specified sum (for example, two cents a gallon) only for fuel sold at retail to transient aircraft.
6. The lessee should have the absolute right to select the fuel supplier.
7. Clear provisions should be included in the lease to cover bulk fuel storage agreements so as not to restrict the lessee or to proliferate the number of storage units.

Landing and parking fees. Landing fees have long been a problem at airports, especially those open to the public. Many operators have found that the administrative costs of collecting landing fees for many types of aircraft cancel most of the revenues. In addition, these funds are so small that they contribute very little income to the business. Many operators have found that landing fees act as a deterrent to itinerant pilots, especially to general aviation aircraft with alternative landing options. In going elsewhere, the aircraft take their additional and perhaps major business activity with them. If landing fees are required, it is suggested that they aren't collected from non-commercial aircraft. Those aircraft involved in commercial passenger or freight operations such as certificated carriers, commuter airlines, charter, and air taxi are normally charged landing fees.

A partnership. The lease for the operation of an aviation business is more than a simple contractual agreement. Both the lessor and the lessee are partners who work for the benefit of the entire community. The agreement is more than a lease; it is a lease, an operating agreement, a partnership agreement, and a community service plan that establishes a mutually beneficial relationship between the two parties and the public that they serve. This kind of relationship is necessary if the airport's service and support facilities in a given community are to grow and to provide a stimulus to the growth of the aviation sector and the overall economy of that community. For aircraft to be really useful in business and personal transportation throughout the network of approximately 15,000 landing facilities in the United States, there must be a sustained growth in the quality of the aircraft-support facilities across the country. The number of aircraft is growing, and more and more individuals and organizations are using aircraft for personal as well as business transportation. The partnership element of the aviation business lease will do a great deal to promote the necessary growth of aircraft support activities. It is apparent that this agreement cannot be one-sided, but must be equitable and represent the interests of both parties.

One innovative solution that has tax benefits is for the building to revert to the airport as soon as it is completed. The FBO then becomes a tenant from the outset. Instead of paying property taxes on the full value of the premises, he or she pays an occupancy or leasehold tax related only to the value of that year's lease payments. Over a 25 or 30 year period, this cuts taxes by a factor of ten or more. The landlord and tenant must provide in the leases for maintenance, repairs, utilities, and insurance on the premises.

Competition with Other FBOs

FAA non-exclusive rights policy. Any airport that has received federal funds from the Aviation Trust Fund must by law be available to all users. This includes being available to all FBOs who are interested and can meet required standards. This means that even airports that hope to be funded must comply with the FAA regulations. Yet the rules also recognize that if new competition would mean neither the old nor the new FBO would have enough business to be viable, there can be some protection for the existing FBO.[28] In many cases the airport minimum standards permit self-fueling and self-maintenance by qualified operators. In cases where the airport standard prevents a certain type of newcomer (such as one offering too few services or too small an area, or one that is undercapitalized), then the FBO needs to be vigilant that the standards are being enforced and applied fairly.

Since an existing FBO at a publicly funded field has limited protection against the granting of leases to new competitors, the best protection may be to provide a full-service, quality operation so that no outside entrepreneur can find any unmet needs.

Through the fence. A "through-the-fence" operation is one on land not owned by the airport owner but with legal or long-standing rights of access through an actual gateway or across an imaginary property line onto the airport. Some airports actively encourage such through-the-fence activities as, for example, corporate aircraft hangars connected in surrounding airport industrial parks. In other cases the through the fence situation may involve only one operator who may have an established aviation business. The problem for the airport operator is that there may not be very much control or revenue (if any) from operations off an airport.

The problem for other FBOs is that the through-the-fence operator may not be paying the true cost of airport facilities. FBOs on the field may be subsidizing the through-the-fence FBO. FBOs already on an airport will generally find that it isn't in their favor if through-the-fence activities are added. FBOs seeking to enter operations at a busy field may find that there is no available airport land and that a through-the-fence easement to adjacent land may be their best alternative. As existing airports use up their available land, this type of situation may become more common, and FBOs need to fully understand both sides of the question.

Financing. As with many other areas of the economy, there is an increasing interest at airports in encouraging the private sector to provide facilities that were previously built by the public airport authority. For example, there are a growing number of air traffic control towers run on contract or under FAA regulation by private companies. As discussed in chapter 8, the reduction in flight service stations has triggered a new service area: private weather systems provided by FBOs. Potential profits for FBOs and/or other private investors are in such areas as the development of business offices on the airfield, restaurants, and hangars. Hangars have often been built by public airport operators, but recent years have seen increasing questioning of why scarce public funds should be used to build facilities that (1) benefit only certain airport users and (2) can be profitable for the private sector. Certain types of portable hangars can be particularly profitable as well as flexible.

FBOs who wish to expand their base of operations should be constantly aware that the lines between public sector and private sector investment at airports are shifting and that this shift may present new opportunities for profit.

Summary

When it is a matter of upkeep and improvement of the physical facilities that make his or her business possible, most FBOs—unless they own the airport—find that they have relatively little direct control. In addition, the health of their business depends on having access to a viable national and international airport network. The attitudes and concerns of airport neighbors can also have a major impact. Sound physical facility planning, therefore, takes into account the airport's wider environment and community attitudes. Airport physical facilities may be grouped into two categories: (1) the public use facilities, such as runways, taxiways, terminals and auto parking, which may be shared by other FBOs, and (2) the private-use facilities that the FBO has the use of through an operating agreement and lease. These facilities may include hangars, ramps, maintenance and office facilities. Public planning for an airport usually starts with a master plan following FAA guidelines. Funding may come from several public sources for the public portions of the airport; the FBO will have to raise private funding. FBOs can benefit greatly—as well as be adversely affected—by the planning and publicity created by an airport's public sponsors. Therefore, it is advisable to stay closely involved with all public actions affecting the field, to understand the planning and funding processes, and to communicate the economic value of the individual FBO operation.

Discussion Topics

1. How is an FBO affected by the operation of those parts of the airport not covered in his or her lease?
2. Why should an FBO be concerned with promoting the airport to the business community and airport neighbors?
3. What are six steps involved in an airport master plan?
4. What might be some of the considerations to be resolved when an FBO seeks financing for developments on leased airport land?
5. What is the most significant environmental issue at most airports and why? What can an FBO do about mitigating it?
6. What is the value of preventive maintenance and how would you set about developing such a program for a combination of repair hangar and office?
7. Identify five operational techniques that can be used to reduce noise around airports. What are their pros and cons from (1) the community's viewpoint; (2) the FBO's viewpoint?

Chapter 13
The Future

Objectives

- ✔ Explain how and why the general aviation industry evolved in a different direction than the airlines.
- ✔ Describe contingency planning and how this technique can assist the FBO owner/manager.
- ✔ Discuss a sample continuing education program that would serve the needs of managers in a mid-sized FBO.
- ✔ Understand the problems inherent with change in any business environment.

Trying to Predict the Future By Looking at the Past Is Like Trying to Drive a Car Using Only the Rear-View Mirror

(Author Unknown)

Introduction

Why do we need to know about the future? For the aviation business owner, a limited view into the future may be sufficient for some purposes. However, for other purposes, the long range must be evaluated. For example, construction of new facilities may involve 20- to 30-year financing. What will the market for these facilities be like in the next few decades? Or there may be reasons right now to get involved in the lease or purchase of a large new aircraft to serve a particular charter market. Can a five-year lease be justified: Will the need for this airplane still be there two or three years from now?

Chapter 1 reviewed the decline in general aviation aircraft production that has taken place since the late 1970s—with shipments falling from over 16,000 units to under 1,000 per year. The causes of this decline were also discussed. Some factors have abated and may no longer have significant impact in the future. Others are still around and most likely will affect future General Aviation trends. Since FBOs service the General Aviation industry, and only a few businesses are servicing major airline accounts, the future of General Aviation and the future of FBOs will tend to go hand in hand.

Forecasting

Predicting the future of general aviation as a whole, and FBOs in particular, is a very uncertain business even for the relatively short range. In the 1970s, the Federal Aviation Administration's forecasting branch expended considerable effort developing a "General Aviation Dynamics" model that calculated the effects on aviation activity from changes in a number of factors. These included the price of avgas, student pilot starts, and many other variables. Past growth trends provided the basis for the relationships in the model.[1] By the mid-1980s, FAA's forecasting for general aviation activity had become very cautious, since historic trends were difficult to enhance. The 1989 national forecasts predicted a decline of 0.1 percent in active General Aviation aircraft between 1988 and 1992, rising to a 0.3 percent growth in the 1992 to 2000 period.[2]

General Aviation hours flown are forecasted to grow at 1.2 percent per annum in over the next twelve years.[3] Other aviation specialists have opted not to even develop numbers for aviation activity; instead, they simply spell out the factors likely to cause downward and upward trends.

Personal and recreational flying in conventional fixed wing aircraft has been the hardest hit segment because so many costs have risen—insurance, fuel, avionics, and maintenance. Business aviation has been more able to absorb these increases as part of the cost of doing business.

A new excitement about the future of general aviation has begun with the signing of the Aviation Revitalization Act in late 1994. Many aviation associations and government officials are expecting the late 1990s to witness the rebirth of general aviation, extending on into the twenty-first century.

Transportation Demand Is a "Derived" Demand

Demand for air transportation, like other forms of transportation, is largely what economists call a **derived** demand; that is, a means to some other end which is in demand. What people are buying when they buy general aviation air transportation is one or more of the following:

1. Face to face contact with people from other places.
2. On-the-spot inspection of facilities, real estate, and processes.
3. Shipment of goods.
4. Conduct of a business, learning or recreational activity while airborne.

The **benefits** of the transaction affect what people buy. When they choose general aviation over other means of accomplishing their purpose, the benefits are generally these:

1. Speed
2. Privacy
3. Control over itinerary
4. Cost advantages
5. Access to maximum number of places compared with airlines

The FBO manager must address the future by constantly considering two things. First, he or she must consider what business they are in. This is not in the business of aircraft provision, repair and instruction so much as in the business of *facilitating people's access to their ultimate (rather than derived) demands or interests.* Second, he or she must consider that as a result of this definition of the business, the competition is not necessarily other providers of transportation, or even other providers of support services for air transportation. The competition is *any other technology or business that facilitates people's access to their ultimate interests.*

What kinds of access do people want, and to what kinds of places and things? In a rapidly changing world, there is no easy answer to these questions, but they are the right questions. As a consequence, the FBO manager of the future must be very aware of economic and social change going on outside as well as within the aviation industry. By the time some other aviation business has started to offer a new service or process, it may be too late for other FBOs to catch up. The FBO manager will need to anticipate, rather than react to, changes in the marketplace.

For the aviation manager, the expectation of change and the definition of what business one should be in as change occurs are essential skills for facing the future. This chapter cannot discuss in-depth all the available "futures" studies and their meaning for aviation. Rather, what it seeks is to identify some major considerations and their possible implications for the FBO of the future.

Trends in the U.S. Economy

As we approach the the twenty-first century, major structural shifts are occurring in many areas of the economy, including the aviation sector. Some of the key trends are:

1. Growth in the service sector, especially "high-tech" such as computers and medical/bio-engineering. Within all types of business there is growing emphasis on service rather than one-time sales.
2. Shifts in manufacturing, including the transfer of some U.S. jobs to overseas locations including Mexico, Pacific Rim nations, and Europe. Recent worldwide trade agreements will only serve to increase this trend.
3. Development of new aircraft designs and aircraft certification regulations. Composite aircraft designs will continue to increase as will the development of new technology, especially in the area of avionics.
4. The homebuilt market area will probably continue its upward trend. Traditional aircraft manufacturing will see new companies entering the arena as well as a resurgence of products from the mainstay companies such as Cessna and Piper.
5. Pervasive application of computers and other multimedia hardware permeate all areas of business.
6. Globalization of the marketplace will continue to expand. Foreign companies will open more offices and manufacturing bases in the United States. U.S. companies will continue their trend of doing more business overseas.
7. Increases in oil and fuel prices due to governmental and environmental pressures to ensure a clean environment.
8. Labor shortages, especially for entry level labor positions. Many military-trained pilots and technicians who were the primary labor supply for the aviation industry are no longer in the pipeline for future replacements; at least not at the levels needed.
9. Airline deregulation's continuing effects in fare wars, mergers, bankruptcies, and consolidation of flight service to a small number of increasingly congested hubs.
10. More regulation and less funding in many areas of the federal government, including more stringent Part 135 and 121 regula-

tions for aviation. The possibility of a partial or fully privatized air traffic control system will grossly effect the general aviation industry in terms of fee assessments.

11. Transportation's role in the context of growing electronic communications.
12. The future of the Aviation Trust Fund at this writing is in question. Whether it will continue to be used to offset the federal deficit or whether the fund will be abolished completely in light of the proposed privatized corporation and fee assessment structure is to be determined.
13. Continued variation and high cost in the insurance industry.

The aviation manager must keep abreast of these and other issues in the economy and constantly be on the lookout for two implications:

- Threats to the business
- Opportunities for new market development

The section that follows discusses in more depth some specific areas that are likely to affect FBOs in the near future.

Current and Future Issues Affecting FBOs

Growth in the Service Sector

Many service companies are purchasing and chartering aircraft for business purposes. Some of the faster growth areas of the economy are in the service sector and these service companies have a high degree of need for fast flexible travel. FBOs need to monitor the changes in their local economy and consider approaching new and growing businesses that may not be familiar with the benefits of general aviation.

The National Business Aircraft Association and the General Aviation Manufacturers Association have been promoting nationally the use of private aircraft to business owners through their campaign "No Plane No Gain." FBO owners and managers should help promote the concept in their local areas.

Overseas Manufacturing

Today the United States makes only 25 percent of the world's automobiles. A decade ago, this figure was 75 percent. The aircraft manufacturing industry is following this trend. Current Boeing aircraft on order for Japan Airlines, for example, are being partially made in Japan. In addition, their quality is very high. Even the People's Republic of China has entered the aircraft manufacturing industry. If manufacturing trends in aviation follow trends in other sectors of industry, we can expect to see continued U.S. innovation, but a gradual transfer of actual production to other countries with cheaper labor. The extremely high degree of customization in much aircraft assembly may be the saving grace of the U.S. small aircraft industry. For avionics and other parts, the trend may grow towards overseas production. This trend has implications for the FBO's maintenance shop's warranty and spare parts situation, as well as for the lucrative aircraft refurbishing and remodeling market.

On the other side of the spectrum, companies like Aerospatiale whose corporate headquarters are in France, have opened up manufacturing facilities in the United States. Even traditional U.S. manufacturers like Mooney Aircraft Company are now owned by Mooney Holding Corporation in France, and Learjet, Inc., owned by Bombardier, Inc. in Montreal, Canada.

An International Economy

The world's international corporations have annual gross sales larger than the gross national product of some countries. Many U.S. companies are now closely tied with other parts of the world. This means a growing need for secure, safe, and speedy air travel between continents. Increasingly, this travel is by corporate aircraft rather than by airline. Servicing these aircraft can be a new source of income for FBOs.

New Aircraft Designs

New aircrafts design and manufacturing processes continue to enter the market. Home-building is on an increase and with the advent of changes in the aircraft certification process, some companies once selling homebuilt "kits" are now selling completed aircraft. This trend may continue. As Cessna reenters the single engine piston aircraft market, the expectation is for an increase in sales across the board. Used aircraft market prices may decline, but this may serve to open up opportunities for new potential aircraft ownership.

Mergers and Acquisitions

U.S. business ownership appears to be becoming more decentralized. Some companies specifically select small communities for plant expansion because of the quality of life offered to their employees. Along with the effects this has on local schools and the housing market, it often has implications in terms of airport and aviation growth. Many businesses are acquiring aircraft with the range for both international and transcontinental flights. FBOs can service these aircraft and meet their special need for constant availability.

Small Airports in Small Communities

For the FBO, the decentralizing pressures that seem to be appearing suggest new market opportunities in the nation's smaller communities that are seeking to attract high-technology and growth industries. There should be growth opportunities for both business and personal aviation, including air-taxi feeder service to the nation's hub airports. The presence of an airport with an innovative and well-run FBO can be an important factor in attracting new companies.

Pervasive Computers

Computers in aviation are likely to become as commonplace as in most other American businesses. To be competitive, FBOs will need to use computers for the financial and administrative aspects of the business, especially as companies become larger and more complex. Being able to pull up the customer's record on a screen is not just efficient; it tends to convince the customer that the entire operation is efficient. "Computer-literate" employees are needed in aviation businesses across the board, as they are in any other business. There are implications for training older employees and those with "computer phobia."

Because of access to computer data banks as well as traditional print media, more information about things within and beyond the FBO business will become more and more readily available. The FBO manager will have to make more decisions about how much time to allocate to sifting through this material to see what its meaning for the business may be. To be competitive, the FBO will almost certainly have to computerize information processes within the business. Care will need to be given to deciding what to collect about performance and how often results should be tabulated. In all this flow of published data, the manager may need to remember once in a while that there is no substitute for going and looking, or "management by walking around."[4]

Chapter 7 discusses the application of computers to the running of an FBO business, and this book refers in almost every other chapter to how computers are coming into use in the rest of the aviation system, for instance:

1. Improved weather services, private and public.
2. Computer diagnostics for aircraft repair.
3. ELT location calculations.

4. Computer disks and video disks for training.
5. Computer brokerage for aircraft.
6. Computer-controlled parts suppliers.
7. Simulation and flight training on computers.
8. Access to national data bases such as the stock market.
9. Personal computers, raising the typical FBO customer's and employee's "computer literacy" and offering at-home access to programs such as flight simulation.
10. Computers in education at all levels.
11. Cockpit computers for increasing numbers of functions.
12. FAA required computerized exams for pilots and Maintenance technicians.

The Labor Market

General aviation will be affected along with most other industries by growing shortages of entry-level labor, as discussed in chapter 5—"Human Resources." This means the likelihood of wage increases as well as the substitution of capital for labor in certain areas. The FBO will bear the additional burden of continuing to be the training and proving ground for employees who, once trained, will move on to better jobs at small airlines and corporate flight departments. The more successful FBOs will adjust their hiring, compensation, and training policies to retain good staff as long as possible.

Airline Deregulation

The Airline Deregulation Act of 1978 continues to affect the entire aviation industry. Within the airline industry there has been a tremendous growth in the number of passengers, varied fares, types of frequent flyer benefits, mergers, failures and consolidations among airlines, and perhaps most significantly for the FBO increased hub-and-spoke patterns of airline route systems. Except between major cities that have direct flights, air trips generally take longer because of the likelihood of one hub stopover. In addition, owing to the declining role of Essential Air Service and declining subsidies, many smaller communities no longer have scheduled air service. Both these deficits in the airline system represent market opportunities for the FBO.

With the advent of low cost, no frills airline operators like Southwest Airlines, United's Shuttle, and Continental Lite, the competition among airlines has become more fierce. Some of the amenities of airline travel such as meal service and prearranged seating are being eliminated. Although this is helping the airlines to offer fares at lower costs to stay competitive, it is concurrently making the benefits of airline travel less attractive, especially to the business traveler. Hence, another opportunity for the FBO to advance the benefits of flying a general aviation aircraft.

New Regulatory Areas

A national trend toward less economic regulation (at least of the nation's transportation industries) appears to be accompanied by a trend toward greater regulation in areas relating to safety and environmental quality. One of the most significant recent regulations affecting FBOs is undoubtedly the introduction of requirements for existing and new underground fuel storage tanks. Most FBOs will have to obtain insurance to demonstrate their financial ability to handle any seepage and cleanup problems. The cost of installing adequately designed tanks is a key factor for any FBO planning expansion or updating of a fuel farm.

Other regulations relate to the training of FBO personnel in safe fueling and fire-fighting at airline airports. Several approved programs are now available. FBOs involved in the disposal of any kind of hazardous waste such as used oil and crop-spraying chemicals must meet more stringent standards that will also be costly.

Aviation Trust Fund

The Aviation Trust Fund, which for many years was used to help offset the federal budget deficit, has come under attack again recently. With the advent of a partial or wholly privatized air traffic control system, airport and airway usage direct fees may used to in the future to subsidize the aviation infrastructure and air traffic control system. Current debate is underway regarding the future of the Aviation Trust Fund.

Insurance

In 1994 the General Aviation Aircraft Product Liability Bill was enacted into legislation by President Bill Clinton. A nine year struggle by the aviation community was finally put to rest with an eighteen year statute of repose bill. How much this will affect the insurance rates has yet to be determined. The expectation is that it will at the least, curb the substantial increases incurred over the past few years, and the possibility of a leveling of current rates in the near future.

Transportation Versus Telecommunications

In future decades, particularly if energy shortages constrain aviation before alternative fuels are feasible, the true competition for FBOs may be telecommunications. The telecommunications industry can sell instant electronic access to people and places at less cost than aviation. While direct contact is still likely to be necessary at certain stages of business relationships, telecommunications technology may be able to help lay the groundwork by screening out alternatives that previously would have taken a personal visit to resolve. Some realtors, for example, are using video to show properties to prospects and only taking them to actually visit those that look most promising. Such an approach is being applied to many other industries and areas of business.

Applying this approach to the FBO's own business suggests such activities as video for brokering aircraft, presenting marketing packages to prospective customers, presenting public relations material about the FBO, accessing information at the parent company or aircraft manufacturer on a real-time basis, accessing real-time weather information, selling how-to manuals for computer or video use, and providing home study flight training floppy disks, CD disks and tapes.

Another affected area is the task of helping a company decide whether it needs a corporate aircraft. The consulting skills of the FBO may need to be tailored to address wider issues such as whether certain telecommunications technology can replace direct travel for some of the company's current or expected access needs. An immediate and inexpensive opportunity is the installation of a computer on-line service for use by charter customers delayed or cancelled by weather.

Public Understanding of the Potential Role of General Aviation

As more people turn to general aviation instead of airline travel, the benefits will become more widely understood and the influence of the industry much greater. Already many legislators have a good grasp of the contribution of general aviation because they would be unable to conduct their election campaigns without the speed and access to small communities provided by private aircraft. Increasingly, this awareness will spread to business decision makers. The result will hopefully be a better understanding of why general aviation should have continued access to the nation's airspace and top airports—an understanding that has not been apparent in recent years. The growth in demand for business aircraft travel creates an opportunity for FBOs to educate key decision makers about the importance of the industry. Every FBO must develop this role.

FBO Opportunities

For the creative and market-oriented FBO, there will be many new business opportunities in the changing future. The unmet needs will be determined not by considering what the FBO likes to do best, but by close contact with existing and potential customers to find out more about their growth, change, and transportation and communication needs. Each unmet need must then be subjected to a rigorous analysis of whether the competition is pursuing this market and whether it can be a profitable line of service for the FBO, given start-up costs and probable sales.

The past decade has seen the elimination of many of the "mom-and-pop" aviation businesses through merger, bankruptcy and retirement, especially at smaller airports. As aircraft range increases, services are needed at less frequent intervals. In order to remain competitive, more capital is needed to sustain an FBO. Therefore, it seems likely that the trend towards larger FBOs, franchises, and chains will continue.

Airport administrators are feeling the pressure to be more self-supporting. Many airports have done little to tap the potential opportunities in this area, partly because it was not necessary. Some airports have good potential for greater revenues from nonaviation activities such as car rentals, restaurants and motels. Another possible service at smaller airports is meeting rooms and small conference centers, so that business people can fly in, conduct business, and leave without arranging ground transportation and spending extra time. Computer, copying, typing, and other services on demand would be an extension of this concept.

Conclusion

"Business as Usual" is the least likely future for the FBO. About 60% of the nation's FBOs have closed down in the past 14 years, according to the FBO Resource Group, a Denver-based consulting firm. In 1980, there were some 10,000 fixed-base operators in the U.S., but today there are about 4,000 and the prediction is that by the year 2000 there will be only 2,000.

There are a number of reasons for this decline, according to the study. For one, there has been no increase in the average aircraft flight hours, and FBOs are caught in a price and volume squeeze. They are unable to raise the fuel prices to increase their profit margins because of competitive pressures, and they are unable to expand their market because of the flat or declining flying activity.

Another factor causing problems for both FBOs and airport operators is the continued growth in governmental regulations, particularly those promulgated by the Environmental Protection Agency. The most expensive of these EPA regulations are the ones concerning underground tanks, spill prevention, and storm water runoff.

Those FBOs that remain will find many new needs to meet and will require an understanding of the major underlying trends in the economy and society in order to seize new opportunities. Qualified staff may be in short supply, and those that are available will be attracted by a competitive salary, fringe benefits, and challenges. The FBO manager will be a true professional by managing, by delegating, and by watching quality at all times while keeping an eye on the bottom line.

Summary

Continued change in the wider economy will likely mean continued change for FBOs. This can either be decline or growth, depending on whether an astute grasp of new opportunities is seized. The strongest growth area seems most likely in the business and executive travel area, particularly if airline travel continues to be more costly and difficult. FBOs need to make a constant effort in several areas: (1) maintaining professional business techniques and personnel practices in order to stay competitive; (2) tuning in to national and local economic trends in order to spot strategic opportunities and threats, and (3) improving the image and understanding of the general aviation industry as a whole so that it gets its share of resources and support.

Discussion Topics

1. How and why has the general aviation industry evolved in a different direction than the airlines?
2. Why is general aviation a key element of the US transportation system? Why is this less true in Europe?
3. Name three problem areas likely to face general aviation managers in the future. How can they be constructively addressed?
4. What is a contingency plan and how can an aviation manager employ contingency planning techniques to help overcome uncertainty about the future?
5. Can good management be learned, or is it inborn? Explain your point of view.
6. What type of continuing education program might best serve the needs of senior managers in a medium sized FBO?
7. What are three problems associated with change in a business organization? How can they be handled?

Notes

Chapter One

1. Nicoll, Dave, *A New Name for a New Game,* Publisher's Memo, Airport Services, June 1988.
2. Letter to author from NATA, February 13, 1989.
3. Kane, Robert M., and Vose, Alan D., *Air Transportation,* Dubuque, Ia.: Kendall/Hunt Publishing Company, 1987.
4. Kane and Vose, op. cit.
5. Kane and Vose, op. cit.
6. Kane and Vose, op. cit.
7. Kane and Vose, op. cit.
8. Constant II, Edward W. *The Origins of the Turbojet Revolution,* Baltimore, MD.: John Hopkins University Press, 1980.
9. Serling, Robert J. and the Editors of Time-Life Books, *The Jet Age,* New York: Time-Life Books, 1982.
10. Delear, Frank J. *Igor Sikorsky—His Three Careers in Aviation,* New York: Dodd, Mead and Company, 1976.
11. *Federal Aviation Administration Aviation Forecasts, Fiscal Years 1989–2000,* United States Department of Transportation/Federal Aviation Administration, Washington, D.C., February 1989.
12. Kane and Vose, op. cit.
13. Kane and Vose, op. cit.
14. *National Airspace System Plan (NAS), Facilities, Equipment and Associated Development,* United States Department of Transportation/Federal Aviation Administration, Washington, D.C.
15. *Airline Deregulation Act,* October 24, 1978.
16. 11, op. cit.
17. National Air Transportation Association, sample advertising from "GAME" plan, reprinted by permission.
18. National Air Transportation Association pamphlet, *FBOs Today. What's Ahead Tomorrow?,* Alexandria, VA., undated.
19. Federal Aviation Administration Advisory Circular 150/5190–2A, *Exclusive Rights at Airports,* Washington, D.C., April 4, 1972.
20. Spanaflight, *Business Flights—A Business Travel Proposition,* Spanaway Airport, Washington.
21. *1980 Survey of Airport Services, 1978 Status and Activity,* United States Department of Commerce, Bureau of the Census, for Federal Aviation Administration, Washington, D.C., November 1980.
22. Telephone conversation, author and Lawrence Burian, NATA, 1988.
23. Results of survey conducted by the Gallup Organization for the Air Transport Association, *The Frequency of Flying Among the General Public,* (ATA), annual.

Chapter Two

1. With apologies to William Shakespeare's *Julius Caesar:* "Some are born great, some achieve greatness, and some have greatness thrust upon them."
2. Christy, Ron and Jones, Billy M. *The Complete Information Bank for Entrepreneurs and Small-Business Managers,* Center for Entrepreneurship and Small Business Management, Wichita State University/ AMACOM, New York, 1988.
3. Brown, Steven W., *13 Fatal Errors Managers Make and How You Can Avoid Them,* Berkley Publishing Group, New York, 1987.
4. Steven C. Brandt, *Entrepreneuring—The Ten Commandments for Building a Growth Company,* New York: Mentor Executive Library, 1982.
5. Thomas J. Peters and Robert H. Waterman, Jr., *In Search of Excellence—Lessons from America's Best-Run Companies,* New York: Warner Books, 1982.

6. Deaver Brown, *The Entrepreneur's Guide,* New York: Ballantine Books, 1980.
7. *Paths Toward Personal Progress/Leaders Are Made, Not Born,* Boston, MA., reprints from Harvard Business Review, 1984.
8. 5, op. cit.
9. Kenneth Lawyer, et al., *Small Business Success: Operating and Executive Characteristics,* Washington, D.C.: Small Business Management Research Report, SBA, 1963
10. 6, op. cit.
11. C. Northcote Parkinson, *The Law,* Boston, Mass.: Houghton Mifflin, 1980.
12. Kenneth Blanchard and Spencer Johnson, *The One-Minute Manager: The Quickest Way to Increase Your Own Prosperity,* New York: William Morrow and Company, 1982.
13. Associated Management Institute Inc. *Seminar Program on Time Management,* Fairchild, CA., 1985.
14. Winston, Stephanie, *The Organized Executive: A Program for Productivity: New Ways to Manage Time, Paper, and People,* Warner Books, New York, 1983.

Chapter Three

1. Jerry Stoltenberg, *Determining Your Natural Market: Practical Market Research for Entrepreneurs In Fifteenth Annual Entrepreneurship Symposium,* School of Business Administration, University of Washington, May 12, 1984.
2. General Aviation Task Force GAME ads (see chapter 1).
3. Peters and Waterman, *In Search of Excellence—Lessons from America's Best-Run Companies,* New York: Warner Books, 1982.
4. *FAA Aviation Forecasts,* Fiscal Years 1988–1999, USDOT/FAA, Feb. 1988.
5. *Business and Commercial Aviation* series on business aviation and the Fortune 1000, Ziff Davis, New York, end of year issue annually.
6. Patton, Carmella L., *Commuter FBO Grabs Corporate Clients with Quick, Quality Work,* ASM, July 1986.
7. Burnham, Frank, *California FBO Finds Profit in the Past,* ASM, November 1985.
8. Nieman, Steve, *Airline Affiliations Spur Business at Flight Schools,* ASM, January 1988.
9. Burnham, Frank, *Prop-Balancing May Be New FBO Profit Source,* ASM, March 1988.
10. Bremer, Karl, *Entrepreneur Seeks FBOs to Manage Airport Motel Chain,* ASM, May 1986.
11. Kilishek, George, *EJA, Atlantic Earn Big Profits from Air Charter,* ASM, September 1987.
12. Bremer, Karl, *Servicing Airliners on the Ground Helps FBOs' Profits Take Off,* ASM, March 1986.
13. *Airliner Deicing Proves Profitable for Minneapolis FBO,* ASM, October 1988.
14. Girsfield, Greg, *FBOs Remove Airfield Snow for Multiple Benefits,* ASM, September 1988.
15. Gilbert, Gordon, *Airports Profit as Hosts for Hotel Development,* ASM, September 1988.
16. Singer, Jennifer, *Air Charter Operators Profit from "Fly-By-Night" Business,* AS, October 1988.
17. Burnham, Frank, *Air Ambulance Services: The Growth of a Rewarding—and Risky—Business,* ASM, April 1985.
18. *In-House Barber Sets FBO A-"Part" from Others,* ASM, December 1986.
19. *Airports Call Pay Phones Profitable,* ASM, December 1987.
20. Schussler, John, *Shared Phone System Gives Airport, Tenants More Features for Less,* ASM, December 1987.
21. *Profitable Holiday Merchandise,* FBO, September/October 1988.

Chapter Four

1. John F. Murphy, *Sound Cash Management and Borrowing,* SBA Management Aids #1.016, Washington, D.C., 1984.
2. *Hobby Loss Revisited—Section 183 Mandates That an Activity Be Carried on for Profit or Demonstrate a Profit Motive,* Taxes and Accounting, Business and Commercial Aviation, May 1987.
3. Informal surveys by J.D. Richardson.
4. J.D. Richardson, *Practical Finance Working Notes,* Piper Aircraft Corporation, Lock Haven, Pa., 1973.
5. 4, op. cit.

6. Steven C. Brandt, *Entrepreneuring—The Ten Commandments for Building a Growth Company,* New York: Mentor Executive Library, 1982.
7. New England Airlines, Block Island, Rhode Island, conversations with Julie F. Rodwell.
8. 6, op. cit.
9. Morris-Davis and Company, *How to Turn Around a Financially Troubled Company,* handbook for Small Business Administration Strategic Business Development Program, 1984.
10. 6, op. cit.
11. Jack H. Feller Jr., *Keep Pointed Toward Profit,* SBA Management Aids #1.003, Washington, D.C., 1983.
12. Julie F. Rodwell, *A Look at Airport Finances at Thirty Airports in the Northwest/Mountain Region,* Combined Airports Conference, Eugene, Oregon, 1983.
13. *Boosting Your Airport Income,* Airports International, June 1984.
14. Milling, Bryan E., *Finding Hidden Profits in Your Accounts Receivable,* ASM, November 1985.
15. Bremer, Karl, *FBOs Earn Travel Agent Commissions Under New Program,* ASM, October 1988.
16. *Venture Capital Rules of Thumb,* Arthur Young Company, 1984.
17. LaRue Tone Hosmer, *A Venture Capital Primer for Small Business,* Washington, D.C., Small Business Administration Management Aids #1.009, 1983.
18. *Fifteenth Annual Entrepreneurship Symposium,* presentation by SeaFirst Bank, Seattle, Washington, University of Washington, May 1984.
19. Worthington, E. R., *Business Loans: How to Get One for Your FBO,* ASM, April 1986.
20. 18, op. cit.

Chapter Five

1. Richard A. Feller, *An Operating and Strategic Manpower Analysis and Plan for the General Aviation Industry,* Washington, D.C.: General Aviation Manufacturers' Association, 1981.
2. Peters and Waterman, *In Search of Excellence—Lessons from America's Best-Run Companies,* New York: Warner Books, 1982.
3. William Olsten, *Pointers on Using Temporary Help Services,* SBA Management Aids #5.004, Washington, D.C., 1983.
4. Steven C. Brandt, *Entrepreneuring: The Ten Commandments for Building a Growth Company,* chs. 5 and 6, New York: Mentor Executive Library, 1982.
5. Career Improvement Group Orientation Seminar, Seattle, Washington, 1984.
6. *Handy Reference Guide to the Fair Labor Standards Act,* Washington, D.C.: United States Department of Labor/Publication 1282, 1981.
7. Civil Rights Act of 1864, USC 1976, Title 28, para 1447.
8. Equal Employment Opportunity Act, United States 1976, Title 20, para 1701 et seq.
9. OSHA Safety and Health Standards, OSHA 2206, United States Department of Labor, March 11, 1983.
10. OSHA, from Seattle regional office information.
11. Prentice Hall Editorial Staff, *Employee Access to Records,* Englewood, NJ.: for American Society for Personnel Administration, 1984.
12. Cessna Pilot Training Manual, Wichita, KS, undated.
13. Jackson Vocational Interest Survey, Sigma Assessment Systems, Port Huron, Michigan.
14. Performax Testing, Performance Systems International, Minneapolis, MN., 1985.
15. Strong Interest Inventory, Consulting Psychologists Press, Inc., Palo Alto, CA 94306.
16. Myers-Briggs Type Indicator, Consulting Psychologists Press, Inc., Palo Alto, CA 94306.
17. Blanchard, Kenneth, PhD and Johnson, Spencer, M.D., *The One Minute Manager,* New York: Berkeley Books, 1982.
18. Strauss, George and Sayles, Leonard, *Personnel: The Human Problems of Management,* Englewood Cliffs, N.J.: Prentice Hall, 1972.
19. Maslow, Abraham, *Motivation and Personality,* 2nd ed., New York: Harper Bros., 1970.
20. Torrey, Charles E. S., *Satisfaction Beyond Money,* Context Shift, Seattle, February 1987.
21. Helen Remick, ed., *Comparable Worth and Wage Discrimination The Possibilities and Political Realities,* Philadelphia, PA.: Temple University Press, 1984.

22. *Flexible Compensation—The Wyatt Approach,* The Wyatt Company, Seattle, WA., 1984.
23. 20, op. cit.
24. 17, op. cit.
25. Rodwell Resources, Seattle, WA.
26. NATA, *Wage and Salary Handbook,* 1988.

Chapter Six

1. Olmi, Antonio, *Selecting the Legal Structure for Your Firm,* SBA Management Aids #6.004, Washington, D.C., 1983.
2. 1, op. cit.
3. Brown, Deaver, *The Entrepreneur's Guide,* New York: Ballantine, 1980.
4. 3, op. cit.
5. 1, op. cit.
6. SBA Office of the General Counsel, *Incorporating a Small Business,* Small Business Adminstration Management Aids #6.003, Washington, D.C., 1983.
7. 6, op. cit.
8. National Air Transportation Association, *1988 Wage and Salary Handook,* Washington, D.C., 1988.
9. Smith, Adam, *An Enquiry into the Nature and Causes of the Wealth of Nations,* Collier Books, 1901.
10. Taylor, Frederick Winslow, *The Principles of Scientific Management,* Norton, 1967.
11. Ouchi, William G., *Theory Z, How American Business Can Meet the Japanese Challenge,* Avon, NY., 1981.
12. Pascale, Richard and Athos, Anthony G. *The Art of Japanese Management: Applications for American Executives,* New York: Warner Books, 1981.
13. Weiss, Andrew, *Simple Truths of Japanese Manufacturing,* Harvard Business Review, July-August 1984.
14. Peters and Waterman, *In Search of Excellence—Lessons from America's Best-Run Companies,* New York: Warner Books, 1982.
15. 3, op. cit.
16. Hurst, David K., *Of Boxes, Bubbles and Effective Management,* Boston, MA.: Harvard Business Review, June 1984.
17. Brandt, Steven C., *Entrepreneuring—The Ten Commandments for Building a Growth Company,* New York: Mentor Executive Library, 1982.
18. 14, op. cit.
19. 14, op. cit.
20. 14, op. cit.
21. Davids, Ralph C., *The Fundamentals of Top Management,* New York: Harper Bros., 1951.
22. Likert, Rensis, *New Patterns of Management,* New York: McGraw-Hill, 1961.

Chapter Seven

1. National Fire Protection Association 232, *Standard for the Protection of Records,* Boston, MA.
2. Piper Accounting System, *Summary Chart of Accounts,* Lock Haven, Pa.: Piper Aircraft Corporation.
3. *There's No Mystery to Accounting,* Dayton, Oh.: Reynolds and Reynolds Company.
4. Peter A. McWilliams, *The Personal Computer Book,* Los Angeles, CA.: Prelude Press, 1983.
5. *How To Get Started With A Small Business Computer,* U.S. Small Business Administration, Pamphlet #MP-14.
6. *Most FBOs Use Computers, Survey Shows,* ASM, August 1986.
7. LaSalle, Peter, *When Does a Computer Make Sense for an Aviation Operation?,* FBO, November/December 1988.
8. Irsfield, Greg *Computer Service Gives FBOs Competitive Edge,* Airport Services, February 1989. 6. 5, op. cit.
9. Christopher Moran, *Preventing Embezzlement,* Small Business Adminstration Management Aids #3.009, Washington, D.C., 1982.
10. Kern, John S., *The Best Safety System Is Your Records System,* ASM, May 1987.

Chapter Eight

1. Advisory Circular #00–34A, Aircraft Ground Handling and Servicing, Washington, D.C.: Federal Aviation Administration, 29 July, 1974.
2. *Specifications and Qualification Procedure—Aviation Jet Fuel Filter/Separators,* Washington, D.C.,: American Petroleum Institute, June 1980.
3. *Airport Equipment Marking for Fuel Identification,* Washington, D.C.: American Petroleum Institute, March 1979.
4. Gilbert, Gordon, *Fueling Training Programs Make FBOs, Skies Safer,* Airport Services Management, February 1988.
5. *Experimental Aircraft Adds New Planes to Autogas STC List,* General Aviation News, April 12, 1984.
6. *Corporate Self-Fueling Threatens FBO Profitability, Airport Tranquillity,* Airport Services Management, August 1983.
7. *Minimum Standards for Commercial Aeronautical Activities on Public Airports,* Federal Aviation Administration Advisory Circular 150/5190, Washington, D.C., August 23, 1966.
8. *Exclusive Rights at Airports,* Federal Aviation Administration Advisory Circular 150/15190–1A, April 4, 1972.
9. National Air Transportation Association survey.
10. National Business Aircraft Association, as quoted in 6, op. cit.
11. Montgomery Aviation, *Front Desk Procedures Manual,* Montgomery, Ala.: Montgomery Aviation, 1985.
12. National Airspace Plan, United States Department of Transportation/Federal Aviation Administration, Washington, D.C.

Chapter Nine

1. *Minimum Standards for Commercial Aeronautical Activities on Public Airports,* FAA Advisory Circular 150/5190–1A
2. Coggin, Robert W. Assist. V.P., Marketing Development, Delta Airlines, *Hub and Spoke Scheduling Versus Direct Flights,* speech at FAA 13th Annual Aviation Forecast Conference, Feb. 1988.
3. 2, op.cit.
4. *Business and Commercial Aviation Magazine,* article in December or January issue based upon surveys by Aviation Data Service of Wichita, KN., annual.
5. *Here Come the 135 Inspectors,* FBO, November/December 1988.
6. See Appendix I for list of Federal Air Regulations, FAR Part 135, *Air Taxi Operators and Commercial Operators,* is to be found in Code of Federal Regulations 14, Parts 60–139, available from United States Government Printing Office, Washington, D.C. 20402.
7. Daniel J. O'Connor, *Airplanes and Income Tax,* Grand Canyon, Arizona, 1984.
8. Business Aviation, Aug. 8, 1988.
9. National Air Transportation Association.
10. 9, op. cit.
11. 9, op. cit.

Chapter Ten

1. *Code of Federal Regulations, 14, Parts 1–200,* published by the Office of the Federal Register National Archives and Records Service, General Services Administration, Washington, D.C., 20402.
2. *Directory of Federal Aviation Administration Certificated Aviation Maintenance Technician Schools,* United States Department of Transportation/Federal Aviation Administration 147–2X, Washington, D.C.
3. *Minimum Standards for Commercial Aeronautical Activities on Public Airports,* Federal Aviation Administration Advisory Circular 150/5190, August 23, 1966.

Chapter Eleven

1. *Aircraft Fuel Storage, Handling, and Dispensing on Airports,* Federal Aviation Administration Advisory Circular 150/5230–4, August 27, 1982.
2. *Aircraft Ground Handling and Servicing,* Federal Aviation Administration Advisory Circular 00–34A, July 29, 1974.
3. Federal Air Regulations, see Appendix I.
4. *General Aviation Ground Operation Safety Handbook,* Chicago, IL.: National Safety Council, 1977.
5. *Fire Inspection Checklist,* from Aviation Ground Operations Safety Handbook, Chicago, IL.: National Safety Council, 1977.
6. National Fire Protection Association-*Aviation Series 400 Fueling, Rescue, Hangars, Oxygen, Painting, Welding, Vehicles, Terminals, Sprinklers,* booklets by NFPA, Quincy, MA.
7. *The Legal Liability of Owners and Operators of Airports,* United States Aircraft Insurance Group (USAIG), undated.
8. Holland, Robert W., *Fuel Storage and the Fixed Base Operator—Options for the 1980s and Beyond,* FBO Magazine, September/October 1988.
9. *EPA Issues Final Underground Storage Tank Rules,* Airport Services, October 1988.
10. *The Underground Storage Tank Guide,* (monthly newsletter) Thompson Publishing Group, 1725 K Street NW, Suite 200, Washington D.C. 20006.
11. ASM Update, *Many FBOs Affected by New Hazardous Waste Rules,* Airport Services Management, October 1985.
12. Griffith, Randy, *Tips on Safe Handling of Agricultural Chemicals at Your Airport,* Airport Services Management, September 1985.
13. Burnham, Frank, *Airports, Crop Dusters Struggle with Toxic Waste Rules, Liability,* Airport Services Management, March 1986.
14. *FBO Hazardous Standards Manual,* National Air Transportation Foundation, Alexandria, Virginia, 1988.
15. *FBOs Must Comply with OSHA Rule on Hazardous Materials Identification,* Airport Services Management, May 1988.
16. National Transportation Safety Board, Code of Federal Regulations, Title 49, Transportation, Effective July 17, 1975:
    Part 800—Statement of Organization and Functions of the Board and Delegations of Authority
    Part 805—Employee Responsibility and Conduct
    Part 821—Rules of Practice in Air Safety Proceedings
    Part 831—Rules of Practice in Aircraft Accident/Incident Investigations
17. See Appendix I on Federal Air Regulations.
18. *Announcement of Availability—International Fire Service Training Association's Manual 206, Aircraft Fire Protection and Rescue Procedures,* Federal Aviation Administration Advisory Circular 150.5200–15, August 26, 1982.
19. Kilishek, George, *FBO Fire Training Evolves to Meet New FAA Requirements,* Airport Services, October 1988.

Chapter Twelve

1. *National Plan of Integrated Airport Systems (NPIAS),* United States Department of Transportation/Federal Aviation Administration.
2. Air Transport Association, annual survey of aviation use conducted by the Gallup Organization, Washington, D.C.
3. Airport and Airway Improvement Act of 1982 as Amended by the Airport and Airway Safety and Capacity Expansion Act Of 1987, PL 100–223, Washington, D.C.: United States Government Printing Office, December 30, 1987.
4. *Potential Closure of Airports,* United States Department of Transportation/Federal Aviation Administration, January 1978.
5. 1, op. cit.

6. *Forecasts of Aviation Activity,* United States Department of Transportation/Federal Aviation Administration 1989.
7. *Citizen Participation in Airport Planning,* Federal Aviation Administration Advisory Circular 150/5050–4, February 5, 1972.
8. *Airport Land Use Compatibility Planning,* Federal Aviation Administration Advisory Circular 150/5050–6, December 30, 1977.
9. Boston-Logan International Airport, Boston, Massachusetts.
10. *Sea-Tac Communities Plan,* Seattle-Tacoma International Airport, Seattle, Washington.
11. *Airport Compatibility Guidelines, Oregon Aviation System Plan, Volume VI,* Oregon Department of Transportation, Aeronautics Division, Salem, OR., 1981.
12. *Airport Landscaping for Noise Control Purposes,* Federal Aviation Administration Advisory Circular 150/5320–14, January 31, 1978.
13. *Noise Control and Compatibility Planning for Airports,* Federal Aviation Administration Advisory Circular 150/5020–1, August 5, 1983.
14. Federal Aviation Administration Part 150—Airport Noise.
15. 3, op. cit.
16. *Airport Master Plans,* Federal Aviation Administration Advisory Circular 150/5070–6.
17. 3, op. cit.
18. *Minimum Standards for Commercial Aeronautical Activities on Public Airports,* Federal Aviation Administration Advisory Circular 150/5190–1, August 23, 1966.
19. *Potential Closure of Airports,* United States Department of Transportation/Federal Aviation Administration, January 1978.
20. *A Model Zoning Ordinance to Limit Height of Objects Around Airports,* Federal Aviation Administration Advisory Circular 150/5190–4, August 23, 1977.
21. John Wiley, *Airport Administration,* Eno Foundation for Transportation Inc., Westport, CT., 1981.
22. *Airspace Utilization Considerations in the Proposed Construction, Alteration, Activation and Deactivation of Airports,* United States Department of Transportation/Federal Aviation Administration Advisory Circular 70–2D, August 1, 1979.
23. Resolution, Spokane Airport Board, In the Matter of Establishing Guidelines for Determining Length of Term for Lessee-Constructed Aeronautical Buildings at Felts Field Airport, November 16, 1983.
24. 3, op. cit.
25. 18, op. cit.
26. 18, op. cit.
27. *Comparison Formula Helps Airports Set Fair Lease Rates,* ASM, July 1987.
28. 3, op. cit.

Chapter Thirteen

1. *General Aviation Dynamics Model,* Battelle Columbus Laboratories for FAA.
2. *FAA Aviation Forecasts, Fiscal Years 1989–2000,* FAA APO 891, March 1989, FAA, Washington DC.
3. *Why Today's Airplanes Won't Cut It (A Visit with Burt Rutan),* Airport Services Management, December 1981.
4. Peters, Thomas J. and Robert H. Waterman, Jr., *In Search of Excellence,* New York: Warner books, 1982.
5. *General Aviation and Energy, A Status Report,* General Aviation Manufacturers' Association brochure, undated.

Suggestions for Further Reading

Chapter One

Aerospace Facts and Figures, Aerospace Industries of America, Washington, D.C., annual.
Airport Services, September 1988; letters to editor about the name FBO.
Analysis of Competition In, and Profile Of, The FBO Industry—The Gellman Report, Philadelphia, Pa.: Gellman Research Associates, December 1979.
Aviation Week and Space Technology, *Business Flying—Servicing the Fleet,* October 17, 1988.
Black, Archibald, *The Story of Flying,* New York: McGraw-Hill, 1943.
Blake, John, *Aviation—The First Seventy Years,* London: Tribune Books, 1973.
Code of Federal Regulations, Parts 1–200, (Aeronautics and Space), United States Government, Washington, D.C., 1984.
Forden, Lesley, *The Ford Air Tours, 1925–31,* Alameda, Calif.: The Nottingham Press, 1973.
Francis, Devon, *Mr. Piper and His Cubs,* Ames, Ia.: Iowa State University Press, 1973.
Fraser, Chelsea, *The Story of Aircraft,* New York: Thomas Y. Crowell, 1939.
GA Gains Against Odds, Airport Services, October 1988.
Garber, Paul, *The National Aeronautical Collections,* 10th ed., Washington, D.C.: Smithsonian Institution, 1965.
Gunston, Bill, and Howard, Frank, *The Conquest of the Air,* New York: Doubleday, 1966.
Harris, Sherwood, *The First to Fly,* Simon & Schuster, 1970.
McDaniel, William H., *Fifty Years of Excellence—The History of Beech,* Wichita, KS.: McCormick-Armstrong Company Publishing Division, 1982.
Membership materials and press kits from:
Aircraft Electronics Association
Aircraft Owners and Pilots Association
Aviation Security Association of America-International
Experimental Aircraft Association
General Aviation Manufacturers Association
Helicopter Association International
International Business Aviation Council
National Association of Flight Instructors
National Business Aircraft Association
Seaplane Pilots Association
National Air Transportation Association Annual Reports, NATA, Alexandria, Virginia.
National Plan of Integrated Airport Systems (NPIAS), Federal Aviation Administration, Washington, D.C.
NBAA Education and Safety Foundation; seminars and workshops on corporate aviation management.
Potential Closure of Airports, Report of the Secretary of Transportation to the United States Congress pursuant to Section 20 of the Airport and Airway Development Act Amendments of 1976 (P.L. 94–353), Washington, D.C., United States Department of Transportation, Federal Aviation Administration, January 1978.
Roseberry, C.R. *The Challenging Skies,* New York: Doubleday, 1966.
Serling, Robert J. *Wrights to Wide-Bodies: the First 75 Years . . . the Growth of U.S. Air Transportation,* ATA, April 1978.
Still, Henry, *To Ride the Wind,* Messner, 1964.

Chapter Two

Bakos, Susan C., *Promoting Teamwork,* ASM, April 1985.
Baran, Richard T., *From Toolbox to Briefcase: Bridging the Aviation Department Managerial Gap,* NBAA Management Aids, March/April 1988.

Baumback, Clifford M., Lawler, Kenneth and Kelly, Pearce C., *How to Organize and Operate a Small Business,* 5th ed., Englewood Cliffs, N.J.: Prentice Hall, 1973.

Becker, Benjamin B., Antonow and Fink, Attorneys, and Tillman, Fred, *Management Checklist for a Family Business,* Small Business Administration Management Aids #3.002, Washington, D.C., 1983.

Business Plan for Retailers, SBA Management Aids #2.011, Washington, D.C., 1983.

Business Plan for Small Service Firms, Small Business Administration Management Aids #2.022, Washington, D.C., 1983.

Didsbury, Jr., Howard F., Editor, *Challenges and Opportunities: From Now To 2001,* World Future Society, Bethesda, MD, 1986.

Doing Business with Government, Conference Notebook prepared by Service Corps of Retired Executives, sponsored by SBA, Seattle, WA.: 1984.

Haimann, Hilgert, *Supervision: Concepts and Practices of Management,* South-Western Publishing Co. 1977.

Haimann, Theo, and Hilgert, Raymond L., *Supervision: Concepts and Practices of Management,* 4th Edition, South-Western Publishing, Cincinnati, OH, 1987.

Hawken, Paul, *The Next Economy: What to do with Your Money and Your Life in the Coming Decade,* Ballantine Books, New York, 1983.

Hennig, Margaret, and Jardim, Anne, *The Managerial Woman,* Pocket Books, New York, 1976.

Hurst, David K., "Of Boxes, Bubbles, and Effective Management", *Harvard Business Review,* Boston, MA.: May–June 1984.

Kamoroff, Bernard, *Small-time Operator—How to Start Your Own Small Business, Keep Your Books, Pay Your Taxes and Stay Out of Trouble,* Laytonville, CA.: Bell Springs Publishing, 1984.

Low, James P., *Association Services for Small Business,* Small Business Administration Management Aids #7.002, Washington, D.C., 1983.

Moskowitz, Milton, and Katz, Michael, *The 100 Best Companies to Work for in America,* Robert Levering, Addison-Wesley Publishing Co., Reading, MA, 1985.

Naisbitt, John, *Megatrends: Ten New Directions Transforming Our Lives,* Warner Books, New York, 1984.

Oncken, William, *Managing Management Time (Who's Got the Monkey),* 1984.

Ouichi, William G., *Theory Z—How American Business Can Meet the Japanese Challenge,* Reading, MA.: Addison-Wesley, 1981.

Pelissier, Raymond F., *Planning and Goal Setting for Small Business,* Small Business Administration Management Aids #2.010, Washington, D.C., 1983.

Peter, Laurence J., and Hull, Raymond, *The Peter Principle,* New York: William Morrow and Company, 1969.

Small Business Decision Making, U.S. Small Business Administration, Pamphlet #MP-19.

Toffler, Alvin, *The Adaptive Corporation,* McGraw-Hill, New York, 1985.

von Oech, Roger, *A Kick in the Seat of the Pants: Using Your Explorer, Artist, Judge & Warrior to be More Creative,* Harper & Row, New York, 1986.

Wantola, Stanley, *Delegating Work and Responsibility,* Small Business Administration Management Aids #3.001, Washington, D.C., 1983.

Weiss, W. H., *Supervisor's Standard Reference Handbook,* Prentice-Hall 1980.

Wiley, John, *Airport Administration,* Eno Foundation for Transportation Inc., Westport, CT., 1981.

Chapter Three

Bremer, Karl, *Cessna Flight Schools Test Potpourri of Marketing Ideas,* ASM, February 1986.

Bremer, Karl, *FAA/GA Industry to Focus on Basics of Flying,* ASM, March 1986.

Bremer, Karl, *FBOs' Advertising Strategies Differ, But Share Success,* AS, July 1988.

Bremer, Karl, *FBO Campaigns to Polish Airport's Tarnished Image,* ASM, August 1986.

Bremer, Karl, *Orlando FBO Offers Customers Toll-Free Trip-Planning Line,* ASM, March 1986.

Britt, Stewart Henderson, *Plan Your Advertising Budget,* Small Business Adminstration Management Aids #4.018, Washington, D.C., 1983.

Burnham, Frank, *How One FBO Makes Helicopters Pay,* ASM June 1986.

Burnham, Frank, *Many-Faceted Program Lures FBO Customers to Airport,* ASM, February 1986.

Burnham, Frank, *Promotional Attitude Keeps Trainers Flying at Long Beach FBO,* ASM, September 1985.

Claus, Karen E., and Claus, R.J., *Signs and Your Business,* Small Business Administration, Management Aids #4.016, Washington, D.C., 1984.
Company Plans to Sell Pilot Supplies Through Store Chain, ASM, April 1985.
Connes, Keith, *Manufacturers Offer Product Lines to Help Retailers,* FBO, September/October 1988.
Dahler, Larry, *The Role of the Support Shop in Providing Total FBO Service,* FBO, November/December 1988.
Dann, Janet, *Changing Economy Pushes Syracuse FBO Into New Markets.*
Dann, Janet, *FBOs Team Up to Provide Marketing, Flight Services,* ASM, July 1985.
Dann, Janet, *National Air-Taxi Franchise to Recruit Local Charter Firms,* ASM, July 1985.
Effective Business Communication, SBA, Small Business Bibliography #92, Washington, D.C., 1982.
Elliot, Jack, *Win Customers with Direct Mail,* ASM, September 1987.
Finding a New Product for Your Company, Small Business Administration Management Aids #2.006, Washington, D.C., 1984.
Fox, Harold W., *Understanding Your Customer,* Small Business Adminstration Management Aids #4.001, Washington, D.C., 1983.
'Game Plan' Effort to Incorporate, Begin Seminars in July, Business Aviation, July 27, 1988.
'Game Plan' Seminar Offers Marketing Communications Tips, Airport Services, September 1988.
Gilbert, Gordon, *Airport Commisssioner Warns of Perils of the Press, Importance of PR,* ASM, March 1985.
Gilbert, Gordon, *Flight School Renovation Doubles Number of Students,* ASM, October 1986.
Gilbert, Gordon, *FBO Open House Acquaints 2,000 with Aviation,* ASM, September 1987.
Gilbert, Gordon, *FBOs See Mail-Order Dealers as Major Parts Competition,* ASM, November 1987.
Gilbert, Gordon, *GA Business Franchises: Link to Profits or Ball-and-Chain?*, ASM, April 1986.
Gilbert, Gordon, *'Game Plan' Seminar Offers Marketing Communication Tips,* ASM, September 1988.
Gilbert, Gordon, *GA Representatives Meet to Discuss Industry Promotion,* ASM, January 1988.
Gould, Douglas P. *Developing New Accounts,* Small Business Adminstration Management Aids #4.010, Washington, D.C., 1983.
Industry-Wide Marketing Can Work Wonders for General Aviation, ASM, February 1988.
Irsfeld, Greg, *Image, Service Help FBOs Keep Customers,* AS, August 1988.
Kilishek, George, *Charter Operation Sells Jet Shares,* ASM, September 1987.
Kilishek, George, *FBOs Tailor Shop, Line Services to Market Needs,* ASM, August 1987.
Kress, George, and Will, R. Ted, *Marketing Checklist for Small Retailers,* SBA, Management Aids #4.012, Washington, D.C., 1984.
Laumer, J. Ford, Jr., Harris, James R., and Guffey, Hugh J. Jr., *Learning About Your Market,* Small Business Administration Management Aids #4.019, Washington, D.C., 1983.
Long Beach Facility Accomodates FBO, Pilots and Aircraft in Style, ASM, August 1985.
Marketing for Small Business, Small Business Adminstration, Small Business Bibliography #89, Washington, D.C., 1978.
Marketing Research Procedures, Small Business Adminstration, Small Business Bibliography #9, Washington, D.C., 1979.
McCaffrey, Mike, with Derloshon, Jerry, *Personal Marketing Strategies,* Englewood Cliffs, N.J.: Prentice Hall, 1983.
McGee, Lynne, *Pay Telephones: Airports Cautiously Eye New Opportunities,* ASM, October 1985.
NATA Moves to Raise Public Awareness about the Necessity of General Aviation, ASM, September 1987.
National Directories for Use in Marketing, Small Business Administration, Small Business Bibliography #13, Washington, D.C., 1981.
NBAA Public Relations for Business, Part 5: Airports . . . and How to Help Them, Washington, D.C., undated.
Nieman, Steve, *Evergreen Aviation Followed Many Paths to Success,* ASM, December 1986.
Outdoor Advertising: Promotional, Revenue Source for Airports, ASM, April 1987.
Postcard Survey Helps Make a Powerful Point, ASM, April 1985.
Quinones, Wendy, *Summer Camp Flying School Nurtures New Crop of Students,* ASM, April 1985.
Schlender, James A., *Business Profile: Kenosha Aero,* FBO, September/October 1988.
Seasonal Cards for Resale, FBO, September/October 1988.
Sell Air Charters By Promoting Benefits of GA, ASM, June 1986.
Singer, Jennifer, *Rural Flight School Capitalizes on Location, Marketing, for Growth,* ASM, September 1988.
Smith, Ivan C., *Tips on Getting More for Your Marketing Dollar,* Small Business Administration Management Aids #4.008, Washington, D.C., 1983.

Smith, Rodney N., *Hawaiian FBO Finds Profit in Pacific Traffic,* ASM, October 1987.
Staats, Alan D., *FBO Trends and Trendy FBOs,* Business and Commercial Aviation, September 1987.
Statistics and Maps for National Market Analysis, Small Business Administration Small Business Bibliography #12, Washington, D.C., 1978.
The Piper Dealer: *Sales and Marketing Plan Guide,* Piper Aircraft Company, Lock Haven, PA., undated.
What Corporate Pilots Want, FBO, November/December 1988.
Worthington, E.R., *How To Sell More Flight Training and Rent More Aircraft,* ASM, February 1986.
Worthington, E.R., *Tips On Marketing Your Overhaul Services,* ASM, March 1986.

Chapter Four

A Study of Business Aviation in 1985, Business Flying, March 1985.
Barker, Phyllis A., *Budgeting in a Small Service Firm,* Small Business Administration Management Aids #1.015, Washington, D.C., 1983.
Bremer, Karl, *Credit-Card Fueler Reduces Labor Costs, Increases Sales,* ASM, February 1987.
Bremer, Karl, *Credit Cards Draw FBO Customers, But Deals Vary,* ASM, February 1987.
Corporate Taxes and the New Law—Congress Estimates That Corporations Will be Paying $125 Billion More in Taxes Under the New Law, Taxes and Accounting, Business and Commercial Aviation, February 1987.
Employee Theft: Is Your FBO an Accomplice?, ASM, October 1985.
Financial Management, SBA Bibliography #87, Washington, D.C., 1979.
Financial Performance Survey: An Economic Profile of the FBO/Air Taxi Industry, NATA, 1986.
Fuel Tax Exemption for FBOs Eliminated, ASM, February 1988.
Gardner, Harrison, *Tunnel Vision Pervades the IRS,* Business and Commercial Aviation, February 1988.
George, Fred, *Chargeback Allocation,* Business and Commercial Aviation, September 1987.
George, Fred, *Is Now the Time to Lease?,* Business and Commercial Aviation, September 1987.
George, Fred *The 1986 Tax Reform Act—Rebuked as Being Detrimental to the Business Aircraft Industry, the Force of PL 99–514's Tornado-Like Reputation Is Greatly Overrated,* Business and Commercial Aviation, May, 1987.
Gilbert, Gordon, *Tax Reform Will Help FBOs Sell, NATA Speaker Says,* ASM, July 1987.
Goulet, Peter G., *Attacking Business Problems with Break Even Analysis,* Small Business Administration Management Aids #1.008, Washington, D.C., 1983.
Hammel, Fred C., *Simple Break Even Analysis for Small Stores,* SBA Management Aids #1.019, Washington, D.C. 1983.
Kolodny, Leonard, *Outwitting Bad Check Passers,* Small Business Administration Management Aids #3.008, Washington, D.C., 1983.
Lennon, Victor A., *What Is the Best Selling Price?,* Small Business Administration Management Aids #1.002, Washington, D.C., 1983.
Litt, Danny S., *Cash Flow in a Small Plant,* SBA Management Aids 1.006, Washington, D.C., 1983.
Moran, Christopher J., *Preventing Embezzlement,* Small Business Administration Management Aids #3.009, Washington, D.C., 1982.
Net Income as Percent of Stockholders' Equity, Business and Commercial Aviation, December 1986.
O'Neal, Cooke, *Credit and Collections,* Small Business Administration Management Aids #1.007, 1983.
Productivity in Small Business Management, Small Business Administration Bibliography #93, Washington, D.C.
Retail Credit and Collections, Small Business Administration Bibliography #31, Washington, D.C., 1983.
Seafirst Bank, *Sources of Small Business Financing,* Seattle, 1984.
The ABC's of Borrowing, Small Business Administration Management Aids #1.001, Washington, D.C., 1983.
What Do You Want, Profit or Cash?, FBO, November/December 1988.
Woelfel, Charles J., *Basic Budgets for Profit Planning,* SBA, Management Aids #1.004, Washington, D.C., 1983.

Chapter Five

Arkin, Joseph, *Control Employee Turnover with the Exit Interview,* ASM, August 1985.
Arkin, Joseph, *Will Flextime Work for You?,* ASM, June 1985.
Bremer, Karl, *How to Hire and Keep Good A&P Mechanics,* ASM, April 1987.
FAA Issues Drug Testing Guidelines, NATA Regulatory Report File 88–308B, January 11, 1989.
Flex News, The Wyatt Company, Seattle, WA., 1984.
Krepela, Rick, *"Are Your Employees Satisfied?"* Airport Services Management, Minneapolis, MN., August 1983.
Levinson, Robert E., *Problems in Managing a Family-Owned Business,* SBA Management Aids #2.004, Washington, D.C., 1984.
Scollard, Gene F., *Setting Up a Pay System,* Small Business Administration, Management Aids #5.006, Washington, D.C., 1983.
Smith, Leonard J., *Checklist for Developing a Training Program,* SBA, Management Aids #5.001, Washington, D.C., 1983.
Trotter, Mary Alice, *Guidelines for Establishing a Drug Testing Policy,* ASM, February 1987.
Weaver (Jr.), Robert A., *Good Communication Avoids Assumptions,* ASM, July 1985.
Weaver (Jr.), Robert A., *Six Reasons Why Supervisors Avoid Making Decisions,* ASM, June 1985.

Chapter Six

Gumpert, D.E. and Boyd, D.P., *Growing Concerns—the Loneliness of the Small Business Owner,* Boston, MA.: Harvard Business Review, November–December 1984.
Selecting the Legal Structure for Your Business, U.S. Small Business Administration, Pamphlet #MP-25.
Shanklin, W.L. and Ryans, J.K. Jr., *Organizing for High-Tech Marketing,* Boston, MA.: Harvard Business Review, November–December 1984.
Tannenbaum, Robert and Schmidt, Warren H., *How to Choose a Leadership Pattern,* in Paths Toward Personal Progress: Leaders Are Made, Not Born, Harvard Business Review Classics, Boston, MA.: Harvard Business Review, 1983.

Chapter Seven

Analyze Your Records to Reduce Costs, U.S. Small Business Administration, Pamphlet #FM-7.
Cooper, Irving M., *Accounting Services for Small Firms,* SBA Management Aids #1.101, Washington, D.C., 1983.
Dealer Uniform Accounting System Manual, Cessna Aircraft Company, Wichita, KS.
Forms for the Nine Key Operations of Business, Moore Business Forms Inc., Seattle, WA.
Gilbert, Gordon, *FBO Computer Software: Sophisticated Help—For Those Who Can Afford It,* ASM, July 1985.
Greene, William C., *Getting the Facts for Income Tax Reporting,* Small Business Administration Management Aids #1.014, Washington, D.C., 1983.
How ASM Readers Are Using Computers, ASM, December 1985.
Kamoroff, Bernard, *Small Time Operator—How to Start Your Own Small Business, Keep Your Books, Pay Your Taxes and Stay Out of Trouble!,* Laytonville, CA.: Bell Springs Publishing, 1984.
Kramer, Edward C., *Can You Use a Minicomputer?,* Small Business Adminstration Management Aids #2.015, Washington, D.C., 1984.
Radics, Stephen P., Jr., *Steps in Meeting Your Tax Obligations,* SBA Management Aids #1.014, Washington, D.C., 1983.
Vurpillat, Victor V., *Computers for Small Business,* Small Business Adminstration Management Aids #2.019, Washington, D.C., 1983.

Chapter Eight

1980 Survey of Airport Services, 1978 Status and Activity, Washington, D.C.: United States Department of Commerce for United States Department of Transportation/Federal Aviation Administration, 1980.
Aarons, Richard N., *Weather Vending Machines Arrive in Pilot Lounges,* January 1987.
Aircraft Fuel Servicing, National Fire Protection Association, 1980.
Aircraft Fuel Storage, Handling, and Dispensing on Airports, United States Department of Transportation/ Federal Aviation Administration, Advisory Circular #150/5230–4, Washington, D.C., August 1982.
American Petroleum Institute Publications and Materials, (bibliography) Washington, D.C., 1984.
Aviation Fuel Inventory Control Guidelines, Exxon Corporation, undated.
Bennett, Jerome, *Automated Weather Observing System Passes San Jose Trial,* Airport Services Management, February 1987.
Boyce, John, *Business Profile: Kansas City Aviation Center,* FBO Magazine, November/December 1988.
Bremer, Karl, *FBO's Experience Offers Lessons in Hangar Construction,* Airport Services Management, July 1986.
Carbon Monoxide Is Threat to Aircraft Refuelers, Airport Services Management, June 1984.
Condon, Maureen, *Weather Program Brings Added, Easy-to-Use Service to Midcoast's Customers,* Airport Services Management, March 1985.
Entrepreneur Seeks FBO's to Manage Airport Motel Chain, Airport Services Management, May 1986.
FAA Finalizes Fueling Regulations, NATA Regulatory Report, November 30, 1987.
FBOs Discover Value of Battery-Powered Ramp Equipment, Airport Services Management, May 1985.
General Aviation Ground Operation Safety Handbook, National Safety Council, Chicago, IL., 1977.
Gilbert, Gordon, *Choosing a Weather System That Meets Your FBO's Needs,* Airport Services Management, June 1986.
Gilbert, Gordon, *Satellite Systems Bring Down Cost of Weather Services,* Airport Services Management, June 1987.
Hastings, Karen Lynn, *Aircraft Cosmetic Care: Confessions of an FBO 'Detailer',* July 1985.
Irsfeld, Greg, *FBO Car Rentals Serve Corporate Fliers' Needs,* Airport Services Management, June 1988.
Kilishek, George, *Home-Built Aircraft: Profit Source for FBOs?,* Airport Services Management, July 1987.
Kucharski, Ed, *Well-Grounded Procedures,* letter to Airport Services Management, April 1985.
Line Service Training Program, International Learning Systems, Box 4160, Greenwich, Connecticut.
Long Beach Facility Accommodates FBO, Pilots and Aircraft in Style, Airport Services Management, August 1985.
Minnesota FBO Lures Business Through Limousine Link, Airport Services Management, July 1988.
Most FBOs Offer Weather Data Free, Mini-Survey Shows, Airport Services Management, October 1987.
New Aviation Fuel Company to Expand Dealer Network, Airport Services Management, February 1988.
Schlender, Jim, *Fuel Operations Management,* FBO Magazine, September/October 1988.
Worthington, E. R. , *Flight Training Options Reflect Shifting GA Market,* Airport Services Management, September 1986.
Worthington, E.R., *Managing Your Line Service Department,* Airport Services Management, February 1986.

Chapter Nine

Aarons, Richard N., *Wanted: A Good Used-Aircraft Broker,* Business and Commercial Aviation, June 1987.
Aircraft Management Can Up FBO Profits, NATA Speakers Say, Airport Services Management, June 1987.
Aircraft Management Firm Not Affiliated with Any One FBO, Airport Services Management, September 1987.
Airplane Simulator and Visual System Evaluation, United States Department of Transportation/Federal Aviation Administration 120–40, Washington, D.C., March 31, 1983.
AOPA Loan Program Spurs Plane Buying, Airport Services Management, October 1986.
Burnham, Frank, *Aerial Firefighting Comes of Age as a Professional—and Profitable—Service,* Airport Services Management, October 1985.
Burnham, Frank, *Flight Simulation: Hindrance or Help in Teaching to Fly?,* Airport Services Management, October 1987.

Business Aviation and the Fortune 500, Business and Commercial Aviation, annual.
Business Flights—A Business Travel Proposition, Spanaway, WA.: Spanaflight, undated brochure.
Certification: Pilot and Flight Instructors, Federal Aviation Administration Advisory Circular, 61–65A, August 1980.
Company Stresses Security in Selling Aircraft Charters, Airport Services Management, August 1986.
FAA Issues Proposal on Mode C Requirement and Controlled Airspace Common Floor, NATA Initial Report File 88–305, February 29, 1988.
FAA Proposes Major Revision of Commercial Operator Regulations, NATA Regulatory Report, Nov. 10, 1988.
FBOs Motivate Flight Instructors to Sell Training, Airport Services Management, August 1987.
Federal Aviation Regulations Part 35: Additional Maintenance Requirements for Aircraft Type Certificated for Nine or Less Passenger Seats, Federal Aviation Administration Advisory Circular 135–7, October 24, 1978.
Federal Aviation Regulations Part 61 (revised) Certification: Pilot and Flight Instructors, Federal Aviation Administration Advisory Circular 61–83 A, November 3, 1980.
Federal Aviation Regulation Part 103: Ultralight Operations.
Federal Aviation Regulations, Part 137—Agricultural Aircraft Operations, Washington, D.C.: Federal Aviation Administration, 1984.
Federal Aviation Regulations, Part 141 (revised)-Pilot Schools, Washington, D.C.: Federal Aviation Administration, 1984.
Federal Aviation Administration Statistical Handbook of Aviation Annual, Federal Aviation Administration Advisory Circular, undated.
Forming and Operating a Flying Club, Federal Aviation Administration Advisory Circular 00–25, March 24, 1969.
George, Fred, *The Pearls (and Perils) of Partnership,* Business and Commercial Aviation, October 1987.
Gilbert, Gordon, *Advisory Council Gives Cessna, Dealers, Input on Factory Decisions, Better Understanding of Policies,* Airport Services Management, May 1985.
Gilbert, Gordon, *Reducing Your Aircraft Rental Liability,* Airport Services Management, April 1987.
Industry Barometer Results, National Air Transportation Association, annual.
Infanger, John F. *Tennessee Valley Airways,* FBO, September/October 1988.
Kilishek, George T., *Air Taxi Success Takes More Than a Plane and a Dream,* Airport Services Management, October 1986.
Line-Oriented Flight Training Programs, Federal Aviation Administration Advisory Circular 120–35, August 11, 1981.
List of Certificated Pilot Schools, Federal Aviation Administration Advisory Circular140–2R, 1983.
Making Borrowed Ideas Pay Off, Windsock, Number 1 1988.
Minimum Needs for Airport Fire Fighting and Rescue Services, Federal Aviation Administration Advisory Circular A5–71–1, United States Department of Transportation/Federal Aviation Administration, Washington, D.C.
NATA Legislative Report,*VA Flight Training Bills Introduced,* August 17, 1988.
Nationally Scheduled Federal Aviation Administration-Approved Industry-Conducted Flight Instructor Refresher Clinics, Federal Aviation Administration Advisory Circular 61–83 A, November 3, 1980.
Nieman, Steve, *Airline Affiliations Spur Business at Flight Schools,* Airport Services Management, January 1988.
Patton, Carmella L., *Flight School Expands with Creation of Aerobatics Course,* Airport Services Management, May 1986.
Pilot Certificates: Aircraft Type Ratings, Federal Aviation Administration Advisory Circular 61–89, December 22, 1981.
Pilot School Certification, Federal Aviation Administration Advisory Circular 141–1.
Piper Offers New Trainer Aircraft, Airport Services Management, July 1988.
Planning and Purchasing Handbook, Business and Commercial Aviation, April issue each year.
Programs for Training of Fire Fighting and Rescue Personnel, Federal Aviation Administration Advisory Circular 139–49–1.
Reporting Requirements for Air Carrier, Commercial Operators, Travel Clubs, and Air Taxi Operators of Large and Small Aircraft, Federal Aviation Administration Advisory Circular 120–30A, September 8, 1976.
State and Regional Disaster Airlift (SARDA) Planning, Federal Aviation Administration Advisory Circular 11–7A, June 3, 1974.

Truth in Leasing, Federal Aviation Administration Advisory Circular 91–37A, January 16, 1978.
The Ultralight Vehicle, Federal Aviation Administration Advisory Circular 103–7, January 30, 1984.
Ultralight Vehicle Operations—Airports, Air Traffic Control and Weather, Federal Aviation Administration Advisory Circular 103–6, June 23, 1983.
Waivers—Airshow/Contests/Races, Federal Aviation Administration Advisory Circular 91–45B, August 5, 1981.
Worthington, E.R., *How To Sell More Flight Training and Rent More Aircraft,* Airport Services Management, February 1986.

Chapter Ten

1988 Blue Book, ASM, June 1988.
AAR Technical Service Center—West Will Expand. . . , The Weekly of Business Aviation, August 8, 1988.
Acceptable Methods, Techniques, and Practices—Aircraft Alterations, Federal Aviation Administration Advisory Circular #43.13–2A, June 9, 1977, AWS-340.
Acceptable Methods, Techniques, and Practices—Aircraft Inspection and Repair, Federal Aviation Administration Advisory Circular #43.13–1A, April 17, 1972, AWS-340.
Aircraft Engine Type Certification Handbook, Federal Aviation Administration Advisory Circular 33–2A, June 15, 1972, AWE-100.
Airframe and Powerplant Mechanics Airframe Handbook, Federal Aviation Administration Advisory Circular 65–15A, April 12, 1976.
Airframe and Powerplant Mechanics Certification Guide, Federal Aviation Administration Advisory Circular 65–11A, January 30, 1976.
Airframe and Powerplant Mechanics General Handbook, Federal Aviation Administration Advisory Circular 65–9A, April 12, 1976.
Announcement of Availability—Summary of Airworthiness Directives, Federal Aviation Administration Advisory Circular 39–6J, 1988.
Approved Aircraft Inspection Program, Federal Aviation Administration Advisory Circular 135–10, September 17, 1981.
Bremer, Karl, *How to Hire and Keep Good A&P Mechanics,* ASM, April 1987.
Bremer, Karl, *Streamline Your Aircraft Repair Shop with a Computer,* ASM, January 1988.
Burnham, Frank, *Avionics Businesses Tread Narrow Path Through Industry Ills and Competitors,* ASM, January 1986.
Burnham, Frank, *Prop Balancing May Be New FBO Profit Source,* ASM, March 1988.
Certification of a Repairman (General), Federal Aviation Administration Advisory Circular 65–24, February 1, 1983.
Certification of Repairman (Experimental Aircraft Builders), Federal Aviation Administration Advisory Circular 65–23, September 28, 1979.
Certification Procedures for Products and Parts, Federal Aviation Administration Advisory Circular 21.303–1A, August 10, 1972.
Continuous Airworthiness Maintenance Programs, Federal Aviation Administration Advisory Circular 120–16B, August 8, 1980.
Dahler, Leroy, *The Role of the Support Shop in Providing Total FBO Service,* FBO, November/December 1988.
Duncan Leases Space from Other FBOs for Avionics Shops, ASM, May 1987.
FBO Coupon Plan Helps Keep 'Em Hopping in the Shop, ASM, June 1985.
FBOs See Mail-Order Dealers as Major Parts Competition, ASM, November 1987.
Federal Aviation Administration Certificated Maintenance Agencies Directory, Federal Aviation Administration Advisory Circular 140–7D, Washington, D.C., October 1983.
Federal Aviation Administration Designated Maintenance Technician Examiner Directory, Federal Aviation Administration Advisory Circular 183–32C, June 24, 1982.
Gilbert, Gordon, *Aggressive Marketing Launches New Maintenance Shop into Black,* ASM, November 1985.
Guide for Developing and Evaluating Repair Station Inspection Procedures Manual, Federal Aviation Administration Advisory Circular 145–3, February 13, 1981.
Installation of Used Engines in New Production Aircraft, Federal Aviation Administration Advisory Circular 21–19, April 26, 1982.

Instruction for Completion of Federal Aviation Administration Form 338 (Office of Management 04-R0060—Major Repair and Alteration (Airframe, Powerplant, Propeller or Appliance) Federal Aviation Administration Advisory Circular 43.9–1D, September 5, 1979.
Inventory Management, U.S. Small Business Administration, brochure #MP 22.
Irsfeld, Greg, *Salvaged Parts Help FBOs Meet Customer Needs,* ASM, November 1988.
Kilishek, George, *Avionics Shops' Focus Shifting from Sales to Service,* ASM, December 1986.
King, Frank, *Aviation Maintenance Management,* Southern Illinois University Press.
Maintenance Aspects of Owning Your Own Airplane, Federal Aviation Administration-P-8740–15A, United States Department of Transportation/Federal Aviation Administration, AFO-800–0783.
Maintenance Certification Procedures, Federal Aviation Administration Advisory Circular 121–16, November 9, 1970.
Maintenance Operations, NBAA Business Management Guide, (undated).
Moldeven, Meyer, *Fixing Production Mistakes,* Small Business Adminstration Management Aids #2.011, Washington, D.C., 1983.
Patton, Carmella, *Helicopter Shop Evolved from a Changing Industry,* ASM, August 1986.
Plane Sense, Federal Aviation Administration Advisory Circular 20–5E, Washington, D.C., 1981.
Preventive Maintenance, Federal Aviation Administration Advisory Circular 43–12A, October 28, 1983.
Productivity Management in Small Business, Small Business Administration, Small Business Bibliography #93, Washington, D.C.
Quinones, Wendy, *Aircraft Refurbisher Invested Hard Work, Capital in Success,* ASM, March 1987.
Setting Up a Quality Control System, Small Business Administration Management Aids #2.012, Washington, D.C., 1983.
Small Aircraft Parts Data Service Being Developed, ASM, March 1987.
Techniques for Productivity Improvement, U.S. Small Business Administration, brochure #MP 24.
The Continued Airworthiness of Older Airplanes, Federal Aviation Administration Advisory Circular 91–60, June 13, 1983.
Worthington, E. R., *Tips on Marketing Your Overhaul Services,* ASM, March 1986.

Chapter Eleven

Air Ambulance Standards Critical to Avoid Liability, Airport Services, June 1988.
Air Taxi Operators Must Comply With Fire-Blocking Rule, Airport Services Management, February 1988.
Barbash, Gabriel, *Medical Response to Airfield Crash Depends on Thorough Planning,* Airport Services Management, April 1986.
Be a Protected Pilot, Seattle, WA.: AVEMCO brochure, undated.
Bremer, Karl, *All You Wanted to Know About Buried Fuel Tanks (But Were Scared to Ask),* Airport Services Management, November 1987.
Bremer, Karl, *Consider Your Situation When Choosing a Tank Type,* Airport Services Management, November 1987.
Bremer, Karl, *Introducing the New FAR Part 139,* Airport Services Management, February 1988.
Bremer, Karl, *Plan Ahead for Emergencies That Involve Hazardous Substances,* Airport Services Management, April 1986.
Burian, Lawrence L., *Can We Stop Products Liability Costs From Dealing Our Industry a Fatal Blow?,* Airport Services Management, July 1985.
Burnham, Frank, *Do General Aviation Airports Need Better Crash-Fire-Rescue?* Airport Services Management, April 1985.
Business Life Insurance, Small Business Administration, Management Aids #2.009, 1984.
Cebula, Andrew V., *Part 139 Training,* NATA News, October 1988.
Clay, Max, *Pollution Liability Insurance Still a Viable Option for FBOs,* Industry Interview, AirTran News, August 1987.
Daley, Michael J., *Protecting Your Airport Against Environmental Hazards,* Airport Services Management, June 1987.
FAA Finalizes Fueling Regulations, NATA Regulatory Report, November 30, 1987.

FAA Issues New Security Access Rule, NATA Regulatory Report, January 20, 1989.
FBOs Must Comply With EPA's Community Right-to-Know Requirement, NATA Regulatory Report, February 29, 1988.
Fuel Tank Leak Tests Aren't Infallible, Illinois Operator Says, Airport Services, June 1988.
GA Product Liability Legislation Dies in the 100th Congress, NATA Legislative Report, November 3, 1988.
Gilbert, Gordon, *Fueling Training Programs Make FBOs, Skies, Safer,* Airport Services Management, February 1988.
Gilbert, Gordon, *Reducing Your Aircraft Rental Liability,* Airport Services Management, April 1987.
Goffman, Joseph, *Product Liability Legislation Is Disincentive for Safety,* Airport Services Management, March 1987.
Greene, Mark R., *Insurance Checklist for Small Business,* Small Business Adminstration Management Aids #2.018, Washington, D.C., 1983.
Hanson, John Jr., *How to Make Your Airport's Parking Lot Safe,* Airport Services Management, April 1986.
Hazard Communication Standard Compliance Manual for Fixed Base and Air Taxi Operators, National Air Transportation Foundation, 1988.
How to Obtain a Good Weather Briefing, General Aviation Accident Prevention Program, Federal Aviation Administration-P-8740–30, United States Department of Transportation/Federal Aviation Administration, 1980.
International Aviation Theft Bureau, Alert Magazine, April 1984.
Irsfield, Greg, *Above-Ground Tanks Help FBOs Meet New EPA Financial Rules,* Airport Services, December 1988.
Kern, John S., *The Best Safety System Is Your Records System,* AirTran News, May 1987.
Kilishek, George, *FBO Insurance Gets Cheaper, More Available,* Airport Services Management, December 1987.
Korzeniowski, George, *Tips on Planning a Security System For Your Operation,* Airport Services Management, March 1985.
NATA Members: Take Part in New Risk Retention Group, AirTran News, August 1987.
Ombudsmen Help FBOs Comply With Hazardous Waste Law, Airport Services Management, April 1987.
Ongoing Planning, Practice, Airport Services Management, April 1986.
Proposal Would Require More Safety Equipment on Part 135 Planes, Business Aviation, July 4, 1988.
Robert E. Breiling Associates, *Business Jet Accident Analysis for Corporate Aviation, Annual Turbine Aircraft Accident Review, Business Turboprop Accident Analysis for Corporate Aviation, Twin Turbine Helicopter Accident Analysis for Corporate Aviation,* Boca Raton, Florida, 1988.
Scatena, Carl, *Underground Tank Removal: A Precise Procedure Must Be Followed . . . Or Else,* AirTran News, May 1987.
Schaden, Richard F., *Better Airplane Design Will Lessen Product Liability,* Airport Services Management, August 1986.
Tank Financial Responsibility Requirement Finalized, NATA Regulatory Report, November 3, 1988.
Tank Test Available to NATA Members, AirTran News, November 1987.
Ten Questions an FBO Should Ask about His Insurance, Aviation Underwriting Specialists advertisement, undated.
The Impact of Rising Airport Liability Insurance Premiums on Airport Facilities and on Airport Capacity, Report of the Administrator of the FAA to the Senate and House Appropriations Committees Pursuant to House Report 99–831, July 1987.
Tudor, David V., *Communicating Chemical Hazards to FBO Employees,* AirTran News, September 1987.
U.S. Transportation Fatalities Rise Slightly in 1987, National Tranpsortation Safety Board, Safety Information press release, May 16, 1988.
White, David W., *Effective CFR (Crash-Fire-Rescue) Requires Ongoing Planning, Practice, Airport Services Management,* April 1986.

Chapter Twelve

Airport Fee Legislation Introduced, NATA, Initial Report File 88–104, April 7, 1988.
Airport Management Concepts Shifting Dramatically in United States, Air Transport World, June 1982.
Airport Safety Self-Inspection, Federal Aviation Administration Advisory Circular 150/5200–18, February 5, 1972.
Airport, Tenants Should Write Lease That Meets Their Changing Needs, ASM, May 1986.
'Airtel' Prospers, Improves Airport's Community Relations, ASM, February 1988.
AOPA Surveys the American Public, FBO, November/December 1988.
Baker, John L., *Massport Proposal Bodes Ill for All Aviation,* ASM, May 1988.
Barol, David, *Economic Impact Studies: How to Get More for Less,* ASM, May 1986.
Campbell, George E., *Airport Management and Operations,* Baton Rouge, LA.: Claitors Publishing Division, 1974.
Collogan, David, *Preserving GA's Access to ALL Airports,* Business and Commercial Aviation, March 1987.
Establishment of Airport Action Groups, NBAA Inc., FYI #87–23, September 22, 1987.
Estimated Airplane Noise Levels in A-Weighted Decibels, Federal Aviation Administration Advisory Circular 36–3B, November 20, 1981.
FAA Calls For Computer-Controlled Security Systems At Air Carrier Airports, ASM, May 1988.
Gilbert, Gordon, *Helicopter Noise Rules: Not the Sounds of Silence,* Business and Commercial Aviation, September 1987.
Gilbert, Gordon, *New Airports Won't Come Easy,* ASM, May 1988.
Gilbert, Gordon, *Short Runways Debated as Solution to Airport Congestion,* ASM, March 1985.
Gillfillan, Walter E., and Horonjeff, Robert, *Developing an Airport Master Plan,* Institute of Transportation and Traffic Engineering, University of California, San Francisco, CA., 1970.
Harrison, Kendall, *Study Sheds Light on Airport's Economic Benefits to Community,* FBO, September/October 1988.
How to Create an Airport Support Group, NBAA Inc., SR #87–3, May 28, 1987.
Hoyt, Kendall K., *Airport-Centered Plans,* ASM, July 1988.
Kelleher, William, *Trust Fund Abuse Stifles Capacity Growth,* ASM, July 1987.
Kingston Smith, Frank, *Airport Lease Negotiation Guide for General Aviation Base Operators,* Washington, D.C.: NATA, 1977.
Lewis, Torch, *Let Them Eat Cake,* Business and Commercial Aviation, October 1987.
Pilot 'Roll Book' Reveals Airport's Monetary Impact, ASM, September 1986.
Planning and Design of Airport Terminal Facilities at Non-Hub Locations, Federal Aviation Administration Advisory Circular 150/5360–9, April 14, 1980.
RAA Calls Logan's Proposed Fee Changes Discriminatory, ASM, February 1988.
Runway Length Requirements for Airport Design, Federal Aviation Administration Advisory Circular 150/5325–4, April 5, 1965.
Smith, Donald I., Odegard, John D., and Shea, William, *Airport Planning and Management,* Belmont, CA.: Wadsworth, 1984.
The Continuous Airport System Planning Process, Federal Aviation Administration Advisory Circular 150/5050–5, November 28, 1975.
Wells, Alexander *Airport Planning and Management,* TAB Books, 1986.
Worthington, E. R., *Lease Negotiation Tips for Fixed-Base Operators,* ASM, August 1986.

Chapter Thirteen

AOPA Poll Shows Overwhelming Support of National Aviation Policy. The Weekly of Business Aviation, August 15, 1988.
Aviation Careers Series: Airport Careers, U.S. Department of Transportation, FAA, Document No. GA-300–124–84.
Burnham, Frank, *FAA Plan Forecasts High-Tech Airports, Airways,* ASM, October 1987.
Dennis, Steve, *The Changing Fortunes of the FBO,* FBO, September/October 1988.

Fiftieth Anniversary Issue; *Aviation, Past, Present and Future,* Flying Magazine, September 1977.
Flying the Glass Cockpit, Living with Electronic Flight Instrument Systems; Today in a Boeing 767, Tomorrow in a Bonanza, Aircraft Owners' and Pilots' Association, Pilot, April 1984.
Goffman, Joseph, *Product Liability Legislation Is Disincentive For Safety,* ASM, March 1987.
Midwest ATC: The Federal Aviation Administration Isn't the Only Game in Town, Airport Services Management, August 1983.
NATA's 1988 Wage and Salary Handbook
Parkinson, C. Northcote, *The Law,* see especially the chapter entitled "Plans and Plants," Boston, MA.: Houghton Mifflin, 1980.
Pilot 'Roll Book' Reveals Airport's Monetary Impact, ASM, September 1986.
Smith, Frank Kingston, *An Appreciation of the Social, Economic and Political Issues of General Aviation,* Department of Transportation/FAA, June 1977.
Society of Manufacturing Engineers Say a Use of Composites Could Add 300,000 Jobs by 1985, Aviation Daily, February 25, 1983.
Toffler, Alvin, *Previews and Premises,* New York: William Morrow and Company 1983.
Toffler, Alvin, *The Third Wave,* New York: William Morrow & Company, 1980.
Wackenhut Security Company Wants to 'Privatize' Municipal Services, Seattle Daily Journal of Commerce, May 18, 1984.
Zaharevitz, Walter, *Aviation Career Series: Aviation Maintenance,* Department of Transportation/FAA, Document No. GA-300–123 (Revised 1980)

Appendix I

Summary of Federal Air Regulations

Code of Federal Regulations 14 Parts I to 200, Aeronautics and Space

Introduction

Fixed base operators and their customers are generally very familiar with certain federal air regulations (FARs), such as Part 61, which deals with pilot licensing, and Part 135, which covers air taxi operations. However, some of those in aviation are unaware of the details of some of the other FARs, which number 200 in all. The code of federal regulations is republished each year to reflect any updates and revisions. What follows here is a list of the FARs by title and number.

Subchapter A—Definitions

Part

1 Definitions and abbreviations

Subchapter B—Procedural Rules

11 General rule-making procedures
13 Investigative and enforcement procedures

Subchapter C—Aircraft

21 Certification procedures for products and parts
23 Airworthiness standards: normal, utility, and acrobatic category airplanes
25 Airworthiness standards: transport category airplanes
27 Airworthiness standards: normal category rotorcraft
29 Airworthiness standards: transport category rotorcraft
31 Airworthiness standards: manned free balloons
33 Airworthiness standards: aircraft engines
35 Airworthiness standards: propellers
36 Noise standards: aircraft type and airworthiness certification
39 Airworthiness directives
43 Maintenance, preventive maintenance, rebuilding, and alteration
45 Identification and registration marking
47 Aircraft registration
49 Recording of aircraft titles and security documents
50–59 [Reserved]

Subchapter D—Airmen

Part	
60	[Reserved]
61	Certification: Pilots and flight instructors
63	Certification: Flight crew members other than pilots
65	Certification: Airmen other than flight crew members
67	Medical standards and certification

Subchapter E—Airspace

71	Designation of Federal airways, area low routes, controlled airspace, and reporting points
73	Special use airspace
75	Establishment of jet routes and area high routes
77	Objects affecting navigable airspace

Chapter F—Air Traffic and General Operating Rules

91	General operating and flight rules
93	Special air traffic rules and airport traffic patterns
95	IFR altitudes
97	Standard instrument approach procedures
99	Security control of air traffic
101	Moored balloons, kites, unmanned rockets and unmanned free balloons
103	Ultralight vehicles
105	Parachute jumping
107	Airport security
108	Airplane operator security
109	Indirect air carrier security

Subchapter G—Air Carriers, Air Travel Clubs and Operators for Compensation or Hire: Certification and Operations

121	Certification and operations: Domestic, flag, and supplemental air carriers and commercial operators of large aircraft
125	Certification and operations: Airplanes having a seating capacity of 20 or more passengers or a maximum payload capacity of 6,000 pounds or more
127	Certification and operations of scheduled air carriers with helicopters
129	Operations of foreign air carriers
133	Rotorcraft external-load operations
135	Air taxi operators and commercial operators
137	Agricultural aircraft operations
139	Certification and operations: Land airports serving CAB—certificated air carriers

Subchapter H—Schools and Other Certificated Agencies

Part	
141	Pilot schools
143	Ground instructors
145	Repair stations
147	Aviation maintenance technician schools
149	Parachute lofts

Subchapter I—Airports

150	Airport noise compatibility planning
151	Federal aid to airports
152	Airport aid program
153	Acquisition of U.S. land for public airports
154	Acquisition of U.S. land for public airports under the Airport and Airway Development Act of 1970
155	Release of airport property from surplus property disposal restrictions
157	Notice of construction, alteration, activation, and deactivation of airports
159	National capital airports
169	Expenditure of Federal funds for non-military airports or air navigation facilities thereon

Subchapter J—Navigational Facilities

171	Non-Federal navigation facilities

Subchapter K—Administrative Regulations

183	Representatives of the Administrator
185	Testimony by employees and production of records in legal proceedings, and service of legal process and pleadings
187	Fees
189	Use of Federal Aviation Administration communications system
191	Withholding security information from disclosure under the Air Transportation Security Act of 1974

Subchapter L—M [Reserved]

Subchapter N—War Risk Insurance

198	War risk insurance

Subchapter O—Aircraft Loan Guarantee Program

199	Aircraft loan guarantee program

Appendix II

Aviation Business Promotion Ideas

1. Tailor your promotion efforts to the specific needs of your customers. Doctors, farmers, businesspeople, college students, and homemakers all have different interests.
2. Stress aviation's value to the community: total payroll, total taxes paid, unusual services performed.
3. Series of interviews (newspaper, radio, TV) with local prominent citizen/flyers on "Why I Fly."
4. Interesting vacation or family trips taken by local aviators could be publicized.
5. "Create" news from the preparation efforts for an open house. Examples: painting or refurbishing your buildings (How many gallons of paint? How many worker hours? Who is doing the painting?); polishing up your planes for display; your staff meeting to discuss plans, and so on. Obtain a photographer for coverage.
6. Identify local newspeople/pilots and involve them in developing aviation promotions.
7. Schedule a cross-country competitive flight. Round-robin course, fuel stop, touch down points with the winner determined on the basis of time and fuel economy.
8. Fly your mayor to visit the mayor of an adjacent town to invite him or her to an aviation activity on your airport. Take along a newspaper or TV representative.
9. Provide free flight instruction to a local radio celebrity or public figure.
10. Erect a banner or streamer across a busy intersection in the downtown area or neighborhood shopping center for your open house.
11. Arrange a helicopter rescue demonstration in cooperation with your local hospital.
12. Plan a day honoring the oldest active pilot in your city, county, or state.
13. Working through a local supply source, arrange to "fly in" the refreshments for your (or some other) aviation activity.
14. Consider a planned group flight. Dawn patrols, breakfast flights, fly-ins have all been used successfully.
15. Plan a "March on the Shopping Center" where you supply posters, banners, pennants to turn the whole center into a promotion.
16. Get employees involved in the program by talking to their outside professional and social groups.
17. Join other operators in selecting a "Ms. or Mr. Aviation" from among local pilots. After he or she is selected, go after newspaper and broadcast publicity—"Head Table Guest" appearances at local business luncheons, dinners, and so forth.
18. Consider displaying a new aircraft in a bank lobby, shopping mall, department store, city park, or parking lot. (Arrange for security and salespeople).
19. Offer a special price on a flight instruction program given as a high school or college graduation present.
20. Don't forget the traditional "penny-a-pound rides" as a means of getting people to an open house.
21. Offer free flight instruction to the high school student who submits the best essay on "Why I'd like to learn to fly"; publicize the contest and winner.

22. Hold a week day open house just for women. Get any local 99's or local women pilots to hostess and give demonstration rides. Announce through women's clubs, garden clubs, church groups, and so on; invite the media.
23. When distributing invitations to aviation activities, distribute them where people are: downtown on a busy street corner, outside a local movie as it lets out, at drive-ins, at restaurants, at other types of activities.
24. Consider a "teaser" advertising program on billboards and newspapers. Give part of the message initially, and build upon it later.
25. Share the proceeds of contests and programs with charity or public service groups in order to get them working with you, promoting aviation activities.
26. Tourist or traveler guide published in the area? "What's going on" column in the newspaper? Be sure to get your dates listed with them.
27. Develop an "adult education course" on aviation and offer through a local school.
28. Get a senior high school class, a Boy Scout Troop, or other organization to sell tickets in advance of a promotion in return for a share in the proceeds.
29. If you have a local resort with a landing strip and a good restaurant, arrange a "Fly to Lunch" special. You sell special meal tickets that cover the cost of transportation and meal. Both you and the resort owner promote and benefit.
30. Place your advertisements in a different place—try the society page, the financial page, or maybe even next to the obituary column.
31. Contact local Air National Guard, Air Reserve, and Naval Air Reserve regarding static military aircraft displays and fly-bys. Include opportunity for recruiting booths.
32. Free shuttle bus to your special event from some large shopping center or congregation points.
33. Consider special interest groups. Special activities for doctors, undertakers, salespeople, executives.
34. Rent a tent, if necessary, for space or for other desirable reasons.
35. Get a radio or TV personality to do a remote broadcast from your lounge or line.
36. Try week night aviation activities. Consider "Moonlight Air Rides" to see the lights.
37. Get a local women's store or department store to conduct a fashion show in your hangar. Arrange a backdrop of cleaned and polished planes. Consider a drawing for free air rides.
38. For open houses and large crowds, identify everything in your facility with signs and explanation cards. Consider a mimeographed "Guide to a Walking Tour" so visitors can know what they should see.
39. A winter time (bad weather) activity: a series of movies on flying to keep interest up. May use a school facility or a restaurant's private dining room. Should consider light refreshments.
40. For public activities make your premises attractive: clean up, paint as needed, wear uniforms and jackets, have floral arrangements in office and lounge.
41. Hire a high school or veterans' band or drum and bugle corps for music at special programs.
42. Get a youth group to offer $1.00 car washes on your ramp while people visit the facility; publicize in advance.
43. Try ten-minute simulator "rides" for twenty-five cents.
44. At various professional programs and meetings display pilot aids and accessories. Have someone available to explain their use.
45. Make your lounge or ready room available to bridge groups.
46. Arrange for or provide babysitting service for flying parents.

47. Sponsor a photo contest—your airport, aircraft, or facility is the subject. Winner receives a number of free flying lessons.
48. Introductory business flights to the businessperson who has to travel during the week. He or she feels the convenience and discovers how easy it would be to learn to fly.
49. Consider a special program for flying farmers. Suggest that they each bring a nonflyer.
50. Develop a "trial order" package to promote air cargo shipments. Invite shipping agent or traffic manager to "ride the trip" with you.
51. Work with hospitals and doctors in developing an air ambulance service. Demonstrate with a trial run.
52. Get involved in an air education program with the local high school or junior college.
53. Develop a package of ideas to keep graduates of your flight schools in touch and proud of the association they have with you.
    - Regular meetings with films or slides to spark interest
    - Brochures and mail-outs to provide a regular source of information
    - Periodic special speakers on key aviation topics

Appendix III

Aviation Management Audit

Aviation Management Audit

A Comprehensive Organizational Audit

RICHCO

Management Audit For Aviation Organizations

A systematic comprehensive organization review to be used by aviation managers in analyzing, evaluating and developing their business

Developed by:
John D. Richardson, Ph.D.

Introduction

The management audit is a systematic, checklist approach to the analysis of your organization, its functions, operations, and decisions. The audit reviews your whole business, as well as the separate components.

Just as a healthy person will go to his or her physician for a periodic check-up, managers can use the audit as a means of determining the condition of their businesses. It becomes the means for conducting a systematic, critical and unbiased review and appraisal. The main purpose is to help the manager better the position of his or her company; to improve the overall health of the organization.

There are three major steps in this audit:

1. The compilation of your business data, and the completion of the checklist.
2. The critical review, analysis, and evaluation of all information obtained by the audit.
3. Determining future action required to improve the health and position of the company.

The benefit derived from conducting an audit is directly related to the attitude of the participant. In order to maximize this benefit, you are encouraged to:

1. Consider each item in the audit seriously, thoughtfully, and with a view for the future.
2. Accept that every item may not apply 100 percent to your situation, but look for the value in each topic.
3. Make the audit a useful self-appraisal tool, sharing ideas and views when appropriate.

In order to make the audit a valuable part of your plan for the future, you are encouraged to use the following procedure in completing this booklet:

1. Complete the entire management audit, answering each question with as much objectivity as possible.
2. Next, start at the beginning and review your answers. Assign a plus (+) or minus (–) for each item you feel is a major strength or deficiency in your organization.
3. Complete the summary and evaluation sheet, list those areas in which you would like to initiate some action, and assign priorities to accomplish selected goals.
4. Establish future dates for reviewing the audit and determining your progress.
5. Follow through with additional audits on an annual basis.

It should be remembered that while the audit is comprehensive, it is only suggestive. The audit will not do the thinking for you. It compares your organization relative to a standard or to other organizations. You must then evaluate your findings and determine your action.

Can You??

- Set aside time to review the audit
- Have someone else take those incoming calls
- Review each item carefully and deliberately
- Remember, it's your business and your future you are evaluating

Contents

Part I—Management Functions Audit

Major concern should be focused upon the top-level managerial guidance provided the organization. Are the key management functions of planning, organizing, directing, and controlling being carried out? What is the status of long-range plans?

Management Functions

A. Planning

		Circle Answer	Evaluation (+) (–)
1. Do you regularly set aside time for planning?	1	**Yes No**	2 ______
2. Have you made a specific effort to set objectives for your organization?	3	**Yes No**	4 ______

3. List your current objectives:

____

____

____

____

____

____

____

4. Are your objectives:			
a. definite	5	**Yes No**	6 ______
b. clear-cut	7	**Yes No**	8 ______
c. written	9	**Yes No**	10 ______
d. attainable	11	**Yes No**	12 ______
5. Are objectives understood by those involved in their attainment ?	13	**Yes No**	14 ______
6. Are objectives accepted by those involved in their attainment?	15	**Yes No**	16 ______
7. Are your objectives current?	17	**Yes No**	18 ______
a. What is the date you last devoted time to listing objectives in writing ?		______________	
b. Are your objectives responsive to change?	19	**Yes No**	20 ______
8. Do you make a specific effort to forecast future conditions?	21	**Yes No**	22 ______

Part II—Operations Audit

This portion of the audit is concerned with those activities primarily operational in nature.

Line Operations

Includes that portion of the business aimed at the incoming customer: the meeting, parking, and servicing of the aircraft.

	Circle Answer			Evaluation (+) (–)
1. Is your flight line visible and identified to incoming aircraft?	1	**Yes**	**No**	2 ______
2. Is your flight line operational (easy to understand by the transient)?	3	**Yes**	**No**	4 ______
3. Do tower personnel know the services offered by your business?	5	**Yes**	**No**	6 ______
4. Can the tower direct the transient to your place of business?	7	**Yes**	**No**	8 ______
5. Do you use radio assistance?				
a. for incoming planes?	9	**Yes**	**No**	10 ______
b. for line personnel?	11	**Yes**	**No**	12 ______
6. Do you use vehicles to assist incoming aircraft?	13	**Yes**	**No**	14 ______
7. Do you provide training to line personnel on:				
a. aircraft servicing	15	**Yes**	**No**	16 ______
b. appearance	17	**Yes**	**No**	18 ______
c. attitude	19	**Yes**	**No**	20 ______
d. local services	21	**Yes**	**No**	22 ______
e. sales	23	**Yes**	**No**	24 ______
8. Have you planned for line maintenance?	25	**Yes**	**No**	26 ______
9. What courtesy services are available?				
a. line vehicle	27	**Yes**	**No**	28 ______
b. luggage cart	29	**Yes**	**No**	30 ______
c. courtesy car	31	**Yes**	**No**	32 ______
d. refreshments	33	**Yes**	**No**	34 ______

Part III—Facility Audit

The land, physical facilities, and major equipment.

Facilities

1. Are your facilities:

a. self-owned?	1	**Yes**	**No**	2 ______
b. leased?	3	**Yes**	**No**	4 ______

2. Is your lease for:

a. one year?	5	**Yes**	**No**	6 ______
b. two years?	7	**Yes**	**No**	8 ______
c. five years?	9	**Yes**	**No**	10 ______
d. ten years?	11	**Yes**	**No**	12 ______
e. fifteen years?	13	**Yes**	**No**	14 ______
e. twenty or more years?	15	**Yes**	**No**	16 ______

3. Is your lease with:

a. airport commission?	17	**Yes**	**No**	18 ______
b. city board?	19	**Yes**	**No**	20 ______
c. county supervisors?	21	**Yes**	**No**	22 ______
d. private owner?	23	**Yes**	**No**	24 ______

e. other ____

4. You obtained assistance during lease negotiation from:

a. lease manual	25	**Yes**	**No**	26 ______
b. lawyer	27	**Yes**	**No**	28 ______
c. aviation consultant	29	**Yes**	**No**	30 ______
d. none	31	**Yes**	**No**	32 ______

e. other ____

5. Your lease payments are:

a. annual cash payments?	33	**Yes**	**No**	34 ______

Part IV—Marketing Audit

This part deals with the many activities involved in the total marketing effort of the organization.

Market Facts

That necessary information required for the planning and development of an aggressive marketing program.

1. Do you have an overall plan for collecting market facts?	1	**Yes**	**No**	2 ______
2. Is this plan in writing?	3	**Yes**	**No**	4 ______
3. Was a proper market survey made when the business started?	5	**Yes**	**No**	6 ______
4. If not, should a market survey be made now?	7	**Yes**	**No**	8 ______
5. Have the basic sources of market survey data been studied?	9	**Yes**	**No**	10 ______
6. Does the population growth, new competition, or change in competitor methods justify new ways of serving the market?	11	**Yes**	**No**	12 ______
7. Is the major problem of your business a lack of sales?	13	**Yes**	**No**	14 ______
8. What has been the trend in your sales in recent years?				
a. rapid rise	15	**Yes**	**No**	16 ______
b. steady increase	17	**Yes**	**No**	18 ______
c. about level	19	**Yes**	**No**	20 ______
d. declining	21	**Yes**	**No**	22 ______

9. What factors have been determined as responsible for the trend in sales?

____

____

____

10. Have you identified your trading area?	23	**Yes**	**No**	24 ______
11. Has the character of the population in your trading area changed (aside from growth or decline)?	25	**Yes**	**No**	26 ______
12. Has this change affected sales?	27	**Yes**	**No**	28 ______
13. Does the future for your company, in your market, look:				
a. excellent	29	**Yes**	**No**	30 ______
b. good	31	**Yes**	**No**	32 ______

Part V—Human Resources Audit

The personnel in an organization should be considered its greatest asset. As such. the various programs dealing with personnel management become most important.

Staffing

The process of identifying human resource needs and providing for the steady flow of qualified personnel.

1. Do you have a firm procedure to follow in identifying human resource needs? 1 **Yes No** 2 ______

2. Do you have a personnel plan that is derived from the overall business plan? 3 **Yes No** 4 ______

3. Do you use a budget as part of your personnel planning process? 5 **Yes No** 6 ______

4. For the majority of employee positions:

a. do you use job descriptions? 7 **Yes No** 8 ______

b. do you utilize employee specifications? 9 **Yes No** 10 ______

5. List the recruiting techniques you use:

____

____

____

____

6. Do you use:

a. application blanks 11 **Yes No** 12 ______

b. weighted application blanks 13 **Yes No** 14 ______

c. interviewer's checklist 15 **Yes No** 16 ______

d. employment history form 17 **Yes No** 18 ______

e. education history form 19 **Yes No** 20 ______

f. military service form 21 **Yes No** 22 ______

g. request for information from references 23 **Yes No** 24 ______

h. request for medical examination 25 **Yes No** 26 ______

i. test score profile 27 **Yes No** 28 ______

j. contract of employment 29 **Yes No** 30 ______

Part VI—Administration Audit

Administration includes many key areas and becomes the focal point for most organizational activities.

Insurance

Every business is faced with many risks, ranging from minor to catostrophlc. Managing these risks calls for an understanding of insurance principles and the selection of desired coverages.

1. Has management truly analyzed all the major risks to which the company is exposed? 1 **Yes No** 2 ______

2. What protection has been provided against each of the risks?

Risk	Protection
______	______
______	______
______	______
______	______
______	______
______	______
______	______
______	______

3. Is self-insurance appropriate for your business? 3 **Yes No** 4 ______

4. What risks are being absorbed?

a. ______

b. ______

c. ______

5. Why?

a. ______

b. ______

c. ______

6. Are there any recommendations for reducing risks or getting protection more economically? 5 **Yes No** 6 ______

Part VII—Information Systems

The manager needs a continuous flow of data to advise him or her of the organization's progress and to enable him or her to control its direction toward desired objectives.

Organization

A key element is the recognition of the need for the organization of information.

1. Have you systematically organized the information flow on your business activity? 1 **Yes No** 2 ______

2. Does your information system cover:

a. money? 3 **Yes No** 4 ______

b. personnel? 5 **Yes No** 6 ______

c. material? 7 **Yes No** 8 ______

3. Does your information system:

a. provide an accurate, thorough picture of operating results? 9 **Yes No** 10 ______

b. permit quick comparison of current data with budgeted goals? 11 **Yes No** 12 ______

c. provide a quick comparison of current data with prior years' operating results? 13 **Yes No** 14 ______

d. reveal all possible employee frauds, thefts, waste, and record-keeping errors? 15 **Yes No** 16 ______

e. provide the necessary data for the prompt filing of required reports? 17 **Yes No** 18 ______

f. identify the contribution of each department to the overall organization? 19 **Yes No** 20 ______

g. provide suitable financial statements for use by management and prospective creditors? 21 **Yes No** 22 ______

4. Do you periodically review all procedures, records, forms, and reports that are part of your information system? 23 **Yes No** 24 ______

5. Are your procedures, records, forms, and reports producing the required information at the lowest cost? 25 **Yes No** 26 ______

Money

The information system should cover the movement of money into and out of the business, the reason for its movement and its availability.

6. Do you have a complete accounting system in operation? 27 **Yes No** 28 ______

Part VIII—Finance Audit

Financial skill technically plays a major part in the operation and development of a business. A sound information system is a prerequisite to developing a high level of financial activity.

Financing the Business

A business man may obtain money from many sources to finance his business. He will need to answer questions of how? where? how much? when? why? and cost?

1. In financing your business do you use:

a. equity financing 1 **Yes No** 2 ______

b. loans 3 **Yes No** 4 ______

c. trade credit 5 **Yes No** 6 ______

d. business profits 7 **Yes No** 8 ______

2. To what sources do you turn for financing?

a. aircraft ______

______

b. building expansion ______

______

c. new shop equipment ______

______

d. receivables ______

______

______

3. Are you setting aside adequate reserves for the replacement of depreciating or obsolescent assets? 9 **Yes No** 10 ______

Financial Analysis

The manager must determine the tools needed for financial analysis, ensure that they are available in his organization and intelligently use them on a regular basis.

4. Have you determined the financial tools you need for the analysis of your business? 11 **Yes No** 12 ______

Appendix IV

Part A
Aviation Business Forms and Source Documents

This illustrates some typical business forms and source documents available for use by aviation businesses. For convenience of presentation, they are grouped into three areas; those for operational control purposes, those for marketing purposes, and those for financial purposes. The following pages suggest how these source documents may be organized.

Operational Control Purposes

- Aircraft scheduling books
- Line service slips
- Pilot check-out cards
- Plane cost records
- Applications for training
- Applications for employment
- Aircraft summary sheets
- Unicom log sheets
- Student pilot summary sheet
- Used aircraft appraisal report
- Instructor activity reports
- Contract forms (aerial applicator)
- Aircraft "squawk" card
- Air taxi reports; I, II, III
- Crew data sheets
- Repair tags
- Hangar lease agreement
- Tie-down lease agreement
- Student appointment form
- Flight reports (air taxi)
- Preflight and run-up checks

Marketing Purposes

- Advertising aids
- Student certificates
- Navigation worksheets
- Weather reporting forms
- Stickers and decals
- Aircraft sales calculation sheet
- Guest register
- Prospect worksheet and survey
- Sales department checklist
- Application for credit

Financial Purposes

- Aircraft revenue invoice
- Aircraft rental form
- Time and job ticket
- Time sheet
- Service order form
- Daily summary of shop time
- Invoice (aerial applicator)
- Lease forms
- Charter invoice
- Check forms
- Cash receipts
- Aircraft rental and invoice

- Tach sheets
- Supporting aircraft inventory schedule
- Daily line sales report
- Monthly aircraft report
- Aircraft depreciation record
- Aircraft summary
- Line service invoice
- Aircraft sales invoice
- Parts invoice
- Customer statement
- Bookkeeping system

Part B
Information System Activity Flow Charts

Financial data of the business information system should move through the organization structure in a logical and efficient manner. The accounting system should receive information on all of the transactions that affect the company resources; and all individuals, both in and out of the organization, should understand the transaction so they can take appropriate action. The following pages contain activity flow charts for the overall system and the basic source documents used in aviation businesses:

- Aircraft rental and flight instruction
- Aircraft sales
- Aircraft charter
- Line sales
- Parts sales
- Service sales
- Payroll
- Cash disbursements and purchases
- Cash receipts

The flow chart graphically depicts the processing of data regarding each of the principal business activities. Individual organizations will vary, but the same basic steps should be followed.

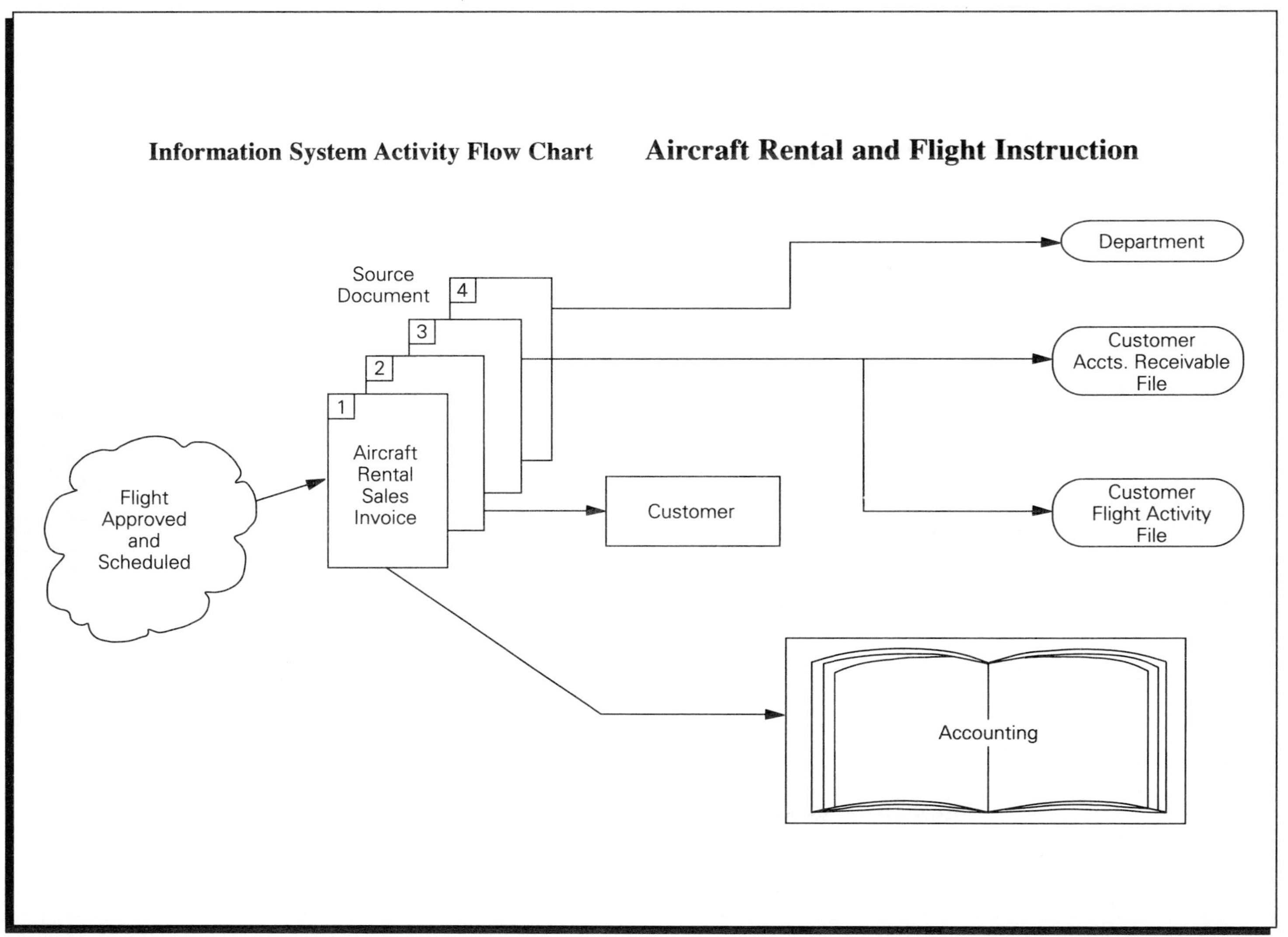
Information System Activity Flow Chart
Aircraft Rental and Flight Instruction
Flight Approved and Scheduled
Source Document
1
2
3
4
Aircraft Rental Sales Invoice
Department
Customer Accts. Receivable File
Customer
Customer Flight Activity File
Accounting

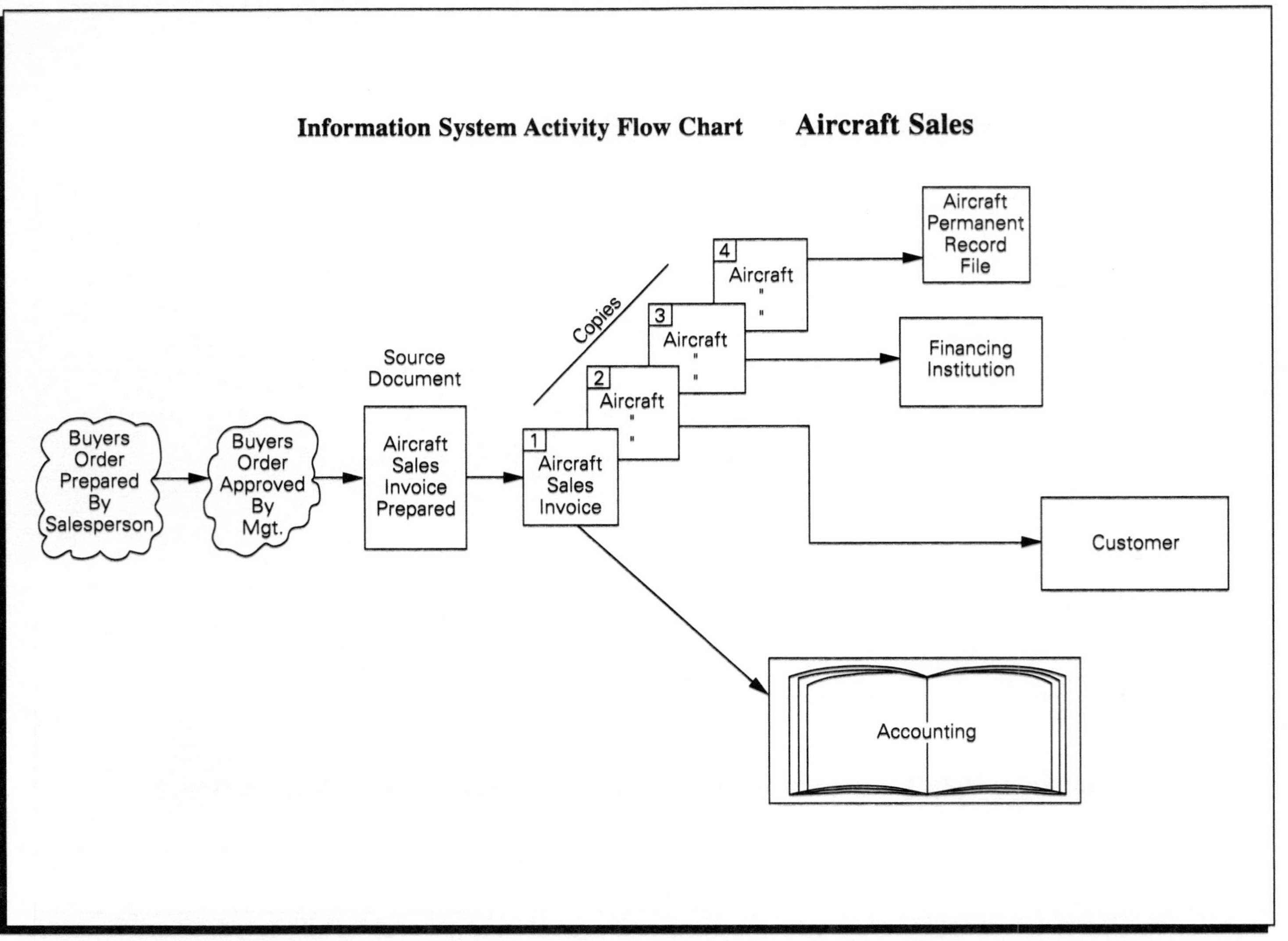
Information System Activity Flow Chart
Aircraft Sales
Buyers Order Prepared By Salesperson
Buyers Order Approved By Mgt.
Source Document
Aircraft Sales Invoice Prepared
1 Aircraft Sales Invoice
2 Aircraft " "
3 Aircraft " "
4 Aircraft " "
Copies
Aircraft Permanent Record File
Financing Institution
Customer
Accounting

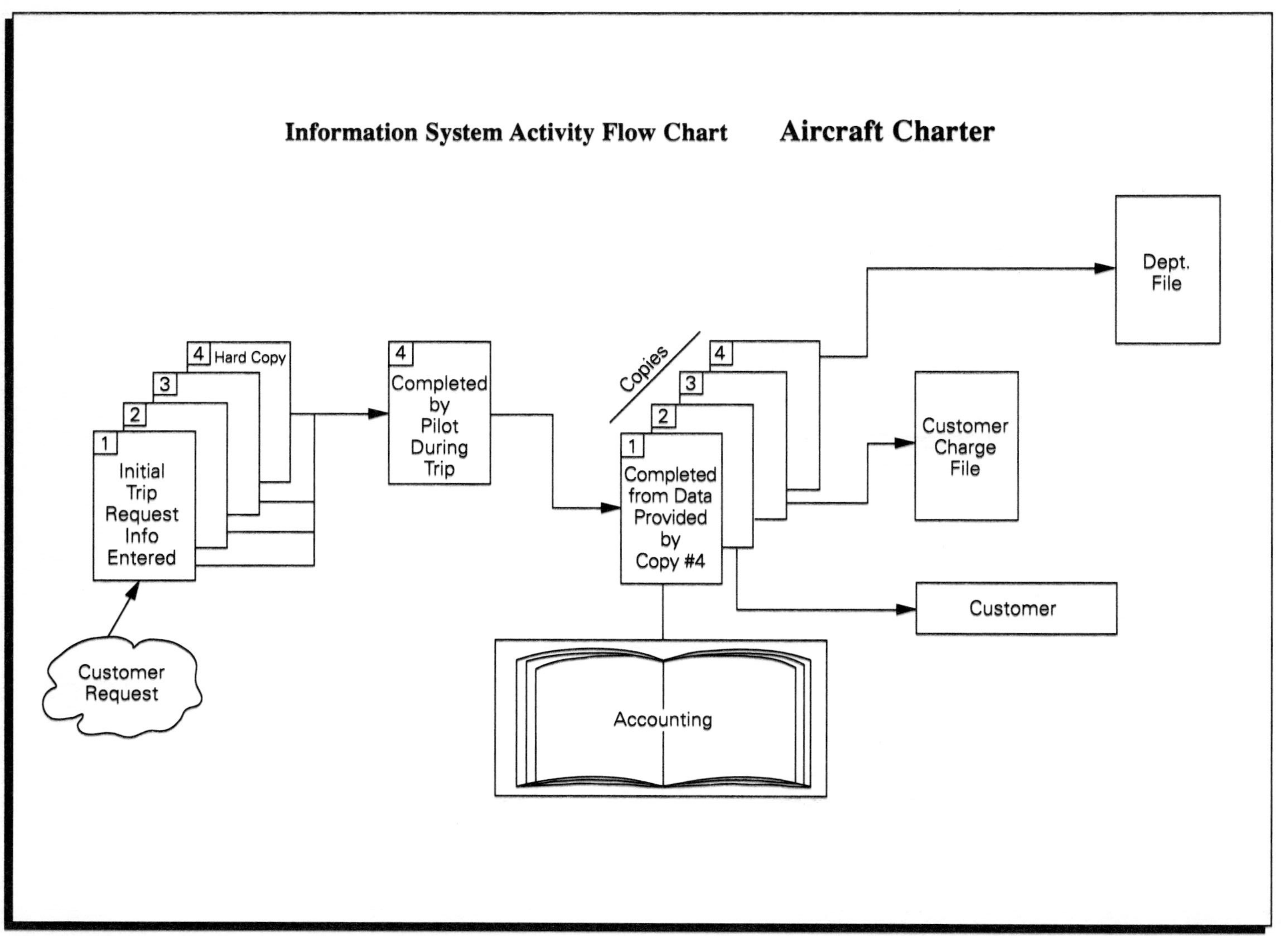
Information System Activity Flow Chart
Aircraft Charter
1
2
3
4
Hard Copy
Initial Trip Request Info Entered
Customer Request
4
Completed by Pilot During Trip
Copies
1
2
3
4
Completed from Data Provided by Copy #4
Dept. File
Customer Charge File
Customer
Accounting

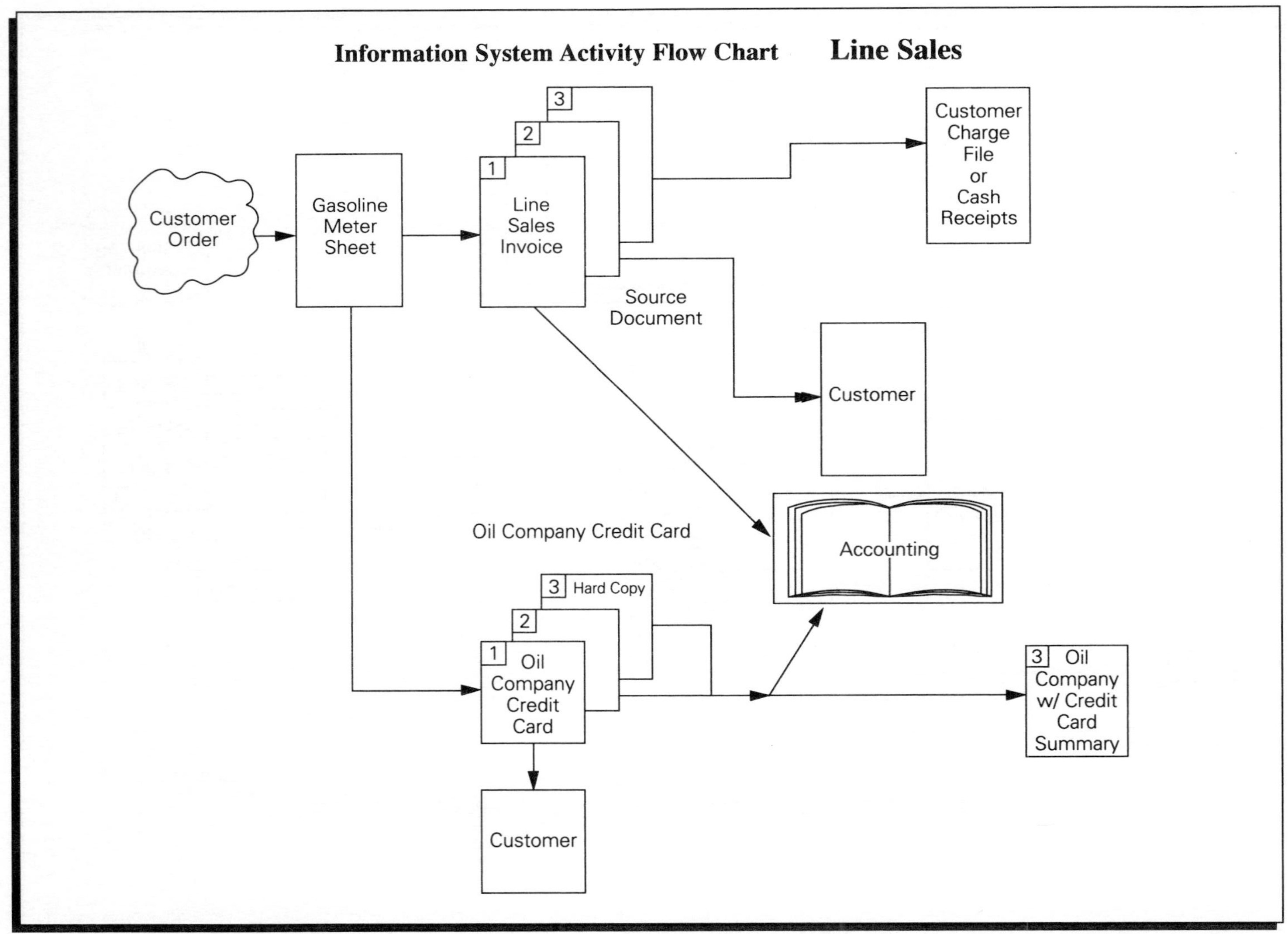
Information System Activity Flow Chart
Line Sales
Customer Order
Gasoline Meter Sheet
1 Line Sales Invoice
2
3
Source Document
Customer Charge File or Cash Receipts
Customer
Accounting
Oil Company Credit Card
1 Oil Company Credit Card
2
3 Hard Copy
Customer
3 Oil Company w/ Credit Card Summary

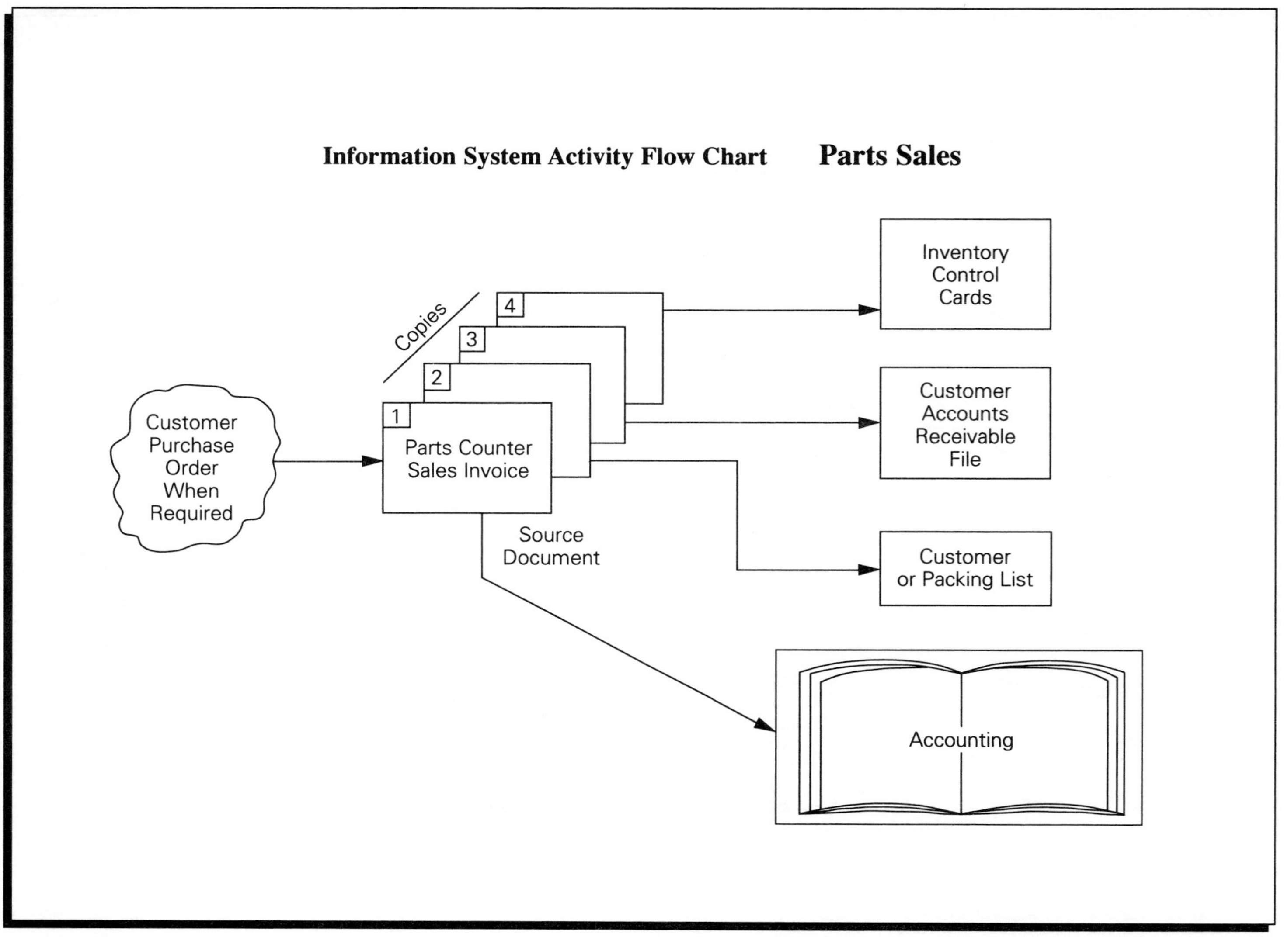
Information System Activity Flow Chart
Parts Sales
Customer Purchase Order When Required
Copies
1
2
3
4
Parts Counter Sales Invoice
Source Document
Inventory Control Cards
Customer Accounts Receivable File
Customer or Packing List
Accounting

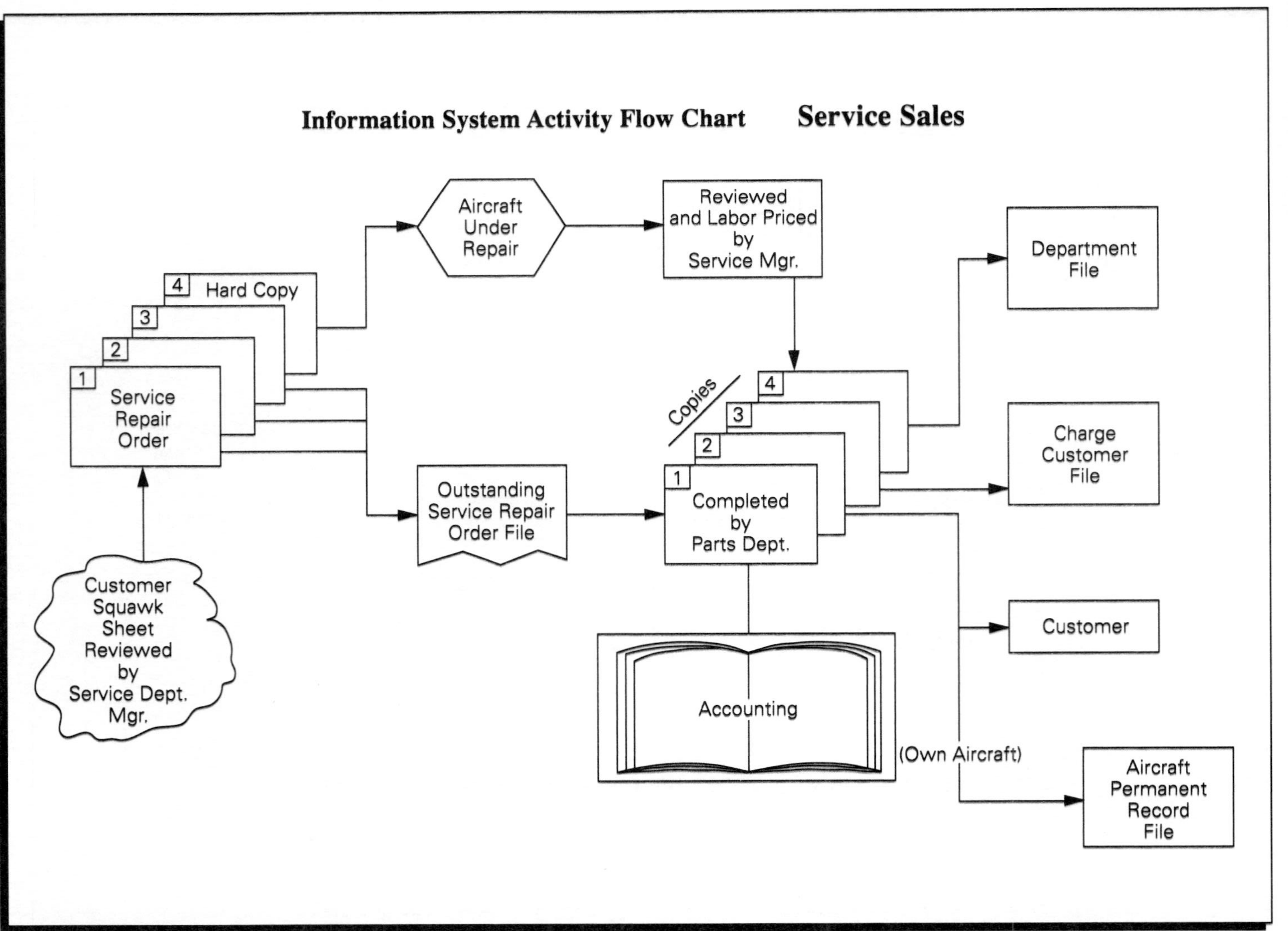
Information System Activity Flow Chart
Service Sales
Service Repair Order
1
2
3
4
Hard Copy
Customer Squawk Sheet Reviewed by Service Dept. Mgr.
Aircraft Under Repair
Outstanding Service Repair Order File
Reviewed and Labor Priced by Service Mgr.
Copies
Completed by Parts Dept.
Accounting
Department File
Charge Customer File
Customer
(Own Aircraft)
Aircraft Permanent Record File

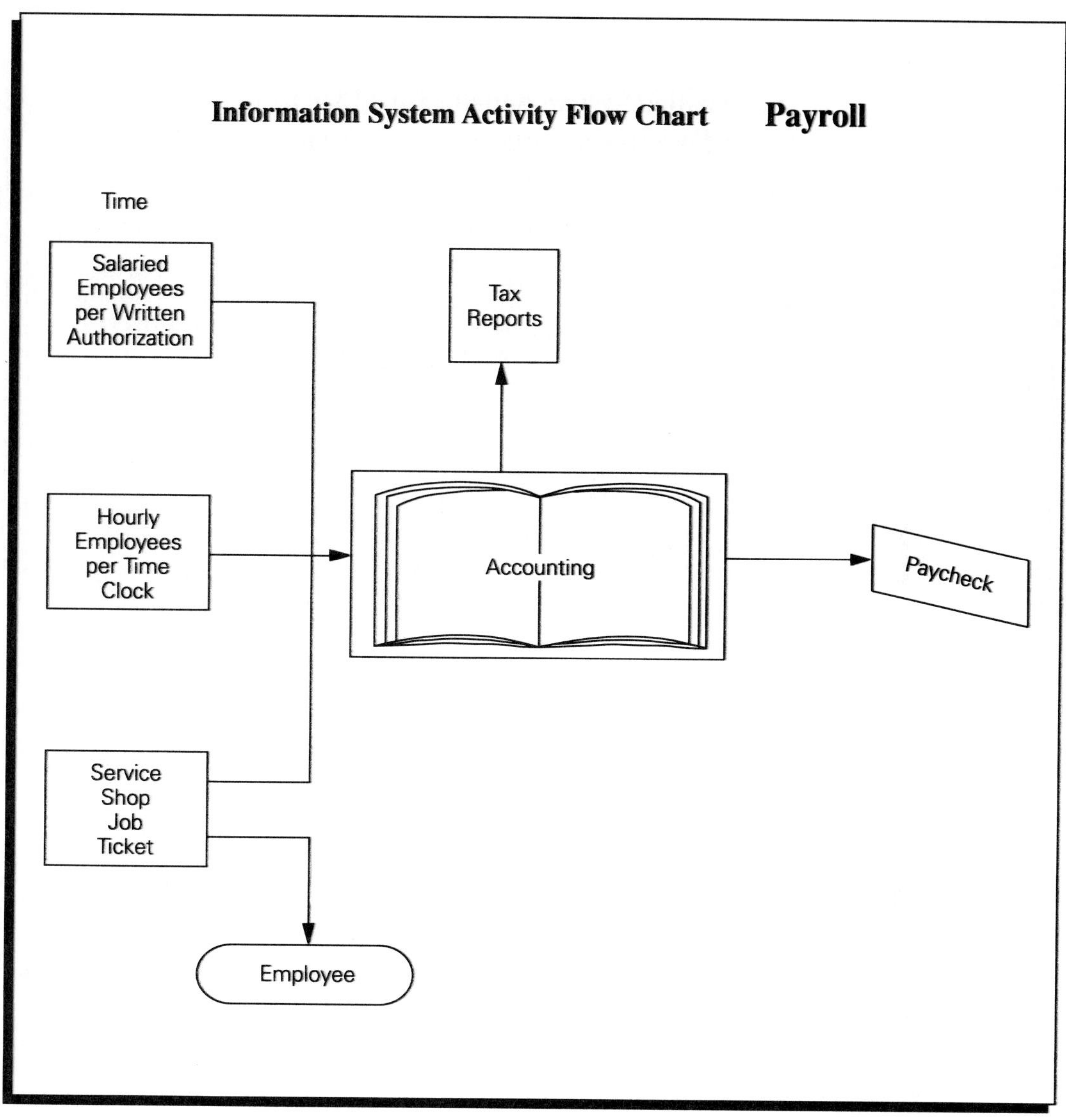
Information System Activity Flow Chart Payroll
Time
Salaried Employees per Written Authorization
Hourly Employees per Time Clock
Service Shop Job Ticket
Tax Reports
Accounting
Paycheck
Employee

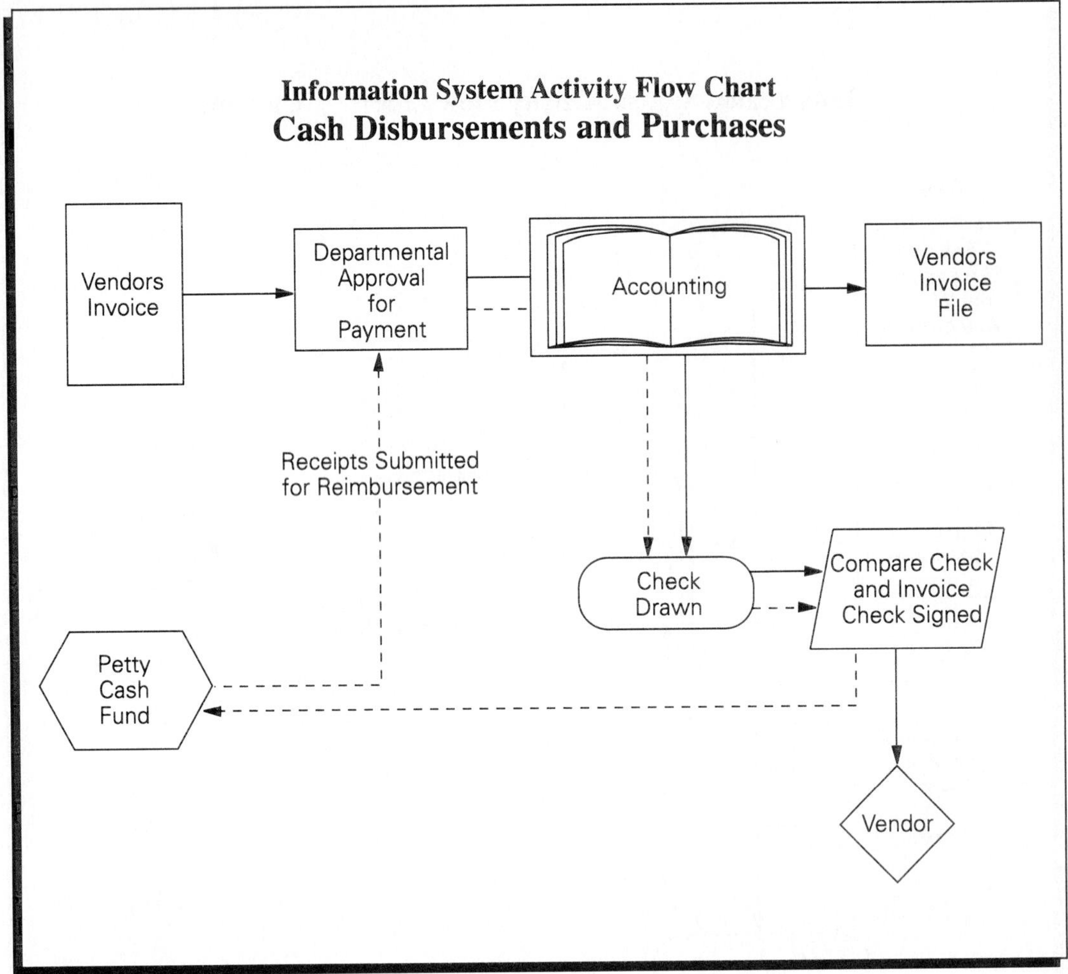
Information System Activity Flow Chart
Cash Disbursements and Purchases
Vendors Invoice
Departmental Approval for Payment
Accounting
Vendors Invoice File
Receipts Submitted for Reimbursement
Check Drawn
Compare Check and Invoice Check Signed
Petty Cash Fund
Vendor

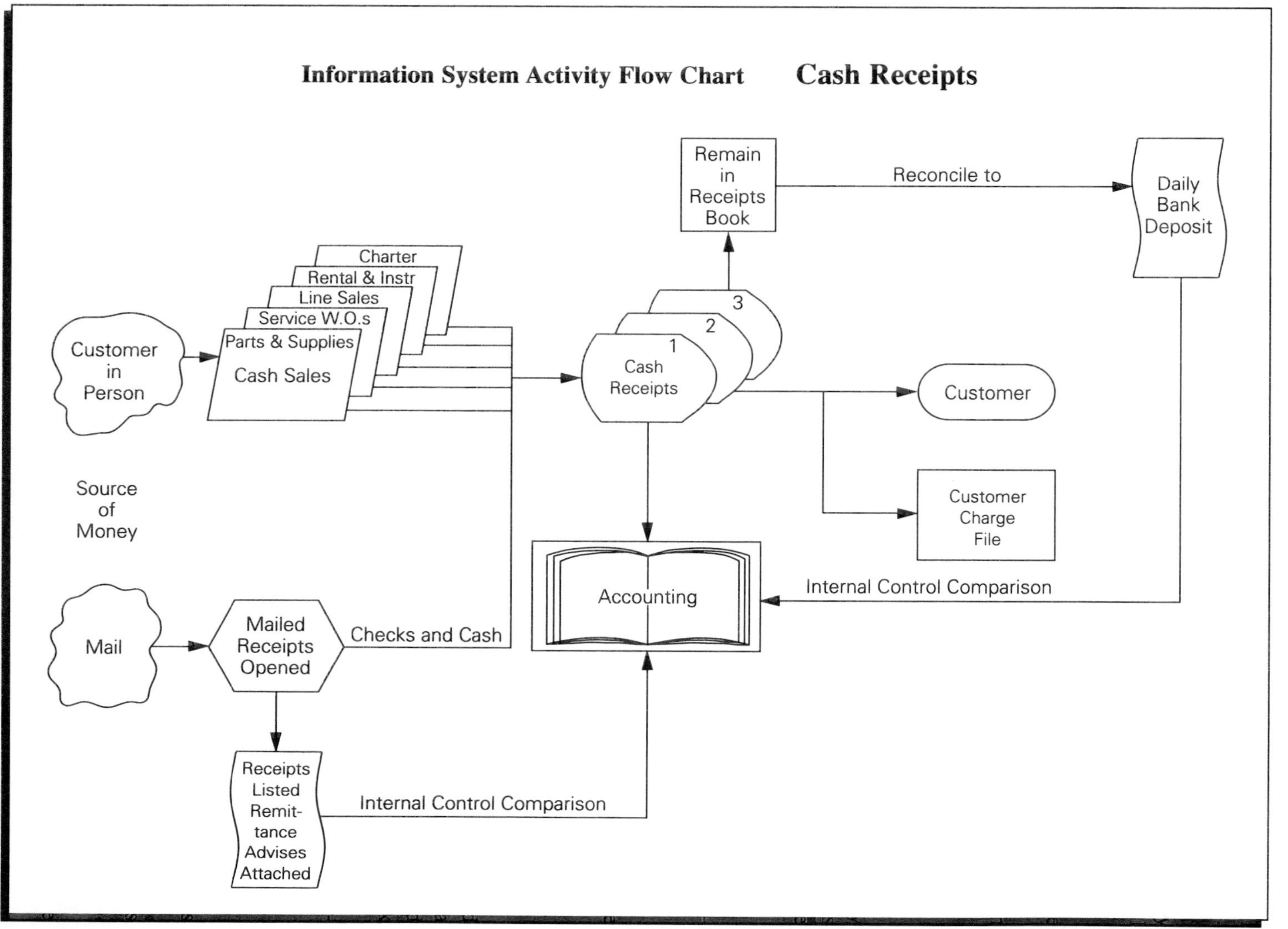
Information System Activity Flow Chart
Cash Receipts
Customer in Person
Charter
Rental & Instr
Line Sales
Service W.O.s
Parts & Supplies
Cash Sales
Source of Money
Mail
Mailed Receipts Opened
Checks and Cash
Receipts Listed Remit-tance Advises Attached
Internal Control Comparison
1
2
3
Cash Receipts
Remain in Receipts Book
Reconcile to
Daily Bank Deposit
Customer
Customer Charge File
Accounting
Internal Control Comparison

Appendix V

Front Desk Procedures Manual

Philosophy of Operation

The reception desk is the "front window" of an aviation business. As such, it represents the organization to the public, to the customer, and to the employees. The basic philosophy of the front desk should be to demonstrate to customers that everything possible will be done to give the best aviation service in the area. The reception desk is the hub for all business conducted by the company and is the public relations center. the primary goal is to see that the customer receives the most efficient and courteous service possible. The secondary goal is to ensure that all company procedures and guidelines are followed in achieving a successful front-desk operation.

Daily Operating Schedule

■ 0000–0600	Reduced operations
■ 0600	Limited services available to early customers
■ 0700	Representatives for each department on hand
■ 0800–1200	All departments and functions staffed at normal capacity
■ 1200–1300	Lunch period
■ 1300–1700	All departments and functions staffed at normal capacity
■ 1700–2000	Limited services available, clean up, and prepare daily reports
■ 2000–2400	Reduced operations

(The specific activity scheduled for each period of the day will be considerably more detailed and with specific activities and individuals indicated for the guidance of desk personnel.)

Customer Reception

The customer may approach the business by foot, by ground vehicle, or by aircraft. The front desk should regard all contacts, from any source, as customers and prepare to treat them in a courteous and efficient manner. Full recognition should be made of the fact that personnel staffing the desk, in the eyes of the customer, are "the company." In order to properly deal with the customer, it is mandatory that the contents of this manual be thoroughly understood and that the organization structure, activities, and personnel be known.

The physical aspects of the front office should be designed to be as attractive as possible and should be kept clean and operational at all times. All personnel should be trained in greeting and dealing with

By permission, Montgomery Aviation Corporation, Montgomery, Alabama.

customers. Every effort should be made to ensure that a pleasant, courteous, and efficient image is projected at all times.

Information and materials shall be kept readily available for customers on:

- Services provided by the company
- Basic price information for materials and services offered
- Key organization personnel—telephone numbers and addresses
- City and local maps
- Motel and hotel accommodations
- Local restuarants, entertainment, and points of interest
- Local transportation services
- Aviation facilities
- Recreation facilities

Departmental Relationships and Responsibilities

In a very real sense the front desk is a representative of and a spokesperson for all the departments in the organization. As such, the front-desk personnel should be very cognizant of the personnel, capabilities, and responsibilities of the departments. The organizational relationships between various departments and the key personnel are depicted in the following chart:

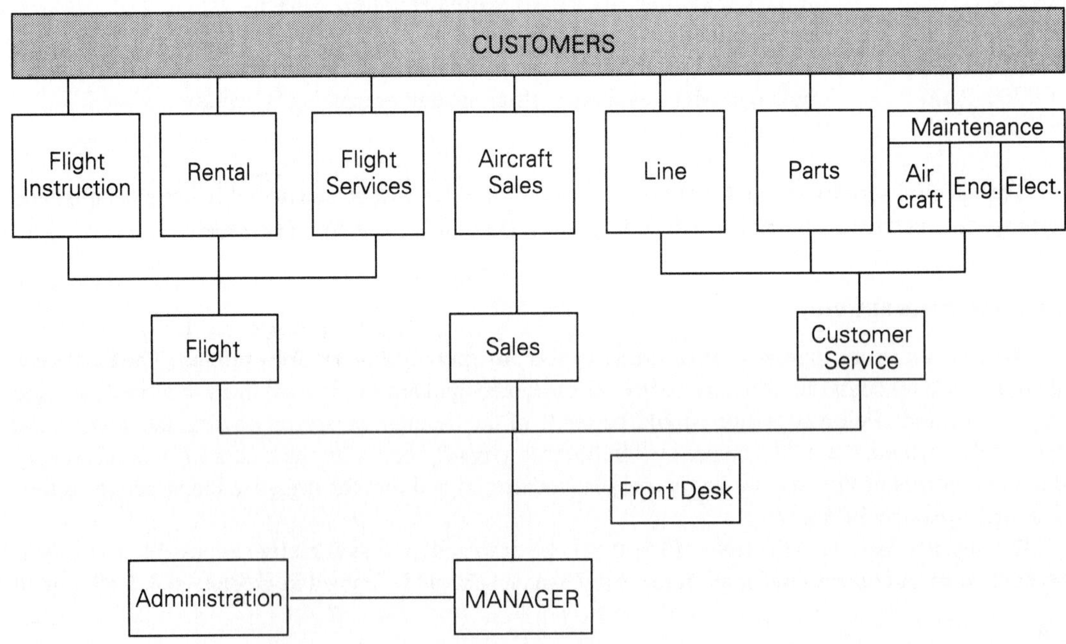

The assigned responsibilities of each of the departments includes the following:

1. *Administrative.* Personnel records and services, accounting, internal records.
2. *Customer services.* Line service, engine and aircraft service, parts, inventory.
3. *Instruction.* Syllabus, records, schedules, course sales.
4. *Flight service.* Rental, charter, special mission, air taxi.
5. *Sales.* New and used aircraft sales, avionics, and related equipment sales.

Information System Requirements

The internal information system has been designed and developed tp provide management with the financial and operational data required for the efficient operation of the business. The front desk is instrumental in the initiation, collection and routing of much of the required data. In addition, front-desk personnel can do much to ensure that departmental data are accurate and timely.

Front-desk personnel will, in the course of work, come in contact with many forms and records. Familiarity with these forms is essential to the successful operation of the front desk.

Following are the forms and records most likely used:

- Gasoline credit cards
- Aircraft rental agreements
- Aircraft schedule sheets
- Aircraft record sheets
- Pilot licenses
- Automobile rental forms
- Cash sales tickets
- Cash drawer forms
- Accident reports
- Approved credit file
- Application for FCC license

Accounting System Information

Many of the forms handled by front-desk personnel must be completed using accounting system numbers and terminology. It is imperative that this be done consistently and accurately. The information system includes a chart of accounts, with assigned numbers, to be used in recording transactions and keeping the necessary records. The most frequently used account numbers for front desk personnel are:

No.	Description of Account	Form or Record	Departmental Codes
707	Pilot supplies	Cash sales	C—Aircraft sales
706	Tie down	Cash sales	D—Parts
701	Gas and oil—internal	Charge customers	E—Service
609	Flight service—internal	Gas sales summary	F—Flight
			G—Line
			Z—General and administration

Interdepartmental Billing

Many products and services normally billed to customers are also used by departments for internal consumption or use. It is necessary that this utilization be clearly identified and the proper billing procedure followed. Typical transactions might include:

Aviation fuel:
- Flight training activity
- Rented aircraft
- Air-taxi operations
- Aircraft sales
- Power line, forest patrol
- Charter
- Air ambulance

Vehicle fuel:
- Fuel trucks
- Line vehicles
- Courtesy car
- Rental car

Service activity:
- Washing aircraft
- Maintenance work
- Telephone charges

It is the responsibility of front desk personnel to ensure that proper action is taken to bill the correct department for each transaction, using the proper forms and the correct account number.

Company Policies and Procedures

The following company policies and procedures should be adhered to by all front-desk personnel:

1. Our company feels that the customer should receive the best aviation service in the area, and a major effort should be exerted to see that this is achieved.
2. Safety, in all aspects of the business, is of primary concern to the company. Safety of all employees, customers, and the public shall be regarded as the standard of operation for all departments.
3. The accident checklist shall be completed as expeditiously as possible for all accidents involving company personnel or equipment.
4. Credit can be extended only to those customers who have established an account with the company. Customers desiring to establish such an account must make application with the management. A list of established credit accounts will be maintained for the guidance of front-desk personnel and all departments.
5. Aircraft can be rented only to pilots who have been approved by a company check pilot. This approval must be based upon:
   a. Demonstration of knowledge of operational features and systems of aircraft (may require oral and written examination of specific aircraft)
   b. Flight check out in the aircraft for the specific type flight activity

6. Prior to each rental period, the individual at the front desk must check to see that the pre-rental requirements have been complied with and the checklist completed. The post-rental checklist will be completed when the aircraft returns.

Emergency Procedures

As the hub of the activity for the organization, the front desk will undoubtedly observe or be notified quickly of emergencies involving company equipment or personnel. Possible emergency situations include:

1. Fire in buildings, equipment, or aircraft
2. Aircraft accidents involving customers, company aircraft, or personnel on the field or away from the field
3. Accidents involving company equipment, vehicles, and personnel
4. Impending hazardous weather situations
5. Loss of power or other utilities affecting business operations

In the event that an emergency situation is reported or observed, front-desk personnel will immediately take the action outlined in the Operational Checklist for the type of situation existing.

Company Personnel Guidelines

The company, in an effort to maintain the image of an efficient, professional activity and to provide individual employees with the opportunity to reach a high level of personal satisfaction, has developed personnel guidelines, procedures, and programs. The front desk has the specific responsibility for understanding and complying with these directives in the operation of front-desk activities and, as the center of activity for the overall organization, to monitor general compliance with the directives. Major emphasis should be given to the following checklists, job descriptions, and personnel programs:

- Handling incoming aircraft customers
- Servicing transient and local aircraft
- Front-desk manager job description
- Flight-line hostess job description
- Line-crew job description
- Front-desk operator job description
- Organization personnel assignments
- Departmental working schedules
- Employee personnel programs

Operational Checklist

To assist front-desk personnel in conducting an efficient and professional operation, the following Operational Checklists are provided. All personnel are encouraged to review these lists periodically and ensure that they are followed when conducting activities in either a normal situation or in an emergency:

A. Aircraft accident procedures
B. General accident procedures
   1. Equipment
   2. Personnel
C. Fire procedures
D. Hazardous weather procedures
E. Procedures for loss of power or other utilities
F. Cash handling procedures
G. Credit handling procedures
H. Renting automobiles
J. Interdepartmental billings
K. Transient pilot services
L. Detailed desk operating checklists:
   1. Cash check out
   2. Closing checklist for afternoon shift
   3. Checklist for night shift
   4. Checklist for early shift
M. Dealing with:
   1. Holdups
   2. Intoxicated persons
   3. Unhappy people
   4. Stolen aircraft

(Specific checklists for individual businesses should be added, similar to the following.)

A. Aircraft Accident Procedures

Accidents occur infrequently, but when they happen, events move rapidly, time is extremely important, and involved personnel can become very emotional. In order to ensure that all required and desirable action is taken as expeditiously as possible, the following steps should be taken:

1. Ensure that all personnel physically involved in the accident are provided immediate medical attention.
   Crash crew Telephone Number ______________________
   Ambulance Telephone Number ______________________
   Doctor Telephone Number ______________________
   Fire Telephone Number ______________________
2. Notify manager with pertinent details.
   What?
   Where?
   Who?
3. Initiate the following action if requested by manager. If unable to contact manager, complete as much as possible and advise manager later.
   a. Provide for physical security of damaged aircraft. Post guards as necessary. Notify nearest FAA GADO office.

b. Develop a list of all personnel concerned. List eyewitnesses and observers. Obtain statements from witnesses.
c. Have pertinent photographs taken.
d. Notify insurance carrier
   Telephone Number ___________________________
e. Notify company counsel
f. Refer any requests for information from news media to FAA and/or to the manager. Maintain good relations.
g. Cooperate with airport management, FAA, and NTSB in all matters related to accident.

B. General Accident Procedures

The organization is concerned with two categories of accidents: (1) those involving equipment and (2) those involving only personnel, such as personal injury due to falling, and so on. The procedures follow essentially the same guidelines:

1. Ensure that all personnel physically involved in the accident are provided immediate attention.
   First Aid Telephone Number ___________________________
   Doctor Telephone Number ___________________________
   Ambulance Telephone Number ___________________________
2. Notify the manager with pertinent details.
   What?
   Where?
   Who?
3. Initiate the following action if requested by manager. If unable to contact manager, complete as much as possible and advise manager later.
   a. Develop a list of all personnel concerned. List eyewitnesses and observers. Obtain statements from witnesses.
   b. Have photographs taken of equipment involved and the damage.
   c. Provide for security of equipment and for movement if required.
   d. Notify insurance carrier.
   e. Notify workmen's compensation agent.

C. Fire Procedures

In the event fire is noted, reported, or suspected in any of the company facilities, equipment, or spaces, comply with the following procedures:

1. Sound fire alarm. Report fire to manager and appropriate department.
2. Report fire to fire station. Telephone Number ___________________________
3. Assure that personnel on the scene are fighting or containing the fire using local equipment.
4. Provide for security of nearby equipment or material, moving if necessary.
5. Maintain constant vigilance for safety of personnel. Provide medical attention to all individuals requiring assistance.
6. After fire is under control, develop a list of all personnel involved, including eyewitnesses and observers—obtain statements from each.
7. Take photographs as needed to record pertinent information.

D. Hazardous Weather Procedures

Company operations, equipment, and personnel are influenced by weather factors, subjecting them to dangers of physical and personal damage. This includes high winds, freezing rain, snow, low visibility, flood, and blowing sand. The front desk, as part of the daily routine, should check the weather situation and remain cognizant of the trends as they might affect aircraft, equipment, buildings, and personnel. The following general procedures shall be used as a guide along with specific activities related to the particular type of weather.

1. Upon receipt of the notice that hazardous weather conditions are coming, alert all departments of the threat and advise the manager of this action.
2. Caution pilots flying or about to fly of the impending threat.
3. Check to see if student activity is being monitored by the flight department.
4. Tour ramp, hangar, and other areas to see if necessary precautionary action has been taken. Aircraft should be secured or stored, doors closed, loose articles or equipment secured or stored. Advise departments on recommendations.
5. Review rental aircraft activity and schedule. Consider canceling as necessary.
6. During period of hazardous weather, monitor the condition of aircraft and facilities to ensure that all possible action is being taken to properly maintain all company property.
7. Notify aircraft owners.

E. Loss of Utilities

The modern aviation activity as a sophisticated business depends heavily upon the uninterrupted supply of all utilities: electricity, water, oil, gas, or telephone. In the event of a utility loss, scheduled or otherwise, it is necessary that action be taken to minimize the effect of the disruption. The following guidelines should be reviewed and appropriate action taken:

1. Review the loss situation and determine the potential threats. For example:
   Loss of water—fire protection, restrooms, water fountains, washing aircraft, and so forth
   Loss of electricity—no lights, no refrigeration, no electric machines or test equipment, no power for doors, no air conditioning, and so on
   Loss of radio—effect on communication, traffic control
   Loss of oil, gas—effect on heat, air conditioning
   Loss of telephone—effect on scheduling, customers
   Loss of alarm systems—fire, security, and so on
2. Take action appropriate to type of loss.
   a. Advise all departments—time and duration, if anticipated.
   b. Alert customers if warning of loss is provided. Provide signs and notices for facilities not operating. Call appropriate utility service department if loss is unscheduled. Notify, request assistance, and attempt to determine time involved.

Appendix VI

Operating Procedure Guide Gordon's Piper Sales

Introduction

The Operating Procedure Guide is designed to provide a positive framework for conducting the day-by-day business of Gordon's Piper Sales. This framework is intended to help create a successful business and guide all personnel in achieving a safer, more efficient operation.

The Guide establishes basic policies, sets the tone for an efficient operation and provides definite guidance in critical areas. It is to become required reading by all employees and a part of the organization's training program. A record is to be kept of all employees receiving and reading this Guide.

General Provisions

Policy

The material contained in this Guide is considered to be the basic framework for operating policy. It is the responsibility of all employees to read and understand the Guide and to implement those portions which are pertinent to or are part of their normal job assignment.

The Guide is considered an effective means for establishing the tone of an efficient aviation organization and providing specific guidelines which have been found to be successful. The two basic concerns are felt to be *safety* and *profitability.*

Safety is considered of prime importance! It is the keystone of a successful business. The field of aviation must place major emphasis upon safe operations because many potential hazards exist, requiring constant surveillance. No activity is to be undertaken, and no personnel or equipment utilized in any effort unless the activity can be carried through to a safe conclusion.

Profitability is the major goal of Gordon's Piper Sales. This goal is subservient to safety, primarily because potential accidents are frequently unforgiving in terms of life and property. Fortunately, it has been found that safe aviation operations are the more profitable ones. The combination of these two elements is found in the well-managed, efficient operation, which achieves the goals of the organization and those of the individual members of the organization.

Both safety and profitability are considered the responsibility of every member of the organization.

Status of This Guide

All operations will be conducted in accordance with the provisions of this Operating Procedure Guide.

Specific operating procedures are available for the individual departments and for the major functions of the business. Questions on procedures not clearly covered will be directed to responsible management.

Basic Procedures

All employees will participate in developing safe operating procedures which guide their daily operations. Safety is everyone's business.

All employees are expected to participate in developing an efficient, effective organization.

All non-pilot employees will be required to read and endorse the safety rules and regulations which relate to their specific job activities.

All company pilot employees will be required to read and comply with flight operation rules.

All student pilots will be required to read and endorse flight operation rules and student procedures.

Renter pilots will be required to read and endorse company flight operation rules and procedures to be followed by renting pilots.

Passengers in company aircraft will be provided a copy of company instructions to passengers.

Safety of Customers and Visitors

It is the responsibility of all employees to assure the personal safety of all customers, passengers, visitors and other persons while on the property.

Facilities and Equipment

All facilities and equipment are to be kept spotlessly clean. This is necessary for an effective aviation business.

Ground equipment will be checked routinely to ensure readiness. Aircraft will be provided all the services required to maintain safe, efficient, operating units.

Planning

Planning is considered essential in maintaining a safe and profitable organization. It is a necessary component of every job and consequently a responsibility of each employee. Each person should plan to conduct his assigned tasks by ensuring that he has the necessary materials on hand and should contribute to overall company plans in every way possible.

Administration

General

A successful business can only be achieved through the combined efforts of all personnel. To achieve the desired level of success every employee should be knowledgeable about all programs and assist in achieving overall organization goals. Individuals will naturally have a primary concern for their assigned duties such as flight line, instruction, sales, etc.

Supervisors will have major responsibilities for their assigned areas, but should also assist in maintaining desired standards throughout the organization.

Personnel

The principal objective of any company is to make a profit. These profits are not for an impersonal company, but for people—people who have put forth their hard earned savings as an investment, or who are contributing their time and talent. People, then, are the source of profit generation and the recipients of profits themselves. In this light, they are the primary factor in determining the success of the organization. This success is determined by individual ability and by collective teamwork.

The goal of this company is to create an environment where the individual and the group can function with maximum effectiveness in achieving individual and company goals of profitability.

Payroll

Payroll record keeping is a necessary administrative procedure, necessary for the company, the individual, and for legal matters. Each employee has the responsibility to assist in accurate time keeping in order to meet internal and external requirements. Labor is a major cost factor and revenue generator; consequently the individual responsibility for total business success becomes a major element in achieving that success.

Credit

It is customary practice for a business to extend credit to customers in good standing. The limit of this credit depends upon several variables such as the product, rating of customer and the capability of the company to carry the credit. Credit is realistically a business operation, not a social activity. All employees should be aware of the problems in extending credit and assist the company in implementing the credit policy and keeping this area within control.

Front Desk Receptionist

Customers arriving by air, by street or via the telephone are frequently given their impression of the organization by the receptionist. This position is a key one in the organization. It is necessary that all employees cooperate with the front desk in conducting day-by-day business in order that the receptionist have the necessary information to do the job properly.

Records

It is the goal of the company to maintain those records and regulations which are necessary for the operation of an efficient, safe organization. The main office will maintain the master copy of all instructions and procedures. Departments will be responsible for maintaining those records, procedures and regulations which relate to their area, and for the successful implementation of individual programs.

Marketing

General

In order to be a successful aviation business, it is necessary that all personnel at Gordon's Piper Sales have a strong marketing orientation. This means that every employee should be customer-oriented, and recognize the importance of understanding and meeting the customers' needs.

Sales

Gordon's Piper Sales makes its various products available to the customer. These are new Piper aircraft, fuel, oil, service, parts, storage, instruction, technical expertise and convenience.

Every employee is a representative of the company at all times and a specific salesperson for his or her assigned area of specialty.

Aircraft sales, as a major company activity, requires special emphasis coupled with aircraft knowledge and selling skills. The sales manager is responsible for conducting an aggressive sales program with a major concern for safety of operations and procedures. Aircraft demonstrations shall be conducted with maximum attention to safety. Prospective buyers will be allowed to fly company aircraft only with qualified company pilots or after meeting normal renter pilot requirements.

Responsibilities

Every employee has the responsibility to acquire the technical skill in his area, as well as the selling skill necessary to deal successfully with the customer.

Training

A special effort shall be made to train all employees in the salesmanship skills required by their job.

Flight Line

General

The primary goal of the flight line is to provide satisfactory, safe, efficient and profitable service to the line customer.

Appearance

The image initially created by the physical appearance of the flight line, its equipment, and the assigned personnel is tremendously important. Every effort will be made to present a pleasing situation to the customer. Flight line personnel are the first to greet customers arriving by air. In addition to creating a favorable initial impression, they must coordinate closely with the front desk receptionist.

The layout of the flight line will be clearly marked for the benefit of all customers and maintained in a neat and attractive manner.

All equipment used on the flight line such as fuel trucks, towing equipment, pumps and other equipment will be kept clean and in good operating condition.

Personnel assigned line duties will be required to wear distinctive clothing when on duty. Such clothing is to assist the customer in identifying line personnel and to create the initial impression of a professional line service interested in serving the customer's needs.

Service

The goal is to anticipate the service needs of prospective line customers and to meet those needs within the resources of the company. These needs typically include:

1. Incoming directions
2. Parking and securing aircraft
3. Fuel and oil
4. Line maintenance
5. Local information
6. Ground transportation
7. Shop maintenance
8. Supporting supplies
9. Weather information
10. Flight planning assistance
11. Departing directions and assistance

Special effort is to be made by all line personnel in greeting and providing service to customers in a professional manner. Standard signals will be used to direct all incoming and departing aircraft.

Facilities

The impression of the total facility upon the customer, either transient or local, is a most important factor. Every effort within available resources will be made to present a favorable image. Such an image includes professional personnel, cleanliness, pleasing appearance and safety consciousness.

Safety

Safety will always be provided primary emphasis at Gordon's Piper Sales. The flight line will be inspected daily to ensure that all assigned equipment is in a fully operational condition. Checklists will be utilized to ensure routine thoroughness of the review of all safety features.

Fire fighting equipment shall be serviced and available at designated key points.

Fuel storage tanks and mobile refueling units will be checked daily for fuel contamination and a written record maintained of such checks.

For each fueling and defueling operation, a grounding cable will be in use and a fire extinguisher readily available. As a standard practice, fuel trucks will always be driven forward, never backed up. When not in use, the trucks will be parked in the designated parking area.

Aircraft will not be towed or moved unless sufficient personnel are present and available to make the move safely.

Customer-owned aircraft will be moved or taxied by qualified personnel only.

The standard procedure is to keep all aircraft, except when in actual use, either hangared or securely chocked and tied down with the controls locked. Line service personnel shall be responsible for securing aircraft and for safeguarding them from the effects of inclement weather.

Training

All line personnel will be required to complete a training program covering the various phases of flight line operations. This program will include:

1. Standard operations and procedures
2. Safety precautions
3. Equipment operations
4. Handling customers

Service

Policy

It will be the general policy of Gordon's Piper Sales to provide aircraft service with the following considerations:

1. Customer satisfaction
2. Quality work
3. Safe shop operation
4. Profitable department

Personnel

Every effort will be made to ensure that properly trained personnel are assigned each job. Supervision will be provided to ensure adequate on-the job review for quality work, timely completion and thorough records.

Training

Service personnel will be provided the training opportunity to become proficient in servicing those aircraft accepted for repair. Continued on-the-job training and upgrading are considered necessary activities.

Quality

An independent service inspection program will be utilized to maintain quality control of all work performed and to release all work at its completion.

Shop and Equipment

Adequate tools and equipment will be provided for the level of work to be accepted by the shop. Assigned personnel will be responsible for properly maintaining the available items and assuring that they will be usable at all times.

The shop layout will be designed in such a manner as to ensure safe, efficient operation. Work will not be accepted if the shop is not properly equipped to handle it, nor will hazardous makeshift arrangements be utilized in lieu of proper equipment.

Every service employee will be responsible for a high level of shop safety, ensuring that safety guards, glasses, shields and procedures are utilized as a routine procedure. Service supervisors will provide assistance in ensuring the operation of a safe shop.

Adequate first-aid equipment will be maintained and available to shop personnel.

Separate storage facilities will be established outside of, and isolated from, other buildings for the storage of oil, grease, paint and other combustible material.

Special precautions will be carried out prior to conducting any painting and welding operations in order to reduce hazards and make the operation safe.

Parts

Parts and parts control play an extremely important role in service activity. The parts inventory represents a major investment of funds, influences customer satisfaction and presents major problems in administration. All employees, both in the service department and elsewhere, are expected to be aware of these problems and to contribute to cooperative means of solving them.

Flight Instruction

General

The primary goal of the Flight Center is to provide flight instruction of the highest quality in the safest possible manner and at an acceptable profit level.

Ground Instruction

The Piper Flite Center coordinated curriculum shall be the basis for the ground instruction offered by this organization. The courses are very flexible and may be offered as a coordinated program, as a classroom program or taught on an individual basis. As a coordinated program it is a highly developed study and flight program, using a step-by-step progression, designed to capitalize on the building block method of learning.

Each student shall have available the necessary books, supplies, and equipment to be utilized during the scheduled ground school.

Flight Instruction

The Piper Flite Center syllabus shall be used as the basis for flight instruction conducted at this organization.

The chief flight instructor shall be responsible for supervising all flight instructors. This includes safety of operations, compliance with regulations, proper record keeping, sound instruction techniques, customer satisfaction and profitable operations.

Each student under instruction will have personally available an Aircraft Owner's Manual for the aircraft in which he or she is training.

Personnel

All flight instructors employed by the company shall hold at least a valid commercial airman certificate and a commercial flight instructor certificate, both of which shall reflect proper ratings in subjects and aircraft categories in which the instructor is to instruct. They shall meet the requirements of FAR Part 141 for flight instructors.

All flight instructors must be current in aircraft and subjects in which they instruct. They must also complete an annual recheck with the chief flight instructor and/or the FAA, demonstrating their continued proficiency in instruction.

Flight instructors must complete extra study in the subject of "the psychology of learning" or a closely related topic.

All ground school instructors shall hold at least a private certificate. Those teaching instrument ground school shall hold a valid instrument ground school certificate.

Operations

All flight instruction operations shall be conducted with a primary concern for the safety of personnel and equipment. The chief flight instructor shall be directly responsible for ensuring the safety of all flight operations.

All student flight operations must be cleared by a flight instructor present on the airport at the time of the flight.

A flight instructor must be inside the aircraft with pre-solo students during engine starts.

In all phases of flight training, the use of checklists will be heavily emphasized as standard operating procedure.

Prior to the first solo flight, each student will be examined concerning knowledge and understanding of:

1. Company flight operation rules
2. Airport traffic rules
3. FAA air traffic rules
4. Aircraft owner's manual
5. Basic safety rules

Student pilots will be checked out prior to each solo flight until they have accumulated a minimum of 10 solo hours.

Aircraft will be operated in accordance with the provisions of the aircraft flight manual and the approved flight syllabus.

Flight Services

General

Gordon's Piper Sales offers the customer a wide variety of flight services including rental, charter, sightseeing, photographic flights and pilot services. The primary goal of Flight Services is to provide customers the desired flight activity of the highest quality with maximum attention to safety, at the desired profit level.

Rental/Charter

The chief pilot is responsible for all rental and charter operations. He or she shall provide for adequate procedures and records to ensure pilot competence and currency, equipment readiness, and satisfactory weather conditions, prior to releasing aircraft.

Aircraft will be rented only to pilots who show:

1. Adequate identification
2. Evidence of financial and personal responsibility
3. Evidence of past experience and proficiency
4. Valid pilot certificate
5. Current medical certificate

In addition to meeting FAA proficiency requirements, renter pilots will be given a flight checkout for specific types of operations, such as:

1. Day VFR local
2. Day VFR cross-country
3. Night VFR local
4. Night VFR cross-country
5. Instrument flight

Specific restrictions may be imposed as deemed necessary by the check pilot. A recheck will be required if the renter pilot's experience is more than 60 days old.

A special emphasis will be placed on the use of checklists by all rental pilots. Failure to use the checklist will result in refusal to rent.

A rental operation will never be allowed to become a "charter" operation due to liability problems.

Charter pilots must meet the following qualifications:

- Single engine: Commercial certificate
Instrument rating
- Multi-engine: Commercial certificate
Instrument rating
Multi-engine rating
- All: Required proficiency levels and
flight checks of current FAR's

Charter flights will be operated under the stipulation of the FAR portions regulating the type flight. The following conditions also apply:

Single engine aircraft:

1. No night IFR is authorized
2. No operation in known icing conditions

3. IFR flight plan routinely
4. Required aircraft equipment

Multi-engine aircraft:

1. Pilot and co-pilot for FAA approved minimums
2. No more than light icing forecast for climb-out and let-down; cruise at non-icing levels
3. IFR in high density areas requires a co-pilot
4. IFR flight plan routinely
5. Required aircraft equipment

Special Missions

The organization may, on occasion, undertake a special flight mission of an aviation services nature. Possible special missions include:

1. Sightseeing
2. Aerial spraying
3. Photographic work
4. Banner towing
5. Power line inspection
6. Forest patrol

Special missions will be approved by the chief pilot and will be undertaken with the same concern for safety, quality of work and profitability as there is for other flight services. By the very nature of the work involved there is additional exposure in this type activity; consequently greater attention will be paid to safety checks and operating procedures related to this exposure. Insurance verification of special coverage should be obtained in each instance.

Ground Operations

General

Ground operations refer to all vehicle and personnel ground activities which are in support of aviation activity and overall company goals. Driving the courtesy car, renting vehicles or assisting customers with luggage are examples. The primary guideline for all employees is to recognize the importance of the customer and to conduct all activities such that his needs are met in a safe and efficient manner.

Vehicle Operation

Operators of all vehicles shall have a valid license for the vehicle being operated and shall have been checked out in the specific piece of equipment. The main office shall maintain a record of qualified personnel.

Vehicles shall be operated below the posted speed limit for the type activity, but never in excess of prudent limits or in a reckless manner.

Private vehicles shall not be permitted upon the aircraft ramp without the permission of, and under the supervision of, line personnel. Permission will normally be granted only for loading and unloading of aircraft.

Control

General

Gordon's Piper Sales is a viable dynamic business facing many challenges. Each business area such as service, instruction or fuel sales has specific goals to be achieved. Controls should be considered as tools to be used in measuring progress toward selected goals. Since goals are individual as well as organizational, controls then become the responsibility of individual employees as well as the organization.

Necessity of Planning

A prerequisite of effective controlling is the development of a plan of action. For each business area there is a plan. A specific number of gallons of fuel will be sold each month. An anticipated number of service hours will be charged out each week. A specific number of aircraft will be sold each month. With a plan for each area, specific controls can be utilized to measure progress toward successful achievement. Each employee has a responsibility to plan for his work area and to contribute to the overall company plan.

Responsibility

Every employee is responsible for exercising control over his assigned work area. The controls used will vary with each specific instance, but will remain a part of each job assignment.

Types of Control

Gordon's Piper Sales uses a variety of controls to assist employees in their work. Controls will vary with each job, but the following are possible tools to be used:

1. *Records*—of sales, expenses, volume, movement, or time
2. *Reports*—routine summaries, special action
3. *Budgets*—of time, or dollars
4. *Prior approval*—for certain designated activities
5. *Financial statements*—by department or entire business

Controls may be designed to cover:

1. Expenses
2. Income
3. Quality of work
4. Financial matters
5. Safety of operation
6. Human Resources
7. Specific operations or activities

Gordon's Piper Sales
Flight Operation Rules

General

All company aircraft will be operated according to the FAA regulations concerning the type of operation being conducted.

Local airport and area traffic procedures and rules will be adhered to as standard operating procedure.

Company flight operation rules for the type pilots, aircraft and weather will be followed at all times.

The chief pilot will be responsible for ensuring that company aircraft are operated in accordance with FAA, airport and company rules, regulations, and procedures.

Individual pilots in charge of aircraft have the ultimate responsibility for complying with the controlling rules and regulations. Company pilots are expected to follow these rules personally and to promote adherence by other pilots using company planes.

Operation of all aircraft belonging to this company must be approved by the chief pilot or his designated representative.

No company aircraft will be operated with any known malfunction unless approved by the chief pilot or his representative.

No off-airport landings will be made unless authorized by the chief pilot.

All cross-country flights will operate on a flight plan as standard operating procedure.

Student Pilots

All student flights will be made in accordance with appropriate FAR's.

All student flights must be cleared by a company flight instructor and be under his supervision. This supervision shall include knowledge of wind direction and velocity, and all other factors affecting the safety of local or destination flight conditions.

Cross-country flights will land only at airports approved by the flight instructor clearing the flight, except in an emergency.

Renter Pilots

All flights by renter pilots must be cleared by the chief pilot or his designated representative. Such clearance will include:

1. Adequate identification
2. Evidence of responsibility
3. Evidence of experience and proficiency
4. Valid pilot certificate
5. Current medical certificate

Flight checks will be made for the specific type operation involved in the rental activity.

Prior to departure the renter pilot shall complete the renter pilot agreement.

When company aircraft are away from the home base, the renter pilot is responsible for making arrangements for and supervising the storage or tie-down of the aircraft.

Sample—Employer Acknowledgment Form

Gordon's Piper Sales

____
Date

To: ____________________________
(employee)

In order to more effectively coordinate the efforts of Gordon's Piper Sales and to create a more efficient activity, it was felt desirable to develop the Operating Procedure Guide.

It is the responsibility of every employee of this company to be aware of the provisions of this Guide and to use them in day-by-day operations. Suggestions for improving the contents and creating a better outline for operations are requested just as is your compliance with the existing Guide expected.

If you have any questions on the manual after reading the contents, please check with your supervisor. This copy of the Guide is for your personal library and for use as a member of the organization. This signed acknowledgment will be kept in your personnel folder.

____
(Signature)

I have read and understood the Company Operating Procedure Guide.

____
(signature)

____
(date)

Appendix VII

Operations Manual
Atlas Aircraft Corporation
Denver, Colorado

Preface

This manual is for the use and guidance of all flight operations, ground operations, and maintenance personnel employed by Atlas Aircraft Corporation. Compliance is mandatory. The chief or director of each duty section is responsible for ensuring the personnel under his control have read, and do comply with, this Manual. Distribution will be made as indicated on the revision record sheet. Revisions pertinent to a duty section, are the responsibility of the chief of that section and will be coordinated with the president of the corporation before printing and distribution.

Distribution:

President	—2	Maint.	—1
Master	—1	Ground Op.	—1
Aircraft	—1 Each	FAA	—2
Flt. Ops.	—2		

Revision Record

Revision Number	Date Inserted	Inserted By	Revision Number	Date Inserted	Inserted By
1.			13.		
2.			14.		
3.			15.		
4.			16.		
5.			17.		
6.			18.		
7.			19.		
8.			20.		
9.			21.		
10.			22.		
11.			23.		
12.			24.		

Courtesy of Atlas Aircraft Corporation, Denver, Colorado

Operations Manual
Atlas Aircraft Corporation
Denver, Colorado

1 February 73

Responsibilities of Officers

President

The president is responsible for the entire operation of the corporation and for coordination of all department activities, to ensure a smooth functioning operation.

Chief Pilot

The chief pilot is responsible for the management of the corporation's policies and compliance with all laws, rates, requirements and regulations governing air taxi (135) operations as applicable to the corporation under its charter and certificate.

He is responsible for the safe and efficient air taxi flight operation of all aircraft owned or leased by the corporation.

He is responsible for the completion and proper disposition of the corporation air taxi operating records. He will act as liason between the FAA and the corporation in all matters pertaining to air taxi operations.

He is responsible, under air taxi operations, for the supervision and scheduling of pilot personnel and aircraft.

The chief pilot will have the authority to hire and/or fire pilot personnel when such action is warranted, and is responsible for their training.

Director of Maintenance

The director of maintenance is responsible for the planning, organizing, and scheduling of maintenance and inspections. He is responsible for the maintenance records and the proper distribution of same. He will act as liason between the corporation and the FAA on maintenance matters.

Supercedes 27 December 1972

Operations Manual
Atlas Aircraft Corporation
Denver, Colorado

31 July 74

Corporation Organization

President .... ______________________
____
____

Chief Pilot .... ______________________
____
____

Director of Maintenance .... ______________________
____
____

Supercedes 15 July 73

Operations Manual
Atlas Aircraft Corporation
Denver, Colorado

1 February 73

Weight and Balance

The pilot in command will be responsible to see that gross weight and center of gravity is within the limits for his particular aircraft. Weight and balance computations will be accomplished in accordance with the manufacturers recommendations or the aircraft flight manual. The gross weight and c.g. condition for each flight shall be entered in appropriate spaces in Form AA-l.

Supercedes 1 May 70

United States of America
Federal Aviation Administration
Washington

Operations Specifications

Atlas Aircraft Corporation is authorized to conduct air taxi operations as an air carrier engaged in air transportation or commercial operation as a commercial operator, utilizing aircraft of 12,500 pounds or less maximum certificated takeoff weight, in accordance with the applicable provisions of Federal Aviation Regulations Part 135, other FARs, and the terms, conditions and limitations contained herein.

Operations are authorized in the following categories and classes of aircraft under the conditions and within the area of operations authorized.

- Airplane Single Engine Land, VFR, Day and Night, Passengers and Cargo
- Airplane Multi-engine Land, VFR and IFR Day and Night, Passengers and Cargo

Area of Operation

- Continental United States, including Alaska and Canada

Other Authorizations or Limitations

- Autopilot Authorization and Limitation

Use of an autopilot (Piper Model Altimatic V) installed in Piper PA-31P, N3TB, is authorized in lieu of a second pilot when passengers are carried under IFR or in actual IFR weather conditions and the pilot holds a current Statement of Competency Letter for instrument flight using autopilot.

- Autopilot Authorization

Use of an autopilot (Piper Model Altimatic V/FD) in Piper PA-23T, N40231, is authorized in lieu of second pilot when passengers are carried under IFR or in actual IFR weather conditions, and the pilot holds a current Statement of Competency Letter for instrument flight using autopilot.

Effective date ____________________

Operations Manual
Atlas Aircraft Corporation
Denver, Colorado

1 February 73

Accident, Incident, or Overdue Aircraft Reports

In the event of an accident, incident, or overdue aircraft, the pilot in command will comply with National Transportation Safety Board Regulation Part 830 and notify the chief pilot or his representative.

Supercedes 1 May 70

Operations Manual
Atlas Aircraft Corporation
Denver, Colorado

1 February 73

Airworthiness of Aircraft

No pilot in command shall accept any company aircraft for flight unless he has determined by checking the Form AA-l Book that the annual and 100-hour inspections are current (Form AA-l), the aircraft weighing and balance (3 yr) and altimeter and static system (2 yr) (stickers on inside cover of Form AA-l Book) are current, all applicable AD's (Form AA-3 on inside cover of Form AA-l Book) are compiled with and that the aircraft is certified airworthy for safe operation by an authorized mechanic.

Supercedes 1 May 70

Operations Manual
Atlas Aircraft Corporation
Denver, Colorado

1 February 73

Mechanical Discrepancy Reporting

1. When a discrepancy is discovered, the pilot in command or mechanic shall make an appropriate entry in the discrepancy reporting section of Form AA-l. The director of maintenance shall assign the corrective maintenance to the proper personnel and instruct them to sign the corrective action on the Form AA-l when completed.

   If there is a malfunction of a piece of equipment, such as radios, lights or other equipment that is not necessary for a particular flight or if a discrepancy is noted in the aircraft or its components that does not affect airworthiness or safety of flight, these items may be deferred. The procedures for handling discrepancies in this category are as follows:

   a. The pilot will note the problem in the discrepancy report column of Form AA-l .

   b. The director of maintenance or his representative will note in the corrective action column that the item is deferred and initial, then transfer that particular discrepancy to the "Deferred Discrepancy Form AA-4."

   c. Deferred discrepancies will be taken care of each 100-hour inspection or as soon as parts become available.

2. Form AA-l Page 409
3. Form AA-4 Page 410

Supercedes 5 April 72

Form AA-1

ATLAS AIRCRAFT CORPORATION—AIRCRAFT FLIGHT LOG

Pilot in Command	Co-Pilot	Type Aircraft	Date	Plane No.

Flite No.	Station		Departure		Arrival		Take-Off		Flying Time		Fuel		Oil Added		Station
	From	To	Time	Tach.	Time	Tach.	Weight	C.G.	Hours	Minutes	Added	Total	Left	Right	
Total Time This Trip															

	Airplane Total Time	Left Engine	Right Engine
Time Forward			
Time This Trip			
Total Time			
Next 100 Hr. Inspection Due			
Next Annual Inspection Due			

AIRCRAFT RELEASE

I hearby certify that the corrective action to all previous discrepancies is in accordance with maintenance requirements and the aircraft is hereby returned to service.

Signature ______________________ Dir. of Maint.

ACCEPTANCE

I have examined the five (5) previous discrepancy reports on this aircraft and do hereby accept this aircraft for service subject to preflight inspection.

Signature ______________________ Pilot in Command

No.	Discrepancy Reports	No.	Sta.	Corrective Action or Comment	Initial

P.I.C. Signature	Empty Weight		Empty Weight C.G.		Max. T/O Weight		Max. Land. Weight	
	Vor. No. 1 Check	360° / 180°	Vor. No. 2 Check	360° / 180°	Date		Station	

Deferred Discrepancies	Form AA-4
Discrepancy	**Corrective Action**

Operations Manual
Atlas Aircraft Corporation
Denver, Colorado

1 February 73

Determination of Previous Aircraft Irregularities

In the Form AA-l, the yellow and pink copies will remain attached until an entered discrepancy has been corrected by an authorized, certificated mechanic. Before accepting an aircraft for a flight the pilot in command will review Form AA-1 and AA-4 for discrepancies, current and deferred, to determine the aircraft airworthiness.

Supercedes 5 April 72

Operations Manual
Atlas Aircraft Corporation
Denver, Colorado

1 February 73

Maintenance Away from Atlas

1. When an aircraft requires maintenance away from Atlas, the following will apply:
   a. The pilot in command will be responsible for the following:
      (1) Notifying the director of maintenance and/or the chief pilot via telephone or most expeditious means of any discrepancy which requires repair before further flight.
      (2) Arrange for the correction of discrepancies by an authorized mechanic and ensure that the appropriate entries are made in the applicable log books or Form AA-1. The forms will be signed with the signature and license number of the mechanic.

Supercedes 5 April 72

Operations Manual
Atlas Aircraft Corporation
Denver, Colorado

1 February 73

Refueling of Aircraft

1. The pilot in command has the responsibility of the following items:
   a. Proper fuel load.
   b. Proper fuel grade.
   c. Sump drains will be checked for water contamination after refueling and on each originating flight.
   d. Check that aircraft is electrostatically protected during refueling.
   e. See that a fire extinguisher is available outside the aircraft during refueling operation.
   f. Determine if the aircraft was damaged during refueling and/or defueling. If aircraft was damaged, he is to take appropriate action.
2. General precautions while refueling are:
   a. No fueling or defueling should be done during electrical storms, occurring within five miles.
   b. Before fueling or defueling, all electrical switches shall be turned off and kept off during said operations.
   c. When passengers are permitted to remain in the cabin while refueling is being accomplished, a responsible cabin attendant or the pilot in command shall remain in the cabin or near the cabin door.
   d. No smoking and no fires or flames shall be permitted within fifty feet of the aircraft being serviced.
   e. In the event that fuel is spilled, extra precautions should be taken to make certain that sufficient time has elapsed for complete dissipation of fumes before the battery master switch or outside power connection is changed; also, if spillage is excessive and ground or ramp is covered with gasoline, flood the area with water and/or chemicals as required, or move the aircraft away from the area.

Supercedes 1 May 70

Operations Manual
Atlas Aircraft Corporation
Denver, Colorado

1 February 73

Flight Locating Procedures

The pilot in command will file a flight plan with Flight Service (VFR) or Air Traffic Control (IFR). Normally these flight plans will be filed prior to flight, however, they may be filed by radio after becoming airborne if necessary. The pilot (PIC) in command is responsible to close VFR flight plans after flight is terminated.

Supercedes 1 May 70

Operations Manual
Atlas Aircraft Corporation
Denver, Colorado

1 February73

Emergency Procedures

In-Flight Emergencies

The pilot in command will utilize the emergency procedures prescribed by the aircraft manufacturer where applicable. Emergencies involving the loss of radio communication will use the appropriate procedures outlined in FAR 91.127. Other emergencies for which an established procedure is not outlined will be handled by the PIC so as to provide the passengers and crew with a maximum level of safety for the existing conditions. This may include, but is not limited to, unscheduled stops for passengers who have become ill, the need for procuring medical assistance, advising ATC of the nature of the emergency, if necessary, and other actions to assure the safety of those on board.

Ground Emergencies

These may be of a varied nature and the PIC will request the assistance of local airport fire and crash crews as necessary. Passenger and crew safety is emphasized and appropriate action will be utilized by the PIC for this purpose.

Reporting of Emergencies

Those emergencies involving deviations from the FAR's will be reported in accordance with FAR 135.7.

Supercedes 1 May 70

Operations Manual
Atlas Aircraft Corporation
Denver, Colorado

1 February 73

Pilot in Command Route Qualifications

1. Atlas Aircraft Corporation pilots in command will not depart on an IFR charter flight unless during the past 12 months he has completed a route flight check administered by an FAA Inspector.
2. When the route check flight has been successfully completed, the pilot will enter the information on the individual Air Taxi Monthly summary form. Example on page 295.

Supercedes 1 May 70

Air Taxi Pilot Monthly Summary

Name ______________________ Certificate and number: ______________

Ratings: ________________ Medical class and date: ________________

Total Hours: ________ ASEL: ________ Night: ________ Instruments: ________

Expiration date of 6 month air taxi IFR check: ______________________

Aircraft qualified in: ________, ________, ________, ________, ________.

Date	Time	Asel	Amel	Day	Nite	WX	Hood	Link	Ladgs Day	Ladgs Nite	Appch	Remarks

Go or No Go Checklist

In accordance with FAA Regulations, and Company Policy, the following minimum installed, and operating properly, equipment list is established for easy reference and guidance in determining capabilities of Atlas Aircraft Corporation aircraft, while operating under FAR Part 135, for the various flight conditions listed.

Day VFR

1. Air speed indicator
2. Altimeter adjustable to barometric pressure
3. Magnetic direction indicator
4. Tachometer—each engine
5. Oil pressure gauge—each engine
6. Stall warning indicator
7. Oil temperature gauge—each engine
8. Manifold pressure gauge—each engine
9. Fuel gauges
10. Fuel pressure indicator or fuel flow indicator—each engine
11. Landing gear position indicator
12. Seat belts—each occupant
13. Fire extinguisher
14. Radio transmitter and receiver
15. Alternate air or carburetor heat (as required)—each engine
16. Oxygen, and oxygen equipment for each occupant, for all flights above 10,000 MSL.

Night VFR or VFR Over-the-Top

1. All equipment required for day VFR
2. Position lights
3. Anticollision lights
4. Flashlight (2 D cell or equivalent)
5. Alternator—each engine
6. Instrument lights
7. Landing light
8. Gyroscopic rate of turn indicator
9. Slip—skid indicator
10. Gyroscopic bank and pitch indicator
11. Gyroscopic direction indicator

IFR

1. All equipment required VFR
2. Clock with sweep second hand
3. Heated pilot tube(s)

4. Alternate static source—instruments
5. Two headsets or one headset and one speaker
6. Two microphones
7. Marker beacon receivers
8. Two navigation receivers
9. Two communication receivers
10. Instrument power failure warning device for each type of power
11. Vertical velocity indicator
12. Free air temperature indicator
13. Three axis auto pilot—single pilot operation

Flight in Positive Control Areas

1. All equipment required for IFR
2. Transponder
3. DME

Light to Moderate Icing

1. All equipment required for IFR
2. Wing and tail de-icing system
3. Propeller de-icing
4. Windshield anti-icing
5. Anti-static wicks
6. Shielded antennas
7. Elevator horn de-icing boot

Appendix VIII[1]

Job Functions for Various Ratings

(a) An applicant for a Class 1, 2, 3, or 4 airframe rating must provide equipment and material necessary for efficiently performing the following job functions:

(1) **Steel structural components**

Repair or replace steel tubes and fittings, using the proper welding techniques when appropriate
Anti-corrosion treatment of the interior and exterior of steel parts
Metal plating or anodizing*
Simple machine operations such as making bushings, bolts, etc.
Complex machine operations involving the use of planers, shapers, milling machines, etc.*
Fabricate steel fittings
Abrasive air blasting and chemical cleaning operations*
Heat treatment*
Magnetic inspection*
Repair or rebuild metal tanks*

(2) **Wood structure**

Splice wood spars
Repair ribs and spars (wood)
Fabricate wood spars*
Repair or replace metal ribs
Interior alignment of wings
Repair or replace plywood skin
Treatment against wood decay

(3) **Alloy skin and structural components**

Repair and replace metal skin, using power tools and equipment
Repair, replace and fabricate alloy members and components such as tubes, channels, cowling, fittings, attach angles, etc.
Alignment of components, using jigs or fixtures as in the case of joining fuselage sections or other similar operations
Make up wooden forming blocks or dies
Fluorescent inspection of alloy components*

(4) **Fabric covering**

Repairs to fabric surfaces
Recovering and refinishing of components and entire aircraft*

[1]Taken from *Federal Aviation Regulation, Part 145—Repair Stations,* U.S. Government Printing Office, Washington, D.C., 1972.

(5) **Control systems**

Renewing control cables, using swaging and splicing techniques
Rigging complete control system
Renewing or repairing all control system hinge point components such as pins, bushings, etc.
Install control system units and components

(6) **Landing gear systems**

Renew or repair all landing gear hinge point components and attachments such as bolts, bushings, fittings, etc.
Overhaul and repair elastic shock absorber units
Overhaul and repair hydraulic-pneumatic shock absorber units*
Overhaul and repair brake system components*
Conduct retraction cycle tests
Overhaul and repair electrical circuits
Overhaul and repair hydraulic system components*
Repair or fabricate hydraulic lines

(7) **Electric wiring systems**

Diagnose malfunctions
Repair or replace wiring
Installation of electrical equipment
Bench check electrical components (this check is not to be confused with the more complex functional test after overhaul)

(8) **Assembly operations**

Assembly of airframe component parts such as landing gear, wings, controls, etc. Rigging and alignment of airframe components, including the complete aircraft and control system
Installation of power plants
Installation of instruments and accessories
Assembly and fitting of cowling, fairings, etc.
Repair and assembly of plastic components such as windshields, windows, etc.
Jack or hoist complete aircraft
Conduct aircraft weight and balance operations (this function will be conducted in draft-free area)*
Balance control surfaces

(b) An applicant for any class of power plant rating must provide equipment and material necessary for efficiently performing the following job functions appropriate to the class of rating applied for:

(1) **Classes 1 and 2**

(i) **Maintain and alter power plants, including replacement of parts**

Chemical and mechanical cleaning
Disassembly operations
Replacement of valve guides and seats
Replacement of bushings, bearings, pins, inserts, etc.
Plating operations (copper, silver, cadmium, etc.)*
Heating operations (involving the use of recommended techniques requiring controlled heating facilities)

Chilling or shrinking operations
Removal and replacement of studs
Inscribing or affixing identification information
Painting of power plants and components
Anticorrosion treatment for parts
Replacement and repair of power plant alloy sheet metal and steel components such as baffles, fittings, etc.*

(ii) **Inspect all parts, using appropriate inspection aids**
Magnetic, fluorescent and other acceptable inspection aids*
Precise determination of clearances and tolerances of all parts
Inspection for alignment of connecting rods, crankshafts, impeller shafts, etc.
Balancing of parts, including crankshafts, impellers, etc.*
Inspection of valve springs

(iii) **Accomplish routine machine work**
Precision grinding, honing and lapping operations (includes crankshaft, cylinder barrels, etc.)*
Precision drilling, tapping, boring, milling and cutting operations
Reaming of inserts, bushings, bearings and other similar components
Refacing of valves

(iv) **Perform assembly operations**
Valve and ignition timing operations
Fabricate and test ignition harnesses
Fabricate and test rigid and flexible fluid lines
Prepare engines for long- or short-term storage
Functional check power plant accessories (this check is not to be confused with the more complex performance test of overhaul)*
Hoist engines by mechanical means
Install engines in aircraft*
Align and adjust engine controls*

Installation of engines in aircraft and alignment and adjustment of engine controls, when completed, must be inspected by either an appropriately rated certificated mechanic or certificated repairman. Persons supervising or inspecting these functions must thoroughly understand the pertinent installation details involved.

(v) **Test overhauled power plants in compliance with manufacturers' recommendations**
The test equipment will be the same as recommended by the manufacturers of the particular engines undergoing test or equivalent equipment that will accomplish the same purpose. The testing function may be performed by the repair station itself, or may be contracted to an outside agency. In either case the repair station will be responsible for the final acceptance of the tested engine.

(2) **Class 3**
Functional and equipment requirements for turbine engines will be governed entirely by the recommendations of the manufacturer, including techniques, inspection methods, and tests.

(c) An applicant for any class of propeller rating must provide equipment and material necessary for efficiently performing the following job functions appropriate to the class of rating applied for:

(1) **Class 1**

(i) **Maintain and alter propellers, including installation and replacement of parts**

Replace blade tipping
Refinish wood propellers
Make wood inlays
Refinish plastic blades
Straighten bent blades within repairable tolerances
Modify blade diameter and profile
Polish and buff
Painting operations
Remove from and reinstall on power plants

(ii) **Inspect components, using appropriate inspection aids**

Inspect propellers for conformity with manufacturer's drawings and specifications,
Inspect hubs and blades for failures and defects, using magnetic or fluorescent inspection devices*
Inspect hubs and blades for failures and defects, using all visual aids, including the etching of parts
Inspect hubs for wear of splines or keyways or any other defect

(iii) **Repair or replace components**

(Not applicable to this class.)

(iv) **Balance propellers**

Test for proper track on aircraft
Test for horizontal and vertical unbalance (this test will be accomplished with the use of precision equipment)

(v) **Test propeller pitch-changing mechanisms**

(Not applicable to this class.)

(2) **Class 2**

(i) **Maintain and alter propellers, including installation and replacement of parts**

All functions listed under paragraph (c) (1) (i) of this appendix when applicable to the make and model propeller for which a rating is sought
Properly lubricate moving parts
Assemble complete propeller and sub-assemblies, using special tools when required

(ii) **Inspect components, using appropriate inspection aids**

All functions listed under paragraph (c) (1) (ii) of this appendix when applicable to the make and model propeller for which a rating is sought.

(iii) **Repair or replace component parts**

Replace blades, hubs, or any of their components
Repair or replace anti-icing devices
Remove nicks or scratches from metal blades
Repair or replace electrical propeller components

(iv) **Balance propellers**

All functions listed under paragraph (c) (1) (iv) of this appendix when applicable to the make and model propeller for which a rating is sought

(v) **Test propeller pitch-changing mechanism**

Test hydraulically, propellers and components

Test electrically operated propellers and components
Test of constant speed devices*

(d) An applicant for a radio rating must provide equipment and materials as follows:

(1) For a Class 1 (Communications) radio rating, the equipment and materials necessary for efficiently performing the job functions listed in sub-paragraph (4) and the following job functions:

The testing and repair of headsets, speakers, and microphones
The measuring of radio transmitter power output

(2) For a Class 2 (Navigation) radio rating, the equipment and materials necessary for efficiently performing the job functions listed in sub-paragraph (4) and the following job functions:

The testing and repair of headsets
The testing of speakers
The repair of speakers *
The measuring of loop antenna sensitivity by appropriate methods
The determination and compensation for quadrantal error in aircraft direction finder radio equipment
The calibration of any radio navigational equipment, en route and approach aids, or similar equipment, appropriate to this rating to approved performance standards

(3) For a Class 3 (Radar) radio rating, the equipment and materials necessary for efficiently performing the job functions listed in subparagraph (4) and the following job functions:

The measuring of radio transmitter power output
The metal plating of transmission lines, wave guides, and similar equipment in accordance with appropriate specifications *
The pressurization of appropriate radar equipment with dry air, nitrogen, or other specified gases

(4) For all classes of radio ratings, the equipment and materials necessary for efficiently performing the following job functions:

- Perform physical inspection of radio systems and components by visual and mechanical methods
- Perform electrical inspection of radio systems and components by means of appropriate electrical and/or electronic test instruments
- Check aircraft wiring, antennas, connectors, relays, and other associated radio components to detect installation faults
- Check engine ignition systems and aircraft accessories to determine sources of electrical interference
- Check aircraft power supplies for adequacy and proper functioning
- Test radio instruments
- Overhaul, test, and check dynamotors, inverters, and other radio electrical apparatus *
- Paint and refinish equipment containers *
- Accomplish appropriate methods of marking calibrations, or other information on radio control panels and other components, as required *
- Make and reproduce drawings, wiring diagrams, and other similar material required to record alterations and/or modifications to radio (photographs may be used in lieu of drawings when they will serve as an equivalent or better means of recording) *
- Fabricate tuning shaft assemblies, brackets, cable assemblies and other similar components used in radios or aircraft radio installations*

- Align tuned circuits (RF and IF)
- Install and repair aircraft antennas
- Install complete radio systems in aircraft and prepare weight and balance reports* (that phase of radio installation requiring alterations to the aircraft structure must be performed, supervised, and inspected by qualified personnel)
- Measure modulation values, noise, and distortion in radios
- Measure audio and radio frequencies to appropriate tolerances and perform calibration necessary for the proper operation of radios
- Measure radio component values (inductance, capacitance, resistance, etc.)
- Measure radio frequency transmission line attenuation
- Determine wave forms and phase in radios when applicable
- Determine proper aircraft radio antenna, lead-in and transmission line characteristics and locations for type of radio equipment to which connected
- Determine operational condition of radio equipment installed in aircraft by using appropriate portable test apparatus
- Determine proper location for radio antennas on aircraft
- Test all types of electronic tubes, transistors, or similar devices in equipment appropriate to the rating

(e) An applicant for any class of instrument rating must provide equipment and material necessary for efficiently performing the following job functions, in accordance with pertinent specifications and manufacturers' recommendations, appropriate to the class of rating applied for:

(1) **Class 1**

(i) **Diagnose instrument malfunctions**

Diagnose malfunctioning of the following instruments:

Rate of climb indicators
Altimeters
Air speed indicators
Vacuum indicators
Oil pressure gauges
Fuel pressure gauges
Hydraulic pressure gauges
De-icing pressure gauges
Pitot-static tube
Direct indicating compasses
Direct indicating tachometers
Accelerometer
Direct reading fuel quantity gauges
Optical (sextants, drift sights, etc.)*

(ii) **Maintain and alter instruments, including installation and replacement of parts**

- Perform these functions on instruments listed under paragraph (e) (1) (i) of this appendix.
- The function of installation includes fabrication of instrument panels and other installation structural components.
- The repair station should be equipped to perform this function. However, it may be contracted to a competent outside agency equipped to perform the function.

(iii) **Inspect, test and calibrate instruments**

Perform these functions on instruments listed under paragraph (e) (1) (i) of this appendix, on and off the aircraft, when appropriate.

(2) **Class 2**

(i) **Diagnose instrument malfunctions**

Diagnose malfunctioning of the following instruments:

Tachometers
Synchroscope
Electric temperature indicators
Electric resistance type indicators
Moving magnet type indicators
Resistance type fuel indicators
Warning units (oil-fuel)
Selsyn systems and indicators
Self-synchronous systems and indicators
Remote indicating compasses
Fuel quantity indicators
Oil quantity indicators
Radio indicators
Ammeters
Voltmeters

(ii) **Maintain and alter instruments, including installation and the replacement of parts**

- Perform these functions on instruments listed under paragraph (e) (2) (i) of this appendix.
- The function of installation includes fabrication of instrument panels and other installation structural components. The repair station should be equipped to perform this function. However, it may be contracted to a competent outside agency equipped to perform the function.

(iii) **Inspect, test and calibrate instruments**

- Perform these functions on instruments listed under paragraph (e) (2) (i) of this appendix, on and off the aircraft, when appropriate.

(3) **Class 3**

(i) **Diagnose instrument malfunctions**

Diagnose malfunctioning of the following instruments:

Turn and bank indicators
Directional gyros
Horizon gyros
Autopilot control units and components*
Remote reading direction indicators*

(ii) **Maintaining and alter instruments, including installation and replacement of parts**

- Perform these functions on instruments listed under (e) (3) (i) of this appendix.
- The function of installation includes fabrication of instrument panels and other installation structural components. The repair station should be equipped to perform this function. However, it may be contracted to a competent outside agency equipped to perform the function.

(iii) **Inspect, test and calibrate instruments**

- Perform these functions on instruments listed under paragraph (e) (3) (i) of this appendix, on and off the aircraft, when appropriate.

(4) **Class 4**

(i) **Diagnose instrument malfunctions**

Diagnose malfunctioning of the following instruments:

Capacitance type quantity gauge
Other electronic instruments
Engine analyzers

(ii) **Maintain and alter instruments, including installation and replacement of parts**

- Perform these functions on instruments listed under paragraph (e) (4) (i) of this appendix.
- The function of installation includes fabrication of instrument panels and other installation structural components. The repair station should be equipped to perform this function. However, it may be contracted to a competent outside agency equipped to perform this function.

(iii) **Inspect, test and calibrate instruments**

- Perform these functions on instruments listed under paragraph (e) (4) (i) of this appendix, on and off the aircraft, when appropriate.

(f) An applicant for a Class 1, 2, or 3 accessory rating must provide equipment and material necessary for efficiently performing the following job functions, in accordance with pertinent specifications and the manufacturers' recommendations:

(1) *Diagnose accessory malfunctions.*
(2) *Maintain and alter accessories, including installation and the replacement of the parts.*
(3) *Inspect, test, and, where necessary, calibrate accessories.*

Note: When an asterisk (*) is shown after any job function listed in this appendix it indicates that the applicant need not have the equipment and material on the premises for performing this job function provided he or she contracts that particular type work to an outside agency having such equipment and material.

APPENDIX IX

Guidelines for Leases or Agreements

Guidelines for Leases or Agreements Granting Commercial Franchise Privileges for Aeronautical / Non-aeronautical Activities at Public Airports Affected by Federal Agreements

1. Background
   a. The federal interest in promoting civil aviation and the FAA responsibility related thereto has been established and augmented by various legislative actions which authorize programs for granting funds, property, and other assistance to local communities for the development of airport facilities. In each instance, the recipient public agency assumes certain obligations, either by contract or by restrictive covenants in deeds, pledging it to maintain and operate its airport facilities safely and efficiently and in accordance with specified conditions.
   b. The legal obligations and conditions assumed by airport owners in consideration of the federal benefits arise through the following:
      (1) Grant agreements issued under the Federal Airport Act of 1946 or the Airport and Airway Development Act of 1970.
      (2) Surplus airport property instruments of transfer, issued pursuant to Section 13g of the Surplus Property Act of 1944, as amended by Pl. 80–289 in 1947. [Surplus airport property conveyances prior to 1947 were handled by WAA (now GSA) as prescribed in Regulation 16, generally referred to as WAA—Reg. 16.]
      (3) Deeds of conveyance issued under Section 16 of the Federal Airport Act of 1946 or under Section 23 of the Airport and Airway Development Act of 1970 (nonsurplus federal land).
      (4) AP-4 Agreements and Section 308a of the Federal Aviation Act of 1958 (exclusive rights).
2. General
   a. The prime obligation of the owner of a federally assisted airport is to operate the airport for the use and benefit of the public. Coincidental with that obligation are the legal obligations of the agreements imposed by the federal government. The sponsor, through these agreements, provides, among other assurances, that with regard to leases or other agreements at the airport:
      (1) The airport will be available for public use on fair and reasonable terms and without unjust discrimination.
      (2) Airport users will be charged for facilities and services under a fee and rental structure which will make the airport as self-sustaining as possible under the circumstances.

Source: FAA, Airports Division NW/Mountain Region. Seattle, WA 1985

(3) No exclusive right will be granted or permitted which is prohibited by Section 308(a) of the Federal Aviation Act of 1958 and its successors.

(4) The airport will be bound by the assurances contained in Title VI of the Civil Rights Act of 1964, as implemented by Part 21 of the Regulations of the Office of the Secretary of Transportation.

(5) All revenue derived from the use of the obligated airport property will be used for the operation, maintenance, or development of the airport. Fair market rental values must be charged for the use of federal surplus property.

b. The sponsor's responsibility for operation is to make available to the public the landing areas, taxiways, parking areas, and other public areas. There is, however, no requirement that the use of the airport be provided free of charge. A cost or fee may be imposed on users in order to recover the costs of providing these facilities. The charge may be a landing fee (which is similar to the toll charge on a highway, bridge, or tunnel) or an indirect charge. Quite frequently the airport owner recovers this use charge indirectly as part of the consideration received from commercial tenant operators who provide direct services to users of the public areas. It may, for example, take the form of a gallonage fee, in which case fuel consumption is regarded as a measure of relative usage or benefit derived from the availability of the public landing area. It may also take the form of a monthly flat charge or a variable charge using the volume of business—rather than fuel gallonage—as the yardstick of benefit derived by patrons from the availability of the public landing areas.

In addition to those charges usually sought to be recovered from a user and/or tenant, there is normally an intent to recover some element of rent for the occupancy of specific premises granted by the airport owner to a private enterprise by lease, license, permit, or other contract.

3. Agreements for leasing airport property

a. The type of document, form of lease, or other written instrument used to grant airport privileges is the sole responsibility of the airport owner. Because of the variety of state laws affecting this type of agreement and because of possible infringement upon the realm of authority of the legal profession, the FAA has not deemed it wise to attempt to prepare and publish a model form of lease. Also, it is quite likely that the provisions required in any one particular lease may be of little value or concern in a lease at another location for various reasons. However, it has been found through experience that generally a lease for a fixed-base operation and other commercial activities on an airport should adequately cover certain points.

b. Typically, any document for the leasing of airport land or facilities should include the following elements:

(1) Airport property to be leased

(a) The lease agreement should adequately describe the specific portion of the airport property leased. (The leased premises should consist of only that portion of the airport property necessary for the lessee's business operation, such as a hangar, shop, office, and gasoline storage space and must *not* include landing, taxiing, or other common use facilities.)

(b) Aeronautical leases should provide the lessee the right to ingress and egress to and from the leased area.

(2) Rights and privileges granted to aeronautical lessees include, among others:
   (a) For FBOs, the non-exclusive right to conduct certain specified aeronautical activities at the airport.
   (b) The non-exclusive right to use, in common with others, all public airport facilities and improvements of a public nature which are now, or may hereafter be, connected with or appurtenant to landing, taxiing, parking areas, and other common use facilities.
   (c) The right to construct facilities such as hangars, ramps, office, shop, buildings, improvements, and so on required in connection with the services to be provided.

(3) Obligations assumed by lessee include, among others:
   (a) To operate the premises leased for the use and benefit of the public, and
      1) To furnish said service on a fair, equal, and not unjustly discriminatory basis to all users thereof[1]
      2) To charge fair, reasonable, and not unjustly discriminatory prices for each unit or service, provided that lessee may be allowed to make reasonable and nondiscriminatory discounts, rebates, or other types of price reductions to volume purchasers
   (b) The (grantee, licensee, lessee, or permittee, as appropriate) for himself, his heirs, personal representatives, successors in interest, and assigns, as part of the consideration hereof, does hereby convenant and agree (in the case of deeds and leases add "as a covenant running with the land") that in the event facilities are constructed, maintained, or otherwise operated on said property described in this (deed, license, lease, permit, as appropriate) for a purpose for which a DOT program or activity is extended or for another purpose involving the provision of similar services or benefits, the (grantee, licensee, permittee) shall maintain and operate such facilities and services in compliance with all other requirements imposed pursuant to 49 CFR Part 21, Nondiscrimination in Federally Assisted Programs of the Department of Transportation, and as said Regulations may be amended.

   The lessee, for himself, his personal representatives, successors in interest, and assigns, as part of the consideration hereof, does hereby covenant and agree, as a covenant running with the land, that (1) no person on the grounds of race, color, or national origin shall be excluded from participation in, be denied benefits of, or otherwise be subjected to discrimination in the use of said facilities, (2) that in the construction of any improvements on, over, or under such land and the furnishing of services thereon, no person on the grounds of race, color, or national origin shall be excluded from participation in, be denied benefits of, or otherwise be subjected to discrimination, (3) that the lessee shall use the premises in compliance with all other requirements imposed or pursuant to Title 49, Code of Federal Regulations, Department of Transportation, Subtitle A, Office of the Secretary, Part 21, Nondiscrimination in Federally-Assisted programs of the Department of Transportation—Effectuation of Title VI of the Civil Rights Act of 1964, and as said Regulations may be amended.[2]

   That in the event of breach of any of these nondiscrimination covenants,

   ____________*(Name of Sponsor)*____________ shall have the right to terminate the license, lease, permit, etc., and to re-enter and repossess said land and facilities thereon, and hold the same as if said lease had never been made or issued; provided, however, that the (licensee, lessee, permitee) allegedly in breach shall have the right to contest said alleged breach under applicable Federal Aviation Administration procedures, and any sanctions under or termination of (license, lease, permit), shall be withheld pending completion of such procedures.

- (c) To provide and maintain sufficient fixtures and equipment to meet public demand for services offered.
- (d) To provide and maintain an adequate staff of employees with skills, licenses, and certificates appropriate to the activities conducted.
- (e) To maintain accurate and acceptable records which are to be made available for examination by the lessor.
- (f) To operate during specified minimum hours and to conform to all rules, regulations, fixed-base operator's standards and ordinances adopted by the lessor or other applicable government bodies including, but not limited to, safety, health, and sanitary codes.
- (g) To demonstrate evidence of financial stability and good credit rating.
- (h) To meet indemnity and insurance minimums.

(4) Rights and privileges reserved to the lessor include, among others:

- (a) For FBO leases, the right to further develop or improve the landing area of the airport as the lessor sees fit, regardless of the desires or view of the lessee, and without interference or hindrance.
- (b) The right, but not the obligation, to maintain and keep in repair the landing area of the airport and all publicly owned facilities of the airport, together with the right to direct and control all activities of lessee in this regard.
- (c) The right to take any action the lessor considers necessary to protect the aerial approaches of the airport against obstruction, together with the right to prevent the lessee from erecting, or permitting to be erected, any building or other structure on the airport which, in the opinion of the lessor, would limit the usefulness of the airport and constitute a hazard to aircraft.
- (d) The right to temporarily close the airport or any of the facilities thereon for maintenance, improvement, or for the safety of the public.
- (e) The right to approve or deny any sub lease of the premises leased.

(5) Other rights and obligations of the lessee and lessor to be ascertained include:

- (a) Who is to provide maintenance of leased area.
- (b) Who is to provide utilities (such as heat, electricity, and water) to the leased area and who is to pay charges therefor.
- (c) The disposition of structures and improvements erected by the lessee. (Is title to pass to lessor at some future time?)
- (d) The period of the lease and whether options for renewal are to be granted. Typically, lease periods should not exceed five years unless substantial capital investments are involved.
- (e) The amount of the rent to be charged and the method of computation; monthly, yearly, or percentage of lessee's gross net sales.

(f) Frequency of review and basis of adjustment of rental amount.

(g) Provisions for termination and surrender of lease, including:

1) Grounds on which lease may be terminated.

2) Rights and obligations of parties upon termination.

3) Obligation of lessee to surrender premises upon termination.

4) Right of lessor to re-enter premises upon termination.

(h) Provisions for breach of covenants, including:

1)Procedure by which either party is to give other party notice of breach.

2) Length of time allowed to rectify breach.

3) Method for settling dispute as to whether breach has occurred.

(i) Provisions covering fire damages to premises, including:

1) Responsibility for restoration and/or repair of damaged premises.

2) Time allowed for restoration and repair.

3) Abatement of rent if premises rendered untenantable.

(6) Other provisions to be included in lease agreements for aeronautical use:

(a) It is clearly understood by the lessee that no right or privilege has been granted which would operate to prevent any person, firm, or corporation operating aircraft on the airport from performing any service on its own aircraft with its own regular employees (including, but not limited to, maintenance and repair) that it may choose to perform.[1]

(b) It is understood and agreed that nothing herein contained shall be construed to grant or authorize the granting of an exclusive right forbidden by Section 308 of the Federal Aviation Act of 1958 or for aeronautical activities, such as, but not limited to:[2]

1) Charter operations

2) Pilot training

3) Aircraft rental

4) Aerial photography

5) Crop dusting

6) Sale of aviation petroleum products

7) Air carrier operations

8) Aircraft sales and services incidental thereto

9) Any other activity which, because of direct relationship to the operation of aircraft, can be regarded as an aeronautical activity.

(c) During the time of war or national emergency, lessor shall have the right to lease the landing area or any part thereof to the United States Government for military or naval use and, if such lease is executed, the provisions of this instrument insofar as they are inconsistent with the provisions of the lease to the government, shall be suspended.[3]

(d) This lease shall be subordinate to the provisions of any existing or future agreement between the lessor and the United States relative to the operation or maintenance of the airport, the execution of which has been or may be required as a condition precedent to the expenditure of federal funds for development of the airport. Failure of the lessee or any occupant to comply with the requirements of any existing or future agreement between the lessor and the United States, which failure shall continue after reasonable notice to make appropriate corrections, shall be cause for immediate termination of lessee's rights hereunder.[4]

(7) Other considerations

(a) Airport manager and/or related duties should not be incorporated in FBO lease agreements. The airport should establish standard rental/lease rates and apply them equally to all and handle the airport manager duties by separate contract. This allows the airport owner to change airport managers or his duties without affecting the basic lease rates.

(b) Provisions not specifically *NOTED* in b. of "agreements for leasing airport property" are not mandatory, but are strongly recommended as being in the best interests of the airport and the sponsor.

(c) Leases not containing the required provisions [1], [2], [3], or [4], should be amended at the first opportunity.

4. Through-the-fence-operations

a. There are instances when the owner of a public airport proposes to enter into an agreement which permits access to the public landing area by aircraft based on land adjacent to, but not part of, the airport property. This type of an arrangement has frequently been referred to as a "through-the-fence-operation," even though the perimeter fence may be an imaginary one.

The obligation to make an airport available for the use and benefit of the public does not impose any requirement to permit access by aircraft from adjacent property. On the contrary, the existence of such an arrangement has been recognized as an encumbrance upon the airport property itself. Orders governing administration of ADAP indicate that a sponsor's title to airport land so encumbered does not meet the land interest requirement for a federal aid project unless the sponsor retains the legal right to, and in fact does, require the off-site property owner or occupant to conform in all respects to the requirements of any existing or proposed grant agreement.

b. The owner of a public airport is entitled to seek recovery of his initial and continuing costs of providing a public use landing area. Historically, he has been urged—in the interests of promoting general aviation—to refrain from direct assessment of user charges except for those engaged as common carriers for hire. Since enactment of the Airport and Airway Development Act of 1970, the owners of airports receiving federal funds have been required to establish a fee and rental structure designed to make the airport as self-sustaining as possible. Most public airports seek to recover a substantial part of airfield operating costs indirectly, through various arrangements relating to commercial activities. The development of aeronautical enterprises on land uncontrolled by the owner of the public airport cannot but result in a competitive advantage to the detriment of on-base operators on whom the airport owner relies for service to the flying public. To equalize this imbalance, the airport owner should attempt to obtain from any off-base enterprise a fair return for its use of the landing area.

c. Arrangements that permit aircraft to gain access to a public landing area from off-site properties introduce safety considerations with additional hazards, and complicate the control of vehicular and aircraft traffic. The construction of additional taxiways, the protection of additional intersections along airport perimeter roads, and frequently the basic airport layout itself, when designed to accommodate landing area access from multiple perimeter locations, presents a substantial and continuing burden for the sole benefit and convenience of such landholding neighbors. Depending on the volume and type of flight activity, the hazards of such an arrangement may well result in severe curtailment of the user potential of the airport.

d. The FAA, almost without exception, discourages and opposes any agreements which grant access to the public landing areas by aircraft normally stored and serviced on adjacent property. Typically, exceptions are considered in the following circumstances:

   (1) Where a bona fide airport tenant has already leased a site from the airport owner and has negotiated airfield use privileges, but also desires to move aircraft to and from a hangar or manufacturing plant on adjacent off-airport property. In this case, actual access will be gained through the area provided by the airport.

   (2) Where an individual or corporation actually residing or doing business on an adjacent land tract proposes to gain access to the landing area solely for aircraft used incidental to such residence or business without offering any aeronautical services to the public, provided that the airport owner is prepared to accommodate the normal expansion of aeronautical services to the public on publicly owned areas of the airport. This situation is commonly encountered where an industrial airpark is developed in conjunction with the airport.

   (3) Where there is insufficient land for further development of aeronautical activities.

e. Any agreement for a "through-the-fence-operation," in addition to the normal lease provisions above, must include a provision making the lease and such operations subject to the same obligations (present and future agreements with the federal government, rules, regulations, and so on) as tenants on airport property (see (6)(d) above).

   (1) Provision must also be made to assure that the lessee contributes his or her fair share toward the cost of operation, maintenance, and improvement of the airport, and that no benefits accrue to the lessee which would give him or her an advantage over an on-airport operator.

       One method of determining a fair return to the airport from off-airport use would be to utilize a percentage of the on-airport tiedown rate, if no other equitable method is available, such as percentage of gross sales, etc. This type of arrangement has the advantage of an automatic inflation factor that would keep off-airport charges in line with on-airport charges.

   (2) It is suggested that on all airports having or anticipating agreements with the federal government, any such proposal be submitted to the FAA for review and comment prior to its finalization.

   (3) A suggested permit is included as Exhibit A.

Notes

[1] Required in leases/agreements for aeronautical services at airports subject to continuing obligations under FAAP/AIP agreements.

[2] Required in all leases/agreements involving federal agreements executed after July 2, 1964.

[3] Only required leases/agreements at airports acquired in whole or in part under a Federal Surplus Property Transfer (unless the National Emergency Use Provision of the Surplus Transfer document has been specifically released by the FAA).

[4] Required in leases in aeronautical operations from adjoining non-airport property ("through-the-fence-operations").

Language provided in [2], [3], and [4], should be used verbatim.

Exhibit A

INGRESS AND EGRESS PERMIT

____ AIRPORT

The (Grantor) for the consideration hereinafter specified, grants to ____________________, (Grantee) the right of ingress and egress into and upon a portion of the ____________________ Airport in ____________________County, ____________________, from property owned or occupied by Grantee which adjoins said Airport on the ______________ side near the ______________ end. The boundaries of said Airport are described in ____________________ recorded in Volume _______ of Deed Records for __________ County ______________, at Page _______ thereof. Ingress and egress hereunder shall be limited to a ______________ foot portion of the ______________ Airport boundary, as shown on drawing attached hereto marked Exhibit A.

This permit shall be for a term of ____________ ( ) years commencing on the ____________ day of _________, 19 ______, and terminating on the ______________ day of _________, 19 ______.

As part of the consideration for granting this permit, Grantee agrees to pay Grantor [______________ (______ ¢) per gallon for all aviation fuel sold or used by Grantee]. [The sum of $ ____________ per month] or [$ ____________________] or [other basis]. Payment shall be made on or before the ________________of each month. Grantee agrees to permit Grantor to audit books and records at any reasonable time and place for the purpose of verifying the amount due the Grantor.

Grantee agrees to comply with all airport rules and regulations adopted by the Grantor relative to the ____ Airport.

Grantee shall save and hold Grantor harmless from any claim or liability arising out of its activities, and shall procure and continue in effect public liability and property damage insurance in minimum amounts as follows:

(a) $________ when the claim is one for damage to or destruction of property and $ _____ to any claimant in any other case.

(b) $ ________ for any number of claims arising out of a single occurrence.

Certificate evidencing such insurance and bearing endorsements requiring ______ days' written notice to Grantor prior to any change, cancellation, or expiration shall be furnished to Grantor prior to exercise by Grantee of its right of entry hereunder. However, Grantee assumes no tort liability either to Grantor or to any other party for damages or injury other than through its own negligence or lack of due care.

Grantee agrees to observe all applicable federal and state statutes and rules and regulations in its operations upon the property abutting said ______________ Airport and in any operation carried on by Grantee or under its supervision or direction upon the airport. Grantee further agrees and covenants to at all times maintain its abutting property, and the improvements thereon, and to conduct its operation, both on and off the Airport, in a reasonably neat and clean fashion, and not to permit the accumulation of rubbish or junk airplane or automobile parts or other material in an unsightly manner. Grantee agrees that if it fails to so maintain its abutting property, Grantor shall have the right, after ______ days' written notice, to come upon the property of Grantee and cause the same to comply with this provision, and to charge the expense thereof to Grantee, or, at the option of the Grantor, to terminate the rights of Grantee hereunder.

Grantee further agrees not to use any portion of the Airport property for the permanent storage of aircraft or other personal property of Grantee, or of personal property for which Grantee is acting as bailee, and Grantee agrees that if Grantor shall at any time demand the removal of personal property located upon the Airport, which personal property is under the control of Grantee and grantee shall fail to remove the same within a period of ____________ (   ) hours after such demand, then Grantor may remove the same and charge the cost of such removal to Grantee.

This permit shall not be sold, assigned, or otherwise transferred by operation of law or otherwise by Grantee to any other person, corporation, association, partnership, municipal corporation or body politic, and this permit shall not pass with any sale, lease, or other disposal of land abutting upon said ____________________________ Airport, and shall automatically terminate in the event of the bankruptcy or dissolution of Grantee, or in the event Grantee shall dispose of its interest in said lands abutting upon the ____ Airport, provided, however, the Grantor may by its express written approval permit the assignment hereof.

Grantee agrees to conduct its operation, both on Airport and on adjoining premises, for the use and benefit of the public, and particularly[a]:

a. To furnish good, prompt, and efficient services adequate to meet all the demands for its service at the Airport;

b. To furnish said service on a fair, equal, and nondiscriminatory to all users thereof; and

c. To charge fair, reasonable, and nondiscriminatory prices for each unit of sale or service, provided that the Grantee may be allowed to make reasonable and nondiscriminatory discounts, rebates, or other similar types of price reductions to volume purchasers.

The Grantee, for himself, his personal representatives, successors in interest, and assigns, as part of the consideration hereof, does hereby covenant and agree, as covenant running with the land, that (1) no person on the grounds of race, color, or national origin shall be excluded from participation in, be denied the benefits of, or otherwise subjected to discrimination in the use of said facilities, (2) that in the construction of any improvements on, over, or under such land and the furnishing of services thereon, no person on the grounds of race, color, or national origin shall be excluded from participation in, denied benefits of, or otherwise subjected to discrimination, (3) that the lessee shall use the premises in compliance with all other requirements imposed by or pursuant to Title 49, Code of Federal Regulations, Department of Transportation, Subtitle A, Office of the Secretary, Part 21, Nondiscrimination in Federally-assisted programs of the Department of Transporation—Effectuation of Title VI of the Civil Rights Act of 1964, and as said Regulations may be amended. That in the event of breach of any of the preceding nondiscrimination covenants, ________*(Name of Sponsor)*________ shall have the right to terminate the license, lease, permit, etc., and to reenter and repossess said land and the facilities thereon, and hold the same as if said lease had never been made or issued.

It is clearly understood by the Grantee that no right or privilege has been granted which would operate to prevent any person, firm, or corporation operating aircraft on the Airport from performing any services on its own aircraft with its own regular employees (including, but not limited to, maintenance and repair) that it may choose to perform.

It is understood and agreed that nothing herein contained shall be construed to grant or authorize the granting of an exclusive right forbidden by Section 308 of the Federal Aviation Act of 1958 or for aeronautical activities such as, but not limited to:

a. Charter operations
b. Pilot training
c. Aircraft rental
d. Aerial photography
e. Crop dusting
f. Sale of aviation petroleum products
g. Air carrier operations
h. Aircraft sales and service incidental thereto
i. Any other activity which, because of its direct relationship to the operation of aircraft, can be regarded as an aeronautical activity

Grantor reserves the right to further develop or improve the landing area of the Airport as it sees fit, regardless of the desires or view of the Grantee, and without interference or hindrance.

Grantor reserves the right, but shall not be obligated to Grantee, to maintain and keep in repair the landing area of the Airport and all publicly-owned facilities of the Airport, together with the right to direct and control all activities of Grantee in this regard.

During the time of war or national emergency, Grantor shall have the right to lease the landing area or any part thereof to the United States Government for military or naval use and, if such lease is executed, the provisions of this instrument insofar as they are inconsistent with the provisions of the lease to the Government, shall be suspended[b].

Grantor reserves the right to take any action it considers necessary to protect the aerial approaches of the Airport against obstruction, together with the right to prevent Grantee from erecting, or permitting to be erected, any building or other structure on or adjacent to the Airport which, in the opinion of the Grantor, would limit the usefulness of the Airport or constitute a hazard to aircraft.

This permit shall be subordinate to the provisions of any existing or future agreement between Grantor and the United States, relative to the operation or maintenance of the Airport, the execution of which has been or may be required as a condition precedent to the expenditure of Federal funds for the development existing or future agreement between Grantor and the United States, which failure shall continue after reasonable notice to make appropriate corrections, shall be cause for immediate termination to Grantee's rights hereunder.

IN WITNESS WHEREOF the parties hereto set their hands and seals this ____________ day of _________________, 19____.

GRANTOR:

____

____

GRANTEE:

by _________________________________

[a] Required where aeronautical services are to be provided.

[b] Required where airport was acquired in whole or in part under Federal Surplus Property Transfer (unless National Emergency Use Provision has been specifically released by the FAA).

APPENDIX X

Model Lease from National Air Transportation Association

Sample

Lease and Operating Agreement

This Lease and Operating Agreement (this "Agreement") entered into as of the __________ day of ________ , 19____ , by and between the Anytown Airport Commission, a body politic and corporate created by the Council of Anytown ("Lessor"), and ____________________ , a __________________ corporation with authority to do business with the State of ______________________("Lessee").

Witnesseth:

WHEREAS, Lessor now owns, controls and operates the Anytown Airport (the "Airport") in the City and County of Anytown, State of _________________________________ ;

WHEREAS, fixed base operation services are essential to the proper accommodation of general and commercial aviation at the Airport; and

WHEREAS, Lessor desires to make such services available at the Airport and Lessee is qualified, ready, willing and able to provide such services;

NOW, THEREFORE, in consideration of the premises and the mutual covenants contained in this Agreement, the parties hereby agree as follows:

Article One
Term

The term of this Agreement shall be for a period of twenty-five (25) years, commencing on the _________ day of _________ , 19____ , and continuing through the_________ day of _______ , 20 ________ (the "Termination Date"), unless earlier terminated under the provisions of this Agreement. Lessee shall have the option, exercisable upon at least one hundred eighty (180), but not more than three hundred sixty-five (365), days' notice to Lessor prior to the Termination Date, to extend the term of the Agreement for an additional period of __________ (______) years from and after the Termination Date, upon the same terms and conditions as are contained in this Agreement.

Article Two

Leased Premises

Lessor hereby leases to Lessee, and Lessee hereby leases from Lessor, the following premises, identified and shown on Exhibit A, attached hereto and made a part hereof, including leasehold improvements constructed by Lessee pursuant to Article Five of this Agreement (the "Premises"), together with the right of ingress and egress for both vehicles and aircraft:

A. Real Property as follows:
(Legal description of real property)

B. Improvement on said real property, as follows:

1. **Hangar Number 1:** An area comprising approximately__________ (______) square feet of usable space under roof (the "Hangar").

2. **Ramp and Apron Area:** An area adjacent to Hangar Number 1, comprising approximately __________ (________) square feet.

3. **General Aviation Terminal:**

   a. An area comprising approximately ___________ (_________) square feet of space within the General Aviation Terminal.

   b. An area comprising of approximately___________ (________) square feet on the ramp side of the General Aviation Terminal.

   c. An area comprising approximately__________ (________) square feet of space north of the General Aviation Terminal.

C. Fuel Storage Area: Above and below-ground fuel storage comprising approximately__________ (________) square feet of land containing ________ (________) ________ (________) gallon fuel tanks.

Article Three

Rights and Obligations of Lessee

A. **Required Services.** Lessee is hereby granted the nonexclusive privilege to engage in, and Lessee agrees to engage in, the business of providing full and complete fixed base operation services at the Airport, __________________________ (________) hours per day, every day, as follows:

1. Aircraft ground guidance within the uncontrolled areas adjacent to the Premises, and ramp service, including sale and into-plane delivery of aviation fuels, lubricants and other related aviation products.

2. Apron servicing of, and assistance to, aircraft, including transient parking, storage and tiedown service, for both based and transient aircraft upon or within facilities leased to Lessee or aircraft parking areas designated by Lessor.

3. Repair and maintenance of based and transient aircraft. Lessee agrees to maintain and operate a repair station approved by the Federal Aviation Administration (the "FAA"), with ratings as follows:

a. Engine, airframe and accessories—Classes I, II and III.

b. Avionics—Classes I and II.

4. Customary accommodations for the convenience of users, including pilot lounge area, information services, direct telephone service connections to the Flight Service Station and the United States Weather Bureau, and courtesy vehicle ground transportation to and from other terminals at the Airport.

5. Equipment and trained personnel to remove disabled aircraft with a gross landing weight of twelve thousand five hundred (12,500) pounds or less from those portions of the Airport provided and made available by Lessor for aircraft and related operations, including aircraft runways, taxiways, ramps, aprons and parking spaces, and areas directly associated therewith, which are not leased by Lessee or any other tenant on the Airport ("Air Operations Area"). Lessee shall perform such removal services on request.

6. Sales of avionic and engine parts and instruments and accessories.

*7. Lessee acknowledges that no right or privilege has been granted which would operate to prevent any person, firm or corporation operating aircraft on the Airport from performing services on its own aircraft, with its own employees, including maintenance and repair services.

B. **Authorized Services.** In addition to the services required to be provided by Lessee pursuant to Paragraph A, above, Lessee is authorized, but not required, to provide the following services and to engage in the following activities:

1. Ramp service at other Airport locations, including into-plane delivery of aircraft fuel, lubricants and other related aviation products; loading and unloading of passengers, baggage, mail and freight; and providing of ramp equipment, aircraft cleaning and other services for air carriers and other persons or firms.

2. Special flight services, including aerial sightseeing, aerial advertising and aerial photography.

3. The sale of new and used aircraft, aircraft parts, navigation equipment, and new and used radio and electronic equipment.

4. The demonstration of aircraft for sale.

5. Flight training, including ground school.

6. Aircraft rental.

7. Aircraft charter operations conducted by Lessee or a subcontractor of Lessee.

8. Any other general aviation services not specifically provided for herein which are approved in advance by Lessor. Lessor's approval of such services shall not be unreasonably withheld.

C. **Operating Standards.** In providing any of the required and/or authorized services or activities specified in this Agreement, Lessee shall operate for the use and benefit of the public and shall meet or exceed the following standards:

1. Lessee shall comply with the minimum operating standards or requirements, promulgated by Lessor, applicable to each of Lessee's activities on the Airport.

*Must be included in all leases governing aeronautical services on airports receiving federal aid.

*2. Lessee shall furnish service on a fair, reasonable and nondiscriminatory basis to all users of the Airport. Lessee shall furnish good, prompt and efficient service adequate to meet all reasonable demands for its services at the Airport. Lessee shall charge fair, reasonable, and nondiscriminatory prices for each unit of sale or service; provided, however, that Lessee shall be allowed to make reasonable and nondiscriminatory discounts, rebates or other similar types of price reductions to volume purchasers.

3. Lessee shall select and appoint a full-time manager of its operations at the Airport. The manager shall be qualified and experienced, and vested with full power and authority to act in the name of Lessee with respect to the method, manner and conduct of the operation of the fixed base services to be provided under this Agreement. The manager shall be available at the Airport during regular business hours, and during the manager's absence a duly authorized subordinate shall be in charge and available at the Airport.

4. Lessee shall provide, at its sole expense, a sufficient number of employees to provide effectively and efficiently the services required or authorized by this Agreement.

5. Lessee shall control the conduct, demeanor and appearance of its employees, who shall be trained by Lessee and who shall possess such technical qualifications and hold such certificates or qualifications as may be required by any governmental authority in carrying out assigned duties. It shall be the responsibility of Lessee to maintain close supervision over its employees to assure a high standard of service to customers of Lessee.

6. Lessee shall meet all expenses and payments in connection with the use of the Premises and the rights and privileges herein granted, including taxes, permit fees, license fees and assessments lawfully levied or assessed upon the Premises or property at any time situated therein and thereon. Lessee may, at its sole expense and cost, contest any tax, fee or assessment.

7. Lessee shall comply with all federal, state and local laws, rules and regulations which may apply to the conduct of the business contemplated, including rules and regulations promulgated by Lessor, and Lessee shall maintain in effect and post in a prominent place all necessary and/or required licenses or permits.

8. Lessee shall be responsible for the maintenance and repair of the Premises and shall keep and maintain the Premises in good condition, order and repair, and shall surrender the same upon the expiration of this Agreement, in the condition in which they are required to be kept, reasonable wear and tear and damage by the elements not caused by Lessee's negligence excepted.

9. It is expressly understood and agreed that, in providing required and authorized services pursuant to this Agreement, Lessee shall have the right to choose, in its sole discretion, its vendors and suppliers.

D. **Signs.** During the term of this Agreement, Lessee shall have the right, at its expense, to place in or on the Premises a sign or signs identifying Lessee. Said sign or signs shall be of a size, shape and design, and at a location or locations, approved by Lessor and in conformance with any overall directional graphics or sign program established by Lessor. Lessor's approval shall not be withheld unreasonably. Notwithstanding any other provision of this Agreement, said sign(s) shall remain the property

*Must be included in all leases governing aeronautical services on airports receiving federal aid.

of Lessee. Lessee shall remove, at its expense, all lettering, signs and placards so erected on the Premises upon termination of this Agreement.

E. **Trade Fixtures.** During the term of this Agreement, Lessee shall have the right, at its expense, to place in or on the Premises trade fixtures, furnishings, personal property, equipment and materials necessary to perform any services required or authorized hereunder. Said trade fixtures, furnishings, personal property, equipment and materials shall remain the property of the Lessee.

*F. **Nonexclusive Right.** It is not the intent of this Agreement to grant to Lessee the exclusive right to provide any or all of the services described in this Article III at any time during the term of this Agreement. Lessor reserves the right, at its sole discretion, to grant others certain rights and privileges upon the Airport which are identical in part or in whole to those granted to Lessee. Lessor does, however, covenant and agree that:

1. It shall enforce all minimum operating standards or requirements for all aeronautical endeavors and activities conducted at the Airport.

2. Any other operator of aeronautical endeavors or activities will not be permitted to operate on the Airport under rates, terms or conditions which are more favorable than those set forth in this Agreement; and

3. It will not permit the conduct of any aeronautical endeavor or activity at the Airport except under an approved lease and operating agreement.

Article Four

Appurtenant Privileges

A. **Use of Airport Facilities.** Lessee shall be entitled, in common with others so authorized, to the use of all facilities and improvements of a public nature which now are or may hereafter be connected with or appurtenant to the Airport, including but not limited to, the use of landing areas, runways, taxiways, navigational aids, terminal facilities and aircraft parking areas designated by Lessor.

B. **Maintenance of Airport Facilities. Lessor shall maintain all public and common or joint use areas of the Airport, including the Air Operations Area, in good repair, and shall make such repairs, replacements or additions thereto as it considers, in its sole discretion, necessary for the safe and efficient operation of the Airport.

C. **Aerial Approaches. Lessor reserves the right to take any action it considers necessary to protect the aerial approaches of the Airport against obstruction, together with the right to prevent Lessee from erecting, or permitting to be erected, any building or other structure on or adjacent to the Airport which, in the opinion of Lessor, would limit the usefulness of the Airport or constitute a hazard to aircraft.

D. **Non-competition.** Lessor shall not engage directly or indirectly in any of the activities described in Paragraphs A and B or Article Three of this Agreement.

*Must be included in all leases governing aeronautical services on airports receiving federal aid.

**Recommended for inclusion in all leases governing aeronautical services on airports receiving federal aid.

Article Five
Leasehold Improvements

A. **Required Improvements.**

1. As part of the consideration for the privileges herein granted, Lessee agrees to construct or otherwise make improvements to the Premises in an amount not less than $______, including all fees and costs associated therewith, but excluding the cost of tools, equipment, inventory or accessories installed or stocked on the Premises. The leasehold improvements are to include not less than ________ (________) square feet of additional hangar space, major renovation and modification of existing office space, pilot's lounge, customer service, shop and maintenance areas. Lessee agrees that it shall, within ninety (90) calendar days from the effective date of this Agreement, submit to Lessor, for approval, detailed plans and specifications for all of the proposed leasehold improvements. Lessor agrees that it shall either approve the plans and specifications as submitted, or transmit proposed revisions to Lessee, within thirty (30) calendar days of receipt of the plans and specifications from Lessee.

2. Upon receiving final approval of the plans and specifications from Lessor, Lessee shall engage one or more qualified contractors to construct said improvements. Construction shall commence within sixty (60) calendar days of Lessee's receipt of Lessor's final approval of the plans and specifications and shall be scheduled for completion not later than one hundred eighty (180) calendar days after commencement of construction. It is agreed and understood that leasehold improvements undertaken pursuant to this provision shall become the property of Lessor upon final completion of construction.

3. **Storage Tanks.** Any underground storage tanks constructed by Lessee shall meet all local, state and federal requirements.

Article Six
Payments

A. **Rent and Fees.** In consideration of the rights and privileges granted by this Agreement, Lessee agrees to pay to Lessor during the term of this Agreement the following:

1. **Rent.** A rental of $______ per annum for the Premises.

2. **Fees.**

a. A sum of $ ________ per gallon on all aviation fuel sold by Lessee at retail, excepting federal (including military), state and municipal government contract and retail fuel used by Lessee in the operation of its business.

b. A sum equal to ____ % of the adjusted gross receipts from all businesses conducted and carried on by Lessee at the Airport. The term "adjusted gross receipts" as used in this Agreement shall mean the aggregate amount of all sales made, and services performed, for cash, on credit or otherwise, of every kind, name and nature. Adjusted gross receipts shall also include the aggregate value of all goods, wares and merchandise received for property or services, at the selling price thereof, as if the same had been sold for cash. There shall be excluded from adjusted gross receipts (i) all fuel sales; (ii) all sales of new and used aircraft; (iii) all sales to federal (including military), state and municipal government entities; (iv) federal, state and municipal sales taxes, or other similar taxes, separately stated and collected from customers; and (v) bad debts.

B. **Payments.**

1. The rental payment specified in Paragraph A. 1, above, shall be paid monthly in advance in the sum of $ _______ per month, the first payment to be made on or before the first day of __________ , 19____ , and a like payment to be made on or before the first day of each month thereafter during the term of this Agreement. It is understood and agreed that the rental payments specified in Paragraph A.1, above, and in the preceding sentence, may be adjusted pursuant to Paragraph G, below, and that each such adjustment shall result in a change in the annual and monthly rental payments.

2. The fees specified in Paragraph A.2, above, shall be paid to Lessor on or before the twentieth (20th) day following the end of each month such fees are collected, together with a report of Lessee's retail fuel sales and adjusted gross receipts during the preceding month. It is understood and agreed that the fees specified in Paragraph A.2, above, may be adjusted pursuant to Paragraph G, below, and that each such adjustment shall result in a change in the calculation of the monthly payments of fees.

C. **Landing Fees.** Lessee shall collect landing fees from aircraft using Lessee's facility in accordance with a schedule of landing fees established by Lessor. Fees so collected shall be reported and paid monthly to Lessor, less a ____ % handling charge to be retained by Lessee, at the same time as the fees paid to Lessor pursuant to Paragraphs A.2 and B.2, above.

D. **Parking Fees.** Lessee shall collect aircraft parking fees, in accordance with a schedule of parking fees established by Lessor, for all aircraft parked in public parking areas adjacent to the Premises, elsewhere on the ramp or apron area adjacent to the Premises, or on such areas as may be designated by Lessor from time to time. Fees so collected shall be reported and paid monthly to Lessor, less a ____ % handling charge to be retained by Lessee, at the same time as the fees paid to Lessor pursuant to Paragraphs A.2 and B.2, above.

E. **Delinquency Charge.** A delinquency charge of % per month shall be added to payments required by Paragraphs A, B, C and D, above, which are rendered more than ten (10) days delinquent.

F. **Place of Payment.** All payments due Lessor from Lessee shall be delivered to the place designated in writing by Lessor.

G. **Renegotiation of Rent and Fees.** The rent and fees specified in Paragraphs A.l and A.2, above, shall be renegotiated during the last six (6) months of each five (5) year period of this Agreement, the increases or decreases in the rent and fees resulting from such re-negotiation to be effective as of the commencement of the succeeding five (5) year period.

It is understood and agreed that (a) no increase in such rental or fees shall exceed ____ % of the rental or fees then being paid by Lessee hereunder, and (b) no such increase shall be required if Lessee is prohibited by law or regulation from passing such increase on to its customers.

H. **Records.** Lessee shall provide and maintain accurate records of retail fuel sales and adjusted gross receipts derived under this Agreement, and landing and parking fees collected, for a period of three (3) years from the date the record is made. Such records shall be maintained according to generally accepted accounting principles. Lessor or its duly authorized representatives shall have the right at all reasonable times during business hours, and at its own expense, to inspect the books, records and receipts of Lessee, and to verify Lessee's fuel sales and adjusted gross receipts, and landing and parking fees collected.

I. **Annual Statement.** Within sixty (60) days after the end of each calendar year, Lessee shall furnish to Lessor a statement of fuel sales and adjusted gross receipts generated, and landing and parking fees collected, during the preceding calendar year, certified by an officer of Lessee as to its accuracy. Lessor reserves the right to audit said statement and Lessee's books and records, including examination of the general ledger and all other supporting material, at any reasonable time during business hours, for the purposes of verifying the reported fuel sales and adjusted gross receipts, and landing and parking fees collected.

If the audit establishes that Lessee has understated or overstated fuel sales or adjusted gross receipts, or landing or parking fees collected, by ____ % or more, the entire expense of said audit shall be borne by Lessee. Any additional payment due from Lessee shall forthwith be paid to Lessor, with interest thereon at ____ % per month from the date such amount originally became payable to Lessor. Any overpayment by Lessee shall be credited against further payments due to Lessor. Either party may refer the results of the audit for resolution in accordance with Paragraph J, below.

J. **Disputes.** In the event that any dispute may arise as to fuel sales, adjusted gross receipts, or landing or parking fees collected, the amount claimed due by Lessor shall be paid forthwith and the dispute shall be submitted to a certified public accountant, agreeable to both parties, who shall determine the rights of the parties hereunder in conformity with generally accepted accounting principles. The fees due said accountant for such services shall be paid by the unsuccessful party, or in the event the determination is partially in favor of each party, the fee shall be borne equally by the parties.

Article Seven
Utilities

Lessee shall have the right to use the utility service facilities located on the Premises at the commencement of the term of this Agreement. In addition, should Lessee's operations require additional utility service facilities, Lessor shall, at its expense, extend such facilities to the Premises. Lessor's obligation under this provision shall be limited to utilities extended by a public utility company to Lessor's property line, and nothing herein shall obligate Lessor to provide any utility to Lessee that is not otherwise available to Lessor at its property line. If Lessor is unable to provide utility service facilities due to the imposition of any limit on consumption or on the construction of additional utility facilities, or the allocation or curtailment of utility facilities or service by law or regulation, it shall have no obligation hereunder.

Lessee agrees to pay the cost of all utilities. In the event Lessee fails to pay any utility bill when due, lessor may, at its option, pay the same and collect from Lessee the amounts so disbursed, plus interest at the rate of ____ % per month or fraction thereof.

Article Eight
Insurance

A. **Required Insurance.** Lessee shall obtain and maintain continuously in effect at all times during the term of this Agreement, at Lessee's sole expense, the following insurance:

1. **Comprehensive general liability insurance** protecting Lessor against any and all liability arising by reason of Lessee's conduct incident to the use of the Premises, or resulting from any accident occurring on or about the roads, driveways or other public places, including runways and taxiways, used by Lessee at the Airport, caused by or arising out of any wrongful act or omission of Lessee, in the minimum amount of $________ ;

2. **Passenger liability insurance** in the minimum amount of $ ________________ per seat, and $ ________________ per occurrence;

3. **Hangar keeper's liability insurance** in the minimum amount of $ ____________ ;

4. **Product liability insurance** in the minimum amount of $ ____________ ;

5. **Professional liability insurance** in the minimum amount of $ ____________ ;

6. **Fire and extended coverage insurance** on all fixed improvements erected by Lessee on or in the Premises to the full insurable value thereof, and

7. **Environmental impairment liability insurance** in the minimum amount of $ ____________ per occurrence and $ ____________ total.

The insurance specified in Paragraphs A.2 through A.7, above, shall name Lessor as an additional insured.

B. **Notice.** Lessor agrees to notify Lessee in writing as soon as practicable of any claim, demand or action arising out of an occurrence covered hereunder of which Lessor has knowledge, and to cooperate with Lessee in the investigation and defense thereof.

Article Nine
Idemnification

To the extent not covered by insurance carried in favor of Lessor, Lessee shall keep and hold harmless Lessor from and against any and all claims, demands, suits, judgments, costs and expenses asserted by any person or persons, including agents or employees of Lessor or Lessee, by reason of death or injury to persons or loss of or damage to property, resulting from Lessee's operations, or anything done or omitted by Lessee under this Agreement except to the extent that such claims, demands, suits, judgments, costs and expenses may be attributed to the acts or omissions of Lessor, its agents or employees.

Article Ten
Casualty

In the event that any fixed improvements erected on the Premises by Lessee, pursuant to Paragraph A of Article Five of this Agreement, are damaged or destroyed by fire or other casualty, Lessee shall immediately repair the improvements and restore them to a condition at least as good as existed immediately before the casualty. While the improvements are being so repaired and restored, the rent hereunder shall abate only if the Premises are rendered untenantable by such damage.

In the event that any fixed improvements erected on the Premises by Lessor are damaged or destroyed by fire or other casualty, the rent hereunder shall not abate provided the Premises are not rendered untenantable by such damage. If the Premises are rendered untenantable, and Lessor elects to repair the Premises, the rent shall abate for the period during which such repairs are being made, provided the damage was not caused by acts or omissions of Lessee, its employees, agents or invitees, in which case the rent shall not abate. If the Premises are rendered untenantable, and Lessor elects not to repair the Premises, this Agreement shall terminate.

Article Eleven

Condemnation

If the entire leased Premises, or such portion thereof as will make the Premises unsuitable for the operation of Lessee's business, are taken under the exercise of the power of eminent domain by Lessor, Lessor shall pay to Lessee the sum of $ ___________ , representing the fair market value of the leasehold, as liquidated damages, and not as a penalty.

Article Twelve

Lessee as Independent Contractor

In conducting its business hereunder, Lessee acts as an independent contractor and not as an agent of Lessor. The selection, retention, assignment, direction and payment of Lessee's employees shall be the sole responsibility of Lessee, and Lessor shall not attempt to exercise any control over the daily performance of duties by Lessee's employees.

Article Thirteen

Assignment

This Agreement, or any part thereof, may not be assigned, transferred or subleased by Lessee, by process or operation of law or in any other manner whatsoever, without the prior written consent of Lessor, which consent shall not be withheld unreasonably.

Article Fourteen

*Nondiscrimination

A. Notwithstanding any other provision of this Agreement, during the performance of this Agreement, Lessee, for itself, its heirs, personal representatives, successors in interest and assigns, as part of the consideration of this Agreement does hereby covenant and agree, as a covenant running with the land, that:

1. No person on the grounds of race, color, religion, sex or national origin shall be excluded from participation in, denied the benefits of, or otherwise be subjected to discrimination in the use of the Premises;

2. In the construction of any improvements on, over or under the Premises, and the furnishing of services therein or thereon, no person on the grounds of race, color, religion, sex or national origin shall be excluded from participation in, or denied the benefits of, such activities, or otherwise be subjected to discrimination;

3. Lessee shall use the Premises in compliance with all other requirements imposed by or pursuant of Title 49, Code of Federal Regulations ("C.F.R."), Department of Transportation, Subtitle A, Office of the Secretary, Part 21, Nondiscrimination in Federally Assisted Programs of the Department of Transportation—Effectuation of Title Vl of the Civil Rights Act of 1964, and as said regulations may be amended.

4. In the event of breach of any of the above nondiscrimination covenants, Lessor shall have the right to terminate this Agreement and to reenter and repossess the Premises and hold the same as if

*Must be included in all leases governing aeronautical services on airports receiving federal aid.

said Agreement had never been made or issued. This provision does not become effective until the procedures of 49 C.F.R. Part 21 have been followed and completed, including expiration of appeal rights.

**B. Lessee assures that it will undertake an affirmative action program, as required by 14 C.F.R. Part 152, Subpart E, to ensure that no person shall, on the grounds of race, creed, color, national origin, or sex, be excluded from participating in any employment, contracting or leasing activities covered in 14 C.F.R. Part 152, Subpart E. Lessee assures that no person shall be excluded on these grounds, from participating in or receiving the services or benefits of any program or activity covered by Subpart E. Lessee assures that it will require that its covered organizations provide assurance to the Lessee that they similarly will undertake affirmative action programs and that they will require assurances from their suborganizations, as required by 14 C.F.R. Part 152, Subpart E, to the same effect.

Lessee agrees to comply with any affirmative action plan or steps for equal employment opportunity required by 14 C.F.R., Part 152, Subpart E, or by any federal, state, or local agency or court, including those resulting from a conciliation agreement, a consent decree, court order, or similar mechanism. Lessee agrees that a state or local affirmative action plan will be used in lieu of any affirmative action plan or steps required by 14 C.F.R. 152, Subpart E, only when it fully meets the standards set forth in 14 C.F.R. 152.409. Lessee agrees to obtain a similar assurance from its covered organizations, and to cause them to require a similar assurance of their covered suborganizations, as required by 14 C.F.R. Part 152, Subpart E.

Article Fifteen

***Requirements of the United States

This agreement shall be subject and subordinate to the provisions of any existing or future agreement between Lessor and the United States, or any agency thereof, relative to the operation or maintenance of the Airport, the execution of which has been or may be required as a condition precedent to the expenditure of federal funds for the development or operation of the Airport; provided, however, that Lessor shall, to the extent permitted by law, use its best efforts to cause any such agreements to include provisions protecting and preserving the rights of Lessee in and to the Premises, and to compensation for taking thereof, interference therewith and damage thereto, caused by such agreement or by actions of Lessor or the United States pursuant thereto.

Article Sixteen

Default and termination

A. **Termination by Lessee.** This Agreement shall be subject to termination by Lessee in the event of any one or more of the following events:

1. The abandonment of the Airport as an airport or airfield for any type, class or category of aircraft.

**Must be included in the leases of all lessees having fifty (50) or more employees and conducting aeronautical activities on airports receiving federal aid.

***Recommended for inclusion in all leases governing aeronautical services on airports receiving aid.

2. The default by Lessor in the performance of any of the terms, covenants or conditions of this Agreement, and the failure of Lessor to remedy, or undertake to remedy, to Lessee's satisfaction, such default for a period of thirty (30) days after receipt of notice from Lessee to remedy the same.

3. Damage to or destruction of all or a material part of the Premises or Airport facilities necessary to the operation of Lessee's business.

4. The lawful assumption by the United States, or any authorized agency thereof, of the operation, control or use of the Airport, or any substantial part or parts thereof, in such a manner as to restrict Lessee from substantially conducting business operations for a period in excess of ninety (90) days.

B. **Termination by Lessor.** This Agreement shall be subject to termination by Lessor in the event of any one or more of the following events:

1. The default by Lessee in the performance of any of the terms, covenants or conditions of this Agreement, and the failure of Lessee to remedy, or undertake to remedy, to Lessor's satisfaction, such default for a period of thirty (30) days after receipt of notice from Lessor to remedy the same.

2. Lessee files a voluntary petition in bankruptcy, including a reorganization plan, makes a general or other assignment for the benefit of creditors, is adjudicated as bankrupt or if a receiver is appointed for the property or affairs of Lessee and such receivership is not vacated within thirty (30) days after the appointment of such receiver.

3. Lessee's abandonment of the Premises.

C. **Force Majeure; Waiver.**

1. Neither party shall be held to be in breach of this Agreement because of any failure to perform any of its obligations hereunder if said failure is due to any act of God, fire, flood, accident, strike, riot, insurrection, war, or any other cause over which that party has no control; provided however, that the foregoing provision shall not apply to failures by Lessee to pay fees, rents or other charges to Lessor.

2. The waiver of any breach, violation or default in or with respect to the performance or observance of the covenants and conditions contained herein shall not be taken to constitute a waiver of any subsequent breach, violation or default in or with respect to the same or any other covenant or condition hereof.

D. **Payment for Leasehold Improvements.** In the event of any cancellation or termination of this Agreement, for any cause other than a breach or default by Lessee, Lessor shall, within thirty (30) days of the date of such termination or cancellation, pay Lessee, for all of the leasehold improvements installed or constructed by Lessee pursuant to Paragraph A of Article Five of this Agreement, a cash price equal to Lessee's unamortized costs for said improvements. Lessee agrees that, for purpose of this provision, it shall amortize the actual direct cost of such improvements on a straight-line basis, commencing with the effective date of this Agreement and extending for the twenty-five (25) year term hereof.

Article Seventeen
Arbitration

Except as provided in Paragraph J of Article Six of this Agreement, all claims or disputes arising out of or relating to this Agreement shall be settled by arbitration in accordance with the Commercial Arbitration Rules of the American Arbitration Association then obtaining. Notice of the demand for arbitration shall be filed in writing with the other party to the Agreement and with the American Arbitration Association and shall be made within a reasonable time after the claim or dispute has arisen. The award rendered by the arbitrator or arbitrators shall be final, and judgment may be entered upon it in accordance with applicable law in any court having jurisdiction thereof.

Except by written consent of the person or entity sought to be joined, no arbitration arising out of or relating to the Agreement shall include, by consolidation, joinder or in any other manner, any person or entity not a party to the Agreement, unless it is shown at the time the demand for arbitration if filed that (a) such person or entity is substantially involved in a common question of fact or law; (b) the presence of such person or entity is required if complete relief is to be accorded in the arbitration; and (c) the interest or responsibility of such person or entity in the matter is not insubstantial.

The agreement of the parties to arbitrate claims and disputes shall be specifically enforceable under the prevailing arbitration law.

Pending final decision of the arbitrator or arbitrators, the parties shall proceed diligently with the performance of their obligations under this Agreement.

Article Eighteen
Miscellaneous Provisions

A. **Entire Agreement.** This Agreement constitutes the entire understanding between the parties, and as of its effective date supersedes all prior or independent agreements between the parties covering the subject matter hereof. Any change or modification hereof must be in writing and signed by both parties.

B. **Severability.** If a provision hereof shall be finally declared void or illegal by any court or administrative agency having jurisdiction, the entire Agreement shall not be void, but the remaining provisions shall continue in effect as nearly as possible in accordance with the original intent of the parties.

C. **Notice.** Any notice given by one party to the other in connection with this Agreement shall be in writing and shall be sent by registered mail, return receipt requested, with postage and registration fees prepaid:

1. If to Lessor, addressed to:

____

____

____

2. If to Lessee, addressed to:

____

____

____

Notices shall be deemed to have been received on the date of receipt as shown on the return receipt.

D. **Headings.** The headings used in this Agreement are intended for convenience of reference only and do not define or limit the scope or meaning of any provision of this Agreement.

E. **Governing Law.** This Agreement is to be construed in accordance with the laws of the state of____________________ .

IN WITNESS WHEREOF, the parties have executed this Agreement as of the day and year first above written.

LESSOR: ______________________________

By: ______________________________

Title: ______________________________

LESSEE: ______________________________

By: ______________________________

Title: ______________________________

Glossary of Aviation Management Terms

AAAE—American Association of Airport Executives.

Accident—An event that occurs even though a reasonable person would not have foreseen its occurrence.

Account—Record of day-to-day changes in items that appear on the balance sheet or income statement.

Account Entry Convention—Debits are entered on the left-hand side, credits on the right. Debit entries equal credit entries.

Account Payable—An obligation to pay an amount to a creditor.

Account Receivable—An amount that is owed to the business, usually by one of its customers as a result of the ordinary extension of credit.

Accountability—The holding of oneself or another totally responsible for results, good or bad.

Accounting—The recording, classifying, summarizing and interpreting of financial data.

Accounting, Cost—The process of collecting labor and overhead costs and attaching them to products.

Accounting Period—The period of time over which an income statement summarizes changes in the owner's equity.

Accounting System—A formal communications network that supplies relevant information for planning control, decision making and evaluation.

Accrual Concept—Net income is measured as the difference between revenues and expenses rather than between cash receipts and expenditures.

Accrued Federal Income Taxes—Accruals for currently payable federal income taxes.

Accrued Personnel Compensation—Accruals for unpaid compensation to personnel.

Acid Test Ratio—The ratio of cash and near-cash items to the total current liabilities.

Act of Bankruptcy—Any of the acts specified by national bankruptcy law which, when committed by the debtor within the specified time period, is proper grounds for declaring a debtor a bankrupt.

Activity—Used in aviation to refer to any kind of movement, e.g., cargo flights, passenger flights, passenger enplanements. Without clarification it has no specific meaning.

Acts of God—Natural phenomena (such as lightning and floods) that are considered impossible to prevent or control, and are usually insurable because they are impersonal in nature.

Actuary—A mathematician who uses probability theory to calculate degrees of risk for use in insurance rate-making.

ADAP—See AIP

Advance from Associated Companies—Net amounts due associated companies for notes, loans and advances that are not settled currently.

Advertising—Nonpersonal selling techniques designed to inform customers and induce them to purchase the product or service being advertised.

Advisory—Advice and information provided to assist pilots in the safe conduct of a flight and aircraft movement.

Advisory Circular—A document published by the Federal Aviation Administration (FAA) giving guidance on aviation issues.

Aerial Application—Aerial application in agriculture consists of those activities that involve the discharge of materials from aircraft flight and miscellaneous collection of minor related activities that do not require the distribution of any materials.

Aerobatic Flight—An intentional maneuver involving an abrupt change in an aircraft's attitude—an abnormal attitude or abnormal acceleration not necessary for normal flight.

Aerodrome—Airport facility (not usually used for seaplane facilities).

Aeronautical Chart—A map used in air navigation containing all or part of the following: Topographic features, hazards and obstructions, navigation aids, navigation routes, designated airspace, and airports.

Agency—The relationship that exists between a person identified as a principal and another by virtue of which the latter may make contracts with a third person on behalf of the principal.

Agent—One who is authorized by a principal or by operation of law to make contracts with third parties on behalf of the principal.

AIP—Airport Improvement Program. A program originally called the Airport Development Aid Program and established by the Airport and Airway Development Act of 1970 to provide federal funding for certain airport improvements and new airport development. The original legislation expired in 1975, was renewed in 1976, expired in 1980, and was renewed for one year in 1981 and replaced by the Airport Improvement Program in 1982 and subsequent years.

Air Cargo—All commercial air express and air freight including air mail and air parcel post (cargo = freight + mail).

Air Carrier—A person who undertakes directly by lease, or other arrangement, to engage in air transportation.

Air Defense Identification Zone/ADIZ—The area of airspace over land or water, extending upward from the surface, within which the identification, the location, and the control of aircraft are required in the interest of national security.

Air Navigation Facility (NAVAID)—Although generally referring to electronic radio wave transmitters (VOR, NDB, ILS), includes any structure or mechanism designed to guide or control aircraft involved in flight operations.

Air Route Traffic Control Center (ARTCC)—FAA-manned facility (21 nationwide) established to provide air traffic control services to aircraft operating in controlled airspace, enroute between terminal areas. Although designed to handle aircraft operating IFR, some advisory services are provided to participating VFR aircraft when controller workloads permit. The primary tool of the ARTCC is the Air Route Surveillance Radar. The FAA recently announced plans for a $9 billion refurbishment of the national airspace system that will make major changes.

Air Taxi—Air carriers that provide on-demand unscheduled service to any destination the passenger desires. Air taxis are not certificated by the CAB but are controlled under FAR Parts 135 and 298.

Air Traffic—Aircraft operating in the air or on an airport surface, exclusive of loading ramps and parking areas.

Air Traffic Control—A service operated by appropriate authority to promote the safe, orderly and expeditious flow of air traffic.

Air Traffic Hub—Air traffic hubs are not airports; they are the cities and Standard Metropolitan Statistical Areas requiring aviation services and may include more than one airport. Communities fall into four classes as determined by each community's as percentage of the total enplaned passengers.

Airborne Speed—Often called "wheels-off, wheels-on speed." The average speed of an aircraft while airborne, in terms of great circle distances. It is calculated by dividing the sum of airport-to-airport distances in statute miles, by the number of airborne hours.

Aircraft—A device that is used or intended to be used for flight in the air.

Aircraft Accident (Incident to Flight)—An aircraft accident incident to flight is that which occurs between the time the engine or engines are started for the purpose of flight until the aircraft comes to rest with all engines stopped for complete or partial deplaning or unloading. It excludes death or injuries to persons on board which result from illness, altercations and other incidents not directly attributed to flight operations.

Aircraft Classes—For the purpose of Wake Turbulence Separation Minima, ATC classifies aircraft as heavy, large, and small as follows:

1. *Heavy*—Aircraft capable of takeoff weights of 300,000 pounds or more whether or not they are operating at this weight during a particular phase of flight.
2. *Large*—Aircraft of more than 12,500 pounds, maximum certificated takeoff weight, up to 300,000 pounds.
3. *Small*—Aircraft of up to 12,500 pounds maximum certificated weight.

Aircraft Contacted—Aircraft with which the Flight Service Stations have established radio communications contact. One count is made for each en route, landing or departing aircraft contacted by Flight Service Stations regardless of the number of contacts made with an individual aircraft during the same flight.

Aircraft Gate Position—An aircraft operational stand close to the terminal building and related to a specific gate.

Aircraft Industry—The industry primarily engaged in the production of aircraft, aircraft engines and parts, aircraft propellers and parts, and aircraft auxiliary equipment. A sector of the aerospace industry.

Aircraft Miles—(or *plane miles*) The miles computed in airport-to-airport distances for each inter-airport hop actually completed, whether or not performed in accordance with the scheduled pattern.

Aircraft Mix—The classification of aircraft into groups which are similar in size and operational characteristics. (See also **Fleet Mix.**)

Aircraft Operation—An aircraft arrival or departure from an airport with FAA airport traffic control service. There are two types of operations—local and itinerant.

1. *Local operations* are performed by aircraft which:
   a. Operate in the local traffic pattern or within sight of the tower.

b. Are known to be departing for, or arriving from, flight in local practice areas located within a 20-mile radius of the control tower.
c. Execute simulated instrument approaches or low passes at the airport.

2. *Itinerant Operations:* All aircraft arrivals and departures other than local operations.

Aircraft Revenue Hours—The airborne hours in revenue service computed from the moment an aircraft leaves the ground until it touches down again.

Aircraft and Traffic Servicing Expenses—Compensation of ground personnel and other expenses incurred on the ground to protect and control the in-flight movement of aircraft, to schedule and prepare aircraft crews for flight assignment, to handle and service aircraft while in line operation, and service and handle traffic on the ground. Requires issuance of documents establishing the air carrier responsibility to provide air transportation and in-flight expenses of handling and protecting all nonpassenger traffic including passenger baggage.

Aircraft Type—A term used to group aircraft—fixed wing, rotorcraft, glider, dirigible, balloon, etc. These types may be further subdivided.

Airfield—A defined area on land or water including any buildings, installations and equipment intended to be used either wholly or in part for the arrival, departure and movement of aircraft.

Airframe—The fuselage, booms, nacelles, cowlings, fairings, airfoil surfaces (including rotors but excluding propellers and rotating airfoils of engines), and landing gear of an aircraft and their accessories or controls.

Airline Operations Area—An area close to the aircraft gate position(s) required for the airline operations personnel and equipment.

Airman's Information Manual/AIM—A publication designed primarily as a pilot's operational and instructional manual for use in the National Airspace System of the United States.

Airplane—An engine-driven fixed-wing aircraft heavier than air that is supported in flight by the dynamic reaction of the air against its wings.

Airport—An area of land or water that is used or intended to be used for landing and takeoff of aircraft and includes its buildings and facilities, if any.

Airport, Basic Transport—An airport designed to accommodate turbojet-powered aircraft up to 60,000 pounds gross weight. This includes most aircraft commonly referred to as "business jet."

Airport, Basic Utility: Stage I—An airport designed to accommodate about 75 percent of the airplanes under 12,500 pounds. These airports primarily serve small population communities, remote areas, and locations with tow levels of aircraft activity.

Airport, Basic Utility: Stage II—An airport designed to accommodate about 95 percent of the airplanes under 12,500 pounds. These airports primarily serve medium-sized population communities with a potential for increased aviation activities.

Airport Elevation/Field Elevation—The highest point of an airport's usable runways measured in feet from mean sea level.

Airport, General Utility—An airport that can accommodate all aircraft under 12,500 pounds. These airports primarily serve communities located on the fringe of a metropolitan area, or a relatively large population community remote from metropolitan areas.

Airport Lighting—Various lighting aids that may be installed on an airport.

Airport Roads—A network of public and non-public roads within the airport boundary providing access to the various airport buildings or areas.

Airport Rotating Beacon—A visual NAVAID operated at many airports. At civil airports alternating white and green flashes indicate the location of the airport, and whether it is open and usable. The total number of flashes are 12 to 15 per minute. At military airports, the beacons flash alternately white and green if open, but are differentiated from civil beacons by dual-peaked (two quick) white flashes between the green flashes. Normally, operation of an airport rotating beacon during the hours of daylight means that the reported ground visibility at the airport is less than three miles and/or the reported ceiling is less than 1,000 feet and therefore, an ATC clearance is required for landing or takeoff.

Airport Surveillance Radar (ASR)—Radar providing position of aircraft by azimuth and range data without elevation data. It is designed for a range of approximately 50 miles. Also called ATC Terminal Radar.

Airport Traffic Control Tower—A central operations facility in the terminal air traffic control system, consisting of a tower cab structure, including an associated IFR room if radar equipped, using air/ground communications and/or radar, visual signaling and other devices, to provide safe and expeditious movement of terminal air traffic.

Airship—An engine-driven, light-than-air aircraft that can be steered.

Airside—That portion of the airport facility where aircraft movements take place, airline operations areas, and areas that directly serve the aircraft (taxiway, runway, maintenance, and fueling area). (See **Landside.**)

Airspace—The space lying above the earth or above a certain area of land or water which is necessary to conduct aviation operations. (See **Controlled Airspace.**)

Airspeed—The speed of an aircraft relative to its surrounding air mass.

Airway Beacon—Used to mark airway segments in remote mountain areas. The light flashes Morse Code to identify the beacon site.

Airway/Federal Airway—A control area or portion thereof established in the form of a corridor, the centerline of which is defined by radio navigational aids.

All-cargo Aircraft—A configuration of an aircraft type which carries cargo and mail only. Some all-cargo aircraft can be rapidly switched to passenger service by the installation of portable seats.

Allocated Expenses—Those which are not directly attributable to any one department but are divided by formula among the various departments of the operation.

Allocation—Assigning one or more items of cost or revenue to one or more segments of an organization according to benefits received, responsibilities or other logic.

ALP—Airport Layout Plan.

ALS—Approach Light System.

Alternate Airport—An airport at which an aircraft may land if landing at the intended airport becomes inadvisable.

Altimeter Setting—The barometric pressure reading used to adjust a pressure altimeter for variations in existing atmospheric pressure or to the standard altimeter setting (29.92).

Ambient Noise Level—Background noise level, exclusive of the contribution made by aircraft.

Amortization—Paying off an investment expenditure.

AMOS—Automatic Meteorological Observation Station.

ANCLUC—Airport Noise Control and Land Use Compatibility planning study. (See **Part 150.**)

Annuity—A guaranteed income for life with payments received at regular intervals; a type of investment offered by insurance companies.

Antitrust—Statutory prohibition of contracts in restraint of trade.

Appreciation—Increase in the market value of an asset over time.

Approach Clearance—Air traffic control service provided by an approach control facility for arriving and departing VFR/IFR aircraft and, on occasion, en route aircraft. At some airports not served by an approach control facility, the ARTCC provides limited approach control service.

Approach Control Service—Air traffic control service provided by a terminal area traffic control facility for arriving and departing IFR aircraft, and, on occasion, VFR aircraft.

Approach Sequence—The order in which aircraft are positioned while on approach or awaiting approach clearance.

Approach Speed—The recommended speed contained in aircraft manuals used by pilots when making an approach to landing. This speed will vary for different segments of an approach as well as for aircraft weight and configuration.

Approach Surface—An imaginary surface longitudinally centered on the extended runway centerline and extending outward and upward from each end of the primary surface. It is applied to each end of a runway based on the type of available or planned approach.

Apron—A defined area on the airside of the terminal building where aircraft are maneuvered and parked and where activities associated with the handling of flights can be carried out. (Also known as *ramp*.)

Arbitration—The settlement of disputes by one or more mediators whose decision is final.

Area Navigation (RNAV)—A method of navigation that permits aircraft operations on any desired course within the coverage of station-referenced navigation signals or within the limits of self-contained system capability.

ARP—Airport Reference Point.

Arrival Time—The time an aircraft touches down on arrival.

Arriving (Passenger, Baggage, Cargo, Mail)—A passenger (baggage, cargo, mail) arriving at the terminal by air, whether terminating, transit, or transfer.

Asset—Property or property right. Current assets are either currently in the form of cash or will be so converted in a short period, usually under a year. Fixed assets are tangible properties of long life, generally used in the production of goods/services.

Asset Turnover—The ratio of sales to total assets available.

Assets—The items on the balance sheet of a business showing the book value of its resources.

Assets, Net—The sum of all recorded assets after reducing such amount by allowance or reserve for bad debts, depreciation, and amortization, but before deducting any liabilities, mortgages or other indebtedness.

Assignment—A transfer of the title or ownership of a right.

ATA—Air Transport Association.

ATC—Air Traffic Control or Alaska Transportation Commission, depending on context. The Alaska Transportation Commission regulates intrastate aviation.

ATC Clears—Used to prefix an ATC clearance when it is relayed to an aircraft by other than an air traffic controller.

ATCT—Air Traffic Control Tower. (See **Control Tower.**)

Attachment—The seizure of property to pay a debt.

Audit—A review of accounting records for accuracy.

Authority—The power to make decisions, command, and delegate responsibility to others.

Autogyro—A plane that derives its lift from airfoils that rotate without engine power.

Automated Radar Terminal Systems/ARTS—The generic term for the ultimate in functional capability afforded by several automation systems.

Automatic Altitude Reporting—That function of a transponder which responds to Mode C interrogations by transmitting the aircraft's altitude in 100-foot increments.

Automatic Direction Finder/ADF—An aircraft radio navigation system which senses and indicates the direction to a L/MF non-directional radio beacon (NDB) ground transmitter.

Automatic Terminal Information Service/ATIS—The continuous broadcast of recorded noncontrol information in selected terminal areas. Its purpose is to improve controller effectiveness and to relieve frequency congestion by automating the repetitive transmission of essential but routine information, e.g., "Los Angeles Information Alpha. 1300 Greenwich Weather, seven one, wind two five zero at five, altimeter two niner six, ILS runway two five left approach in use, runway two five right closed, advise you have Alpha."

Available Seat—Miles (ASMs)—The aircraft miles flown in each flight stage multiplied by the number of seats available on that stage for revenue passenger use.

Avgas—AViation GASoline. Fuel used in reciprocating (piston) aircraft engines. Avgas is manufactured in the following grades: 80/87, 100LL, 100/130, and 115/145. Some aircraft are now permitted to use automobile gas or mogas. (80 not readily available anymore.)

Aviation Weather Service—A service provided by the National Weather Service (NWS) and FAA which collects and disseminates pertinent weather information for pilots, aircraft operators and ATC.

Bad Check Laws—Laws making it a criminal offense to issue a bad check with intent to defraud.

Baggage—The personal property or other articles of a passenger transported in connection with his journey. Unless otherwise specified, it includes both checked and unchecked baggage.

Baggage Claim Area—An area provided in the terminal building for the claiming of checked baggage from the airlines by passengers on arrival.

Baggage Make-up Area—The area where checked baggage for departing flights is loaded into containers or onto baggage carts.

Baggage Stripping Area—The area where checked baggage from arriving flights is unloaded from baggage containers or baggage carts. (Also referred to as "*baggage breakdown area.*")

Balance—The beginning balance is the amount in an account at the start of the accounting period. New—the amount in an account at the end of an accounting period; the amount reported on the next balance sheet.

Balance Sheet—A financial statement that reports the assets and liabilities of a company at a specific point in time.

Balloon—A lighter-than-air aircraft that is not engine-driven.

Balloon Payment—A final loan payment, often larger than the previous payments.

Bankruptcy—A procedure by which someone unable to pay his or her debts may be declared bankrupt, after which all assets in excess of exemption claims are surrendered to the court for distribution to creditors, and the debtor is given a discharge that releases him or her from the unpaid balance on most debts.

Based Aircraft—An aircraft permanently stationed at an airport, usually by some form of agreement between the aircraft owner and airport management. Most states have specific definitions of based aircraft. Records vary in accuracy, depending upon counting method used.

Baseline—With respect to an environmental factor, the amount of pollution or impact present in the ambient. With respect to aviation activity forecasts, the probable level of activity if unusual shifts in trend do not occur.

Bearing—The horizontal direction to or from any point, usually measured clockwise from true north, magnetic north or some other reference point, through 360 degrees.

Behavioral Science—The study of human social and individual activity.

Below Minimums—Weather conditions below the minimums prescribed by regulations for the particular action involved, e.g., landing minimums, takeoff minimums.

Beneficiary—The person to whom the proceeds of an insurance policy are payable; a person for whose benefit property is held in trust; or a person given property in a will.

Bill of Lading—A document issued by a carrier reciting the receipt of goods and the terms of the contract of transportation. Regulated by the Federal Bills of Lading Act or the Uniform Commercial Code.

Bill of Sale—A writing signed by the seller saying that the property therein described has been sold to the buyer.

Blimp—A lighter than air craft normally powered by aircraft engines, and having no rigid framework.

Board of Directors—A group elected by stockholders to provide guidance for a corporation.

Book Value—The dollar value of a company's assets minus its liabilities.

Brake Horsepower—The power delivered to the propeller shaft (main drive or main output) of an aircraft engine.

Braking Action (Good, Medium, Fair, Poor, Nil)—A report of conditions on the airport movement area providing a pilot with the degree/quality of braking that he might expect.

Breakeven Point—The level of output/sales where operating revenues cover expenses.

BRL—Building Restriction Line; setback line for construction at airports.

Broadcast—Transmission of information for which an acknowledgment is not expected.

B.S.—Broadcast Station. Public or private radio broadcasting station (AM or FM).

BSL—Building Setback Line.

Budget—A plan of action expressed in dollars; a financial plan. An expense budget is the part of the total budget relating to expenses of one or more departments.

Business Transportation—The use of a personal or corporate aircraft for purposes of business travel, but not for hire. Sometimes described as executive or corporate travel.

CAB—Civil Aeronautics Board, eliminated January 1, 1985 under the terms of the Airline Deregulation Act of 1978. Remaining functions transferred to United States Department of Transportation and other federal agencies. Formerly regulated scheduled and charter air service.

Calibrated Airspeed—Indicated airspeed of an aircraft, corrected for position and instrument error.

Capacity—The maximum volume of flight activity which an airport element can accommodate without saturation.

Capital—Money, goods, information, land and equipment used to produce other goods and services.

Capital Budgeting—Long term planning for capital goods acquisition.

Capital Gains or Losses, Operating Property—Gains or losses on retirements of operating property and equipment, flight equipment, expendable parts or miscellaneous materials and supplies when sold or otherwise retired in connection with a general retirement program and not as incidental sales performed as a service to others.

Capital Stock—The declared money value of the outstanding stock of the corporation.

Capital, Total—Owners equities plus creditors' equities.

Carousel—A mechanically driven rotating baggage claim or sorting device which is oval or circular in shape and on which baggage remains until physically removed.

Cash—General and working funds available on demand which are not formally restricted or earmarked for specific objectives.

Cash Budget—A schedule of expected cash receipts and disbursements.

Cash Flow—The amount of cash flowing in and out of a business in a given period.

Cash Surrender Value—The sum total paid to the insured if he surrenders his policy to the insurer.

CAT I (one)—Category I ILS approach procedure which provides for approach to a Height Above Touchdown (HAT) of not less than 200 feet, except in unusual terrain, and with Runway Visual Range (RVR) of not less than 1800 feet.

CAT II (two)—Category II ILS approach procedure which provides for approach to a Height Above Touchdown of not less than 100 feet and with Runway Visual Range of not less than 1200 feet. Installed only at major airports.

CAT IIIA (three-A)—Category III ILS approach which provides for approach with no decision height minimum and a runway visual range of not less than 700 feet. Installed only at major airports.

Ceiling—The height above the earth's surface of the lowest layer of clouds or obscuring phenomena that is reported as "broken," "overcast" or "obscured" and not classified as "thin" or "partial."

Celestial Navigation—The determination of geographical position by reference to celestial bodies. Normally used in aviation as a secondary means of position determination.

Center's Area—The specified airspace within which an Air Route Traffic Control Center (ARTCC) provides air traffic control and advisory service.

Central Tendency Error—A rating error in which the employer is reluctant to rate the employee at the outer ends of the scale.

Certificated—See **Air Carrier**.

CFR—Crash-Fire-Rescue (e.g., facilities, equipment, station).

Chain of Command—The hierarchy of managers and subordinates.

Charter—A non-scheduled flight offered by either a supplemental or certificated airline.

Charter Revenues—Revenues from nonscheduled air transport services in which the party receiving the transportation obtains exclusive use of an aircraft and the remuneration paid by such party accrues directly to, and the responsibility for providing transportation is that of, the accounting air carrier. Passenger charter revenues are from charter flights carrying only passengers and their personal baggage. Freight charter revenues are from charter flights carrying either (1) freight only or (2) passengers and freight simultaneously.

Chattel Mortgage—A mortgage that carries a lien on the movable property of a business firm.

Check—An order by a depositor on his bank to pay a sum of money to a payee; a bill of exchange drawn on a bank and payable on demand.

CIP—Capital Improvement Program.

Circling Approach—A descent in an approved procedure to an airport for a circle-to-land maneuver.

Civil Rights Act—A national law passed in 1964 establishing the right to equal employment in business and unions. It is designed to eliminate discrimination because of race, color, religion, sex or national origin.

Classification Method—A job evaluation system in which the job hierarchy is divided into a number of pay groups or grades, with written definitions for each grade, and each job assigned to a particular grade.

Clear Air Turbulence/CAT—Turbulence encountered in air where no clouds are present. This term is commonly applied to high-level turbulence associated with wind shear.

Clear of Traffic—Previously issued traffic is no longer a factor.

Clear Zone—The ground areas beneath the inner end of the runway approach surface. Height restrictions are involved.

Cleared for Approach—ATC authorization for an aircraft to execute any standard or special instrument approach procedure for that airport. Normally an aircraft will be cleared for a specific instrument approach procedure.

Cleared as Filed—The aircraft is cleared to proceed in accordance with the route of flight filed in the flight plan.

Cleared to Land—ATC authorization for an aircraft to land. It is predicated on known traffic and known physical airport conditions.

Cleared for Takeoff—ATC authorization for an aircraft to depart. It is predicated on known traffic and known physical airport conditions.

Clearway—A clearway is an area available for the continuation of the takeoff operation which is above a clearly defined area connected to and extended beyond the end of the runway. The area over which the clearway lies need not be suitable for stopping aircraft in the event of an aborted takeoff. Clearways are applicable for use only in the takeoff operations of turbine-engined airplanes.

Climbout—That portion of flight operation between takeoff and the initial cruising altitude.

Closed Runway—A runway that is unusable for aircraft operations. Only the airport management/military operations office can close a runway.

COBOL—Common Business Oriented Language. A programming language specifically designed for business data processing applications.

Codes/Transponder—The number assigned to a particular multiple pulse reply signal transmitted by a transponder.

Coinsurance—A clause commonly found in fire insurance policies which limits the liability of insurance companies unless the insured has a minimum percent of the value of the property insured.

Commercial Operator—A person who, for compensation or hire, engages in the carriage by aircraft in air commerce of persons or property, other than as an air carrier or foreign air carrier or under the authority of Part 375. Where it is doubtful that an operation is for "compensation or hire," the test applied is whether the carriage by air is merely incidental to the person's other business or is, in itself, a major enterprise for profit.

Commission—A fee paid to an agent or employee for transacting some business or performing a service, usually a percentage of the money involved in the transaction.

Committed Costs—Those fixed costs arising from the possession of plant and equipment and a basic organization and, thus, affected primarily by long-run decisions as to the desired level of capacity.

Common IFR Room—A highly automated terminal radar control facility. It provides terminal radar service in an area encompassing more than one major airport which accommodates instrument flight operations.

Communication—The exchange of information between two or more persons for the purpose of bringing about understanding.

Communication, Distortion—A term used to signify, a loss of accuracy in a message.

Communication, Feedback—The response that the receiver makes upon decoding and interpreting the meaning of the source's message.

Communication, Two-way—Communication and feedback between the source and receiver.

Commuter—An airline that provides scheduled air transportation at least five times per week over specified routes using light aircraft. Although not issued a certificate of public convenience and necessity, commuters are controlled by the FAA through safety requirements, insurance requirements, and aircraft size limitations. The principal pertinent regulations are FAR 298 and FAR 135.

Commuter Operator—Operators of small aircraft of a maximum size of 60 seats who perform at least five scheduled round trips per week between two or more points or carry mail. They operate under Part 298, FAR 135, and at times FAR 121.

Comparable Worth—Evaluation of the worth of dissimilar jobs by assigning points for skill level and conditions of job.

Compass Locator—A low power, low or medium frequency (L/MF) radio beacon installed in conjunction with the outer or middle marker of an instrument landing system (ILS). It can be used for navigational distances of approximately 15 miles or as authorized in the approach procedure.

Composite Flight Plan—A flight plan which specifies VFR operation for one portion of flight and IFR for another portion. It is used primarily in military operations.

Concessionaire—An individual firm, company, or organization permitted by the airport authority to locate or carry on business at the airport for the convenience of its users.

Concourse—The landside part of a departure and/or arrival facility, which usually includes circulation space and departure lounges.

Conditioned Sales Contract—A written document conveying to a lender, title to purchased goods until the debt associated with them has been resolved by the borrower.

Conical Surface—An imaginary surface extending outward and upward from the periphery of the horizontal surface of an airport at a slope of 20 to 1 for a horizontal distance of 4,000 feet. (See **Horizontal Surfaces.**)

Conservatism, Doctrine of—An asset is recorded at the lower of two possible values, or an event is recorded in such a way that the owner's equity is lower than it otherwise would be.

Consideration—The legal term for the compensation granted by one party in a contract in return for some service or product. This is essential to the creating of a binding contract.

Consignment—An agreement whereby a customer formally assigns his aircraft to a dealer's stock for a period of time, in hopes that the dealer will be able to sell it for a commission. The owner retains title but the dealer has exclusive right to his commission if the aircraft is sold during the time period.

Consistency, Doctrine of—All events of the same character are treated in the same fashion from one period to another.

Constrained Operational Activity—Present or forecast aircraft activity which is limited due to economic, environmental, operational or physical factors. Unconstrained forecasts assume no such limits but express the demand that would exist in an absence of capacity problems.

Construction Work in Progress—Accumulated direct and indirect costs for constructing and readying property and equipment for installation in operations. May include accumulated costs for uncompleted overhauls.

Consumer Goods—Those goods sold to an individual buyer for his own use rather than resale.

Continuous Budget—A budget which perpetually adds a month or quarter in the future as the month or quarter just ended is dropped.

Contract—A legally enforceable agreement between two or more competent parties, requiring one party to perform some service in exchange for some form of consideration; the written evidence of such an agreement.

Contract Operator—An air carrier operating on a private for-hire basis, as distinguished from a public or common air carrier, holding a commercial operator certificate (issued by the FAA under FAR 121) authorizing the carrier to operate aircraft over 12,500 pounds for the transportation of goods or passengers for compensation or hire.

Contribution Approach—A method of preparing income statements which separates variable costs from fixed costs in order to emphasize the importance of cost behavior patterns for purposes of planning and controlling.

Contribution Margin—Excess of sales price over variable expenses. Also called *marginal income*. May be expressed as a total, a ratio, or on a per-unit basis.

Control Areas—The airspace designated as Federal Airways, additional Control Areas, and Control Area Extensions but not including the Continental Control Area.

Control Sector—An airspace area of defined horizontal and vertical dimensions for which a controller, or group of controllers, has air traffic control responsibility, normally within an air route traffic control center or an approach control facility.

Control Tower—A central operations facility in the terminal air traffic control system consisting of a tower cab structure (including an associated IFR room if radar-equipped) using air/ground communications and/or radar, visual signaling, and other devices to provide safe and expeditious movement of terminal air traffic. (See **ATCT**.)

Control Zones—Areas of controlled airspace which extend upward from the surface and terminate at the base of the Continental Control Area. Control zones that do not underlie the Continental Control Area have no upper limit. A control zone may include one or more airports and is normally a circular area with a radius of five statute miles and any extensions necessary to include instrument departure and arrival paths. (See also **Control Areas.**)

Controllable Cost—A cost which may be directly regulated at a given level of managerial authority, either in the short run or in the long run.

Controlling—The evaluation of performance and, if necessary, correction of what is being done to assure attainment of results according to plan.

Convenience Goods—Goods utilized in our day-to-day living. These refer particularly to nondurable goods.

Corporation—An artificial being, or business entity, which is legally separate from the person(s) who own(s) it.

Correlation Analysis—A statistical total that measures the degree of dependency between two or more variables and the average amount of change in one variable associated with a unit increase in another. In *simple* correlation, a dependent variable is related to just one independent variable. In *multiple* correlation, the dependent variable is related to two or more independent variables.

Cost Accounting—A quantitative method that accumulates, classifies, summarizes and interprets information for three major purposes: (1) operational planning and control, (2) special decisions, and (3) product costing.

Cost Center—The smallest unit of activity or area of responsibility for which cost data are accumulated.

Cost Concept—Accounting ordinarily values the resources of a business at cost rather than market value.

Costs of Carrying—The unavoidable costs of carrying inventory. They are primarily interest on investment, obsolescence write-offs, insurance, and space costs. Overstocking may raise these costs to dangerous levels.

Cost of Goods Sold—Cost of the merchandise sold to customers during a given accounting period.

Costs of Net Carrying—These include expensive expediting, loss of sales, and loss of customer goodwill associated with carrying too little inventory. They are more difficult to measure than costs of carrying, and they are potentially more harmful.

Course—The intended direction of flight in the horizontal plane measured in degrees from north.

Credit Entry—An entry on the right-hand side of an account. The record of a decrease in any asset account. The record of an increase in an equity account.

Credit Rating—A measure used by credit bureaus to determine an individual's ability or willingness to pay his debts based on the individual's history of resolving debts and his current financial position.

Critical Engine—The engine which, upon failure, would most adversely affect the performance or handling qualities of an aircraft.

Crosswind Component—The wind component measured in knots at 90 degrees to the longitudinal axis of the runway.

Cruise—Used in an ATC clearance to authorize a pilot to conduct flight at any altitude from the minimum IFR altitude up to and including the altitude specified in the clearance. The pilot may level off at any intermediate altitude within this block of airspace. Climb/descent within the block is to be made at the discretion of the pilot. However, once the pilot starts descent and reports leaving an altitude in the block he may not return to that altitude without additional ATC clearance.

Cruising Altitude/Level—An altitude or flight level maintained during en route level flight.

Current Assets—Cash and other resources expected to be realized in cash, or sold, or consumed within one year. Cash marketable securities receivables and inventories.

Current Liabilities—Obligations, the liquidation of which is expected to require the use, within one year, of current assets or the creation of other current liabilities. Accounts payable; unpaid taxes and other debts within one year.

Current Notes Payable—Face value of notes, drafts, acceptances, or other similar evidences of indebtedness payable on demand or within one year including the portion of long-term debt due within one year of the balance sheet dale.

Current Ratio—A measure of liquidity. Total current assets divided by total current liabilities.

Cycle—An interval of time in which one of a recurring set of actions is completed.

Cyclic Maintenance—Repair or reconstruction projects using CIP funds which are performed at selected pre-defined intervals, usually several years apart.

Data—A collection of numbers, letters, or symbols that can be processed, maintained or produced by a management information system.

Data Management—The procedures and programs associated with planning, organizing, maintaining and controlling the data base.

Data Processing—The accumulation, classification, analysis, and reporting of large quantities of information by mechanical equipment.

dB—Decibel(s).

dBA—Decibel(s), measured on the A-weighted scale to factor out anomalies.

Debit Entry—A left-hand entry. The record of an increase in any asset record. The record of a decrease in an equity account.

Debt-Equity Ratio—The debt-equity ratio shows the percent of the business that is financed by creditors in relation to that financed by owners. It is computed by dividing total liabilities by total owners' equity.

Debt-to-Total Capital Ratio—Debt divided by total capital, i.e., equities of creditors divided by total equities.

Decentralization—An extension of delegation; the situation which results from a systematic delegation of results expected throughout the organization, to the lowest possible level.

Decibel—The standard unit of noise measurement relating to a logarithmic scale in which 10 units represents a doubling of acoustic energy.

Decision Making—Choosing between alternate courses of action.

Deferred Charges—Debit balances in general clearing accounts, including prepayments, chargeable against operations over a period of years, capitalized expenditures of an organizational or developmental character, and property acquisition adjustments.

Deferred Credits—Credit balances in general clearing accounts including premiums on long-term debt securities of the air carrier.

Deferred Federal Income Taxes—Credit balance of deferred income tax credits and debits arising from different treatment for tax and book accounting purposes of airworthiness reserve or self-insurance reserve provisions, depreciation allowances under provisions of sections 167 and 168 of the Internal Revenue Code, and pre-operating, aircraft integration, route extension, or other developmental expenses.

Deflation—A decline in the general level of prices.

Delegation—The assignment of authority and duties of others at a lower organizational level.

Department—Generally, a group of executives and employees engaged in performing a single function or a group of closely related functions.

Departure Control—A function of an air traffic control facility providing air traffic control service for departing IFR and, under certain conditions, VFR aircraft.

Departure Lounge—A common area used for assembling originating passengers who have passed ticket and baggage check-in and the necessary government and security controls, together with transfer and transit passengers. (See **Concourse.**)

Departure Time—The time an aircraft becomes airborne.

Deplanement—A passenger disembarkation from a (commercial) flight.

Depreciation—The general conversion of the depreciable cost of a fixed asset into expense, spread over its remaining life. There are numerous methods, all based on a periodic change to an expense account and a corresponding credit to a reserve account.

Depreciation, Accelerated—A depreciation schedule which is higher in earlier years of the life of an asset and lower in the later years as compared with the straight line.

Depreciation, Accumulated—A fixed asset valuation account, showing the total amount of depreciation accumulated to date.

Depreciation, Double-Declining Balance Method—An accelerated method of depreciation, similar in its effect to the years' digits method.

Depreciation, Flight Equipment—Charges to expense for depreciation of airframes, aircraft engines, airframe and engine parts, and other flight equipment.

Depreciation, Purpose of Account—To write off the cost of the asset to the years over which it is used.

Depreciation, Straight-Line—Charging off of an equal fraction of an asset's cost each year of its life.

Design Hour—The design hour is an hour close to peak but not absolute peak, which is used for airport planning and design purposes. It is usually the peak hour of the average day of the peak month or the 37th busiest hour of the year (90th percentile).

Developmental and Preoperating Costs—Costs accumulated and deferred in connection with alterations in operational characteristics such as the development and preparation for operation of new routes, and the integration of new types of aircraft or services.

DH/Decision Height—During a precision approach, the height (or altitude) at which a decision must be made to either continue the approach or execute a missed approach.

Direct—Straight line flight between two navigational aids, fixes, points or any combination thereof.

Direct Costing—That type of product costing which charges fixed manufacturing overhead immediately against the revenue of the period in which it was incurred, without assigning it to specific units produced. Also called *variable costing and marginal costing.*

Direct Labor—All labor which is obviously related and specifically and conveniently traceable to specific products.

Directing—Getting members of a group to accomplish their tasks by integrating their efforts in the interest of individuals and group objectives.

Direction Finder/DF—A radio receiver equipped with a directional sensing antenna used to take bearings on a radio transmitter.

Directors—The persons vested with control of the corporation, subject to the elective power of the shareholders.

Discipline—Systematic, corrective action taken when rules and regulations are violated, in order to effect a behavior change.

Discount—Amount by which the face value of a financial instrument exceeds the sales price.

Discounted Interest—A deduction from principal for finance charges at the time a loan is made. The remaining amount is repaid through installment payments.

Displaced Threshold—A threshold that is located at a point on the runway other than the designated beginning of the runway.

Distance Measuring Equipment/DME—Equipment (airborne and ground) used to measure, in nautical miles, the slant range distance of an aircraft from the DME navigation aid.

Distribution Costs—Nonmanufacturing costs of marketing, shipping, warehousing, billing, financing, etc.

Dividends—Includes dividends payable, in cash or in stock, to preferred and common stockholders, declared but not necessarily paid during the accounting period. The current liability is created by the declaration, the amount ordinarily being charged to retained earnings.

DME—Distance Measuring Equipment.

Dollar Cost Averaging—A method of buying stocks in installments by investing the same fixed dollar amount in the same long-term growth stock at regular intervals over a long period of time, making the average cost per share less than the average price paid per share.

Domestic Flight—A flight within a single country.

Domestic Passenger (Baggage, Cargo, Mail)—A passenger (baggage, cargo, mail) transported wholly on a domestic flight.

Double-Entry Accounting—The usual type of accounting in which two aspects of each event are recorded.

Down Payment—The initial amount of the purchase price of an item bought on credit that the purchaser pays in cash.

Drag Chute—A parachute device installed on certain aircraft which is deployed on landing roll to assist in deceleration of the aircraft.

Earnings Per Share—Net earnings divided by the number of shares outstanding.

Earnings, Retained—Cumulative increase in the stockholders' equity as a result of company operations.

EAS—See **Essential Air Service.**

Economic Man Theory—The principal that money is the primary factor in human motivation.

Economic Order Quantity (EOQ)—The amount of inventory which should be ordered at one time in order to minimize the associated annual costs of the inventory.

Economy Service—In domestic operations, transport service established for the carriage of passengers at fares and quality of service below coach service.

Ego or Esteem Needs—The needs for self-confidence, independence and achievements and job knowledge combined with a second group of ego needs for status recognition, appreciation and respect.

ELT/Emergency Locator Transmitter—A small battery-operated radio transmitter attached to the aircraft. In the event of a crash, the impact triggers the ELT, which transmits a signal on 121.5 MHz and 243 MHz. It aids in locating downed aircraft by radiating a downward sweeping audio tone, 204 times per second. It is designed to function automatically after an accident.

Employment Requisition—A request for a qualified applicant usually initiated by line personnel.

Enplanement—A passenger boarding of a (commercial) flight.

En Route—The route of flight from point of departure to point of destination, including intermediate stops (excludes local operations).

En Route Airspace—Controlled airspace above and/or adjacent to terminal airspace.

En Route Air Traffic Control Services—Air traffic control service provided aircraft on IFR flight plans, generally by centers, when these aircraft are operating between departure and destination terminal areas. When equipment capabilities and controller workload permit, certain advisory/assistance services may be provided to VFR aircraft.

En Route High Altitude System—Includes the controlled airspace in the high altitude stratum which is generally defined as the airspace from 18,000 to 45,000 feet.

En Route Low Altitude System—Includes the controlled airspace in the low altitude stratum, which is generally defined as the airspace between 700 feet or 1200 feet above ground level (AGL) up to 18,000 above sea level (ASL).

Entrepreneur—One who undertakes risks and responsibilities, and combines the basic factors of production in an effort to create an economic unit known as a business.

EPA—U.S. Environmental Protection Agency.

Equities—Claims against assets by owners or by creditors. The amount of one's investment in an ownership position. In regard to real property, it is calculated as the market value minus claims against the property, such as a first mortgage balance.

Equities, Owners'—Claims against assets by owners.

Essential Air Service—Derives from Section 419 of the Airline Deregulation Act of 1978 which bears this name and relates to points having certificated service at the time of the Act or being on a carrier's certificate between July 1968 and October 1978.

Exception Principle—A policy by which exceptions to the rule or to standard operation procedures are passed up the chain of command for solution.

Excise Tax—Specialty tax designed strictly for revenue-raising purposes and levied against luxury items.

Execute Missed Approach—Instructions issued to a pilot making an instrument approach which means continue inbound to the missed approach point and execute the missed approach procedures as described on the Instrument Approach Procedure Chart or as previously assigned by ATC.

Executive Transportation—Any use of an aircraft by a corporation, company or other organization for the purposes of transporting its employees and/or property not for compensation or hire and employing professional pilots for the operation of the aircraft.

Expected Value—A weighted average of all the conditional values of an act. Each conditional value is weighed by its probability.

Expense, Accrued—A liability account arising from expenses that are incurred prior to the related expenditure; i.e., accrued wages.

Expense, Operating—The costs associated with sales and administrative activities as distinct from those associated with production.

Expense, Prepaid—An expense recognized after a relevant expenditure; an expense for future benefits.

Extended Coverage—A clause providing protection against additional perils; it is appended to normal fire insurance contracts.

Extended Over-water Operation—An operation over water at a horizontal distance of more than 50 nautical miles from the nearest shore line.

FAA—Federal Aviation Administration.

Facility—A term commonly employed when referring to an area or areas and/or system(s) where particular handling functions take place.

Factor Comparison Method—A job evaluation system which compares jobs by making judgments about which jobs contain more of a certain compensatable factor than others. Jobs are compared to one another, one factor at a time. (See **Comparable Worth.**)

Fair Credit Reporting Act—A federal statute designed to protect consumers, and applicants for jobs and insurance, from false information supplied by credit bureaus and third persons.

Fair Market Price—The amount of money a buyer is willing to offer and a seller willing to accept (assuming both are fully informed and act voluntarily and intelligently).

FAR—Federal Air Regulations, administered by FAA. Some of the most common are FAR 121 (creating rules for certificated carriers), FAR 135 (operating rules for air taxis and most commuters), and FAR 36 (noise rules). See Appendix I.

FBO (Fixed Base Operator)—An operator of one or more aircraft who has a permanent fixed aviation service facility at an airport. FBOs usually engage in aviation activity such as flight instruction, fuel sales, repairs, aircraft rental and sales, and air charter.

Feathered Propeller—A propeller whose blades have been rotated so that leading and trailing edges are nearly parallel with the aircraft flight path to stop or minimize drag and engine rotation. Normally used to indicate shutdown of a reciprocating or turboprop engine due to malfunction.

Federal Airway—A path through the navigable airspace of the United States, identified by an area on the surface of the earth, designated or approved by the FAA Administrator as suitable for interstate, overseas or foreign commerce.

Federal Insurance Contribution Act (FICA)—An act that combined Social Security old age, survivors, disability and hospital insurance taxes into a single tax.

Federal Trade Commission (FTC)—The federal regulatory agency charged with responsibility for policing unfair trade practices.

Feedback—The data supplied by monitoring system for purposes of investigation, evaluation and follow up including possible changes to a program.

Feeder Route—A route depicted on instrument approach procedure charts to designate routes for aircraft to proceed from the en route structure to the Initial Approach Fix (IAF).

Feeder System—This usually involves air taxi and/or commuter (regional) air carriers operating short to medium haul flights into larger air terminals. Passengers and freight can then connect with the larger carriers for a longer flight. Many carriers have interline agreements to ensure that this service be provided with minimum inconvenience to the customer. Some feeder systems include an even closer relationship, e.g., the Allegheny commuter system, the Alaska Airlines sub-contract systems.

Fidelity Insurance—Insurance designed to protect against financial loss resulting from the dishonesty of an employee.

Fifo—The First-In-First-Out method of inventory method of inventory valuation, which assumes that the goods that enter inventory first are the first to be sold. (See **Lifo.**)

File—An organized collection of information directed toward some purchase; for example, a file of savings account data or airline passenger records.

Final Approach IFR—The flight path of an aircraft which is inbound to the airport on an approved final instrument approach course, beginning at the point of interception of that course (Final Approach Fix) and extending to the airport or the point where circling for landing or missed approach is executed.

Finance Charge—The fee, consisting of both interest and charges for carrying costs, that is paid by a borrower for the privilege of using credit.

Fix—A geographical position determined by visual reference to the surface, by reference to one or more radio NAVAIDs, by celestial plotting or by another navigational device.

Fixed Assets—The land, plant and equipment, and other physical productive assets of a firm that are expected to have a useful life in excess of one year.

Fixed Costs—Those costs a business firm expects to incur regardless of the level of actual output, and whose magnitude is not subject to fluctuation during the planning period.

Fixed-wing Aircraft—Aircraft having wings fixed to the airplane fuselage and outspread in flight, i.e., nonrotating wings.

Flameout—Unintended loss of combustion in turbine engines resulting in the loss of engine power.

Flap Extended Speed—The highest speed permissible with wing flaps in a prescribed extended position.

Fleet Mix—The proportion of aircraft types or models at an airport. (See also **Aircraft Mix.**)

Flexible Budget—A budget, usually referring to overhead costs only, which is prepared for a range, rather than for a single level of activity; one which can be automatically geared to changes in the level of volume; also called *variable budget.* Direct materials and direct labor are sometimes included in the flexible budget.

Flight Crewmember—A pilot, flight engineer, or flight navigator assigned to duty in an aircraft during flight time.

Flight Equipment—Airframes, aircraft engines, and other flight equipment used in the in-flight operations of aircraft. (See **Flight Equipment-cost.**)

Flight Equipment-cost—Total cost to the air carrier of complete airframes, fully assembled engines, installed aircraft propellers and rotary wing aircraft rotors and similar assemblies, installed airborne communications and electronic navigational equipment and other similar assemblies, complete units of miscellaneous airborne flight equipment and costs of modification, conversion or other improvements to leased flight equipment.

Flight Level—A level of constant atmospheric pressure related to a reference datum of 29.92 inches of mercury. Each is stated in three digits that represent hundreds of feet. For example, flight level 250 represents a barometric altimeter indication of 25,000 feet; flight level 255, an indication of 25,500 feet.

Flight Path—A line, course, or track along which an aircraft is flying or intended to be flown.

Flight Plan—A description or outline of a planned flight which a pilot submits to the FAA, usually through a Flight Service Station. The flight plan includes information on aircraft type, identification, airspeed and altitude to be flown (initially), time of departure, origin and destination airports, estimated time en route, number of passengers and amount of fuel on board, aircraft's color and equipment, and name of the pilot. Flight plans are optional for all VFR flights, but are required for IFR flights in controlled airspace, including all scheduled passenger flights.

Flight Recorder—A general term applied to any instrument or device that records information about the performance of an aircraft in flight or about conditions encountered in flight. Flight recorders may make records of airspeed, outside air temperature, vertical acceleration, engine RPM, manifold pressure and other pertinent variables for a given flight.

Flight Service Station (FSS)—An FAA-operated air-ground voice communications station which relays clearances, requests for clearances and position reports between en route aircraft and the *Air Route Traffic Control Center.* In addition, the FSS provides preflight briefing for either VFR or IFR flights, gives in-flight assistance, broadcasts weather once each hour, monitors radio navigational facilities, accepts VFR flight plans and provides notification of arrival, and broadcasts notices to airmen (NOTAMS) concerning local navigational aids, airfields and other flight data. As part of the National Airspace Plan (NAS) the FSS have been reduced in number and automated.

Flight Time—The time from the moment the aircraft first moves under its own power for the purpose of flight until the moment it comes to rest at the next point of landing ("Block-to-block" time).

Flight Visibility—The average forward horizontal distance, from the cockpit of an aircraft in flight, at which prominent unlighted objects may be seen and identified by day and prominent lighted objects may be seen and identified by night.

Flight Watch—A shortened term for use in air-ground contacts on frequency 122.0 MHz to identify the flight service providing En Route Flight Advisory Service.

Flooring—A wholesale credit line for a dealer with a financing source, for the purpose of buying new or used aircraft. Simple interest is usually used to compute the cost of the line and the aircraft is the collateral for the loan.

Flow—Direction of activity. (See **Outbound, Inbound.**)

Flow Chart—A graphic representation of the major steps in a process. The illustrative symbols may represent documents, machine steps or human actions involved in the process.

Flow Control—Measures designed to adjust the flow of traffic into a given airspace, along a given route, or bound for a given airport so as to ensure the most effective utilization of the airspace.

Fly-by—A usually low-altitude flight past a predesignated place by one or more airplanes.

Flying Operations Expenses—Expenses incurred directly in the in-flight operation of aircraft and expenses attaching to the holding of aircraft and aircraft operational personnel in readiness for assignment to an in-flight status.

Flyover—A low-altitude flight over a public gathering or place by one or more airplanes.

Food, Drug and Cosmetic Act—A federal statute prohibiting the interstate shipment of misbranded or adulterated foods, drugs, cosmetics and therapeutic devices.

Forecast—In budgeting, a projection of what costs and revenues should be. In aviation activity, a projection of future traffic.

Foreman—Generally, a first line supervisor who is one level above the hourly wage employees.

Formal Organization—The organization resulting from use of prescribed communication channels, standardized methods, clearly defined jobs and stated chains of command.

Formation Flight—More than one aircraft which, by prior arrangement between the pilots, operate as a single aircraft with regard to navigation and position reporting. Separation between aircraft within the formation is the responsibility of the flight leader and the pilots of the other aircraft in the flight. This includes transition periods when aircraft within the formation are maneuvering to attain separation from each other to effect individual control and during join-up and breakaway.

Freight—Property other than express and passenger baggage transported by air.

Freight Revenues—Revenues from the transportation by air of property other than express or passenger baggage. These revenues are from individually-waybilled shipments carried in scheduled service (belly cargo) as well as all-cargo flights.

Fringe Benefits—Insurance plans, pensions, vacations, and similar benefits for employees.

FSS—See **Flight Service Station.**

Fuel Dumping—Airborne releases of usable fuel. This does not include the dropping of fuel tanks.

Fuel Taxes—Excise taxes paid by aircraft operators on the aviation gasoline and jet fuel they purchase.

Functional Organization—An internal business organization that divides authority and responsibility on the basis of function, thereby making each function somewhat autonomous.

FY—Fiscal Year.

Game Theory—The mathematical process of selecting an optimum strategy in the face of an opponent who has a strategy of his/her own.

Garnishment—The name given in some states to attachment proceedings.

Gate—A point of passenger access to the apron/ aircraft from the terminal building or extension thereto and vice versa.

Gate Lounge—An area adjacent to a gate used for assembling departing passengers for a flight departure.

General and Administrative Expenses—Expenses of a general corporate nature and expenses incurred in performing activities which contribute to more than a single operating function such as general financial accounting activities, purchasing activities, representation at law, and other general operational administration not directly applicable to a particular line function.

General Aviation (GA)—Refers to all civil aircraft and operations which are not classified as air carrier or commuter. The types of aircraft used in general aviation activities cover a wide spectrum from corporate multi-engine jet aircraft piloted by professional crews to amateur-built single-engine piston acrobatic planes, balloons and dirigibles.

General Partnership—A partnership in which the partners conduct, as co-owners, a business for profit, and each partner has a right to take part in the management of the business and has unlimited liability.

Glide Path (On/above/below)—Used by ATC to inform an aircraft making a Precision Approach Radar (PAR) approach of its vertical position (elevation) relative to the descent profile. The terms "slightly" and "well" are used to describe the degree of deviation; e.g., "slightly above glidepath." Trend information is also issued with respect to the elevation of the aircraft and may be modified by the terms "rapidly" and "slowly," e.g., "well above glidepath, coming down rapidly."

Glide Slope—Provides vertical guidance for aircraft during approach and landing. It can be an electronic component that provides vertical guidance (by instrument reference) during ILS approaches. It can also be provided by visual ground aids such as VASI for nonprecision VFR approaches.

Glider—A heavier-than-air aircraft, that is supported in flight by the dynamic reaction of the air against its flying surfaces and whose free flight does not depend principally on an engine.

GNP (Gross National Product)—The market value of the total output of goods and services produced by the nation's economy before deduction of depreciation charges and other allowances for business and institutional consumption of durable goods. It includes the purchase of goods and services by consumers and government, gross private domestic investment, and net exports.

Go Ahead—Proceed with your message. Not to be used for any other purpose.

Go Around—Instructions for a pilot to abandon his approach to a landing.

Goodwill—An intangible asset representing the difference between the purchase price and the value of the tangible assets purchased.

Grapevine—Informal communication network.

Gross Profit—That profit earned on sales after deducting the cost of the goods sold but before deducting other business expenses.

Ground Property and Equipment—Property and equipment other than flight equipment, land, and construction work in progress.

Ground Service Equipment—Equipment used for servicing aircraft on the apron.

Ground Speed—The speed of an aircraft relative to the surface of the earth.

Grounding—A voluntary determination by a carrier or carriers or an order from the Federal Aviation Administration to refrain from flying a particular type of aircraft as a result of suspected or actual malfunction of such aircraft, until the cause can be determined and appropriate corrective action taken.

Group Dynamics—Forces within the group situation which determine the behavior of the group and its individual members.

Gyroplane—A rotorcraft whose rotors are not engine-driven except for initial starting, but are made to rotate by action of the air when the rotorcraft is moving; and whose means of propulsion, consisting usually of conventional propellers, is independent of the rotor system.

HAA—Height Above Airport. Indicates the height of the minimum descent altitude (MDA) above the published airport elevation.

Halo Effect—The tendency of supervisors to assume that an employee who is good, bad, or average in one respect is equally good, bad, or average in all others.

Handoff—Transfer of radar identification of an aircraft from one controller to another, either within the same facility or inter-facility. Actual transfer of control responsibility may occur at the time of the handoff, or at a specified time, point or altitude.

Hangar Keeper Liability Insurance—Insurance to cover the liability potential of an aircraft not owned by the FBO but in his care and custody, such as storage, tie-down, service, etc.

HAT—Height Above Touchdown. Indicates the height of the decision height (DH) or minimum descent altitude (MDA) above the highest runway elevation in the touchdown zone (first 3,000 feet of runway).

Helicopter/copter—Rotorcraft that, for all its horizontal motion, depends principally on its engine-driven rotors.

Helipad—The part of the landing and takeoff area designed for helicopters.

Heliport—An area of land, water, or structure used or intended to be used for the landing and takeoff of helicopters.

Heuristic—A problem-solving approach by which the computer attacks a problem by a trial-and-error method.

Hierarchy of Needs—A theory of motivation developed by A. H. Maslow which set forth categories of human needs according to priority.

High-speed Taxiway—A taxiway with design geometrics allowing use at high speeds.

HIRL—High Intensity Runway Lighting.

Hold/holding Procedure—A predetermined maneuver which keeps aircraft within a specified air space while awaiting further clearance from air traffic control. Also used during ground operations to keep aircraft within a specified area or at a specified point while awaiting further clearance from air traffic control.

Holding Fix—A specified fix identifiable to a pilot by NAVAIDS or visual reference to the ground used as a reference point in establishing and maintaining the position of an aircraft while holding.

Homing—Flight toward a NAVAID, without correcting for wind, by adjusting the aircraft heading to maintain a relative bearing of zero degrees.

Horizontal Surface—An imaginary surface consisting of a horizontal plane 150 feet above the established airport elevation, the perimeter of which is constructed by swinging arcs of specified radii from the center of each end of the primary surface of each runway and connecting the adjacent arcs of lines tangent to those arcs.

Hub—The center of an air service network (hub-and-spoke pattern). Airports are defined as large hubs, medium hubs, small hubs, and non-hubs. Destination points for essential air service. These are the most common but not sole uses of "hub."

Hub-and-spoke System—System used by airlines in which air traffic is routed to a major airport (hub) from markets (shorter routes within the airline's system or served by other carriers) and consolidated for longer flights with higher load factors.

Hull Insurance—Coverage against physical damage to the aircraft itself, in flight or on the ground.

Human Relations—A term applied to the interactions of people and including the study of human behavior at work and efforts to take action in order to produce improved work results.

Human Resource Planning—The process by which a company plans for the continuous and proper staffing of the organization.

Human Resources—Human behavior and skills evaluated as an economic asset.

HVOR—High-altitude VOR. (See **VOR**.)

IFR—Instrument Flight Rules that govern flight procedures under instrument meteorological conditions (limited visibility or other operational constraints).

IFR Aircraft/IFR Flight—An aircraft conducting flight in accordance with instrument flight rules.

IFR Conditions—Weather conditions below the minimum for flight under visual flight rules.

Imaginary Surface—Any of several surfaces established with relation to an airport and each runway for the purpose of determining whether an object is an obstruction to air navigation. (See also **Approach Surface, Conical Surface, Horizontal Surface, Primary Surface, Transitional Surface.**)

IMC—Instrument Meteorological Conditions.

Inbound—Activity originating beyond the study area or location under discussion and terminating there.

Incentives—External stimuli to an individual which tend to initiate, speed up, or inhibit certain activities.

Incidental Revenues, Net—Revenues less related expenses from services incidental to air transportation, such as sales of service, supplies, and parts, and rental of operating property and equipment.

Income

Net Income (after income taxes)—Net income (before income taxes) less federal income taxes.

Net Income (before income taxes)—Net operating income plus or minus "other income and expense."

Net Operating Income—Total net sales less total operating costs.

Other Income and Expense—Includes interest income, royalty income, capital gains and losses, interest expense, cash discounts, etc.

Income Before Taxes—Net sales minus cost of goods sold minus operating expenses minus nonoperating expenses.

Income Statement—A financial form that serves as a record of all income and expense transactions occurring over a specific period of time, usually one year.

Income Taxes for the Period—Provisions for federal, state, local and foreign taxes, which are based upon net income.

Indirect Labor—All labor which is not specifically associated with or cannot be practically traced to specific units of output.

Industrial Goods—Those goods sold to the buyer for the services they will supply to him.

Industrial/Special—Any use of an aircraft for specialized work allied with industrial activity; excluding transportation and aerial application. (Examples: pipeline patrol, survey, advertising photography, helicopter hoist, etc.)

Informal Leader—The most influential member of the informal group, informally selected by its members.

Informal Organization—An organization of members with common social interests, not prescribed by forman organization, and existing as an addition to the formal organization.

Information—A collection of words or other data, especially as derived from the processing of data. Information can be derived from data to the extent that the data are accurate, timely and relevant to the subject under consideration.

Initial Approach Fix/IAF—The fix(s) depicted on instrument approach procedure charts that identifies the beginning of the initial approach segment(s).

Inner Marker/IM/Inner Marker Beacon—A marker beacon used with an ILS (Category II) precision approach located between the middle marker and the end of the ILS runway, transmitting a radiation pattern keyed at six dots per second and indicating to the pilot, both aurally and visually, that he is at the designated decision height (DH), normally 100 feet above the touchdown zone elevation, on the ILS CAT II approach. It also marks progress during a CAT III approach.

Instructional Flying—Any use of an aircraft for the purpose of formal instruction with the flight instructor aboard or with the maneuvers on the particular flight(s) specified by the flight instructor.

Instrument Approach—An approach conducted with guidance provided by radar and/or radio navaids.

Instrument Flight Rules/IFR—Rules governing the procedure for conducting instrument flight. Also a term used by pilots and controllers to indicate a type of flight plan.

Instrument Landing System (ILS)—A precision landing aid consisting of localizer (azimuth guidance), guide slope (vertical guidance), marker beacons (range and approach fix information), and approach light system.

Instrument Operation—The arrival at or departure from an airport of an aircraft operating in accordance with an IFR Flight Plan or the provision of IFR separation from other aircraft by a terminal traffic control facility.

Instrument Runway—A runway equipped with electronic and visual navigation aids for which a precision or nonprecision approach procedure having straight-in landing minimums has been approved.

Insurable Risk—A potential financial calamity that insurance companies deem profitable to insure; normally, such a risk will not be associated with a possible widespread disaster such as an earthquake, and the amount of the potential loss must be easily measurable.

Insurance—A plan of security against risks by charging the loss against a fund created by the payments made by policyholders.

Intangible Assets—Assets possessing no physical characteristics, but whose value lies in the legal rights or in the name and reputation of the company.

Interest—Charge for the use of money. A charge made for allowing someone else to use one's money, usually a percentage of the amount being used. Specifically, for a borrower, the cost of borrowing money; for an investor, the payment received from a bank or similar institution for lending money to it.

Interline Transfer—The transfer of passengers, baggage, cargo, or mail between flights of different airlines.

Internal Control—The coordinated methods and measures in an organization designed to: (a) promote efficiency, (b) encourage adherence to prescribed management plans and policies, (c) check the accuracy and validity of organization data and (d) safeguard assets.

International—International flights involve an origin in one country and a destination in another. U.S. carriers require Presidential approval for international flights.

International Civil Aviation Organization (ICAO)—A specialized agency of the United Nations whose objective is to develop the principles and techniques of international air navigation and to foster planning and development of international civil air transport.

International and Territorial Operations—Operators of aircraft flying between the 50 states of the United States and foreign points, between the 50 states and U.S. possessions or territories, and between foreign points. Includes both the combination passenger/cargo and the all cargo carriers engaged in international and territorial operations.

Interregional—Activity involving an origin in one region and a destination in another.

Intersecting Runways—Two or more runways which cross or meet within their lengths.

Intersection—(1) A point defined by any combination of courses, radials or bearings of two or more navigational aids; (2) used to describe the point where two runways cross, a taxiway and a runway cross, or two taxiways cross.

Interstate—Activity with an origin in one state and a destination in another.

Interstate Air Carrier—An air carrier which conducts operations across state boundaries.

Interview, Employment—The process used in selection by which an applicant is interviewed in order to determine qualifications for the job.

Interview, Evaluation—An interview by a supervisor with an employee in order to discuss his performance appraisal or work performance.

Interview, Nondirective—An interview where the individual is urged to talk about himself, not following a list of specific questions.

Interview, Patterned—An interview where specific questions are asked by the interviewer in order to get an outline listing of the individual's qualifications.

Intraline Transfer—The transfer of passengers, baggage, cargo, or mail between flights of the same airline. Also known as *on-line*.

Intraregional—Activity entirely within regional boundaries.

Intrastate—Activity entirely within state boundaries.

Intrastate Air Carrier—An air carrier which conducts operations solely within the boundaries of a state. The operating rights of these carriers are state-granted and not subject to federal economic regulation.

Inventory—Goods being held for sale, and material and partly finished products which upon completion will be sold.

Inventory, Periodic Method—An inventory accounting system that requires a physical count of inventory to determine the ending amounts of raw materials, work in process and finished goods, and hence also the cost of goods sold.

Inventory, Perpetual Method—An inventory accounting system whereby a continuous record is kept which tracks raw materials, work in process, finished goods and cost of goods sold on a day-to-day basis.

Inventory Turnover—The number of times the average inventory of a firm is replaced during a given period.

Invoice—Bill for goods delivered, or services rendered.

ISER—Institute of Social and Economic Research.

Itinerant Operation—Any aircraft arrival and/or departure other than a local operation.

Jamming—Electronic or mechanical interference which may disrupt the display of aircraft on radar or the transmission/reception of radio communications/navigation.

Jet Blast—The high-velocity movement of air behind a jet engine in operation.

Jet Fuel—Kerosene used as the fuel in turbine-powered aircraft. This kerosene is commonly referred to as "jet fuel," in contrast to the "aviation gasoline" used in piston-engine aircraft.

Jet Routes—A high altitude route system, at or above 18,000 feet MSL, predicated on a network of designated high altitude VHF/UHF facilities.

Jet Stream—A migrating stream of high-speed winds present at high altitudes.

Jettisoning of External Stores—Airborne release of external stores, e.g., tiptanks, ordinances.

Job Analysis—Any technique for collection, classifying, and analyzing information concerning the characteristics and requirements of general work assignments.

Job Description—The objectives, authority, and responsibility and relationships with others required by the person occupying a specific position.

Job Enrichment—Upgrading the responsibility, scope and challenge of work.

Job Evaluation—A formalized system for determining the worth, in monetary terms, of jobs within an organization. (See **Comparable Worth.**)

Joint-use Facility—An airport terminal building used by more than one passenger or cargo operator.

Journal—Records of transactions or activities kept in chronological order.

Jumbo (Jet)—DC-10, B-747, L-1011, C-5A, and future similar or larger widebody aircraft.

Known Traffic—With respect to ATC clearances, means aircraft whose altitude, position and intentions are known to ATC.

Labor Turnover—The gross movement of wage and salary workers into and out of employee status with respect to individual establishments.

Land Cost—The initial cost and the cost of improving land owned or held in perpetuity by the owner.

Landing Area—Any locality either on land or water, including airports and intermediate landing fields, which is used, or is intended to be used, for the landing and take-off of aircraft, whether or not facilities are provided for the shelter, servicing, or repair of aircraft, or for receiving or discharging passengers or cargo.

Landside—That portion of the airport utilized for all activities except aircraft movement (See **Airside**). The landside generally includes the following elements: vehicular access roads and parking, passenger terminal, cargo terminal, aircraft hangars, FBOs, fuel storage area, CFR equipment, and maintenance facilities. Also referred to as *terminal area.*

Large Regionals—Certificated air carriers with annual operating revenues of between $10,000,000 and $75,000,000.

Lateral Separation—The lateral spacing of aircraft at the same altitude by requiring operation on different routes or in different geographical locations.

LDN (Day-night Average Sound Level)—The 24-hour equivalent sound level (Leq) with a 10-decibel penalty applied to nighttime (10:00 P.M. to 7:00 A.M.) levels.

Lead Time—The time interval between placing an order and receiving delivery.

Leadership—The ability to direct the activities of others toward the solving of a problem or the accomplishment of a goal.

Leadership, Benevolent Authoritative—A leadership pattern by which the manager keeps all decision-making at his level but which takes into consideration the human aspects of his subordinate group.

Leadership, Consultive—A pattern of leadership by which the manager consults with subordinates in order to arrive at a decision.

Leadership, Exploitive/Authoritative—A pattern of leadership by which the leader relies heavily on force to compel his subordinates to obey his will.

Leadership, Participative—A pattern of leadership by which the manager encourages subordinates to work together as a team in contributing ideas to help solve mutual problems.

Leadership, Situational—An approach to studying leadership which centers on the essence of the leadership role and the skills necessary for a particular situation. Different situations involving different groups require different leadership abilities.

Lease—An agreement between the owner of property and a tenant by which the former agrees to give possession of the property to the latter in consideration of the payment of rent, under specific terms. (Parties—landlord or lessor, tenant or lessee.)

Ledger—A group of accounts.

Legal Entity—A legal person, artificially created by law, possessing most of the rights and privileges of a real person. This description applies to corporations.

LEQ (Equivalent Sound Level)—The equivalent A-weighted sound level for a specified period of time.

Leverage—Operating with a significant ratio of liabilities to gross assets.

Liability—The equity of a creditor.

Liability, Current—Obligation that becomes due within a short time, usually one year.

Liability Insurance—Protects the insured against the loss arising by reason of the liability imposed by law for the negligent or wrongful act of himself or those for whom he is responsible, or against liability assumed by contract.

Lifo—The Last-In-First-Out method of inventory valuation which assumes that the goods that enter inventory last are the first to be sold.

Light Gun—A hand-held direction light signaling device which emits a brilliant narrow beam of white, green, or red light as selected by the tower controller. The color and type of light transmitted can be used to approve or disapprove anticipated pilot actions where radio communication is not available. The light gun is used for controlling traffic operating in the vicinity of the airport and on the airport movement area.

Lighted Airport—An airport where runway and obstruction lighting is available.

Limited Partnership—A partnership in which at least one partner has a liability limited to the loss of the capital contribution that he has made to the partnership, and such a partner neither takes part in the management of the partnership nor appears to the public to be a partner.

Line Authority—Authority which is exerted downward over subordinates.

Line Organization—An internal business organization structure characterized by the strict, vertical flow of authority and the lack of assistants at the various executive levels.

Line and Staff Organizations—The internal business organization structure that much resembles the line organization, with the exception that it employs staff members, or assistants, to assist the regular line supervisors.

Linear Programming—A mathematical approach to problems which contain many interacting variables, which basically involves combining limited resources to maximize profits or minimize costs.

Liquidity—Ability to meet current obligations. The ease with which an investment can be converted to cash.

LIRL—Low Intensity Runway Lights.

L/MF—Low to Medium Frequency.

Load—Any item carried in an aircraft other than those included in the basic operating weight.

Load Factor, Passenger—The ratio of passenger seats occupied to the total seat capacity of the aircraft.

Loading Bridge—An adjustable protected passageway bridging the space between a terminal building or a pier and an aircraft passenger door.

Local Operation—Any operation performed by an aircraft which: (a) operates in the local traffic pattern or within sight of the tower; (b) is known to be departing for, or arriving from, flight in local practice areas located within a 20-mile radius of the control tower; or (c) executes a simulated instrument approach or low pass at the airport.

Local Traffic—Aircraft operating in the traffic pattern or within sight of the tower, or aircraft known to be departing or arriving from flight in local practice areas or aircraft executing practice instrument approaches at the airport.

Localizer—The component of an ILS which provides course guidance to the runway. The localizer may be used as part of a complete ILS, or by itself.

Long Haul—Flights greater than 1,500 miles.

Longitudinal Separation—The longitudinal spacing of aircraft at the same altitude by a minimum distance expressed in units of time or miles.

Long-term Debt—The face value or principal amount of debt securities issued or assumed by the company which has not been retired or cancelled and is not payable within 12 months of the balance sheet date.

Long-term Prepayments—Prepayments of obligations, applicable to periods extending beyond one year.

Loran—Long Range Navigation aid operating in the 1750–1950 KHZ (LORAN A) or 100–110 KHZ (LORAN C and D) frequency band.

Loss Payee—The third party named as the one to whom the loss may be paid, as his interest in the property may appear.

Low Approach—An approach over an airport or runway following an instrument approach or a VFR approach including the go-around maneuver where the pilot intentionally does not make contact with the runway.

LVOR—Low altitude VOR.

Mach Number—The ratio of true airspeed to the speed of sound.

Magnetometer—A device which permits the identification of metallic substances on passengers.

Maintenance, Direct (expense)—The costs of labor, materials, and outside services consumed directly in periodic maintenance operations and the maintenance, repair, or upkeep of airframes, aircraft engines, other flight equipment, and ground property and equipment.

Maintenance, Indirect (expense)—Overhead or general expenses of activities involved in the repair and upkeep of property and equipment, including inspections of equipment in accordance with prescribed operational standards. Includes expenses related to the administration of maintenance stocks and stores, the keeping of maintenance operations records, and the scheduling, controlling, planning, and supervision of maintenance operations.

Majors—Certificated air carriers with annual operating revenues of $1,000,000,000 or more.

MALS—Medium (intensity) Approach Light System.

Management—The process of combining and guiding the factors of production to achieve the desired goals of the business firm.

Management Development—The development of managers for advancement or for improved performance in present position.

Management by Exception—The established managerial principle of providing management only with facts that reflect an exceptional condition requiring attention and action, for example, preparation of a budgetary report when the variance between actual and estimated expenses exceeds a predetermined percentage. When results occur within a normal range, they are not reported.

Management Information System—One that supports managerial decision making by supplying relevant information when required.

Management by Objectives—A concept combining performance appraisal for managers and employees with a process of developing and refining organizational goals.

Management Philosophy—The pattern of beliefs, attitudes and values of those who establish and manage an organization. In managing human resources it refers to management's system of beliefs about the nature of people and about the determinants of cooperation in an organization and is reflected in the way managers deal with subordinates.

Management Prerogative—The right of a manager to decide certain issues if he/she is to manage effectively.

Management Science—A specialty concerned with applying scientific techniques, especially those embodying advanced mathematics, to management problem-solving. Among the common techniques used in management science are linear programming, probability theory, information theory, game theory, Monte Carlo methods and queuing theory. Also referred to as *operations research.*

Margin on Sales—The ratio of net income to sales.

Marginal Analysis—The determination of the point at which the cost of an extra unit of input will exactly pay for itself.

Marker Beacon—A VFR navigational aid which transmits a narrow directional beam. It is associated with an airway or an instrument approach.

Marketing—The process by which goods and services are distributed. The overall selling effort of a company.

Master Plan—A long-range comprehensive plan to guide airport development.

Mayday—The international radiotelephony distress signal. When repeated three times, it indicates imminent and grave danger and that immediate assistance is requested.

Medium Haul—Flights between 500 and 1,500 miles.

Medium Regionals—Certificated air carriers with annual operating revenues of less than $10,000,000.

Merchandise Inventory—The inventory held by a retailer or wholesaler which is intended solely for resale.

Merchandising Mix—The proportions in which personal sales promotion and nonpersonal sales promotion techniques are utilized by a business firm in marketing its goods.

Merit Rating—Formal periodic evaluating of employee's performance of his job.

MGW—Maximum Gross (takeoff) Weight of an aircraft or type of aircraft.

Microwave Landing System (MLS)—An instrument landing system operating in the microwave spectrum which provides lateral and vertical guidance to aircraft having compatible avionics equipment.

Middle Marker (MM)—A marker beacon that defines a point along the glide slope of an ILS. It is usually located approximately 3,500 feet from the runway threshold.

Military Operation—An operation by military aircraft.

Minimum Descent Altitude (MDA)—The lowest altitude, expressed in feet above sea level, to which descent is authorized on final approach or during circling-to-land maneuvering in execution of a standard instrument approach procedure where no electronic glide slope is provided.

Minimums/minima—Weather condition requirements established for a particular operation or type of operation; e.g., IFR takeoff or landing, alternate airport for IFR flight plans, or VFR flight.

MIRL—Medium Intensity Runway Lighting.

Missed Approach—A prescribed procedure to be followed by aircraft that cannot complete an attempted landing at an airport.

Modal Split—Division of travel between modes of transport, often expressed as a percentage.

Model—The general characterization of a process, object, or concept in terms of mathematics. A model enables a relatively simple manipulation of variables to be accomplished in order to determine how the process, object or concept would behave in different situations.

Morale or Attitude Surveys—Fact finding and analytical techniques which obtain and evaluate information concerning the attitude of individuals and groups. The intent of such surveys is to determine the level of morale within the organization.

Mortgage—A pledge of real estate as security for a loan.

Motion Study—Analysis of motions performed and determination of improvements so that work can be accomplished more efficiently.

Motivation—The willingness to work towards achievement of a goal or a reward.

Motivation, Maintenance Seekers—Those individuals usually preoccupied or dissatisfied with factors such as pay, benefits, supervision, working conditions, company policy and administration.

Movement—Usually synonymous with the term operation (i.e., a takeoff or a landing).

MSL—Mean Sea Level.

Multiple Insurers—Insurers who agree to divide a risk so that each is only liable for a specified portion.

National Airspace System (NAS)—The common network of U.S. airspace, air navigation facilities, equipment and services, airports or landing areas, aeronautical charts, information and services, rules, regulations and procedures, technical information, manpower and material. Included are system components shared jointly with the military.

National Flight Data Center (NFDC)—A facility in Washington, D.C., established by FAA to operate a central aeronautical information service for the collection, validation, and dissemination of aeronautical data in support of the activities of government, industry, and the aviation community.

National Plan of Integrated Airport Systems (NPIAS)—This plan identifies airports and needed development projects of national importance. To qualify for federal funding under AIP, an airport must be included in the NPIAS. There are about 3,200 airports in the NPIAS (and about 6,500 public-use airports nationwide). All air carrier and commuter airports are in the NPIAS, as well as about 2,000 general aviation airports.

National Search and Rescue Plan—An interagency agreement which provides for the effective utilization of all available facilities in all types of search and rescue missions.

Nationals—Certificated air carriers with annual operating revenues of between $75,000,000 and $1,000,000,000.

Navaid—See **Air Navigation Facility.**

Navigable Airspace—Airspace at and above the minimum flight altitudes prescribed in the FARs including airspace needed for safe takeoff and landing.

NDB—Non-Directional Beacon. Radio navigation aid operating in the 190–1750 KHz frequency band.

NEF—Noise Exposure Forecast.

Negative—"No," "Permission not granted" or "That is not correct" as used in air traffic control.

Negligence—For liability insurance purposes, any careless act on the part of the insured for which he may be subject to punishment under the law.

Negotiable Instruments—Drafts, promissory notes, checks and certificates of deposit in such form that greater rights may be acquired thereunder than by taking an assignment of a contract right; called negotiable commercial paper by the code.

Net Income—Revenues minus expenses, taxes, interest paid, and depreciation. The earnings of a company after allowing for all legitimate business expenses, including taxes.

Net Income After Special Items—The net gain of the business, i.e., the net of operating profit or loss, nonoperating income and expenses, income taxes, and special items.

Net Income Before Income Taxes—Operating profit or loss plus or minus nonoperating income and expenses, net. This is the net income before income taxes and special items.

Net Income Percentage—Net income divided by net sales.

Net Present Value Method—A method of calculating the expected utility of a given project by discounting all expected future cash flows to the present, using some predetermined minimum desired rate of return.

Net Worth—The difference between assets and liabilities for a person, family or business. If the dollar value of assets is greater than that of liabilities, there is a positive net worth. In a business, net worth may also be known as "partnership share" or "owner's equity."

Night—The time between the end of evening civil twilight and the beginning of morning civil twilight, as published in the American Air Almanac converted to local time.

NIPTS—Noise Induced Permanent Threshold Shift.

NOAA—National Oceanic and Atmospheric Administration.

Noise Abatement—A procedure for the operation of aircraft at an airport which minimizes the impact of noise on the environs of the airport.

Noise Contour—A line on a map connecting points of equal noise exposure.

Non-current Liabilities—Obligations the liquidation of which is not expected to require the use, within one year, of current assets or the creation of current liabilities.

Non-directional Beacon (NDB)—An electronic ground station transmitting in all directions in the low and mid-range frequency spectrum; provides azimuth guidance to aircraft equipped with direction finder receivers. These facilities are often established with ILS outer markers to provide transition guidance to the ILS system.

Nonprecision Approach Procedure—A standard instrument approach procedure in which no electronic glide slope is provided.

Nonrevenue Flights—Flights and flight stages involving training, test, technical, positioning for scheduled flights, ferry, company business, publicity and forced returns for which no remuneration is received.

Non-scheduled—See **Charter.**

NOS—National Ocean Survey.

Note—A written promise to repay a loan.

Notes and Accounts Receivable—Notes receivable and amounts due on open accounts.

Note Receivable—A debt that is evidenced by a note or other written acknowledgment.

Notice to Airmen (NOTAM)—A notice containing information (not known sufficiently in advance to publicize by other means) concerning the establishment, condition or change in any component (facility, service, procedure of, or hazard) in the National Airspace System, the timely knowledge of which is essential to personnel concerned with flight operation.

NTSB—National Transportation Safety Board. An agency of the U.S. government established to investigate serious accidents involving all modes of transportation. The Board also makes recommendations on safety measures and practices and is the repository of aviation accident statistics.

NWS—National Weather Service.

O & D—Origin and Destination.

OAG—Official Airline Guide. Publishes all North American, world, and cargo scheduled flights.

Obstruction Light—A light, or one of a group of lights, usually red or white, frequently mounted on a surface structure or natural terrain to warn pilots of the presence of an obstruction.

OFAW—Obstacle-Free Area Width. Pertains to runway or taxiway.

Operating Expenses—Those expenses incurred because of the productive operations of the business firm.

Operating Profit or Loss—The profit or loss from performance of an activity, based on overall operating revenues and overall operating expenses. Does not include nonoperating income and expenses or special items and is before income taxes.

Operating Property and Equipment—Land and units of tangible property and equipment that are used in air transportation services and services incidental thereto.

Operating Property and Equipment, Net, as a Percent of Cost—The cost of operating property and equipment less related depreciation and overhaul reserves as a percent of the total cost of operating property and equipment before deducting such reserves.

Operating Revenues—Revenues from the performance of air transportation and related incidental services. Includes (1) transport revenues from the carriage of all classes of traffic in scheduled and nonscheduled services including the performance of aircraft charters, and (2) nontransport revenues consisting of federal subsidy (where applicable) and the net amount of revenues less related expenses from services incidental to air transportation.

Operational Maintenance—Airport maintenance performed on a regular basis as required throughout the year.

Operations—An operation is a landing or a takeoff. (See **Touch-and-Go.**)

Opportunity Cost—The maximum alternative earning that might have been obtained if the productive good, service, or capacity had been applied to some alternative use.

Order Point—That level of inventory which should trigger a reorder of goods. It is usually measured by the safety stock plus average usage during lead time.

Organization Chart—A diagram of positions and their relationships to one another in an organization.

Organization, Formal—The official relationships or the positions in an organization generally shown on an organization chart and described in job descriptions.

Organization, Informal—The network of informal personal and social relationships that exists within an organization which is quite distinct from the formal organizational structure.

Organizing—The grouping of component activities, assigning each grouping to a manager, and establishing authority relationships among the groupings.

Originating Flight—A flight, designated by a flight number, commencing at the airport in question.

Originating Passenger (Baggage, Cargo, Mail)—A passenger (baggage, cargo, mail) commencing transport by air at the airport in question.

Other Accrued Taxes—Accruals for taxes, exclusive of federal income taxes, constituting a charge borne by the air carrier.

Other Current and Accrued Liabilities—Accruals for liabilities against the air carrier for personnel vacations, dividends declared but unpaid on capital stock, and other miscellaneous current and accrued liabilities.

Other Current Assets—Prepayments of rent, insurance, taxes, etc., which if not paid in advance would require the expenditure of working capital within one year, and other current assets not provided for in specific objective accounts.

Other Deferred Charges—Unamortized discount and expense on debt; unamortized capital stock expense; and debits, not provided for elsewhere, the final disposition of which must await receipt of additional information.

Other Deferred Credits—Unamortized premium on debt and credits, not provided for elsewhere, the final disposition of which must await receipt of additional information.

Other Investments and Receivables—Notes and accounts receivable not due within one year and investments in securities issued by others excepting associated companies.

Other Noncurrent Liabilities—Liabilities under company administered employee pension plans and for installments received from company personnel under company stock purchase plans, advances from associated companies and noncurrent liabilities.

Other Nonoperating Income and Expenses Net—Capital gains or losses on retirement of nonoperating property and equipment and investments in securities of others, interest and dividend income, and other nonoperating items except capital gains or losses on operating property and interest expense.

Other Paid in Capital—Premium and discount on capital stock, gains or losses arising from the reacquisition and the resale or retirement of capital stock, and other paid-in capital.

Other Temporary Cash Investments—Securities and other collectible obligations acquired for the purpose of temporarily investing cash, other than those issued by the United States Government or associated companies.

Other Use Flying—Use of general aviation aircraft for purposes other than those in specific categories, such as business, personal, air taxi.

Outbound—Activity originating at the study area or location under discussion and terminating outside it.

Outer Marker/OM—One component of an ILS, one of two marker beacons used for an ILS approach, normally four to seven miles from the runway threshold. It provides the pilot with an audio and visual signal. (See also **Middle Marker.**)

Out-of-Pocket Costs—Costs which entail current or near-future outlays for the decision at hand.

Out of Trust—A condition whereby a dealer sells equipment upon which there is a lien without immediately paying off the lien holder. This is a felony.

Over—My transmission is ended; I expect a response.

Overall Aircraft Revenue Hours, Scheduled Service—Aircraft hours are the airborne hours computed from the moment an aircraft leaves the ground until it touches the ground at the end of the flight.

Overall Capacity per Aircraft—The average overall carrying capacity (tons) offered for sale per aircraft in revenue services, derived by dividing the overall available ton-miles by the overall aircraft miles flown in revenue services.

Over Allowance—The amount allowed on a trade-in aircraft above the realistic blue book value.

Overhead Rate—Method of allocating overhead to the various products manufactured.

Package Policy—An insurance contract (normally property) that combines several types of coverage. A homeowner's policy, for example, combines property coverage with liability and medical coverage.

PANCAP—Practical ANnual CAPacity. An extension of PHOCAP, PANCAP allows an airfield to be overloaded for short periods of time during the year ("overload" being a period of time when demand exceeds PHOCAP).

PAR—Precision Approach Radar. Equipment that may be used to monitor certain nonradar approaches, but is primarily used to conduct precision approaches where the radar controller issues specific verbal instructions to the pilot.

PAR Approach—A precision instrument approach wherein the air traffic controller issues guidance instructions, for pilot compliance, based on the aircraft's position in relation to the final approach course (azimuth), the glide slope (elevation), and the distance (range) from the touchdown point on the runway as displayed on the controller's radar scope.

Parallel Runways—Two or more runways at the same airport whose centerlines are parallel. In addition to runway number, parallel runways are designated as L (left) and R (right) or, if three parallel runways, L (left), C (center) and R (right).

Part 150—Noise regulation and abatement program; replaces **ANCLUC**.

Participative Management—A management style characterized by the superior delegating decision-making to subordinates, who in turn participate in setting goals for themselves.

Partnership—A noncorporate business venture of two or more persons.

Passenger Boarding—The checking and entry of passengers into an aircraft prior to its departure.

Passenger Disembarkation—Exit of passengers from an aircraft after its arrival.

Passengers—The sum of enplanements plus deplanements. May or may not also include intransit passengers (where such occur).

PATWAS—Pilots Automatic Telephone Weather Answering Service. A recorded telephone weather briefing service. In some locations, pilots using touch-tone telephones may obtain weather information for specific routes.

PAX—Passengers.

Payback—The measure of the time needed to recoup, in the form of cash inflow from operations, the initial dollars invested. Also called *payout* and *payoff*

Payload—The weight of passengers, baggage, cargo, and mail, including both revenue and nonrevenue items.

Payroll—Includes the gross earning paid in the calendar year to all employees on the payroll. Includes all forms of compensation directly to workers, such as salaries, wages, commissions, dismissal pay, all bonuses, vacation and sick leave pay and compensation in kind, prior to such deductions as employees' Social Security, contributions, withholding taxes, group insurance, union dues, and savings bonds.

Peak—A defined period during which the highest traffic activity occurs (or is expected to occur) at an airport or in an airport terminal. See also **Design Hour.**

Peak-day Activity—That level of activity, existing or forecast, which is representative of typical peak-day conditions; demand levels in excess of the peak-day value may occasionally occur as atypical highs.

Peak-hour Demand—That level of activity, existing or forecast, which is representative of typical peak-hour conditions; demand levels in excess of the peak-hour value may occasionally occur as atypical highs.

Peak Month—The month of the year during which the highest traffic activity occurs or is expected to occur.

People Mover—A mechanical system for assisting the horizontal or vertical movement of people over relatively long distances, usually within passenger terminals and piers, e.g., moving sidewalks, escalators, etc.

P/E Ratio—The ratio (expressed as a multiple) of the price of a share of stock to the company's earnings per share.

Performance Appraisal—The formal system of appraising an employee on work performance periodically and in writing.

Performance Appraisal, Checklist—A method where the evaluator indicates the individual performance factors describing individual performance by checking yes or no to various statements.

Personal and Pleasure Flying—Any use of an aircraft for personal purposes not associated with a business or profession, and not for hire. This may include maintenance of pilot proficiency.

Personnel Management—The functions of creating, developing, and utilizing human resources within an organization. This definition includes work-group behavior, communication, motivation, leadership and other related human relation subjects.

PHOCAP—Practical HOurly CAPacity. The number of aircraft movements that the runways can handle corresponding to a tolerable level of delay.

Physical Inventory, Taking of—Counting all merchandise on hand, usually at the end of an accounting period.

Physiological Needs—The basic human bodily needs consisting of the need for food, water, clothing and shelter.

Pier—A terminal building extension protruding into the apron area, giving protected passenger access to aircraft gate positions.

Pilot Preflight Briefing—A service provided by a Flight Service Station to assist pilots in flight planning. Briefing items may include weather information, Notices to Airmen, military activities, flow control information and other items as requested.

Pilot Weather Report/PIREP—A report of meteorological phenomena encountered by pilots of aircraft in flight. (See **PIREP**.)

Pilot's Discretion—Used in conjunction with altitude assignments. Means that Air Traffic Control has offered the pilot the option of starting climb or descent whenever he wishes and may conduct the maneuver at any rate he wishes. He may temporarily level off on any intermediary altitude. However, once he has vacated an altitude he may not return to that altitude.

PIREP—PIlot Report (designator "UA"). A report furnished by the pilot of an aircraft concerning meteorological conditions encountered in flight.

Piston Planes—An aircraft operated by engines in which pistons moving back and forth work upon a crankshaft or other device to create rotational movement.

Place—In reference to aircraft size, number of seats including pilot(s) (e.g., a four-place aircraft).

Planning—The function of management that determines what shall be done, how it shall be done, why it shall be done, and by whom.

Planning Grant Program (PGP)—A program authorized by the Airport and Airway Development Act of 1970 to provide federal grants to airport sponsors for airport master planning and to planning agencies for airport system planning. Objectives of the program were promotion of effective location and development of individual airports and the development of an adequate National Airport System Plan.

Point System—A method of job evaluation where each of the factors in a job description is assigned points according to a standardized scale.

Policy—The paper evidencing the contract of insurance.

Position/Progress Report—A report over a known location as transmitted by the pilot of an aircraft to ATC.

Positive Control—The separation of all air traffic within designated airspace, by air traffic control.

Positive Control Areas—Airspace wherein aircraft are required to be operative under Instrument Flight Rules.

Posting—Transfer of an entry from the journal to a ledger account.

Power of Attorney—A written authorization to an agent by the principal.

Precipitation—Any or all forms of water particles (rain, sleet, hail or snow), that fall from the atmosphere and reach the surface.

Precision Approach—An instrument approach utilizing both vertical and horizontal guidance.

Precision Approach Radar/PAR—Radar equipment in some ATC facilities serving military airports, which is used to detect and display the azimuth, range and elevation of an aircraft on the final approach course to a runway.

Premium—Money paid for insurance protection or to buy an annuity.

Prepaid Interest—Interest paid in advance of the due date. Up to two years' mortgage interest may be deducted from taxable income in the year of purchase, provided that such interest is actually paid then.

Price—The consideration of a sale of goods.

Primary Surface—An imaginary surface longitudinally centered on a runway. When the runway is paved, the primary surface extends 200 feet beyond each end of the runway.

Prime Rate—The lowest loan interest rate charged by all banks at any given time. It is usually available to special customers.

Principal—One who employs an agent to act on his behalf; the person who as between himself and the surety is primarily liable to the third person or creditor.

Private-Use Airport—An airport which is not open for the use of the general public but only by permission.

Privately-Owned Airport—An airport which is owned by a private individual or corporation.

Probability Theory—A measure of the likelihood of the occurrence of a chance event, used to predict the behavior of a group rather than a single item in the group.

Problem Solving—Expressing in concise, quantified terms the relative advantages and disadvantages of pursuing a possible future course of action, or the relative advantages of any one of several alternative methods of operation.

Productivity—Average total number of employees divided into the indicated performance and financial measures for the year.

Profile Descent—An uninterrupted descent (except where level flight is required for speed adjustment) from cruising altitude level to interception of a glide slope or to a minimum altitude specified for the initial or intermediate approach segment of a nonprecision instrument approach. The profile descent normally terminates at the approach gate or where the glide slope or other appropriate minimum altitude is intercepted.

Profit—In ordinary accounting terms, profit is the excess of sales revenues after deducting all related expenses.

Profit and Loss Account—A temporary account to which are transferred revenue and expense accounts at the end of an accounting period.

Proforma Statement—A financial statement forecasting revenues and expenses likely to be incurred in the future.

Progressive Discipline—Discipline that is imposed on an individual in several stages of increasing severity, each one moving closer to the separation stage, but each step in turn designed to effect a behavior change prior to such a move.

Prohibited Area—An area of designated airspace within which the flight of aircraft is prohibited.

Promissory Note—An unsecured, short-term debt instrument in which the maker promises to pay the payee a specified sum at a certain time.

Promotion and Sales Expenses—Costs incurred in promoting the use of air transportation, generally, and creating a public preference for the services of particular air carriers. Includes the functions of selling, advertising and publicity, space reservations, and developing tariffs and flight schedules for publication.

Proprietor—The owner of an unincorporated business.

Public-Use Airport—An airport which is open for the use of the general public.

Publicly-Owned Airport—An airport which is owned by a city, state, county, regional agency or the federal government.

Purchase Agreement—A written document between a buyer and a seller giving the terms of a sale transaction.

Quantity Discount—A reduction in unit price inversely proportional to the size of the order. Usually constrained by the Robinson-Patman Act.

Queuing Theory—A form of probability theory useful in studying delays or lineups at servicing points.

Radar Advisory—Air Traffic Control provision of advice and information based on radar observations.

Radar Beacon—A radar transmitter that upon receiving a radar signal emits a signal which reinforces the normal reflected signal or which introduces a code into the reflected signal, especially for identification purposes.

Radar Contact—The term used by air traffic control to inform the pilot of an aircraft that it has been identified on radar display. Radar service may be provided until radar identification is lost or radar service is terminated. When a pilot is informed of "radar contact" he automatically discontinues reporting over compulsory reporting points.

Radar Separation—Radar spacing of aircraft in accordance with established minima.

Radar Service—A term which encompasses one or more of the following services based on the use of radar which can be provided by a controller to a pilot of a radar identified aircraft.

1. *Radar Separation*—Radar spacing of aircraft in accordance with established minima.
2. *Radar Navigational Guidance*—Vectoring aircraft to provide course guidance.
3. *Radar Monitoring*—Radar following of an aircraft in flight whose primary navigation is being performed by the pilot. To observe and note deviations from its authorized flight path, airway, or route.
4. The radar monitoring of instrument approaches with precision approach radar (PAR) or radar monitoring of simultaneous ILS approaches, including advice and instructions, whenever an aircraft nears or exceeds the prescribed PAR safety limit or simultaneous ILS no transgression zone.

Radial—A magnetic bearing extending from a VOR/VORTAC/TACAN navigation facility.

Radio—A device used for communication, and a term used to refer to a Flight Service Station, e.g., "Seattle Radio" is used to call the Seattle Flight Service Station.

Rail—Runway Alignment Indicator Light.

Ramp—See **apron.**

RAPCON—Radar Approach Control Facility (Air Force).

RATCF—Radar Approach Control Facility (Navy).

Rate of Return on Stockholder Equity—The ratio (expressed as a percentage) of (a) net income after special items to (b) stockholder equity. A measure of the return upon the capital invested in the business by the stockholder. These rates of return are calculated on net income after special items inclusive of investment tax credits not allocated to cost of service and exclusive of such investment tax credits.

Rate of Return on Total Investment—The ratio (expressed as a percentage) of (a) net income after special items but before interest expense to (b) total investment, long-term debt, advances, stockholder equity-net less unamortized discount and expense on debt.

Ratio Analysis—Means of evaluating performance of an enterprise by examining the relationships between various figures such as net sales to working capital.

Real-Time Processing—Paralleling data processing with a physical process in such a manner that the results of the data processing are immediately useful to the physical operation. In managerial problem solving, the realtime system must operate with sufficient speed to provide answers within the time that a decision must be made.

Recourse—An agreement signed by the dealer in regard to a retail contract, whereby the dealer agrees to honor the contract should the retail customer fail to make proper payments. This obligation to the financing source by the dealer only exists if recourse is agreed to by the dealer and usually he will enjoy at least 1 percent override on the contract for assuming this contingent liability.

Recruitment—The process by which an organization seeks out and attracts personnel desired for positions within the organization.

Registered Aircraft—Aircraft registered by FAA (required for all U.S. active aircraft). FAA records of registered aircraft are by address of owner as opposed to **based aircraft.**

REIL—Runway End Identifier Lights.

Relevant Range—The band of activity in which budgeted sales and expense relationships will be valid.

Reliability—The consistency with which an employment test yields the same score throughout a series of measurements.

Reliever Airport—A metropolitan area general aviation airport with facilities and services suitable for attracting and diverting general aviation activity away from major air carrier airports. The immediate benefit is reduced congestion and additional capacity at the air carrier facility.

Rent—Payment one receives for allowing someone else to use his property.

Replacement Value—The amount of money that would have to be paid today to replace an object with a new one; this value is acceptable to property insurers only when used to determine the amount of insurance needed for physical structures such as a building. Also called *replacement cost.*

Report—Used to instruct pilots to advise ATC of specified information, e.g., "Report passing Hamilton VOR."

Reporting Form—Insurance whereby the premium varies as the exposure varies—inventory or usage.

Reporting Point—A geographical location in relation to which the position of an aircraft is reported.

Resale Price Maintenance Agreement—An agreement that the buyer will not resell a trademark or brand name article below a stated minimum price which agreement, by virtue of fair trade laws, is valid not only as between the contracting parties but in some states may also bind other persons in the trade who know of the agreement although they do not sign it.

Reserves for Obsolescence and Deterioration—Expendable Parts—Accruals for losses in the value of expendable parts.

Reserves for Overhaul—Accumulated provisions for overhauls of flight equipment.

Reserves for Uncollectible Accounts—Accruals for estimated losses from uncollectible accounts.

Responsibility—The creation of an obligation on the part of subordinates for satisfactory performance.

Restricted Area—Airspace designated under Federal Aviation Regulations within which the flight of aircraft, while not wholly prohibited, is subject to restrictions. Most restricted areas are designated joint use and IFR/VFR operations in the area may be authorized by the controlling ATC facility when it is not being utilized by the using agency.

Retail Paper—A consumer time payment contract usually figured on discount or add-on interest.

Retained Earnings—Corporate profits that are not paid out in cash dividends, but are reinvested in the company to foster its growth.

Retained Earnings Adjustments—Charges or credits to unappropriated retained earnings, other than dividends, that reflect transfers to paid-in capital accounts or appropriations.

Retained Earnings Appropriated—Retained earnings segregated for contingencies and other special purposes, including retained earnings segregated in connection with self-insurance plans.

Retained Earnings Unappropriated—The cumulative net income or loss from operations of the air carrier less dividends declared on capital stock and amounts appropriated for special purposes.

Return on Investment (rate of return)—The most widely used single measure of a firm's operating efficiency. It is the ratio of net income to invested capital or asset turnover.

Revenue—An increase in owners' equity arising from operations.

Revenue, Operating—Revenue associated with sales of goods and services.

Revenue Passenger Mile (RPM)—One revenue passenger transported one mile in revenue service.

Revenue Ton Mile (RTM)—One ton of revenue traffic transported one mile.

Risk—The possibility of loss now or in the future. With regard to insurable risk, it is the chance of financial loss from perils named in the insurance contract. With regard to investment risk, it is the chance for financial loss due to uncertainty about the future. With regard to common risk, it is the chance of financial loss due to recessions, unemployment, inflation, etc.

Robinson-Patman Act—A federal statute designed to eliminate price discrimination in interstate commerce.

Roger—I have received all of your last transmission.

Rotor—Horizontal airfoils and their hub on a helicopter.

Route—A defined path, consisting of one or more courses, in a horizontal plane, which aircraft traverse over the surface of the earth.

Route Segment—As used in Air Traffic Control, a part of a route that can be defined by two navigational fixes, two NAVAIDS, or a fix and a NAVAID.

RPM—Revenue Passenger Miles.

Runway—A defined rectangular area on a land airport prepared for the landing and takeoff run of aircraft along its length. Runways are normally numbered in relation to their magnetic direction rounded off to the nearest 10 degrees, e.g., Runway 25 is nearest 250 degrees.

Runway Gradient—The average slope, measured in percent, between two ends or points on a runway. Runway gradient is depicted on government airport sketches when total runway gradient exceeds 0.3 percent.

Runway Safety Area—A cleared, drained, graded, and preferably turfed area symmetrically located about the runway. Under normal conditions, the runway safety area is capable of supporting snow removal, fire fighting and rescue equipment, and of accommodating the occasional passage of aircraft without causing major damage.

Runway in Use/Active Runway/Duty Runway—Any runway or runways currently being used for takeoff and landing. When multiple runways are used, they arc all considered "active" runways.

RVR—Runway Visual Range.

Safety Advisory—Safety advisories are issued by ATC to pilots of aircraft under their control if ATC is aware the aircraft is at an altitude which, in the controller's judgment, places the aircraft in unsafe proximity to terrain, obstructions or other aircraft. The controller may discontinue issuance of further advisories if the pilot responds that he is taking action to correct the situation or that he has the other aircraft in sight.

Sales—Net of returns, allowances and discounts; the dollar value of shipments less returns and allowances, including dealer's commission, if any.

Sales Contract—The portion of a purchase agreement designed to protect a creditor against defaults on payments.

Sales Mix—The relative combination of the quantities of a variety of company products that compose total sales.

Salesmanship—The art of determining the needs of the prospect and then filling these needs with a product or service from the company's mix.

Satellite—A building surrounded by aircraft gate positions, separated from the terminal building and reached by surface, underground, or above ground connection.

SAWS—State Aviation Weather Service. A statewide aviation weather reporting program utilizing persons trained and certified by the National Weather Service, and equipped by the FAA. These observers are used at locations that lack other means of reporting weather information (i.e., FAA, NWS, military), and are compensated for each report made.

Scheduled Air Carrier—See **Certificated.**

SDF—Simplified Directional Facility. Used for nonprecision approaches, the SDF provides a final approach similar to that of an ILS localizer except that the SDT course may be offset from the runway (usually not more than 3 degrees).

Search and Rescue/SAR—Services which seek missing aircraft and provide aid to those found that are in need of assistance. It is a cooperative effort using the facilities and services of available federal, state and local agencies. The U.S. Coast Guard is responsible for coordination of search and rescue for the Maritime Region and the U.S. Air Force is responsible for search and rescue for the Inland Region.

Seasonal Trends—Changes in an economic index that are caused by, or related to, changes in the seasons of the year.

Secondary Airport—An airport receiving approach control service as a satellite to a primary approach control facility, or one at which control is exercised by the approach control facility under tower en route control procedures.

Section 401 (of the Federal Aviation Act of 1958 as amended by the Airline Deregulation Act of 1978)—Provides for the issuance of a certificate of public convenience and necessity by the CAB, to carriers engaged in scheduled or charter, interstate and overseas air transportation. The certificate previously had stated the regular defined routes and destinations to be served by a fixed level of service. However, beginning January 1, 1982 carriers with 401 certificates received freedom to enter new markets without federal approval.

Section 406 (of the Federal Aviation Act of 1958 as amended by the Airline Deregulation Act of 1978)—Provides for the compensation (subsidy) of regional air carriers. Rates paid are subject to the conditions peculiar to air transportation and to the particular air carrier or class of air carrier.

Section 419 (of the Federal Aviation Act of 1958 as amended by the Airline Deregulation Act of 1978)—"Small Community Air Service. Guaranteed Essential Air Service." Provides for the guarantee of a minimum level of air service to eligible communities. (See **EAS.**)

SEL—Sound Exposure Level.

Selection—The methods and procedures by which a personnel department chooses individuals for positions within the organization.

Self-Actualization or Fulfillment Needs—The desire to realize one's potential.

Self-Insurance Reserves—Accruals through charges against income for uninsured losses.

Separation—The spacing of aircraft by ATC to achieve their safe and orderly movement in flight and while taking off and landing.

Separation Minima—The minimum longitudinal, lateral, or vertical distances by which aircraft are spaced through the application of air traffic control procedures.

Service Roads—Public or restricted roads within the airport boundary, primarily used for service purposes.

Severe Weather Avoidance Plan/SWAP—A plan to re-route air traffic to avoid severe weather in the New York ARTCC area in order to provide the least disruption to the ATC system when large portions of airspace are unusable due to severe weather.

Short Haul—Flights of less than 500 miles.

Short Takeoff and Landing Aircraft/STOL—Aircraft which, within its approved operating weight, are capable of operating from a "short takeoff and landing" runway in compliance with applicable STOL characteristics, airworthiness operations, noise and pollution standards.

Shutdown Cost—A fixed cost which continues to be incurred even when there is no activity.

Simple Interest—Interest charged on the unpaid balance of a loan which diminishes as the principal is reduced.

Simulation—A problem-solving technique utilizing a mathematical model that represents a physical system or phenomenon and that can be varied so that the original can be analyzed and understood by study of the behavior of the model.

Social Responsibilities of Management—Those managerial responsibilities to employees, the local community, the state, the nation and the human race.

Sociogram—A method of charting relationships within a work group.

Source Document—The original record of any transaction, internal or external, which occurs in the firm's operation.

Span of Control—The number of subordinates a manager can effectively supervise. This term is sometimes called the span of management.

Special Funds—Special funds not of a current nature and restricted as to general availability. Includes items such as sinking funds, pension funds under the control of the air carrier, equipment purchase funds, and funds segregated as part of a plan for self-insurance.

Special Income Credits and Debits, Net (special items)—Extraordinary credits and debits that are of sufficient magnitude that inclusion in the accounts for a single year would materially distort the total operating revenues or total operating expenses if included therein.

Special Income Tax Credits and Debits, Net—Income taxes applicable to special income credits or debits and other extraordinary income tax items not allocable to income of the current accounting year.

Special VFR Conditions—Weather conditions in a control zone which are less than basic VFR and in which some aircraft are permitted flight under Visual Flight Rules.

Specialty Goods—Goods that are purchased only on occasion, are usually expensive, and are generally classed as luxuries.

Speed Brakes/Dive Brakes—Moveable aerodynamic devices on aircraft that reduce airspeed during descent and landing.

Squawk (Mode, Code, Function)—Activate specific modes/codes/functions on the aircraft transponder, e.g., "Squawk three/alpha, two one zero five, low."

SSD—Service Segment Data.

Standard Terminal Arrival Route/STAR—A preplanned instrument flight rule (IFR) air traffic control arrival route published for pilot use in graphic and/or textual form. STARs provide transition from the en route structure to a fix or point from which an approach can be made.

Static Budget—A budget prepared for only one level of activity and, consequently, one which does not adjust automatically to changes in the level of volume.

Statistics—A branch of mathematics involving the collection, analysis, interpretation, and presentation of masses of numerical data.

Step-Variable Costs—Those variable costs which change abruptly at intervals of activity because their acquisition comes in indivisible chunks.

Stockholder Equity—The aggregate book value of holders of the air carrier's stock in assets owned by the air carrier.

STOL—Short Takeoff and Landing—A term applied to aircraft with specific performance capabilities. These include the ability to operate out of very short (often unprepared) airfields. STOL aircraft are useful in operations where terrain makes approach and departure paths difficult, or where steep approach and departure angles are desired to minimize noise effects.

Straight-in Approach—A descent in an approved procedure in which the final approach course alignment and descent gradient permits authorization of straight-in landing minimums.

Subordination Agreement—A party with a high priority legal position in regard to key assets of a corporation voluntarily relinquishes his preferred position in favor of another party—such as a lending institution.

Subrogation—Insurer is substituted for the insured and acts in his behalf, thereby the insurer can seek reimbursement from any negligent third parties who may have caused the loss.

Sunk Cost—A cost which has already been incurred and which, therefore, is irrelevant to the decision-making process. Also called *historical cost.*

Sunset—Provisions in the Airline Deregulation Act of 1978 for the orderly termination of the CAB's economic authority over air carrier operations. The established dates for termination of authority include the following: December 31, 1981—routes flown by certificated carriers; January 1, 1983—fares, tariffs of certificated carriers; January 1, 1985—complete termination of CAB as an agency. Remaining functions such as consumer protection have been passed to other agencies.

Supervision—The function of leading, coordinating and directing the work of others.

Supplemental Air Carrier—One of a class of air carriers holding certificates authorizing them to perform passenger and cargo charter services supplementing the scheduled service of the certificated air carriers. They are sometimes referred to as nonscheduled carriers.

Supportive Management—A managerial style where the supervisor builds and maintains his subordinates' sense of personal worth and importance, and attempts to help subordinates achieve their goals.

Surplus, Capital—An increase in owners' equity not generated through the company's earnings.

Surplus, Earned—Obsolescent name for retained earnings.

Surveillance Approach—An instrument approach wherein ATC issues instructions for pilot compliance based on aircraft position in relation to the final approach course (azimuth) and the distance (range) from the end of the runway as displayed on the controller's radar scope. The controller will provide recommended altitudes on final approach if requested by the pilot.

Synergism—Separate but related parts producing a sum greater than its components. It is sought for in organizing.

TACAN/TACtical Air Navigation—An ultra-high, electronic rhotheta frequency air navigation aid which provides suitably equipped aircraft a continuous indication of bearing and distance to the TACAN station.

Taxable Income—For federal income tax purposes, the amount of income, less exemptions, on which income tax is determined.

Tax Write-off—An investment loss that can offset against one's gross income when determining adjusted gross income.

Taxi into Position and Hold—Used by ATC to instruct a pilot to taxi onto departure runway, assume takeoff position and hold. It is not authorization for takeoff and is used when takeoff clearance cannot immediately be issued because of traffic or other reasons.

Taxiway—A defined path over which aircraft can taxi from one airfield area to another.

Taxiway Safety Area—An area symmetrically located about the taxiway that performs the same function for airplanes on the taxiway as the runway safety area does for airplanes on the runway.

Tenancy at Will—The holding of land for an indefinite period that may be terminated at any time by the landlord or by the landlord and tenant activity together.

Tenancy from Year to Year—A tenancy which continues indefinitely from year to year until terminated.

Tenancy for Years—A tenancy for a fixed period of time, even though the time is less than a year.

Term Insurance—Nonpermanent insurance in which protection is provided only for the length of the specified term, after which all benefits cease to exist.

Terminal Airspace—The controlled airspace normally associated with aircraft departure and arrival patterns to/from airports within a terminal system and between adjacent terminal systems in which tower enroute air traffic control service is provided.

Terminal Control Area (TCA)—The controlled airspace extending upward from the surface or higher to specified altitudes within which all aircraft are subject to positive air traffic control procedures.

Terminal, Cargo—A building or facility located between landside loading/unloading docks and apron within which cargo processing takes place.

Terminal, Passenger—A building or facility located between curbside and apron within which passenger and baggage processing takes place.

Terminal Radar Service Area/TRSA—Airspace surrounding designated airports wherein ATC provides radar vectoring, sequencing and separation on a full-time basis for all IFR and participating VFR aircraft. Service provided in a TRSA is called Stage III Service.

Terminating Flight—A flight, designated by a flight number, ending at the airport in question.

Terminating Passenger (Baggage, Cargo, Mail)—A passenger (baggage, cargo, mail) terminating transportation by air at the airport in question.

Test, Performance—An employment test which measures what an applicant can actually do.

T-hangar—A T-shaped aircraft hangar which provides shelter for a single airplane. Usually constructed in rows TLT.

The Rule of 78—A method used by banks and finance companies for determining the amount of rebate due to the borrower when he elects to pay off his discount interest contract early. It is analogous to "The Sum of the Year's Digits" in that, like accelerated depreciation, it determines the use one gets from the commodity, in this case the funds loaned. For example: The sum of the digits 1 + 2 + 3 . . . to 12 is 78. The first month 12/78 of the total interest is earned, the second month 11/78, etc. The amount to be remitted for the twelfth (12th) month of an early payment is 1/78.

Theory X—A theory of human behavior described by Douglas McGregor representing the traditional approach to motivating performance by management. It states that because of man's inherent dislike of work he must be motivated by use of negative or external motivation.

Theory Y—The modern approach to motivation as described by Douglas McGregor. It states that work can be a source of satisfaction and that man is most effectively motivated through the use of positive and internal motivation.

Threshold—The physical or effective end of runway pavement.

Threshold Crossing Height/TCH—The height of the glide slope above the runway threshold.

Time Study—The determination of the time necessary to perform a task. Several different methods are available.

Ton—A short ton (2,000 pounds).

Ton-Mile—One short ton—transported one statute mile. Ton-miles are computed by summation of the products of the aircraft miles flown on each interairport hop multiplied by the number of tons carried on that hop.

Total Flight Services—The sum of flight plans originated and pilot briefs, multiplied by two, plus the number of aircraft contacted.

Total General Services and Administration Expenses—Passenger service, aircraft and traffic servicing, promotion and sales, and general and administrative expenses.

Touchdown—The point at which an aircraft first makes contact with the landing surface. When used with a precision radar approach (PAR), it is the point where the glide path intercepts the landing surface.

Touchdown Zone—The first 3,000 feet of the runway beginning at the threshold. The area is used for determination of Touchdown Zone Elevation in the development of straight-in landing minimums for instrument approaches.

Touch-and-Go—A touch-and-go operation is used for flight training or proficiency and is an operation in which the aircraft lands and begins takeoff roll without stopping. It is counted as two operations. Such operations affect runway capacity differently than separate landings and takeoffs.

Track—The actual flight path of an aircraft over the surface of the earth.

Traffic Forecast—A forecast determining for certain future years the total traffic in passenger, cargo, mail, and aircraft movements.

Traffic Pattern—The traffic flow that is prescribed for aircraft landing at, taxiing on, and taking off from an airport. The usual components of a traffic pattern are upwind leg, crosswind leg, downwind leg, and final approach.

1. *Upwind Leg*—A flight path parallel to the landing runway in the direction of landing.
2. *Crosswind Leg* A—flight path at right angles to the landing runway at its departure end.
3. *Downwind Leg*—A flight path parallel to the landing runway in the direction opposite to landing.
4. *Base Leg*—The flight path at right angles to the landing runway off its approach end.
5. *Final Approach*—A flight path in the direction of landing along the extended runway centerline.

Traffic in Sight—A term used by pilots to inform a controller that previously reported traffic is in sight.

Transaction—Each business event that is recorded in the accounting records.

Transfer Passenger (Baggage, Cargo, Mail)—A passenger (baggage, cargo, mail) arriving by one flight and continuing the journey by another flight. (See also **Interline Transfer, Intraline Transfer.**)

Transient Operations—That portion of itinerant operations performed by aircraft other than those based at the airport in question.

Transition—The general term that describes the change from one phase of flight or flight condition to another, e.g., transition from en route flight to the approach or transition from instrument flight to visual flight.

Transitional Surface—An imaginary surface extending outward and upward at a right angle to the runway centerline plus the runway centerline extended at a slope of 7 to 1 from the sides of the primary surface and from the sides of the approach surfaces.

Transponder—The airborne radar beacon receiver/transmitter portion of the Air Traffic Control Radar Beacon System (ATCRBS) which automatically receives radio signals from interrogators on the ground and selectively replies with a specific reply pulse or pulse group only to those interrogations being received on the mode to which it is set to respond.

Treasury Stock—The cost of capital stock issued by the air carrier which has been reacquired by it and not retired or cancelled.

Turbine-powered Aircraft—Includes aircraft with either turbojet, turbofan, turboprop, or turboshaft engines.

Turbofan Planes—Aircraft operated by a turbojet engine whose thrust has been increased by the addition of a low-pressure compressor (fan). The turbofan engine can have an oversized low-pressure compressor at the front with part of the flow by-passing the rest of the engine (front-fan or forward-fan) or it can have a separate fan driven by a turbine stage (aft-fan).

Turbojet Planes—Aircraft operated by jet engines incorporating a turbine-driven air compressor to take in and compress the air for the combustion of fuel, the gases of combustion (or the heated air) being used both to rotate the turbine and to create a thrust-producing jet.

Turboprop Planes—Aircraft in which the main propulsive force is supplied by a gas turbine-driven conventional propeller. Additional propulsive force may be supplied from the discharged turbine exhaust gas.

Turboshaft Helicopter—A helicopter powered by one or more gas turbine engines.

Turnover—The percentage of the work force who quit, are fired, or are otherwise separated from the payroll for a given period.

TVOR—Terminal VOR.

TWEB—Transcribed WEather Broadcast. Weather information, recorded continuously and updated periodically, which is broadcast over L/MF (NDB) and VOR facilities. Pilots may listen to a TWEB by tuning in the appropriate facility.

Under the Hood—Indicates that the pilot is using a hood to restrict visibility outside the cockpit while simulating instrument flight. An appropriately rated pilot is required in the other control seat of the aircraft while this operation is being conducted.

Under Influence—The influence that is asserted upon another person by one who dominates that person.

Unfair Competition—Employing competitive methods that have been declared unfair by statute or by an administrative agency.

Unicom—Frequencies authorized for aeronautical advisory services to private aircraft. Only one such station is authorized at any landing area. The frequency 123.0 MHz is used at airports served by an airport traffic control tower or a Flight Service Station, and 122.8 MHz is used for other landing areas. Services available are advisory in nature, primarily concerning the airport services and airport utilization.

United States Government Securities—Investment in transferable obligations of the United States Government.

Unity of Command—Only one supervisor for each employee.

Universal Agent—An agent authorized by the principal to do all acts that can lawfully be delegated to a representative.

Utility—The useful and necessary characteristics of all products that are usable by consumers, namely, form, time, place and possession.

Utility Aircraft—An aircraft designed for general purpose work.

Validity—The extent to which a test measures what it is designed to measure.

Variable Costs—Those costs whose total magnitude varies directly with the level of production.

Vector—A heading issued to an aircraft to provide navigational guidance by radar.

Vertical Separation—Separation established by assignments of different altitude or flight levels.

Vertical Takeoff and Landing Aircraft/VTOL—Aircraft capable of vertical climbs and/or descents and of using very short runways or small areas for takeoff and landings. These aircraft include, but are not limited to, helicopters.

VFR—Visual Flight Rules that govern flight procedures in good weather, with conditions usually being at least a 1,000 foot ceiling and three miles visibility.

VFR Aircraft—An aircraft conducting flight in accordance with Visual Flight Rules (VFR).

VHF—Very High Frequency.

VHF/DF—Very High Frequency—Direction Finder.

Victor Airway—Designated air route between two points, using radials from appropriate VOR facilities and including the airspace within parallel lines four nautical miles each side of the airway centerline.

Visibility—The ability, as determined by atmospheric conditions and expressed in units of distance, to see and identify prominent unlighted objects by day and prominent lighted objects by night. Visibility is reported as statute miles, hundreds of feet or meters.

Visitor—A non-passenger, non-employee using the terminal (e.g., a well-wisher accompanying a departing passenger, a greeter meeting an arriving passenger, or a sightseer).

Visual Approach—An approach wherein a pilot operating an aircraft on an IFR flight plan, in VFR conditions, under the control of an air traffic control facility, with air traffic control authorization, may proceed to the airport of destination in VFR conditions.

Visual Flight Rules/VFR—Rules that govern the procedures for conducting flight under visual conditions. The term "VFR" is also used in the United States to indicate weather conditions that are equal to or greater than minimum VFR requirements. In addition, it is used by pilots and controllers to indicate type of flight plan.

Visual Separation—A means employed by ATC to separate IFR aircraft in terminal areas. There are two ways to effect this separation:

1. The tower controller sees the aircraft involved and issues instructions, as necessary, to ensure that the aircraft avoid each other
2. A pilot sees the other aircraft involved and upon instructions from the controller provides his own separation by maneuvering his aircraft as necessary to avoid it.

VMC—Visual Meteorological Conditions.

VOR—Very High Frequency Omnirange Station; a ground-based radio (electronic) navigation air transmitting radials in all direction in the VHF frequency spectrum; provides azimuth guidance to pilots by reception of electronic signals. VORs operate in the 108–117.85 MHz frequency band.

VORTAC—Co-located VOR and TACAN.

Vortices/Wing Tip Vortices—Circular patterns of air created by the movement of airfoils through the air. Air flowing around and about the tips of airfoils tend to roll up into two rapidly rotating vortices cylindrical in shape. These are the most predominant parts of aircraft wake turbulence and their rotational force is dependent upon wing loading, gross weight and speed of the generating aircraft. Vortices from medium to heavy aircraft can be of extremely high velocity and hazardous to smaller aircraft.

V/STOL—Vertical or short takeoff and landing aircraft.

VTOL—Vertical takeoff and landing aircraft.

Wage and Salary Administration—Maintaining a logical salary and/or wage structure.

Wake Turbulence—Phenomena resulting from the passage of an aircraft through the atmosphere. The term includes vortices, thrust stream turbulence, jet blast, jet wash, propeller wash and rotor wash, both on the ground and in the air.

Wide-body Aircraft—A term used for high-capacity aircraft of the types Boeing 747, Douglas DC-10, Lockheed 1011, Airbus A-300B, or similar (i.e., aircraft with double aisles in the passenger cabin and seating.

Wind Shear—A change in wind speed and/or wind direction in a short distance, resulting in a tearing or shearing effect. It can exist in a horizontal or vertical direction and occasionally in both.

Work Measurement—A means of determining the amount of work that should be produced by an individual or group of employees in some specified time period. It is used for establishing the amount of time it should take or will take to perform the work assigned.

Work Stoppage—An incident of labor-management strife arising from disputes over wages, hours, rules, and/or conditions of work, as well as from jurisdictional problems of craft representation of airline employees. A strike or lockout. Such incidents may or may not affect normally scheduled airline services.

Working Capital—Investable funds that are not currently tied up in long-term assets; it is equal to current assets minus current liabilities. The excess of current assets over current liabilities; or those funds used to finance day-to-day operations.

Workmen's Compensation—A system providing for payments to employees because they have been injured from a risk arising out of the course of their employment or because they have contracted an occupational disease, payment being made without consideration of the negligence of any party.

Index